Dictionary of Battles and Sieges

Dictionary of Battles and Sieges

A Guide to 8,500 Battles from Antiquity
through the Twenty-first Century

Volume 2
F–O

Tony Jaques

Foreword by Dennis Showalter

GREENWOOD PRESS
Westport, Connecticut • London

Library of Congress Cataloging-in-Publication Data

Jaques, Tony.
   Dictionary of battles and sieges : a guide to 8,500 battles from antiquity through the twenty-first century /
Tony Jaques ; foreword by Dennis Showalter.
      p. cm.
   Includes bibliographical references and index.
   ISBN 0–313–33536–2 (set : alk. paper)—ISBN 0–313–33537–0 (vol. 1 : alk. paper)—ISBN 0–313–33538–9
(vol. 2 : alk. paper)—ISBN 0–313–33539–7 (vol. 3 : alk. paper)   1. Battles—History—Encyclopedias.   2. Sieges—
History—Encyclopedias.   3. Military history—Encyclopedias.   I. Title.
   D25.J33 2007
   355.403—dc22   2006015366

British Library Cataloguing in Publication Data is available.

Library of Congress Catalog Card Number: 2006015366
ISBN: 0–313–33536–2 (set)   ISBN-13: 978–0–313–33536–5 (set)
        0–313–33537–0 (vol. 1)   978–0–313–33537–2 (vol. 1)
        0–313–33538–9 (vol. 2)   978–0–313–33538–9 (vol. 2)
        0–313–33539–7 (vol. 3)   978–0–313–33539–6 (vol. 3)

First published in 2007

Greenwood Press, 88 Post Road West, Westport, CT 06881
An imprint of Greenwood Publishing Group, Inc.
www.greenwood.com

Printed in the United States of America

The paper used in this book complies with the
Permanent Paper Standard issued by the National
Information Standards Organization (Z39.48–1984).

10 9 8 7 6 5 4 3 2 1

This dictionary is dedicated to the memory of my father, Pat Jaques, 1903–1980.

Contents

F

Fada ▎ 1987 ▎ Libyan-Chad War

On the day of Chadian victory at **Zouar**, government troops and Goukouni Oueddei's rebels joined in a fierce attack on Fada, 400 miles to the southeast, where a Libyan brigade was routed with claimed 780 killed and 120 armoured vehicles destroyed. Libya bombed Fada next day, trying to destroy captured war supplies, and in March attempted to advance on Fada from **Ouadi Doum** (2 January 1987).

Faddiley ▎ 583 ▎ Anglo-Saxon Conquest of Britain

See **Fethanleag**

Faenza ▎ 490 ▎ Goth Invasion of Italy

King Theodoric of the Ostrogoths defeated Odoacer, the German ruler of Italy, on the **Sontius** and at **Verona** in 489, then besieged him in his capital in **Ravenna**. A powerful sortie by Odoacer broke the siege and at Faenza he beat the Ostrogoths and advanced into northern Italy. However, a subsequent Ostrogoth victory at the **Adda** drove Odoacer back to a long siege at Ravenna.

Faesulae ▎ 225 BC ▎ Gallic Wars in Italy

Responding to pressure from Roman expansion in the north, Insubrian Gauls and their Boii allies crossed the Apennines and advanced as far as Clusium. The Gauls then lured a local Roman force into a trap at Faesulae (modern Fiesole) near Florence, killing 6,000. The arrival of Consul Lucius Aemilius Papus drove the invaders towards the coast and defeat at **Telamon** and later at **Clastidium**.

Faesulae ▎ 405 ▎ Goth Invasion of the Roman Empire

The great Roman-Vandal General Flavius Stilicho repulsed the Visigoths at **Pollentia** and **Verona**, then faced a fresh invasion by Goths and Vandals under Radagaisus, who attacked Florence. At nearby Faesulae (modern Fiesole), supported by Sarus the Goth and Uldin the Hun, Stilicho destroyed the invaders and Radagaisus was executed. The survivors retreated to join Alaric's warband.

Faial ▎ 1812 ▎ War of 1812

Pursued to neutral Faial in the Portuguese Azores, the American privateer *General Grant* (Captain Samuel Reid) was attacked by the British ships *Plantagenet* (Captain Robert Floyd), *Rota* (Captain Philip Somerville) and *Carnation* (Captain George Bentham). After repulsing a hard-fought attack and inflicting about 300 casualties, Reid had to scuttle his ship (26–27 September 1812).

Faid Pass ▎ 1943 ▎ World War II (Northern Africa)

Germany reinforced its Panzer army in Tunisia and General Jurgen von Arnim launched his offensive by driving the French from Faid Pass. Two weeks later, the German tanks stormed out of the pass and smashed through thin American defence, capturing many tanks and men. Sbeitla and Sidi Bou Zid fell and the Americans retreated to **Kasserine** (30 January–2 February & 14–16 February 1943).

Fair Garden | 1864 | American Civil War (Western Theatre)

Ten days after being repulsed east of Knoxville, Tennessee, near **Dandridge**, Union General Samuel B. Sturgis met an advancing Confederate force under Generals William T. Martin and John T. Morgan further west at Fair Garden, near Sevierville. Supported by Colonel Edward M. McCook, Sturgis defeated the Confederates but incurred heavy losses and retired next day (27 January 1864).

Fair Oaks | 1862 | American Civil War (Eastern Theatre)

See **Seven Pines**

Fair Oaks | 1864 | American Civil War (Eastern Theatre)

In a diversion east of Richmond, Virginia, Union General Benjamin F. Butler advanced north from **New Market Road** against Confederate General Richard H. Anderson on the Nine Mile Road near Fair Oaks. Butler was driven off by a counter-attack and other Union forces were no more successful the same day, southwest of Petersburg at **Hatcher's Run** (27–28 October 1864).

Falaise | 1944 | World War II (Western Europe)

While a German counter-attack failed around **Mortain**, British and Canadians from **Caen** and Americans from **Avranches** attempted to encircle two enemy armies. However, severe fighting held open the gap between Falaise and Argentan and 20,000 men escaped before the Allied trap closed. The Germans lost perhaps 560 tanks, 9,000 guns, 10,000 killed and 50,000 captured (13–20 August 1944).

Falan | 1389 | Wars of Scandinavian Union

See **Falkoping**

Falkirk | 1298 | William Wallace Revolt

Recovering from defeat at **Stirling**, Edward I of England led a large force against Scottish nationalist Sir William Wallace. At Falkirk, the Scots volunteer army resisted the King's cavalry on marshy ground but was destroyed in one of the first major victories by English longbowmen. Wallace fled to France and was executed in 1305 after another Scottish defeat at **Stirling** (22 July 1298).

Falkirk | 1746 | Jacobite Rebellion (The Forty-Five)

English General Henry Hawley was advancing to relieve the Jacobite siege of **Stirling** when he met the rebels under Charles Stuart—Bonnie Prince Charlie—and Lord George Murray to the southeast at Falkirk. In a confused 20-minute action during a rainstorm, the Hanoverians were driven off with heavy losses in men and equipment and the siege continued (17 January 1746).

Falkland Islands | 1914 | World War I (War at Sea)

Returning home via South America, German Admiral Maximilian von Spee sank two British cruisers off **Coronel**, then met Admiral Frederick Doveton Sturdee's pursuing battle squadron near the Falkland Islands. A decisive one-sided action saw four German cruisers sunk, with von Spee himself lost. The fifth cruiser escaped into the Pacific and was later destroyed (8 December 1914).

Falkoping | 1389 | Wars of Scandinavian Union

During a time of rebellion among local nobles, Queen Margaret of Denmark invaded Sweden and, on the Plain of Falan, near Falkoping, her forces defeated and captured King Albert of Sweden and his son, ending the Folkung Dynasty. As a result of the battle, Denmark, Norway and Sweden came under one crown and the Scandinavian Union continued for 130 years (24 February 1389).

Fallen Timbers | 1794 | Little Turtle's War

General Anthony Wayne was determined to secure the Ohio Valley and established **Fort**

Recovery on the Wabash before marching north against Miami, Shawnee and other tribes. Attacking at Fallen Timbers, a forest clearing on the Maumee near modern Toledo, Wayne's regulars used bayonets to secure a decisive victory. The Indians of the northwest soon sued for peace (20 August 1794).

Falling Waters ∎ 1861 ∎ American Civil War (Eastern Theatre)
See **Hoke's Run**

Fallujah ∎ 1941 ∎ World War II (Middle East)
After besieging Iraqi forces were repulsed at **Habbaniyah**, west of Baghdad, a British relief column (Habforce) arrived from Transjordan under General George Clarke and attacked the Iraqis at nearby Fallujah on the Euphrates. The Iraqi army was heavily defeated and pro-Axis leader Rashid Ali fled. Habforce entered Syria next month and attacked Vichy forces at **Palmyra** (19–21 May 1941).

Falside ∎ 1547 ∎ Anglo-Scottish Royal Wars
See **Pinkie**

Faluja ∎ 1948–1949 ∎ Israeli War of Independence
Following the fall of **Huleiqat**, northeast of Gaza, Jewish commander Shimon Avidan attacked an Egyptian Brigade further east at the village of Faluja and nearby Iraq al-Manshiyya, commanded by General Taba Bey and (later President) Gamel Abdul Nasser. Despite repeated heavy attacks, the "Faluja Pocket" held out and armistice saw them permitted to withdraw (22 October 1948–7 January 1949).

Famagusta ∎ 1570–1571 ∎ Venetian-Turkish War in Cyprus
In renewed war against Venice, Sultan Selim II sent Lala Mustafa with a large force to Cyprus, where he captured **Nicosia**, then besieged Famagusta. Before help arrived from Europe, Governor Marc Antonio Bragadino negotiated a safe capitulation, but he was then murdered and

his men were enslaved. The Turks were later defeated in October 1571 at **Lepanto** (15 September 1570–1 August 1571).

Famaillá ∎ 1841 ∎ Argentine Civil Wars
With his army virtually destroyed at **Quebracho Herrado** (November 1840), Unitarist General Juan Galo Lavalle was pursued to Tucumán, where he made a final stand 20 miles to the southwest at Famaillá against General Manuel Oribe. Lavalle was heavily defeated, then killed fleeing to Bolivia (8 October), ending opposition in the north and east to Dictator Manuel de Rosas (19 September 1841).

Famars ∎ 1793 ∎ French Revolutionary Wars (1st Coalition)
See **Valenciennes**

Fancheng ∎ 219 ∎ Wars of the Three Kingdoms
Just months after Cao Cao of Wei was driven out of Hanzhou by defeat at **Dingjun**, his cousin Cao Ren was defeated and besieged at Fancheng by Guan Yu of Shu. Cao Cao's relief army under Yu Jin was destroyed by floods, but Guan Yu was badly beaten by a second force under Xu Huang. Guan Yu was pursued and executed and Sun Quan seized the middle Yangzi, leading to battle in 222 at **Yiling**.

Fangtou ∎ 369 ∎ Wars of the Sixteen Kingdoms Era
With northern China wracked by war between states, Emperor Fei of the Eastern Jin sent Huan Wen north across the Yellow River to invade the Xianbei state of Former Yan and besiege Fangtou. With his supplies cut and facing attack by Former Qin, Huan withdrew but was pursued and routed by General Murong Chui. Huan's expedition is said to have cost 30,000 men (August–November 369).

Fano ∎ 271 ∎ Roman-Alemannic Wars
When Alemanni tribesmen invaded northern Italy, they defeated Emperor Aurelian at **Placentia** and advanced southwards towards Rome. On the Metaurus at Fano, however, Aurelian's

regrouped forces caught the invaders and inflicted a decisive defeat. The capital was saved and Aurelian pursued the Alemanni back north, where he caught and annihilated the survivors at **Pavia**.

Fao I 1986 I Iraq-Iran War
See **Al Faw**

Farah I 1719 I Persian-Afghan Wars
Campaigning against Asadullah Khan, leader of the Abdali Afghans who had defeated the Persians at **Herat**, Mahmud Ghilzai of Kandahar, a nominal vassal of the Shah, besieged the rebel at Farah, in western Afghanistan. Asadullah was defeated and killed, along with 3,000 of his men. Mahmud Ghilzai secured Afghanistan, then invaded Persian territory and seized **Kerman**.

Fariskur I 1250 I 7th Crusade
The French Crusade of King Louis IX was driven back from an advance on Cairo by a costly defeat at **Mansura** (8 February) and attempted to withdraw to **Damietta**, on the eastern Nile Delta. At Fariskur, the retreating army was routed, with thousands of prisoners enslaved or executed. The King himself was taken prisoner and ransomed, ending his disastrous expedition to Egypt (6 April 1250).

Farka I 1896 I British-Sudan Wars
See **Firket**

Farmah I 640 I Muslim Conquest of Egypt
See **Pelusium**

Farmville I 1865 I American Civil War (Eastern Theatre)
As defeated Confederates withdrew west from **Petersburg**, Virginia, pursuing Union troops crossed **High Bridge** and advanced units under General Andrew A. Humphreys met Confederate commander Robert E. Lee at Cumberland Church, near Farmville. The Union forces were repulsed and Lee was able to continue west towards **Appomattox Court House** (7 April 1865).

Farnham I 893 I Viking Wars in Britain
Danish invaders who landed in Kent advanced into Wessex, but at Farnham near Guildford, they were heavily defeated by Alfred's son Edward, who recovered the booty they had seized. Driven north across the Thames, the Danes were besieged at Thorney Island by Prince Edward and Aethelred of Mercia, who forced them to give hostages and abandon Kent, withdrawing to Viking East Anglia.

Farquhar's Farm I 1899 I 2nd Anglo-Boer War
See **Nicholson's Nek**

Farrukhabad I 1750 I Pathan War
On a massive offensive in northern India against Safdar Jang, Subadar of Awadh, Pathan leader Ahmad Khan Bangesh led a surprise attack on the Mughal army outside Farrukhabad, near the upper Ganges, where the Subadar's General, Naval Rai, was defeated and killed. The Pathans secured a second victory over Safdar Jang himself to the northwest at **Kasganj** (3 August 1750).

Farrukhabad I 1751 I Pathan War
When a Bangash attack on northern India was defeated at **Qadirganj**, Rohilla Pathans who went to aid their Sunni Muslim brethren were routed near Farrukhabad by Marathas under Gangadhar Jaswant and Jawahir Singh Jat. After Pathan General Sadulla Khan fled and Bahadur Khan was killed, along with a claimed 10,000 Rohillas, the invasion was driven back across the Ganges (28 April 1751).

Farrukhabad I 1804 I 2nd British-Maratha War
British commander General Sir Gerard Lake repulsed Maharaja Jaswant Rao Holkar of Indore at **Delhi** (2 November), then pursued the Maratha army down the Ganges towards Farrukhabad, where he destroyed the Maratha cavalry in a one-sided disaster. Holkar fled to his ally the Raja of **Bharatpur** and Lake marched west to aid the siege of **Dieg** (17 November 1804).

Farsetmore I 1567 I O'Neill Rebellion
See **Letterkenny**

Fategarh I 1858 I Indian Mutiny
Preparing for the British advance from Cawnpore to **Lucknow**, General Sir Colin Campbell sent Brigadier Adrian Hope northwest to the Ganges, where he captured the vital bridge at Kali Nadi and the following day attacked nearby Fategarh. In the face of a decisive cavalry charge led by Colonel Hope Grant, the rebels fled across the Ganges, abandoning the town and its fort (2 January 1858).

Fatehabad I 1041 I Afghan Wars of Succession
In the aftermath of disaster at **Dandanaqan** in Turkmenistan (May 1040), Ghaznavid Sultan Masud ibn Mahmud withdrew to India and was deposed and killed by his brother Muhammad, who immediately marched west to claim Afghanistan. At Fatehabad, near Jalalabad, Masud's son Maudad routed the rebels, executed Muhammad and his sons, then secured himself as Sultan (March 1041).

Fatehabad I 1879 I 2nd British-Afghan War
Amid renewed hostilities following British victory at **Peiwar Kotal**, General Sir Charles Gough (brother of Commander-in-Chief Sir Hugh) marched against Khugiani tribesmen in eastern Afghanistan. Gough's heavily outnumbered force defeated 5,000 Afghans in a fierce fight east of **Kabul** at Fatehabad, 14 miles southwest of Jalalabad. However, Major Wigram Battye was killed (2 April 1879).

Fatehpur I 1799 I Maratha Territorial Wars
Supported by Irish-born General George Thomas, Vama Rao of Hariana invaded Jaipur and took a strong defensive position to the northwest at Fatehpur, where he was attacked by the Rajput army of Partab Singh led by General Raja Roraji Khavis. Although heavily outnumbered, Thomas achieved a remarkable victory, though the arrival of Rajput reinforcements forced him to withdraw.

Fatehpur I 1857 I Indian Mutiny
As General Sir Henry Havelock marched out of Allahabad to recapture **Cawnpore**, rebel leader Nana Sahib tried to intercept a column under Major Sydenham Renaud and found himself facing Havelock's full force at Fatehpur. The rebels were driven off in a brief action. The British suffered few losses and, after plundering Fatehpur, advanced through **Aong** and **Pandu Nadi** (12 July 1857).

Fatehpur Sikri I 1527 I Mughal Conquest of Northern India
See **Khanua**

Fathkelda I 1724 I Mughal-Hyderabad War
See **Shakarkhelda**

Fatshan Creek I 1857 I 2nd Opium War
Determined to punish China for seizing men off the ship *Arrow*, British Admiral Sir Michael Seymour, with Commodore Henry Keppel, destroyed war junks at Escape Creek (25 May), then attacked the main Chinese fleet at nearby Fatshan Creek, south of Guangzhou. Every ship in the Chinese fleet was destroyed or captured and the British advanced to capture **Guangzhou** itself in December (1 June 1857).

Faughart I 1318 I Rise of Robert the Bruce
See **Dundalk**

Faventia I 82 BC I Sullan Civil War
While Gaius Marius the Younger lost south of Rome at **Sacriportus**, his allies Papirius Carbo and Caius Norbanus advanced from the north. After a series of costly skirmishes, Carbo was routed at Faventia (modern Faenza) by Sullan General Quintus Caecilius Metellus. Norbanus fled to Rhodes, Carbo played no further major part, and Sulla returned south to defeat Marius at the **Colline Gate**.

Favorita ∎ 1797 ∎ French Revolutionary Wars (1st Coalition)
See **La Favorita**

Faya Largeau ∎ 1983 ∎ Chad Civil Wars
After Goukouni Oueddei's Libyan-backed rebels overwhelmed the northern city of Faya Largeau (23 June), their advance was checked at **Abéché** by government troops, who counter-attacked and retook Faya with very heavy losses on both sides (30 July). Massive Libyan bombing regained the city (10 August), though Faya was abandoned by Libya after defeat at **Ouadi Doum** in March 1987.

Fehmarn ∎ 1644 ∎ Thirty Years War (Franco-Habsburg War)
See **Kolberg Heath**

Fehrbellin ∎ 1675 ∎ Scania War
Swedes invading Brandenburg under Count Karl Gustav Wrangel were repulsed at **Rathenow** and three days later were surprised northwest of Berlin at Fehrbellin by Elector Frederick William and Field Marshal Georg von Derfflinger. The Elector's much smaller force won a great victory and he went on to capture Swedish Pomerania. However, he had to return it when war ended (28 June 1675).

Fei River ∎ 383 ∎ Wars of the Sixteen Kingdoms Era
Fu Jian of the Kingdom of Former Qin unified much of northern China, then led a massive army south against the Eastern Jin, with their capital at Nanjing. In a famous action at the Fei River (Feishui) in Anhui, the smaller Jin Imperial army under Xie An and Xie Xuan inflicted a terrible defeat, killing Qin commander Fu Jung. Fu Jian fled north and his empire soon collapsed.

Feldkirch ∎ 1799 ∎ French Revolutionary Wars (2nd Coalition)
As French commander André Masséna crossed the Rhine in Switzerland, General Nicolas Oudinot attacked General Friedrich von Hotze's Austrians just inside Austria at Feldkirch and was driven back

from well-entrenched positions. Masséna himself joined the attack, but was again heavily repulsed and withdrew through **Zurich**. He resumed the offensive in September (7–23 March 1799).

Fellin ∎ 1560 ∎ Livonian War
Ivan IV of Russia renewed his war against Livonia, sending Andrei Kurbsky, who defeated the Livonian Order in Estonia at **Oomuli**, then besieged fortified Fellin (modern Viljandi), further north. Grandmaster Wilhelm Furstenberg surrendered the city after almost three weeks and was taken to Moscow. The Order never recovered and was secularised the following year (4–20 August 1560).

Fenes ∎ 1660 ∎ Transylvanian National Revolt
See **Gilau**

Fenghuangcheng ∎ 1894 ∎ Sino-Japanese War
Campaigning in southern Manchuria, the Japanese fell back from **Caohekou** to defend Fenghuangcheng (Fengcheng) against the Amur army of Tatar General Yiketang'a. Repulsed nearby (9 December), the Chinese launched a massive assault but were attacked in the rear and decimated by General Naobumi Tatsumi. The Japanese then moved west against **Haicheng** (14 December 1894).

Fengtian ∎ 783 ∎ Later Tang Imperial Wars
During war against rebellious provinces in northeast China, troops in the capital Chang'an mutinied and Emperor Dezong fled 50 miles northeast to Fengtian, where he was besieged by Zhi Ci. Garrison commander Hun Zen led a brilliant five-week defence, including destruction of a huge siege tower, until an Imperial army under Li Huaiguang arrived and the mutineers were defeated.

Ferdiddin ∎ 1901 ∎ Wars of the Mad Mullah
Driven off with heavy losses by part of the first British Somaliland expedition at **Samala**,

Muhammad Abdullah Hassan withdrew south towards Ferdiddin, near Damot, where he was met days later by the main force of largely Somali levies under General Eric Swayne. The Mullah suffered high losses and fled to Italian territory, though Swayne lost the following year at **Erego** (17 June 1901).

Fère-Champenoise ▌ 1814 ▌ Napoleonic Wars (French Campaign)
See **La Fère-Champenoise**

Ferghana ▌ 102 BC ▌ Wars of the Former Han
See **Dayuan**

Ferkeh ▌ 1896 ▌ British-Sudan Wars
See **Firket**

Ferozeshah ▌ 1845 ▌ 1st British-Sikh War
When a large Sikh army crossed the Sutlej into British East Punjab, they were repulsed by British General Sir Hugh Gough at **Mudki**, then retired northwest to Ferozeshah, near Ferozepur, where they were attacked three days later. In some of the hardest fighting in India, Lal Singh repulsed the first British assault, but was finally driven out at great cost to both sides (21–22 December 1845).

Ferrara ▌ 1815 ▌ Napoleonic Wars (The Hundred Days)
King Joachim I of Naples (Marshal Murat) prematurely declared war after Napoleon Bonaparte's return from Elbe and led a Neapolitan army against Austria in northern Italy to capture Bologna. Attempting to cross the Po towards Mantua, he was beaten at Ferrara by General Vincenz Bianchi and had to withdraw south, where he was routed (3 May) at **Tolentino** (12 April 1815).

Ferrol ▌ 1805 ▌ Napoleonic Wars (3rd Coalition)
See **Cape Finisterre**

Ferrybridge ▌ 1461 ▌ Wars of the Roses
Returning from **Mortimer's Cross** too late to prevent defeat at **St Albans**, Edward Duke of York pursued the Royalists into Lancashire and sent John Radcliffe Lord Fitzwalter to Ferrybridge, where he was surprised and killed. Later that day, John Mowbray Duke of Norfolk counter-attacked to kill Lancastrian leader John Baron Clifford and the Yorkists won next day at **Towton** (28 March 1461).

Festubert ▌ 1915 ▌ World War I (Western Front)
Despite terrible losses at **Aubers**, four days later, British commander Sir Douglas Haig attacked again further south towards Festubert, west of La Bassée, to support the French offensive in **Artois**. A massive bombardment helped secure some initial success and Festubert was captured, though the British lost almost 16,000 men and the attack soon ground to a halt (15–27 May 1915).

Fethanleag ▌ 583 ▌ Anglo-Saxon Conquest of Britain
Ceawlin of the West Saxons was advancing along the Upper Severn after his great victory at **Deorham**, when he was halted at Fethanleag (modern Faddiley) near Nantwich, Cheshire, by Britons under Brochmael, Prince of Powys. Ceawlin was heavily defeated and his brother Cutha was killed. The West Saxon King was later overthrown and defeated at **Wodnesbeorg** in 592 by his nephew Coel.

Fetterman Massacre ▌ 1866 ▌ Red Cloud's War
Sent to protect a wood train under attack five miles from **Fort Phil Kearney**, Wyoming, the impetuous Captain William Fetterman and 82 other soldiers were lured into an ambush on nearby **Lodge Trail Ridge** by perhaps 2,000 Sioux under Crazy Horse and Red Cloud. They fought back bravely, inflicting heavy Indian losses, but the entire detachment was wiped out (21 December 1866).

Fez ∎ 1911 ∎ French Colonial Wars in North Africa

When Sultan Mulai Hafid of Morocco was besieged in Fez by tribal rebels, his troops under French Colonel Emile Mangin held the city and eventually drove off a final massive assault (11 May). Fez was then relieved by French forces under General Robert Monier from Casablanca and Colonel Jean Broulard from Tangiers and the rebels were forced to withdraw (12 March–22 May 1911).

Fez ∎ 1912 ∎ French Colonial Wars in North Africa

Moroccan soldiers in the French garrison at Fez mutinied and were put down by General Robert Monier, after which the city came under siege by Moroccan forces opposed to Sultan Mulai Hafid. A relief column under Colonel Henri Gouraud arrived to destroy the nearby Moroccan camp with artillery and a French Protectorate was soon declared (17 April–1 June 1912).

Fidenae ∎ 426 ∎ Roman-Etruscan Wars

After losing to the Etruscans near Fidenae at **Cremera** (477), Rome renewed the war against Fidenae and, early in the campaign, King Tolumnius of Veii was killed, reputedly in single combat. Following subsequent Roman failure, Aemielius Mamercus was appointed Dictator in command and Fidenae was taken by storm and looted. A few years later, Rome advanced upstream against **Veii** itself.

Field of Blood ∎ 1119 ∎ Crusader-Muslim Wars
    See **Antioch, Syria**

Figueras ∎ 1794 ∎ French Revolutionary Wars (1st Coalition)

French General Jacques Dugommier repulsed a Spanish invasion of France, then advanced into Catalonia and was killed by a cannonball (17 November) while attacking General Amarillas Comte de la Union in defensive lines at Banyuls, covering Figueras. De la Union was killed (20 November) as General Dominique de Perignon stormed the pass at Banyuls and Figueras itself fell a week later (17–20 November 1794).

Figueras ∎ 1811 ∎ Napoleonic Wars (Peninsular Campaign)

When Spanish insurgent leader Juan Antonio Martínez seized the Catalonian town of Figueras, near the French border, he was immediately besieged by Marshal Jacques Macdonald. The garrison held out in the hope of relieving French pressure on the siege of **Tarragona**, but no help came. The starving garrison surrendered three days after a sortie was heavily repulsed (9 April–19 August 1811).

Fihl ∎ 635 ∎ Muslim Conquest of Syria

Following great Arab victories at **Ajnadin** and the **Yarmuk**, the Byzantine General Baanes attempted to halt the Muslim advance towards **Damascus**. At Fihl, in the eastern Jordan Valley (near the site of ancient Pella) Arab General Khalid ibn al-Walid drove him back and seized the nearby town of Basain (modern Beth Shan). Khalid then continued on through **Marj as-Suffar** (23 January 635).

Finisterre ∎ 1747 ∎ War of the Austrian Succession
    See **Cape Finisterre**

Finland ∎ 1939–1940 ∎ Russo-Finnish War
    See **Winter War**

Finschhafen ∎ 1943 ∎ World War II (Pacific)
    See **Huon Peninsula**

Finta ∎ 1653 ∎ Moldavian Civil War

In a struggle for the throne of Moldavia, Prince Vasile Lupu was driven out by rival George Stefan, aided by Wallachian and Transylvanian troops. Supported by his Cossack son-in-law, Timus, Lupu was briefly restored, before a decisive battle on the road to Tirgoviste at Finta saw Lupu defeated and exiled. Stefan then resumed the throne (17 November 1653).

Fiodoroivskoy | 1812 | Napoleonic Wars (Russian Campaign)
  See **Vyazma**

Firadz | 634 | Muslim Conquest of Iraq
  Muslim General Khalid ibn al-Walid advancing up the Euphrates from **Ain Tamar** destroyed the hostile Bani Tughlib, then pursued the Persian army up to Firadz, close to the frontier of the Byzantine Empire. There he routed a combined Roman-Sassanian army but wisely did not advance further. Khalid was soon summoned to join the Muslim offensive in Syria at **Ajnadin** (January 634)

Firket | 1896 | British-Sudan Wars
  At the start of Britain's campaign to reconquer the Sudan after the fall of **Khartoum**, General Herbert Kitchener's British-Egyptian-Sudanese army attacked the Mahdists at Firket, south of Akasha. The Dervish army was driven out by a surprise dawn assault with about 1,000 killed, including commander Hammuda Idris. Kitchener then advanced through **Hafir** to Dongola (7 June 1896).

First of June | 1794 | French Revolutionary Wars (1st Coalition)
  To protect a desperately needed food convoy from North America, French Admiral Louis Villaret de Joyeuse took his fleet to sea and drew off the British force of Admiral Richard Howe. After four days of running battle, the decisive struggle was joined off Ushant and the French lost seven ships captured and one sunk. Howe won, but the food convoy arrived safely (29 May–1 June 1794).

Firth of Forth | 1708 | War of the Spanish Succession
  Hoping to promote rebellion against England, French Admiral Claude Chevalier de Forbin sailed to the east coast of Scotland with 10,000 soldiers and James Stuart the Old Pretender. Intercepted at the Firth of Forth by Admiral Sir George Byng, Forbin escaped with just a single ship captured. His withdrawal ended French hopes of provoking a Scottish rising (13 March 1708).

Fish Creek | 1885 | 2nd Riel Rebellion
  General Frederick Middleton took command of Canadian forces against rebellion in Saskatchewan and marched on the rebel headquarters at Batoche, southwest of Prince Albert. But to the south at Fish Creek, he was ambushed by rebel leader Gabriel Dumont. Although the Méti and Indians inflicted about 50 casualties, Middleton cautiously continued his advance on **Batoche** (24 April 1885).

Fishdam Ford | 1780 | War of the American Revolution
  In pursuit of guerrilla General Thomas Sumter after his defeat at **Fishing Creek** (18 August), British cavalry under Major James Wemyss marched west against the rebels at Moore's Hill, in Chester County, South Carolina, where they collided to the south at Fishdam Ford. Wemyss was wounded and repulsed in a confused action, but Sumter was further pursued to **Blackstocks** (9 November 1780).

Fisher's Hill | 1864 | American Civil War (Eastern Theatre)
  Following defeat at the **Opequon**, Confederate commander Jubal A. Early retreated along the Shenandoah to Fisher's Hill, just south of Strasburg, Virginia, where he was attacked by pursuing Union General Philip Sheridan. Early was badly beaten—losing 1,200 casualties, 1,000 prisoners and 16 guns—and he soon suffered further defeat at **Tom's Brook** and **Cedar Creek** (21–22 September 1864).

Fishguard | 1797 | French Revolutionary Wars (1st Coalition)
  Shortly after a failed French invasion of Ireland at **Bantry Bay**, Captain Jean-Baptiste Laroque landed 1,400 French troops and ex-convicts near Fishguard in southwestern Wales. With insufficient food and weapons, the demoralised French under American adventurer Colonel William Tate surrendered next day to John Campbell Lord Cawdor without a shot fired (23 February 1797).

Fish Hook | 1970 | Vietnam War
  See **Cambodia**

Fishing Creek ▌ 1780 ▌ War of the American Revolution

Immediately after routing the rebels at **Camden**, British commander Charles Earl Cornwallis sent cavalry leader Colonel Banastre Tarleton after partisan Colonel Thomas Sumter, marching north with loot from **Wateree Ferry**. Catching Sumter at Fishing Creek, South Carolina, Tarleton virtually destroyed his force and recovered British prisoners as well as the looted supplies (18 August 1780).

Fish River ▌ 1781 ▌ 1st Cape Frontier War

When Xhosa crossed the Fish River into Dutch South Africa's Zuurveld (modern Bathurst and Albany), eastern border commander Adriaan van Jaarsveld attacked with 92 whites and 40 Khoi. Rarabe's brother Langa withdrew, but other Chiefs would not. After two months of fighting along the Fish, the Xhosa were driven out, ending the first Frontier War (23 May–19 July 1781).

Fish River ▌ 1819 ▌ 5th Cape Frontier War

The Xhosa Prophet Nxele was heavily repulsed attacking **Grahamstown** in Cape Colony and withdrew east pursued by British Colonel Thomas Willshire and Boers under Andries Stockenstrom. At the mouth of the Fish River, Nxele attacked the Boers and was driven off with terrible losses. He then surrendered near Trompettersdrif and later drowned while escaping from custody (13 August 1819).

Fish River ▌ 1851 ▌ 8th Cape Frontier War

While British forces advanced to the **Waterkloof**, further south Colonel George Mackinnon led 1,000 troops and 300 Mfengo levies against Xhosa on the Fish, 30 miles northeast of Grahamstown. In a serious incident, an isolated company under Captain William J. Oldham was attacked with 32 killed and 21 wounded, although Mackinnon eventually secured the area (September 1851).

Fismes ▌ 1814 ▌ Napoleonic Wars (French Campaign)

As General Gebhard von Blucher's Prussian-Russian army advanced towards the French capital, they met a force under Marshal Auguste Marmont at Fismes, west of **Rheims**, where Marmont was repulsed in a sharp action. As a result, Napoleon Bonaparte abandoned Rheims, while the Allies felt they could ignore the French Emperor and continue the drive on Paris (17 March 1814).

Fiume ▌ 1919 ▌ D'Annunzio's Insurrection

Italy and Yugoslavia disputed post-war possession of the Dalmation port of Fiume and Italian adventurer Gabriele D'Annunzio led volunteers to seize the city. When the Treaty of Rapallo declared Fiume independent, D'Annunzio declared war on Italy but withdrew under Italian bombardment. Benito Mussolini annexed Fiume in 1923 (12 September–27 December 1919).

Five Forks ▌ 1865 ▌ American Civil War (Eastern Theatre)

With Union forces attacking his defences southwest of **Petersburg**, Virginia, Confederate commander Robert E. Lee ordered General George Pickett to hold the crossroads at Five Forks, northwest of **Dinwiddie Court House**. Union commander Philip Sheridan secured a brilliant victory—taking over 5,000 prisoners—which is said to have decided the fate of Petersburg (1 April 1865).

Flamanda ▌ 1916 ▌ World War I (Balkan Front)

While August von Mackensen campaigned down the Danube from **Tutrakan** towards **Constanta**, Romanian commander Alexandru Averescu attempted a counter-offensive further upriver between Zimnicea and Flamanda. The Romanian crossing into Bulgaria was a disorganised shambles and, after defeat near Flamanda, their offensive was abandoned (29 September–3 October 1916).

Flamborough Head ▌ 1779 ▌ War of the American Revolution

American John Paul Jones led a small squadron against a Baltic convoy off Yorkshire near Flamborough Head, where his converted merchantman *Bonhomme Richard* engaged the British frigate *Serapis* under Captain Richard Pearson. In one of America's most famous naval actions, Jones forced Pearson to surrender as his own ship sank, then took the captured convoy to Texel (23 September 1779).

Flanders **|** 1914 **|** World War I (Western Front)

In bloody action fought across Flanders, the Allies and Germans struggled for advantage, from the **Yser** in the north, through **Langemark**, **Ypres**, **Gheluvelt**, **Nonne Boschen**, **Messines** and **Armentières** to **La Bassée**. After shocking losses on both sides, the line stabilised, marking the end of mobility and the start of trench warfare (10 October–30 November 1914).

Flanders **|** 1918 **|** World War I (Western Front)

On the offensive against the northern end of the **Hindenburg Line**, King Albert of Belgium, with General Sir Herbert Plumer and French under Jean Degoutte, advanced between Lille and the coast against General Friedrich von Arnim. Passchendaele, Dixmude and Armentières were quickly taken and the Allies then advanced on **Courtrai** (28 September–10 October 1918).

Flanders Ridges **|** 1917 **|** World War I (Western Front)

See **Ypres**

Fleetwood Hill **|** 1863 **|** American Civil War (Eastern Theatre)

See **Brandy Station**

Flers-Courcelette **|** 1916 **|** World War I (Western Front)

General Sir Henry Rawlinson led a fresh assault in the Battle of the **Somme**, attacking on an extended front northeast from **Pozières**, supported by the first use of tanks on the Western Front. The Allies secured considerable territory, capturing Martinpuich, Flers and Courcelette, but suffered very heavy losses before German reinforcements stabilised the front (15–22 September 1916).

Fleurus **|** 1622 **|** Thirty Years War (Palatinate War)

Withdrawing after defeat at **Höchst** in June, Protestants under Count Ernst von Mansfeld and Christian of Brunswick marched west towards Bergen-op-Zoom, besieged by General Ambrogio de Spinola. At Fleurus, near Charleroi, Spanish General Gonzalo Fernández de Cordoba was defeated attempting to block them. Six weeks later (4 October) Bergen was relieved (29 August 1622).

Fleurus **|** 1690 **|** War of the Grand Alliance

Following French defeat at **Walcourt** at the hands of Prince George Frederic of Waldeck, command was given to Duke Francois Henri of Luxembourg, who gained his revenge at Fleurus, northeast of Charleroi. Waldeck's German-Spanish-English army was decisively defeated, with massive losses in casualties and prisoners, and Luxembourg went on to secure Flanders (1 July 1690).

Fleurus **|** 1794 **|** French Revolutionary Wars (1st Coalition)

The Austrian-British-Hanoverian army of Friedrich Josias Prince of Saxe-Coburg, advancing to relieve the siege of **Charleroi**, arrived one day late to prevent its surrender and launched a large-scale attack on French positions to the northeast at Fleurus. Coburg was routed after a counter-attack led by General Jean-Baptiste Jourdan and Austria abandoned the Netherlands (26 June 1794).

Fleury (1st) **|** 1916 **|** World War I (Western Front)

General Konstantin Schmidt von Knobelsdorf renewed the offensive northeast of **Verdun**, launching a massive bombardment with gas around Fleury and nearby fortifications at Thiaumont. However, a French counter-attack under General Charles Mangin prevented a breakthrough to Souville and the German offensive stalled, with troops diverted to the **Somme** (23 June–1 July 1916).

**Fleury (2nd) I 1916 I World War I
(Western Front)**

In a third attack northeast of **Verdun**, Germans again tried to break through around Fleury towards **Souville**. General Robert Nivelle's defence held firm and the Germans were repulsed. Generals Erich von Falkenhayn and Konstantin Schmidt von Knobelsdorf were replaced and a lull followed until the French offensive towards **Douaumont** (1 August–6 September 1916).

**Flodden I 1513 I Anglo-Scottish
Royal Wars**

Despite a previous cross-border raid being beaten at **Broomhouse** in August, James IV of Scotland invaded England, where Henry VIII sent Thomas Howard Earl of Surrey to meet him in a bloody engagement at Flodden, south of the Tweed near Branxton. While both sides lost heavily, King James and 12 earls were killed in a disastrous defeat and the Scots withdrew (9 September 1513).

**Florence I 405 I Goth Invasion of the
Roman Empire**
See **Faesulae**

**Florence I 1529–1530 I 2nd Habsburg-
Valois War**

When Spain and France made peace in Italy, Florence continued the war and was besieged by Imperial Prince Philibert of Orange. The Florentine Francisco Ferrucci broke out after ten months but was routed at Gavinana in the Pistoia Mountains, where both Ferrucci and Philibert were killed (2 August). Florence then surrendered, ending the Republic (14 October 1529–12 August 1530).

Flores I 1591 I Anglo-Spanish Wars
See **Azores**

**Flores Fight I 1839 I Texan Wars
of Independence**
See **San Gabriels, Texas**

Flores Sea I 1942 I World War II (Pacific)
See **Madoera Strait**

**Florida, Bolivia I 1814 I Argentine War of
Independence**

Sent to organise resistance in the Santa Cruz area of modern Bolivia, Argentine guerrilla leader Ignacio Warnes, under General Juan Antonio Alvarez de Arenales, met and defeated a Spanish Royalist force at Florida, then marched 50 miles northeast to seize the city of Santa Cruz. After subsequent Argentine defeats in the east of the country, Warnes was killed at **Parí** (25 May 1814).

Florida, USA I 1814 I War of 1812

While escorting a British convoy from Havana to Bermuda, the brig *Epervier* (Commander Richard Wales) was attacked off the coast of Florida by the American sloop *Peacock* (Captain Lewis Warrington). Wales was forced to strike his colours when the smaller British ship was dismasted and heavily damaged with eight killed and 15 wounded. However, the convoy escaped (29 April 1814).

Florina I 1912 I 1st Balkan War
See **Monastir**

**Florina I 1916 I World War I
(Balkan Front)**

With Romania about to enter the war, Allied forces under General Maurice Sarrail attempted a diversionary offensive into Serbia from **Salonika**. Bulgarians and Germans on the western flank launched a massive pre-emptive attack against the Serbs around Florina, but after heavy fighting, the Serbs held firm and the struggle died down until a new advance towards **Monastir** (15–27 August 1916).

Florina I 1947 I Greek Civil War

Determined to establish a headquarters in northern Greece, Communist commander Markos Vaphiadis led about 650 men against Florina, where a fifth column rising failed to eventuate and he was repulsed after five hours. When Vaphiadis attacked again four days later, a stronger government force with air support drove him off with heavy losses (28 May & 1 June 1947).

Florina I 1949 I Greek Civil War

Communist leader Nikos Zakhariadis took command from "defeatist" Markos Vaphiadis after **Kastoria** and sent over 4,000 men against Florina, where they secured part of the town. Attacked by government forces, with massive air support, the insurgents were driven out with over 1,000 casualties. They then withdrew south to their stronghold around **Vitsi** (12–16 February 1949).

Flowing Springs I 1864 I American Civil War (Eastern Theatre)
See **Summit Point**

Flushing I 1809 I Napoleonic Wars (5th Coalition)

As part of the diversionary expedition to **Walcheran** Island guarding Antwerp, British forces led by General Sir John Pitt Lord Chatham laid siege to Flushing, held by a 5,000-strong garrison under General Louis-Claude Monnet. After a bold defence, Monnet was forced to capitulate, for which he was court-martialled. However, the British expedition overall was a costly disaster (2–15 August 1809).

Focsani I 1789 I Catherine the Great's 2nd Turkish War

Russian forces under General Alexander Suvurov advanced into Turkish Wallachia, where they joined with Austrian Prince Friedrich Josias of Saxe-Coburg to attack the Turks under Mustapha Pasha at Focsani in Moldavia (modern Romania). The Turkish camp fell by storm with heavy losses and the routed survivors fled, abandoning a massive booty of cannon and stores (20 July 1789).

Focsani I 1917 I World War I (Balkan Front)
See **Maracesti**

Foggia I 1943 I World War II (Southern Europe)

While Anglo-American forces landed in southwestern Italy at **Salerno**, British General Sir Bernard Montgomery raced up the east coast after landing at Messina and Taranto, heading for the strategic airfield at Foggia. Montgomery seized Foggia—the same day **Naples** fell—to bring southern Europe within range of Allied bombers. He then advanced north against **Termoli** (1 October 1943).

Foix I 1812 I Napoleonic Wars (Peninsular Campaign)

With French forces in Spain occupied with the siege of **Valencia**, Spanish General Pedro Sarsfield led a cheeky raid across the border and temporarily seized and ransomed the French town of Foix, 45 miles south of Toulouse on the Ariege in the foothills of the Pyrenees. Although the action had little strategic value, it was a welcome boost to Allied morale (19 February 1812).

Folck's Mill I 1864 I American Civil War (Eastern Theatre)
See **Cumberland**

Fombio I 1796 I French Revolutionary Wars (1st Coalition)
See **Piacenza**

Fondouk Pass I 1943 I World War II (Northern Africa)

As British forces broke through the **Mareth Line** into southern Tunisia, American tanks and infantry under General Charles Ryder circled west towards Fondouk Pass. Despite heavy air support, the attack failed against intense German defence. British and Americans then combined to smash their way through the Pass but too late to cut off the retreating Axis army (27–30 March & 8–9 April 1943).

Fontaine-Française I 1595 I 9th French War of Religion

When Phillip II of Spain refused to recognise Henry IV of France and supported the dubious claim of his own daughter Elizabeth, Henry declared war on Spain. A Spanish invasion of French Burgundy from Milan was repulsed at Fontaine-Française, northeast of Dijon, but a further Spanish invasion from the Netherlands seized territory in the northwest (9 June 1595).

Fontana Fredda ▎ 1809 ▎ Napoleonic Wars (5th Coalition)
See **Sacile**

Fontenailles ▎ 841 ▎ Frankish War of Succession
See **Fontenoy, France**

Fontenatum ▎ 841 ▎ Frankish War of Succession
See **Fontenoy, France**

Fontenay ▎ 1793 ▎ French Revolutionary Wars (Vendée War)
Royalist leader Maurice d'Elbée secured victory at **Thouars** for the counter-revolution in western France, then advanced south towards Fontenay-le-Comte. At nearby Pissotte, the rebels were routed by Republican General Francois Chalbos, with d'Elbée wounded. A fresh attack nine days later drove Chalbos out and the Royalists captured valuable arms and stores (16 & 26 May 1793).

Fontenoy, Belgium ▎ 1745 ▎ War of the Austrian Succession
Having initially respected the neutrality of the Austrian Netherlands, Louis XV of France and Marshal Maurice de Saxe took an army into Flanders to besiege Tournai. Five miles southeast at Fontenoy, Saxe defeated a large English-Austrian-Dutch-Hanoverian relief force under William Augustus Duke of Cumberland. He then went on to take Tournai and all of Flanders (11 May 1745).

Fontenoy, France ▎ 841 ▎ Frankish War of Succession
Amid protracted civil war for the Frankish crown following the death of Charlemagne, Emperor Lothair I met his brothers Ludwig the German and Charles the Bold at Fontenoy, near Auxerre in central France. The decisive battle which became known as the "Judgement of God" saw Lothair suffer a heavy defeat, leading to the Treaty of Verdun and partition of the empire (25 June 841).

Foochow ▎ 1884 ▎ Sino-French War
See **Fuzhou**

Foochow ▎ 1926 ▎ 1st Chinese Revolutionary Civil War
See **Fuzhou**

Forbach ▎ 1870 ▎ Franco-Prussian War
See **Spicheren**

Force Z ▎ 1941 ▎ World War II (Pacific)
See *Prince of Wales* and *Repulse*

Ford ▎ 1864 ▎ American Civil War (Eastern Theatre)
See **North Anna**

Ford of the Biscuits ▎ 1594 ▎ O'Donnell's Rebellion
In a prelude to the Tyrone Rebellion, Irish rebels Hugh O'Donnell and Cormac O'Neill (brother of the Earl of Tyrone) ambushed government troops sent to relieve Enniskillen, Ulster. At the nearby River Arney, the English under Sir Henry Duke and Sir Edward Herbert were defeated and lost over 100 men. The battle was named for biscuit rations spilled in the fighting (7 August 1594).

Formigny ▎ 1450 ▎ Hundred Years War
At the conclusion of a five-year truce, France invaded English Normandy and Sir Thomas Kyriel took a fresh army to support Edmund Beaufort Duke of Somerset. Marching from Cherbourg to relieve **Caen**, Kyriel was routed and captured at Formigny by Count Arthur of Richemont and Count Charles of Clermont. Defeat at Formigny led directly to England losing Normandy (15 April 1450).

Fornham ▎ 1173 ▎ Anglo-Norman Rebellion
With Henry II of England away in France, Robert Beaumont Earl of Leicester and his Flemish mercenaries joined with Hugh Bigod Earl of Norfolk supporting the King's eldest son "Young King Henry." A Royalist army under Richard de Lucy and Humphrey de Bohun utterly defeated the rebellious Barons at Fornham St Genevieve in Suffolk and Leicester was captured (16 October 1173).

Fornovo I 1495 I Italian War of Charles VIII

Charles VIII of France marching north from his conquest of Naples was blocked by the mercenary army of Milan and Venice under Giovanni Gonzago. At Fornovo, west of Parma, French Generals Louis de la Trémouille and Gian Giacomo Trivulzio drove the Italians off. Charles continued his withdrawal to France and defeat at **Aversa** the next year cost him Naples (6 July 1495).

Fort Alabama I 1836 I 2nd Seminole Indian War

See **Thonotosassa**

Fort Anderson I 1863 I American Civil War (Eastern Theatre)

On campaign against the Union army in North Carolina, General James Longstreet sent Confederate Generals Daniel H. Hill and James J. Pettigrew against the powerful Union base at New Bern, at the mouth of the Neuse. At Fort Anderson, the Confederates were heavily repulsed by Colonel Hiram Anderson and withdrew north to **Washington**, North Carolina (13–15 March 1863).

Fort Anderson I 1865 I American Civil War (Eastern Theatre)

See **Wilmington**

Fort Anne I 1777 I War of the American Revolution

British General John Burgoyne pursuing Colonel Pierce Long down Lake Champlain from **Fort Ticonderoga** was too slow to trap the Americans at Skenesboro and sent Colonel John Hill against Fort Anne, where Long was reinforced by Colonel Henry van Rensselaer. Hill suffered a costly defeat, but with Burgoyne approaching, the rebels burned the fort and continued south (8 July 1777).

Fort Apalachicola I 1816 I 1st Seminole Indian War

See **Negro Fort**

Fort Balaguer I 1813 I Napoleonic Wars (Peninsular Campaign)

In one of the few successes of the disastrously incompetent Allied siege of **Tarragona**, General Sir John Murray sent Colonel William Prevost south against French-held Fort Balaguer, guarding the coast road from Valencia. While Prevost succeeded in capturing the fort, a few days later the attack on Tarragona was abandoned and Murray withdrew by sea to Alicante (3–7 June 1813).

Fort Bisland I 1863 I American Civil War (Lower Seaboard)

On the offensive in western Louisiana, Union forces under General Nathaniel P. Banks advanced up the Bayou Teche against Confederate General Richard Taylor and Colonel Tom Green at Fort Bisland, west of Berwick City. Heavy fighting forced Taylor to withdraw his outnumbered force northwest through a skilled rearguard action further upstream at **Irish Bend** (12–13 April 1863).

Fort Blakely I 1865 I American Civil War (Western Theatre)

See **Blakely**

Fort Bowyer I 1814 I War of 1812

On the offensive in the Gulf of Mexico, British Commodore William Percy and Colonel Edward Nicholls attacked Fort Bowyer (modern Fort Morgan) guarding Mobile Bay, held by a small force under Major William Lawrence. Landing after heavy bombardment, the British were badly beaten with 160 killed and the sloop *Hermes* sunk before they retreated to **Pensacola** (12–15 September 1814).

Fort Bowyer I 1815 I War of 1812

Following defeat at **New Orleans**, British forces under Admiral Sir Alexander Cochrane and General John Lambert attacked Fort Bowyer (modern Fort Morgan) at the mouth of Mobile Bay, which had repulsed an earlier assault. Major William Lawrence's garrison was overwhelmed and the British were threatening Mobile itself when news arrived that the war was over (8–12 February 1815).

Fort Brooke ▌ 1863 ▌ American Civil War (Lower Seaboard)

Two Union ships under Captain Alexander A. Semmes led an expedition into Hillsborough Bay, Florida, where they bombarded Fort Brooke, just east of Tampa, defended by Captain John Westcott. A landing party then captured two Confederate ships on the nearby Hillsborough River and a third was scuttled before the Union expedition withdrew (16–18 October 1863).

Fort Carey ▌ 1780 ▌ War of the American Revolution
See **Wateree Ferry**

Fort Carillon ▌ 1758 ▌ Seven Years War (North America)
See **Fort Ticonderoga**

Fort Caspar ▌ 1865 ▌ Cheyenne-Arapaho Indian War
See **Platte Bridge**

Fort Clinton ▌ 1777 ▌ War of the American Revolution

Campaigning north from New York City, British General Sir Henry Clinton attacked American fortresses on the Hudson. Fort Montgomery, held by Governor George Clinton, fell quickly, but nearby Fort Clinton, under his brother James Clinton, was strongly defended. It eventually fell after heavy losses on both sides, though the offensive failed to help the British at **Saratoga** (6 October 1777).

Fort Constantine ▌ 1836–1837 ▌ French Conquest of Algeria
See **Constantine**

Fort Darling ▌ 1862 ▌ American Civil War (Eastern Theatre)
See **Drewry's Bluff**

Fort Davidson ▌ 1864 ▌ American Civil War (Trans-Mississippi)

Confederate General Sterling Price started a large-scale expedition across Missouri by attacking Fort Davidson, at Pilot Knob north of Ironton, defended by General Thomas Ewing. The heavily outnumbered garrison inflicted over 1,500 casualties before escaping under cover of dark and the Union army regrouped to meet Price in western Missouri at **Lexington** (27 September 1864).

Fort Dearborn ▌ 1812 ▌ War of 1812

When American General William Hull was blockaded by the British in **Detroit**, he unwisely ordered Captain Nathan Heald to evacuate Fort Dearborn, on the site of modern Chicago. After abandoning the fort, the militia garrison and civilians were attacked by Potawatomi Indians. Many were massacred, though Heald was among the prisoners. Detroit surrendered next day (15 August 1812).

Fort Defiance ▌ 1836 ▌ 2nd Seminole Indian War

With the great Seminole leader Osceola threatening Fort Defiance outside Micanopy, Florida, garrison commander Major Julius Heilman led a bold counter-offensive, attempting an ambitious double envelopment. The Indians were repulsed after some hard fighting, but Heilman lacked the resources to complete his strategy and he returned to the fort (9 June 1836).

Fort del Or ▌ 1580 ▌ Geraldine Rebellion

Supporting James Fitzmaurice and his cousin Gerald Fitzgerald Earl of Desmond against Anglo-Scots colonisation of Ulster, Spanish and Italians under Sebastiano di San Guiseppe landed at Smerwick, where they were besieged in Fort del Or by Lord Arthur Grey de Wilton. After being forced to surrender, a reported 600 were massacred, though San Guiseppe survived (7–10 November 1580).

Fort De Russy ▌ 1864 ▌ American Civil War (Trans-Mississippi)

Union commander Nathaniel P. Banks opened his campaign up the Red River in Louisiana by sending Generals Andrew J. Smith and Joseph Mower against the partly completed Confederate Fort de Russy, below Alexandria. A bold assault from the landward side forced garrison commander Colonel William Byrd to surrender and Banks continued upriver towards **Mansfield** (14 March 1864).

Fort Donelson I 1862 I American Civil War (Western Theatre)

On the offensive in western Kentucky, Union General Ulysses S. Grant captured **Fort Henry** on the Tennessee River, then marched ten miles east against Fort Donelson on the Cumberland, held by Confederate Generals John B. Floyd, Gideon Pillow and Simon B. Buckner. After heavy fighting and naval bombardment, the fort and 12,000 men surrendered unconditionally (11–16 February 1862).

Fort Donelson I 1863 I American Civil War (Western Theatre)

Determined to disrupt Union shipping on the Cumberland, in Tennessee, Confederate commander Joseph Wheeler, supported by Generals Nathan B. Forrest and John A. Wharton, attacked Fort Donelson and nearby Dover. The heavily outnumbered garrison under Colonel Abner C. Harding refused to surrender and heavy fighting saw Wheeler forced to withdraw (3 February 1863).

Fort Drane (1st) I 1836 I 2nd Seminole Indian War

Amid fighting around Fort Drane, near Irvine, south of modern Gainesville, Florida, the great Seminole Chief Osceola launched an unexpected attack on the fortress itself. Most unusual for the time, Osceola attacked at night, but following two hours of fierce fighting after midnight, he was driven off and withdrew with only a few captured horses. The fort was later abandoned (20 April 1836).

Fort Drane (2nd) I 1836 I 2nd Seminole Indian War

Seminole Indians who occupied abandoned Fort Drane, south of Gainesville, Florida, were

later attacked in the open by Major Benjamin Pierce from nearby Fort Defiance. Chief Osceola narrowly escaped capture in heavy fighting before Pierce was forced to withdraw to Micanopy. Two months later, Osceola was lured out of the everglades and seized under a flag of truce (21 August 1836).

Fort Driant I 1944 I World War II (Western Europe)

As part of the assault on **Metz**, American forces under General LeRoy Irwin failed trying to storm the powerful Fort Driant. A second assault after massive bombardment penetrated tunnels under the fort before it too was repulsed with over 500 casualties. A third assault took the city of Metz, but Driant held out for another two weeks (27 September, 3–13 October & 9 November–8 December 1944).

Fort Duquesne I 1758 I Seven Years War (North America)

Three years after the British disaster at **Monongahela**, Brigadier John Forbes led a fresh advance on the French at Fort Duquesne (modern Pittsburgh, Pennsylvania). A patrol by Major James Grant was surrounded and suffered heavy losses (14 September). By the time a full attack was prepared, French Captain Francois-Marie de Lignery blew up the fort and fled (23 November 1758).

Fort Erie I 1812 I War of 1812

In a courageous raid across the Niagara River with 100 men in two longboats, American Captain Jesse Elliott seized two British brigs under the guns of Fort Erie. *Caledonia* (Lieutenant Robert Irvine) was sailed across river to Black Rock, but *Detroit* (Lieutenant Frederic Rolette)—the former American vessel *Adams*—was grounded mid-river, then stripped and destroyed (8–9 October 1812).

Fort Erie (1st) I 1814 I War of 1812

American General Jacob Brown led a fresh offensive across the southern Niagara River, taking 3,500 men into Canada to attack Fort Erie, which had been recaptured by the British a year earlier in the offensive following victory at **Stoney Creek**. Major Thomas Buck surrendered the strategic fort and the Americans marched north against General Sir Phineas Riall at **Chippewa** (2–3 July 1814).

Fort Erie (2nd) I 1814 I War of 1812

Advancing against the Americans on the Canadian shore of the Niagara days after victory at **Lundy's Lane**, British General Sir Gordon Drummond besieged General Edmund Gaines at Fort Erie. A major assault was repulsed with heavy losses (15 August) and, after a bloody sortie (17 September), General George Izard blew up the fort and withdrew across the river (4 August–5 November 1814).

Fort Fisher I 1864 I American Civil War (Eastern Theatre)

In an expedition against the vital Confederate port of Wilmington, North Carolina, Admiral David D. Porter and General Benjamin F. Butler led a combined Union assault on nearby Fort Fisher. Butler was driven off by a determined Confederate Division led by General Robert F. Hoke and the garrison under Colonel Charles Lamb. He was later relieved of command (7–27 December 1864).

Fort Fisher I 1865 I American Civil War (Eastern Theatre)

A renewed attempt on Fort Fisher, below Wilmington, North Carolina, saw Union General Alfred H. Terry, supported by Admiral David D. Porter, defeat Confederate General Robert F. Hoke under General Braxton Bragg. Colonel Charles Lamb surrendered the fort after heavy shelling and infantry assault and Terry ascended the Cape Fear against **Wilmington** (13–17 January 1865).

Fort Foster I 1836 I 2nd Seminole Indian War
See **Thonotosassa**

Fort Foureau I 1900 I French Conquest of Chad
See **Kousséri**

Fort Frontenac I 1758 I Seven Years War (North America)

Two years after British defeat at **Oswego** on Lake Ontario, British Colonel John Bradstreet regained the southern shore of the lake and sailed against Fort Frontenac (modern Kingston) guarding the entrance to the St Lawrence. After a bold assault, French Commandant Pierre Jacques Payen de Noyan surrendered his small garrison and a massive supply of guns and stores (27 August 1758).

Fort George, Florida I 1781 I War of the American Revolution
See **Pensacola**

Fort George, Quebec I 1813 I War of 1812

Colonel Winfield Scott invaded Canada across the Niagara River on Lake Ontario and attacked the British at Fort George, supported by the American fleet under Commodore Isaac Chauncey. With over 350 casualties, British General John Vincent spiked his guns and withdrew west, counter-attacking within days at **Stoney Creek**. America abandoned the fort in December (27 May 1813).

Fort Harrison I 1864 I American Civil War (Eastern Theatre)
See **New Market Heights**

Fort Hatteras I 1861 I American Civil War (Eastern Theatre)

On campaign against blockade-runners off North Carolina, Union General Benjamin F. Butler and Admiral Silas H. Stringham attacked the Confederate Forts Hatteras and Clark on Hatteras Island, held by Colonel William F. Martin. Following a bold amphibious attack, which cost just a handful of Union casualties, Martin surrendered the forts and about 700 men (28–29 August 1861).

Fort Henry I 1862 I American Civil War (Western Theatre)

With the Confederates defeated in eastern Kentucky at **Mill Springs**, a separate Union force under General Ulysses S. Grant advanced in western Kentucky against Fort Henry on the Tennessee River, defended by General Lloyd Tilghman. The fort surrendered to Flag-Officer Andrew H. Foote after bombardment from the river and Grant marched east against **Fort Donelson** (6 February 1862).

Fort Hindman I 1863 I American Civil War (Western Theatre)
See **Arkansas Post**

Fort Huger I 1863 I American Civil War (Eastern Theatre)
See **Suffolk**

Fort Itala I 1901 I 2nd Anglo-Boer War
Over-confident after victory at **Blood River Poort**, days later Boer commander Louis Botha marched into Natal and sent his brother Christiaan against Fort Itala, east of Dundee, defended by Major Archibald Chapman. A reckless frontal assault by the Boers was driven off with costly losses and, after a further repulse at nearby Fort Prospect, the commando withdrew north (26 September 1901).

Fort Jesus I 1696–1698 I Later Portuguese Wars in East Africa
See **Mombasa**

Fort King I 1840 I 2nd Seminole Indian War
On patrol outside Fort King, near modern Ocala, Florida, 18 men under Captain Gabriel Rains were ambushed by a much larger Seminole force led by Halleck Tustenuggee. In fierce fighting, with four soldiers and three Indians killed, Rains was severely wounded but got his men back to the fort. For his courage, he was later brevetted Major. Tustenuggee was also wounded (28 April 1840).

Fort Laramie I 1854 I Sioux Indian Wars
Marching east from Fort Laramie, in southeastern Wyoming, 24-year-old Lieutenant John Grattan unwisely attempted to arrest some Brulé Sioux who had killed an emigrant's cow. Chief

Conquering Bear was fatally wounded in an exchange of fire and, in retribution, Grattan and his entire detachment of 29 were killed. The army was avenged a year later at **Ash Hollow** (18 August 1854).

Fort Lee I 1776 I War of the American Revolution
With **Fort Washington** on Manhattan Island secured by General William Howe, General Charles Earl Cornwallis crossed the Hudson against Fort Lee, just recently reinforced by American General George Washington. Attacking with 4,000 British and Hessian troops, Cornwallis seized Fort Lee and valuable military supplies, although Washington led his troops to safety (20 November 1776).

Fort Loudoun I 1760 I Cherokee Indian Wars
When Governor William Lyttelton of South Carolina unwisely provoked war against the Cherokee, Chief Oconostota besieged Fort Loudoun, near Vonore, Tennessee, held by Colonel Paul Demeré. Captain John Stuart negotiated a surrender, but the 200-strong garrison was butchered as they left for **Fort Prince George**. Stuart was captured and Demeré was tortured to death (8 August 1760).

Fort Loyal I 1690 I King William's War
Following French success against **Schenectady** and **Salmon Falls**, Rene Robinau de Portneuf and Augustine de Courtmanche soon led Canadians and Indians against Fort Loyal at Falmouth, near modern Portland, Maine, held by Captain Sylvanus Davis. When a British sortie was destroyed the garrison surrendered, but over 100 were butchered and Davis was held prisoner (16–20 May 1690).

Fort Macon I 1862 I American Civil War (Eastern Theatre)
Union General Ambrose E. Burnside led an expedition against the North Carolina coast, where he captured the key town of **New Bern**, on the Neuse, then sent Brigadier General John G. Parke southeast to the Atlantic against Fort

Macon. When his heavy guns arrived, Parke smashed the fort's defences and Colonel Moses J. White surrendered about 400 men (23 March–25 April 1862).

Fort McAllister I 1863 I American Civil War (Lower Seaboard)

In a naval assault on Fort McAllister, at Genesis Point outside Savannah, Georgia, three Union ironclads under Captain Percival Drayton, supported by gunboats and mortar schooners, bombarded the fortress, held by Captain George W. Anderson. The Union squadron was eventually forced to withdraw and Fort McAllister was not taken until almost two years later (3 March 1863).

Fort McAllister I 1864 I American Civil War (Western Theatre)

When Union commander William T. Sherman reached Savannah (10 December) after his "March to the Sea" through Georgia, General William B. Hazen attacked Major George W. Anderson at strategic Fort McAllister, southwest of the city. A bold assault saw Hazen take the fort by storm and, on the night of 20/21 December, the Confederates evacuated Savannah (13 December 1864).

Fort McHenry I 1814 I War of 1812

British General Robert Ross advanced to seize **Baltimore**, while Admiral Sir Alexander Cochrane's naval squadron moved upriver to bombard the city's defences at Fort McHenry, held by Major George Armistead. Ross was defeated and killed on land and, when the bombardment of the fort next day failed to make any impression, the entire force withdrew (13–14 September 1814).

Fort Meigs I 1813 I War of 1812

With Americans defeated west of Lake Erie at **Frenchtown** in January, British General Henry Proctor took a large force from Amherstburg up the Maumee to attack General William Harrison at the powerful new stockade at Fort Meigs. Proctor crushed part of a relief force under General Green Clay (**Dudley's Defeat**), but he lacked resources to take the fort and withdrew to Canada (1–5 May 1813).

Fort Mercer I 1777 I War of the American Revolution

After capturing Philadelphia with victory at **Brandywine**, British General Sir William Howe attacked Fort Mercer, on the west bank of the Hudson, held by Colonel Christopher Greene. During a poorly planned assault, Hessian General Car von Donop was heavily repulsed and killed (22 October). When **Fort Mifflin** opposite fell, Fort Mercer was finally evacuated (22 October–21 November 1777).

Fort Mifflin I 1777 I War of the American Revolution

Having captured Philadelphia following victory at **Brandywine**, British General Sir William Howe and his brother Admiral Richard Howe bombarded Fort Mifflin, downstream on the east bank of the Hudson, held by Colonel Samuel Smith (later, Major Simeon Thayer). The Americans withdrew after massive casualties and Howe turned against **Fort Mercer** (10 October–15 November 1777).

Fort Mims I 1813 I Creek Indian War

Creek under Red Eagle (William Weatherford) took advantage of America's war with Britain and followed action at **Burnt Corn** by attacking Major Daniel Beasley at Fort Mims, north of Mobile, Alabama. More than half the 500 militia and civilians in the fort were killed in a brutal assault. In November, the Americans were avenged at **Tallaseehatchee**, **Talladega** and **Autossee** (30 August 1813).

Fort Montgomery I 1777 I War of the American Revolution
See **Fort Clinton**

Fort Moultrie I 1776 I War of the American Revolution
See **Fort Sullivan**

Fort Necessity I 1754 I Seven Years War (North America)

Threatening Fort Duquesne (modern Pittsburgh, Pennsylvania), Colonel George Washington and about 150 Virginia militia defeated a French patrol at **Youghiogany**, but were driven back to Fort Necessity, near modern Uniontown, by French and Indians under Captain Louis Coulon de Villiers. Washington capitulated after nine hours' fighting and his force was released (3 July 1754).

Fort Niagara I 1759 I Seven Years War (North America)

British General John Prideaux advanced along the Mohawk to Lake Ontario and sailed west to besiege the strong French fortress at Niagara, defended by Captain Pierre Pouchot. Sir William Johnson took command after Prideaux was killed by a shell and, when Captain Francois-Marie de Lignery died in a failed relief attempt, Pouchot surrendered next day (June–25 July 1759).

Fort Niagara I 1813 I War of 1812

When American General John Boyd burned Newark before abandoning Fort George on the Niagara River and crossing back into America, British commander Sir Gordon Drummond sent Colonel John Murray across the river against Fort Niagara, where Captain Nathaniel Leonard was said to be drunk. Murray seized the fort at bayonet-point and took 350 prisoners (18 December 1813).

Fort Ninety-Six I 1781 I War of the American Revolution

General Nathanael Greene, pursuing the British into South Carolina, marched west towards the Savannah to besiege the powerful Fort Ninety-Six, held by Colonel John Cruger. Greene lost about 150 casualties and was unable to take the fort. He withdrew when Colonel Lord Francis Rawdon arrived with reinforcements, though the garrison was later evacuated to **Charleston** (22 May–19 June 1781).

Fort Oswego I 1756 I Seven Years War (North America)

See **Oswego**

Fort Peddie I 1846 I 7th Cape Frontier War

After victory at **Burnshill**, Xhosa forces advanced south into eastern Cape Colony against Colonel Martin Lindsay at Fort Peddie. Although a British supply train was destroyed at the Fish River (21 May), a massive assault on the fort was heavily repulsed (28 May). The garrison held out until Colonel Henry Somerset arrived to defeat the Xhosa at nearby **Gwanga** (30 April–7 June 1846).

Fort Phil Kearney I 1866–1867 I Red Cloud's War

Built in July 1866 to protect the Bozeman Trail from Wyoming to the goldfields of Montana, Fort Phil Kearney, south of modern Sheridan, immediately came under attack and was besieged following the **Wagon Box Fight** (August 1867). Despite being relieved, the so-called Fort Perilous became untenable and was finally abandoned in August 1868 as part of a truce with the Indians.

Fort Pillow I 1864 I American Civil War (Western Theatre)

Raiding Union communications, Confederate General Nathan B. Forrest destroyed **Paducah**, Kentucky, and within weeks marched west from Jackson against Fort Pillow, Tennessee, on the Mississippi, held by Major Lionel F. Booth. With Booth killed in heavy fighting, Major William F. Bradford surrendered and the Confederates reportedly murdered many black prisoners (12 April 1864).

Fort Pitt I 1763 I Pontiac's War

Near the start of Pontiac's War against the British, his Indian allies laid siege to Fort Pitt (modern Pittsburgh), commanded by the Swiss-born Captain Simeon Ecuyer. After intermittent assaults, there was a concentrated five-day attack (27 July–1 August) before the Indians withdrew to support the action at **Bushy Run**. The fort was relieved a week later (22 June–10 August 1763).

Fort Prince George I 1760 I Cherokee Indian Wars

When Governor William Lyttelton of South Carolina seized several Cherokee Chiefs and sent them to Fort Prince George as hostages, the fort came under siege by Chief Oconostota. After Captain Richard Cotymore was lured out and fatally wounded (16 February 1760), the Indian hostages were killed. But Oconostota lacked the forces to take the fort and turned northwest against **Fort Loudoun**.

Fort Prospect I 1901 I 2nd Anglo-Boer War
See **Fort Itala**

Fort Pulaski I 1862 I American Civil War (Lower Seaboard)

In an advance on Savannah, Georgia, Union forces under General David Hunter and Captain Quincy A. Gillmore attacked Fort Pulaski, on Cockpit Island, guarding the river approaches to the Confederate city. Although casualties were minimal, Gillmore's new rifled artillery caused heavy damage and Colonel Charles H. Olmstead surrendered the fort and 360 men (10–11 April 1862).

Fort Recovery I 1791 I Little Turtle's War
See **St Clair's Defeat**

Fort Recovery I 1794 I Little Turtle's War

Determined to secure the Ohio Valley, General Anthony Wayne advanced to the site of **St Clair's Defeat** in 1791 on the Wabash, southwest of modern Celina, and established Fort Recovery, which was soon besieged. An attack by Little Turtle of the Miami was heavily repulsed, after which the great Chief was replaced and he did not command the decisive action at **Fallen Timbers** (30 June 1794).

Fort Rice I 1865 I Cheyenne-Arapaho Indian War

A Cheyenne-Sioux force campaigning in North Dakota attacked strategic Fort Rice, on the Missouri south of Mandan, held by a strong garrison under Colonel John Pattee. About 300 warriors made repeated assaults but were heavily repulsed by steady infantry fire and howitzers. They then withdrew west into Montana and attacked two army columns on the **Powder River** (28 July 1865).

Fort Ridgely I 1862 I Sioux Indian Wars

Little Crow of the Santee Sioux led a rising in Minnesota, where he slaughtered settlers, then advanced on Fort Ridgely, south of modern Fairfax. A patrol was ambushed at nearby Redwood Ferry, with Captain John Marsh among the 24 killed. However, Fort Ridgely was reinforced by Lieutenant Tim Sheehan and repulsed two costly assaults by Little Crow and Big Eagle (20–22 August 1862).

Forts Jackson and St Philip I 1862 I American Civil War (Lower Seaboard)

Union Flag-Officer David G. Farragut advanced up the Mississippi towards the Confederate city of New Orleans, where he attacked the key defences at Forts Jackson and St Philip, defended by General Johnson K. Duncan and Commander John K. Mitchell. When Farragut's squadron passed the defences and seized **New Orleans** itself, these downstream forts surrendered (16–28 April 1862).

Fort St David I 1746 I 1st Carnatic War
See **Negapatam**

Fort St David I 1746–1748 I 1st Carnatic War

Having captured the main British base in southeastern India at **Madras**, French Governor General Joseph Dupleix marched south against Fort St David. The beleaguered garrison was reinforced by British Admiral Thomas Griffin (March 1747) and was later saved by Admiral Edward Boscawen, who went on to attack Dupleix at **Pondicherry** (19 December 1746–11 August 1748).

Fort St David I 1758 I Seven Years War (India)

As warfare resumed against Britain in India, newly arrived French Governor-General Comte Thomas Lally took a large force against the powerful British Fort St David, south of Pondicherry. After severe artillery damage and the arrival of a French fleet, the demoralised and poorly led garrison surrendered. Lally then moved inland to besiege **Tanjore** (29 April–2 June 1758).

Fort St George ▌ 1758–1759 ▌ Seven Years War (India)
See **Madras**

Fort St Joseph ▌ 1781 ▌ War of the American Revolution
When Spain entered the war, Governor Don Bernardo de Galvez of Lousiana captured **Mobile** in British West Florida (March 1780) then, to avenge an attack at **St Louis**, sent Captain Eugenio Pourré and a mixed force up the Mississippi towards Detroit. Pourré surprised and briefly seized the British garrison at Fort St Joseph, claiming the area for Spain before returning downstream (12 February 1781).

Fort St Philip ▌ 1862 ▌ American Civil War (Lower Seaboard)
See **Forts Jackson and St Philip**

Fort Sanders ▌ 1863 ▌ American Civil War (Western Theatre)
General James Longstreet, attempting to capture Knoxville, Tennessee, from Union commander Ambose E. Burnside, was checked to the south at **Campbell's Station** (16 November), then stormed Fort Sanders, to the northwest. Entangled in Union defences, Longstreet's force lost about 500 casualties and 300 prisoners and he withdrew northeast through **Bean's Station** (29 November 1863).

Fort Schlosser ▌ 1813 ▌ War of 1812
A cheeky raid across the Niagara River into New York State saw a small British force of militia and regulars under Colonel Thomas Clark attack Fort Schlosser, midway down the river opposite Chippewa. They withdrew after causing some damage and a larger-scale British assault occurred a few days later further south at **Black Rock** (5 July 1813).

Fort Schuyler ▌ 1777 ▌ War of the American Revolution
See **Fort Stanwix**

Fort Shelby ▌ 1814 ▌ War of 1812
See **Prairie du Chien**

Fort Sinquefield ▌ 1813 ▌ Creek Indian War
Two days after the massacre at **Fort Mims**, about 100 other Creeks under Prophet Francis (Hillis Hadjo) attacked nearby Fort Sinquefield, west of the Alabama near Grove Hill, held by 30 civilians and militia under Lieutenant James Bailey. Facing a spirited defence, the Indians were driven off with 11 killed—including Francis—and the garrison withdrew to Fort Madison (2 September 1813).

Fort Sitibaldi ▌ 1817 ▌ 3rd British-Maratha War
See **Sitibaldi**

Fort Smith ▌ 1863 ▌ American Civil War (Trans-Mississippi)
See **Devil's Backbone**

Fort Stanwix ▌ 1777 ▌ War of the American Revolution
Supporting the British offensive from Canada, Colonel Barry St Leger advanced down the Mohawk against Fort Stanwix (modern Rome, New York), held by Colonels Peter Gansevoort and Marnius Willett. A relief column was repulsed downstream at **Oriskany**, but when General Benedict Arnold's main force approached, St Leger abandoned his siege and retreated (3–23 August 1777).

Fort Stedman ▌ 1865 ▌ American Civil War (Eastern Theatre)
In a final offensive east from besieged **Petersburg**, Virginia, a dawn attack by General John B. Gordon captured Union Fort Stedman, very close to the Confederate Line. But the fort surrendered after a powerful counter-attack by Generals John G. Parke and John F. Hartranft. Gordon withdrew with 3,500 men lost, including 1,900 captured and Petersburg fell a week later (25 March 1865).

Fort Stephenson ▌ 1813 ▌ War of 1812
Repulsed from **Fort Meigs**, west of Lake Erie in May, British General Henry Proctor made a further half-hearted assault (28 July) then advanced up the Sandusky in Ohio against Fort Stephenson, held by Major George Croghan.

Following an ineffective bombardment, Proctor and his Indian allies were driven off. Naval defeat on **Lake Erie** the next month ended his campaign (1 August 1813).

Fort Stevens I 1864 I American Civil War (Eastern Theatre)

Confederate General Jubal A. Early, invading Maryland after victory at **Lynchburg**, defeated a Union force at the **Monocacy**, then advanced on Washington. However, the delaying action enabled veterans under Generals Horatio G. Wright and Alexander McCook to reinforce the capital and, after defeat to the northwest at Fort Stevens, Early fell back through **Snicker's Ferry** (11–12 July 1864).

Fort Sullivan I 1776 I War of the American Revolution

With North Carolina Loyalists defeated at **Moore's Creek Bridge**, British Admiral Sir Peter Parker and General Henry Clinton took an expedition against South Carolina, bombarding Colonel William Moultrie at Fort Sullivan outside Charleston Harbour. The British fleet was damaged and driven off in a humiliating defeat and the position was renamed Fort Moultrie (28 June 1776).

Fort Sumter I 1861 I American Civil War (Lower Seaboard)

In the opening action of the war, Confederate General Pierre G. T. Beauregard demanded the surrender of the Union garrison of Fort Sumter in Charleston Harbour, South Carolina, defended by Major Robert Anderson, who capitulated following a heavy bombardment. While the shelling caused no casualties, the ensuing war cost the lives of over 620,000 soldiers (12–13 April 1861).

Fort Sumter I 1863 I American Civil War (Lower Seaboard)

See **Charleston Harbour**

Fort Texas I 1846 I American-Mexican War

As the war began, Mexican Generals Francisco Meija and Pedro de Ampudia bombarded and besieged Major Jacob Brown at Fort Texas, on the Rio Grande opposite Matamoros. Although Brown was killed, Captain Edgar Hawkins held off the Mexicans until relieved by General Zachary Taylor advancing through **Palo Alto**. Nearby modern Brownsville is named for Brown (3–9 May 1846).

Fort Ticonderoga I 1758 I Seven Years War (North America)

British General James Abercrombie renewed the offensive from Lake George in eastern New York, leading a strong force against Fort Ticonderoga (French Fort Carillon) where Marquis Louis de Montcalm had established effective defensive lines. Abercrombie withdrew after losing almost 2,000 men in a foolhardy frontal assault and was replaced by General Jeffrey Amherst (8 July 1758).

Fort Ticonderoga I 1759 I Seven Years War (North America)

A year after a costly British repulse at Fort Ticonderoga, on Lake Champlain in eastern New York, General Jeffrey Amherst led a fresh assault against the French position, now held by Chevalier Francois-Charles de Bourlamaque. The French blew up the magazine and withdrew after a brief action. A few days later Amherst also captured Crown Point, ten miles to the north (26 July 1759).

Fort Ticonderoga I 1775 I War of the American Revolution

At the start of the war, Americans Colonel Benedict Arnold and Major Ethan Allen attacked Fort Ticonderoga, on Lake Champlain, held by Captain William Dalaplace and 50 men. Surprised at dawn, Dalaplace surrendered and the Americans secured about 80 guns for the continuing siege of **Boston**. A detached company then marched north against **Crown Point** (10 May 1775).

Fort Ticonderoga I 1777 I War of the American Revolution

British General John Burgoyne launched a fresh offensive from Canada into New York, where he attacked the powerful Fort Ticonderoga, on the western shore of Lake Champlain, held by General Arthur St Clair. Heavily bombarded from the landward side, St Clair was forced to abandon the fort, evacuating by land and water through **Hubbardton** and **Fort Anne** (5–6 July 1777).

Fort Wagner I 1863 I American Civil War (Lower Seaboard)

Following a diversionary attack on the defences of **Charleston Harbour**, South Carolina, at **Grimball's Landing**, Union General Quincy Gillmore attacked further east at Fort Wagner, on Morris Island. The Union assault was repulsed by General Pierre G. T. Beauregard after costly fighting and the fort remained under siege until eventual Confederate evacuation (10 July–7 September 1863).

Fort Washington I 1776 I War of the American Revolution

Just weeks after victory at **White Plains**, British General William Howe attacked the isolated American Fort Washington, on the northern end of Manhattan Island, held by Colonel Robert Magaw. General George Washington reached nearby **Fort Lee** with reinforcements, but after intense fighting, Magaw surrendered, yielding massive supplies of guns and ammunition (16 November 1776).

Fort Wayne I 1790 I Little Turtle's War
See **Harmar's Defeat**

Fort White I 1850 I 8th Cape Frontier War

Defeated at **Boomah Pass**, near the Keiskamma River, British survivors withdrew to nearby Fort White, south of Burnshill, where they came under siege by the great Xhosa Chief Sandile. A force of just 120 men under Captain John Mansergh of the 6th Regiment of Foot held off the Xhosa for two days with steady volley fire and Sandile eventually had to withdraw (25–26 December 1850).

Fort William Henry, Maine I 1696 I King William's War

In the final North American action of the war, Pierre le Moyne d'Iberville led a land and sea attack against Fort William Henry at Pemaquid, near modern Bristol, Maine, held by Captain Pascoe Chubb. Supported by Abnaki Indians under Jean-Vincent de Saint Castin, d'Iberville forced the British garrison to surrender and they were transported to Boston (14–15 August 1696).

Fort William Henry, New York I 1757 I Seven Years War (North America)

Marquis Louis de Montcalm marching south from Ticonderoga took a large French and Indian force against Fort William Henry, at the head of Lake George in eastern New York. After heavy bombardment, Colonel George Monro surrendered in return for safe withdrawal, but the garrison were treacherously massacred by the Indians. Montcalm destroyed the fort and withdrew (4–9 August 1757).

Fort Zeelandia I 1661–1662 I Chinese Conquest of Taiwan

Defeated by the Manchu at **Nanjing** in 1659, Ming General Zheng Chenggong (known as Koxinga) withdrew to Dutch-held Taiwan and attacked Fort Zeelandia, in the southwest, near Tainan. A long siege cost about 1,600 Dutch lives before Governor Fredrik Coyet surrendered. The Ming held the island until defeat by the Manchu in July 1683 at **Penghu** (1 May 1661–1 February 1662).

Forum Gallorum I 43 BC I Wars of the Second Triumvirate

During renewed war after the murder of Julius Caesar, Decimus Brutus was besieged by Mark Antony at **Mutina** (modern Modena). At nearby Forum Gallorum, Antony ambushed and defeated a relief army under Gaius Vibius Pansa, who was fatally wounded. Antony was then attacked and routed by Aulus Hirtius and was forced back to his camp outside Mutina (14 April 43 BC).

Forum Trebronii I 251 I 1st Gothic War
See **Abrittus**

Fossalta I 1248 I Imperial-Papal Wars

Amid continuing warfare between the cities of northern Italy, pro-Papal Guelfs were forced out of Florence, triggering a major offensive by Bologna against Ghibelline leader Enzio (Hensius), son of Emperor Frederick II. At Fossalta, Philip Ugoni of Brescia led the Guelfs to a great victory. Enzio was captured and spent his remaining 22 years as a prisoner in Bologna (26 May 1248).

Foule Point I 1811 I Napoleonic Wars (5th Coalition)

Arriving at **Mauritius** to find it had already fallen, three French frigates under Captain Francois Roquebert headed for Madagascar, where they were attacked off Foule Point by Captain Charles Schomberg with three frigates and a brig. Sharp fighting saw Roquebert defeated and killed, while one other French ship surrendered at Tamatave and the third fled back to France (20 May 1811).

Four Courts I 1922 I Irish Civil War

When Irish Republican forces seized Dublin's Four Courts, they came under heavy attack by government forces under General Patrick Daly, supported by General Emmet Dalton. In action which marked the start of the war, artillery smashed the buildings, which were taken by storm. Commander Ernie O'Malley surrendered, though other forces held out in **O'Connell Street** (28–30 June 1922).

Four Days Battle I 1666 I 2nd Dutch War

After unwisely despatching Prince Rupert away down the English Channel, English Admiral George Monck was attacked off North Foreland by a large Dutch fleet under Mihiel de Ruyter. Monck was almost overwhelmed before

Rupert's return on the third day prevented total disaster. The English retreated to the Thames having lost 23 ships, while de Ruyter lost only four (11–14 June 1666).

Four Lakes I 1858 I Yakima Indian Wars

When a small Federal force was defeated at **Pine Creek** by Indians in Washington resisting removal to a reservation, Colonel George Wright took 600 men against rebel tribes in the Columbia Basin. At Four Lakes, just southwest of Spokane, Wright defeated a force of Coer d'Alanes, Spokanes and Palouses, with decisive victory a few days later on the **Spokane Plain** (1 September 1858).

Fowltown I 1817 I 1st Seminole Indian War

At war with the Seminole in southwestern Georgia, General Edmund Gaines ordered Major David Twigg against Chief Neamathla's village at Fowltown. Both sides suffered casualties in a sharp action and, after the Indians attacked an army patrol on the Apalachicola River, General Andrew Jackson invaded Spanish Florida and marched towards **Pensacola** (21 November 1817).

Foz d'Aronce I 1811 I Napoleonic Wars (Peninsular Campaign)

Marshal Michel Ney, retreating from the failed French invasion of Portugal, fought rearguard actions against Arthur Wellesley Lord Wellington at **Redhina**, **Cazal Novo** and **Condeixa**. However, with **Coimbra** occupied by the allies, Ney was forced northeast through Foz d'Aronce on the Ceira. In a rare reverse, he was driven back under shellfire at the cost of heavy losses (15 March 1811).

Fraga I 1134 I Early Christian Reconquest of Spain

During his offensive against Muslim Spain, King Alfonso I of Aragon—El Batallador, the fighter—won great victories at **Saragossa** and **Cutanda**. Besieging Fraga, west of Lérida, he suffered his first defeat at the hands of the brilliant new General Yahya Ben Gania and reinforcements from Cordova. Alfonso died two months later, apparently from battle wounds (17 July 1134).

France I 1940 I World War II (Western Europe)

As Germany swept into **Belgium** and the **Netherlands**, Panzers stormed across France from the **Ardennes** and raced for the coast. There were bold counter-attacks at **Laon** and **Arras**, but Paris fell, leaving perhaps 400,000 by-passed men to surrender on the useless Maginot Line. As the **Channel Ports** fell, survivors evacuated through **Dunkirk** and France capitulated (10 May–21 June 1940).

Frankenau I 1914 I World War I (Eastern Front)

See **Orlau-Frankenau**

Frankenhausen I 1525 I German Peasants' War

On campaign against peasant armies in Thuringia, Langrave Philipp of Hesse secured victory at Fulda (3 May), then was joined by Saxon troops advancing on rebel-held Mühlhausen. To the east at Frankenhausen, rebel leader Thomas Muntzer suffered a bloody, decisive defeat and was later tortured to death. Mühlhausen quickly surrendered, effectively ending the war in Thuringia (15 May 1525).

Frankfort on the Oder I 1631 I Thirty Years War (Swedish War)

Gustavus Adolphus advanced up the River Oder to divert the Imperial siege of Magdeburg and drove Catholic General Haimbald von Schaumberg back on Frankfort. The Swedish King took the city by storm and, although von Schaumberg escaped with some of the Imperial cavalry, the garrison was killed or captured and Frankfort was sacked, helping trigger the outrage at **Magdeburg** (13 April 1631).

Franklin I 1863 I American Civil War (Western Theatre)

Following Confederate victories south of Nashville, Tennessee, at **Thompson's Station**

and **Brentwood**, Confederate General Earl Van Dorn advanced on Franklin, defended by General Gordon Granger. A flank counter-attack by Union cavalry under General David S. Stanley almost led to disaster before Van Dorn was finally defeated and withdrew south to Spring Hill (10 April 1863).

Franklin I 1864 I American Civil War (Western Theatre)

As Confederate commander John B. Hood pursued General John M. Schofield north across Tennessee, he failed to trap the Union army at **Spring Hill**, then met Schofield again further north on the Harpeth River at Franklin. Leading a bloody front assault against strong defences, Hood suffered more than 6,000 casualties, yet continued his ill-fated advance on **Nashville** (30 November 1864).

Frastenz I 1499 I Swabian War

In their final struggle for freedom, the Swiss cantons defeated the Habsburg cities of the Swabian League at **Schwaderloch**, then Confederation forces under Heinrich Wolleb stormed the Germans heavily entrenched at Frastenz, on the River Ill, south of Feldkirch. The Swiss captured the camp in the face of heavy artillery fire at the cost of over 4,000 Swabian casualties (20 April 1499).

Fratesci I 1659 I Wallachian-Turkish War

Campaigning against the Turks close to the Danube, Mihnea III Radu of Wallachia defeated an Ottoman force at Fratesci, just north of Giurgiu. However, he was later overwhelmed and the battle was said to be the last victory over the Turks in Romania for more than 200 years. It was quickly followed by the Ottoman conquest of Transylvania in 1660 at **Gilau** and **Nagyvarad** (23 November 1659).

Fraubrunnen I 1375 I Guglers' War

During a truce in the Hundred Years War, Enguerrand VII, Sire de Coucy, took a large army of English and French mercenaries into Swiss Aargau, which he claimed from Duke Leopold III of Austria. After several failures, his troops (known as Guglers for their hooded cloaks) were decisively defeated at Fraubrunnen, northeast of Bern, by a Swiss-Bernese army and de Coucy withdrew (27 December 1375).

Frauenberg I 1525 I German Peasants' War

Peasant commander Wendel Hipler took the offensive in Franconia and seized Würzburg, then besieged nearby Frauenberg, held by Conrad III von Thuenguen (Bishop of Würzburg and Duke of Franconia). A failed assault by Florian Geyer cost over 400 casualties and the fortress held out until relieved by Georg Truchsess von Waldburg (5 June) after victory at **Königshofen** (15 May 1525).

Fraustadt I 1706 I 2nd "Great" Northern War

As Charles XII of Sweden marched against Russians under General George Ogilvie at Grodno in eastern Poland, Saxon-Russian reinforcements under General Johann Schullenberg were utterly routed at Fraustadt (modern Wschowa), southwest of Leszno, by Swedish General Karl Gustav Rehnskjold. The Russians at Grodno then withdrew without a battle (3 February 1706).

Frayser's Farm I 1862 I American Civil War (Eastern Theatre)

See **White Oak Swamp**

Fredericia I 1657 I 1st Northern War

Attacking the Danish mainland, Swedish forces under Count Karl Gustav Wrangel besieged the city of Fredericia in eastern Jutland. When Danish Grand Marshal Andre Bilde was killed, his garrison of over 3,000 surrendered and Denmark quickly sued for peace. However, war soon broke out again and Wrangel captured **Funen**, then besieged **Copenhagen** (24 October 1657).

Fredericia I 1849 I 1st Schleswig-Holstein War

In resumed hostilities against Frederick VII of Denmark, Schleswig and Holstein rebels and their German allies, led by Prussian General Eduard von Bonin, defeated the Danes at **Duppel**, then besieged Fredericia in eastern Jutland. A courageous Danish sortie then caused heavy German losses and Prussia made a separate armistice, leaving the Duchies to fight alone (5 May–6 July 1849).

Fredericksburg I 1862 I American Civil War (Eastern Theatre)

General Ambrose E. Burnside took command of the Union army after **Antietam**, advancing across Virginia against General Robert E. Lee to attack over the Rappahannock at Fredericksburg. After terrible losses in a frontal assault, which cost 13,000 Union and 5,000 Confederate casualties, Burnside was forced to withdraw. However, Lee was unable to follow up his victory (11–15 December 1862).

Fredericksburg I 1863 I American Civil War (Eastern Theatre)

On a fresh offensive into Virginia, Union commander Joseph Hooker crossed the Rappahannock at Fredericksburg and left General John Sedgewick to capture the town from Confederate General Jubal A. Early. Early was defeated and driven out, although at nearby **Salem Church** he helped repulse Sedgewick's attempt to reinforce Hooker at **Chancellorsville** (3 May 1863).

Fredericktown I 1861 I American Civil War (Trans-Mississippi)

Union Colonel Joseph B. Plummer resolved to secure southeast Missouri and marched west from the Mississippi against Fredericktown, which had already been seized by Colonel William P. Carlin from Pilot Knob. Confederate General M. Jeff Thompson's Missouri State Guard was badly defeated in battle nearby, then fled south towards Greenville and dispersed (21 October 1861).

Fredrikshald I 1718 I 2nd "Great" Northern War

Returning from exile after his disastrous defeat at **Poltava** in 1709, Charles XII of Sweden raised a fresh initiative against Danish Norway. While besieging Fredrikshald (modern Halden), he was shot dead and the campaign was abandoned, though naval action continued at **Osel** and **Grengam**. Persistent claims that the King was assassinated led to his exhumation as late as 1917 (22 December 1718).

Fredrikshamn | 1789 | 2nd Russo-Swedish War

A year after a previous ill-prepared venture was repulsed off **Hogland**, Gustav III of Sweden again assaulted Russian Fredrikshamn (modern Hamina) on the Gulf of Finland to open the way to St Petersburg. Gustav's army was heavily repulsed and the King withdrew after a Swedish naval defeat the same day in the **Svenskund**. He was beaten again a week later at sea off **Hogfors** (24 August 1789).

Fredrikshamn | 1790 | 2nd Russo-Swedish War

Gustav III of Sweden led a third attempt to capture Fredrikshamn (modern Hamina), on the Gulf of Finland, and to threaten St Petersburg, attacking a Russian flotilla at sea nearby. When the Russians withdrew short of ammunition, Gustav did not immediately follow up his victory and a Swedish assault on the port two days later was repulsed with heavy losses (15 & 17–18 May 1790).

Freeman's Farm | 1777 | War of the American Revolution

See **Saratoga, New York (1st)**

Freiberg, Saxony | 1762 | Seven Years War (Europe)

In the final action of the war, Prince Henry Ludwig, brother of Frederick II of Prussia, attacked a Saxon-Austrian force under Marshal Jean-Baptiste Serbelloni at Freiberg, southwest of Dresden. Supported by the great Prussian General Friedrich von Seydlitz, Prince Henry secured this relatively minor victory and the war soon came to an end (29 October 1762).

Freiburg, Württemberg | 1644 | Thirty Years War (Franco-Habsburg War)

After Baron Franz von Mercy's Bavarians captured Freiburg, Louis II Duke d'Enghien joined with Marshal Henri de Turenne in an heroic assault against entrenched positions. The French suffered terrible losses in two failed attacks and were repulsed attacking Mercy's rearguard as he withdrew. However, d'Enghien claimed the victory and secured the middle Rhine (4, 5 & 9 August 1644).

Freiburg, Württemberg | 1713 | War of the Spanish Succession

When Austria alone resumed the war against France, Marshal Claude Villars crossed the Rhine and, after capturing **Landau**, laid siege to Freiburg. Villars entered the city (30 September) after defeating Imperial commander Prince Eugène of Savoy in the field. Six weeks later the Governor surrendered the citadel and the war finally came to an end (22 September–13 November 1713).

Frenchman's Butte | 1885 | 2nd Riel Rebellion

Canadian cavalry General Thomas Strange pursued the Cree Indian Big Bear (Mistahimaskwa) west after victory at **Batoche**, attacking the elusive rebels two weeks later at Frenchman's Butte, in northwest Saskatchewan, near Fort Pitt, north of Lloydminster. However, the government forces were outflanked and repulsed and the Cree escaped further north towards **Loon Lake** (28 May 1885).

Frenchtown | 1813 | War of 1812

Determined to regain the initiative on Lake Erie after the loss of **Detroit**, American General James Winchester seized Frenchtown (modern Munroe, Michigan) on the Raisin River. A counter-attack across the ice by British Colonel Henry Proctor and Indians under Roundhead saw Winchester suffer heavy losses. He and 500 men surrendered and some were murdered (21 January 1813).

Fresnay | 1420 | Hundred Years War

Thomas Montacute Earl of Salisbury, advancing south from Alencon in northwestern France, took several towns, then besieged

Fresnay. A large Franco-Scottish relief force marching north from Le Mans under Marshal Pierre de Rieux (alias Rochefort) was routed by John Holland Earl of Huntingdon, who inflicted perhaps 3,000 casualties. Rieux was captured and Fresnay surrendered (3 March 1420).

Freteval | 1194 | French War of Richard I

Ransomed from captivity on his way home from the Crusades, Richard I—the Lion Heart—regained control of England, then sailed for France to recover land taken by his former Crusader ally King Phillip II Augustus. At Freteval, east of Le Mans, Richard defeated Phillip's army and forced him to yield the English domains. After a brief peace, their struggle resumed in 1198 at **Gisors** (3 July 1194).

Freyer's Farm | 1904 | German Colonial Wars in Africa

With Herero rebels fighting in the north of German Southwest Africa, Nama tribesmen in the south joined in and, at Freyer's Farm, east of Bersheba, Jakob Morenga ambushed a pursuing 30-strong detachment under Lieutenant Baron Oscar von Stempel. Four German officers were killed in the attack, including von Stempel, marking the start of the so-called Herero War (30 August 1904).

Frezenberg | 1915 | World War I (Western Front)

When British forces fell back to new defensive lines northeast of **Ypres** after action at **Gravenstafel** and **St Julien**, Duke Albrecht launched a fresh attack east of Ypres on the Frezenberg Ridge. In the offensive's turning point, new British commander Sir Herbert Plumer's stubborn defence held firm. The Germans soon made one final attempt at **Bellewaarde** (8–13 May 1915).

Fribourg | 1340 | Burgundian-Swiss Wars

Despite defeat at **Laupen** near Bern in 1339, the rival Swiss city of Fribourg and its Austrian and Burgundian allies continued the inter-city war until the Bernese army of Lord John of Bubenberg and Rudolf von Erlach drove the Fribourgers to their city wall and inflicted a heavy defeat. Two days later, Fribourg was stormed and much of it was burned to the ground (24–26 April 1340).

Friedberg, Bavaria | 1796 | French Revolutionary Wars (1st Coalition)

On the day that Austria defeated France at **Amberg**, another Austrian force under General Maximilian Latour fared less well further south at Friedberg, near **Augsburg**. Latour was routed by French General Jean Victor Moreau, although a further French defeat in the north at **Würzburg** forced Moreau to begin withdrawing towards the Rhine through **Biberach** (24 August 1796).

Friedberg, Hesse | 1796 | French Revolutionary Wars (1st Coalition)

Generals Jean-Baptiste Jourdan and Jean-Baptiste Kléber led a renewed French advance east of the Rhine, concentrating their forces north of Frankfurt against Austrian General Alexander Wartensleben, who had been ordered by Archduke Charles Louis to hold Friedberg. The Austrian right wing was routed in heavy fighting nearby and Wartensleben fell back on Frankfurt (10 July 1796).

Friedland | 1807 | Napoleonic Wars (4th Coalition)

A fresh spring offensive in eastern Prussia following the winter carnage at **Eylau** saw Russians under General Levin Bennigsen advance against Napoleon Bonaparte on the Alle River at nearby Friedland (modern Pravdinsk) without waiting for General Anton Lestocq's Prussians. The Russians lost massive casualties in a one-sided disaster and Tsar Alexander I sued for peace (14 June 1807).

Friedlingen | 1702 | War of the Spanish Succession

When Elector Maximilian Emanuel of Bavaria joined forces with France, Austrian commander Prince Louis Margrave of Baden was driven back across the Rhine from **Landau** by Duke Claude de Villars. In the Black Forest at Friedlingen, the French infantry was initially repulsed before a cavalry attack defeated Prince Louis.

Villars was created a Marshal of France (14 October 1702).

Friedrichstadt ▌ 1850 ▌ 1st Schleswig-Holstein War

Abandoned by Prussia after failure at **Fredericia** in mid-1849, Schleswig and Holstein fought on alone against Danish reoccupation and, after decisive defeat at **Idstedt** in July, the rebel Duchies made a final effort to storm the well-fortified town of Friedrichstadt on the Eider. They were bloodily repulsed after a week and the war ended with Danish rule reimposed (29 September–6 October 1850).

Frigidus ▌ 394 ▌ Later Roman Military Civil Wars

When the Frankish Roman General Arbogastes murdered Valentinian II, he had his ally Eugenius appointed Emperor. But aided by desertion in the opposing army, Theodosius, Emperor in the east, defeated the usurpers at the Frigidus River, east of Aquileia, near the Adriatic. Eugenius was executed, Arbogastes committed suicide, and the empire was briefly reunited (6 September 394).

Froeschwiller ▌ 1793 ▌ French Revolutionary Wars (1st Coalition)

Generals Charles Pichegru and Louis Lazare Hoche recovered from French defeat at **Kaiserslautern** and weeks later attacked Austrian General Dagobert Wurmser between Haguenau, on the Moder, north of Strasbourg, and the nearby village of Froeschwiller (Wörth). A confused five-day action saw Wurmser beaten and withdraw north to lose again at **Wissembourg** (18–22 December 1793).

Froeschwiller ▌ 1870 ▌ Franco-Prussian War

See **Wörth**

Frog Lake ▌ 1885 ▌ 2nd Riel Rebellion

While Canadian Indians besieged **Battleford**, the Cree Kapapamahchakwew (Wandering Spirit) and Ayimisis (son of Big Bear) attacked the settlement at Frog Lake, on the North Sas-

katchewan just inside Alberta, killing Indian agent Thomas Quinn and eight others. Wandering Spirit eluded defeat the following month at **Frenchman's Butte** but was eventually hanged for the deed (2 April 1885).

Frontenac ▌ 1758 ▌ Seven Years War (North America)

See **Fort Frontenac**

Frontier ▌ 1958 ▌ Algerian War

Determined to cut the flow of men and arms into Algeria, France built a 200-mile electrified fence along the Tunisian border and sent large forces to prevent the ALN breaking through. A series of brutal actions, collectively known as the Battle of the Frontier, cost the insurgents perhaps 6,000 killed or captured and gave France a significant tactical and strategic victory (January–June 1958).

Frontiers ▌ 1914 ▌ World War I (Western Front)

As German forces swept through Belgium towards France, French commander Joseph Joffre invaded Alsace and Lorraine, then turned north to try and stop the German onrush. The principal actions of the Battles of the Frontiers were fought at **Lorraine**, **Ardennes**, **Charleroi** and **Mons**, with a key siege at **Namur** and the famous rearguard action at **Le Cateau** (14–27 August 1914).

Front Royal ▌ 1862 ▌ American Civil War (Eastern Theatre)

After victory in the Shenandoah at **McDowell**, Confederate General Thomas "Stonewall" Jackson attacked Front Royal, Virginia. Supported by Colonel Richard Taylor's Louisiana Tigers, Jackson stormed the town and, at nearby Cedarville, forced the surrender of almost 900 Union troops, including commander Colonel John R. Kenly. He then marched north on **Winchester** (23 May 1862).

Front Royal ▌ 1864 ▌ American Civil War (Eastern Theatre)

See **Cedarville**

Fryeburg | 1725 | Dummer's War

Amid skirmishing with Indians in northern New England, Governor William Dummer of Massachusetts offered a bounty for Indian scalps. A raiding party under Captain John Lovewell was ambushed by Abnaki near modern Fryeburg, Maine, where Lovewell and 19 others were killed. The Indians also suffered heavy losses and withdrew. The fight effectively ended the war (8 May 1725).

Fucine Lake | 89 BC | Roman Social War

Fighting Rome over rights of citizenship, the Marsi and Samnite tribes of central Italy led an armed revolt, during which Roman commander Lucius Porcius Cato was attacked by the Marsi at the now-drained Fucine Lake (modern Fucino), in the Apennines near Arezzano. Cato was defeated and killed, but later the same year, the Italian allies were heavily defeated at **Asculum** and **Pompeii**.

Fuengirola | 1810 | Napoleonic Wars (Peninsular Campaign)

As a diversion to lure French General Francois Sébastiani from Malaga, a British-Polish force from Gibraltar under Andrew Lord Blayney landed by sea at nearby Fuengirola. Blayney intended to re-embark and attack unprotected Malaga, but he left it too late and was trapped at Fuengirola. Sébastiani routed the landing force and took Blayney prisoner (13–15 October 1810).

Fuentarrabia | 1638 | Thirty Years War (Franco-Habsburg War)

Prince Henry II de Bourbon Prince of Condé resolved to help France against Imperial Spain in the lowlands, invading Spain itself to assist Catalan rebels and in the futile hope of advancing towards Madrid. Outside the frontier fortress of Fuentarrabia, at the mouth of the Bidassao River, he was routed and his expedition ended in disaster, although France continued to aid the rebellion against Madrid.

Fuentarrabia | 1836 | 1st Carlist War

Following success near San Sebastian at **Hernani**, General Sir George de Lacy Evans of the British Legion took 5,000 men east against Spanish Carlists at Fuentarrabia. However, over-caution by General William Reid allowed the Carlists to secure a key bridge near the town. The bridge was taken after bloody fighting, though heavy losses forced Evans to abandon his offensive (11–13 July 1836).

Fuentarrabia | 1837 | 1st Carlist War
See **Irun**

Fuente de Cantos | 1810 | Napoleonic Wars (Peninsular Campaign)

Despite defeat at **Villagarcia**, a month later Spanish General Pedro La Romana renewed his advance towards Seville, supported by General George Madden's Portuguese cavalry. Facing a massive counter-attack by Marshal Édouard Mortier, La Romana began to withdraw, but at Fuente de Cantos, his rearguard under Madden and General Martin La Carrera was heavily defeated (15 September 1810).

Fuentes d'Onoro | 1811 | Napoleonic Wars (Peninsular Campaign)

As a French relief army approached the Allied siege of **Almeida**, Arthur Wellesley Lord Wellington marched south to the heights of Fuentes d'Onoro. In two separate engagements Marshal André Masséna was repulsed with heavy losses and withdrew. Meanwhile, the garrison of Almeida broke out and France lost its last foothold in Portugal (3 & 5 May 1811).

Fujigawa | 1180 | Gempei War

Recovering from disastrous defeat at **Ishibashiyama**, Minamoto Yoritomo quickly gathered a fresh army and again marched on Japan's ruling Taira. Securing a base at Kamakura, he surprised Taira Koremori at the Fujigawa, west of Mount Fuji. In the first major Minamoto victory, the Taira fled to Kyoto, but soon recovered to defeat Yoritomo's uncle Yukiie at the **Sunomata** (9 November 1180).

Fulford | 1066 | Norwegian Invasion of England

Harold Godwinson Earl of Wessex was no sooner elected King of England than he faced an invasion of Northumbria by Harald Hadrada of Norway, supported by Harold's own estranged brother Tostig. Just outside of York at Fulford, Harold's loyal brothers Edwin and Morcar were defeated and the King rushed north to meet the invaders at **Stamford Bridge** (20 September 1066).

Funen I 1658 I 1st Northern War

Having captured **Fredericia** and Danish Jutland, Charles X of Sweden and Count Karl Gustav Wrangel took advantage of an extreme winter to cross the frozen Little Belt and attack Funen Island. Despite Danish attempts to smash up the ice with artillery fire, Funen fell after heavy fighting. The Swedes then marched east to capture Zealand and besiege **Copenhagen** (February 1658).

Fuqiao I 494 BC I Wars of China's Spring and Autumn Era

Determined to avenge the death of his father He-lü, of wounds after defeat at **Zuili** (496 BC), Fuchai of Wu took a large army into neighbouring Yue. A decisive battle at Fuqiao, near the mouth of the Yangzi, saw Fuchai inflict a crushing defeat on the army of Yue. King Goujian was forced to accept a humiliating peace, but he eventually recovered and struck back at the **Lizhe**.

Furnes I 1297 I Franco-Flemish Wars

When Guy de Dampierre Count of Flanders declared for Edward I of England, he was immediately attacked by Philip IV of France. Edward I took a force to assist his Flemish ally. However, before he arrived, Count Guy was defeated at Furnes (modern Veurne) and died in captivity. Philip conquered Flanders, though five years later, the Count's son defeated the invaders at **Courtrai**.

Furth I 1632 I Thirty Years War (Swedish War)

See **Alte Veste**

Fusan I 1592 I Japanese Invasion of Korea

See **Pusan**

Fushimi I 1868 I War of the Meiji Restoration

After the restoration of Imperial government in Japan, former Tokugawa Shogun Yoshinobu let his supporters persuade him to march on the court at Kyoto. Just southeast at Fushimi and Toba, the 10,000-strong Shogunal army was heavily defeated by 6,000 "Imperial" troops from Satsuma and Choshu. Yoshinobu retreated to Edo, where his allies were routed at **Ueno** (27 January 1868).

Fustat I 640–641 I Muslim Conquest of Egypt

See **Babylon, Egpyt**

Futtehabad I 1041 I Afghan Wars of Succession

See **Fatehabad**

Futtehabad I 1879 I 2nd British-Afghan War

See **Fatehabad**

Futtehpore I 1799 I Maratha Territorial Wars

See **Fatehpur**

Futtehpore I 1857 I Indian Mutiny

See **Fatehpur**

Fuzhou I 1884 I Sino-French War

After a failed French attack on **Chilung** in Taiwan, Admiral Amédée Courbet sailed up the Min in Fujian against the shipyards and arsenal at Fuzhou. He destroyed Chinese ships on the river, then bombarded the city, causing massive damage. China formally declared war a few days later. The attack cost Courbet ten killed and 48 wounded while the Chinese lost over 2,000 casualties (23 August 1884).

Fuzhou I 1926 I 1st Chinese Revolutionary Civil War

While Nationalist commander Chiang Kai-shek advanced in central China towards **Wuchang**, his General, He Yingqin, on the coast at Shantou (Swatow) repulsed an invasion by Zhou Yinren, then counter-attacked into Fujian. The key city of

Fuzhou on the Min Delta finally fell and He Yingqin soon supported the advance further north against **Hangzhou** (13 October–9 December 1926).

Fyvie ▌ 1644 ▌ British Civil Wars

James Graham Marquis of Montrose and 800 Royalists withdrawing into the Highlands after the sack of **Aberdeen** in September were surprised at nearby Fyvie by Covenanter forces under Archibald Campbell Marquis of Argyll. Although outnumbered five to one, Montrose drove off four attacks before withdrawing. He defeated Argyll two months later at **Inveraray** (24 October 1644).

G

Gadebusch I 1712 I 2nd "Great" Northern War

Swedish General Magnus Stenbock repulsed a Danish invasion of Sweden at **Helsingborg**, then took his army south to protect Swedish territory in Germany. Attacked at Gadebusch in Mecklenberg by Frederick IV of Denmark, who was aided by Saxon cavalry, Stenbock's outnumbered force achieved a remarkable victory. He was defeated the following May at **Tonning** (20 December 1712).

Gaeta I 1435 I Aragon's Conquest of Naples

Determined to press his claim to Naples, Alfonso V of Aragon besieged nearby Gaeta, held for Genoa by Francisco Spinola. With the city almost starved into surrender, Genoese Admiral Biagio Assereto arrived and, off nearby Isla de Ponza, Alfonso was routed and captured, along with his two brothers. Alfonso was later released and defeated René of Anjou to secure **Naples** (5 August 1435).

Gaeta I 1860–1861 I 2nd Italian War of Independence

Advancing from victory at the **Volturno**, near Capua, Giuseppe Garibaldi and Piedmontese General Enrico Cialdini besieged the last remaining forces of Francis II of Naples at the port of Gaeta, northwest of Naples. Francis abdicated after the city fell to Cialdini (created Duke of Gaeta) and Victor Emmanuel was proclaimed the first King of unified Italy (3 November 1860–13 February 1861).

Gafsa I 1943 I World War II (Northern Africa)
See **El Guettar**

Gafulford I 825 I Later Wars of Wessex

In his campaign to restore the authority of the Kingdom of Wessex, overshadowed by Mercia, King Egbert of Wessex campaigned in Cornwall against the local southern Welsh. In alliance with Devon he won a sharp victory at Gafulford (modern Galford in Devon), securing eastern Cornwall for Wessex. He then turned against Mercia at **Ellandun**.

Gaines' Mill I 1862 I American Civil War (Eastern Theatre)

Continuing his offensive east of Richmond after **Beaver Dam Creek**, Confederate General Robert E. Lee initiated the third of the **Seven Days' Battles**, attacking General Fitz-John Porter north of the Chickahominy at Gaines' Mill, Virginia. Lee's superior force was defeated with greater losses, but Richmond was saved as the Union began withdrawing through **Savage's Station** (27 July 1862).

Gainsborough I 1643 I British Civil Wars

Francis Williams Baron Willoughby and Oliver Cromwell marched to relieve the Royalist siege of Gainsborough, Lincolnshire, and defeated and killed Colonel Sir Charles Cavendish. When new Royalist forces appeared under William Cavendish Earl of Newcastle, Cromwell's Ironsides cavalry withdrew, though Willoughby's infantry were lost with the eventual fall of the town (28 July 1643).

Gaixial I 202 BC I Chu-Han War

Amid warlord rivalry after the collapse of the Qin (Ch'in) Dynasty, Liu Bang broke the truce agreed after **Chenggao** (204 BC) and resumed war against Xiang Yu. After a bloody campaign, Xiang Yu suffered a crushing defeat at Gaixial (Kai-hsia) in Anhui and committed suicide. Liu Bang established the 215-year Western Han Dynasty as Emperor Gao Zu, the first commoner to rule China.

Gajalhatti Pass I 1790 I 3rd British-Mysore War

See **Sathinungulum**

Galaxidi I 1821 I Greek War of Independence

In order to secure the Gulf of Corinth, Turkish Admiral Kara Ali sent the Egyptian squadron under Ismael Djebel Akhdar (Ismael Gibraltar), east from Patras to attack Galaxidi (modern Galaxídhion). The Ottoman ships destroyed the town and port with long-range guns and captured 34 ships, though the action could not delay the fall of **Tripolitza** just a few days later (1 October 1821).

Galiabur I 1920 I Wars of the Mad Mullah

During a major campaign against Muhammad Abdullah Hassan of Somaliland, British forces secured inland forts around **Baran**, while a naval party under Captain Gilbert Hewett led an assault on the coastal fort at Galiabur, west of Las Khoria. About 200 Dervishes fought to the death before Galiabur fell, securing the north coast. The Mullah fled inland to **Taleh** (6 February 1920).

Galicia I 1914 I World War I (Eastern Front)

A huge campaign across southeast Poland and modern Ukraine saw Austrian forces advance through **Krasnik** and **Komárow**, while further south Russians crossed the **Zlota Lipa** and

Gnila Lipa and took **Lemberg** after **Rawa Russka** and **Gorodok**. Austria abandoned Galicia except **Przemysl** at the cost of 400,000 men, while Russia lost 250,000 (18 August–21 September 1914).

Gallabat I 1889 I Sudanese-Ethiopian War

Determined to avenge defeat at **Debra Sina** in 1887, Yohannes IV of Abyssinia took a massive army against Mahdist General Zaki Tamal on the Atbara at Gallabat, opposite Metemma. Abyssinians over-ran the Mahdist positions, but when Yohannes was killed his army withdrew and were massacred as they fled. Gallabat is reputedly the last major battle fought with edged weapons (9 March 1889).

Gallabat I 1940 I World War II (Northern Africa)

Soon after Italy joined the war, Italian forces had entered Sudan from Ethiopia and British General William Slim later mounted a counteroffensive near Gallabat. Despite initial success, lack of air cover and armour eventually forced Slim to withdraw after heavy fighting. Two months later, a renewed British advance succeeded further north through **Agordat** (6–9 November 1940).

Gallinero I 1832 I Mexican Civil Wars

Supporting a rising against President Anastasio Bustamente, General Esteban Moctezuma seized San Luis Potosi after victory at **Poza de las Carmelos** in June, then met Bustamente and 4,000 men at nearby Puerto del Gallinero. After heavy losses on both sides, Moctezuma withdrew with about 2,000 casualties. Bustamente reoccupied San Luis Potosi, but soon lost **Puebla** (17 September 1832).

Gallipoli I 1354 I Byzantine-Ottoman Wars

Ottoman forces under Suleyman Pasha (son of Sultan Orchan) won a civil war for Byzantine Emperor John VI Cantacuzenus in Thrace at **Didymoteichon** (1352), then refused to evacuate the Gallipoli Isthmus. When a great earthquake shattered the walls of Gallipoli two years later, Suleyman seized the city, which became the beachhead for Turkish conquest in Europe (2 March 1354).

Gallipoli ▌ 1366 ▌ Byzantine-Ottoman Wars

When Pope Urban V declared a crusade against the Ottomans, one of the few who actively campaigned was Count Amadeus VI of Savoy, who led a fleet of galleys and 1,500 men to the Dardanelles. A sharp action captured Gallipoli (modern Gelibolu) but Amadeus withdrew after a bloody incursion into the Black Sea, handing the city to the Byzantines (24 August 1366).

Gallipoli ▌ 1416 ▌ Venetian-Turkish Wars

In response to a new Venetian campaign of conquest in Dalmatia, Ottoman Sultan Mehmed I sent his fleet of over 100 ships under Cali Bey from Gallipoli. However, in a brilliant surprise attack, Venetian Admiral Pietro Loredan destroyed the Turkish fleet at Gallipoli. Emperor Manuel II then intervened to arrange a short-lived peace (29 May 1416).

Gallipoli ▌ 1915–1916 ▌ World War I (Gallipoli)

Following the navy's failure to storm the **Dardanelles Narrows**, British and French forces landed on Gallipoli Peninsula at **Helles** and **Anzac** and later at **Suvla Bay**. After failed offensives including **Krithia**, **Sari Bair** and **Scimitar Hill**, evacuation ended the disastrous campaign, which had cost each side perhaps 250,000 casualties, many lost to disease (25 April 1915–9 January 1916).

Galveston ▌ 1862 ▌ American Civil War (Trans-Mississippi)

While blockading the Texas Coast, Union Admiral David G. Farragut captured **Sabine Pass** outside Port Arthur, then ordered Commander William B. Renhsaw to force the surrender of Galveston, to the west, defended by Colonels Joseph J. Cook and Xavier B. Debray. The port surrendered after a brief exchange of fire, but was lost again a few months later (4 October 1862).

Galveston ▌ 1863 ▌ American Civil War (Trans-Mississippi)

Confederate commander John B. Macgruder led a dawn attack on New Year's Day, surprising Galveston, Texas, which had previously surrendered without much struggle. Colonel Isaac S. Burrell's garrison fought hard before surrendering and naval Commander William B. Renshaw died scuttling his flagship. However, most of the Union squadron escaped to resume the blockade (1 January 1863).

Gámeza ▌ 1819 ▌ Colombian War of Independence

As Republican commander Simón Bolívar advanced through western Colombia, General Francisco de Santander's division met Spanish Colonel José María Barreiro at the Gámeza River near Tunja. Barreiro was driven back from the bridge, but held an inaccessible fortress at the nearby Peña de Tópaga. Bolívar withdrew to Tasco and attacked again at **Pantano de Vargas** (12 July 1819).

Gammelsdorf ▌ 1313 ▌ Habsburg Wars of Succession

Following the death of Henry VII of Germany in 1313, the Habsburg Frederick of Austria and the Wittelsbach candidate Louis of Bavaria both claimed the crown. In the ensuing civil war, Louis defeated Frederick at Gammelsdorf, west of the Isar from Landshut, and was crowned as Louis IV. The costly dispute continued until Frederick's eventual defeat at **Mühldorf** (November 1313).

Gamonal ▌ 1808 ▌ Napoleonic Wars (Peninsular Campaign)

Napoleon Bonaparte invaded Spain with a large army and sent Marshal Nicolas Soult to threaten Madrid. Between the Ruevena and Arlanzon Rivers east of Burgos at Gamonal, Soult surprised and virtually destroyed a Spanish army under General Ramon Patigno Count Belvedere, inflicting massive casualties and taking all his guns. Soult later seized Burgos (10 November 1808).

Ganale Doria ┃ 1936 ┃ 2nd Italo-Ethiopian War

While Italian forces in northern Ethiopia prepared to attack in the **Tembien**, General Rudolfo Graziani in the south advanced from Dolo against Ras Desta, son-in-law of Emperor Haile Selassie. Attacking along the Ganale Doria with large-scale use of mustard gas, Graziani routed the Ethiopians and drove the survivors into the desert, then captured the ruins of Negelli (12–15 January 1936).

Gandamak ┃ 1809 ┃ Afghan Wars of Succession
  See **Nimla**

Gandamak ┃ 1842 ┃ 1st British-Afghan War
  See **Jagdalak**

Gandarus ┃ 38 BC ┃ Roman-Parthian Wars
  See **Gindarus**

Gandesa ┃ 1874 ┃ 2nd Carlist War

As Don Alfonso de Bourbon, brother of the Spanish pretender Don Carlos VII, assembled his forces northwest of Tortosa, Liberal commander Colonel Eulogio Despujol attacked a strong position at Gandesa, held by Carlist Colonel Tomás Segarra. The Carlists were driven out with over 100 men killed in a costly defeat. Don Alfonso soon led an offensive south against **Cuenca** (4 June 1874).

Gandzha ┃ 1588 ┃ Turko-Persian Wars

In the wake of the costly Turkish capture of **Tabriz**, new Turkish commander Ferhad Pasha defeated the Persians near **Baghdad**, then joined the Governor of Shirwan to invade Karabagh in Azerbaijan. Following fierce fighting, Ferhad besieged and captured Gandzha (later Kirovabad). Shah Abbas made peace in 1590, ceding Tabriz and Shirwan to the Turks.

Gandzha ┃ 1826 ┃ Russo-Persian Wars
  See **Yelizavetpol**

Ganesh Khind ┃ 1817 ┃ 3rd British-Maratha War
  See **Kirkee**

Gangiri ┃ 1857 ┃ Indian Mutiny
  See **Kasganj**

Gangut ┃ 1714 ┃ 2nd "Great" Northern War
  See **Hango**

Gannoruwa ┃ 1638 ┃ Later Portuguese Colonial Wars in Asia

With a disastrous Portuguese expedition destroyed at **Radenivela** in 1630, Captain-General Diego de Mello de Castro led over 6,000 men on a fresh invasion against the Kingdom of Kandy, in central Ceylon. The Portuguese troops, supported by Indian and African mercenaries, captured and burned the capital, Kandy, but a few miles west at Gannoruwa, de Mello's force was surrounded and destroyed.

Ganzak ┃ 591 ┃ Byzantine-Persian Wars

When Persian General Bahram Chobin seized the Sassanid Persian throne, Emperor Maurice sent a large army to support the legitimate ruler, Chosroes II. After a fierce skirmish near Lake Urmiah, Bahram was caught and routed at Ganzak (modern Takht-i-Suleiman, Azerbaijan) by Byzantines led by Narses. Bahram fled to the Turks and was soon assassinated. Restoration of Chosroes ended the war.

Gaoping ┃ 954 ┃ Wars of the Five Dynasties

During rivalry after the fall of Tang (907), Shizong of Later Zhou took an army against Liu Min of Eastern Han. At Gaoping, in southeast Shanxi, the Han suffered a decisive defeat and Zhou besieged the Han capital at Taiyuan until driven off by the intervention of Liao. Zhou secured much of northern China and unification was completed when its rulers were replaced in 960 by the new Song Dynasty.

Gaouz I 1918 I French Colonial Wars in North Africa

Marshal Louis Lyautey responded to attacks on convoys around **Khenifra** in central Morocco by sending a new offensive under Colonel Paul Doury, who used artillery and aircraft to assault 1,500 Berbers at Gaouz, south of Errachidia. While Doury lost 200 killed, the Moroccans suffered very heavy casualties. The tribal chiefs began to submit and by 1921, Zaian resistance was over (9 August 1918).

Garcia I 1841 I Colombian War of Supreme Commanders

As fighting continued in Antioquia, Colombian government forces under General Eusebio Borrero fought an inconclusive action at **Itagüí** and were surprised a month later at the hacienda of Garcia by Colonel Juan Gregoria Sarria for General José María Obando. Borrero was defeated and captured, but after a few months Obando himself was finally beaten at **La Chanca** (12 March 1841).

Garcia Hernandez I 1812 I Napoleonic Wars (Peninsular Campaign)

In the aftermath of his victory at **Salamanca**, Arthur Wellesley Lord Wellington sent cavalry to pursue the French and, at Garcia Hernandez, General George Anson and the German Legion of General Eberhardt von Bock caught up with General Maximilian Foy. A remarkable victory saw the French routed and Wellington continued towards Madrid (23 July 1812).

Garhakota I 1858 I Indian Mutiny

General Sir Hugh Rose relieved the British garrison at **Sagar**, then marched 25 miles east against Garhakota, one of the most powerful fortresses in central India. However, Rose took insufficient men to properly invest the place and a poorly handled action allowed the rebels to escape after brief resistance. Rose then returned to Sagar to prepare his advance on **Jhansi** in March (12 February 1858).

Gariach I 1411 I MacDonald Rebellion

See **Harlaw**

Garibpur I 1971 I 3rd Indo-Pakistan War

Before the official start of the war, Indian Colonel Raj Kumar Singh entered East Pakistan with 14 tanks to cut communications south of Jessore and seized the village of Garibpur. Pakistani Brigadier Mohammad Hayat counter-attacked in force, but was driven off with 11 tanks destroyed. Singh held Garibpur and the Pakistanis abandoned nearby Chaugacha (20–22 November 1971).

Garigliano I 457 I Roman-Vandal Wars

Facing continuing raids against Italy by the Vandals of North Africa, new Emperor Majorian surprised a Vandal-Berber raiding party returning with loot from Campania. At the mouth of the Garigliano, many of the raiders were slaughtered before they could return to their ships, or were driven into the sea and drowned. Gaiseric, the Vandal, was avenged a few years later at **Cape Bon**.

Garigliano I 1139 I Norman-Papal War

In order to punish King Roger II of Sicily for supporting former anti-pope Anacletus, Pope Innocent II excommunicated the King and, supported by Robert of Capua, unwisely took an army against him in southern Italy. On the Garigliano, near Gallucio, the Papal army was utterly destroyed. Innocent was captured and had to recognise Roger's rule over Sicily and southern Italy (22 July 1139).

Garigliano I 1503 I Italian War of Louis XII

Eight months after defeat at **Cerignola**, the French camped at the Garigliano, near Cassino, facing Spanish commander Gonsalvo de Cordoba. After weeks of stalemate, with costly French and Italian losses from skirmishing and swamp fever, Cordoba was reinforced. He attacked across the river to destroy the Allies and seize Gaeta, ending French claims to Naples (27 December 1503).

Garigliano ▌ 1944 ▌ World War II (Southern Europe)

Diverting from the Allied landing at **Anzio**, British General Sir Richard McCreery and French under General Alphonse Juin crossed the Garigliano near Minturno, at the western end of the **Gustav Line** across Italy. General Fridolin von Senger was driven back, but German reinforcements stopped the Americans on the **Rapido** and halted the offensive west of **Monte Cassino** (17–19 January 1944).

Garnett's and Golding's Farms ▌ 1862 ▌ American Civil War (Eastern Theatre)

In a lesser action during the **Seven Days' Battles**, east of Richmond, Virginia, Confederate General John B. Magruder sent a flank attack south of the Chickahominy at Garnett's and Golding's Farms. Confederate forces under General Robert A. Toombs and Colonel George T. Anderson were repulsed and Magruder fought again next day at **Savage's Station** (27–28 June 1862).

Garo Pass ▌ 1904 ▌ British Invasion of Tibet

See **Karo Pass**

Garrapata ▌ 1876 ▌ Colombian Civil Wars

When Conservatives in Antioquia and Tolima rose in rebellion, they were defeated at **Los Chancos**, then rebel General Marcelino Vélez faced Liberal government Generals Santos Acosta and Sergio Camargo in Tolima at Garrapata. Despite superior numbers, Vélez was defeated, leading to a temporary armistice, followed by further losses at **La Donjuana** and **Manizales** (20–22 November 1876).

Garris ▌ 1814 ▌ Napoleonic Wars (Peninsular Campaign)

As Arthur Wellesley Lord Wellington closed in on **Bayonne** in southwestern France, General Jean Isidore Harispe attempted to defend the River Bidouse, southeast of the city at Garris. With about 500 men lost, including 200 captured, Harispe destroyed the bridges and with-drew southeast through Saint Palais. However, Wellington rebuilt the bridges and crossed the following day (15 February 1814).

Gartalunane ▌ 1489 ▌ Scottish Barons' Rebellion

Facing renewed Baronial rebellion, James IV of Scotland sent John Lord Drummond to relieve Colin Campbell Earl of Argyll, besieged in Dumbarton by Robert Lord Lyle and Mathew Stewart, son of Sir John Stewart Earl of Lennox. Near Dumbarton at Gartalunane (modern Gartloaning), Drummond surprised and routed Lennox and the rebellion collapsed (11–12 October 1489).

Garua ▌ 1914–1915 ▌ World War I (African Colonial Theatre)

British Colonel Charles Carter marched from Nigeria into northern German Cameroon where he attacked Garua, on the upper Benue. He was driven off with over 300 casualties, but a second Anglo-French expedition led by Colonel Frederick Cunliffe besieged the fortress and forced Hauptmann von Crailsheim to surrender, leaving Germany only the fortress at **Mora** (30 August 1914 & 10 June 1915).

Gate Pa ▌ 1864 ▌ 2nd New Zealand War

Within weeks of conquering the Waikato at **Orakau**, General Sir Duncan Cameron marched east to the Bay of Plenty, where Rawiri Puhirake had provocatively built a fortified pa near Tauranga. With 1,700 men and artillery, the British fought their way into Gate Pa, but were driven out with 120 casualties. Rawiri slipped away into the night and was soon killed at **Te Ranga** (29 April 1864).

Gaugamela ▌ 331 BC ▌ Conquests of Alexander the Great

In one of the greatest battles of the ancient world, Alexander the Great returned from Egypt and defeated a huge Persian army under King Darius III at Gaugamela, between Nineveh and Arbela in modern Iraq. Persian casualties in the battle were enormous and Alexander entered

Babylon a few days later, making himself master of Persia. Darius was killed fleeing across central Iran (1 October 331 BC).

Gavdos ▮ 1941 ▮ World War II
(War at Sea)
See **Cape Matapan**

Gavere ▮ 1453 ▮ Franco-
Burgundian Wars
Consolidating his hold on the Low Countries after the Hundred Years War, Philip Duke of Burgundy took a large army against Ghent, which had risen in protest against increased taxes. South of the city at Gavere he crushed the Ghent Militia, with 10,000 reported killed, and imposed a massive financial penalty, which cowed other cities until Liège rose in revolt at **Montenaeken** (23 July 1453).

Gavilán ▮ 1817 ▮ Chilean War
of Independence
When a Patriot force under Juan Gregoria Las Heras advanced through **Potrerillos** to capture Gavilán, northeast of Concepción, Spanish General José Ordóñez attacked from nearby Talcahuano and met with initial success. Heavy Patriot reinforcements then arrived from Arauco under Bernardo O'Higgins and Ordóñez had to withdraw, with heavy losses in men, guns and munitions (4 May 1817).

Gavinana ▮ 1529–1530 ▮ 2nd Habsburg-
Valois War
See **Florence**

Gawilgarh ▮ 1803 ▮ 2nd British-
Maratha War
British General Arthur Wellesley won at **Assaye** (24 September) and **Argaum** (28 November) against Maratha leaders, Daulat Rao Sindhia of Gwalior and Raja Raghuji Bhonsle of Berar, then pursued the Raja's defeated force to the hill fortress of Gawilgarh, east of Burhanpur. The fortress fell by storm after heavy bombardment, effectively ending the fighting in central India (15 December 1803).

Gaza ▮ 332 BC ▮ Conquests of Alexander
the Great
Alexander the Great moved south from the capture of **Tyre** to besiege Gaza, the last major settlement before entering the desert route to Egypt. Raising a massive earth rampart around the city, he used powerful siege machines to demolish the walls before the final assault. The citizens were slaughtered and garrison commander, Batis, was tortured to death (September–November 332 BC).

Gaza ▮ 312 BC ▮ Wars of the Diadochi
In the war between the successors of Alexander the Great, Antigonus secured Syria with victory at **Tyre**. However, Ptolemy of Egypt later returned to attack Gaza, held for Antigonus by his son Demetrius Poliorcetes. Demetrius was completely defeated and fled to Cilicia, but when Antigonus prepared a massive counter-offensive Ptolemy withdrew, leaving Syria to his rival.

Gaza ▮ 1239 ▮ Later Crusader-
Muslim Wars
When Theobald of Champagne, King of Navarre, arrived in Palestine with a French army, he led a Crusader offensive against fortresses in the south, where a large contingent under Count Henry of Bar recklessly advanced without support. Surprised near Gaza by the massive Ayyubid army of Emir Rukn ad-Din, Count Henry's force was routed and he was killed (13 November 1239).

Gaza ▮ 1244 ▮ Later Crusader-
Muslim Wars
See **La Forbie**

Gaza ▮ 1516 ▮ Ottoman-Mamluk War
See **Yaunis Khan**

Gaza (1st) ▮ 1917 ▮ World War I
(Middle East)
With Turkey driven out of Sinai at **Rafa**, British commander Archibald Murray entered Palestine and sent General Charles Dobell against the opposing line between Gaza and Beersheba, held by Colonel Friedrich von Kressenstein. Despite

initial success, poor communication led to premature British withdrawal with over 4,000 men lost, though Murray claimed it as victory (26–27 March 1917).

Gaza (2nd) ▮ 1917 ▮ World War I (Middle East)

Despite bloody losses at Gaza, British commander Archibald Murray sent General Charles Dobell on a frontal assault against the newly reinforced Turkish line between Gaza and Beersheba. The ill-conceived assault failed at a cost of over 6,000 British casualties and Murray was replaced by General Sir Edmund Allenby, who won with a flank attack at **Beersheba** in October (17–19 April 1917).

Gaza (3rd) ▮ 1917 ▮ World War I (Middle East)

See **Sheria**

Gaza ▮ 1956 ▮ Arab-Israeli Sinai War

Campaigning in northern Sinai after the fall of **Rafa**, Israelis under Colonel Aharon Doron advanced on large Egyptian and Palestinian troop concentrations around Gaza, where they met unexpectedly fierce resistance. Following sharp fighting, Egyptian Governor General Fuad al Dijani surrendered Gaza to avoid further losses, effectively ending war in the north (2–3 November 1956).

Gaza ▮ 1967 ▮ Arab-Israeli Six Day War

At the start of the Sinai Campaign, Israeli Colonel Yehudi Resheff, with a reinforced mechanised brigade, advanced through Khan Yunis towards Gaza, held by a Palestinian division under General Mohammed Hasni. Heavy hand-to-hand fighting developed before the Jews seized Gaza City and the key Ali Montar Ridge, giving Israel the much-disputed Gaza Strip (5–6 June 1967).

Gazala ▮ 1942 ▮ World War II (Northern Africa)

After a four-month stalemate, German commander Erwin Rommel launched a massive attack on the British defensive line, south from Gazala, shielding **Tobruk**. Turning the desert flank at **Bir Hacheim**, Rommel stormed into the British rear and, after brutal action in the **Cauldron**, General Neil Ritchie withdrew into Egypt through **Mersah Matruh** to **El Alamein** (26 May–13 June 1942).

Gdansk ▮ 1308 ▮ Wars of the Teutonic Knights

When Margrave Waldemar of Brandenberg besieged Gdansk, Prince Ladislav of Poland appealed to the Teutonic Order and Gunter von Schartzburg seized the city (renamed Danzig) and killed the inhabitants. The Knights then refused to relinquish Pomerania, moving their headquarters from Venice to nearby Marienburg. They were defeated by Ladislav at **Plowce** in 1331 (14 November 1308).

Gdansk ▮ 1577 ▮ Gdansk War

See **Danzig**

Gdansk ▮ 1626–1630 ▮ 2nd Polish-Swedish War

See **Danzig**

Gdansk ▮ 1733–1734 ▮ War of the Polish Succession

See **Danzig**

Gdansk ▮ 1807 ▮ Napoleonic Wars (4th Coalition)

See **Danzig**

Gdansk ▮ 1813–1814 ▮ Napoleonic Wars (War of Liberation)

See **Danzig**

Gdansk ▮ 1945 ▮ World War II (Eastern Front)

See **Danzig**

Gdov ▮ 1614 ▮ Russo-Swedish Wars

With Russia's invasion of Sweden repulsed near Novgorod at **Bronnitsa**, King Gustavus Adolphus himself led a force into Russia and attacked Gdov, east of Lake Peipus, which had been captured by forces of Tsar Michael.

Gustavus took the city by storm after two bloody assaults and returned next year to continue his offensive further south against **Pskov** (July–10 September 1614).

Gebora I 1811 I Napoleonic Wars (Peninsular Campaign)

During Marshal Nicolas Soult's siege of **Badajoz**, he sent a veteran French force, led by Marshal Édouard Mortier, north across the Guadianna to attack a Spanish relief army under General Gabriel Mendizabal. Surprised near the Gebora River, Mendizabal was routed with heavy losses in men and guns and his survivors fled to reinforce the garrison at Badajoz (19 February 1811).

Gedaref I 1898 I British-Sudan Wars

As Dervish forces withdrew up the Blue Nile after defeat at **Omdurman** (2 September), about 4,000 men under Emir Saadallah were intercepted at Gedaref by Colonel Charles Parsons, who had marched across the Atbara from eastern Sudan. The Dervishes were defeated in hard fighting with about 500 dead and Parsons then held Gedaref against a counter-attack by Ahmed Fedil (22 September 1898).

Gefrees I 1809 I Napoleonic Wars (5th Coalition)

Archduke Charles of Austria won at **Aspern-Essling** (22 May), then sent a diversionary expedition through Saxony into Bavaria. Near Gefrees, northeast of Beyreuth, Austrian Field Marshal Michael von Kienmeyer and General Paul Radivojevich inflicted a sharp defeat on General Androche Junot. However, news of Austrian defeat at **Znaim** brought the campaign to an end (8 July 1809).

Geisberg I 1793 I French Revolutionary Wars (1st Coalition)

See **Wissembourg**

Gela I 1943 I World War II (Southern Europe)

At the start of the Allied invasion of **Sicily**, American General George Patton landed in the southwest between Licata and Cape Scaramia. Heaviest fighting was around Gela, where Italians and German General Paul Conrath counter-attacked in force. Supported by accurate naval gunfire, General Terry Allen secured the bridgehead and Patton swept north towards **Palermo** (10–12 July 1943).

Gelt I 1570 I Dacre's Rebellion

Leonard Dacre of Gilsland gathered a northern rising in support of the imprisoned Mary Queen of Scots, but on the banks of the Gelt, near Carlisle, his 3,000 Borderers were utterly defeated by an English army under Henry Lord Hunsdon and Sir John Forster. Dacre fled to France, while English forces ravaged Teviotdale and the Border to stamp out insurrection (20 February 1570).

Gelves I 1510 I Spanish Colonial Wars in North Africa

See **Los Gelves**

Gemaizeh I 1888 I British-Sudan Wars

When Mahdist General Osman Digna threatened the Red Sea port of Suakin, despite his defeat at **Handoub**, Governor Sir Charles Holled-Smith appealed to Cairo and Sir Francis Grenfell brought British-Sudanese-Egyptian reinforcements. Taking the offensive, Grenfell attacked Osman at Gemaizeh, just west of Suakin, and the Dervishes were driven off with perhaps 500 killed (20 December 1888).

Gemas I 1942 I World War II (Pacific)

In an attempt to stall the Japanese in northwest Johore, Australian General Gordon Bennet took position at the Gemencheh near Gemas, where he ambushed the invaders and inflicted costly losses. But after very heavy fighting against Japanese reinforcements, and with his coastal flank threatened at **Muar**, Bennet had to fall back through Yong Pen towards **Singapore** (14–20 January 1941).

Gemauerthof I 1705 I 2nd "Great" Northern War

After capturing the fortresses of **Dorpat** and **Narva**, Russian Marshal Boris Sheremetev marched into Courland to hold the Swedes, while Tsar Peter took the main Russian army into Poland. In a bloody action at Gemauerthof, near Jelgava in Latvia, Sheremetev's superior force was beaten by General Adam Lewenhaupt, who then secured a strong defensive position at Riga (16 July 1705).

Gembloux I 1578 I Netherlands War of Independence

A fresh offensive in the Netherlands saw Spanish Viceroy Don John of Austria and his nephew Alexander Farnese drive the Dutch out of Namur and attack them in retreat at nearby Gembloux. The Dutch force under new commander Antoine de Goignies suffered a terrible rout, with thousands killed for just a handful of Spanish casualties. Don John soon attacked again at **Rymenant** (31 January 1578).

Generals I 1824 I Peruvian War of Independence
See **Ayacucho**

Geneva I 1602 I Swiss Religious Wars

In a final attempt to recapture Calvinist Geneva, Duke Charles Emmanuel of Savoy, with Spanish aid, sent 2,000 mercenaries under Charles d'Albigny, who took the city by surprise and scaled the outside walls. However, in a small yet significant victory for the Reformation, they were repulsed by Isaac Mercier. Savoy later recognised Geneva as an independent city (21–22 December 1602).

Genil I 1319 I Later Christian Reconquest of Spain

Following the death of Ferdinand IV of Castile, his brothers Juan and Pedro became joint regents for the infant Alfonso XI and undertook an offensive against the Muslim military leader Ismail, who had seized the throne of Granada. Juan and Pedro were defeated and killed in a bitter battle at the River Genil, throwing Castile into civil war between rival claimants to the Regency.

Genoa I 1522 I 1st Habsburg-Valois War

A month after the disastrous French defeat at **Bicocca** and the subsequent withdrawal from Lombardy, the Spanish-German army of General Prospero Colonna attacked Genoa, the last remaining substantial French possession beyond the Alps. Colonna stormed and pillaged Genoa in a sudden assault, giving the Imperialists effectively control of northern Italy (30 May 1522).

Genoa I 1684 I Franco-Genoese War

To punish Genoa for building ships for Spain and selling munitions to the Ottoman Governor of **Algiers**, Louis XIV of France sent Admiral Abraham Duquesne to bombard the city, accompanied by Secretary for War, Jean Baptiste Colbert Marquis de Seignelay. After suffering considerable damage, Genoa was humbled and had to abandon its long alliance with Spain (May 1684).

Genoa I 1746–1747 I War of the Austrian Succession

Austrian Marquis Anton Otto Botta d'Adorno attacked France and Spain in northern Italy, where he seized the great port of Genoa (6 September 1746). But, in a courageous insurrection against Austrian tyranny he was thrown out (5–10 December). Austro-Sardinian forces then laid the city under siege, which fatally drained their resources and ultimately failed (January–June 1747).

Genoa I 1795 I French Revolutionary Wars (1st Coalition)

A large-scale naval engagement off the city of Genoa saw a British squadron, under Admiral Sir William Hotham, clash with Admiral Pierre Martin and the French were driven off with two ships captured. Although Captain Horatio Nelson claimed the Admiral had been derelict in failing to pursue, Parliament voted Hotham thanks. He soon met Martin again off the **Hyères** (13 March 1795).

Genoa **|** 1800 **|** French Revolutionary Wars (2nd Coalition)

Amid renewed Austrian fighting in northern Italy, Baron Michael von Melas attacked French General André Masséna and drove him into siege at Genoa, confined by British ships and Austrian troops under General Karl Ott. Napoleon Bonaparte arrived too late over the Alps and Masséna negotiated a conditional surrender, allowing him to keep his men and guns (20 April–4 June 1800).

Genoy **|** 1820 **|** Colombian War of Independence

With Colombian independence assured by victory at **Boyacá**, Patriot forces in the south, under General Manuel Valdés, crossed the Juanambú towards Popayán, held by Spanish Colonel Sebastián Calzada. At Genoy, just north of Pasto, Valdés was heavily defeated by Royalist Colonel Basilio García and was forced to withdraw. Armistice later that year secured peace (2 February 1820).

Geok Tepe **|** 1879 **|** Russian Conquest of Central Asia

Having conquered the Khanate of **Khokand**, Russia faced resistance in southern Turkmenistan by tribesmen known as Tekkes. Russian artillery, under General Nikolai Pavlovich Lomakin, badly damaged their stronghold at Geok Tepe, but the Russians were repulsed with heavy losses in men, material and prestige. The town fell two years later amid heavy bloodshed (28 August 1879).

Geok Tepe **|** 1881 **|** Russian Conquest of Central Asia

With Russian expansion in Turkmenistan checked by Tekke tribesmen, General Mikhail Skobelev led a fresh campaign, which bombarded and stormed their stronghold of Dengil-Tepe at Geok Tepe. Skobelev allegedly refused to accept surrender and up to 20,000 Tekkes were reported killed. The brutal victory virtually completed Russia's conquest of central Asia (12 January 1881).

Georgegarh (1st) **|** 1801 **|** Maratha Territorial Wars

Major Louis Bourquein invaded Haryana for Sindhia, then left Captain Lewis Smith to besiege the strong fortress of Georgegarh near Jhajjar. Irish-born adventurer George Thomas drove off Smith and routed Sindhia's rearguard under veteran General Puran Singh. Bourquein returned with a large force, but was heavily defeated outside Georgegarh and withdrew (25–29 September 1801).

Georgegarh (2nd) **|** 1801 **|** Maratha Territorial Wars

Following Sindhia's defeat in Haryana, General Pierre Perron sent Colonel Pedron and 30,000 men to besiege Irish-born adventurer George Thomas at Georgegarh, near Jhajjar. A relief force under Raja Vaman Rao was driven off (18 October) but, after massive defections among his Marathas, Thomas abandoned his guns and fought his way out to **Hansi** (October–10 November 1801).

Georgia Landing **|** 1862 **|** American Civil War (Lower Seaboard)

Union General Godfrey Weitzel led an offensive on the Lafourche in western Louisiana, advancing south through **Donaldsonville** on the Mississippi against Confederate forces under General Alfred A. Mouton. With over 200 men captured in a running action near Georgia Landing, Mouton was forced to withdraw further south to nearby Labadieville (27 October 1862).

Gerberoi **|** 1080 **|** Norman Dynastic Wars

William of Normandy conquered Saxon England at **Hastings**, then faced rebellion at home by his son Robert, supported by Philip I of France. Besieged in Philip's castle at Gerberoi, near Beauvais northwest of Paris, the rebels were defeated, reputedly after Robert wounded his father in single combat. Robert was forgiven, but was later imprisoned after losing to his brother Henry at **Tinchebrai** in 1106.

Gerchsheim ▮ 1866 ▮ Seven Weeks' War

Within days of Prussian victory at **Aschaffenburg**, General Erwin von Manteuffel led the advance southeast through **Tauberbischofsheim** and **Werbach**, then sent Generals August von Goeben and Karl von Wrangel against Gerchsheim. After costly losses on both sides, with further losses the same day at nearby **Helmstadt**, Prince Karl of Bavaria retreated east through **Würzburg** (25 July 1866).

Gergovia ▮ 52 BC ▮ Rome's Later Gallic Wars

Having captured **Avaricum** in central Gaul in March, Julius Caesar marched into the Auvergne to attack Gergovia (near modern Clermont-Ferrand), the fortified capital of Arverni Chieftain Vercingetorix. Despite surprising nearby Gallic camps, the Romans were repulsed in an uncoordinated attack, losing over 700 men. Caesar withdrew north and later that year routed Vercingetorix at **Alesia**.

Germanikeia ▮ 778–779 ▮ Byzantine-Muslim Wars
 See **Hadath**

Germantown ▮ 1777 ▮ War of the American Revolution

When British General Sir William Howe secured Philadelphia (26 September) after victory at **Brandywine**, General George Washington counter-attacked at Germantown, five miles to the north. A confused action saw Washington repulsed with over 1,000 casualties, including 400 prisoners. After further action at **White Marsh**, he withdrew to winter quarters in Valley Forge (4 October 1777).

Germiston ▮ 1900 ▮ 2nd Anglo-Boer War
 See **Elandsfontein**

Gerona ▮ 1285 ▮ French-Aragonese War

When Pedro III of Aragon claimed Sicily in the aftermath of the **Sicilian Vespers**, Pope Martin IV encouraged Philip III of France to invade Aragon, where he besieged Gerona, held by Viscomte Raymond de Cardona, which fell after heavy losses to disease on both sides. Following naval disaster at **Las Hormigas,** the isolated French garrison surrendered in October (26 June–7 September 1285).

Gerona ▮ 1808 ▮ Napoleonic Wars (Peninsular Campaign)

The fortress of Gerona, blocking the coastal route from France to Barcelona, withstood attack by French General Philibert Duhesme in June 1808, then faced a better-equipped siege by Duhesme from the south and General Honoré Reille in the north. A Spanish relief army under Count Raimondo Caldagues routed Reille and Duhesme was forced to withdraw (18–20 June & 24 July–20 August 1808).

Gerona ▮ 1809 ▮ Napoleonic Wars (Peninsular Campaign)

Having withstood two previous sieges, the Catalonian city of Gerona under General Mariano Alvarez de Castro was besieged by French General Laurent Gouvion Saint-Cyr and later Marshal Pierre Augereau. Both sides suffered terrible losses in repeated assaults and in failed relief attempts by Spanish General Joachim Blake, before the heroic garrison finally fell (24 May–11 December 1809).

Gertruydenberg ▮ 1588–1589 ▮ Netherlands War of Independence

Sir John Wingfield was appointed Governor of Gertruydenberg (modern Geertruidenberg, near Breda), then held the city against Alexander Farnese Duke of Parma, even sending aid to his brother-in-law, Peregrine Bertie Lord Willoughby, besieged at **Bergen**. But the Dutch suspected Wingfield would treacherously surrender Gertruydenberg to Spain and he finally capitulated (1588–10 April 1589).

Gertruydenberg ▮ 1593 ▮ Netherlands War of Independence

In one of his great sieges, Prince Maurice of Orange invested Gertruydenberg (modern Geertruidenberg, near Breda) using special matting to support his guns on the soft ground. As at **Steenwijk**, he used his troops to dig siege positions. After a Spanish relief attempt under Count Ernst von Mansfeld was driven off, the powerful fortress surrendered (26 March–24 June 1593).

Gesher I 1948 I Israeli War of Independence

Advancing south of the Sea of Galilee to support the Syrians further north around **Deganiya**, Iraqi forces attempted to cross the Jordan near Gesher, just south of its junction with the Yarmak. The Iraqis were heavily defeated by Israel's Golani Brigade, though they later regrouped and advanced west across the Jordan further downriver towards **Jenin** (15–22 May 1948).

Gestilren I 1210 I Swedish Wars of Succession

Amid continuing rivalry for Sweden's throne, Sverker II seized power in 1196, when Knut Eriksson died. After years of Sverker's tyrannical rule, Knut's son Erik raised a large force in Norway and returned to reclaim the crown. Despite Danish support, Sverker was defeated and killed at Gestilren, west of Tidaholm near Lake Vattern, and Erik Eriksson was proclaimed King (17 July 1210).

Gettysburg I 1863 I American Civil War (Eastern Theatre)

Marching north across the Potomac to Gettysburg in Pennsylvania, Confederate commander Robert E. Lee attacked General George G. Meade's Union army in a defensive position south of town. In the bloodiest battle on American soil, Lee was decisively defeated with terrible losses and began his retreat southwest through **Williamsport**, cautiously pursued by the shattered victors (1–3 July 1863).

Ghagra River I 1529 I Mughal Conquest of Northern India

See **Gogra**

Ghallaghurga I 1762 I Indian Campaigns of Ahmad Shah

See **Kup**

Ghazhdewan I 1512 I Mughal-Uzbek Wars

See **Ghujduwan**

Ghazi-ud-din-Nagar I 1857 I Indian Mutiny

Approaching rebel-held **Delhi**, British Brigadier Archdale Wilson was met by a mutineer force at the nearby village of Ghazi-ud-din-Nagar on the Hindan. Despite being badly affected by extreme heat, the British troops defeated the rebels and repulsed a counter-attack next day. Joined by General Sir Henry Barnard, they then advanced on the strategic position at **Badli** (30–31 May 1857).

Ghazni I 998 I Afghan Wars of Succession

When Amir Sebuktigin of Bokhara died (997), his son and successor Isma'il found himself at war with his ambitious older brother, Mahmud of Balkh. Isma'il was defeated in heavy fighting near the capital Ghazni and Mahmud seized the throne. While Isma'il lived in comfortable captivity, Mahmud built an empire, which eventually stretched from the Punjab to Persia (March 998).

Ghazni I 1117 I Eastern Muslim Dynastic Wars

Intervening in a disputed succession in Afghanistan, the Seljuk Sultan Sanjar of Khorasan took a large army against Malik Arslan Shah of Ghor. Outside Ghazni at Shahrabad, Malik Arslan suffered a terrible defeat and his brother Bahram Shah was installed as a Seljuk vassal. Malik Arslan later attempted to return from exile in Lahore (1118) but was defeated and executed by his brother.

Ghazni I 1148 I Ghor-Ghazni Wars

Saif-ud-Din of Ghor invaded the Afghan kingdom of Ghazni, where he defeated the army of Bahram Shah, who fled to India. He then annexed Ghazni before Bahram returned and defeated the Ghurid Prince. Saif-ud-Din surrendered in return for his life, but was tortured to death. His death was later avenged by his brother, Ala-ud-Din Husain, who defeated Bahram and destroyed Ghazni.

Ghazni ▌ 1151 ▌ Ghor-Ghazni Wars

Determined to gain control of Afghanistan, Ala-ud-Din Husain of Ghor invaded Ghazni and defeated the army of Bahram Shah, who fled. In revenge for the torture and execution of his brother at Ghazni in 1148, Ala-ud-Din then destroyed Ghazni city, burning it to the ground and earning the nickname Jahan-Suz (the burner). His victory effectively ended the Ghaznavid Dynasty in Afghanistan.

Ghazni ▌ 1839 ▌ 1st British-Afghan War

Britain was concerned over Russian influence in Afghanistan and sent General Sir John Keane, who led his 20,000-strong force against Ghazni, held by Afzal Khan for Amir Dost Muhammad. Keane took the powerful fortress by storm after blowing up the gate in a brilliant assault, then advanced to Kabul to restore Shah Shuja (7 August). Dost Muhammad fled (21–23 July 1839).

Ghaznigak ▌ 1888 ▌ Afghan Civil Wars

Amir Abdur Rahman consolidating his authority in northern Afghanistan despatched forces under General Shulam Haidar and Sandar Abdullah against his cousin Ishaq Khan, Governor of Afghan Turkestan. Ishaq was defeated in battle at Ghaznigak, east of Balkh near Tashqurghan (modern Kholm), and fled to Russia, where he died soon afterwards (27 September 1888).

Gheluvelt ▌ 1914 ▌ World War I (Western Front)

Despite losses at **Langemark**, German forces launched a massive attack on Gheluvelt, east of Ypres. The most important action of the First Battle of **Ypres** saw the town seized, then lost to a bold British counter-attack. The courageous defence is said to have saved Ypres, though Gheluvelt was lost in a subsequent German offensive to the northwest through **Nonne Boschen** (29–31 October 1914).

Gheria, Bengal ▌ 1740 ▌ Mughal Wars of Succession

The incompetent Mughal Nawab Safaraz Khan of Bengal faced rebellion by Ali Vardi Khan, Governor of Bihar, and marched out from his capital at Murshidabad to face the rebels. Safaraz Khan was killed in the decisive battle near the Ganges at Gheria and his generals immediately proclaimed Ali Vardi Khan as Nawab of Bengal, Bihar and Orissa (10 April 1740).

Gheria, Bengal ▌ 1763 ▌ Bengal War

British Major Thomas Adams restored Mir Jafar as Nawab of Bengal, then took his mixed force against the usurper Mir Kasim, who established a strong defensive position on the Plain of Gheria near Jangipur at Sooty. Following very hard fighting, with costly losses on both sides, Mir Kasim was driven out and withdrew to his stronghold on the Ganges at **Udaynala** (2 August 1763).

Gheria, Bombay ▌ 1756 ▌ War against Malabar Pirates

On campaign against pirates on India's Malabar Coast, south of Bombay, British Admiral Charles Watson and Colonel Robert Clive, with Maratha support, followed capture of **Savandrug** by attacking the pirate stronghold at Gheria (modern Vijayadurg). Forcing his way into the harbour, Watson took the fortress from the rear and Chief Tulaji Angria was finally defeated (13 February 1756).

Ghoaine ▌ 1842 ▌ 1st British-Afghan War

Advancing from Kandahar in southern Afghanistan towards Ghazni against Akbar Khan (son of deposed Amir Dost Muhammad), British General William Nott was blocked by Afghan General Shems-ud-Din at Karabagh, near Ghoaine, two miles from Ghazni. Nott inflicted a heavy defeat, capturing all the Afghan guns, and continued his advance through **Maidan** to Kabul (30 August 1842).

Ghujduwan ▌ 1512 ▌ Mughal-Uzbek Wars

After the Uzbek leader Ubaid Khan defeated the Mughal Babur of Kabul at **Kul-i-Malik**, near

Samarkand in Uzbekistan, Shah Ismail Safawi of Persia sent General Najm-i Thani to aid his former ally. At Ghujduwan (modern Gizhdivan), northeast of Bokhara, the Mughals and Persians were heavily defeated. Babur then turned his attention to conquests in India (12 November 1512).

Giants I 1813 I Napoleonic Wars (War of Liberation)
 See **Leipzig**

Giao-chao I 602 I Sino-Vietnamese Wars
 Facing renewed rebellion in Annam, in northern Vietnam, where Li Bon had been crushed at **Chu Dien**, Sui Emperor Wen Di sent the famous General Liu Fang, who took a large force and attacked the rebels in Giao-chao, near Hanoi. Having secured victory and restored order, he then marched south and reimposed control over King Sambhuvarman of Champa at **Tra-khe**.

Gibbet Rath I 1798 I Irish Rebellion
 Soon after the Irish rising began, General Sir Ralph Dundas tried to negotiate terms with rebels in Kildare. But, just east of the town on the Curragh, at Gibbet Rath, rebels attempting to surrender were attacked by General Sir James Duff, who claimed they had fired on his men. The ensuring massacre saw about 350 rebels killed. Duff reported three of his troops also died (29 May 1798).

Gibeon I 1915 I World War I (African Colonial Theatre)
 Renewing the invasion of German Southwest Africa after defeat at **Sandfontein**, General Jan Smuts led a southern force towards Gibeon, where Major Duncan McKenzie tried to encircle Germans under Hauptmann Bogislav von Kleist. The South Africans failed to cut the railway and, after the heaviest fighting of the campaign, the Germans escaped north towards **Windhoek** (25–26 April 1915).

Gibraltar I 207 BC I 2nd Punic War
 With Carthage under pressure in Spain, the city of Gades (Cadiz) threatened to ally itself with Rome and Punic Admiral Adherbal arrived to arrest the leaders. A Roman squadron sent from Carteia under Laelius attacked the Carthaginian ships in the turbulent Straits of Gibraltar, where the heavier Roman ships inflicted a costly defeat, sinking three triremes. The three surviving vessels escaped to Carthage.

Gibraltar I 1607 I Netherlands War of Independence
 Dutch Admiral Jacob van Heemskerk led a bold attack on Gibraltar, taking his outgunned ships against a large Spanish fleet under Admiral Don Juan Alvarez d'Avila. During the bloody battle, both admirals were killed, though the Dutch leader's death was kept from his captains, who went on to achieve a stunning victory. The Spanish fleet was destroyed without Dutch loss (25 April 1607).

Gibraltar (1st) I 1704 I War of the Spanish Succession
 Stubbornly assaulting Spanish Gibraltar, the Anglo-Dutch fleet under Admirals Sir George Rooke and Sir George Byng laid down a bombardment, then Prince George of Hesse landed with 1,800 men and Governor Diego de Salinas surrendered the fortress next day. A French counter-attack was then repulsed off **Malaga** and at the war's end the rock was ceded to Britain (23–24 July 1704).

Gibraltar (2nd) I 1704–1705 I War of the Spanish Succession
 A Franco-Spanish force under Marshal Count René de Tessé resolved to retake Gibraltar and besieged the strategic island, held by marines under Prince George of Hesse. A small French squadron was surprised and destroyed by Admiral Sir John Leake (29 October 1704), but the siege was not raised until Leake returned and defeated the French fleet off **Marbella** (September 1704–5 April 1705).

Gibraltar I 1779–1783 I War of the American Revolution
 When Spain entered the war, French and Spanish forces under Louis Duc de Crillon besieged

Gibraltar, brilliantly defended by General George Eliott. Reinforced following British victory off **Cape St Vincent** (16 January 1780), Eliott drove off a massive land and sea assault (13 September 1782). Gibraltar was saved and Eliott was made Baron Heathfield (24 June 1779–6 February 1783).

Gien ∎ 1652 ∎ War of the 2nd Fronde
See **Blenau**

Giessen ∎ 1797 ∎ French Revolutionary Wars (1st Coalition)
See **Kirchberg**

Gijon ∎ 1936 ∎ Spanish Civil War
As the war started, Nationalist Colonel Antonio Pinilla at Gijon held out in the Simancas Barracks against Asturian miners, who eventually broke in using dynamite. Ordering no surrender, Pinilla called down shellfire from the Nationalist Cruiser, *Almirante Cervera*, offshore and both sides died in the bombardment. The miners then turned against nearby **Oveida** (19 July–16 August 1936).

Gijon ∎ 1937 ∎ Spanish Civil War
Soon after the fall of **Bilbao** and **Santander**, Nationalist forces under Generals Antonio Aranda and José Solchaga converged on Gijon in Asturias, the last remaining Republican stronghold in northern Spain. Republican resistance was crushed and the Nationalists seized the city, securing the whole northern coast and its vital resources for the rebel cause (1 September–21 October 1937).

Gila River ∎ 1857 ∎ Apache Indian Wars
Leading the Gila Expedition in Southern Arizona, Colonel Benjamin Bonneville, supported by Colonel Dixon S. Miles and Captain Richard Ewell, advanced down the Gila and, north of Mount Turnbull, found a large camp of Coyotera Apache. A co-ordinated attack saw 45 killed and about 36 captured for the loss of nine wounded soldiers. The Apache soon sued for peace (27 June 1857).

Gilau ∎ 1660 ∎ Transylvanian National Revolt
When Crimean Tatars drove Prince George Rákóczi II out of Transylvania, his supporters restored him, then faced a Turkish army under Pasha Ahmed Sidi of Buda invading Transylvania in force. In the west at Fenes, near Gilau, west of Cluj, Rákóczi was defeated and died of his wounds two weeks later aged just 39. The Turkish offensive then continued against **Nagyvarad** (22 May 1660).

Gilbert Islands ∎ 1943 ∎ World War II (Pacific)
At the start of the Allied offensive in the Central Pacific, American General Holland Smith invaded the Gilbert Islands, seizing **Makin** with relative ease then **Tarawa** 100 miles south, where there were shocking losses on both sides. Capture of the Gilberts provided important airfields for land-based aircraft to support the next advance north into the **Marshall Islands** (20–24 November 1943).

Gilead ∎ 635 ∎ Muslim Conquest of Syria
See **Fihl**

Gilgal Creek ∎ 1864 ∎ American Civil War (Western Theatre)
See **Marietta**

Gilgit ∎ 747 ∎ Tang Imperial Wars
Despite withdrawing after **Dafeichuan** (670), Tang China eventually regained the remote northwest and General Gao Xianzhi later led 10,000 men across the Pamirs against the Tibetan client-state of Gilgit (Little Balur). A brutal action saw 5,000 Tibetans killed and a garrison was established to restore Chinese control in the Pamir region. In 751, Gao was halted in Central Asia at **Talas**.

Gimrah ∎ 1832 ∎ Russian Conquest of the Caucasus
Facing rebellion in Muslim Dagestan, west of the Caspian, Russian Baron Grigori Rosen, supported by General Franz Kluge-von-Klugenau, drove Imam Ghazi Muhammad to a

final stand at Gimrah, west of modern Buinaksk. Imam Ghazi and most of his followers were killed when Gimrah fell by storm. However, another Imam was elected and resistance continued for 25 years (29 October 1832).

Gindarus I 38 BC I Roman-Parthian Wars

When Pacorus of Parthia invaded Roman Syria, supported by Roman General Quintus Labienus, Mark Antony, despite continuing civil war, sent an army under Ventidius Bassus, who executed Labienus. Ventidius defeated Parthian General Phranipates, then defeated and killed Pacorus at Gindarus, west of the Euphrates, and Parthia withdrew from Syria (9 June 38 BC).

Gindrinkers Line I 1941 I World War II (China)

See **Kowloon**

Gingee I 1648 I Bijapur-Maratha Wars

Mohammad Adil Shah resolved to expand the power of Muslim Bijapur and sent General Mustafa Khan against Gingee, west of Pondicherry, held by the Rupa Nayak. During a long siege, the Maratha leader, Shahji Bhonsle, was captured and Mustafa Khan died. Muhammad Khan then continued the siege to capture the city and reputedly enough treasure to load 89 elephants (28 December 1648).

Gingee I 1689–1698 I Mughal-Maratha Wars

Attacking the Maratha kingdoms of central India, Emperor Aurangzeb sent General Zulfiqar Khan to besiege King Rajaram at Gingee fortress, west of Pondicherry. Despite his troops being under attack in the field, Aurangzeb refused to make peace. When Rajaram escaped to Vellore, a new Mughal commander and fresh forces scaled the walls to end the nine-year siege (17 February 1698).

Gingee I 1750 I 2nd Carnatic War

Having routed Nawab Mohammad Ali of Arcot near **Tiruvadi**, French Colonel Louis d'Auteil attacked Gingee, 50 miles inland from Pondicherry, defended by 10,000 of the Nawab's men. In a remarkable feat, a storming party under the Marquis Charles de Bussy blew in the gates with an explosive charge to capture the most powerful fortress in southeast India (11 September 1750).

Gingee I 1752 I 2nd Carnatic War

Over-confident after victory at **Seringham**, Governor Thomas Saunders of Madras sent Major James Kinneer, with just 200 European troops and about 2,000 Sepoys, against Gingee, inland from Pondicherry, the most powerful fortress in southeast India. Intercepted by a French column under Colonel Jacques Kerjean, Kinneer was overwhelmed and repulsed with heavy losses (6 August 1752).

Gingindlovu I 1879 I Anglo-Zulu War

British commander Lord Frederick Chelmsford advancing to relieve Eshowe, in southern Zululand, met perhaps 10,000 Zulus under Somopo and Dabulamanzi (brother of King Cetshwayo) near Gingindlovu. Cut down by volley fire and Gatlings, the Zulus fled with about 1,200 killed. Chelmsford lost 13 killed and 48 wounded and **Eshowe** was relieved next day (2 April 1879).

Ginniss I 1885 I British-Sudan Wars

When General Charles Gordon was killed by Mahdists and the British relief expedition withdrew from **Khartoum**, new Khalifa Abdullah el-Taaishi advanced down the Nile and threatened Kosheh, south of Akasha. Arriving with reinforcements, General Sir Frederick Stephenson routed the main Dervish army in a dawn attack at nearby Ginniss and drove them upstream (30 December 1885).

Giornico I 1478 I Swiss-Milanese Wars

After Charles of Burgundy was killed at **Nancy** (January 1477), Swiss under Hans Waldmann and Adrian von Bubenberg attacked the Lady Bona of Savoy, widow of former Burgundian ally Duke Galeazzo Sforza of Milan. Repulsed at Bellinzona, the Swiss withdrew to Giornico, in the Leventina Valley, where the Milanese army was routed and the valley became Swiss (28 December 1478).

Girgil **I** 1847 **I** Russian Conquest of the Caucasus

At war with Imam Shamil of Dagestan, Count Mikhail Vorontsov besieged the rebel position at Girgil, while Shamil attacked the Russians in the field. After a heavy bombardment, the village fell by storm—at the cost of about 500 Russian casualties—and Vorontsov marched against **Saltah**. Girgil was captured again a year later by Prince Moisie Argutinsky (13–20 June 1847).

Girishk **I** 1795 **I** Afghan Wars of Succession

While Zaman Shah of Kabul was campaigning against the Sikhs in the Sind, he was attacked in the rear by his brother Mahmud Mirza. Marching rapidly west, Zaman heavily defeated his brother at Girishk, on the Helmand River northwest of Kandahar. Mahmud fled to Persia, but five years later he returned to overthrow and blind his brother at **Kabul**.

Giron **I** 1829 **I** Peruvian-Colombian War
See **Tarqui**

Gisikon **I** 1653 **I** Swiss Peasant War

Locked in conflict with the city aristocracies, Swiss peasants fought an inconclusive battle at **Wohlenschwyl**. The following day, part of their army, under Christian Schybi, was heavily defeated at Gisikon by General Zweier von Evebach and the garrison of nearby Lucerne. The rising was crushed after a further peasant defeat days later at **Herzogenbuchsee** and Schybi was executed (4–5 June 1653).

Gisikon **I** 1845 **I** Sonderbund War

Fighting against Catholic separatists of the Sunderbund League, the Protestant forces of Switzerland under General William Henry Dufour captured Fribourg and Zug. Then, in the main fighting of the conflict, they defeated the Catholics at Gisikon with fewer than 100 dead on either side. Nearby Lucerne fell next day and

the 25-day war came to an end (23 November 1845).

Gisors **I** 1198 **I** French War of Richard I

Returned from the Crusades, Richard I of England—the Lion Heart—regained his French domains at **Freteval** (1194), then faced war against Phillip II. Near Beauvais at Gisors, the French King narrowly escaped death, when his knights were routed and thrown into the Epte by a collapsing bridge. Richard had little other success and died six months later at **Chalus** (28 September 1198).

Gissar **I** 1511 **I** Mughal-Uzbek Wars
See **Pul-i-Sanghin**

Gitschin **I** 1866 **I** Seven Weeks' War

Facing a Prussian invasion of Bohemia by Prince Friedrich Karl, Austrian Count Edouard von Clam-Gallas was repulsed at **Münchengratz** and fell back on Gitschin (modern Jicin) with Crown Prince Albert of Saxony. With no aid from the main Austrian army concentrating at **Königgratz**, Clam-Gallas suffered a heavy defeat and was relieved of his command (29–30 June 1866).

Giurgiu **I** 1595 **I** Wallachian-Turkish War

Ottoman Grand Vizier Sinan Pasha, advancing into Romania against Prince Michael the Brave of Wallachia, overcame defeat at **Calugareni** to attack Bucharest and capture **Tirgovist**. However, Michael and Sigismund Bathory of Transylvania pursued Sinan to the Danube, where the Ottoman rearguard was smashed while crossing the river at Giurgiu. Wallachia was restored (27 October 1595).

Giurgiu **I** 1854 **I** Crimean War

Russian General Mikhail Gorchakov marching up the Danube from the siege of **Silistria** encountered a large Turkish force at Giurgiu under Colonel Robert Cannon (in the Sultan's service as Bahram Pasha). After very heavy fighting, and with a Turkish flotilla arriving up the river, the Russians withdrew towards Budapest and the focus of fighting moved to Armenia and the Crimea (7 July 1854).

Givenchy I 1914 I World War I (Western Front)

To relieve the French in **Arras** and support their winter offensive in **Champagne**, British commander Sir John French ordered an attack on strategic Givenchy, west of **La Bassée**, where Indian troops took the town before being driven out by artillery. Reinforcements arrived and Givenchy was retaken and held as extreme winter conditions ended the advance (18–22 December 1914).

Givenchy I 1915 I World War I (Western Front)

With French forces bleeding in a battle of attrition in **Artois**, British General Sir Henry Rawlinson attacked north of the La Bassée canal around Givenchy to coincide with a new French advance. The British attack was repulsed with heavy losses, as was a simultaneous British supporting action near **Bellewaarde** bringing the Second Battle of Artois to an end (15–16 June 1915).

Gladsmuir I 1745 I Jacobite Rebellion (The Forty-Five)

See **Prestonpans**

Glasgow I 1864 I American Civil War (Trans-Mississippi)

As Confederate General Sterling Price marched west through Missouri, he sent General Joseph O. Shelby's "Iron Brigade" north across the Missouri River against Glasgow, defended by Colonel Chester Harding. Badly defeated, Harding was forced to surrender and Shelby seized large quantities of arms and supplies before continuing west to rejoin Price at **Lexington** (15 October 1864).

Glatz I 1760 I Seven Years War (Europe)

Austrian Marshal Gideon von Loudon destroyed a Prussian force at **Landshut** in Silesia (23 June), then marched southeast to besiege the fortress town of Glatz (modern Klodzko, Poland), while Frederick II of Prussia tried to divert the Austrians by besieging **Dresden**. On the same day that von Loudon took Glatz by storm,

Frederick left for Silesia to defend **Liegnitz** (June–29 July 1760).

Glencoe I 1692 I First Jacobite Rebellion

Amid the final doomed Scottish resistance to the accession of William III, the Macdonalds of Glencoe in Argyleshire were slow to acknowledge the Protestant King and suffered a surprise attack by Royalists under Captain Robert Campbell of Glenlyon. While most Macdonalds escaped, 38 were killed in a massacre, which came to symbolise the cause of Jacobite rebellion (13 February 1692).

Glendale I 1862 I American Civil War (Eastern Theatre)

See **White Oak Swamp**

Glen Fruin I 1603 I Later Scottish Clan Wars

In the culmination of a long-running feud, Alexander Colquhoun of Luss was commissioned by James VI of Scotland to pursue the troublesome Alasdair MacGregor of Glenstrae. In Glen Fruin, at Strone, Colquhoun's force was surrounded and over 200 were killed. The government outlawed and later hanged MacGregor and 11 Chiefs. His clan name was proscribed for over 150 years.

Glenlivet I 1594 I Huntly Rebellion

Renewing the rebellion crushed at **Corrichie**, the Catholic nobles, George Gordon Earl of Huntly and Francis Hay Earl of Errol, faced King James VI, who marched north, then sent Archibald Campbell Earl of Argyll forward to Glenlivet. Argyll was routed, but the rebels withdrew as the Scottish King advanced. James destroyed Huntly Castle and Huntly fled aboard (4 October 1594).

Glen Lochy I 1544 I Scottish Clan Wars

See **Shirts**

Glen Malure I 1580 I Geraldine Rebellion

James Eustace Viscount Baltinglass supported the Catholic Fitzgeralds of Munster by raising a rebellion in Leinster aided by Fiach MacHugh O'Byrne. At Glen Malure, in County Wicklow, O'Byrne defeated Lord Arthur Grey de Wilton, Lord Deputy of Ireland. However, the English quickly recovered to overcome the rebels and their Italian allies at **Fort del Or** near Smerwick (25 August 1580).

Glenshiel I 1719 I War of the Quadruple Alliance

A failed invasion to support rebellion in Scotland saw a Spanish fleet with 6,000 men scattered by a storm and only about 300 landed to help defend Glenshiel, west of Inverness. Royalist General Joseph Wightman routed the Jacobite leaders, George Keith Earl of Marischal and William Murray Marquis of Tullibardine, and the captured Spaniards were sent home (10 June 1719).

Glentrool I 1307 I Rise of Robert the Bruce

Robert the Bruce of Scotland recovered from defeat to raise a fresh army, which took a defensive position at Glentrool, near Newton Stewart, against Aymer de Valance Earl of Pembroke (who had beaten him at **Methven** in June 1306). The English were repulsed in a sharp action over rocky ground and a month later, Bruce won his great victory over Pembroke at **Loudon Hill** (April 1307).

Globe Tavern I 1864 I American Civil War (Eastern Theatre)

A fresh offensive against the Weldon Railroad, south of besieged Petersburg, Virginia, saw Union General Gouvernor K. Warren reach Globe Tavern, where he met Confederate Generals Ambrose P. Hill, Henry Heth and Wiliam Mahone. The Confederates were driven off in bloody fighting, though a probe further south was checked days later at **Reams Station** (18–21 August 1864).

Glorieta Pass I 1862 I American Civil War (Trans-Mississippi)

When Confederate General Henry Hopkins Sibley invaded New Mexico through **Valverde** to capture Santa Fe, part of his force under Major Charles L. Pyron was met to the southeast at Glorieta Pass by advancing Union troops led by Major John C. Chivington. Pyron was forced to withdraw after bitter fighting and Sibley eventually retreated south to San Antonio (26–28 March 1862).

Glorious First of June I 1794 I French Revolutionary Wars (1st Coalition)

See **First of June**

Gloucester I 1643 I British Civil Wars

Following Royalist capture of **Bristol** (26 July), King Charles I took his force against the Parliamentary stronghold at Gloucester, defended by Governor Edward Massey. After a fiercely defended siege, a large relief force from London under Robert Devereux Earl of Essex drove the Royalists off. Returning to the capital, Essex was beaten at **Newbury** (10 August–6 September 1643).

Gloucester Hill I 1951 I Korean War

See **Imjin**

Glowworm I 1940 I World War II (War at Sea)

While the British Navy laid mines off Norway, the destroyer *Glowworm* turned to seek a man lost overboard and encountered a German invasion force. Crippled by a destroyer, *Glowworm* rammed and badly damaged the heavy cruiser *Admiral Hipper* before sinking under gunfire. Captain Gerard Roope was among over 100 men lost and was awarded the war's first Victoria Cross (8 April 1940).

Gnesen I 1656 I 1st Northern War

Despite the defeat of a Swedish force outside Warsaw at **Warka**, Swedish forces under Adolf Johan, brother of King Charles X, continued to campaign west of the capital and met a much larger Polish army under Stefan Czarniecki and Jerzy Lubomirski at Gnesen (Gniezno), near Poznan. The Poles were defeated and Czarniekci was beaten by Charles himself in July at **Warsaw** (27 April 1656).

Gniezno I 1656 I 1st Northern War
See **Gnesen**

**Gnila Lipa I 1914 I World War I
(Eastern Front)**
On a cautious counter-offensive into eastern
Poland, Russian commander Nikolai Ivanov sent
Generals Nikolai Ruzskii and Aleksei Brusilov
west across the **Zlota Lipa** against a reinforced
Austrian force under General Eduard Böhm-
Ermolli on the Gnila Lipa. The Austrians were
driven back on **Lemberg** (Lvov), while Brusilov
circled north through **Rawa Russka** (29–30
August 1914).

**Goa I 1510 I Early Portuguese Colonial
Wars in Asia**
Afonso de Albuquerque expanding Portugal's
presence in India, seized the west coast port of
Goa from Adil Shah, Sultan of Bijapur. A large-
scale Muslim counter-attack a few months later
made Albuquerque abandon the city, but he soon
retook it and later sailed east to seize **Malacca**
(August 1511). Goa remained Portuguese until
annexed by India in 1961 (4 March & 25 November 1510).

**Goa I 1604 I Dutch-Portuguese
Colonial Wars**
Dutch Admiral Steven van de Haghen was
leading an expedition to the East Indies and
reached Portuguese Goa, on the west coast of
India, where he was attacked by a large Spanish-
Portuguese fleet. Van de Haghan drove off the
attack in a fierce action, during which he captured a Portuguese frigate. The Dutch Admiral
then continued east to seize the strategic island
of **Ambon** (29 October 1604).

**Godaveri I 1326 I Wars of the
Delhi Sultanate**
Muhammad Shah II assumed the throne in
Delhi, then faced rebellion in the Deccan by his
cousin Baha-ud-din Garshasp, Governor of
Sagar, who refused to recognise him. When the
rebel advanced on Deogiri, he was defeated at
the Godaveri by Khvaja Jahan and Majir Abu
Rija. He was eventually caught and executed and

Mohammad renamed Deogiri as Daulatabad, his
southern capital.

**Godby I 1918 I Finnish War
of Independence**
See **Aland**

Gode I 1977 I Ogaden War
When Ogaden separatist rebels and Somali
"volunteers" were heavily repulsed by the Ethiopian garrison at Gode (May), Somali President
Siad Barre committed his army to a full invasion
of Ethiopia with massive armoured support.
Within a week, the Somalis had captured Gode
and Ginir and most of central Ogaden. Their
advance in the north was checked at **Jijiga** and
Dire Dawa (July 1977).

Godley Wood I 1814 I War of 1812
See **Baltimore**

**Godolla I 1849 I Hungarian
Revolutionary War**
See **Hatvan**

**Goes I 1572 I Netherlands War
of Independence**
With Zeeland holding out for Spain, Dutch
under Jerome de 't Zeraerts besieged Goes on
South Beveland. A brilliant night exploit saw
veteran Christoforo de Mondragón lead 3,000
men ten miles through chest-deep low tide from
the mainland (only nine drowned) to relieve the
siege. The Dutch withdrew and the garrison of
Goes went west to reinforce **Middelburg** (26
August–21 October 1572).

Gogland I 1788 I 2nd Russo-Swedish War
See **Hogland**

**Gogra I 1529 I Mughal Conquest of
Northern India**
Flushed with success after destroying the
Rajput army at **Khanua** (March 1527), the great
Mughal Babur advanced into Bihar and Bengal
against Sultan Nasrat Ali. Babur won a decisive
victory in a three-day battle at the Gogra (Gha-
gra) where it joins the Ganges. He died soon

afterwards and his son Humayun was left to complete the establishment of the 300-year Mughal Empire (6 May 1529).

Gogunda ∎ 1576 ∎ Mughal Conquest of Northern India
  See **Haldighat**

Gohalwar ∎ 1757 ∎ Indian Campaigns of Ahmad Shah

Afghan ruler Ahmad Shah Durrani was returning home from the sack of **Delhi** in January when his force was attacked by Baba Deep Singh and he sent his son Timur Shah, Governor of Lahore, to punish the Sikhs. A few miles to the north of Amritsar at Gohalwar, the massively outnumbered Sikhs drove off the Afghans, although General Attal Khan slew Baba Deep (11 November 1757).

Goito ∎ 1848 ∎ 1st Italian War of Independence

In support of Italy's rising against Austria, King Charles Albert of Sardinia took command of the Allied forces and at Goito, on the Mincio east of Mantua, he defeated the Austrians under Marshal Josef Radetzky. While the Austrians were driven back across the Adige, they were victorious a few weeks later at **Santa Lucia** and in every other battle of the war (10 April 1848).

Golab ∎ 1656 ∎ 1st Northern War

On a fresh advance into Poland after his previous check at **Jasna Gora**, Charles X of Sweden pursued Polish commander Stefan Czarniecki across the Vistula, south of Warsaw, then attacked him to the southeast at Golab. The Poles were defeated and Charles continued southeast into the Ukraine, where he failed to storm Zamosc (17 February) and fell back towards **Sandomierz** (8 February 1656).

Golan Heights ∎ 1967 ∎ Arab-Israeli Six Day War

Responding to shelling from the Golan Heights, Israeli aircraft savaged Syrian positions and General Dan Laner attacked towards the powerful fortifications at Tel Faher. Israeli tanks broke through after severe fighting, then quickly took the nearby fortress at Tel Azaziat. With Jewish forces threatening the northern Golan, Syria accepted a humiliating ceasefire (9–10 June 1967).

Golan Heights (1st) ∎ 1973 ∎ Arab-Israeli Yom Kippur War

In a surprise assault on the Golan Heights, Syrian forces seized strategic **Mount Hermon** and forced the Israelis back along a wide front with massive superiority in men and tanks. After two days of intense fighting, the Israelis counter-attacked and the Syrians were pushed back to their starting point at the original 1967 ceasefire position, known as the Purple Line (6–9 October 1973).

Golan Heights (2nd) ∎ 1973 ∎ Arab-Israeli Yom Kippur War

After repulsing a surprise Syrian assault across the Golan Heights, Israeli commander Yitzhak Hofi launched a massive counter-attack under Generals Raful Eitan and Dan Laner. Israeli armour smashed through to seize many key positions, but the Syrian defence was bitterly fought and Laner's over-stretched troops were about to face a widespread counter-offensive (10–12 October 1973).

Golan Heights (3rd) ∎ 1973 ∎ Arab-Israeli Yom Kippur War

As an Israeli offensive across the Golan Heights drove deep into Syria, aid came from Jordan and Iraq for a determined Arab counter-attack. After severe fighting, the Arab effort stalled and, when the recapture of **Mount Hermon** brought Israeli forces within artillery range of Damascus, Syria agreed to a ceasefire. Both sides eventually broadly returned to the pre-war border (15–19 October 1973).

Golconda ∎ 1687 ∎ Mughal Conquest of the Deccan Sultanates

Emperor Aurangzeb attacked the Muslim Sultanates of Central India, where he captured **Bijapur**, then besieged Golconda fortress, west of Hyderabad, defended by Sultan Abu-l-Hasan.

The Mughals suffered awful losses in costly sorties and the faulty explosion of two giant mines. Bribery finally opened the gates, ending the independent kingdom of Golconda (28 January–1 October 1687).

Gold Beach I 1944 I World War II (Western Europe)
  See **D-Day**

Goldberg I 1635 I Thirty Years War (Franco-Habsburg War)
  When John George of Saxony declared war on Sweden in Pomerania, his forces were defeated on the Elbe at **Domitz** by the Swedish-German army of Johann Banér. A month later he was defeated again to the northeast at Goldberg, 15 miles south of Gustrow. John George was then driven back into Brandenberg, where his army was defeated again at **Kyritz** (1 December 1635).

Golden Rock I 1753 I 2nd Carnatic War
  See **Trichinopoly (1st)**

Golden Spurs I 1302 I Franco-Flemish Wars
  See **Courtrai**

Golding's Farm I 1862 I American Civil War (Eastern Theatre)
  See **Garnett's and Golding's Farms**

Goldsboro Bridge I 1862 I American Civil War (Eastern Theatre)
  Union General John G. Foster led an expedition deep into North Carolina along the Neuse, where he dispersed Confederate forces at **Kinston** and **White Hall**, then defeated General Thomas L. Clingman's Confederate brigade at Goldsboro Bridge. Foster proceeded to destroy strategic railway facilities, which had been his objective, before returning downstream to New Bern (17 December 1862).

Goliad I 1835 I Texan Wars of Independence
  As fresh Mexican forces entered Texas, General Martin Perfecto de Cos secured Goliad, then marched to San Antonio leaving a garrison of only about 30, who were soon attacked by volunteers under George Collingsworth and Ben Milam. In a brief action with few casualties, the Texans captured the town, along with vital military supplies then used at the siege of **San Antonio** (9 October 1835).

Goliad Massacre I 1836 I Texan Wars of Independence
  See **Coleto Creek**

Gollheim I 1298 I Habsburg Wars of Succession
  After Rudolf of Germany died, the Electors provoked a bitter dispute by passing over his Habsburg son, Albert of Austria, in favour of the more pliable Adolphus of Nassau. Alienated by the King's unwise rule, some German Princes supported Albert to overthrow Adolphus. West of Worms, near Gollheim, the King was defeated and killed, reputedly by Albert's own hand (2 July 1298).

Golomb I 1656 I 1st Northern War
  See **Golab**

Golovchin I 1708 I 2nd "Great" Northern War
  See **Holowczyn**

Golpejerra I 1072 I War of Castilian Succession
  In the war of succession between the sons of Ferdinand I of Castile, Sancho II of Castile defeated his brother, Alfonso VI of Leon, at **Lantada** in 1068, and they met again on the nearby battlefield of Golpejerra, near Carrion. Alfonso was defeated and captured and Sancho crowned himself King of Leon, reuniting Castile, Leon and Galicia (January 1072).

Golymin I 1806 I Napoleonic Wars (4th Coalition)
  Following victories at **Jena** and **Auerstadt**, Napoleon Bonaparte marched into Poland and, on the same day as the battle at **Pultusk**, Marshals Louis Davout and Pierre Augereau met

part of the Russian army under Prince Andréi Gallitzin further north of Warsaw at Golymin. The outcome was indecisive, but the Russians withdrew and the French were bogged in the mud (26 December 1806).

Gona I 1942 I World War II (Pacific)

With Japanese forces driven back across **Papua** over the **Kokoda Trail**, Australian General George Vasey attacked the fortified Japanese position on the northern coast at Gona. Repeated assaults supported by artillery and bombing saw Gona finally taken at heavy cost to both sides. The Australians then turned east against nearby **Buna** (18 November–9 December 1942).

Gonaives I 1802 I Napoleonic Wars (Santo Domingo Rising)

French General Charles Leclerc sent to suppress a rising in **Santo Domingo** by black leader Francois Toussaint l'Ouverture, launched one of the few large battles of the mainly guerrilla campaign on the Plain of Gonaives. While Leclerc seized Gonaives, General Donatien Rochambeau was repulsed at nearby Ravine-à-Coulevres and the rebels held out at **Crête-à-Perriot** (23 February 1802).

Gondar I 1887 I Sudanese-Ethiopian War
See **Debra Sina**

Gondar I 1941 I World War II (Northern Africa)

Despite Italy's surrender in East Africa at **Amba Alagi**, substantial Italian forces continued to hold out in the mountains of Ethiopia. Converging east through Chelga, south through **Wolchefit Pass** and west from Kulkaber, General Charles Fowkes took Gondar after heavy fighting. General Guglielmo Nasi surrendered over 23,000 men and the campaign was finally over (27 November 1941).

Gondra I 1933 I Chaco War

In a massive offensive against Paraguay in the Chaco Boreal, Bolivian forces under the German General Hans Kundt were driven off from the fortress of **Nanawa** and regrouped to attack Paraguayan Colonel Rafael Franco, under siege at nearby Gondra. A renewed assault commencing on 3 August was also repulsed and the offensive soon came to an end (January–9 September 1933).

Gonzales I 1835 I Texan Wars of Independence

Facing growing resistance from Texan citizens, Mexican authorities sent a force to repossess the cannon provided to Gonzales, east of San Antonio, for protection against Indians. Led by Colonels John H. Moore and Joseph E. W. Wallace, the residents used the gun to drive off the Mexicans—their battle banner said "Come and Take it"—and the war for Independence truly began (2 October 1835).

Goodrich's Landing I 1863 I American Civil War (Western Theatre)

In support of besieged **Vicksburg**, Confederate forces further down the Mississippi under Colonel William H. Parsons advanced south from Arkansas and captured a small Union fortress near Lake Providence, Louisiana. Next day, Union marines led by General Alfred W. Ellet arrived at Goodrich's Landing and heavy fighting forced Parsons to withdraw (30 June 1863).

Goodwin Sands I 1511 I Anglo-Scottish Royal Wars

Scottish commander Andrew Barton returning from a cruise against Portugal was intercepted near the Goodwin Sands by English Admiral Lord Thomas Howard and his brother Sir Edward. With Barton killed in action, his two ships were taken as prizes. The resulting quarrel between Henry VIII of England and James IV of Scotland soon led to war and Scottish disaster at **Flodden** (2 August 1511).

Goodwin Sands I 1652 I 1st Dutch War

Prior to official declaration of the war, English Admiral Robert Blake intercepted a Dutch fleet under Admiral Maarten Tromp, which had been sheltering near Dover while waiting for a Dutch East Indies convoy. With Blake joined by the

Downs squadron of Admiral Nehemiah Bourne, Tromp was defeated off the Goodwin Sands and was driven off with the loss of one ship (29 May 1652).

Goodwood ∎ 1944 ∎ World War II (Western Europe)

After finally taking **Caen**, Sir Bernard Montgomery launched a big armoured offensive to the southeast. Operation Goodwood saw over 1,000 British and Canadian tanks attack after massive aerial and artillery bombardment. But Marshal Günther von Kluge halted the controversial offensive after terrible losses on both sides. Montgomery then stalled until the advance on **Falaise** (18–21 July 1944).

Goose Green ∎ 1982 ∎ Falklands War

British troops marching south from **San Carlos** advanced on the Argentine garrison at the grass airfield at Goose Green. Unexpectedly outnumbered, Colonel Herbert Jones was killed taking nearby Darwin. Severe fighting cost 17 British and 50 Argentines killed before Air Commodore Wilson Pedroza surrendered Goose Green and 1,500 Argentines were captured (28–29 May 1982).

Gophna ∎ 166 BC ∎ Maccabean War

The first engagement of the war saw the Seleucid General Apollonius march south from Samaria to suppress the Hebrew rebellion, led by Judas Maccabeus. Avoiding an open battle, the outnumbered Jews attacked their enemy in a narrow valley near Gophna, north of Jerusalem. The Seleucid army was routed and Apollonius died on the battlefield.

Gorakhpur ∎ 1858 ∎ Indian Mutiny

Disheartened by defeat at **Sohanpur**, Faizabad rebels under Mehndi Husain were attacked at Gorakhpur by about 11,000 Gurkhas under General George MacGregor and Nepalese commander Jang Bahadur. With the rebels routed and pursued across the Rapti, order was restored in Gorakhpur and Jang Bahadur marched west into Oudh to support the British at **Lucknow** (6 January 1858).

Goraria ∎ 1857 ∎ Indian Mutiny

On the offensive in central India against the rebel Firuz Shah, Colonel Charles Stuart and Agent Henry Durand attacked the rebels at the village of Goraria, near Mandasur (Mandsaur). The rebels were finally driven out of Goraria after stubborn resistance and a heavy artillery bombardment. Firuz Shah and 2,000 men had meantime abandoned Mandasur (23–24 November 1857).

Goraslau ∎ 1601 ∎ Balkan National Wars

Prince Michael of Wallachia lost his throne at **Bucov** in late 1600, but regained support from Emperor Rudolf II, who sent General George Basta to help recover Transylvania from Sigismund Bathory (restored a year earlier with Basta's aid at **Mirischlau**). At Goraslau, near Zalau in northwest Transylvania, Basta defeated Sigismund, then murdered the hapless Michael (3 August 1601).

Gorazde ∎ 1994–1995 ∎ Bosnian War

With **Sarajevo** invested, heavy fighting developed further east around the Muslim enclave at Gorazde, which eventually also came under Serb siege. While NATO air-strikes forced Serb heavy weapons to pull back, fighting and shelling continued and UN peacekeepers were taken hostage. However, the UN "safe haven" held out until the war's end (March 1994–December 1995).

Gorée ∎ 1758 ∎ Seven Years War (West Africa)

On campaign against French West Africa, Britain captured **Senegal**, but was repulsed from nearby Gorée and sent a stronger force under Commodore Augustus Keppel and Colonel Richard Worge. The island fortress surrendered after a daylong bombardment, yielding 300 prisoners and almost 100 guns. At the end of the war, Gorée reverted to France (29 December 1758).

Gorée ∎ 1804 ∎ Napoleonic Wars (3rd Coalition)

The French West African island of Gorée in Senegal, captured by the British in 1800, was retaken after fighting in 1804 by French Colonel Francois Blanchot de Verly, Governor of St Louis. It was then taken again a few weeks later by troops from a British convict transport. In July 1809 it was used by Major Charles Maxwell as the base to capture St Louis. Senegal was returned to France in 1814.

Gorizio ▌ 1916 ▌ World War I (Italian Front)

See **Isonzo (2nd)**

Gorlice-Tarnow ▌ 1915 ▌ World War I (Eastern Front)

Despite a check in the **Carpathians**, the Austro-German army of General August von Mackensen concentrated southeast of Cracow and attacked General Radko Dmitriev on the axis Gorlice-Tarnow. Massive bombardment saw Mackensen break through the Russian line in just two days and take 140,000 prisoners. The Allies soon seized **Przemysl** and **Lemberg** (1 May–27 June 1915).

Gorni-Dubnik ▌ 1877 ▌ Russo-Turkish Wars

As part of the Russian siege of **Plevna**, south of the Danube, General Ossip Gourko led a large-scale attack against the redoubt of Gorni-Dubnik, 14 miles to the southwest, held by Achmet Hefiz Pasha. The strongpoint fell at a cost of over 3,000 Russian casualties and the nearby redoubt of Telisch fell two days later. Plevna held out another two months (24 October 1877).

Gorodeczno ▌ 1812 ▌ Napoleonic Wars (Russian Campaign)

During the Allied offensive into Russia towards **Smolensk**, a French-Austrian force under General Jean-Louis Reynier and Field Marshal Prince Karl Philipp von Schwarzenberg was challenged at Gorodeczno by Russians led by General Count Alexander Tormazov. The Russians were driven off with heavy losses to both sides and the Allied advance continued (12 August 1812).

Gorodok ▌ 1914 ▌ World War I (Eastern Front)

In the advance on Lemberg (Lvov), Russian forces circled north through **Rawa Russka**, while west of the city around Gorodok, Austrian Generals Moritz Auffenberg and Svetozar Boroevic met Russians under Generals Nicolai Ruzskii and Aleksei Brusilov. Very heavy fighting forced the Austrians back across the San and the exhausted Russians besieged **Przemysl** (6–11 September 1914).

Goryokaku ▌ 1869 ▌ War of the Meiji Restoration

With pro-Tokugawa rebels crushed at **Fushimi**, **Ueno** and **Wakamatsu**, Imperial General Kuroda Kiyotaka took a force to Hokkaido against Enomoto Takeaki, who had established a "Republic" at Goryokaku in Hakodate Bay. Enomoto was forced to surrender after a bloody assault, finally securing peace for Japan and ending the 250-year Tokugawa Shogunate (20–27 June 1869).

Gorzno ▌ 1629 ▌ 2nd Polish-Swedish War

Chancellor Axel Oxenstierna resolved to check Polish raids on outlying Swedish possessions and sent General Hermann Wrangel into northern Poland. Northeast of Torun at Gorzno, a Polish army under General Mikolaj Potocki was decisively defeated. Wrangel then advanced to the walls of Torun (German Thorn) before the threat of Polish reinforcements forced him to withdraw (2 February 1629).

Gotha ▌ 1757 ▌ Seven Years War (Europe)

Frederick II of Prussia withdrew west from **Prague**, leaving General Friedrich von Seydlitz with just 1,900 dragoons to resist Austrian Prince Joseph of Saxe-Hildburghausen and French Duke Charles of Soubise. A comic-opera coup at Gotha, near Erfurt, saw the Austro-French vanguard of 9,500 men routed. The Allied commanders lost again in November at **Rossbach** (17 September 1757).

Gothic Line I 1944–1945 I World War II (Southern Europe)

When Allied forces breached the **Gustav Line** and entered **Rome**, Field Marshal Albert Kesselring fought a bold withdrawal to the Gothic Line, through the **Apennines** to **Rimini** in the east, which fell after heavy fighting. The Germans then counter-attacked south of **Bologna** and the offensive stalled until the spring, when a renewed advance entered the **Po Valley** (August 1944–April 1945).

Gotland I 1563 I Nordic Seven Years War

While raiding against Oland, off southeast Sweden, Danish commander Peder Skram's 32-strong Danish-German flotilla was boldly attacked off Gotland by just 18 Swedish ships under Jakob Bagge. The resulting action was a hard-fought draw, but Skram was dismissed for failing to defeat the outnumbered Swedes. The two fleets met again the following year off **Oland** (11 September 1563).

Gottolengo I 1427 I Venetian-Milanese Wars

Venetian Captain-General Francesco Bussone Count Carmagnola captured **Brescia** in 1426 and continued the war by attacking an outnumbered Milanese army at Gottolengo, northeast of Cremona. The confused battle was broken off with heavy losses on both sides and no clear result. Carmagnola soon gathered his forces for a renewed encounter at nearby **Casa-al-Secco**.

Gqokli I 1818 I Rise of Shaka Zulu

On a bloody offensive after assuming the Zulu throne, the young warrior Shaka moved against his rival Zwide of the Ndwandwe, who had killed the King's mentor, Dingiswayo. In Shaka's first great victory, at Gqokli near Ulundi, Zwide's larger force under Nomahlanjana was routed—with a claimed 7,000 killed out of 12,000. He was finally beaten the following year at **Mhlatuze** (April 1818).

Grahamstown I 1819 I 5th Cape Frontier War

Provoked by British intervention after his victory at **Amalinda**, the Xhosa Chief Ndlambe sent Nxele and 10,000 warriors against the settlement at Grahamstown, defended by Colonel Thomas Willshire and just 450 men. In a battle which virtually saved Cape Colony, the Xhosa were finally repulsed, losing perhaps 1,000 killed. Nxele was defeated in August at the **Fish River** (22 April 1819).

Grahovo I 1858 I Turko-Montenegran Wars

When Prince Danilo II of Montenegro attempted to annexe some border areas of Herzegovina, he provoked a fresh Turkish invasion by Hussein Pasha. The Turks were heavily defeated in the northwest at Grahovo by Danilo's brother Mirko Petrovich, losing 3,000 men killed and all their guns. The Powers then intervened to secure peace and Danilo was later assassinated (13 May 1858).

Grammos I 1948 I Greek Civil War

Following success at **Roumeli**, 40,000 government troops began a large offensive against the stronghold on Mount Grammos, but were driven off and General Kalogeropolous was relieved. General Thrasyvoulos Tsakalotos attacked again and, after heavy losses on both sides, Markos Vaphiadis led a brilliant rebel withdrawal into Albania. He soon came back at **Kastoria** (14 June–22 August 1948).

Grammos I 1949 I Greek Civil War

Ten days after victory in the northwest at **Vitsi**, huge government forces under Marshal Alexandros Papagos, with intense air support, attacked and overwhelmed the final insurgent stronghold around Mount Grammos. Communist leader Nikos Zakhariadis and about 8,000 survivors crossed into Albania then dispersed into exile. A ceasefire on 16 October ended the war (25–30 August 1949).

**Grampians ∎ 84 ∎ Roman Conquest
of Britain**
See **Mons Graupius**

Gran ∎ 1683 ∎ Turkish-Habsburg Wars
See **Esztergom**

**Gran ∎ 1685 ∎ Later Turkish-
Habsburg Wars**
See **Neuhausel**

**Granada, Nicaragua ∎ 1855 ∎ National
(Filibuster) War**

The American Filibuster William Walker defeated a Legitimist force in western Nicaragua at **La Virgen** in September, then bypassed the concentration further north at Rivas by sailing along the lake to land and advance on Granada. Walker surprised and stormed the city and, after executing Legitimist leader Ponciano Corral at Leon, effectively seized power in Nicaragua (13 October 1855).

**Granada, Nicaragua ∎ 1856 ∎ National
(Filibuster) War**

Attacking the American William Walker, who had seized power in Nicaragua, the Central American allies under Mariano Paredes advanced from **Masaya** to besiege nearby Granada. After shocking losses on both sides to wounds and disease (Paredes died of cholera), Walker burned and abandoned Granada and José Victor Zavala pursued him to **Rivas** (24 November–13 December 1856).

**Granada, Spain ∎ 1491–1492 ∎ Final
Christian Reconquest of Spain**

In the final campaign of the Reconqista, Ferdinand V of Castile and Aragon launched his massive army against the heavily fortified city of Granada, the last remaining Muslim possession in Spain. Abu Abdallah (Boabdil), King of Granada, surrendered the city after a long and brutal siege and eight centuries of Muslim rule in Spain came to an end (April 1491–2 January 1492).

**Grand-Couronné ∎ 1914 ∎ World War I
(Western Front)**
See **Nancy**

**Grandella ∎ 1266 ∎ Angevin Conquest
of the Two Sicilies**
See **Benevento**

**Grande Ronde Valley ∎ 1856 ∎ Yakima
Indian Wars**

While campaigning against Indians in the Columbia Basin resisting removal to reservations, Colonel Benjamin F. Shaw took 400 volunteers from Washington into northern Oregon against Walla Wallas, Cayuse and Umatillas in the Grande Ronde Valley, west of modern La Grande. Shaw's men killed 40 Indians and destroyed a large village. Fighting resumed in 1858 at **Pine Creek** (17 July 1856).

**Grand Gulf ∎ 1863 ∎ American Civil War
(Western Theatre)**

Union Admiral David D. Porter preparing to assault Confederate **Vicksburg** on the Mississippi led a squadron of ironclads against Confederate batteries downstream at Grand Gulf, Mississippi, commanded by General John S. Bowen. Though Porter's gunboats were driven off after a heavy exchange of fire, the main Union forces landed further south near **Port Gibson** (29 April 1863).

**Grand Port ∎ 1810 ∎ Napoleonic Wars
(5th Coalition)**

Determined to recover the Indian Ocean island of Mauritius, British Commodore Samuel Pym, supported by Captain Nesbit Willoughby, landed on Isle de la Passe (13 August). But in a sea-battle off Grand Port, French Commodore Victor Duperre sank or captured all four British frigates. The expedition had to withdraw and **Mauritius** was not retaken until later in the year (23 August 1810).

Grandson ∎ 1476 ∎ Burgundian-Swiss War

Provoked by a Swiss invasion of Lorraine and defeat at **Héricourt**, Charles the Bold of Burgundy took an army into Switzerland, where he captured Grandson on Lake Neuchatel and hanged the garrison (28 February). Facing a powerful Swiss counter-attack northeast of the town, his troops panicked and fled, abandoning their arms and baggage. He lost again at **Morat** in June (2 March 1476).

Granicus I 334 BC I Conquests of Alexander the Great

Alexander the Great opened his war against Persia by crossing the Dardanelles to the Granicus (modern Kocabas), on the Sea of Marmara, where he met and decisively defeated a smaller scratch force under local Satraps and Greek mercenary commander Memnon. The Persians fled and the mercenaries were largely massacred, though Memnon escaped with the Persian fleet to **Miletus** (May 334 BC).

Granson I 1476 I Burgundian-Swiss War
See **Grandson**

Grantham I 1643 I British Civil Wars

Advancing towards Newark, Nottinghamshire, New Model Army commanders Francis Willoughby Lord Parham, Sir John Hotham and Oliver Cromwell were surprised at nearby Grantham by Royalist cavalry under General Charles Cavendish. The Royalists were driven off with substantial losses in a confused action, but the Parliamentary advance on Newark was abandoned (13 May 1643).

Grant's Hill I 1758 I Seven Years War (North America)
See **Fort Duquesne**

Granville I 1703 I War of the Spanish Succession

In command of a British squadron off northwestern France, Admiral Thomas Dilkes attacked a French convoy of 45 merchant ships and their escort of just three frigates. In a brilliant victory between Granville and Avranches, he drove ashore, captured or destroyed almost the entire fleet. The following year Dilkes was knighted for his part in the great victory off **Malaga** (26–27 July 1703).

Granville I 1793 I French Revolutionary Wars (Vendée War)

Royalist rebel Henri de la Rochejaquelein marched north into Normandy after victory at **Entrammes** (26 October) to support a planned landing by émigrés and attacked the port of Granville, defended by Republican General Jean Pierre Varin and a small garrison. The large Vendéean army was disastrously repulsed and retreated towards the Loire before the British navy arrived (November 1793).

Granville Raid I 1945 I World War II (Western Europe)

Leading an unexpected German offensive late in the war, Admiral Friedrich Huffmeier, commander of occupying forces in the British Channel Islands, sent 600 men in minesweepers and smaller craft from Jersey against the French port of Granville. The raiders, under Lieutenant Carl-Friedrich Mohr, destroyed port facilities and Allied shipping before withdrawing (8–9 March 1945).

Graspan I 1899 I 2nd Anglo-Boer War

As British General Lord Paul Methuen advanced to relieve besieged **Kimberley**, he drove the Boers out of **Belmont**, then attacked Jacobus Prinsloo and Jacobus de la Rey in a position further north at Graspan. The British lost about 200 men in a successful frontal assault and the Boers about 100 before Methuen continued north across the **Modder** towards **Magersfontein** (25 November 1899).

Grass Fight I 1835 I Texan Wars of Independence

While Texan forces maintained a loose blockade of Mexican General Martin de Cos at **San Antonio**, word was received of an approaching mule train with silver to pay the Mexican garrison. A detachment under James Bowie and Ed Burleson attacked the column and, after a sharp skirmish, captured the load. It proved to be grass collected for horses inside the siege (28 November 1835).

Grassy Lick | 1864 | American Civil War (Eastern Theatre)
See **Cove Mountain**

Grathe Heath | 1157 | Danish War of Succession
With three claimants to the Danish throne, Sweyn III Grade invited his rivals to mediation at Roskilde, where he assassinated Knut III Magnussen (9 August). However, Waldemar I escaped to Jutland and, south of Viborg at Grathe Heath, he later defeated Sweyn, who was killed by a peasant during the subsequent pursuit. Waldemar became sole King of all Denmark (23 October 1157).

Grattan Massacre | 1854 | Sioux Indian Wars
See **Fort Laramie**

Graus | 1063 | Early Christian Reconquest of Spain
Having invaded Muslim Saragossa, held by al-Muqtadir, King Ramiro I of Aragon attacked the Pyrennean town of Graus, north of Monson. Concerned by Aragonese expansion, Ramiro's brother Ferdinand I of Castile sent his son Sancho to help the Muslims recover Graus. Aided by Rodrigo Diaz de Bivar—El Cid—Sancho defeated and killed his uncle Ramiro (8 May 1063).

Grave | 1674 | 3rd Dutch War
In command of the counter-attack against French invaders of the Dutch Republic, General Karel Rabenhaupt Baron de Sucha laid siege to Grave, on the Maas northeast of Hertogenbosch, where he had formerly been Governor. The siege lasted over three months—assumed by William III of Orange on 9 October—before the city was finally retaken (15 July–28 October 1674).

Gravelines | 1558 | 5th Habsburg-Valois War
Following the recapture of **Calais**, French forces under Marshal Paul des Thermes advanced into Spanish Flanders, but were driven back by Count Lamoral of Egmont and trapped on the shore at Gravelines, east of Calais, between the Spanish army and the English fleet, which pounded their flank. The French rout led to peace between England, France and Spain and ended the war (13 July 1558).

Gravelines | 1644 | Thirty Years War (Franco-Habsburg War)
Gaston Duke d'Orleans (son of Henry IV) expanded French territory north into the Spanish Netherlands, where he laid siege to Gravelines, supported by Marshals Charles de la Porte Duke de la Meilleraie and Jacques de Gassion plus a Dutch naval blockade. The port fell after two months, followed by other key towns including Bethune, Cassel, Courtrai and **Dunkirk** (May–28 July 1644).

Gravelly Run | 1865 | American Civil War (Eastern Theatre)
See **Lewis's Farm**

Gravelotte | 1870 | Franco-Prussian War
With Marshal Francois-Achille Bazaine defeated at **Mars-la-Tour**, Prussian General Helmut von Moltke attacked at Gravelotte, sending Prince Friedrich Karl of Prussia against Bazaine's right flank at St Privat. Marshal Francois-Antoine Canrobert defended bravely until forced back by numbers. Bazaine then weakly retired east into a strategically disastrous siege at **Metz** (18 August 1870).

Gravenstafel | 1915 | World War I (Western Front)
Opening the Second Battle of **Ypres**, the German Fourth Army under Duke Albrecht attacked in the northeast around Gravenstafel. French troops were forced back by the first use of gas on the Western Front before British and Canadians under General Sir Herbert Plumer checked the advance. The Germans then switched to attack again through nearby **St Julien** (22–23 April 1915).

Gray | 1870 | Franco-Prussian War
German commander Karl August Werder defeated a French force at **Chatillon-le-Duc**, then marched west towards Dijon against Gardes

Mobiles sent to defend the Vingeanne. The French were put to flight, losing a large number of prisoners in fighting near Gray at Talmay and Essertenne. Werder then sent General Gustav von Beyer probing further west towards **Dijon** (27 October 1870).

Greasy Grass | 1876 | Sioux Indian Wars
   See **Little Big Horn**

Great Bridge | 1775 | War of the American Revolution
In the wake of humiliation at **Hampton** (25 October), Virginian Governor John Murray Earl of Dunmore faced an advance on Norfolk itself under American Colonel William Woodford. At the Great Bridge, a causeway south of the town, Captain Charles Fordyce was defeated and killed and Dunmore fell back. When the colonists seized **Norfolk,** he withdrew to ships in the harbour (9 December 1775).

Great Meadows | 1754 | Seven Years War (North America)
Advancing against the French at Fort Duquesne (modern Pittsburgh, Pennsylvania), Colonel George Washington and about 150 Virginia militia encountered a patrol at Great Meadows near the Youghiogany. A sharp action saw the French all killed or captured, including Ensign Joseph Coulon de Villiers killed. Just weeks later, Washington was forced to surrender at **Fort Necessity** (27 May 1754).

Great Plains | 203 BC | 2nd Punic War
   See **Bagradas**

Great Sortie | 1870 | Franco-Prussian War
   See **Villiers**

Great Swamp Fight | 1675 | King Philip's War
In war against Wampanoag Chief Metacomet—known by New England colonists as King Philip—1,000 men under Governor Josiah Winslow of Plymouth, aided by Mohegan Indians, attacked the fortified village of Philip's Narran-gansett ally, Canonchet, at Kingston, Rhode Island. The tribe was devastated in the so-called Great Swamp Fight, although Canonchet escaped (19 December 1675).

Great Wall | 1933 | Manchuria Incident
A sequel to Japan seizing Manchuria at **Mukden** (modern Shenyang) in 1931, saw Japan invade Jehol (Inner Mongolia) to declare the Great Wall their southern boundary. General He Yingqin led a prolonged resistance in the so-called Battle of the Great Wall but, with Beijing itself threatened, China made peace. Jehol was then absorbed into the puppet state of Manchukuo (23 February–31 May 1933).

Great Zab River | 130 BC | Later Syrian-Parthian War
   See **Zab**

Greece | 1940 | World War II (Southern Europe)
Encouraged by German success in the west, Italians invaded Greece from **Albania** under General Sebastiano Visconti-Prasca and later Ubaldo Soddu. They were checked by Greek commander Alexander Papagos, who counter-attacked and entered Albania. Early the next year, German forces invaded Greece and Papagos had to withdraw and surrender (28 October–23 December 1940).

Greece | 1941 | World War II (Southern Europe)
As German forces under Marshal Wilhelm List stormed through the **Balkans** into Yugoslavia and Greece, 75,000 British and Commonwealth troops under General Henry Wilson arrived from the Middle East in a futile attempt to defend Greece. The Greek army was overwhelmed, with more than 250,000 men captured and the badly mauled Allies evacuated to **Crete** (6–30 April 1941).

Greenbrier River | 1861 | American Civil War (Eastern Theatre)
With the Confederates repulsed on **Cheat Summit,** south of Huttonsville, West Virginia,

General Joseph Reynolds advanced 12 miles east towards Confederate General Henry R. Jackson on the Greenbrier River. Reynolds was checked in a sharp action at Bartow, but Jackson suffered greater losses and abandoned Bartow for **Camp Allegheny**, nine miles to the southeast (3 October 1861).

Green Islands I 1944 I World War II (Pacific)

New Zealanders under General Harold Barrowclough captured the **Treasury Islands**, then attacked the Green Islands, northwest of **Bougainville**, occupied by about 120 Japanese. While the main island, Nissan, was taken at the cost of just ten New Zealanders and three American observers killed, the action secured an important strategic airfield to bomb **Truk** and **Rabaul** (15–16 February 1944).

Green River I 1861 I American Civil War (Western Theatre)
See **Rowlett's Station**

Green Spring I 1781 I War of the American Revolution
See **Jamestown Ford**

Grenada I 1779 I War of the American Revolution

French Admiral Charles-Hector Comte d'Estaing, commanding in the West Indies, eluded British Admiral John Byron to seize **St Vincent** (16 June), then sailed south and seized Grenada, along with over 1,000 men and 120 guns. The two fleets met off Grenada and a drawn action saw Byron's ships suffer heavy damage. However, d'Estaing withdrew and later sailed for **Savannah** (2–6 July 1779).

Grenada I 1796 I French Revolutionary Wars (1st Coalition)

Faced by rebellion against British rule in the West Indian island of Grenada, led by French planters and supported by the French in Martinique, British General Sir Ralph Abercromby landed with a small force and recaptured the island after ten days of fighting. The French

mulatto leader Fedon was hanged along with a number of rebel planters (June 1796).

Grenada I 1983 I American Invasion of Grenada

When left-wing military forces seized power in Grenada, US President Ronald Regan sent an intervention force of 7,000, supposedly to protect American civilians. When the Grenadian army and 700 Cuban militia resisted fiercely, 19 Americans and perhaps 60 locals and Cubans were killed and many were wounded before order was restored and free elections were ensured (25–27 October 1983).

Grengam I 1720 I 2nd "Great" Northern War

Following Russian victory at sea near **Osel**, off Estonia, Admiral Mikhail Golitsyn's galleys attacked Swedish commander Erik Sjoblad near Grengam in the southern Aland Islands. Lured onto shallow reefs, the Swedes were attacked and boarded, with four frigates and over 400 men captured. The victory further strengthened Russia's position and hastened an end to the war (27 July 1720).

Grevena I 1947 I Greek Civil War

Driven off from **Konitsa**, near the Albanian border, a large Communist force advanced southeast towards Grevena. Very severe fighting saw over 300 insurgent casualties and also heavy government losses before the attack was finally driven off. However, the insurgents gradually secured considerable territory in the area and, months later, attacked further south at **Metsovo** (22–25 July 1947).

Grijon I 1809 I Napoleonic Wars (Peninsular Campaign)

With French Marshal Nicolas Soult driven through northern Portugal by an Anglo-Portuguese counter-offensive by General Sir Arthur Wellesley, his rearguard under General Julien Mermet took a defensive position just south of Oporto, at Grijon. Wellesley's cavalry suffered a sharp check on the nearby heights of

Carvalho before Mermet withdrew and **Oporto** fell next day (11 May 1809).

Grimball's Landing I 1863 I American Civil War (Lower Seaboard)

Union General Alfred H. Terry renewed the offensive against **Charleston Harbour**, South Carolina, leading a diversionary landing on the western side of James Island. Terry repulsed an attack by Confederate General Johnson Hagood at Grimball's Landing before withdrawing. The main offensive was launched two days later, further east against **Fort Wagner** (16 July 1863).

Griswoldville I 1864 I American Civil War (Western Theatre)

As Union commander William T. Sherman marched through Georgia from Atlanta to **Savannah**, his right wing under General Charles C. Walcutt was attacked at Griswoldville, just east of Macon, by militia under Generals Pleasant J. Philips and Joseph Wheeler. The Georgians were repulsed with 600 men lost and Wheeler attacked days later at **Buck Head Creek** (22 November 1864).

Grochow I 1831 I Polish Rebellion

When Poland deposed Duke Constantine, brother of Tsar Nicholas I, Russian Field Marshal Hans von Diebitsch took 100,000 men as far as Grochow on the eastern outskirts of Warsaw, where he was finally halted by Prince Michael Radziwill. Both sides suffered massive losses and the Russian invaders withdrew a few days later after another bloody encounter at **Praga** (19–20 February 1831).

Grodek I 1914 I World War I (Eastern Front)
See **Gorodok**

Grodno I 1708 I 2nd "Great" Northern War

Charles XII of Sweden and General Carl Gustav Rehnskjold invaded Russian Lithuania and Charles personally took a vanguard of only 800 cavalry to seize the strategic bridge on the Nema at Grodno from 2,000 Russians. Believing the entire Swedish army had arrived, Tsar Peter I fled Grodno and, after a failed counter-attack, the Russians withdrew to the Berezina (26 January 1708).

Grodno I 1915 I World War I (Eastern Front)

Just days after the fall of **Brest-Litovsk**, Germans under General Hermann von Eichhorn converged north on Grodno (in modern Byelorussia), which was surrounded by strong fortresses. After fighting their way into the city, the Germans were driven out by a powerful counter-attack. The Russian rearguard was then repulsed and the Germans continued northeast towards **Vilna** (1–4 September 1915).

Groenkloof I 1901 I 2nd Anglo-Boer War

Facing Boer commandos in the eastern Cape Colony, a strong counter-insurgency column under Colonel Harry Scobell attacked commandant Johannes Lotter in camp at Groenkloof, near the village of Pietersburg, west of Cradock. Surprised at dawn, the Boers lost 60 casualties and another 60 captured. Lotter and seven other prisoners were later executed (4–5 September 1901).

Groenkop I 1901 I 2nd Anglo-Boer War
See **Tweefontein**

Grol I 1627 I Netherlands War of Independence

Dutch Captain-General Frederick Henry (son of William of Orange) led his first siege in the prolonged war, attacking the Spanish-held town of Grol (modern Groenlo), northwest of Winterswijk, with a force of 30,000 Dutch, French and English troops. When a mine was exploded the attackers stormed Grol, which was forced to surrender (19 July–9 August 1627).

Groningen I 1580 I Netherlands War of Independence
See **Hardenberg Heath**

Groningen I 1594 I Netherlands War of Independence

Continuing his successful campaign in northern Holland, Prince Maurice of Orange besieged the fortified city of Groningen, which had previously held out against Dutch forces. Supported by English General Sir Francis Vere, Maurice overwhelmed the stubborn pro-Spanish garrison, forcing the city's surrender. Catholicism was officially banned (April–15 July 1594).

Groningen I 1672 I 3rd Dutch War

While France entered the Dutch Republic from the south through **Tolhuis** and **Nijmegen**, Bishop Christof Bernhard van Galen of Munster invaded the north on behalf of Louis XIV and besieged Groningen, defended by General Karel Rabenhaupt Baron de Sucha. After more than a month Van Galen was unable to take the fortress city and withdrew (22 July–26 August 1672).

Groote Keeten I 1799 I French Revolutionary Wars (2nd Coalition)

At the beginning of the British-Russian expedition to Holland, General Sir Ralph Abercromby, supported by General John Moore, made a strongly opposed landing in the north at Groote Keeten, which cost over 500 British casualties. Fortunately, Frederick Augustus Duke of York arrived with reinforcements before battle three weeks later at **Bergen-aan-Zee** (27 August 1799).

Grossbeeren I 1813 I Napoleonic Wars (War of Liberation)

Defeated at **Lützen** and **Bautzen**, Prussia and Russia attempted to attack Napoleon Bonaparte's lieutenants, including Marshal Nicolas Oudinot, advancing against Berlin. At nearby Grossbeeren, General Friedrich von Bulow's Prussians and Swedes under former French Marshal Jean Baptiste Bernadotte defeated Oudinot and forced him to withdraw (23 August 1813).

Gross-Gorschen I 1813 I Napoleonic Wars (War of Liberation)

See **Lützen**

Gross-Jagersdorf I 1757 I Seven Years War (Europe)

While Prussia's Anglo-Hanoverian allies were defeated in the west at **Hastenbeck**, 100,000 Russians under Marshal Stefan Apraksin invaded East Prussia against General Hans von Lehwald. The heavily outnumbered Prussians suffered a costly defeat at Gross-Jagersdorf, southeast of Königsberg. Apraksin's hungry army later mutinied and returned to Russia (30 July 1757).

Grotniki I 1439 I Hussite Wars

When Hussite Polish magnates formed a confederation against 15-year-old King Ladislaw III, Regent Bishop Zbigniew Olenski of Cracow sent a large force against them at Grotniki, southwest of Posnan. Rebel leader Spytek of Melsztyn, the Castellan of Belz, was defeated and killed, crushing the resistance and virtually ending the Hussite cause in Poland (4 May 1439).

Groveton I 1862 I American Civil War (Eastern Theatre)

At the start of the decisive battle known as Second **Bull Run**, Confederate General Thomas "Stonewall" Jackson surprised a Union force under Generals Rufus King and John Gibbon to the west at Groveton, Virginia. With both sides suffering costly losses, Union commander John Pope moved towards Jackson in apparent pursuit and was drawn into the main battle next day (28 August 1862).

Grumentum I 207 BC I 2nd Punic War

As the Carthaginian Hannibal in Italy awaited his brother Hasdrubal marching from Spain, he was attacked southeast of Salerno outside Grumentum (modern Saponara di Grumento) by superior Roman forces under Gaius Claudius Nero and Quintus Fulvius Flacco. An inconclusive action allowed Hannibal to continue towards Apulia, while Nero marched north to defeat Hasdrubal at the **Metaurus**.

Gruneberg I 1761 I Seven Years War (Europe)

On a fresh Allied offensive in the west, Duke Ferdinand of Brunswick led a Prussian-British force into Hesse. At Gruneberg, just east of Giessen, he was defeated by French forces under Marshal Victor-Francois Broglie, who captured 2,000 prisoners. Ferdinand was forced to withdraw, but had his revenge a few months later at **Vellinghausen** (21 March 1761).

Grunwald **|** 1410 **|** Later Wars of the Teutonic Knights
   See **Tannenberg**

Guadalajara, Mexico **|** 1858 **|** Mexican War of the Reform
Recovering from the terrible Liberal defeat at **Ahualalco** (29 September), commander Santos Degollado besieged Guadalajara, which fell by assault after a month (27 October). However, six weeks later Degollado faced 4,000 Conservative government troops under Generals Miguel Miramón and Leonardo Márquez. A sharp defeat forced him to evacuate the city (September–14 December 1858).

Guadalajara, Mexico (1st) **|** 1860 **|** Mexican War of the Reform
Liberal commander Pedro Ogazón regrouped after loss at **Colima** (December 1859) to attack Guadalajara, successfully defended by a 3,000-strong garrison under General Adrián Woll. General José López Uraga then tried to take the city, but he was defeated and captured wounded. When President Miguel Miramón arrived to complete the Liberal rout, Ogazón had to withdraw (April–25 May 1860).

Guadalajara, Mexico (2nd) **|** 1860 **|** Mexican War of the Reform
Six weeks after victory at **Silao**, new Liberal commander Jesús González Ortega besieged and bombarded nearby Guadalajara, stoutly defended by General Severo del Castillo. President Miguel Miramón sent a relief force under General Leonardo Márquez, but before he arrived Castillo was forced to surrender. Márquez himself lost at nearby **Calderón** (26 September–3 November 1860).

Guadalajara, Spain **|** 1937 **|** Spanish Civil War
Despite Nationalist failure around Madrid at **Corunna Road** and **Jarama**, Mario Roatta's Italians attacked to the northeast towards Guadalajara, supported by Spanish General José Moscardó. The Nationalists took and then lost Brihuega before the line was stabilised. Republican General Enrique Jurado from Madrid later counter-attacked at **Brunete** and **Teruel** (8–23 March 1937).

Guadalaviar **|** 75 BC **|** Sertorian War
   See **Turia**

Guadalcanal—Land **|** 1942–1943 **|** World War II (Pacific)
After American victory at **Midway**, General Alexander Vandergrift landed on Guadalcanal against General Haruyoshi Hyakutake. A bloody, escalating six-month campaign cost 25,000 Japanese and 6,000 American casualties, with major actions at the **Tenaru** and **Matanikau** Rivers and at **Bloody Ridge**, before the Japanese finally evacuated the island (7 August 1942–9 February 1943).

Guadalcanal—Naval (1st) **|** 1942 **|** World War II (Pacific)
When Admiral Hiroake Abe's bombardment force was met off Guadalcanal by Admiral Daniel Callaghan, a brief night action saw an American cruiser and four destroyers lost and two Japanese destroyers sunk. After dawn, a damaged Japanese battleship was sunk by aircraft and an American cruiser was torpedoed with 700 men lost. Battle resumed next night (13 November 1942).

Guadalcanal—Naval (2nd) **|** 1942 **|** World War II (Pacific)
Returning to bombard Guadalcanal, Admiral Nobutake Kondo lost a battleship and a destroyer in a brutal night action, which also cost Admiral Willis Lee three destroyers sunk and a cruiser damaged. Meanwhile, Admiral Raizo Tanaka's destroyers landed some troops though he lost all 11 of his troop-ships, which were

never again used to reinforce Guadalcanal (14–15 November 1942).

Guadalete ▍ 711 ▍ Muslim Conquest of Spain

While Roderic, last Visigothic King of Spain, was campaigning in the north, a small Muslim force under Tarik ibn Ziyad invaded from North Africa and advanced into Cadiz Province, supported by rival Goth leader Achila. Near the town of Xeres (Jerez) at Lake Janda, the Arabs won a great victory and Roderic was killed. The battle is mistakenly best known as Guadalete (19 July 711).

Guadalquivir ▍ 211 BC ▍ 2nd Punic War
See **Baetis**

Guadeloupe ▍ 1759 ▍ Seven Years War (Caribbean)

General Sir Peregrine Hopson and Commodore John Moore regrouped after loss at **Martinique** and sailed to French Guadeloupe, where they landed after a heavy bombardment. However, the assault stalled through inertia and losses to disease, including Hopson himself. General John Barrington eventually took the island, which was returned to France after the war (23 January–1 May 1759).

Guadeloupe ▍ 1794 ▍ French Revolutionary Wars (1st Coalition)

Having taken the French West Indian islands of **Martinique** and **St Lucia**, British Admiral Sir John Jervis and General Sir Charles Grey landed on Guadeloupe, where General Georges Collot surrendered after a week. General Victor Hugues later counter-invaded and, though Jervis and Grey returned, French reinforcements landed and the island was retaken (12 April–10 December 1794).

Guadeloupe ▍ 1798 ▍ Franco-American Quasi War

In undeclared war with Revolutionary France, three American ships in the West Indies under Captain Alexander Murray were surprised off Guadeloupe by French frigates *l'Insurgente* (36) and *La Volontaire* (44). The American schooner *Retaliation* (Lieutenant William Bainbridge) surrendered after a powerful broadside. *L'Insurgente* was taken two months later off **Nevis** (20 November 1798).

Guadeloupe ▍ 1800 ▍ Franco-American Quasi War

A year after his victory off **Nevis**, American Captain Thomas Truxton in *Constellation* pursued and attacked the powerful French frigate *La Vengeance,* off Guadeloupe. French Captain F. M. Pitot withdrew after a bloody, five-hour drawn action, though *Constellation* was too badly damaged to pursue. A treaty soon ended America's undeclared war with Revolutionary France (1 February 1800).

Guadeloupe ▍ 1810 ▍ Napoleonic Wars (5th Coalition)

Although Britain captured the West Indian island of Guadeloupe in 1794, it was immediately recovered by French Governor Victor Hugues. In 1810 Britain sent a fresh expedition under General Sir George Beckwith and Guadeloupe fell within a week. An immediate French attempt to recapture the island failed, but it was returned to France in 1815 (27 January–5 February 1810).

Guad-el-Ras ▍ 1860 ▍ Spanish-Moroccan War

Marshal Leopoldo O'Donnell wanted to punish the Moors for attacking Spanish possessions in North Africa and secured **Tetuán** (4 February), then advanced east against entrenched positions behind the Guad-el-Ras. The Moors were decisively defeated and British diplomatic pressure brought the war to an end, with Morocco giving Spain the Atlantic coast territory, known as Ifni (23 March 1860).

Gualcho ▍ 1828 ▍ Central American National Wars

After securing Honduras following victory over Central American Federal forces at **La Trinidad**, General Francisco Morazán marched into El Salvador and routed Federal General

Vicente Dominquez on the Rio Lempa at Gual-cho. Morazán occupied San Miguel, but could not break the Federal siege of San Salvador and withdrew, later returning for victory at **San Antonio** (6 July 1828).

Gualqui I 1819 I Chilean War of Independence

See **Hualqui**

Guam I 1898 I Spanish-American War

Early in the war, the American warship *Charleston* (Captain Henry Glass) and three transports left Honolulu to seize Guam. After a token bombardment of Fort Santa Cruz, Spanish Governor Juan Marino (who had no knowledge of the state of war or Spain's naval defeat at **Manila**) surrendered the island, giving the United States its first possession in the Pacific (21 June 1898).

Guam I 1941 I World War II (Pacific)

As war started, Japanese attacked the naval station on Guam, held with nothing larger than machine-guns by 427 marines and sailors and 247 native troops. After two days of bombing, which sank a minelayer in the harbour, 5,400 Japanese landed and brief fighting cost 17 military and about 40 civilians killed. Governor Captain George J. McMillin (USN) then surrendered (8–10 December 1941).

Guam I 1944 I World War II (Pacific)

Bloody fighting on **Saipan** in the **Mariana Islands** delayed the attack on Guam, 150 miles to the southwest, fiercely defended by 19,000 Japanese under General Takeshi Takashina. Landing after a massive naval bombardment, General Roy Geiger virtually annihilated the garrison, although guerrilla resistance continued for months. The last survivor held out until 1972 (21 July–10 August 1944).

Guanajuato (1st) I 1810 I Mexican Wars of Independence

Militant priest Miguel Hidalgo initiated peasant rebellion at **Dolores**, then marched on Guanajuato, where the Intendente Juan Antonio de Riano attempted to defend the Alhondiga de Granaditas (granary). De Riano was killed, along with perhaps 300 Spanish soldiers and civilians, and Hidalgo marched towards Mexico City and the **Monte de las Cruces** (28 September 1810).

Guanajuato (2nd) I 1810 I Mexican Wars of Independence

Two weeks after beating Miguel Hidalgo at **Aculco**, Royalist commander Félix María Calleja marched north from Querétaro against Revolutionary General Ignacio Allende at Guanajuato. A six-hour action saw the large rebel army defeated, losing about 1,000 killed and 22 cannon, followed by executions and vengeance. Allende escaped to fight two months later at **Calderón** (23 November 1810).

Guandu I 200 I Wars of the Three Kingdoms

Amid the decline of the Han Dynasty, the warlord Yuan Shao took a large force south across the Yellow River and met his rival Cao Cao (Ts'ao Ts'ao) near Guandu, northwest of modern Kaifeng. Cao Cao held the numerically superior force, which fell apart when he cut their supplies. When Yuan Shao died (202), Cao Cao fought his sons and eventually ended Yuan power in 207 at **White Wolf Mountain**.

Guangchang I 1934 I 2nd Chinese Revolutionary Civil War

Mao Zedong's Communists in Jiangxi repulsed four "encirclement campaigns," before facing a massive new Nationalist offensive under German General Hans von Seekt. The Red Army suffered severe casualties trying to defend Guangchang to protect their capital to the south at Ruijin (Juichin). These losses triggered the decision to break out on the Long March to Yan'an (11–28 April 1934).

Guangzhou I 879 I Huang Chao Rebellion

Bandit warlords threatened the Tang Empire and Huang Chao demanded control of the international trade port of Guangzhou (Canton).

When it was refused, he attacked the city in force, killing Military Governor Li Tiao. The ensuing sack of the great city reportedly cost more than 100,000 killed, including many foreign merchants. Huang then returned north to capture Luoyang and Chang'an.

Guangzhou ▌ 1841 ▌ 1st Opium War

Superintendent Captain Charles Elliot secured the **Bogue Forts**, then sent General Sir Hugh Gough up the Zhujiang with 15 warships under Captain Sir Humphrey Fleming Senhouse to besiege Guangzhou itself. Following a Chinese assault at Whampoa, Gough attacked and Commissioner Yishan capitulated. The British withdrew, but months later renewed the war at **Xiamen** (25–30 May 1841).

Guangzhou ▌ 1857 ▌ 2nd Opium War

After the British sank junks at **Fatshan Creek**, Anglo-French troops under James Lord Elgin and Baron Jean-Baptiste Gros advanced on Guangzhou (Canton), supported by Admiral Charles Rigault de Genouilly and General Sir Charles van Straubenzee. Imperial Commissioner Ye Mingshen yielded after brief bombardment. In May 1858, the Allies secured the **Dagu Forts** (28–30 December 1857).

Guangzhou ▌ 1927 ▌ 2nd Chinese Revolutionary Civil War

While Chiang Kai-shek's Nationalists campaigned in northern China against the warlords, a Communist insurrection broke out in Guangzhou (Canton), where a Soviet was proclaimed under General Ye Ting. Kuomintang General Zhang Fakui brutally suppressed the rising with terrible destruction and thousands were executed (11–14 December 1927).

Guangzhou ▌ 1938 ▌ Sino-Japanese War

As Japan's army drove deep into China towards **Wuhan**, their navy determined to cut overseas supply lines and attacked the southeast coast. Xiamen (Amoy) fell to amphibious assault (12 May) and troops, with massive naval and air cover, later landed at Bias Bay (Daya Bay) to advance on Guangzhou (Canton). The city fell by storm and the Chinese withdrew (12–21 October 1938).

Guánica ▌ 1898 ▌ Spanish-American War

With war in Cuba virtually over, American General Nelson A. Miles took 3,300 men against Puerto Rico, landing at the southern port of Guánica. Supported by General Guy V. Henry, Miles defeated the Spanish garrison, killing four without loss to himself, then started east towards Ponce. However, news of peace arrived and Puerto Rico was later ceded to the United States (25 July 1898).

Guantánamo Bay ▌ 1898 ▌ Spanish-American War

American Admiral William T. Sampson blockaded **Santiago de Cuba**, then detached Commander Bowman H. McCalla with two ships further east against Guantánamo Bay. A bold assault enabled McCalla to establish a strong position on Fisherman's Point (McCalla's Hill) and victory a few days later at **Cuzco** isolated the Spanish forces at Guantánamo City (6 June 1898).

Guararapes ▌ 1648 ▌ Dutch-Portuguese Colonial Wars

Following Dutch capture of **Recife** in Brazil in 1630, traders faced continuing Portuguese attack and came under full siege from August 1645. Reinforced by a Dutch fleet under Witte Cornelius de With, commander Sigismund von Schoppe attacked the Portuguese at nearby Guararapes. He was driven off with 500 dead and 500 wounded and Recife remained under siege (17–18 April 1648).

Guararapes ▌ 1649 ▌ Dutch-Portuguese Colonial Wars

Under long-term siege at **Recife** in Brazil, Dutch forces made a second attack on the Portuguese at nearby Guararapes and managed to secure the town. Next day, they were routed in a counter-attack under Portuguese commander Francisco Barreto, losing almost 1,000 dead. Recife remained under siege another five years and finally fell in January 1654 (18–19 February 1649).

Guarda I 1812 I Napoleonic Wars (Peninsular Campaign)

While the Allies besieged **Badajoz** in the south, French Marshal Auguste Marmont advanced through northern Portugal and met a Portuguese force under Generals Sir Nicholas Trant and John Wilson in Upper Beira at Guarda. The Portuguese militia were routed but, with the fall of Badajoz, Marmont's offensive had little strategic value and he eventually withdrew (14 April 1812).

Guard Hill I 1864 I American Civil War (Eastern Theatre)

See **Cedarville**

Guarina I 1547 I Spanish Civil War in Peru

See **Huarina**

Guastalla I 1734 I War of the Polish Succession

Louis XV of France supported his father-in-law, former King Stanislas Leszcynski of Poland, by sending troops into Lombardy, where Marshal François de Coigny recovered from defeat at the **Secchia** to counter-attack days later near Luzarra at Guastalla. New Imperial commander Friedrich Ludwig of Württemberg was defeated and killed and Austria retired behind the Po (19 September 1734).

Guatemala City I 1829 I Central American National Wars

With El Salvador secured after victory at **San Antonio** in late 1828, Liberal General Francisco Morazán of Honduras continued on into Guatemala and besieged Federal President Manuel Jose Arce in Guatemala City. When garrison commander Mariano Aycinena capitulated and Arce was deposed, Morazán became President. In 1834, he moved the Federal capital to San Salvador (13 April 1829).

Guatemala City I 1840 I Central American National Wars

Determined to reunite the Central American Federation, President Francisco Morazán of Salvador repulsed a Honduran invasion at **San Pedro Perulapán**, then invaded Guatemala. With just 800 men he seized the capital, but next day was thrown out by a Guatemalan counter-attack under José Rafael Carrera. Morazán went into exile but seized Costa Rica in 1842 at **Cartago** (18–19 March 1840).

Gubat I 1885 I British-Sudan Wars

See **Abu Kru**

Gubel I 1531 I Swiss Religious Wars

See **Zug**

Guélémou I 1898 I Franco-Mandingo Wars

On a final offensive against Mandingo warrior Samory Touré, French forces seized the key city of **Sikasso**, in modern Mali (1 May), and Captain Henri-Joseph Gouraud marched in pursuit of Samory on the Cavally, in modern Ivory Coast. Samory was surprised at Guélémou, near Biankouma and captured after a brief struggle. He was exiled to Gabon and died two years later (29 September 1898).

Guelta Zemmour I 1981 I Western Sahara Wars

When Morocco built fortified sand walls to seal off the northwest of Western Sahara, Polisario guerrillas attacked the remote base at Guelta Zemmour near the Mauritanian border. After failed attempts, a massive offensive briefly overran the base in severe fighting. Morocco abandoned Guelta Zemmour and other bases beyond the wall and a decade of intermittent fighting ensued (12–13 October 1981).

Guenes I 1808 I Napoleonic Wars (Peninsular Campaign)

Spanish General Joachim Blake led a futile attempt to counter-attack east towards **Bilbao** after battle at **Valmaseda** (5 November) reaching as far as Guenes, where he unexpectedly met a major French force under Marshal Francois Lefebvre. Only nightfall saved Blake from total disaster and he withdrew west to **Espinosa**, where he was defeated a few days later (7 November 1808).

Guernica ∎ 1833 ∎ 1st Carlist War

Early in the war against Spanish Regent Maria Cristina, Carlists at Guernica under Fernando de Zabala and Simon de La Torre faced attack by Baron Jacobo Maria del Solar de Espinosa. In their first victory against Regulars, the Carlists held out and inflicted over 300 Cristino casualties. They withdrew when reinforcements approached and won again a week later at **Asarta** (21 December 1833).

Guernica ∎ 1937 ∎ Spanish Civil War

While Nationalist forces besieged **Bilbao**, German bombers launched a brutal assault to the northeast on Guernica. More a massacre than a battle, the scale of civilian destruction shocked the world and crystallised support for the Republican cause. The Basque city was abandoned two days later, along with Durango to the south, and Bilbao itself fell after three more weeks (26 April 1937).

Guetaria ∎ 1812 ∎ Napoleonic Wars (Peninsular Campaign)

British Admiral Sir Home Popham joined an offensive against northern Spain to relieve pressure on the Allies around **Salamanca**. He seized **Lequeitio**, but failed to capture nearby Guetaria in early July. A larger attempt, supported by guerrilla leader Jauregui, was driven off by troops from Bayonne under General Pierre-Gabriel d'Aussenac. A third attack in August also failed (19 July 1812).

Guiba ∎ 1916 ∎ World War I (Middle East)

When the pro-Turkish Sultan Ali Dinar of Darfur, in western Sudan threatened British war interests, he was defeated at **Beringia**, near El Fasher, and his Sultanate was annexed. Pursued into southern Sudan by Major Hubert Huddleston, the Sultan was surprised and killed in camp at Guiba (modern Juba), ending the Turkish-inspired resistance in the Sudan (6 November 1916).

Guildford Courthouse ∎ 1781 ∎ War of the American Revolution

Marching into North Carolina against General Nathanael Greene, the British army under General Charles Earl Cornwallis crossed the Catawba at **Cowan's Ford**, then advanced on Greene in a well-prepared defensive position at Guildford. Greene withdrew after brutal fighting, yet the victory had cost Earl Cornwallis heavy losses and he began retreating towards Wilmington (15 March 1781).

Guiledge ∎ 1973 ∎ Guinea-Bissau War

After ten years of largely guerrilla warfare, independence forces in Portuguese Guinea secured modern artillery and anti-aircraft missiles and launched a large-scale conventional siege of the southern command base at Guiledge. Deprived of air supremacy, the garrison was badly defeated, greatly boosting the rebel cause. Within 18 months Portugal had recognised independent Guinea-Bissau (May 1973).

Guilin ∎ 1852 ∎ Taiping Rebellion

The Taiping army withdrawing through Guangxi from **Yung'an**, besieged Guilin (Kweilin), recently reinforced by Imperial General Xiang Rong. When the main government army arrived, its commander Wulantai was killed in the first attack. General Qin Dingsan then continued the bloody assault and, after 33 days, the Taiping withdrew northeast through **Quanzhou** (18 April–19 May 1852).

Guiling ∎ 353 BC ∎ China's Era of the Warring States

When the army of Wei invaded Zhao and besieged the capital Handan, the neighbouring state of Qi sent an army under Tian Ji and Sun Bin into Wei, forcing them to abandon the siege and withdraw to defend their own country. At Guiling (modern Heze, Shandong), the army of Wei was routed with commander Pang Juan captured. The successful Qi generals defeated Wei again in 341 BC at **Maling**.

**Guilin-Liuzhou I 1944 I World War II
(China)**

As Japan's **Ichigo** offensive swept through southeast China, General Yasuji Okamura's army drove south from **Hengyang** towards Guilin and west from Guangzhou to Liuzhou. The huge combined action saw Guilin fall (10 November) and Liuzhou the next day. The capture of Nanning two weeks later secured the important land route to French Indo-China (21 October–11 November 1944).

**Guillemont I 1916 I World War I
(Western Front)**

Supposedly to distract German attention from the hard-pressed Romanian front, British and French forces taking part in the Battle of the **Somme** attacked Guillemont, just southeast of **Delville Wood**. Heavy fighting secured the strong fortress, though stubborn German defence eventually prevented the Allies from capturing several other nearby positions (3–6 September 1916).

**Guimaraes I 1128 I Portuguese War
of Succession**

See **Sao Mamede**

Guinegate I 1479 I Franco-Austrian War

When Charles Duke of Burgundy died, Louis XI of France invaded the Netherlands and was met by a large army under Archduke Maximilian, son of the Emperor Frederick III and son-in-law of the late Duke. At Guinegate, south of St Omer, French General Philip de Crèvecoeur des Querdes repulsed the Imperial cavalry, but was defeated by Flemish and German infantry (7 August 1479).

**Guinegate I 1513 I War of the
Holy League**

In alliance with Emperor Maximilian I, Henry VIII of England invaded France from Calais and besieged the fortified town of Thérouanne, south of St Omer (22 June). French cavalry sent by King Louis XII were routed at nearby Guinegate by English and German troops (known as the "Battle of the Spurs" from the haste of the

French flight). Thérouanne fell a week later (16 August 1513).

**Guise I 1914 I World War I
(Western Front)**

With the outnumbered British Expeditionary Force withdrawing southwest from **Mons** through **Le Cateau**, French commander Charles Lanzerac launched an unexpected offensive into the flank of General Karl von Bulow's advancing army. The Germans suffered a sharp check in heavy fighting between Guise and St Quentin as the Allies withdrew south to the **Marne** (29 August 1914).

**Gujarat, India I 1178 I Later Muslim
Conquest of Northern India**

Muhammad of Ghor launched a fresh invasion of northern India from Afghanistan and overthrew the Ghaznevid rulers of Punjab, who had ruled since victory at **Waihand** in 1008. However, his invasion of Gujarat was decisively repulsed by the Hindu Raja Bhimdev II. The defeat in Gujarat was a rare setback for Muslim expansion and secured the kingdom against further Muslim attack.

**Gujarat, Pakistan I 1797 I Punjab
Campaigns of Shah Zaman**

See **Gujrat**

**Gujranwala I 1761 I Indian Campaigns
of Ahmad Shah**

Afghan Governor Khwaja Abed Khan of Lahore recovered from the defeat of an Afghan army at **Sialkot** in August to besiege the victorious Sikhs at Gujranwala, northeast of Lahore. He was, in turn, besieged by Sikh General Charat Singh, who led a massive attack on the Afghan camp. Khwaja Abed lost almost all his guns and baggage and fled back to his capital (September 1761).

**Gujrat, Pakistan I 1797 I Punjab
Campaigns of Shah Zaman**

After Shah Zaman of Kabul was defeated by the Sikhs near **Amritsar**, he left Ahmad Khan Shahanchi as Governor at Rohtas, who soon advanced across the Jehlum to pre-empt a Sikh attack. In the northern Punjab at Gujrat, a coalition of Sikh leaders routed the Afghans, killing a reported 3,000. Ahmad Khan was executed and his head was sent to Ranjit Singh in Ramnagar (29 April 1797).

Gujrat, Pakistan ▎ 1849 ▎ 2nd British-Sikh War

In the aftermath of costly battles against Sikhs at **Ramnagar** and **Chilianwallah**, British commander Sir Hugh Gough was reinforced by General William Whish from the fall of **Multan** and they advanced and crushed the Sikh army at Gujrat, west of Sialkot. Devastated by artillery fire, Sher Singh and his father Chattar Singh surrendered and Britain annexed the Punjab (21 February 1849).

Guler ▎ 1696 ▎ Mughal-Sikh Wars

Amid warfare in the northern Punjab against Sikh Guru Gobind Singh, Mughal commander Dilawar Khan's son Rustam Khan was routed crossing the Sutlej. Dilawar then sent General Hussain Khan against rebel Raja Gopal of Guler and his Sikh allies. In battle with the Guru and Raja Ram Singh of Jaswan near Guler, southeast of Pathankot, Hussain was defeated and killed (20 March 1696).

Gulina ▎ 1834 ▎ 1st Carlist War

Soon after suffering a costly attack at **Alsasua**, Spanish Liberal commander Vicente Jenaro de Quesada in Vitoria ordered Brigadier Linares from Pamplona in an attempt to trap Carlist General Tomás Zumalacárregui. Just northwest of Pamplona at Gulina, Zumalacárregui attacked Linares and both sides suffered about 600 casualties before Zumalacárregui was driven off (17 June 1834).

Gulnabad ▎ 1722 ▎ Persian-Afghan Wars

Having seized Afghanistan, Mahmud Ghilzai of Kandahar took a large force into Persia and advanced on Isfahan. Shah Sultan Husain sent Grand Vizier Muhammad Kuli Khan Shamlu and Sayid Abdullah, Wali of Arabia, to meet the invaders at nearby Gulnabad. However, the Persians were destroyed, with a reported 25,000 killed. Mahmud then seized **Isfahan** and the crown (8 March 1722).

Gumbinnen ▎ 1914 ▎ World War I (Eastern Front)

General Max von Prittwitz was encouraged at **Stalluponen** and days later met Russia's invasion of eastern Prussia under General Pavel Rennenkampf near Gumbinnen (modern Guziew). The poorly co-ordinated German attack lost 6,000 prisoners and Prittwitz ordered withdrawal. He was replaced as commander by Paul von Hindenberg, who soon won at **Tannenberg** (20 August 1914).

Gumburu ▎ 1903 ▎ Wars of the Mad Mullah

During a third expedition against Muhammad Abdullah Hassan of Somaliland, Colonel Alexander Cobbe advanced from Obbia to Galadi, then sent Colonel Arthur Plunkett to Gumburu to rescue a patrol. Ambushed by a massive Dervish force, the British were routed with over 200 killed, including Plunkett. Dervish losses were also high and they soon lost at **Daratoleh** (17 April 1903).

Gundet ▎ 1875 ▎ Egyptian-Ethiopian War

Egyptians under the Danish officer Soren Adolph Arendup marching southwest into the Abyssinian highlands from Massawa, on the Red Sea, were surprised at night by the army of Yohannes IV of Ethiopia at Gundet, north of Adowa. Although other Egyptians under Rustem Bey arrived to help, Arendup and Rustem were defeated and killed on the second day (15–16 November 1875).

Gunib ▎ 1859 ▎ Russian Conquest of the Caucasus

Russia's final campaign to subjugate Dagestan saw Muslim rebel Imam Shamil driven from his fortress at Vedeno, southeast of Grozny, to take refuge with 400 followers on nearby Mount Gunib, under siege by Prince Aleksandr Bariatinsky. A bloody assault took the position by storm and Shamil surrendered. Resistance ended and he died in Russia in 1871 (21 August–6 September 1859).

Guns I 1532 I Turkish-Habsburg Wars

During renewed Turkish invasion of Hungary following repulse at **Vienna**, Sultan Suleiman I advanced and ravaged much of the country while Vizier Ibrahim Pasha besieged Guns (modern Koszeg), held by Nicolas Jurischitz. Despite extensive mining, every assault was repulsed and Ibrahim withdrew in return for nominal submission. Suleiman later abandoned his expedition (9–28 August 1532).

Gunzburg I 1805 I Napoleonic Wars (3rd Coalition)

Napoleon Bonaparte's Grand Army crossed the Rhine in massive force and swung south to cut off the Austrian invasion of Bavaria, under General Karl Mack von Leiberich. Threatened with encirclement at **Ulm**, Mack attempted to break out east across bridges at the junction of the Danube and Gunz near Gunzburg, where he was repulsed by Marshal Michel Ney (9 October 1805).

Gura I 1876 I Egyptian-Ethiopian War

Advancing inland from Massawa on the Red Sea, Egyptian Sirdar Muhammad Rateb Pasha took a strong entrenched position to the southwest at Gura, then rashly marched out to meet the approaching army of Yohannes IV of Ethiopia. Although the Egyptians were routed, with 3,500 casualties, Yohannes withdrew two days later after a costly assault on the fort (7 & 9 March 1876).

Gura I 1990–1991 I Eritrean War of Independence
See **Dekemhare**

Guraganj I 1857 I Indian Mutiny
See **Arrah**

Gurdas Nangal I 1715 I Mughal-Sikh Wars

Sikh leader Banda Singh Bahadur ravaged northern Punjab, then took a powerful defensive position at the village of Gurdas Nangal, near Gurdaspur, against siege by Mughal General Abdus-Samad Khan, later reinforced by a massive army under Qamr-ud-Din Khan. Starved into surrender, Banda and over 700 Sikhs were taken to Delhi for execution (April–7 December 1715).

Gurdaspur I 1715 I Mughal-Sikh Wars
See **Gurdas Nangal**

Gurganj I 1221 I Conquests of Genghis Khan

Attacking the Khwarezmian Empire, which once covered Afghanistan, Transoxonia and much of Uran, the Mongol Genghis Khan destroyed **Samarkand**, then sent his sons Jochi and Ogedei to besiege the former capital Gurganj (modern Urgench), south of the Aral Sea. After a desperate defence, the inhabitants surrendered when the city caught fire. They were all massacred or enslaved (April 1221).

Gurrumkonda I 1791 I 3rd British-Mysore War

Nizam Ali of Hyderabad supported Britain in renewed war against Tipu Sultan of Mysore, sending Hafiz Farid-ud-din against Gurrumkonda in the hills northeast of Kolar. A relief force under Tipu's son Fath Ali and General Ghazi Khan killed Hafiz Farid-ud-din, but siege was renewed by Sikander Jal and Captain Andrew Read and was sustained until the end of the war (December 1791).

Guru I 1904 I British Invasion of Tibet

Britain suspected Russian intervention in Tibet and sent Colonel Francis Younghusband and a military escort of 1,000 under General James Macdonald. The road was blocked at Guru by up to 2,000 poorly armed Tibetans and the resulting massacre saw 600 Tibetans killed and about 300 wounded. The British then advanced through **Red Idol Gorge** to **Gyantse** on the way to Lhasa (31 March 1904).

Gustav Line I 1943–1944 I World War II (Southern Europe)

Advancing up Italy from **Naples** and **Termoli**, Anglo-American forces faced the fomidable

Gustav Line, along the **Garigliano** and **Rapido** in the west, through **Monte Cassino** to the **Sangro**. A landing in the rear at **Anzio** stalled, but the Allies broke through after a massive air offensive on supply lines. Rome was taken and the Germans fell back to the **Gothic Line** (November 1943–May 1944).

Guyana | 1813 | War of 1812

In action off the Demarara River in Guyana, the American sloop *Hornet* (Captain James Lawrence) attacked the British sloop *Peacock* (Commander William Peake). A brief, but bloody action, saw Peake killed and his badly damaged ship sank soon after it was forced to surrender. Among his passengers captured was General Thomas Hislop, en route to command in India (24 February 1813).

Guzów | 1607 | Zebrzydowski's Rebellion

Polish nobles led by Mikolaj Zebrzydowski, Palatine of Cracow, regrouped after defeat at **Janowiec** (October 1606) and renewed rebellion against Sigismund III. His patience exhausted, the King sent Hetmen Jan Karol Chodkiewicz and Stanislas Zolkiewski, who won at Guzów, near Radom. The rebels were later pardoned again and Sigismund eased his constitutional reforms (6 July 1607).

Gwalior | 1780 | 1st British-Maratha War

In a diversion south of Agra following his capture of **Ahmadabad**, General Thomas Goddard detached Captain William Popham against the powerful Maratha fortress of Gwalior, near Lashkar, held for Mahadji Sindhia. In a remarkable night-time assault—aided by treachery—Popham's small force scaled the walls and the surprised garrison of Ambuji Ingle quickly surrendered (3 August 1780).

Gwalior | 1858 | Indian Mutiny

Despite defeat at **Kalpi** (23 May), rebel leaders Tantia Topi, Rao Sahib and the Rani of Jhansi took 12,000 men and seized Gwalior from Maharajah Sindhia. A bold counteroffensive saw General Sir Hugh Rose win at nearby **Morar**, kill the Rani at **Kotah-Ki-Serai**, then take Gwalior by bloody assault. Tantia Topi and Rao Sahib fled, but both were eventually caught and hanged (20 June 1858).

Gwanga | 1846 | 7th Cape Frontier War

When British Colonel Henry Somerset arrived to relieve **Fort Peddie**, east of Grahamstown in eastern Cape Colony, he attacked the besieging forces of Mhala and Siyolo at nearby Gwanga. Unwisely accepting battle in the open, the Xhosa were destroyed by cavalry. Intermittent fighting continued until 1847, when Sandile surrendered and the British annexed Kaffrari (7 June 1846).

Gwozdiec | 1531 | Polish-Moldavian War

Hospodar Petrylo of Moldavia intervened in the disputed Hungarian succession, invading southern Poland in support of the Turkish cause. At the head of a Polish counter-offensive, Grand Hetman Jan Tarnowski attacked and defeated the Moldavians at Gwozdiec, near Kolmyya in modern Ukraine. However, as he withdrew northeast he was massively outnumbered and besieged at **Obertyn**.

Gwynn Island | 1776 | War of the American Revolution

Virginian Governor John Murray Earl of Dunmore burned and abandoned **Norfolk** after defeat at **Great Bridge** (December 1775), then took his ships 40 miles north to Gwynn Island, near the Rappahannock. Attacked six months later by Americans from Williamsburg under General Andrew Lewis, Dunmore was routed and driven off. He eventually returned to England (8–10 July 1776).

Gyantse | 1904 | British Invasion of Tibet

Concerned about possible Russian intervention in Tibet, a British force under General James advanced through **Guru** and **Red Idol Gorge** to Gyantse, where they occupied Chang Lo Mission outside the nearby fortress. After weeks of siege and counter-siege, the British were reinforced. When truce talks failed, they stormed Gyantse, then advanced to Lhasa to end the war (12 April–6 July 1904).

Gytheum I 194 BC I Spartan-Achaean Wars

Facing renewed hostility by Nabis of Sparta, the Achaean League and Roman allies won at **Argos**, then Titus Quinctius Flamininus and his brother Lucius led an attack on the powerful Spartan fortress at Gytheum. Garrison commander Gorgopas surrendered after heavy fighting and loss of this arsenal persuaded Nabis to sue for peace. Fighting resumed two years later at **Mount Barbosthene**.

Gyula I 1566 I Turkish-Habsburg Wars

When Ottoman Sultan Suleiman I and Grand Vizier Sokollu Mehmet invaded Hungary, Suleiman himself besieged **Szigetvar** in the southwest, while Pertev Pasha and 30,000 men were sent east against the important fortress of Gyula. Commander László Kerecsény held out for two months until he was forced to surrender after most of his garrison had been killed (August–September 1566).

H

Haarlem ❙ 1572–1573 ❙ Netherlands War of Independence

Advancing into Holland after taking **Mons**, Don Fadrique Alvarez (son of the Duke of Alva) and 30,000 men besieged commander Wigbold Ripperda at the powerful Protestant city of Haarlem, west of Amsterdam. William of Orange failed attempting to break the siege and Haarlem capitulated after seven months. The surviving garrison were butchered (11 December 1572–12 July 1573).

Habbaniyah ❙ 1941 ❙ World War II (Middle East)

Pro-Axis forces seized **Iraq**, then attacked the Royal Air Force base at Habbaniyah, 40 miles west of Baghdad with artillery and armour. A small scratch force under Air Vice Marshal Harry Smart and Colonel Ouvry Roberts drove off the Iraqis with repeated air-strikes and a bold counter-attack. Days later, relief arrived and the Iraqis were soon defeated at nearby **Fallujah** (30 April–6 May 1941).

Habry ❙ 1422 ❙ Hussite Wars

Sigismund of Hungary led a massive German crusade into Bohemia against the heretic Hussites, but was beaten southeast of Prague at **Nebovidy** by Jan Zizka and had to retreat southeast from nearby **Kutna Hora**. When he attempted to make a stand near Habry, Sigismund suffered a terrible defeat at the hands of the Hussites and his routed army fled south to **Nemecky Brod** (8 January 1422).

Hacketstown ❙ 1798 ❙ Irish Rebellion
See **Carlow**

Hadad ❙ 1562 ❙ Turkish-Habsburg Wars

In continuing war over Hungary, Emperor Ferdinand I sent forces to assist Menyhart Balassa, a Transylvanian noble rebelling against John Sigismund Zapolya, who ruled Transylvania and part of Hungary as a Turkish vassal. John was defeated in battle in northern Romania at Hadad (modern Ardud) and Ferdinand agreed to pay the Sultan a tribute for Zapolyai Hungary (4 March 1562).

Hadaspur ❙ 1802 ❙ Maratha Territorial Wars
See **Poona**

Hadath ❙ 778–779 ❙ Byzantine-Muslim Wars

On a fresh offensive into northern Syria, Byzantine General Michael Lachanodrakon besieged Germanikeia (modern Maras) northeast of Adana, then marched northeast to al-Hadath, where he defeated an Arab army then sacked the city and ravaged the countryside. Abbasid Caliph al-Mahdi retaliated with forces which captured **Samalu** then humbled Constantinople after victory at **Nicomedia**.

Hadden Rig ❙ 1542 ❙ Anglo-Scottish Royal Wars

Thomas Howard Duke of Norfolk led a force north against Scotland and sent Sir Robert Bowes and 3,000 cavalry towards Berwick, where they were heavily defeated at nearby Hadden Rig by George Gordon Earl of Huntly and Lord George Home. Bowes and about 600 men were captured and the victory encouraged a Scots advance to battle in November at **Solway Moss** (August 1542).

Hadley ∎ 1676 ∎ King Philip's War

With the Narrangansett destroyed in the **Great Swamp Fight** (December 1675), Major John Talcott led a strong force of Connecticut colonists and Mohegan Indians scouring Massachusetts for the Wampanoag Chief Metacomet (King Philip). Near Hadley, Talcott beat a large force of Philip's men and won again at Marlborough. Philip died two months later at **Mount Hope** (12 June 1676).

Hadong ∎ 1950 ∎ Korean War

As Allied forces withdrew to the **Pusan Perimeter** in southeast Korea, fresh troops were sent forward to Chinju to stall the North Korean advance and Colonel Harold Mott took a green battalion southwest to the strategic junction at Hadong. Ambushed in a mountain pass, the Americans were routed with over 300 killed and 100 captured, one of their worst single-action losses of the war (27 July 1950).

Hadrianopolis ∎ 378 ∎ 5th Gothic War

See **Adrianople**

Haelen ∎ 1914 ∎ World War I (Western Front)

While German forces besieged the Belgian border fortress of **Liège**, a cavalry force under General Georg von de Marwitz swept around to the northwest against the town of Haelen on the Gette, held by a small force under General Lèon Ernest de Witte. The Germans were driven off, but a week later Haelen and **Tirlement** fell as the main invasion advanced on Brussels (12 August 1914).

Haemus ∎ 981 ∎ Byzantine Wars of Tsar Samuel

See **Mount Haemus**

Haengju ∎ 1593 ∎ Japanese Invasion of Korea

Within days of victory north of Seoul at **Pyokjekwan**, the Japanese counter-attacked against Korean General Kwon Yul at Haengju fortress, west of Seoul on the Han River. The massively outnumbered Koreans secured victory in an heroic action and Konishi Yukinaga soon sued for peace. Seoul was abandoned and most of the Japanese army left for home (March 1593).

Hafir, Iraq ∎ 633 ∎ Muslim Conquest of Iraq

Advancing into Persian Mesopotamia from **Akraba** in January, Muslim General Khalid ibn al-Walid and Muthanna defeated and killed Hormuz, the local Satrap, near the springs at Hafir, southwest of Basra, capturing massive arms and treasure. Arabs called it "Battle of the Chains," claiming Persian troops had been chained together to prevent retreat. Khalid soon won again at **Mazar** (March 633).

Hafir, Sudan ∎ 1896 ∎ British-Sudan Wars

With General Herbert Kitchener's British-Egyptian-Sudanese army advancing up the Nile to reconquer the Sudan, Mahdist commander Emir Wad Bashara attempted to block the rapids of Hafir, just north of Dongola. After two days of fighting, additional British artillery was brought up to clear the rapids. Kitchener secured Dongola and advanced towards the **Atbara** (17–19 September 1896).

Hagelsberg ∎ 1813 ∎ Napoleonic Wars (War of Liberation)

On the same day that Napoleon Bonaparte defeated the Allies at **Dresden**, a small French force under General Jean-Baptiste Girard came under attack far to the northwest on the Lubnitz River, at Hagelsberg. Prussian General Karl Friedrich Hirschfeld, with Cossack support, routed the heavily outnumbered French and Girard was driven back into Magdeburg (27 August 1813).

Haguenau ∎ 1793 ∎ French Revolutionary Wars (1st Coalition)
See **Froeschwiller**

Hahozaki ∎ 1274 ∎ Mongol Wars of Kubilai Khan
See **Hakata Bay**

Haicheng ∎ 1894–1895 ∎ Sino-Japanese War
Japanese General Taro Katsura advanced into southern Manchuria through **Fenghuangcheng** to seize strategic Haicheng, then held it against repeated attacks by Chinese General Song Qing. A Japanese sortie suffered badly at **Kangwachai**, but after a final repulse at Haicheng, Song withdrew and Katsura marched northwest towards **Niuzhuang** (13 December 1894–28 February 1895).

Haicheng ∎ 1900 ∎ Russo-Chinese War
As Russians drove north into Manchuria from **Port Arthur** (modern Lüshun), Yingkou fell and General Fleisher attacked Haicheng, held by 4,000 Chinese Regulars and 1,000 Boxer militia. While the city fell after heavy shelling, Fleisher lacked the forces to sustain the advance towards Mukden (modern Shenyang) and had to await reinforcements before continuing on through **Shaho** (11–12 August 1900).

Haidru ∎ 1813 ∎ Afghan-Sikh Wars
See **Attock**

Haifa ∎ 1948 ∎ Israeli War of Independence
Without waiting for expiry of the United Nations Mandate in Palestine, Jewish forces under Moshe Carmel attacked the key port city of Haifa, where British General Hugh Stockwell tried to maintain order. The civilian population of perhaps 50,000 Arabs fled and the city fell after intense fighting. Nearby Acre fell a few days later and Zionists further south attacked **Jaffa** (21–23 April 1948).

Haikalzai ∎ 1842 ∎ 1st British-Afghan War
While Akbar Khan, son of deposed Amir Dost Muhammad, besieged **Kabul**, other Afghans besieged **Kandahar**, defended by British General William Nott. An ill-prepared relief force under Brigadier Sir Richard England was shamefully repulsed at Haikalzai with over 100 men lost, but a second attempt reached Kandahar on 10 May and Nott advanced towards Kabul (28 March 1842).

Hail ∎ 1921 ∎ Saudi-Rashidi Wars
Having fought Kuwait at **Jahrah** in 1920, Abd al-Aziz (Ibn Saud) of Riyadh turned against the Rashidi capital Hail, destabilised by assassination of the Emir. Supported by his Ikhwan ally Faisal al-Dawish, Aziz seized the city and its new ruler Muhmmad ibn Talal. Aziz then made himself Sultan of Nejd and, a few years later, attacked the Hashemites at **Mecca** and **Medina** (2 November 1921).

Hailar ∎ 1900 ∎ Russo-Chinese War
See **Ongon**

Hairini ∎ 1864 ∎ 2nd New Zealand War
See **Rangiaowhia**

Haiyang ∎ 1894 ∎ Sino-Japanese War
Japanese Admiral Sukeyuki Ito disembarked troops in Korea to attack **Pyongyang**, then sailed north against the Chinese fleet under Admiral Ding Ruchang off the Yalu, near Haiyang Island. Although Ito's flagship *Matsushima* suffered heavy damage and casualties, he lost no ships. Four Chinese vessels were sunk and the rest retreated damaged to **Port Arthur** (modern Lüshun) (17 September 1894).

Haji Pir ∎ 1965 ∎ 2nd Indo-Pakistan War
Responding to incursions into northern Kashmir, Indian forces advanced into Pakistani territory behind a prolonged artillery bombardment. In heavy fighting against Pakistani regulars and Azad-Kashmiri elements, the Indians secured Bharat Gali, then seized the strategic high altitude pass at Haji Pir. Pakistan struck

back in force further south around **Chhamb** (21–28 August 1965).

Hajipur ▌ 1760 ▌ Seven Years War (India)

As Mughal Emperor Shah Alam II withdrew south through Bengal, pursued by Major John Caillaud after defeat at **Sherpur**(22 February), Patna itself was threatened by Imperial ally Khadem Husain Khan of Purnea. A small British-Sepoy force under Captain Ranfurlie Knox marched northeast to defeat Khadem Husain at Hajipur and further action a week later secured Patna (16 June 1760).

Haj Omran ▌ 1983 ▌ Iraq-Iran War

Iran was halted in central Iraq at **Amara** and **Mehran** and swung its effort north into Kurdistan, supported by anti-Baghdad Iraqi Kurds. When they took the major army base at Haj Omran, northeast of Arbil, Iraq launched a heavy counter-offensive. However, their tanks were limited by mountainous terrain and large areas were lost. In October, Iran attacked further south towards **Panjwin** (22–29 July 1983).

Hakata ▌ 941 ▌ Sumitomo Uprising

Japanese provincial Governor Fujiwara Sumitomo turned against the government and raided along the Inland Sea coast of Honshu. In response, the Imperial court sent a large force under Ono Yoshifuru and Minamoto Tsunemoto, who drove the rebel out of his base in Iyo to Dazaifu in Kyushu. At nearby Hakata, Sumitomo was decisively defeated and fled back to Iyo, where he was executed.

Hakata Bay ▌ 1274 ▌ Mongol Wars of Kubilai Khan

In a large-scale assault on Japan, Kubilai Khan sent a Mongol-Korean force under Zhao Liangbi, which landed on Kyushu at Hakata Bay, near modern Fukuoka. Beaten by Japanese defence led by Shoni Sukeyoshi, the invaders lost thousands more when a great storm arose and wrecked the Mongol fleet. A second invasion was repulsed seven years later at the same site (19 November 1274).

Hakata Bay ▌ 1281 ▌ Mongol Wars of Kubilai Khan

Another massive assault on Japan by Kubilai Khan saw a huge Mongol-Korean force under Hong Dagu land on Kyushu just north of Hakata Bay, site of a previous failure. Following two months of inconclusive assault and delayed reinforcements, a typhoon—Kamikaze, or Divine Wind—destroyed the Mongol fleet, with thousands drowned as they fled (21 June–16 August 1281).

Hakodate ▌ 1869 ▌ War of the Meiji Restoration

See **Goryokaku**

Hakozaki ▌ 1274 ▌ Mongol Wars of Kubilai Khan

See **Hakata Bay**

Hakusukinoe ▌ 663 ▌ Sino-Korean Wars

See **Paekchon**

Halabja ▌ 1988 ▌ Iraq-Iran War

Iranian forces and their Kurdish allies renewed the offensive in Iraqi Kurdistan, where they captured Halabja, southeast of **Suleimaniya**. Iraqi aircraft immediately attacked with cyanide and nerve gas, killing perhaps 5,000, mainly civilians, and maiming thousands. While the world was shocked, Iraq soon began to win the war at **Al Faw** and many Kurds fled into Iran and Turkey (16 March 1988).

Halai ▌ 1894 ▌ 1st Italo-Ethiopian War

As Italian forces tried to secure Ethiopia, they faced rebellion in the north by former ally Batha Agos of the Okulé-Kusai, who besieged Halai, near Saganeiti, in modern Eritrea. Attacked in the rear by a column under Major Pietro Toselli, Batha Agos was defeated and killed. The survivors fled to Tigre and fought at **Coatit**. A year later, Toselli was killed at **Amba Alagi** (18 December 1894).

Haldighat ❙ 1576 ❙ Mughal Conquest of Northern India

Mughal Emperor Akbar, facing rebellion by Pratap Singh, the Rajput Rana of Mewar, sent his General Man Singh of Jaipur and 5,000 horsemen into the Punjab. Near the Haldighat Pass, northwest of Udaipur at Gogunda, Pratap Singh was heavily defeated and fled to the hills of Aravilli. However, within ten years he had recovered most of Mewar (18 June 1576).

Halfaya Pass ❙ 1941 ❙ World War II (Northern Africa)

See **Sollum-Halfaya**

Haliartus ❙ 395 BC ❙ Corinthian War

Fearing that Thebes, Athens, Corinth and Argos were about to ally against them, Sparta sent a small force under the famous General Lysander to secure the central Greek city of Haliartus, in Boeotia. When trapped between the city's garrison and a Theban army attacking from the rear, the Spartans were heavily defeated and Lysander was killed. Sparta was avenged the following year at **Coronea**.

Halicarnassus ❙ 334 BC ❙ Conquests of Alexander the Great

After victory at the **Granicus**, Alexander the Great advanced through Asia Minor via **Miletus** to besiege Halicarnassus (modern Bodum), held by the Persian Satrap Orontopates and Greek mercenary commander Memnon. The city fell after a difficult siege and Alexander restored his ally Ada, former Satrap of Caria. Ptolemaeus was then left to subdue the province (September–November 334 BC).

Halidon Hill ❙ 1333 ❙ Anglo-Scottish War of Succession

Advancing into Scotland to support his ally Edward Baliol besieging **Berwick**, Edward III of England faced a large relief army under Sir Archibald Douglas, Regent for the boy-King David II. Douglas was defeated and killed in a one-sided disaster at nearby Halidon Hill and the English King restored Baliol to the Scottish throne, receiving in return much of the Scottish lowlands (18 July 1333).

Halka ❙ 1939 ❙ Russo-Japanese Border Wars

See **Khalkan Gol**

Halle ❙ 1806 ❙ Napoleonic Wars (4th Coalition)

While Napoleon Bonaparte was routing the main Prussian army at **Auerstadt** and **Jena**, a separate Corps under Prince Eugene of Württemberg was held further north on the Saal at Halle, west of Leipzig. A short, sharp action saw Marshal Jean Baptiste Bernadotte drive the Prussians out of a poorly prepared defensive position and they withdrew north towards the Elbe (17 October 1806).

Hallue ❙ 1870 ❙ Franco-Prussian War

A mid-winter French offensive on the Somme saw General Louis Léon Faidherbe attempt to recapture **Amiens**, taking position to the northeast on the Hallue, where he bravely repulsed an attack by General Edwin von Manteuffel. But with German reinforcements approaching, Faidherbe withdrew north towards Arras. Within days he attacked towards Péronne at **Bapaume** (23 December 1870).

Halmstad ❙ 1563 ❙ Nordic Seven Years War

With the loss of strategic **Alvsborg** to Frederick II of Denmark, Erik XIV of Sweden marched south into Danish Halland and attempted to seize Halmstad. After a costly failure, Erik left his troops to depart for Stockholm and was widely accused of cowardice. Meanwhile, the withdrawing Swedish army was decisively defeated two weeks later near Halmstad at **Mared** (23 October 1563).

Halys ❙ 585 BC ❙ Median-Lydian War

Cyaxeres of the Medes extended his empire into Armenia, where he sustained a prolonged conflict with Alyattes of Lydia. War reached its climax in a semi-legendary confrontation on the Halys (modern Kizil Irmak). When a solar eclipse halted fighting, the combatants made peace and the Halys remained the border until Lydia invaded in 547 BC and was defeated at **Pteria** (28 May 585 BC).

Halys **I** 82 BC **I** 2nd Mithridatic War

Provoking renewed war against King Mithridates VI of Pontus, Lucius Licinius Murena, Roman Propaetor in Asia, advanced into Cappadocia and took Comana. However, he had to fall back on the Halys (modern Kizil Irmak) when Pontic General Gordius was reinforced by Mithridates himself. Murena was heavily defeated and Roman commander Lucius Sulla intervened to restore peace.

Hama **I** 1925 **I** Druze Rebellion

Encouraged by Druze capture of **Suwayda** in southern Syria, rebellion against the French Mandate soon broke out in the north at Hama, led by Fawzi al-Qawukji, a dissident Syrian Legion officer. Aided by other dissidents and Bedouin he seized the city, but it was massively bombarded with over 300 killed. Al-Qawukji fled and the French soon bombarded **Damascus** itself (4–7 October 1925).

Hamad **I** 1920 **I** Saudi-Kuwait War

During a border war between Abd al-Aziz (Ibn Saud) of Riyadh and Salim ibn Mubarak of Kuwait, Salim sent 400 troops south into disputed territory, where they were met by Faisal al-Dawish and his Ikhwan warriors. At the Wells of Hamad, inland from Dawhat Bilbul near Karya al Ulya, the Kuwaitis were routed and Faisal continued north towards **Jahrah** (May 1920).

Hamadan **I** 1220 **I** Conquests of Genghis Khan

After invading the Khwarezmian Empire, which once covered Afghanistan, Transoxonia, and much of Iran, the Mongol Genghis Khan destroyed its capital **Samarkand**, then sent Generals Jebei and Subetai in pursuit of Sultan Mohammad II. Muhammad was defeated in battle near Hamadan and fled to the Caspian where he died. The Mongol generals returned a year later and destroyed Hamadan.

Hamadan **I** 1503 **I** Persian-Turkoman Wars

In his war with the Turkomans, Shah Ismail Safawi of Persia routed the Sultan Alwand at **Sharur** and, two years later, completed his conquest at Hamadan in the west of modern Iran. Sultan Murad of the Ak Kyunlu (White Sheep) Turkoman confederacy suffered a decisive defeat and the fall of the Turkoman Dynasty secured Ismail effective control of Persia (20 June 1503).

Hamadan **I** 1630 **I** Turko-Persian Wars

Five years after Turkish forces were repulsed outside **Baghdad**, Grand Vizier Khuzrev Pasha led a fresh invasion into Persian Kurdistan. Having captured Mosul, he met and defeated a large Persian army under Zaynal Khan near Hamadan, in western Persia. The city then fell to Khuzrev's siege, although he was later driven back from an advance against Baghdad (5 May 1630).

Hamadan **I** 1731 **I** Turko-Persian War

When Shah Tahmasp II of Persia was repulsed at **Erivan**, Governor Ahmad Pasha of Baghdad took another Turkish army, which seized Kermanshah (30 July) then threatened Hamadan. Tahmasp marched south to relieve Hamadan, but 20 miles northeast at Korijan he was routed and had to accept a humiliating peace. The Shah was later deposed by General Nadir Kuli (15 September 1731).

Hamaguri Gomon Incident **I** 1864 **I** War of the Meiji Restoration
See **Kyoto**

Hamburg **I** 1813–1814 **I** Napoleonic Wars (War of Liberation)

French Marshal Louis Davout seized Hamburg following the battle of **Luneberg**, but steadfastly refused to surrender the great German city, even after the first abdication of Napoleon Bonaparte in April 1814. It required a written order directly from King Louis XVIII before the determined Marshal agreed to withdraw (30 May 1813–27 May 1814).

Hamburger Hill **I** 1969 **I** Vietnam War
See **Dong Ap Bia**

Hamel I 1918 I World War I (Western Front)

During a large-scale raid across the front line, Australians and Americans under Australian General John Monash attacked the town of Le Hamel, 12 miles east of Amiens, which had been seized by the Germans three months earlier to create a salient. The surprise assault was a remarkable success and straightened the German line prior to the major Allied offensive from **Amiens** (4 July 1918).

Hamirpur I 1858 I Indian Mutiny

See **Budhayan**

Hammelburg I 1866 I Seven Weeks War

On the offensive against Austria's German allies, Prussian General Edouard von Falckenstein invaded Bavaria and, after victory at **Wiesenthal** and **Zella**, sent General Gustav von Beyer against part of General Friedrich von Zoller's army at Hammelburg. As at **Kissingen** on the same day, the Bavarians were defeated and Zoller and Prince Karl of Bavaria were forced to retire (10 July 1866).

Hampden I 1814 I War of 1812

Leading a British expedition to the Penebscot River in Maine, General Sir John Sherbrooke and Admiral Edward Griffiths captured the fort at Castine. Colonel Henry John and naval Captain Robert Barrie then advanced upriver to Hampden and defeated American militia General John Blake (3 September). Blake surrendered next day and the British withdrew (26 August–9 September 1814).

Hampton I 1775 I War of the American Revolution

British Governor John Murray Earl of Dunmore took the offensive in Virginia and sent naval Captain John Squires against Hampton, on the James River. Reinforced next day by Minutemen under Colonel William Woodford, the town militia sank or captured all six British ships. After further defeats at **Great Bridge** and

Gwynn Island Dunmore was driven out of Virginia (24–25 October 1775).

Hampton Roads I 1862 I American Civil War (Eastern Theatre)

In the first action between iron-clads, the Confederate ship *Monitor* under Captain Franklin Buchanan met the converted Union vessel *Merrimac* (renamed *Virginia*), commanded by Lieutenant John L. Worden in Hampton Roads, Virginia. With Buchanan badly wounded, Lieutenant Catesby Jones renewed the duel and Worden eventually withdrew with over 400 casualties (8–9 March 1862).

Han, China I 645 BC I Wars of China's Spring and Autumn Era

Near the start of the great rivalry between the Jin (Chin) and Qin (Ch'in) states along the valley of the Yellow River, Jin Prince Hui was met in battle near the Han River by Qin Lord Mu. Hui was defeated and taken prisoner. Following intervention by the Zhou Royal court, Hui was released but Jin-Qin rivalry continued. The Qin soon turned south and also clashed with the Chu (September 645 BC).

Han, Korea I 1950 I Korean War

After the rapid fall of **Seoul**, South Korean Generals Yu Jai Hyung and Kim Hong-il bravely organised defence on the Han River, just south of the city, where North Korean commander Lee Kwon Mu attacked towards Yongdung-po. Having rebuilt demolished bridges and broken through in the west at Inchon, the invaders stormed the Han and drove south towards **Osan** (29 June–3 July 1950).

Hanau I 1635–1638 I Thirty Years War (Franco-Habsburg War)

Resisting Imperial siege, Scots commander Sir James Ramsay defended Hanau on the Main from Autumn 1635 until June 1636, when he was relieved by Landgrave William of Hesse-Cassel and Swedes, under Sir Alexander Leslie. The siege was immediately renewed and Ramsay capitulated. He seized Hanau again in

December 1637, but was captured and died of wounds (1635–12 February 1638).

Hanau **|** 1813 **|** Napoleonic Wars (War of Liberation)

As Napoleon Bonaparte withdrew towards the Rhine after defeat at **Leipzig**, a Bavarian army under Prince Karl Philipp von Wrede attempted to cut off his retreat at Hanau, near Frankfurt. Bonaparte broke through to cross the Rhine and the following day his rearguard under Marshal Édouard Mortier completed the Bavarian defeat, with the Prince severely wounded (30–31 October 1813).

Hancock **|** 1862 **|** American Civil War (Eastern Theatre)

In a mid-winter attempt to cut Union rail and river traffic on the upper Potomac, Confederate General Thomas "Stonewall" Jackson attacked the garrison at Hancock, on the Pennsylvania–Maryland border, stubbornly defended by General Frederick W. Lander. After a failed bombardment, Jackson was forced to withdraw into West Virginia, where he captured Romney (5–6 January 1862).

Handan **|** 259–258 BC **|** China's Era of the Warring States

After crushing a Zhao army at **Changping**, Qin (Ch'in) General Bai Qi laid siege to the well-fortified capital, Handan. As a result of political intrigue, Bai Qi committed suicide, but the siege continued. Zhao sought aid from Wei, whose king sent an army under General Jin Bi. But when Jin Bi hesitated to help, the King's brother Wuji killed him and led an attack which routed the besieging army of Qin.

Handan **|** 1945 **|** 3rd Chinese Revolutionary Civil War

Communist General Liu Bocheng routed a Kuomintang incursion of **Shangdang** (15 October), then moved east to meet Nationalist forces advancing north along the Beijing–Hankou railway. After heavy fighting around Handan, Nationalist General Gao Shuxun defected with

over 10,000 men and two other corps were beaten, with General Ma Fawu captured (31 October 1945).

Handoub **|** 1888 **|** British-Sudan Wars

When Mahdist General Osman Digna raided towards Handoub in eastern Sudan, Major Herbert Kitchener, Governor in Suakin, marched north with 450 Sudanese troops and irregulars. Near Handoub, they defeated the Dervishes and killed about 300, although Kitchener withdrew badly wounded. His successor defeated Osman again in December at **Gemaizeh** (17 January 1888).

Hangchow **|** 1275–1276 **|** Mongol Wars of Kubilai Khan

See **Hangzhou**

Hangchow **|** 1861 **|** Taiping Rebellion

See **Hangzhou**

Hangchow **|** 1863–1864 **|** Taiping Rebellion

See **Hangzhou**

Hangchow **|** 1926–1927 **|** 1st Chinese Revolutionary Civil War

See **Hangzhou**

Hanging Rock **|** 1780 **|** War of the American Revolution

American Colonel Thomas Sumter attacked British outposts north of **Camden**, where he sent Major William Davie against Hanging Rock, South Carolina, held by a Tory force under Colonels Thomas Brown and Morgan Bryan and Major John Carden. Reinforced by Sumter from **Rocky Mount**, the rebels inflicted about 200 casualties before withdrawing as reinforcements arrived (6 August 1780).

Hango **|** 1714 **|** 2nd "Great" Northern War

With Charles XII of Sweden exiled in Turkey, Tsar Peter's newly created fleet entered the Gulf of Finland under Admiral Feodor Apraxin and met Swedish Admiral Johan Ehrenskjold off Cape Hango east of Ahvenanmaa (Aland). The outgunned Russians overwhelmed the Swedes, giving the Tsar his first naval victory—"**Poltava at sea**"—and aiding his conquest of Finland (6 August 1714).

Hangzhou ∎ 1275–1276 ∎ Mongol Wars of Kubilai Khan

The Mongol Kubilai Khan attacked southern China, where **Xiangyang** fell after a long siege and General Bayan advanced on the Song capital Hangzhou (then Lin'an). Regent Jia Sidao was defeated west of Hangzhou and the Dowager Empress Xie surrendered the city and the young Emperor Gong Zong. The Song Dynasty finally fell in 1279 after defeat at **Yashan** (July 1275–January 1276).

Hangzhou ∎ 1861 ∎ Taiping Rebellion

Despite losing **Anqing**, Taiping commander Li Xiucheng invaded Zhejiang and besieged Hangzhou, where the walls of the starving city were taken by storm (28 December). The Manchu garrison held out in the inner city, but after bloody fighting, Governor Wang Yuling and thousands of others killed themselves. Li then advanced northeast on **Shanghai** (26 October–31 December 1861).

Hangzhou ∎ 1863–1864 ∎ Taiping Rebellion

On a fresh offensive against the Taiping in Zhejiang, Imperial commander Zuo Zongtang laid siege to Hangzhou and gradually captured the surrounding towns, including Fuyang to the southwest. In the final assault, General Jiang Yili and French commander Paul d'Aiguebelle destroyed part of the walls and took the city by storm, followed by a terrible sack (20 September 1863–31 March 1864).

Hangzhou ∎ 1926–1927 ∎ 1st Chinese Revolutionary Civil War

Northern warlord Sun Zhuanfang lost **Nanchang** (November 1926), yet regrouped to launch a fresh offensive under Meng Zhaoyue, who drove Zhou Fengqi out of Hangzhou.

Chiang Kai-shek sent a large Nationalist army under Bai Chongxi and heavy losses outside Hangzhou forced Meng to evacuate. Chiang then turned north against **Shanghai** (22 December 1926–16 February 1927).

Hanigalbat ∎ 681 BC ∎ Assyrian Wars

See **Khanigalbat**

Hankou ∎ 1852 ∎ Taiping Rebellion

See **Wuchang**

Hankou ∎ 1911 ∎ 1st Chinese Revolution

When China's revolution began at **Wuchang**, nearby Hankou also fell to Republican forces (12 October 1911). Imperial troops then counter-attacked under Yin Zhang and Duan Qirui, supported by Admiral Sa Zhening. Very heavy fighting forced rebel commander Huang Xing to abandon Hankou and the Imperials turned on nearby **Hanyang** (27–30 October 1911).

Hanling ∎ 532 ∎ Wei Dynastic Wars

The warlord Erzhu Rong appointed a puppet Emperor in the Wei court at Luoyang and beat rebel Ge Rong at **Ye** (528), near modern Anyang. But four years later, their successors Erzhu Zhao and Gao Huan met near Ye at Hanling. Gao won a decisive victory and appointed his own Emperor. In 534, Wei split into rival kingdoms which fought a brutal war including battles at **Shayuan**, **Heqiao** and **Yubi**.

Hanna ∎ 1916 ∎ World War I (Mesopotamia)

Despite disastrous losses at **Sheik Sa'ad** and the **Wadi**, General Sir Fenton Aylmer's Anglo-Indian force trying to relieve besieged **Kut-al-Amara**, made a third attack on the Tigris just downstream at the defile of Hanna. An ill-conceived British frontal assault was driven off with almost 3,000 casualties and Aylmer withdrew. Another attempt in March was repulsed at **Dujaila** (21 January 1916).

Hanoi ∎ 1426–1427 ∎ Sino-Vietnamese War

See **Dong-do**

Hanoi I 1873 I French Conquest of Indo-China

With French adventurer Jean Dupuis campaigning in northern Vietnam (Tonkin), Lieutenant Francis Garnier invaded with just 200 men and captured the citadel of Hanoi in a sharp action without French loss. Chinese Black Flag forces then intervened and, when Garnier was killed in a sortie (21 December), France made peace and withdrew to southern Vietnam (20 November 1873).

Hanoi I 1882 I French Conquest of Indo-China

On a fresh advance into northern Vietnam (Tonkin) after the death of Francis Garnier, French Captain Henri Rivière took just 230 men from Saigon to attack Hanoi. Carrying 250 reinforcements, his ships then bombarded the citadel and took it by storm after Governor Hoang Dieu hanged himself to avoid capture. A year later, Rivière captured **Nam Dinh**, but was killed near **Hanoi** (25 April 1882).

Hanoi I 1883 I Sino-French War

Captain Henri Rivière captured **Hanoi** and **Nam Dinh** in northern Vietnam (Tonkin), then faced intervention by Chinese Black Flag forces under Liu Yongfu, who opened an offensive against Hanoi. On a sortie with 450 men towards Phu Hoai, the French were ambushed and routed at the nearby Pont de Papier. They lost 50 killed (including Rivière) and another 76 wounded (19 May 1883).

Hanover I 1863 I American Civil War (Eastern Theatre)

As Confederate commander Robert E. Lee crossed the Potomac, he unwisely permitted General James "Jeb" Stuart to take his cavalry raiding behind General George G. Meade's Union army. Southeast of **Gettysburg** at Hanover, Pennsylvania, Stuart was defeated and almost captured by General Judson Kilpatrick. His cavalry played little part in the main battle next day (30 June 1863).

Hanover Court House I 1862 I American Civil War (Eastern Theatre)

After directing the Union siege of **Yorktown**, early in the Peninsula campaign, General Fitz-John Porter met Confederate General Lawrence O'Bryan Branch near Hanover Court House, north of Richmond, Virginia. While Porter claimed he inflicted over 900 casualties, including 700 men captured, the Union army was eventually forced to withdraw through the **Seven Days' Battles** (27 May 1862).

Hanover Junction I 1864 I American Civil War (Eastern Theatre)

See **North Anna**

Hansan I 1592 I Japanese Invasion of Korea

Despite disaster off southern Korea at **Sachon** (8 July), Japan sent a large naval force west from Pusan under Admiral Wakizaka Yasuharu, to support the war in the north. Ambushed off Hansan Island by Korean commander Yi Sun-shin, the Japanese fleet was devastated. Only 14 ships escaped out of 73 and a second action two days later off **Angolpo** completed the Japanese debacle (14 August 1592).

Hansi I 1037–1038 I Muslim Conquest of Northern India

On a fresh invasion of India, Sultan Masud ibn Mahmud of Afghanistan left Ghazni and, against the advice of his ministers, attacked Hansi, the old capital of Hariyana northwest of Delhi. Overcoming stubborn resistance he breached the city walls, then stormed and sacked the city, slaughtering the men and enslaving the women and children (20 December 1037–1 January 1038).

Hansi I 1801–1802 I Maratha Territorial Wars

Irish adventurer George Thomas, who became virtual ruler of an area northwest of Delhi, had to abandon **Georgegarh** and fled to his capital at Hansi, where he was attacked by a Franco-Maratha army under Major Louis Bourquein. After heavy fighting Thomas negotiated a surrender and withdrew with his fortune, but died before he could board the ship home (21 November 1801–1 January 1802).

Hanwella ∎ 1803 ∎ 1st British-Kandyan War

When Britain attempted to intervene in the Kingdom of **Kandy**, in central Ceylon, a claimed 12,000 Kandyan troops under Pilima Talauva attacked Lieutenant Charles W. Mercer at the small fortress of Hanwella, east of Colombo. Later relieved and reinforced by Captain William Pollard, the fort held out and Colombo was saved, though the war was already virtually over (3–6 September 1803).

Hanyang ∎ 1852 ∎ Taiping Rebellion
See **Wuchang**

Hanyang ∎ 1911 ∎ 1st Chinese Revolution

China's revolution began at **Wuchang** and nearby Hanyang also fell to Republican forces (12 October 1911). An Imperial counter-attack then retook **Hankou** and General Feng Guozhang launched a massive assault on Hanyang. The city fell after huge losses on both sides, but Wuchang held out until the fall of **Nanjing** in early December led to establishment of a Republic (20–27 November 1911).

Happo ∎ 1592 ∎ Japanese Invasion of Korea
See **Okpo**

Happrew ∎ 1304 ∎ William Wallace Revolt

Twelve months after defeat at **Roslin**, a strong English force under Sir John de Segrave, Sir Robert Clifford and Sir William Latimer was sent against the Scottish rebels. At Happrew, just west of Peebles, they defeated Sir William Wallace and Sir Simon Fraser and a year later Wallace was captured and executed. Fraser was beheaded after defeat in 1306 at **Kirkincliffe** (March 1304).

Hara ∎ 1638 ∎ Shimabara Rebellion

Roused by poverty and oppression, mainly Christian Japanese peasants in the Amakusa-Shimabara region of western Kyushu rebelled against Masuda Shiro. Besieged in Hara Castle, near Shimabara, by Itakura Shigemasa and later Matsudaira Nobutsuna, the rebel stronghold was finally taken by storm. Shiro and up to 35,000 men, women and children were massacred (12 April 1638).

Haraiya ∎ 1858 ∎ Indian Mutiny

British forces under Colonel Francis Rowcroft renewing the British offensive north of the Gaghara opposite Faizabad attacked about 4,000 rebels under Mehndi Husain at Haraiya, east of his previous defeat at **Amorha** (5 March). The rebels were utterly crushed in the final decisive action and fled, leaving Rowcroft to advance and secure the Gorakhpur District (18 June 1858).

Hard ∎ 1499 ∎ Swabian War

In their final struggle for freedom, the Swiss cantons marched against the Habsburg cities of the Swabian League and advanced to Hard, on the Upper Rhine at Lake Constance near Bregenz, where a reputed 10,000 Germans were put to flight. The Swiss were victorious again in a smaller engagement a month later at **Bruderholz** (20 February 1499).

Hardaumont ∎ 1916 ∎ World War I (Western Front)
See **Louvement**

Hardenberg Heath ∎ 1580 ∎ Netherlands War of Independence

Georges van Lalaing Count Rennenberg turned against William of Orange and declared for Spain. He was then besieged at Groningen by William's ally, Bartold Entens, and Viceroy Alexander Farnese sent a force of pro-Spanish Dutch under Martin Schenck van Neuenaar. To the south at Hardenberg Heath, Count Albert of Hohenloe was routed and Groningen was relieved (17 June 1580).

Harenc ∎ 1097 ∎ 1st Crusade
See **Albara**

Harenc I 1098 I 1st Crusade

Just weeks after Duqaq of Damascus was defeated at **Albara** attempting to relieve besieged **Antioch, Syria**, his brother Ridwan of Aleppo (the titular ruler of Antioch) led a second relief army, which captured Harenc, just east of the city. In a bold offensive, Crusader heavy cavalry rode out to meet the Muslim force, which was badly defeated. Antioch fell five months later (9 February 1098).

Harer I 1977–1978 I Ogaden War

Somali forces sweeping into Ethiopa's northern Ogaden through **Jijiga** advanced on Harer and took part of the ancient walled city. But they were driven out in heavy fighting and defence of the besieged city was the turning point of the war. With a huge airlift of Soviet armour and Cuban troops, Ethiopia began its counteroffensive by relieving the siege at Harer (October 1977–February 1978).

Harfleur I 1415 I Hundred Years War

With France wracked by the Burgundian-Armagnac civil war, newly crowned King Henry V of England took an army to claim the French throne and landed near modern Le Havre to besiege Harfleur. Although the English suffered heavily from casualties and disease, the port surrendered after four weeks. Henry marched to victory a month later at **Agincourt** (19 August–22 September 1415).

Harfleur I 1416 I Hundred Years War

Following the English victory at **Agincourt** (October 1415), Bernard of Armagnac Constable of France took a large force to besiege English-occupied Harfleur. A decisive battle off the port saw the blockading French fleet of Count Jean of Dunois and Robinet de Braquemont destroyed by English ships under Sir Walter Hungerford. The siege was lifted a few days later (15 August 1416).

Hargeisa I 1988 I Somalian Civil War

After years of insurgency against the military government of President Siad Barre, Isaaq rebels in northern Somalia seized Burao (27 May), then attacked and captured Hargeisa, Somalia's second largest city. Massive bombing destroyed much of Hargeisa, after which the rebels withdrew. Barre then began a brutal campaign to displace and repress the northern clans (31 May–June 1988).

Harkany I 1687 I Later Turkish-Habsburg Wars

Charles V of Lorraine inflicted a costly Turkish defeat at **Vienna** then, while campaigning in Hungary, captured **Buda** for the Holy League and used superior fire-arms to defeat a large Turkish army at Harkany, south of the famous battlefield of Mohacs. In the wake of the Turkish rout, Grand Vizier Suleiman Pasha was executed for failure and Sultan Mehmed IV was deposed (12 August 1687).

Harlaw I 1411 I MacDonald Rebellion

Rising against Regent Robert Stewart Duke of Albany, Donald MacDonald Lord of the Isles gathered a Highland army and was met in bloody battle at Harlaw, near Aberdeen, by Alexander Stewart Earl of Mar and Aberdeen militia under Provost Sir Robert Davidson. While both sides claimed victory, the Highlanders withdrew and Lowland dominance was established (24 July 1411).

Harlem Heights I 1776 I War of the American Revolution

British forces landed on Manhattan Island at **Kip's Bay** to attack General George Washington in New York City and General Alexander Leslie faced an American defensive line next day at Harlem Heights, held by Colonels Thomas Knowlton and Archibald Crary. While Knowlton and Major Andrew Leitch were killed in a costly action, the British advance was successfully delayed (16 September 1776).

Harmar's Defeat I 1790 I Little Turtle's War

Advancing into the Ohio Valley from Fort Washington (Cincinnati), General Josiah Harmar and 1,500 regulars and militia suffered three humiliating defeats near modern Fort Wayne,

Indiana, at the hands of Miami Chief Little Turtle and the Shawnee Blue Jacket. Harmar was forced to retreat and later resigned. A fresh expedition next year was destroyed in **St Clair's Defeat** (18–22 October 1790).

Harpasus I 229 BC I Pergamum-Seleucid Wars

Attalus I of Pergamum was determined to expand his kingdom in western Anatolia and defeated the Seleucid Antiochus Hierax in Lydia at **Lake Koloe**. He then marched further south into Caria for a decisive victory against Hierax on the Harpasus. After being repulsed in Mesopotamia by his brother Seleucus II, Hierax fled into exile, while Attalus went on to secure much of Seleucid Asia Minor.

Harper's Ferry I 1862 I American Civil War (Eastern Theatre)

After victory in Virginia at **Bull Run**, Confederate commander Robert E. Lee crossed the Potomac, leaving General Thomas "Stonewall" Jackson to besiege Harper's Ferry, West Virginia. Following a brief bombardment, Colonel Dixon S. Miles surrendered more than 12,000 men (before he was killed by a stray shell) and Jackson marched north towards **Antietam** (12–15 September 1862).

Harra I 683 I Muslim Civil Wars

During instability following the death of Umayyad Caliph Mu'awiya, a revolt was raised in Arabia by Abdullah, son of Zubair, the conqueror of Egypt. New Caliph Yazid I sent an army under General Muslim, which captured **Medina**. When Muslim died, the Umayyad army, led by his successor Hosein ibn Numair, defeated Abdullah ibn Zubair in the Harra, then besieged **Mecca** (26 August 683).

Harran I 610 BC I Babylon's Wars of Conquest

Following destruction of **Nineveh** and the death of King Sin-shar-ishkun, Assyrian General Ashur-uballit took his army west to Harran (Carrhae) on the Balikh in southeast Turkey, where he assumed the throne. Attacked by Na-bopolassar of Babylon and Cyaxares of Media, the Assyrians were eventually forced to abandon Harran. The survivors were finally beaten five years later at **Carchemish**.

Harran I 53 BC I Roman-Parthian Wars
See **Carrhae**

Harran I 1104 I Crusader-Muslim Wars

In a fresh offensive on the Upper Euphrates, Bohemund I of Antioch, just released from captivity, joined with Baldwin of le Bourg and Joscelin of Edessa against the city of Harran. At nearby Carrhae, site of a Roman disaster in 53 BC, the Crusaders were routed by Soqman, ruler of Mardin and Jekermish, Atabeg of Mosul. Baldwin and his cousin Joscelin were captured (May 1104).

Harrison's Landing I 1861 I American Civil War (Eastern Theatre)
See **Ball's Bluff**

Hartebeestmund I 1905 I German Colonial Wars in Africa

Campaigning in German Southwest Africa, Nama leader Jakob Morenga, who had routed a German column at **Freyer's Farm**, ambushed Captain von Koppy's pursuing cavalry on the Orange River at Hartebeestmund. In their worst single action of the so-called Herero War, the Germans lost 43 casualties. The Nama were soon defeated at **Vaalgras** and **Van Rooisvlei** (24 October 1905).

Hartley Wood I 1554 I Wyatt's Rebellion
See **Wrotham Heath**

Hartsville, Tennessee I 1862 I American Civil War (Western Theatre)

Confederate General John H. Morgan led a bold expedition northeast of Nashville, Tennessee, where he marched north through Lebanon against Colonel Absalom B. Moore guarding the Cumberland at Hartsville. Crossing the river before dawn, Morgan surprised the Union troops and forced their surrender, capturing Moore and about 1,800 men, plus large quantities of supplies (7 December 1862).

Hartville, Missouri I 1863 I American Civil War (Trans-Mississippi)

On his first expedition into southwestern Missouri, Confederate General John S. Marmaduke was repulsed at **Springfield**, **Missouri** and turned east towards Hartville, where he was met west of the town by approaching Union troops under Colonel Samuel Merrill. Bloody fighting forced Merrill back on Hartville, but Marmaduke suffered greater losses and retreated into Arkansas (11 January 1863).

Harvest Moon I 1965 I Vietnam War
See **Phuoc Ha**

Hasankale I 1048 I Seljuk Wars of Expansion

As Seljuk Turks invaded Armenia, Ibrahim Inal, kinsman of Sultan Toghril Beg, met and defeated a largely foreign Byzantine army under Katakalon Kekaumenos and Liparit IV, Duke of Trialeti, near Pasinler, outside Hasankale. The Seljuks then marched west to plunder Erzurum. Duke Liparit was later released from captivity and Constantine IX agreed to peace (18 September 1048).

Hasanpur I 1720 I Mughal Wars of Succession

Following the murder of his brother Husain Ali Khan, the Mughal king-maker Abdullah Khan proclaimed Prince Ibrahim Emperor in Delhi, then faced the Imperial army under Mohammed Shah and General Amin Khan. Abdullah was crushed in battle at Hasanpur, on the Jumna south of Delhi, where he and the Prince Ibrahim were captured and died in prison (13 November 1720).

Hasbain I 1408 I Hundred Years War
See **Othée**

Hasenbuhl I 1298 I Habsburg Wars of Succession
See **Gollheim**

Hashin I 1885 I British-Sudan Wars

General Sir Gerald Graham was determined to open the road from the Red Sea to the Nile and marched west from Suakin to the village of Hashin, where a large Mahdist force, loyal to Osman Digna, was driven off in heavy fighting. While Graham lost 60 men killed and wounded, the Dervishes suffered perhaps 500 killed. They were defeated again two days later at **Tofrek** (20 March 1885).

Haslach I 1805 I Napoleonic Wars (3rd Coalition)

During Napoleon Bonaparte's advance on **Ulm**, General Pierre Dupont de L'Etang became isolated on the north bank of the Danube near Haslach. In a remarkable action on the nearby Michelberg Heights, Dupont attacked a massively superior Austrian force under Archduke Ferdinand then withdrew, taking almost as many prisoners as his entire command (11 October 1805).

Hastenbeck I 1757 I Seven Years War (Europe)

Advancing towards Prussia, French Marshal Louis Letellier (later Duke d'Estrées) invaded Hanover against William Augustus Duke of Cumberland. After an indecisive struggle at Hastenbeck, on the Weser near Hameln, the Anglo-Hanoverian army was beaten when Cumberland withdrew prematurely to the Elbe. He later disgracefully agreed to declare Hanover neutral (26 July 1757).

Hastings, England I 1066 I Norman Conquest of Britain

When William of Normandy landed near Pevensey, Sussex, with a well-armed force to claim the English throne, King Harold II hurried back from defeating a Norwegian invasion of Yorkshire at **Stamford Bridge**. In England's most celebrated battle, Harold was killed and his army was crushed on Senlac Hill near Hastings. William soon conquered the entire kingdom (14 October 1066).

Hastings, Vietnam I 1966 I Vietnam War
See **Song Ngan**

Hatcher's Run I 1864 I American Civil War (Eastern Theatre)

Leading a Union advance to cut the Boydton Plank Road, southwest of besieged **Petersburg**, Virginia, General Winfield Scott Hancock was met at Hatcher's Run by Confederate General Henry Heth and cavalry under General Wade Hampton. The Union thrust was bloodily repulsed, though another attack a few months later was more successful (27–28 October 1864).

Hatcher's Run I 1865 I American Civil War (Eastern Theatre)

In a fresh Union assault on the strategic Boydton Plank Road, southwest of besieged **Petersburg**, Virginia, Generals Andrew A. Humphreys and Gouvernor K. Warren attacked near Hatcher's Run in support of cavalry under General David M. Gregg. Confederate General John B. Gordon was initially repulsed before he eventually halted the Union advance (5–7 February 1865).

Hatchie Bridge I 1862 I American Civil War (Western Theatre)

Confederate General Earl Van Dorn attempting an offensive in northern Mississippi, was driven off from **Corinth** and escaped across the Tennessee border, pursued by Union General Edward O. C. Ord. Both sides lost about 500 men in a holding action at Hatchie Bridge, near Middleton, but Van Dorn was able to avoid destruction and returned to Holly Springs, Mississippi (5 October 1862).

Hat Creek I 1876 I Sioux Indian Wars
See **War Bonnet Creek**

Hateley Field I 1403 I Percy's Rebellion
See **Shrewsbury**

Hatfield Chase I 633 I Anglo-Saxon Territorial Wars
See **Heathfield**

Hat Mon I 42 I Wars of the Later Han
See **Lang Bac**

Hatra I 199 I Wars of Emperor Severus
See **Atra**

Hatteras I 1861 I American Civil War (Eastern Theatre)
See **Fort Hatteras**

Hattin I 1187 I 3rd Crusade

Guy of Jerusalem faced an invasion of Palestine by Saladin of Egypt and rashly decided to advance east from well-watered area near Saffuriya, through arid country, to relieve Tiberius on the Sea of Galilee. Near the Horns of Hattin, the Crusaders were utterly annihilated. Saladin went on to retake most major cities of the Holy Land, including **Jerusalem**, triggering the Third Crusade (4 July 1187).

Hatvan I 1849 I Hungarian Revolutionary War

Following defeat at **Kapolna**, new Hungarian commander General Artur Gorgey assumed the offensive and, east of Budapest at Hatvan, was attacked by Austrian forces under General Franz von Schlick. After costly losses on both sides, Schlick was driven west from Hatvan. Further Imperial defeats at **Isaszeg**, **Waitzen** and **Nagy Sallo** soon forced the Austrians out of Hungary (2 April 1849).

Hausen I 1809 I Napoleonic Wars (5th Coalition)

Encouraged by French reverses in Spain, Austria invaded Bavaria to attack Marshal Louis Davout on the Danube, where Prince Herman Hohenzollern found himself facing the French rearguard under Generals Louis Friant and Louis St Hillaire, south of Regensburg between Hausen and Teugen. Hohenzollern was repulsed and Archduke Charles lost next day at **Abensberg** (19 April 1809).

Havana I 1555 I Sack of Havana

When pirates sacked Havana in 1538, they accepted a ransom not to burn the city. But a few years later, in one of the largest pirate attacks in the Caribbean, the Huguenot pirate, Jacques de Sores, led four ships, which surprised and plundered the city, then put it to the torch. As a result of this assault, and a further attack in 1558, the fortress of Castillo del Morro was built to protect the harbour.

Havana I 1748 I War of the Austrian Succession

English Admiral Charles Knowles patrolling in the West Indies for a Spanish treasure ship was intercepted near Havana by an equal force under Admiral Don Andres Reggio. An indecisive action saw Knowles capture one Spanish ship and another was driven ashore and burned. However, he was court-martialled and reprimanded for slowness in bringing his squadron to action (1 October 1748).

Havana I 1762 I Seven Years War (Caribbean)

When Spain entered the war, Admiral Sir George Pocock and General Sir George Keppel Earl Albemarle landed on Cuba and besieged Havana, where Castillo del Morro held out heroically until the death of fortress commander Don Luis de Velasco. General Juan de Prado soon surrendered the island and a massive booty. Spain later regained Cuba in return for Florida (6 June–14 August 1762).

Havelberg I 1631 I Thirty Years War (Swedish War)

See **Werben**

Havré I 1572 I Netherlands War of Independence

With Louis of Nassau under siege in **Mons** by Don Fadrique Alvarez (son of the Duke of Alva), Huguenot commander Jean de Hangest Sieur de Genlis returned from France with 7,000 men to support William of Orange. However, just east of Mons at Havré, in modern Belgium, the relief force was routed by Spanish troops under Chiappin Vitelli. Genlis was executed and Mons fell two months later (19 July 1572).

Havrincourt I 1918 I World War I (Western Front)

See **Épéhy**

Haw River I 1781 I War of the American Revolution

As General Nathanael Greene fell back through North Carolina before the advancing British army, he sent General Andrew Pickens and Colonel Henry Lee against Colonel John Pyle and about 300 Loyalist militia on the Haw River. Pyle's force was virtually destroyed in a brief action and, as a result, there was no Loyalist support in the coming battle at **Guildford Courthouse** (25 February 1781).

Haw's Shop I 1864 I American Civil War (Eastern Theatre)

Union cavalry under General David M. Gregg advancing to cover General Ulysses S. Grant crossing the Pamunkey, northeast of Richmond, Virginia, were blocked at Haw's Shop, west of Hanovertown, by Generals Fitzhugh Lee and Wade Hampton. A large-scale cavalry action saw Gregg eventually halted, but Grant's army was already approaching **Totopotomoy Creek** (28 May 1864).

Hayfield Fight I 1867 I Red Cloud's War

Working in a hayfield outside Fort C. F. Smith, near modern Yellow Tail on the Big Horn River in Montana, 30 soldiers and civilians were attacked by 300 Sioux and Cheyenne under Crazy Horse. Armed with repeating rifles, the troopers drove the Indians off with heavy losses. A similar attack was repulsed next day 90 miles to the southeast in the **Wagon Box Fight** (1 August 1867).

Haynes' Bluff I 1863 I American Civil War (Western Theatre)

See **Snyder's Bluff**

Hazarasp I 1017 I Eastern Muslim Dynastic Wars

When rebels killed Shah Abul Abbas Mamun of Khwarezm, his brother-in-law, Mahmud of Ghazni marched to the Oxus River and in a two-day battle at Hazarasp, northwest of Bokhara, defeated and captured the rebels Kumar-Tash Sharabi, Alptagin and Sayyadtagin. Mahmud had all three trampled to death by elephants and appointed his General Altuntash as Khwarezm-shah (3 July 1017).

Heartbreak Ridge I 1951 I Korean War

Continuing their offensive in the east, over-confident South Korean and United Nations forces advanced from **Bloody Ridge** to attack North Korean and Chinese troops well dug in along Heartbreak Ridge, south of Mundung-ni. The area was finally cleared at the cost of 3,700 Allied and perhaps 25,000 Communist casualties and truce talks resumed (13 September–13 October 1951).

Heathfield I 633 I Anglo-Saxon Territorial Wars

Concerned by the growing power of Christian King Edwin of Northumbria, the Pagan Penda of Mercia and the Christian Caedwallan of Gwynned invaded southern Northumbria, where they defeated and killed Edwin at Heathfield (modern Hatfield Chase), near Doncaster. The defeat split Northumbria into Deira and Bernicia, until victory the following year at **Heavenfield** (14 October 633).

Heavenfield I 634 I Anglo-Saxon Territorial Wars

Caedwallan of Gwynned (North Wales) joined Mercia to kill Edwin of Northumbria at **Heathfield** (October 633), but was soon defeated and killed by Edwin's nephew and successor Oswald, son of Aethelfrith, at Heavenfield (Hefenfelth), near Hexham. Oswald's victory restored Northumbria and led to a period of renewed power. The battle site was subsequently named Oswald's Cross.

Hecatombaeum I 226 BC I Cleomenic War

After victory in Arcadia at **Ladoceia**, Cleomenes III of Sparta became dictator after a coup, then invaded Achaea against Aratus of Sicyon. At Hecatombaeum, near Dyme, Cleomenes secured a decisive victory. The Achaean League sued for peace and began to break up. However, Sparta's aggression provoked intervention by Antigonus III of Macedon, who later beat Cleomenes at **Sellasia**.

Hechuan I 1258 I Mongol Conquest of China
See **Diao Yu**

Hedgeley Moor I 1464 I Wars of the Roses

Despite the terrible Lancastrian defeat at **Towton**, their cause continued in northern England, where Yorkist John Neville Lord Montagu came under attack leading a force north from Newcastle. At Hedgeley Moor near Alnwick, Lancastrian Henry Beaufort Duke of Somerset was driven off, with Sir Ralph Percy killed. Three weeks later, Montagu beat Somerset again at **Hexham** (25 April 1464).

Hefei I 1853–1854 I Taiping Rebellion
See **Luzhou**

Heidelberg I 1622 I Thirty Years War (Palatinate War)

When defeat at **Höchst** drove the Protestant army west across the Rhine, Johan Tserclaes Count Tilly of Bavaria besieged Heidelberg, defended by German-Dutch-English forces under Henry van de Merven and Sir Gerard Herbert. The city fell by assault after eleven weeks and the citadel capitulated three days later. Tilly then turned against **Mannheim** (June–19 September 1622).

Heigoutai I 1905 I Russo-Japanese War
See **Sandepu**

Heijo I 1894 I Sino-Japanese War
See **Pyongyang**

Heiligerlee I 1568 I Netherlands War of Independence

The first major action of the Netherlands War saw Count Louis of Nassau and his brother Adolphus lead a force against Count John of Aremberg, Stadtholder of Friesland, and Spanish troops under Gonzales de Braccamonte. Near Heiligerlee, east of Groningen, the Imperial forces were defeated, with Aremberg and Adolphus both killed, reputedly in single combat (23 May 1568).

**Heilsberg I 1807 I Napoleonic Wars
(4th Coalition)**

On a spring offensive in eastern Prussia following **Eylau** (8 February), Russian General Levin Bennigsen was blocked by Marshals Nicolas Soult and Jean Lannes south of Königsberg, at Heilsberg (modern Lidzbark Warminski). Despite Marshal Joachim Murat's cavalry, the Russians could not be dislodged. Both armies withdrew to meet again four days later at **Friedland** (10 June 1807).

**Hejaz I 1812–1813 I Turko-
Wahhabi War**

When Wahhabi forces seized most of Arabia and ended the annual pilgrimage, new Ottoman Sultan Mahmud II authorised Viceroy Muhammad Ali of Egypt to send an expedition into the Hejaz. Led by Ali's brilliant son Ibrahim, the Egyptian-Turkish army captured Medina (1812) and Mecca (1813) and restored the Hashemite Dynasty. Turkey ruled the Hejaz until the Arab Revolt of 1916.

**Hejaz I 1916 I World War I
(Middle East)**

With support from Britain and France, Sharif Hussein, Emir of Mecca, proclaimed the Arab Revolt against Turkey and launched his campaign in the Hejaz. The Arabs captured **Jeddah** (17 June) and Mecca (4 July), as well as **Yanbu** (27 July) and **Taif** (22 September), but could not take the key city of **Medina**. When Hussein declared himself Caliph in 1924, he was defeated by the Saudis at **Taif**.

**Hel I 1939 I World War II
(Western Europe)**

At the start of the war, German forces bombarded the Polish naval base at Hel, on a peninsula near Danzig, where garrison commander Wlodzimierz Steyer held out, despite the surrender of nearby **Westerplatte**. After the fall of **Warsaw**, amid renewed heavy hand to hand fighting, Admiral Józef Unger surrendered, ending the last Polish resistance in the north (1 September–2 October 1939).

**Helena, Arkansas I 1863 I American
Civil War (Western Theatre)**

Confederate forces under General Theophilus H. Holmes attempting to relieve pressure on besieged **Vicksburg**, Mississippi, attacked Helena, far up the river in Arkansas, courageously defended by Union General Benjamin Prentiss. Despite superior numbers, Holmes was driven off with the loss of about 400 casualties and 1,200 men captured and Helena remained in Union hands (4 July 1863).

**Helena, France I 431 I Roman-
Frankish Wars**

When Clodion, King of the Franks, began to expand his territory south into Gaul, he was surprised at Helena (Helesme, northeast of Cambrai in modern France) by a large army under Flavius Aetius, Roman Military Governor of Gaul. Clodion (Chlodio) was heavily defeated, though he subsequently managed to capture Cambrai and advance his border to the River Somme.

**Helgeaa I 1026 I Norwegian Wars
of Succession**

Olaf II Haraldsson of Norway and Anund Jakob of Sweden joined forces to threaten Denmark and, in response, the Danish Knut II returned from England to meet their combined fleets at the mouth of the Helge River, in southern Sweden. Knut secured a sharp victory and, after a subsequent battle at **Stangebjerg**, Olaf fled into exile. Knut then seized the throne of Norway.

**Helgoland I 1864 I 2nd Schleswig-
Holstein War**

In support of Prussia's invasion of Denmark, Austrian Captain Wilhelm von Tegetthof's small squadron and some Prussian gunboats attacked Danish Commodore Edouard Svenson, blockading Hamburg and the Elbe and Weser estuaries. Battle off Helgoland saw the Allies driven off and the Austrian flagship Schwarzenberg severely damaged, but the blockade was broken (8 May 1864).

Helgoland Bight ▮ 1914 ▮ World War I (War at Sea)

At the start of the war, Commodore Reginald Tyrwhitt led cruisers and destroyers against German shipping off Helgoland, which drew six German cruisers into action. Admiral Sir David Beatty arrived with a battle squadron and Germany lost three cruisers sunk and three damaged for few British casualties. In 1916, Beatty became commander of the Grand Fleet (27–28 August 1914).

Helicopter Valley ▮ 1966 ▮ Vietnam War
See **Song Ngan**

Heliopolis ▮ 640 ▮ Muslim Conquest of Egypt

As they advanced up the eastern branch of the Nile from Pelusium into Byzantine Egypt, the small Muslim force of Amr ibn al-As was reinforced by the powerful General Abdullah ibn Zubair for a decisive battle at Heliopolis, near modern Cairo. Byzantine General Augustalis Theodorus was defeated and the Muslims went on to besiege the nearby citadel of **Babylon, Egypt** (August 640).

Heliopolis ▮ 1800 ▮ French Revolutionary Wars (Middle East)

After Britain and Turkey repudiated a negotiated French withdrawal from Egypt, General Jean-Baptiste Kléber renewed the fighting and defeated a Turkish force under Ibrahim Bey at Heliopolis, then recaptured nearby Cairo. Although Kléber was assassinated by a Muslim fanatic three months later, the French held out in Egypt until a new Allied invasion in March 1801 (20 March 1800).

Helles ▮ 1915–1916 ▮ World War I (Gallipoli)

Following the navy's failure to storm the **Dardanelles Narrows**, a hastily assembled British force under General Aylmer Hunter-Weston landed around Cape Helles at the tip of the Gallipoli Peninsula, with another landing further north at **Anzac**. After a badly delayed advance, the Allies were repulsed trying to attack at **Krithia**. Helles was evacuated on 9 January 1916 (25 April 1915).

Hellespont ▮ 324 ▮ Roman Wars of Succession

Emperor Constantine renewed the war against Valerius Licinius, Emperor in the East, and defeated his rival at **Adrianople**, then immediately besieged him in Byzantium. Constantine's young son Crispus won a two-day naval battle in the Hellespont and Admiral Amandus retreated after heavy losses. Defeat at sea persuaded Licinius to withdraw across the Bosphorus to **Chrysopolis** (July 324).

Helmed ▮ 1501 ▮ 1st Muscovite-Lithuanian War

Determined to avenge defeat by the Livonian Order in August at the **Seritsa**, Prince Ivan III of Moscow sent a massive army under Daniil Shchenya against the fortress of Helmed (near Dorpat in modern Latvia). The Order's army was annihilated and the Russians ravaged eastern Livonia. War dragged on and Russian forces met the knights again a year later at **Lake Smolino** (24 November 1501).

Helmstadt ▮ 1866 ▮ Seven Weeks War

Prussia secured victory at **Aschaffenburg** and General Erwin von Manteuffel then proceeded southeast through **Werbach**. While General August von Goeben attacked **Gerchsheim**, General Gustav von Beyer set off through Helmstadt for Neubrunn. Bavarian commander Prince Luitpold was heavily defeated and the combined Prussian forces advanced on **Würzburg** (25 July 1866).

Helsingborg ▮ 1362 ▮ Wars of the Hanseatic League

The ambitious Waldemar IV Atterdag of Denmark captured **Visby** on the Baltic island of Gotland (July 1361) and found himself at war with the cities of the Hanseatic League, which were Allied with Sweden and Norway. The Allied fleet under John Wittenborg of Lubeck captured **Copenhagen**, but was destroyed off nearby Helsingborg. In the ensuing peace, Waldemar retained Gotland (8 July 1362).

Helsingborg I 1710 I 2nd "Great" Northern War

With the Swedish army destroyed at **Poltava** (July 1709), Frederick IV of Denmark sent a 15,000-strong force under Count Christian Reventlow into Swedish Scania in November 1709. Swedish General Magnus Stenbock raised a fresh army and at Helsingborg crushed the invasion, forcing the Danes to withdraw before he marched south to defend Swedish land in Germany (10 March 1710).

Helsingfors I 1918 I Finnish War of Independence

See **Helsinki**

Helsinki I 1918 I Finnish War of Independence

When pro-Bolshevik forces rose against the government and seized Helsinki (28 January) a bitter civil war ensued. A German division under General Rudiger von de Golz eventually landed and marched on the capital. Bombarded by artillery and Admiral Alexander Meurer's ships offshore, Helsinki was retaken and a Finnish offensive soon seized **Vyborg** (12–13 April).

Helsinki I 1939 I Russo-Finnish War

The first day of Russia's undeclared war on Finland saw bombers raid 16 locations, most notably Helsinki, which suffered 91 killed and about 250 wounded. Despite further bombing later—particularly three very costly raids in February 1944—Helsinki remained one of three European combatant capitals (with London and Moscow), not occupied by an enemy (30 November 1939).

Helvetia I 1900 I 2nd Anglo-Boer War

On a new Boer offensive in the eastern Transvaal, Ben Viljoen and Chris Müller took 700 men in a night assault against Helvetia, north of Machadodorp, held by 250 under Major Edward Collen. The badly wounded Collen lost about 40 men and surrendered. Viljoen captured the 4.7-inch gun, "Lady Roberts," then burned the camp and marched south against **Belfast** (28–29 December 1900).

Hemmingstedt I 1500 I Wars of the Kalmar Union

Resolved to expand his influence, John I of Denmark led a force of North German nobles and mercenaries against rebellious peasant farmers in Holstein. But, on flooded fields at Hemmingstedt in Ditmarschen (in modern Germany), the outnumbered farmers secured a decisive victory. The battle led the nobility of Sweden to overthrow John, who had seized the throne at **Rotebro** (17 February 1500).

Hengist's Down I 837 I Viking Raids on Britain

See **Hingston Down**

Hengyang I 1944 I World War II (China)

As part of Japan's **Ichigo** offensive, General Isamu Yokoyama drove deep into Hunan, where he seized **Changsha**, then advanced south against Hengyang, held by General Fang Zianjue. Supported by American bombers, Hengyang held out under siege for 48 days before the Chinese were forced to withdraw. Yokoyama then continued south towards **Guilin** (23 June–8 August 1944).

Hennebont I 1341–1342 I Hundred Years War

In a disputed succession in Brittany, Charles of Blois captured his rival Jean de Montfort, then attacked Countess Jeanne de Montfort at Hennebont, northeast of Lorient. After repulsing a bloody assault and subsequent siege, she was relieved by Sir Walter Manny, sent by Edward III of England, and withdrew to **Brest**. Manny then defeated the Spanish at **Quimperlé** (December 1341–June 1342).

Hennersdorf I 1745 I War of the Austrian Succession

Despite defeat at **Hohenfriedberg** and **Sohr**, Austrian Prince Charles of Lorraine gathered reinforcements and marched into Prussia to threaten Berlin. Turning to face Frederick II of Prussia at Hennersdorf, 12 miles east of Gorlitz, the Austro-Saxon army suffered another terrible defeat. Following a further loss at **Kesseldorf**, Empress Maria Theresa sued for peace (24 November 1745).

Henni ▌ 1911 ▌ Italo-Turkish War
See **Sidi El Henni (1st)**

Heqiao ▌ 538 ▌ Wei Dynastic Wars
After destroying an invasion by Eastern Wei at **Shayuan** (537), Yuwen Tai of the Western Wei launched a counter-offensive east, which captured Luoyang. In severe fighting at the Yellow River near Heqiao (Ho-ch'iao), Yuwen suffered a decisive defeat and withdrew. Five years later, Yuwen attempted a fresh advance on Luoyang and was defeated again at **Mangshan** (13 September 538).

Heraclea, Anatolia ▌ 806 ▌ Byzantine-Muslim Wars
When Nicephorus deposed Empress Irene and resumed war against Caliph Harun al-Rashid, the Muslim leader again invaded Anatolia and, after defeating a Byzantine army at **Crasus**, led a reputed 135,000 men against Heraclea (modern Eregli). Following a decisive action, he took Heraclea by storm, then nearby Tyana. Threatened by Bulgaria in the west, Nicephorus sued for peace (September 806).

Heraclea, Anatolia ▌ 1097 ▌ 1st Crusade
Crusaders under Bohemund defeated the Seljuk Turk, Kilij Arslan, at **Dorylaeum** in July, then seized his capital at Iconium. However, they found their way through eastern Turkey to Syria blocked by the local Emirs of Cappadocia. At Heraclea (modern Eregli), a well-timed charge by heavy cavalry dispersed the Turks and the Crusaders continued towards the key city of **Antioch** (August 1097).

Heraclea, Anatolia (1st) ▌ 1101 ▌ Crusader-Muslim Wars
Sultan Kilij Arslan and Malik Ghazi, Danishmend Turkish Emir of Sebastea, moved south from their great victory at **Mersivan** in July and reached Heraclea in southern Anatolia to cut off the advance by Count William of Nevers. The French troops of the so-called Nivernais Crusade were surrounded and virtually annihilated, though Count William and a handful escaped to Antioch (August 1101).

Heraclea, Anatolia (2nd) ▌ 1101 ▌ Crusader-Muslim Wars
Within weeks of Crusader defeats at **Mersivan** and Heraclea, another Christian army set out for southern Anatolia under William IX of Aquitaine and Hugh of Vermandois. The so-called Aquitanian Crusade was also ambushed and routed at Heraclea by Sultan Kilij Arslan and Malik Ghazi of Sebastea. Duke William escaped but Vermandois was fatally wounded (September 1101).

Heraclea, Lucania ▌ 280 BC ▌ Pyrrhic War
Invited by the Greek city of Tarentum to help check Roman domination of Italy, King Pyrrhus of Epirus invaded with a large army, including war elephants never before seen in Italy. On the Plain of Heraclea, west of modern Taranto, Pyrrhus routed Valerius Laevinus. The victory induced more Greek cities to join Pyrrhus against the Romans and he soon won another costly victory at **Asculum**.

Heraclea, Propontis ▌ 313 ▌ Roman Wars of Succession
See **Tzirallum**

Herat ▌ 208 BC ▌ Early Syrian-Parthian War
See **Arius**

Herat ▌ 1221–1222 ▌ Conquests of Genghis Khan
After destroying the Khwarezmian cities of **Merv** and **Nishapur**, the Mongol Tolui (youngest son of Genghis Khan) captured Herat in Khorasan. He spared the population, but when the citizens rebelled after Mongol defeat at **Parwan Durrah**, Mongol General Eljigidei was sent to punish the city. Herat (in modern

Afghanistan) surrendered after a long siege and the citizenry were massacred.

Herat ∎ 1383 ∎ Conquests of Tamerlane

Early in his campaign of conquest, the Turko-Mongol Tamerlane marched southwest to put down rebellion in Khorasan, then including parts of Iran and Afghanistan. The city of Herat fell to his overwhelming force and he went on to capture Zaranj, Kandahar and Isfizar (where living captives were cemented into towers) as he consolidated his control before turning west against Persia and Azerbaijan.

Herat ∎ 1507 ∎ Mughal-Uzbek Wars

The Uzbek conqueror Muhammad Shaybani Khan drove the Mughal Babur from **Samarkand** in 1498 and later marched southwest into Khorasan to attack Herat, which was held by the Timurid Mughal Mirza Zunnin. When Mirza Zunnun was killed in a fierce battle outside the city, Shaybani captured Herat. The following year, he marched east against Babur himself at **Kandahar**.

Herat ∎ 1528 ∎ Persian-Uzbek Wars

Having defeated the Persians and their Mongol allies at **Kul-i-Malik** and **Ghujduwan** in 1512, the Uzbek leader Ubaid Khan marched into Khorasan and besieged Persian commander Husein Khan Shamlu at Herat (in the west of modern Afghanistan). The starving garrison was on the verge of surrendering after seven months when the Uzbeks were defeated at **Damghan** and Ubaid withdrew.

Herat ∎ 1588–1589 ∎ Mughal-Uzbek Wars

The great Uzbek leader Abdullah Khan II expanded his power on the Oxus, where he captured Balkh (1568) Gissar and Samarkand (1575), then advanced into Khorasan to attack the Mughal city of Herat. Emperor Akbar made peace with the Uzbeks, conceding Balkh, but ten years later, Abdullah faced counter-attack by Persia at **Rabat-i-Pariyan** (June 1588–February 1589).

Herat ∎ 1598 ∎ Persian Reconquest of Khorasan

See **Rabat-i-Pariyan**

Herat ∎ 1719 ∎ Persian-Afghan Wars

When Asadullah Khan of Herat declared independence, he faced a huge Persian army under Safi Kuli Khan. Near Herat at Kariz, Asadullah's outnumbered Abdali Afghans won an unlikely victory, when the Persians were confused by friendly artillery fire. Safi was captured and Asadullah went on to seize much of Khorasan. Later that year, he was killed at **Farah** by Mahmud Ghilzai of Kandahar.

Herat ∎ 1729 ∎ Persian-Afghan Wars

Shah Tahmasp II resolved to recover Persia from its Afghan conquerors and captured **Meshed** in 1726. He later advanced towards Herat, held by Abdali Afghans under Allah Yar Khan, who marched northwest to meet the invaders. After defeat at nearby Kafir Qala, Kusuya, Rabat-i-Paryan and Shakiban, Allah Yar Khan finally pledged allegiance to Tahmasp and retained Herat (May 1729).

Herat ∎ 1731–1732 ∎ Persian-Afghan Wars

While Shah Tahmasp II besieged **Erivan** in Turkish Armenia, Abdali Afghans in Herat under Dhul-Fiqar overthrew the Persian nominee Yar Allah Khan. General Nadir Kuli (later Nadir Shah) marched over 1,500 miles east to Herat, which surrendered after a long siege. Yar Allah Khan was then restored. Meanwhile, Tahmasp was defeated at **Hamadan** (May 1731–27 February 1732).

Herat ∎ 1750 ∎ Persian-Afghan Wars

Following the death of Nadir Shah of Persia, the Afghan ruler Ahmad Shah Durrani took 70,000 men against Herat in western Afghanistan, held for Nadir's teenage son Shah Rukh, by General Emir Shah. The city fell after a long siege and Emir Shah was killed in a final stand in the citadel of Herat. A Persian attempt to retake the city the following year was defeated at **Torbat-i-Jam**.

Herat ∎ 1837–1838 ∎ Persian-Afghan Wars
Encouraged by Russia, Shah Muhammad of Persia attacked Herat, in western Afghanistan, held by about 4,000 Afghans under Vizier Yar Muhammad, advised by British Major Eldred Pottinger. A heavy assault was repulsed (23 June) and after Britain failed to secure peace, a British landing at Karrack on the Persian Gulf forced a Persian withdrawal (23 November 1837–9 September 1838).

Herat ∎ 1856 ∎ Persian-Afghan Wars
Although the Treaty of Peshawar established peace between Britain and Afghanistan, Shah Nasiruddin of Persia unexpectedly invaded and captured Herat, triggering war with Britain in the Persian Gulf. After defeat at **Bushire** in December the Persians withdrew, appointing Afghan Sultan Ahmad Khan (nephew of Dost Muhammad) their Governor of Herat (25 October 1856).

Herat ∎ 1863 ∎ Persian-Afghan Wars
Amir Dost Muhammad of Afghanistan annexed Kandahar following the death of his disloyal brother Kohandil Khan, then marched against Herat, held by his nephew Ahmad Khan in the name of the Shah Nasir ad-Din of Persia. Ahmad Khan died during the siege, but a few days after capturing Herat, Dost Muhammad himself also died, triggering a bloody war of succession (June 1863).

Herat ∎ 1870 ∎ Later Afghan War of Succession
In the final act of the struggle for Afghan succession, the brilliant General Yakub Khan and his younger brother Ayub Khan rebelled against their father, the restored Amir Sher Ali, who declined to recognise Yakub as his heir apparent. The brothers seized Herat in a surprise attack, but with British encouragement, Sher Ali pardoned his son and made him Governor of Herat (6 May 1870).

Herat ∎ 1978 ∎ Afghan Civil War
When the city of Herat rose against the Kabul government of President Muhammad Daoud, aided by massive army defection, Kandahar commander General Sayed Mukharam led a large-scale assault, supported by air-strikes. The revolt in Herat was brutally put down with about 5,000 killed, leading directly to a military uprising in **Kabul** and the overthrow of Daoud (March 1978).

Herbsthausen ∎ 1645 ∎ Thirty Years War (Franco-Habsburg War)
   See **Mergentheim**

Herdonea ∎ 212 BC ∎ 2nd Punic War
   As he withdrew from **Capua**, the Carthaginian General Hannibal defeated a Roman blocking force at the **Silarus**, then a few days later advanced on Herdonea (modern Ordona), south of Foggia, besieged by the praetor, Gnaeus Fulvius Flaccus. With a larger and more experienced force, Hannibal inflicted a decisive defeat. Fulvius fled and his army of about 18,000 was largely destroyed.

Herdonea ∎ 210 BC ∎ 2nd Punic War
   One year after Roman capture of **Capua**, Gnaeus Fulvius Centumalus and 22,000 men camped near Herdonea (modern Ordona) were attacked by a larger force under the Carthaginian Hannibal. Taken in the rear by Numidian cavalry, Fulvius was killed and his army was crushed, with perhaps 10,000 killed. Herdonea was then destroyed and shortly afterwards, Hannibal won again at **Numistro**.

Héricourt ∎ 1474 ∎ Franco-Burgundian Wars
   Swiss forces financed by Louis XI of France marched into Lorraine against Charles the Bold of Burgundy and at Héricourt, near Belfort, the Burgundian army of Henry of Neufchatel was heavily defeated. The Swiss occupied Héricourt and many other towns before Charles responded by invading Switzerland itself, where he was defeated in 1476 at **Grandson** and **Morat** (13 November 1474).

Héricourt ∎ 1871 ∎ Franco-Prussian War
   French General Charles-Denis Bourbaki attempting to relieve **Belfort**, won at **Villersexel**,

then led over 100,000 men against General Karl August von Werder's heavily outnumbered siege force on the Lisaine at nearby Héricourt. In extreme winter cold, the French were driven off with 6,000 casualties and retreated through **Pontarlier**. Belfort held out until war's end (15–17 January 1871).

Hermaeum ∎ 255 BC ∎ 1st Punic War

In order to relieve the Carthaginian siege of Clupea (modern Kelibia) in northeast Tunisia, a fresh Roman fleet under Consuls Marcus Aemilius and Servius Fulvius sailed from western Sicily and off Hermaeum, near Cape Bon, inflicted massive damage on the Carthaginian navy. The siege of Clupea was lifted, but the Roman fleet was later virtually destroyed in a storm off Camarina in Sicily.

Hermannstadt ∎ 1442 ∎ Turkish-Hungarian Wars

Turkish commander Mezid Bey was sent by Ottoman Sultan Murad II into Transylvania, where he besieged Hermannstadt (modern Sibiu) defended by Hungarians under Janos Hunyadi. After the Turks lost a reported 20,000 men, including Mezid Bey and his son killed, they were forced to withdraw. Later that year another Ottoman force was defeated at **Vasaq** (18 March 1442).

Hermannstadt ∎ 1916 ∎ World War I (Balkan Front)

Encouraged by Russia's **Brusilov Offensive** in Galicia, Romania entered the war against the Central Powers and invaded Transylvania. However, German General Erich von Falkenhayn counter-attacked against the southern column at Hermannstadt (Sibiu). Romanian commander General Ioan Culcer was surprised and defeated and withdrew into the mountains (26–29 September 1916).

Hernani ∎ 1836 ∎ 1st Carlist War

In an attempt to relieve the Carlist siege of **San Sebastian**, Spanish forces and the British Legion under General Sir George de Lacy Evans, supported by naval gunfire, attacked the besieging army on nearby heights at Hernani. Bloody fighting drove the Carlists out of their defensive positions and raised the siege, though victory cost the Allies more than 600 men out of 5,000 (5 May 1836).

Hernani ∎ 1837 ∎ 1st Carlist War
See **Oriamendi**

Herrings ∎ 1429 ∎ Hundred Years War
See **Rouvray**

Hertogenbosch ∎ 1629 ∎ Netherlands War of Independence

To avenge the loss of **Breda** in 1625, Frederick Henry of Orange took more than 25,000 men against the fortress of Hertogenbosch held by Antonius Baron Schets van Grobbendonck. Having driven off a large relief army under the Count Henry de Berg, the Stadtholder stormed the outer fortresses of St Isabella and St Anthony and Grobbendonck was forced to capitulate (1 May–14 September 1629).

Hertogenbosch ∎ 1794 ∎ French Revolutionary Wars (1st Coalition)
See **Bois-le-Duc**

Herzogenbuchsee ∎ 1653 ∎ Swiss Peasant War

Swiss peasant leader Nicolas Leuenberger rose against the city aristocracies and fought an inconclusive battle at **Wohlenschwyl**, then gathered a force of perhaps 8,000 Emmenthal peasants to oppose Sigismund von Erlach of Bern near Herzogenbuchsee, east of Solothurn. The peasants were defeated and the rising was cruelly crushed, with Leuenberger executed (8 June 1653).

Hesheng ∎ 1926 ∎ 1st Chinese Revolutionary Civil War

While Nationalist commander Chiang Kaishek campaigned southwest of Wuchang through **Pingjiang** and **Tingsiqiao**, his General Zhang Fakui's "Ironsides" spearheaded fighting along the railway further east. Advancing through **Tingzu**, they defeated Wu Beifu trying to hold the strategic Hesheng Bridge, then drove north for **Wuchang** (28–30 August 1926).

Hessich-Oldendorf I 1633 I Thirty Years War (Swedish War)

Duke George of Brunswick-Luneburg and Swedish Marshal Dodo von Knyphausen advanced to the Weser, where they besieged Hameln, then faced a large relief force under Field Marshal Jost Maximilian von Gronsfeld and Count Johann Merode. Northwest of Hameln at Hessich-Oldendorf, the approaching Imperial army suffered a decisive defeat and von Gronsfeld was captured (8 July 1633).

Hetsugigawa I 1587 I Japan's Era of the Warring States

See **Toshimitsu**

Hexham I 1464 I Wars of the Roses

Henry Beaufort Duke of Somerset rallied the Lancastrians after defeat at **Hedgeley Moor** (25 April) and marched towards Newcastle, accompanied by Henry VI and Margaret of Anjou. To the west at Hexham, he was met and routed by John Neville Lord Montagu. Somerset and many others were executed, while Margaret fled to France. Henry went into hiding and was later captured (15 May 1464).

Hibera I 215 BC I 2nd Punic War

See **Ibera**

High Bridge I 1865 I American Civil War (Eastern Theatre)

As defeated Confederate forces withdrew west from **Petersburg**, Virginia, heavy fighting developed on the Appomattox around High Bridge, where Union General Theodore Read was surprised by Confederates under General Thomas L. Rosser. While Read was killed and lost many prisoners, Union General Andrew A. Humphreys continued the pursuit towards **Farmville** (6–7 April 1865).

Highnam I 1643 I British Civil Wars

After taking Malmesbury by assault (21 March), Parliamentary commander Sir William Waller surprised Welsh troops under Edward Somerset Lord Herbert of Raglan, who had supported the unsuccessful Royalist siege of Gloucester. Two miles west of Gloucester at Highnam, Herbert's force was utterly destroyed, with over 600 killed and 1,000 captured (24 March 1643).

Higueruela I 1431 I Later Christian Reconquest of Spain

When dissident Muslim nobleman Ridwan Venegas asked John II of Castile to support Ibn al-Maw as King of Granada, John sent his Constable Álvaro de Luna to impose their nominee. Close to Granada at Higueruela, the Castilians defeated the army of Mohammad IX and forced Granada to accept the ursurper as Yusuf IV. But within a year he lost favour and was killed (1 July 1431).

Hill 60, Flanders I 1915 I World War I (Western Front)

Just before the German offensive against **Ypres**, British forces exploded a massive mine to seize strategic Hill 60, southeast of the city and held off counter-attacks. Two weeks later the Germans launched a gas-led assault which was initially repulsed before the position fell to a second attempt. Hill 60 was not finally regained by the Allies until September 1918 (17–21 April & 1–5 May 1915).

Hill 60, Gallipoli I 1915 I World War I (Gallipoli)

Supporting the Allied offensive from **Suvla Bay** against **Scimitar Hill**, Australian, New Zealand and Indian forces under General Vaughan Cox attacked on the southern flank at Hill 60 (Kaiajik Aghala), commanding the road from Suvla Bay to Anzac Cove. Two costly assaults secured the lower slopes, but the Allies failed to drive the Turks from the summit (21–22 & 27 August 1915).

Hill 203 I 1904 I Russo-Japanese War

General Maresuke Nogi launched one of the hardest fought actions of the Japanese siege of **Port Arthur** when he stormed 203-metre Hill, defended by Colonel Nikolai Tretyakov. After capturing the strategic hill at a cost of about 10,000 Japanese and 3,000 Russian lives, Nogi immediately installed siege guns to destroy the remaining warships in the harbour (26 November–5 December 1904).

Hill 304 I 1916 I World War I (Western Front)
See **Le Mort-Homme**

Hillabee I 1813 I Creek Indian War
Amid revenge for the massacre at **Fort Mims**, Indians were slaughtered at **Tallaseehatchee** and **Talladega** in Alabama before General James White, with Tennessee Militia and some Cherokee, attacked Hillabee village, 20 miles further east. White's forces killed 68 Hillabee warriors without loss. A few days later more Indians died in the much larger massacre at **Autossee** (18 November 1813).

Hillah I 1920 I Iraqi Revolt
See **Rustumiyah**

Hillsman Farm I 1865 I American Civil War (Eastern Theatre)
See **Sayler's Creek**

Hill's Plantation I 1862 I American Civil War (Trans-Mississippi)
On the offensive against Confederates west of the Mississippi in Arkansas, Union Colonel Charles Hovey attacked General Thomas C. Hindman and Colonel William Parsons at Hill's Plantation on the Cache, east of Augusta. After an initial repulse, Hovey was reinforced by General William P. Benton and the defeated Confederates withdrew southwest to Little Rock (7 July 1862).

Himera I 480 BC I Carthaginian Invasion of Sicily
As Carthage expanded her power in the central Mediterranean, the great Carthaginian leader Hamilcar landed on the north coast of Sicily at Panormus (modern Palermo) and marched east against Himera, held by Theron of Acragas. When a relief army under Gelo of Syracuse ar-

rived, Hamilcar was defeated and killed and his ships were burned. The victory saved Sicily from Carthage for 70 years.

Himera I 409 BC I Carthaginian-Syracusan Wars
Determined to avenge his grandfather's death at Himera in 480 BC, Hannibal led a fresh Carthaginian invasion of Sicily to capture **Selinus**, then besieged Himera in the north. A naval force under Diocles of Syracuse managed to evacuate half the city's population before it was taken by storm. A claimed 3,000 were executed and Himera was burned. Hannibal died at **Acragas** in 406 BC.

Himera I 383 BC I 3rd Dionysian War
See **Cronium**

Himera River I 311 BC I Agathoclean War
In a fresh Carthaginian offensive in southern Sicily against the Tyrant Agathocles, Hamilcar (son of Gisco) and 45,000 men advanced to Ecnomus, near the mouth of the Himera, where Agathocles attacked their camp. In a fierce counter-attack, Hamilcar reportedly inflicted 7,000 casualties for just 500 men lost. The badly defeated Tyrant withdrew under siege to **Syracuse** (June 311 BC).

Hindan I 1857 I Indian Mutiny
See **Ghazi-ud-din-Nagar**

Hindenburg Line I 1918 I World War I (Western Front)
Following victory at the **Marne**, **Albert** and **Bapaume**, Allied forces attacked Germany's Hindenburg Line behind the Western Front. Widespread fighting included battles at **St Mihiel**, **Épéhy**, **Argonne**, **Canal du Nord**, **Cambrai-St Quentin**, **Flanders**, **Courtrai** and **Le Cateau**, as the Allies broke through towards the **Selle** and **Sambre** (12 September–11 November 1918).

Hingston Down I 837 I Viking Raids on Britain
King Egbert of Wessex lost to Vikings in Dorset at **Carhampton**, but two years later he

took a big army into Cornwall to fight a large-scale Danish landing, which was supported by the West Welsh, who were taking the opportunity to resist West Saxon rule. Just west of the Tamar near Callington at Hingston Down (Hengestdune) Egbert won a great victory and secured control of Cornwall.

Hipponium I 48 BC I Wars of the First Triumvirate
See **Vibo**

Hippo Regius I 430–431 I Roman-Vandal Wars
Two years after beating the Suevi at **Merida**, in southern Spain, the Vandal Gaiseric took 20,000 warriors plus their families to Africa, where Roman Governor John Bonifacius was defeated, then besieged at Hippo Regius (modern Bone, Algeria). The city fell after 14 months, when a relief attempt from Constantinople under Aspar failed. Gaiseric gradually secured most of North Africa, including **Carthage**.

Hira I 633 I Muslim Conquest of Iraq
Muslim General Khalid ibn al-Walid advanced into Persian Mesopotamia along the west bank of the Euphrates from **Ullais** and besieged the walled city of Hira, southeast of modern Nadjak. Hira fell by assault, reportedly after Khalid filled in the moat with the bodies of his slain weak camels. Persia's attempt to recover this key city in 634 resulted in the brutal Battle of the **Bridge** (May 633).

Hirsov I 1773 I Catherine the Great's 1st Turkish War
With the Turks destroyed at **Turtukai** in June, Russian General Alexander Suvorov was sent down the Danube between Matchin and Silistria, where he took a position near the Boriu River and the fortress of Hirsov. Supported by General Mikhail Miloradovich, he brilliantly defeated an attack by 10,000 Turkish cavalry and infantry, though the victory had little strategic value (4 September 1773).

Hittin I 1187 I 3rd Crusade
See **Hattin**

Hiuchi I 1183 I Gempei War
Determined to avenge humiliation at **Fujigawa**, Taira Koremori marched north from Kyoto against Minamoto Yoshinaka, who had resumed the war against Japan's ruling clan. Blocked by the mountain fortress at Hiuchi, Komemori took the position by siege, reputedly by destroying its drinking water, but the delay contributed to his disastrous defeat weeks later at **Kurikara** (17–20 May 1183).

Hjortensjon I 1543 I Dacke's Rebellion
Nils Dacke led a peasant revolt in southern Sweden against King Gustavus I and secured considerable success before he failed in a siege of Kalmar. He was later attacked and decisively defeated by the Royal army at Hjorten Lake, near Hogsby. The wounded rebel was then hunted down and executed, ending the last provincial resistance to the Lutheran Swedish state (20 March 1543).

Hjorungavag I 985 I Scandinavian National Wars
Amid the confused alliances of Scandinavian warfare, Jomsburg Vikings under Vagn Akason, supporting King Sweyn Forkbeard of Denmark, sailed against Haakon Jarl of Norway. Lured into an ambush off Hjorungavag, near Alesund, Norway, the outnumbered Jomsburgs met Haakon's entire fleet and were utterly defeated. Fifteen years later, they helped the Norwegians defeat Sweyn at **Svolde**.

Hlobane I 1879 I Anglo-Zulu War
In order to destroy a Zulu position on the Hlobane plateau in northern Zululand, Major Redvers Buller attacked from the east, supported by Colonel John Russell advancing from the west. After bloody fighting on the steep rocky slopes, with 94 British soldiers and over 100 Natal African auxiliaries killed, a massive Zulu force appeared and Buller retreated west to **Khambula** (28 March 1879).

Hlophekhulu I 1888 I Zulu Rebellion

In support of uSuthu Chief Dinuzulu, Shingana gathered forces further south and raided "loyal" Zulus. When Colonel Henry Stabb marched north from Eshowe with 200 white Regulars and 1,500 African levies, a major attack at Hlophekhulu saw the rebels routed with about 300 killed. The rising collapsed and Dinuzulu and his uncles Shingana and Ndabuko were exiled on St Helena (2 July 1888).

Hoa Binh I 1951–1952 I French Indo-China War

Encouraged by success at **Nghia Lo**, General Jean de Lattre de Tassigny sent paratroops to cut the Viet Minh supply route at Hoa Binh, on the Black River 40 miles west of Hanoi (14 November). When Viet Minh General Vo Nguyen Giap attacked, both sides poured men into a battle of attrition until new French commander Raoul Salan ordered a bloody retreat (9 December 1951–24 February 1952).

Hoa-Moc I 1885 I Sino-French War
See **Tuyen-Quang**

Hobkirk's Hill I 1781 I War of the American Revolution

Rebel commander Nathanael Greene pursuing the British into South Carolina after battle at **Guildford Courthouse** in March, paused to await reinforcements just north of Camden at Hobkirk's Hill, where he was attacked and routed by Colonel Lord Francis Rawdon. However, Rawdon had no choice but to evacuate Camden (10 May) and retreated towards **Charleston** (25 April 1781).

Ho-ch'iao I 538 I Wei Dynastic Wars
See **Heqiao**

Hochkirch I 1758 I Seven Years War (Europe)

Returning to Saxony after victory at **Zorndorf** in August, Frederick II of Prussia advanced against a superior Austrian army under Marshal Leopold von Daun at Dresden. Frederick was surprised in a dawn attack further east at Hoch-kirch and only just managed to escape after massive losses in men and guns. Von Daun also suffered heavy losses and eventually withdrew (13 October 1758).

Hochkirchen I 1813 I Napoleonic Wars (War of Liberation)
See **Bautzen**

Ho-chou I 1258 I Mongol Conquest of China
See **Diao Yu**

Höchst, Frankfurt I 1622 I Thirty Years War (Palatinate War)

Johan Tserclaes Count Tilly of Bavaria and General Gonzalo Fernández de Cordoba destroyed Baden's army at **Wimpfen** (6 May), then pursued Christian of Brunswick to prevent him joining with Count Ernst von Mansfeld. On the Main west of Franskfort at Höchst, the Imperials intercepted and defeated the Brunswickers and Christian joined Mansfeld retreating across the Rhine (20 June 1622).

Höchstädt I 1703 I War of the Spanish Succession

Having beaten the Austrians on the Danube at **Munderkingen** (31 July), French Marshal Claude Villars in the service of Maximilian Emanuel of Bavaria met a second Imperial army under Count Frederick of Styrum at Höchstädt and inflicted a terrible defeat. However, a dispute over the failure to advance on Vienna saw Villars replaced by Marshal Ferdinand Marsin (20 September 1703).

Höchstädt I 1704 I War of the Spanish Succession
See **Blenheim**

Höchstädt I 1800 I French Revolutionary Wars (2nd Coalition)

Austrian General Paul Kray fell back across the Rhine after defeat at **Engen** and **Stockach** and failed to halt the French offensive at **Biberach** and **Erbach** and retired to Ulm, on the Danube. Crossing the river further east to cut off the Austrian withdrawal, French General Jean Victor Moreau defeated Kray at Höchstädt. Kray then abandoned Ulm and Austria soon sought an armistice (19 June 1800).

Höchst im Odenwald ▌ 1795 ▌ French Revolutionary Wars (1st Coalition)

French General Jean-Baptiste Jourdan invaded Germany and was defeated near Höchst, 25 miles northeast of **Mannheim**, by Austrian Count Charles von Clerfayt. Jourdan was then driven back across the Rhine. His loss is blamed on French commander Charles Pichegru, who failed to support Jourdan's force and later betrayed the Republic, defecting to the Austrians (11 October 1795).

Hochuan ▌ 1258 ▌ Mongol Conquest of China

In a large-scale assault on Sung southern China, the Mongol Khan Mongke, a grandson of Genghis Khan, captured Chengtu, then besieged Sung General Wang Chien at Hochuan (Hechuan) in central Szechwan. After four months, Mongke's last assault was repulsed and he died soon afterwards. The war was then suspended until resumed by his brother Kubilai (May–August 1258).

Hof ▌ 1807 ▌ Napoleonic Wars (4th Coalition)

Responding to the Russian mid-winter offensive in eastern Prussia, French Marshal Joachim Murat drove General Levin Bennigsen north and at Hof, near Landsberg, caught up with the Russian rearguard under General Mikhail Barclay de Tolly. Barclay suffered heavy casualties before joining the main Russian force for battle two days later, a few miles north at **Eylau** (6 February 1807).

Hofuf ▌ 1913 ▌ Saudi-Ottoman War

Despite acknowledging Ottoman overlordship as ruler of Nejd, Emir Abd al-Aziz (Ibn Saud) determined to drive Turkey from the eastern Arabian province of al-Hasa and attacked Hofuf. As at **Riyadh**, his men scaled the walls at night and the Governor and 1,200-strong garrison were forced to surrender. Nejd was finally con-

quered, although Aziz reaffirmed Ottoman authority (9 May 1913).

Hogfors ▌ 1789 ▌ 2nd Russo-Swedish War

When a Swedish attempt to invade Finland was repulsed in August on land at **Fredrikshamn** and at sea on the **Svenskund**, Swedish Admiral Karl Ehrensward withdrew his flotilla towards Hogfors (modern Karkkila) in southern Finland, northwest of Helsinki. There he suffered a further defeat and both the navy and army were forced to withdraw to their own frontier (1 September 1789).

Hogland ▌ 1788 ▌ 2nd Russo-Swedish War

Gustav III of Sweden was determined to recover Finland from Russia and landed at Helsinki while his brother, Duke Charles of Sodermanland, sailed west against Fredrikshamn. Off Hogland Island (modern Sursaari), Charles met a Russian squadron under English Admiral Samuel Greig and each side lost one ship before the Swedes withdrew under blockade to Sveaborg, outside Helsinki (17 July 1788).

Hogsby ▌ 1543 ▌ Dacke's Rebellion
See **Hjortensjon**

Hohenfriedberg ▌ 1745 ▌ War of the Austrian Succession

While advancing to recover Silesia, the Austro-Saxon army of Prince Charles of Lorraine was surprised by Frederick II of Prussia at Hohenfriedberg, near Streigau. Frederick inflicted about 6,000 casualties and took over 7,000 prisoners in a brilliant attack. The defeated Austrians withdrew into Bohemia, but rallied and re-entered Silesia, where Frederick beat them at **Sohr** (4 June 1745).

Hohenlinden ▌ 1800 ▌ French Revolutionary Wars (2nd Coalition)

After a failed truce following Austrian defeat at **Höchstädt** (19 June), Archduke John of Austria took over command and marched against the French occupying Bavaria. During a snowstorm, General Jean Victor Moreau destroyed the Austrian army piece-meal at Hohenlinden, east of

Munich, and began his advance towards Vienna. Austria then once again sued for peace (3 December 1800).

Hojuji I 1184 I Gempei War

Minamoto Yoshinaka seized Kyoto after victory at **Shinowara**, then turned against former Emperor Go-Shirakawa, who was plotting with his cousin Minamoto Yoritomo in Kamakura. In a brutal attack on the Hojuji Palace in Kyoto, Yoshinaka destroyed Go-Shirakawa's troops, burned his palace and seized his Imperial person, provoking intervention by Yoritomo next month at **Uji** (January 1184).

Hoke's Run I 1861 I American Civil War (Eastern Theatre)

As Confederate forces assembled in the Shenandoah, Union General Robert Patterson crossed the Potomac at Williamsport and met part of General Thomas J. Jackson's brigade near Martinsburg at Hoke's Run, West Virginia. The outnumbered Confederates fell back, losing about 100 men. Patterson eventually withdrew, enabling the Confederates to concentrate at **Bull Run** (2 July 1861).

Hollandia I 1944 I World War II (Pacific)

To cut off the Japanese in northern New Guinea, American General Robert Eichelberger landed with 80,000 men at Hollandia, bypassing the main Japanese army at **Wewak**. With Japanese aircraft previously destroyed by bombardment, General Masazumi Inada was routed with perhaps 9,000 killed. Another landing took place the same day further east at **Aitape** (22–27 April 1944).

Hollarbrunn I 1805 I Napoleonic Wars (3rd Coalition)

Napoleon Bonaparte captured Vienna, then found his way north blocked by a small Russian rearguard under General Prince Pyotr Bagration at Hollabrunn (sometimes Oberhollarbrunn), northwest of Vienna. Despite heavy casualties, Bagration's delaying action allowed General Mikhail Kutuzov's Russian army to retire, though it was defeated a month later at **Austerlitz** (16 November 1805).

Holme I 905 I Viking Wars in Britain

During a fresh invasion of Wessex and Mercia, Danes from East Anglia marched west, aiding Aethelwald of Mercia claiming the crown of Wessex from his cousin Edward the Elder. Aethelwald had previously been repulsed at **Wimborne** and, at Holme (modern Holmesdale, Surrey), he was defeated and killed. Edward restored peace with Danish East Anglia until his victory at **Tempsford** in 918.

Holowczyn I 1708 I 2nd "Great" Northern War

As Charles XII of Sweden advanced into Russia across the Berezina, he met Prince Alexander Menshikov at Holowczyn on the Babich. Boldly attacking across the shallow river, Charles defeated and dispersed the Russians, who withdrew to the Dneiper. However, Charles was running short of supplies and ammunition and unwisely turned south towards the Ukraine (4 July 1708).

Holy Ground I 1813 I Creek Indian War

Following American victory at **Talladega** and **Autossee**, General Ferdinand Claiborne took 800 infantry and militia and 150 Choctaw allies under Pushmataha against the Creek Indian camp at Holy Ground Creek, near Econochaca on the Alabama. The Creeks lost over 30 killed and the booty seized reportedly included 300 white scalps from the massacre at **Fort Mims** (23 December 1813).

Holy River I 1026 I Norwegian Wars of Succession

See **Helgeaa**

Homildon Hill I 1402 I Anglo-Scottish Border Wars

Following Scottish defeat at **Nesbit**, Archibald Earl of Douglas led a 10,000-strong raid into Northumberland, supported by Murdoch Stewart Earl of Fife. At Homildon Hill near Wooler, the returning Scots were destroyed by

Henry Percy Earl of Northumberland, his son Henry (Hotspur), and George Dunbar Earl of March. The Earls Douglas and Fife were both captured (14 September 1402).

Homs ▌ 1281 ▌ Mongol Invasion of the Middle East

Taking advantage of a fresh Mongol invasion of Syria, Crusaders of the Military Orders and King Leo of Armenia supported the Christian Mongols against the Mamluk Sultan Qalawun. The two large armies met near Homs on the upper Orontes. After a confused battle with heavy losses on both sides, the Mongols withdrew across the Euphrates (30 October 1281).

Homs ▌ 1832 ▌ 1st Turko-Egyptian War

Ibrahim Pasha took **Acre** (27 May), then completed the Egyptian conquest of Syria by taking Damascus (18 June), aided by Emir Bashir II of Lebanon. When Muhammad Pasha of Aleppo tried to stop him on the Orontes at Homs, Ibrahim won a decisive victory, capturing the enemy guns, 3,000 men and eight Pashas. Days later, he turned against the main Ottoman army at **Belen** (8–9 July 1832).

Honain ▌ 630 ▌ Campaigns of the Prophet Mohammed
See **Hunain**

Hondschoote ▌ 1793 ▌ French Revolutionary Wars (1st Coalition)

General Jean Nicolas Houchard led a revitalised French Army of the North, advancing on the British-Hanoverian siege of **Dunkirk**. During a three-day battle ten miles east at Hondschoote, a bayonet attack routed the outnumbered Marshal Count Johann von Walmoden. When Houchard did not follow up, Frederick Augustus Duke of York disengaged and withdrew to Belgium (6–8 September 1793).

Honey Hill ▌ 1864 ▌ American Civil War (Western Theatre)

In support of the Union march through Georgia towards Savannah, General John Hatch sailed up the Broad River to attack the Confederate railway, northeast of **Savannah**. At Honey Hill, near Grahamville, he was heavily defeated and repulsed by Colonel Charles Colcock (under General Gustavus W. Smith) and the line to Charleston remained open (30 November 1864).

Honey Springs ▌ 1863 ▌ American Civil War (Trans-Mississippi)

While on campaign in Indian Territory, Union General James B. Blunt attacked the Confederate depot at Honey Springs, Oklahoma, defended at the nearby Elk Creek by General Douglas H. Cooper and a force comprising mainly American Indians. Cooper was driven off with about 500 casualties and Blunt crossed the Arkansas border to occupy **Fort Smith** (17 July 1863).

Hong ▌ 638 BC ▌ Wars of China's Spring and Autumn Era

In the shifting alliances among rival states around the Yellow River, Duke Xiang of Song joined with Wei, Deng, Xu and Chen, and marched on Zheng to try and force it to rejoin his union. After a fruitless campaign, troops from Chu arrived to reinforce Zheng. At the Hong River, Xiang and his allies were decisively defeated. The Duke died the following year from a wound received.

Hong Kong ▌ 1941 ▌ World War II (China)

When the Japanese swept into **Kowloon**, British forces withdrew to Hong Kong Island and, a week later, the invaders stormed across Lei Yu Mun Strait. Bloody fighting cost about 4,500 British and 2,750 Japanese killed before General Christopher Maltby surrendered to General Takashi Sakai. More than 6,500 British, Indian and Canadian troops were taken prisoner (18–25 December 1941).

Honigfelde ▌ 1629 ▌ 2nd Polish-Swedish War
See **Sztum**

Hooglede ▌ 1794 ▌ French Revolutionary Wars (1st Coalition)

Austrian Count Charles von Clerfayt advancing to relieve the French siege of the Netherlands city of Ypres was repulsed by General Jean-Baptiste Jourdan at Hooglede. A second attack was partially successful at the nearby village of **Roulers**, but Clerfayt was again heavily defeated at Hooglede and had to withdraw. Ypres capitulated the following day (10–16 June 1794).

Hooglhy ∣ 1632 ∣ Later Portuguese Colonial Wars in Asia

At war with the Portuguese in Bengal, Mughal Emperor Shahjahan sent Governor Qasim Khan and a reported 150,000 men to besiege the small trading settlement at Hooghly, defended by only about 300 European troops and 700 Indian Christians. The starving inhabitants fled downriver after three months, followed by years of persecution of Christians (24 June–24 September 1632).

Hook (1st) ∣ 1952 ∣ Korean War

At the western end of the defensive line across Korea, Chinese forces followed a massive artillery assault with a brutal hand-to-hand attack on the strategic crescent-shaped ridge known as The Hook. American marines under Colonel Mike Delaney were driven off before a huge aerial and artillery bombardment enabled them to regain the ridge in bloody fighting next day (26–27 October 1952).

Hook (2nd) ∣ 1952 ∣ Korean War

After relieving American marines who had defended the ridge northwest of Seoul known as The Hook, the Black Watch under Colonel David Rose faced a massive Chinese assault, which overran forward positions. Very heavy fighting saw the ridge regained at the cost of 12 British killed and 93 missing or wounded. The Chinese lost over 100 dead (18–19 November 1952).

Hook ∣ 1953 ∣ Korean War

Determined to seize the strategic ridge known as The Hook, Chinese forces followed two weeks of bombardment with a bloody infantry assault. The last major British action of the war saw the Duke of Wellington's Regiment under Colonel Ramsay Bunbury repulse the attack at the cost of 149 casualties (28 killed). The Chinese lost perhaps 250 killed and 800 wounded (28–29 May 1953).

Hoover's Gap ∣ 1863 ∣ American Civil War (Western Theatre)

As he marched south from Nashville against General Braxton Bragg at Shelbyville, Union General William S. Rosecrans sent a flank advance further east under General George H. Thomas. At Hoover's Gap, Tennessee, northeast of Wartrace, Confederate General Alexander P. Stewart fought a brilliant holding action, but had to withdraw and Bragg fell back through Tullahoma (24–26 June 1863).

Hopton Heath ∣ 1643 ∣ British Civil Wars

Compton Spencer Earl of Northampton advanced from Banbury to relieve the Royalist town of Stafford, then a few days later marched out against Parliamentary forces under Sir John Gell and Sir William Brereton. On nearby Hopton Heath, Northampton inflicted a sharp defeat, capturing eight guns, but he was killed during an over-enthusiastic pursuit (19 March 1643).

Horaniu ∣ 1943 ∣ World War II (Pacific)

As Allied troops landed elsewhere on **Vella Lavella**, west of **New Georgia**, Japanese Admiral Matsuji Ijuin escorted a force to land on the northeast tip of the island. In a night-time destroyer action against Captain Thomas Ryan off Horaniu, the Japanese lost two patrol boats and several troop-carrying barges. However, Ijuin successfully landed most of his force (17–18 August 1943).

Horice ∣ 1423 ∣ Hussite Wars

In continuing war in Bohemia after Imperial defeat at **Nemecky Brod**, former Hussite General Cenek of Wartenberg led well-armed Royalist cavalry against Taborite Hussites under Jan Zizka, who took a defensive position on a steep hill near Horice, north of Hradec Králové. Forced to fight dismounted, the Royalists were routed and the Taborites soon won again at **Strachuv** (20 April 1423).

Hormizdagan | 224 | Persian-Parthian War

With the Sassanian leader Ardashir (Artaxerxes) of Persia expanding his power, Artabanus V of Parthia took an army against his dangerous neighbour. But on the Plain of Hormizdagan (location unknown), he was defeated and killed. Ardashir crushed Parthia and took the title Shah of Shahs. He and his son and successor Shapur then led a campaign of conquest to build the 420-year Sassanian Empire.

Hormuz | 1507–1508 | Portuguese Colonial Wars in Arabia

The great Portuguese commander Afonso de Albuquerque captured **Muscat** in Oman, then took seven ships and 500 men against the vital port of Hormuz, guarding the Persian Gulf. The ruler of Hormuz surrendered when Portuguese bombardment destroyed his fleet, but a mutiny and counter-offensive four months later forced Albuquerque to withdraw (September 1507–January 1508).

Hormuz | 1515 | Portuguese Colonial Wars in Arabia

Repulsed in southern Arabia at **Aden**, the great Portuguese commander Afonso de Albuquerque gathered 27 ships and over 2,000 men for a second offensive against the port of Hormuz. Overwhelmed by the massive assault, the King of Hormuz surrendered and Portugal gained the vital stronghold commanding the Persian Gulf and the trade route between Arabia and Asia (March 1515).

Hormuz | 1622 | Anglo-Portuguese Colonial Wars

Following English victory in the Persian Gulf at **Jask**, East India ships, under Captain John Weddell, defeated Portuguese Admiral Rui Freire de Andrade to capture Kishm (30 January), then besieged nearby Hormuz to support Persian forces attacking on land. Governor Simon de Mello finally surrendered and the 2,000 Portuguese residents were sent to **Muscat** (9 February–22 May 1622).

Horncastle | 1643 | British Civil Wars
See **Winceby**

Hornet vs *Peacock* | 1813 | War of 1812
See **Guyana**

Hornet vs *Penguin* | 1815 | War of 1812
See **Tristan de Cunha**

Hornkranz | 1893 | German Colonial Wars in Africa

When Nama tribesman in German Southwest Africa refused a treaty, Colonel Curt von Francois led a surprise attack on the Khoi camp at Hornkranz, west of Reheboth. Although about 50 women and children were killed, Nama leader Hendrik Witbooi and most his warriors escaped to fight a guerrilla war until defeat at **Naukluf**. Von Francois was recalled the next month (12 April 1893).

Horns of Hattin | 1187 | 3rd Crusade
See **Hattin**

Horokiri | 1846 | 1st New Zealand War

After the raid on **Boulcott's Farm**, outside Wellington, British forces arrested the great Te Rauparaha. Major Edward Last, supported by Ngatiawa allies under Te Rangitake, then pursued his nephew Te Rangihaeata to the nearby Horokiri Valley. Last withdrew after a stubborn action, but Te Rangihaeata soon retreated into remote hills, ending fighting around Wellington (5–7 August 1846).

Horreum Margi | 505 | Gothic War in Italy

Eastern Emperor Anastasius was concerned by Theodoric the Ostrogoth campaigning north from Italy towards the Danube and sent General Sabinian, supported by Bulgarian auxiliaries, to Dacia against Mundo, a descendant of Attila the Hun. At Horreum Margi, near the Margus (modern Morava in Serbia), the Roman-Bulgarian army was totally destroyed by the outnumbered Goth and Hun allies.

Horseshoe Bend I 1814 I Creek Indian War

When Creek Indians renewed their offensive in Alabama after defeat at **Econochaca**, Generals Andrew Jackson and John Coffee led over 2,000 men against 900 Creek and Cherokee under Chief Menawa on the Tallapoosa north of Dadeville. In decisive action at Horseshoe Bend (Tohopeka) about 700 Indians were killed and 500 women and children captured, ending the war (27 March 1814).

Ho-sheng I 1926 I 1st Chinese Revolutionary Civil War

See **Hesheng**

Hostalrich I 1809–1810 I Napoleonic Wars (Peninsular Campaign)

Marshal Pierre Augereau faced continued resistance in Catalonia following the capture of **Gerona** and despatched General Alois Mazzuchelli's Italian brigade southwest against Hostalrich. While the mountain town fell (7 November 1809), the Spanish garrison held the local fortress against a four-month siege by General Joseph Souham before fighting their way out (16 January–12 May 1810).

Hoton Nor I 1731 I Chinese-Mongol Wars

Three decades after the Kangxi Emperor routed the Zunghar Mongols at **Jaomodo** (1696), his son Yongzhen determined to attack new Zunghar ruler Galdan Tseren. Qing General Furdan took an army deep into Mongolia and built a fortress at Khobdo. Lured further into the mountains, his army was ambushed and besieged at Hoton Nor and virtually destroyed. Peace was later agreed (23–27 July 1731).

Hotva I 1638 I Cossack-Polish Wars

See **Zhovnyne**

Hoxne I 870 I Viking Wars in Britain

Danish Vikings under Ivar and Ubba—sons of Ragnar Lodbrok—consolidated their position in southeast England, where they met King Edmund "the Martyr" of East Anglia, at Hoxne (Heglisdune), north of Ipswich in Suffolk. When his force was overwhelmed, Edmund was executed and interred at Beadricesworth, which became known as Bury St Edmund (20 November 870).

Hoyerswerda I 1813 I Napoleonic Wars (War of Liberation)

Advancing across the Spree after victory at **Bautzen**, Napoleon Bonaparte sent Marshal Nicolas Oudinot's division towards Berlin. Marching south in defence, Prussian General Friedrich von Bulow underestimated the French strength and, at Hoyerswerda, northeast of Dresden, was sharply repulsed. Within three months, he had his revenge at **Luckau** and again at **Grossbeeren** (28 May 1813).

Hsiang I 1934 I 2nd Chinese Revolutionary Civil War

See **Xiang**

Hsiang-chi I 757 I An Lushan Rebellion

See **Xiangji**

Hsiang-chou I 758 I An Lushan Rebellion

See **Xiangzhou**

Hsiang-yang I 1206–1207 I Jin-Song Wars

See **Xiangyang**

Hsiang-yang I 1268–1273 I Mongol Wars of Kubilai Khan

See **Xiangyang**

Hsien-yang I 207 BC I Fall of the Qin Dynasty

See **Xianyang**

Hsing-an I 1900 I Russo-Chinese War

See **Xing-an**

Hsinmintun I 1925 I Guo Songling's Revolt

See **Xinmintun**

Hsuchow | 1927 | 2nd Chinese Revolutionary Civil War
See **Xuzhou**

Hsuchow | 1937–1938 | Sino-Japanese War
See **Xuzhou**

Hsu-I | 451 | Wars of the Six Dynasties
See **Xuyi**

Hsü-ko | 707 BC | Wars of China's Spring and Autumn Era
See **Xuge**

Huachi | 1820 | Ecuadorian War of Independence
In a renewed rising in Ecuador, Patriots led by Luis Urdaneta and José Garcia were met just south of Ambato, at Huachi, by Royalist forces under Colonel Francisco González, who won a bloody victory, with about 800 Patriots killed. When Garcia soon lost again at **Tanizahua**, General Antonio José de Sucre took command and defeated González in August 1821 at **Yaguachi** (22 November 1820).

Huachi | 1821 | Ecuadorian War of Independence
Patriot General Antonio José de Sucre followed up victory at **Yaguachi** (19 August), pursuing Spanish commander Melchior Aymerich to Huachi, just south of Ambato, where the Royalists turned and inflicted a bloody defeat. Sucre lost over half his army, including General José Mires captured, but by May 1822 he recovered with victory at **Ríobamba** and **Pichincha** (12 September 1821).

Huaihai | 1948–1949 | 3rd Chinese Revolutionary Civil War
The largest battle in modern China saw perhaps 600,000 Communist troops under Chen Yi and Lin Biao attack an equal Nationalist force around Xuzhou under Liu Zhih and Bai Chongxi. The massive Huaihai offensive sealed the fate of Nationalist rule with perhaps 500,000 men lost at **Nianzhuang**, **Chenguanzhuang** and **Shuangduiji** (7 November 1948–January 1949).

Huaiqing | 1853 | Taiping Rebellion
Having captured **Nanjing**, the Taiping sent Li Kaifang and Lin Fengxiang across the Yellow to besiege Huaiqing (modern Qinyang), northeast of Luoyang, held by Yu Bingdao and Qiu Baoyang. Determined to hold the city, Beijing sent reinforcements under Imperial Commissioner Ne'er Jing'e and the Taiping Northern Expedition had to withdraw west into Shanxi (8 July–1 September 1853).

Hualqui | 1819 | Chilean War of Independence
In bitter action near the war's end, 50 Royalist irregulars led by Vicente Benavides attacked Hualqui (modern Gualqui) on the Bio Bio, 13 miles southeast of Concepción, defended by just 25 Patriots under José Tomás Huerta. Benavides was driven off, losing half his men, and three prisoners later executed. A subsequent loss further south at **Valdivia** soon ended hostilities (20 November 1819).

Huamachuco | 1883 | War of the Pacific
Despite defeat at **Miraflores** in 1881 and the fall of Lima, Peruvian forces continued a guerrilla war against the Chilean army of occupation. The last action of the war saw 3,000 Peruvian irregulars, led by General Andrés Avelino Cáceres, attack 1,600 Chileans under Colonel Alejandro Gorostiaga in the Andes at Huamachuco. Peru suffered a decisive defeat and peace was quickly signed (10 July 1883).

Huamantla | 1847 | American-Mexican War
American General Joseph Lane advancing from Veracruz to relieve the siege of **Puebla**, met a Mexican blocking force 25 miles to the northeast at Huamantla under General Antonio de Santa Anna. The Mexicans were driven off with over 150 killed and, when Major Samuel Walker was killed by a sniper, Lane permitted

his men to rape and sack the town (9 October 1847).

Huanta I 1814 I Peruvian War of Independence

Leading an Indian rising in Cuzco, Mateo Pumacahua sent José Gabriel Bejar, Mariano Angulo and Manuel Hurtado de Mendoza west, to Huamanga, where they raised a large Indian force. But they were defeated at Huanta, 15 miles northwest of Ayacucho, by a Royalist force from Lima under Colonel Vicente Gonzalez. Within four months the Indians lost again at **Matará** (2–3 October 1814).

Huaqui I 1811 I Argentine War of Independence

After defeat at **Suipacha** in Upper Peru (modern western Bolivia), Spanish Royalist General José Manuel de Goyeneche regrouped and broke an armistice by attacking Patriot commander Juan José Castelli in Bolivia at Huaqui (Guaqui), on Lake Titicaca. The Spanish regulars routed the Patriot army, though in September 1812, the Argentines were avenged at **Río Piedras** and **Tucumán** (20 June 1811).

Huara I 1891 I Chilean Civil War

During civil war between Chile's Congress and President José Manuel Balmaceda, Loyalist Colonel Eulogio Robles Pinochet recovered from defeat at **San Francisco** to take a position two days later at Huara between Iquique and Pasagua against Congressist Colonel Estanislao del Canto Arteaga. The advancing rebels were repulsed with 240 dead, but soon won at **Pozo Almonte** (17 February 1891).

Huarina I 1547 I Spanish Civil War in Peru

When Gonzalo Pizarro killed the Viceroy of Peru at **Anaquito** (January 1546), King Charles of Spain appointed Pedro de la Gasca, who sent over 1,000 men under Diego Centeno against the usurper. One of Peru's bloodiest battles, at Huarina on Lake Titicaca, saw 350 Royalists and over 100 Pizarrists killed before Pizarro secured

victory. He was defeated a year later at **Xaquixaguana** (26 October 1547).

Huatai I 450 I Wars of the Six Dynasties

As Wei forces from northern China encroached beyond the Yellow River, Song Emperor Wen lost Huatai (near modern Jixian, Shandong) in 431, but in 450 he sent Wang Xuanmo to retake the town. After three months of siege, Wang withdrew in the face of a massive Wei army, which caught and routed him. Emperor Tuwai of Wei then continued his southern offensive and besieged **Xuyi**.

Huayin I 211 I Wars of the Three Kingdoms

Checked on the Yangzi at **Red Cliffs** (208), the northern warlord Cao Cao (Ts'ao Ts'ao) turned against the warlords of the northwest and advanced on a large combined force under Ma Chao and Hun Sui. Using a bold oblique approach, he attacked and destroyed the Allied army at Huayin, at the junction of the Wei and Yellow Rivers. Victory secured the strategic Wei Valley as far as Chang'an.

Huayna Pucará I 1572 I Tupac Amaru Revolt

Thirty-five years after Manco Capac's failed siege of **Cuzco**, his son Tupac Amaru renewed the revolt and Viceroy Francisco de Toledo launched a large-scale offensive on the Inca mountain stronghold at Vilcabamba. At nearby Huayna Pucará, the Inca army was routed and Vilcabamba fell next day. Tupac Amarau, the last Inca, was pursued and captured and was beheaded at Cuzco (23 June 1572).

Huazhou I 1850 I Taiping Rebellion

At the start of the Taiping rebellion in Guangxi, Chinese Imperial commander Zhou Fengqi sent General Li Dianyuan against rebel leaders Hong Xiuquan and Feng Yunshan at the village of Huazhou in the Penghua Range, northeast of Jintian. Ambushed by Taiping under Meng De-en, General Li was heavily

defeated and fled and the victorious Taiping returned to **Jintian** (4 November 1850).

Hubbardton ∎ 1777 ∎ War of the American Revolution

American General Arthur St Clair withdrew
across Lake Champlain from the fall of **Fort
Ticonderoga**, leaving his rearguard under Colonel Seth Warner at Hubbardton, Vermont. Both
sides suffered heavy losses in a dawn attack
by British forces under Generals Simon Fraser
and Friedrich Riedesel. However, Warner was
defeated and dispersed towards **Bennington**
(7 July 1777).

Hudayda ∎ 1934 ∎ Saudi-Yemeni War

Amid border war with Abd al-Aziz (Ibn Saud)
of Saudi Arabia, Imam Yahya ibn, Muhammad
of Yemen sent forces into disputed territory and
Ibn Saud responded with two invading armies
under his sons Faisal and Crown Prince Saud. A
bold campaign saw Faisal capture the city of al-
Hudayda within three weeks. The ensuing peace
treaty secured the disputed Asir region for Saudi
Arabia.

Hue ∎ 1883 ∎ French Conquest of Indo-China

With France defeated in the north near **Hanoi**
in May, Admiral Amedée Courbet took seven
ships and over 1,000 troops against the Imperial
capital at Hue in central Vietnam (Annam).
Following a massive naval bombardment, the
forts on the nearby Perfume River at Thuan-An
were destroyed and captured. Emperor Hiep Hoa
was forced to accept French overlordship (20
August 1883).

Hue ∎ 1968 ∎ Vietnam War

In the **Tet Offensive**, North Vietnamese and
Viet Cong surprised and took the former Imperial capital Hue. A counter-attack by American
and South Vietnamese saw half the city destroyed by air-strikes, artillery and naval bombardment. Hue was finally retaken at a cost of
over 5,000 Communists and about 500 Allied
troops killed and thousands of civilians executed
(31 January–24 February 1968).

Hue ∎ 1975 ∎ Vietnam War

As North Vietnam's final offensive began in
the central highlands at **Ban Me Thuot**, large
forces attacking in the north took Quang Tri (19
March), then advanced on Hue, which the government ordered held at all cost. Facing Communist shelling and likely encirclement, South
Vietnamese General Ngo Quang Truong abandoned Hue and thousands fled towards **Danang**
(23–25 March 1975).

Huebra ∎ 1812 ∎ Napoleonic Wars (Peninsular Campaign)

Anglo-Portuguese troops under Arthur Wellesley Lord Wellington retreating from their
failed siege of **Burgos**, finally reached the
Huebra. At San Munoz, the rearguard was attacked by French Marshals Nicolas Soult and
Jean-Baptiste Jourdan. However, the artillery
bombardment proved ineffective and the Allies
crossed the river to reach **Ciudad Rodrigo** (17
November 1812).

Huesca ∎ 1096 ∎ Early Christian Reconquest of Spain

See **Alcoraz**

Huesca ∎ 1811 ∎ Napoleonic Wars (Peninsular Campaign)

See **Ayerbe**

Huesca ∎ 1837 ∎ 1st Carlist War

As Spanish pretender Don Carlos V led his
army through Aragon, he was unwisely attacked
at Huesca by pursuing government forces under
General Iribarren and French Foreign Legion
Colonel Joseph Conrad. Taking advantage of a
superior position and failing light, the Carlists
inflicted heavy losses (including Iribarren killed), then continued east through **Barbastro** (24
May 1837).

Huhnerwasser ∎ 1866 ∎ Seven Weeks War

As Prussian Prince Friedrich Karl invaded
Austrian Bohemia through **Liebenau** and
Podol, Austrian forces were sent to defend the
Iser, while General Leopold Gondrecourt met
Prussian advance units under General Herwath

von Bittenfeld at Huhnerwasser. Gondrecourt had to withdraw east after a costly brief action and joined Count Edouard von Clam-Gallas at **Münchengratz** (27 June 1866).

Huilquipamba ∎ 1840 ∎ Colombian War of Supreme Commanders

Almost ten years after victory at **Palmira**, General José María Obando renewed rebellion in the south, but Pasto was occupied by government forces under General Pedro Alcántara Herrán. At nearby Huilquipamba, Obando fled after he was routed by Herrán, supported by Tomás Cipriano de Mosquera and Ecuadorian forces under General Juan José Flores (30 September 1840).

Huirangi ∎ 1861 ∎ 2nd New Zealand War
See **Te Arei**

Huj ∎ 1917 ∎ World War I (Middle East)

British forces under General John Shea advanced from victory at **Beersheba** and attacked a Turkish rearguard—supported by German and Austrian regulars—at Huj, northeast of **Gaza**. A bold cavalry charge secured the German Headquarters, though at the cost of unexpectedly heavy British casualties. Most of the Turkish force escaped north towards **Jerusalem** (8 November 1917).

Hukawng ∎ 1944 ∎ World War II (Burma-India)

Stalled in the Hukawng Valley in northern Burma in late 1943, General Joseph Stilwell's Chinese Divisions were joined by Merrill's Marauders and renewed the offensive against determined resistance under General Shinichi Tanaka. Severe fighting secured Maingkwan-Walawbum (3–7 March) and Shaduzup (29 March), as Stilwell advanced on **Myitkyina** (January–April 1944).

Hulao ∎ 621 ∎ Rise of the Tang Dynasty

With northwest China secured at **Qianshuiyuan** (618), the Tang Dynasty turned against its last rivals. The Emperor's son, Li Shimin, besieged Wang Shichong at **Luoyang**,

then continued east against a Xia relief army under Dou Jiande, encamped at Sishui. Lured out to defeat at nearby Hulao, the Xia lost 3,000 killed and perhaps 50,000 captured, including Dou. Wang quickly surrendered (28 May 621).

Huleiqat ∎ 1948 ∎ Israeli War of Independence

Following the Second Truce, Jewish forces under Ygal Allon renewed the offensive against the Egyptians in the south. Despite initial failure around Gaza, the Israelis attacked the fortified position to the northeast at Huleiqat, which fell by storm after heavy fighting. This opened the way into the Negev towards **Beersheba**, though further east **Faluja** held out under siege (18–20 October 1948).

Hulst ∎ 1642 ∎ Thirty Years War (Franco-Habsburg War)
See **Kempen**

Hulst ∎ 1645 ∎ Netherlands War of Independence

Frederick Henry of Orange determined to secure southern Netherlands, where he captured **Sas van Gent**, then a year later besieged nearby Hulst, about 15 miles northwest of Antwerp. Driving off a Spanish relief army under Baron Johann von Beck and Duke Charles IV of Lorraine, he captured the town's outer defences and forced it to capitulate (October–4 November 1645).

Humaitá ∎ 1868 ∎ War of the Triple Alliance

When President Francisco Solano López of Paraguay was defeated in the southwest at **Tuyutí**, he withdrew from besieged Humaitá, leaving Colonel Paulino Alen and a garrison of about 3,000. An assault by 12,000 men under Brazilian General Manuel Osório was driven off with unexpected losses, but Alen later killed himself and Colonel Francisco Martinez surrendered Humaitá (24 July 1868).

Humblebeck ∎ 1700 ∎ 2nd "Great" Northern War
See **Copenhagen**

Hummelshof ▮ 1702 ▮ 2nd "Great" Northern War

Russian Marshal Boris Sheremetev beat Swedish General Anton von Schlippenbach in Livonia at **Erestfer** in January, then inflicted an even greater defeat north of Valga at Hummelshof, where his 30,000 men overwhelmed Schlippenbach's 8,000. With more than 5,000 casualties and their artillery lost, the defeat ended Swedish mobile force in Livonia, leaving only fixed garrisons (18 July 1702).

Hunain ▮ 630 ▮ Campaigns of the Prophet Mohammed

Immediately after capturing the strategic city of **Mecca**, the Prophet Mohammed took the Muslim army of Medina against other infidel allies of the defeated Koreish of Mecca. In the Hunain Valley to the southeast, Mohammed heavily defeated the Hawazin tribes, who withdrew to siege at Taif. They eventually negotiated acceptance of Islamic authority and the war ended (31 January 630).

Hundred Slain ▮ 1866 ▮ Red Cloud's War
See **Fetterman Massacre**

Hundsfeld ▮ 1109 ▮ Polish-German Wars
See **Psie Pole**

Hungahungatoroa ▮ 1865 ▮ 2nd New Zealand War

Pursuing the religio-military Hauhau on New Zealand's east coast, Major James Fraser, with Captain Charles Westrupp's Forest Rangers and Maori allies, attacked Kereopa and Patara in a major fortified position at Hungahungatoroa, near the Kawakawa. Scaling precipitous cliffs, Fraser secured a decisive victory with over 500 Hauhau captured. He soon won again at **Waerenga** (October 1865).

Hungnam ▮ 1950 ▮ Korean War
See **Koto-ri**

Hungry Hill ▮ 1855 ▮ Rogue River War

With settlers and Indians warring on the Rogue River in southern Oregon, Captain Andrew Jackson Smith led about 250 regulars and volunteers against 100 warriors under Tecumtum at Hungry Hill, between Grave and Cow Creeks. Both sides withdrew after two days of indecisive attack and counter-attack and the war continued until Smith won at **Big Meadow** (31 October–1 November 1855).

Huningue ▮ 1796–1797 ▮ French Revolutionary Wars (1st Coalition)

Following repeated defeat east of Rhine at the hands of Archduke Charles Louis of Austria, French General Jean Victor Moreau withdrew across the river at Huningue, leaving General Pierre-Marie Ferino to hold the strategic crossing. Ferino capitulated after a remarkable three-month siege and was permitted to march out with all his arms and baggage (26 October 1796–19 February 1797).

Huningue ▮ 1815 ▮ Napoleonic Wars (The Hundred Days)

Among French commanders who refused to surrender after **Waterloo** was Baron Joseph Barbanege at Huningue, on the Rhine near Basel. His massively outnumbered force withstood two months' siege before surrendering with full honours to an estimated 25,000 Austrians under Archduke John and Swiss under General Nikolaus Bachmann. The town was razed (26 June– 26 August 1815).

Hunt's Gap ▮ 1943 ▮ World War II (Northern Africa)

German tanks under Colonel Rudolph Lang advancing on the important communication centre at Beja, in northern Tunisia, were delayed at **Sidi Nsir**, which allowed reinforcement of a powerful anti-tank defence 12 miles further west at Hunt's Gap. By the time Lang's armour arrived two days later, he was driven off with very heavy losses and the northern offensive failed (28 February 1943).

Huon Peninsula ▮ 1943 ▮ World War II (Pacific)

With **Salamaua** secured, Australians under General Edmund Herring, with American support, attacked the strategic Huon Peninsula in northeast New Guinea, inland through the Markham Valley and from the sea against Finschhafen. The Japanese counter-attacked at nearby Sattelberg, but General Hotazo Adachi finally had to withdraw west to **Wewak** (22 September–20 December 1943).

Huoyi ▎ 617 ▎ Rise of the Tang Dynasty

With the Sui Dynasty in decline, Li Yuan rebelled in Taiyuan and led a large force down the Fen, where he was blocked at Huoyi by a strong Sui force under Song Laosheng. Lured into taking his troops outside the walls, Song was badly defeated and Huoyi fell. Li marched on to take the capital Chang'an (9 November) and in 618 he proclaimed himself Gaozu, first Emperor of the new Tang Dynasty (8 September 617).

Hürtgen Forest ▎ 1944–1945 ▎ World War II (Western Europe)

After breaching the **Siegfried Line** at **Aachen**, American General Courtney Hodges entered the Hürtgen Forest, where some of the hardest fighting in the west saw over 30,000 American casualties in a battle of attrition. The delay helped Germany prepare the **Ardennes** offensive and the forest was not cleared until a fresh attack finally captured Schmidt (6 October 1944–9 February 1945).

Husainpur ▎ 1720 ▎ Mughal-Hyderabad War

See **Ratanpur**

Hydaspes ▎ 326 BC ▎ Conquests of Alexander the Great

As Alexander the Great marched into India past the stronghold at **Aornos**, Indian Prince Porus attempted to defend the Hydaspes (modern Jhelum) River. Near modern Jalalpur, Alexander secured a brilliant victory over Porus, who used elephants to make up for inferior numbers. Although the victor then occupied the Punjab, his troops mutinied to force a return west and he died en route (May 326 BC).

Hyderabad, India ▎ 1709 ▎ Mughal Wars of Succession

In the decline of the Mughal Empire following the death of Aurangzeb, his eldest son Muazim returned from Afghanistan to defeat Prince Azam at **Jajau**. Muazim (now as Emperor Bahadur Shah) then marched against his other brother, Kambakhsh. In battle outside Hyderabad against General Munim Khan and Prince Jahinshah, Kambakhsh was defeated and died of wounds (3 January 1709).

Hyderabad, Pakistan ▎ 1843 ▎ British Conquest of Sind

When the Baluchi Amirs of Sind (modern Pakistan) besieged the Residency at Hyderabad, Britain launched an opportunistic invasion and sent General Sir Charles Napier to relieve Major James Outram. After a stunning victory at **Miani**, Napier routed Sher Muhammad's siege just outside Hyderabad at Dubba and Britain annexed the Sind (15 February–24 March 1843).

Hyères ▎ 1795 ▎ French Revolutionary Wars (1st Coalition)

Four months after an unsatisfactory action off **Genoa** against Admiral Pierre Martin, Admiral Sir William Hotham met Martin again near the Hyères Islands off Provence. When the outnumbered French tried to run, a disorganised pursuit saw one French ship burned, before the wind changed and the over-cautious Hotham broke off the chase. Soon after, he was relieved of command (13 July 1795).

Hyrcanian Rock ▎ 588 ▎ Byzantine-Persian Wars

While war continued in Mesopotamia between Byzantines and Sassanids, a huge Turkish army invaded Persia. Sassanid King Hormizd IV sent General Bahram Chobin to confront the threat and, after marching east with a small force, he ambushed the Turks at Hyrcanian Rock, a narrow pass leading onto the Iranian Plateau. Attacking from the heights above Bahram secured victory and repulsed the invasion.

Hysiae I 669 BC I Rise of Argos

The city-state of Argos in northeastern Pelo-ponnese reached its peak under the Tyrant Pheidon, who greatly expanded Argive power. In a decisive clash at Hysiae, at the foot of Mount Parthenium, Pheidon routed a Spartan army, perhaps by using newly developed hoplite tactics. While victory gave Argos control over much of Peloponnese, Sparta was avenged in 547 in the Battle of the **Champions**.

I

Ia Drang ❘ 1965 ❘ Vietnam War

After a North Vietnamese attack was beaten at **Plei Me**, US airborne troops launched a large-scale offensive in the nearby Ia Drang Valley, southwest of Pleiku. In their first major battle against North Vietnamese regulars, the Americans suffered almost 300 killed, including 150 lost in a deadly ambush. However, the Communists had up to 2,000 killed and withdrew (14–18 November 1965).

Ialomitsa ❘ 1446 ❘ Turkish-Hungarian Wars

Hungarian Regent Janos Hunyadi intervened in a dispute in Wallachia, taking an army to support Prince Dan III against Vlad the Devil, who had returned with Ottoman forces to regain his Princedom. Hunyadi surprised and destroyed the Turks at the Ialomitsa River and captured Vlad, who was taken to Tirgoviste and executed, along with his eldest son (August 1446).

Iao Valley ❘ 1790 ❘ Hawaiian Wars
See **Kepaniwai**

Ibarra ❘ 1823 ❘ Ecuadorian War of Independence

Soon after liberation of Ecuador at **Pichincha** (May 1822), Pasto city rebelled against President Simón Bolívar and defeated local Governor Juan José Flores. Bolívar took 2,000 men and, northeast of Quito, at Ibarra, utterly routed Royalist leader Agustín Agualongo, killing 600 out of 1,500. General Bartolomé Salom soon

won again at **Catambuco** and brutally crushed the rising (17 July 1823).

Ibeka ❘ 1877 ❘ 9th Cape Frontier War

In a final attempt to regain lost Xhosa land, Galekas under veteran chief Kreili resumed war and 8,000 men attacked a force of Frontier Armed Police at Ibeka, in southeast Transkei but were heavily repulsed. The following day Regulars led by Commandant Charles Griffith arrived and burned Krieli's kraal. The Galeka were beaten again four months later at **N'Axama** (29 September 1877).

Ibera ❘ 217 BC ❘ 2nd Punic War
See **Ebro**

Ibera ❘ 215 BC ❘ 2nd Punic War

Carthaginian General Hasdrubal faced renewed Roman success in northeast Spain and attacked Ibera, opposite Dertosa near the mouth of the **Ebro**, scene of a naval defeat two years earlier. Hasdrubal's Spanish levies faltered in an attempted encirclement and his African troops were routed, giving strategic victory to Scipio the Elder and his brother Gnaeus, who later recaptured **Saguntum**.

Ibiza ❘ 1936 ❘ Spanish Civil War
See **Majorca**

Icamole ❘ 1876 ❘ Diaz Revolt in Mexico

Continuing the insurrection against President Sebastián Lerdo de Tejada, General Porfirio Diaz captured Matamaros, then was intercepted to the northwest at Icamole by government troops from Monterrey under General Carlos Fuero. Despite a courageous attack by Francisco Naranjo, Diaz was defeated and fled. His forces lost again a week later at **San Juan Epatlán** (20 May 1876).

Ice, Battle on the I 1242 I Rise of Russia
    See **Lake Peipus**

Ichigo I 1944 I World War II (China)
    Reinforced to 25 divisions, Japanese commander Shunroku Hata (later Yasuji Okamura) led the massive Ichigo offensive to seize Allied airfields in eastern China and open a land route to French Indo-China. The brilliant offensive started with Kogo, to clear **Central Henan**, then entered the Togo phase south to secure **Changsha**, **Hengyang** and **Guilin-Liuzhou** (April–December 1944).

Ichinotani I 1184 I Gempei War
    The Minamoto brothers, Yoshitsune and Noriyori, destroyed their rebellious cousin Yoshinaka at the **Awazu** and two weeks later marched west against the Taira, who had fled Kyoto with the boy-Emperor Antoku after defeat at **Shinowara**. A brilliant pincer action at Ichinotani, west of Kobe, routed Taira Munemori, who fled with Antoku to the Taira stronghold at **Yashima** (18 March 1184).

Iconium I 1147 I 2nd Crusade
    See **Dorylaeum**

Idistaviso I 16 I Rome's Germanic Wars
    See **Weser**

Idle I 617 I Anglo-Saxon Territorial Wars
    Two years after defeating the Welsh Kingdom of Powys at **Chester**, King Aethelfrith of Northumbria was attacked in the east by the Saxon King Raedwald of East Anglia. Raedwald defeated and killed Aethelfrith on the east bank of the Idle in Nottinghamshire and established Edwin, son of Aella of Deira, as the first Christian King of Northumbria.

Idstedt I 1850 I 1st Schleswig-Holstein War
    Abandoned by Prussia after the failed siege of **Fredericia**, Schleswig and Holstein fought on alone against Danish reoccupation. Decisive battle at Idstedt, a village just north of Schleswig, saw troops from the rebel Duchies under General Karl Wilhelm von Willisen heavily defeated. After rebel failure to capture **Friedrichstadt**, the war ended with Danish rule reimposed (25 July 1850).

Ifni I 1957 I Ifni War
    While campaigning in Spanish Sahara, newly independent Morocco also sent forces against the Spanish enclave of Ifni in the southwest. Heaviest fighting was in the south of Ifni, where an airdrop of Spanish paratroops failed to secure the area. When the Spanish withdrew into Sidi Ifni town, fighting died down. Twelve years later, Ifni was retroceded to Morocco (25 November–4 December 1957).

Iganie I 1831 I Polish Rebellion
    See **Siedlce**

Igualada I 1809 I Napoleonic Wars (Peninsular Campaign)
    Generals Laurent Gouvion Saint-Cyr and Louis-Francois Chabot manoeuvring north of Tarragona attacked the Spanish left, under General Mariano Alvarez de Castro at Igualada, 30 miles northwest of Barcelona. Chabot was initially repulsed before St-Cyr arrived with his main force and Castro was beaten. The Spanish fled southwest towards further defeat days later at **Valls** (17 February 1809).

Iguará I 1895 I 2nd Cuban War of Independence
    Revolutionaries under General Máximo Gómez and Antonio Maceo marched into western Cuba where they met and defeated a Spanish force near Iguará. The Spanish fell back, losing 18 men killed, along with large quantity of rifles and cartridges. However, Gómez could ill-afford his handful of casualties and was pursued by

General Fernando Oliver west towards **Manacal** (3 December 1895).

Ihantala ∎ 1944 ∎ World War II (Northern Europe)

Soviet forces invaded Finland to capture **Vyborg**, then attacked Finnish defensive lines to the northeast at Tali and Ihantala. Supported by German anti-tank guns and aircraft, the Finns won a decisive defensive victory in one of history's major armoured battles. The Russian advance was stopped, but the invaders meanwhile attempted to attack again around **Vuosalmi** (25 June–7 July 1944).

Ile d'Aix ∎ 1758 ∎ Seven Years War (Europe)

While assembling in the Bay of Biscay off the port of Rochefort to escort a large merchant convoy to North America, a French naval squadron was attacked by English Admiral Sir Edward Hawke. Although heavily outnumbered, Hawke's ships drove many of the French vessels ashore on the nearby Ile d'Aix, helping ensure Allied victory weeks later in Nova Scotia at **Louisbourg** (4 April 1758).

Ile de France ∎ 1810 ∎ Napoleonic Wars (5th Coalition)

See **Mauritius**

Ile de Groix ∎ 1795 ∎ French Revolutionary Wars (1st Coalition)

British Admiral Alexander Hood Lord Bridport, assisting the ill-fated émigré landing at **Quiberon**, met a French squadron off L'Orient near Ile de Groix. Pursuing the outnumbered Admiral Louis-Thomas Villaret de Joyeuse as he attempted to retreat, Bridport captured three French ships and inflicted heavy loss of life. He was however accused of excessive caution (23 June 1795).

Ile de Ré ∎ 1627 ∎ 3rd Huguenot Rebellion

In support of French Huguenots, England sent George Villiers Duke of Buckingham against the Ile de Ré, guarding the Protestant port at **La Rochelle**. With insufficient forces, Buckingham failed to capture the island's two fortresses, commanded by Jean de Toiras. And when more French troops landed, the English sailed away a total failure (12 July–29 October 1627).

Ilerda ∎ 78 BC ∎ Sertorian War

With rebel General Quintus Sertorius controlling much of Spain after victory at the **Baetis** and **Anas**, Lucius Manilius, Roman Consul in Narbonnese Gaul, invaded with three Legions and 1,500 cavalry to support Quintus Metellus Pius, Governor of Further Spain. A disastrous defeat near Ilerda saw Manilius routed by the Sertorian Lieutenant Lucius Hirtuleius and he retreated to Gaul.

Ilerda ∎ 49 BC ∎ Wars of the First Triumvirate

Julius Caesar marched into Spain with 40,000 men against supporters of his rival Pompey and met their army of about 70,000 under Lucius Afranius and Marcus Petreius at Ilerda (modern Lérida), northwest of Tarragona. Caesar drove his enemy into siege with a great campaign of manoeuvre, then forced their surrender. He returned to Italy after capturing **Massilia** in Gaul (2 May–2 July 49 BC).

Ilescas ∎ 1936 ∎ Spanish Civil War

As the Nationalist army advanced towards **Madrid**, a diversionary force under General Fernando Barrón captured Ilescas, south of the capital on the road to Toledo. Republican General José Asenio was drawn into the battle, but he was eventually driven back by Nationalist reinforcements. Meantime, the main force advanced west of Madrid through **Navalcarnero** (18–23 October 1936).

Ilha de Redencão ∎ 1866 ∎ War of the Triple Alliance

Crossing the upper Parana into Paraguay, 900 Brazilians under Colonel João Carlos Vilagran Cabrita landed and dug in on a low bank, then known as Ilha de Redencão, near Itapirú. Five days later, Paraguayan Colonel José Eduvigis Díaz attacked with 1,300 men. He was driven off in bloody hand-to-hand fighting with over 600 killed and fell back on **Estero Bellaco** (10 April 1866).

Ilipa ∎ 206 BC ∎ 2nd Punic War

The Carthaginians Mago and Hasdrubal Gisco, attempting to recover territory lost in Spain, gathered a large army at Ilipa (modern Alcalá del Río) near Seville, where they faced Roman General Publius Scipio the Younger. Scipio routed the Carthaginians in a brilliant tactical victory, although a sudden rainstorm prevented pursuit. This decisive action effectively drove Carthage out of Spain.

Illig ∎ 1904 ∎ Wars of the Mad Mullah

Soon after British troops beat Muhammad Abdullah Hassan inland at **Jidballi** (10 January), two ships attacked Illig on Somaliland's east coast. A Naval brigade and troops under Captain Horace Hood from the cruiser *Hyacinth* took Fort Illig at bayonet point and killed about 60 Dervishes for only three British dead. The Mullah fled to Italian territory and signed a peace, which lasted until 1908 (21 April 1904).

Illyricum ∎ 261 ∎ Roman Military Civil Wars

A year after the capture of Emperor Valerian at **Edessa**, his former General Macrianus rebelled against his successor Gallienus and invaded the west with his son Fulvius Junius Macrianus, as usurper. Reaching the Danube, father and son were defeated and killed in Illyricum, near the border with Thrace, by Gallienus' General Aureolus. The second son, Quietus, was killed in the east by the Palmyreans.

Iloilo ∎ 1899 ∎ Philippine-American War

Soon after war started at **Manila**, American General Marcus P. Miller delivered an ultimatum to General Martin Delgado at Iloilo, further south on Panay. Delgado, who had seized the town from Spain, refused to surrender and Miller bombarded the town with naval guns. The American then landed and secured Iloilo (which had been looted and burned) and also took nearby Jaro (10 February 1899).

Ilomantsi ∎ 1944 ∎ World War II (Northern Europe)

Soviet forces invading Finland suffered terrible losses at **Ihantala** and **Vuosalmi**, but attempted a new offensive north of Lake Ladoga around Ilomantsi. Despite superiority in men and material, two Russian Divisions were encircled and virtually destroyed. Russia then granted Finland an armistice (5 September), which preserved independence and ended the Continuation War (2–9 August 1944).

Ilorin ∎ 1897 ∎ British Conquest of Northern Nigeria

Sir Charles Goldie of the Royal Niger Company determined to secure northern Nigeria and destroyed the Nupe at **Bida**, then turned west against Emir Sulaymanu at Ilorin. Once again, ill-armed warriors were destroyed by Maxim guns and artillery and the Emirate was brought under British protectorate. In 1903, British forces attacked further north at **Kano** and **Sokoto** (16 February 1897).

Ilu ∎ 1942 ∎ World War II (Pacific)
See **Tenaru**

Ilurci ∎ 211 BC ∎ 2nd Punic War

With Roman forces campaigning against the Carthaginian Hasdrubal in Andalusia, Publius Scipio was killed on the **Baetis** after being forced to split his forces. Shortly afterwards his brother Gnaeus Scipio was defeated and killed by another Carthaginian army at Ilurci (modern Lorca), west of Cartagena. Rome then withdrew north of the Ebro, effectively conceding southern Spain.

Imbembesi ∎ 1893 ∎ Matabele War
See **Bembesi**

Imjin ∎ 1592 ∎ Japanese Invasion of Korea

With the fall of Seoul after victory at **Chongju** in June, Japanese Generals Konishi Yukinaga and Kato Kiyomasa advanced to the Imjin, where Korean General Kim Myung attempted a defence. When the Japanese feigned withdrawal, some Koreans were lured across the river and destroyed. King Songju withdrew and Kato marched northeast, while Konishi advanced on **Pyongyang** (15 July 1592).

Imjin I 1951 I Korean War

Despite being driven out of **Seoul** (14 March), Communist Chinese troops launched a fresh offensive to retake the South Korean capital and found their way blocked to the north by Commonwealth forces at the Imjin River. Both sides suffered heavy loses, including the famous stand by the Gloucestershire Regiment, but the line held, as it did further east around **Kapyong** (22–25 April 1951).

Immae I 218 I Roman Military Civil Wars

Marcus Macrinus became Roman Emperor by conspiring in the murder of his predecessor Caracalla, then faced a conspiracy by Varius Avitus Bassianus, claiming to be the illegitimate son of his cousin Caracalla. Macrinus was in turn overthrown and killed after defeat at Immae, north of Antioch. Bassianus became Emperor as Elagabalus, but proved equally ineffectual (8 June 218).

Immae I 271 I Roman-Palmyrean War

Determined to reassert Roman authority in the east after defeat of Valerian at **Edessa** in 260, Emperor Aurelian led a major force against Zenobia, warrior Queen of Palmyra, whose empire extended beyond Syria to include Egypt and northern Mesopotamia. Palmyrean General Zabdas marched north from Antioch to the Orontes at Immae and was heavily defeated. He lost again a year later at **Emessa**.

Imola I 1797 I French Revolutionary Wars (1st Coalition)

With the Austrians and Piedmontese defeated in northern Italy, French General Claude Victor took a force against Rome. Advancing south from Imola, southeast of Bologna, supported by General Jean Lannes, Victor smashed into a Papal force under Austrian General Michael Colli. The Papal troops were driven back with heavy losses and Rome was occupied (3 February 1797).

Imphal I 1944 I World War II (Burma-India)

Japanese commander Renya Mutaguchi's huge offensive into India was stopped at **Kohima**, while further south Generals Masafumi Yamauchi and Genzo Yanagida converged to cut off General William Slim's army at Imphal (29 March). The campaign's decisive action saw the siege of Imphal broken and Mutaguchi had to withdraw with over 50,000 casualties (22 March–26 June 1944).

Imus I 1896 I Philippines War of Independence

Spanish General Ernesto Aguirre defeated Emilio Aguinaldo in Cavite at **Zapote Bridge**, then returned with a larger force and attacked the Revolutionary leader in a strongly entrenched position at Imus, 12 miles southwest of Manila. Aguinaldo defeated the 500 Spanish in a bold flanking movement as they crossed the river. Two months later he won again at **Binakayan** (5 September 1896).

Imus I 1897 I Philippines War of Independence

Having captured **Dasmariñas**, south of Manila, Spanish General José Lachambre was heavily reinforced and took 15,000 men against Revolutionary leader Emilio Aguinaldo at the Imus. In brutal fighting—with 250 Spanish and 400 rebels killed, including Aguinaldo's brother Crispulo—the entrenched positions were taken at bayonet point. Aguinaldo fell back on **Naic** (25 March 1879).

Inab I 1149 I Crusader-Muslim Wars

The great Muslim leader Nur-ed-Din led a massive offensive against the Crusader Principality of Antioch, where he besieged the Christian fortress of Inab, east of the River Orontes. Raymond of Antioch approached with a small relief army, supported by the Assassin leader Ali ibn Wafa, but they were ambushed near Inab with both Raymond and Ali killed (29 July 1149).

Inchon I 1904 I Russo-Japanese War

See **Chemulpo**

Inchon I 1950 I Korean War

On a bold offensive behind enemy lines, General Edward Almond landed almost 70,000 men on the west coast at Inchon, where the surprised garrison was overwhelmed with just 20 Marines and perhaps 300 North Koreans killed. The Americans then seized Kimpo Airfield and raced east towards **Seoul**, supported by the army advancing north from the **Pusan Perimeter** (15–18 September 1950).

Inda Silase I 1989 I Ethiopian Civil War

Encouraged by Eritrean success at **Afabet** in March 1988, Tigrayan rebels in northern Ethiopia abandoned guerrilla tactics and launched a large-scale conventional attack on the town of Inda Silase. Aided by Eritrean forces, they destroyed an Ethiopian army of perhaps 20,000 men and the government effectively abandoned Tigray. In May the rebels advanced on **Addis Ababa** (19 February 1989).

Indaw I 1944 I World War II (Burma-India)

Behind Japanese lines in northern Burma, British Chindits led by General Orde Wingate (later General Walter Lentaigne) attacked forces under General Yoshihide Hayashi (later General Kaoru Takeda) north of Indaw around the fiercely held fortified positions Aberdeen, White City and Broadway. With Indaw secured, the Allies advanced northeast on **Mogaung** (5 March–27 April 1944).

Independence I 1862 I American Civil War (Trans-Mississippi)

A small Confederate force under Colonels John T. Hughes and Gideon W. Thompson renewed the offensive in western Missouri, where they attacked Independence, just east of Kansas City. The garrison under Colonel James Buel surrendered after a brief action in which Hughes was killed. A few days later Thompson supported another victory to the southeast at **Lone Jack** (11 August 1862).

Independence I 1864 I American Civil War (Trans-Mississippi)

On his march across Missouri, Confederate General Sterling Price advanced across the **Little Blue River** to reach Independence, just outside Kansas City, where he was attacked by pursuing Union forces led by General Alfred Pleasonton. His rearguard under General James Fagan fought a bold holding action, then marched southwest to join Price at the **Big Blue River** (22 October 1864).

Indi I 1676 I Mughal Conquest of the Deccan Sultanates

With Bijapur weak under the infant Sultan Sikander Adil Shah, Mughal Viceroy Bahadur Khan led an invasion against the Regent Buhlul. The Sultanate was forced to cede some fortresses, but at Indi, northeast of Bijapur city, the Mughals suffered a terrible defeat, with Governor Islam Khan Rum of Malwa among many killed. A fresh invasion in 1679 stalled at the fortress of **Bijapur** (23 June 1676).

India Muerta I 1845 I Argentine-Uruguayan War

While Argentine forces intervened in Uruguay against President Fructuso Rivera and besieged **Montevideo**, General Justo José Urquiza (who had defeated Rivera at **Arroyo del Sauce** in January 1844) attacked him again at India Muerta, northeast of Montevideo near Lazcano in Rocha. Rivera was decisively defeated and withdrew into Brazilian territory (27 March 1845).

Indian Key I 1840 I 2nd Seminole Indian War

After looting **Caloosahatchee** (July 1839), a group of so-called "Spanish" Seminole under Chakaika took the war to the offshore islands and attacked unsuspecting Indian Key, midway along the Florida Keys near Marathon. Thirteen white settlers were killed, including the noted botanist Dr Henry Perrine. Chakaika then burned the little settlement and escaped with his plunder (7 August 1840).

Indore I 1801 I Maratha Territorial Wars

In a bloody war between rival Maratha Princes, Daulat Rao Sindhia of Gwalior launched a major assault on Maharaja Jaswant Rao Holkar of Indore to avenge his defeat at **Ujjain** (2 July). Outside Indore, Daulat Rao inflicted a crushing defeat and seized and sacked Holkar's capital. However, he failed to follow up his victory and a year later was utterly defeated near **Poona** (14 October 1801).

Indus I 458 I Hun Invasion of India

As Huns from Central Asia attempted to enter India, a huge army was met at the Indus by Skandagupta, last ruler of the once-great Gupta Empire. A decisive battle along the river inflicted heavy losses and checked the advance of the "White Huns." But within a few years, they attacked again, penetrating deep into the dying Gupta Empire. By 500 AD they were well established in Malwa.

Indus I 1221 I Conquests of Genghis Khan

Deserted by his Afghan allies after victory at **Parwan Durrah**, Prince Jalal-ud-din of Khwarezm faced a huge offensive by the Mongol Genghis Khan, who pursued him to the banks of the Indus. Near modern Kalabagh, Jalal-ud-din was heavily defeated and his General Amin Malik was killed. The Prince and his survivors reputedly escaped by swimming their horses across the River (24 November 1221).

Ingavi I 1841 I Bolivian-Peruvian War

President Agustín Gamarra of Peru was overconfident after Bolivian defeat in Peru at **Yungay** (January 1839) and rashly took an army into Bolivia, where he met a smaller Bolivian force under General José Ballivián at Ingavi, near Viachi. A complete rout saw Gamarra defeated and killed, ending the war and ensuring Bolivian Independence with Ballivián as the new President (18 November 1841).

Ingavi I 1935 I Chaco War

After advancing north into the Chaco Boreal through victory at **Yrendagüe** and **Ybibobo** in December 1934, Paraguayan forces were checked by a Bolivian counter-offensive at **Boyuibé**. But, in a final action further east at Ingavi, Bolivian Colonel Julio Bretel was defeated and surrendered. Peace was signed a week later and three years of negotiation won Paraguay most of the Chaco (7 June 1935).

Ingogo I 1881 I 1st Anglo-Boer War

Despite defeat at **Laing's Nek**, British General Sir George Colley quickly advanced from Newcastle, Natal, with about 400 men to attack Boer General Nicolaas Smit at Ingogo (Schuinshoogte). Colley lost 64 killed and 77 wounded in heavy fighting for just 18 Boer casualties, but managed to withdraw to nearby Mount Prospect. He was soon defeated again at **Majuba Hill** (8 February 1881).

Ingolstadt I 1525 I German Peasants' War

Following victory over a peasant army at **Königshofen** , forces representing German nobility ravaged the countryside in pursuit of rebels and Ludwig IV, Elector Palatine, attacked Florian Geyer and 600 of his Black Troop at the town of Ingolstadt, southeast of Würzburg. The castle was stormed and burned with all but a handful slain. Geyer escaped and was later killed in the pursuit (June 1525).

Ingosten I 1899 I French Colonial Wars in North Africa

A French "scientific expedition" into central Algeria under geologist Georges Flamand was escorted by Captain Theodore Pein and shadowed by Captain Marcel Germain. Ambushed by about 300 Arabs at Ingosten, Pein repulsed the Tidikelt, killing more than 50 before Germain arrived. Next day, the French occupied **In Salah** and imposed a fine on the town (28 December 1899).

Ingur I 1855 I Crimean War

When Turks under Omar Pasha (Michael Lattas) landed on the Black Sea coast of Georgia at Sukhumi, they advanced to the Ingur River, where they attacked a 12,000-strong Russian force under Prince Knyaz Bagration-Muhranski. While the Russians were defeated and forced back with 400 men lost, the Turkish counter-offensive was too late to relieve Russia's siege of **Kars** (6 November 1855).

Inhlobane ∎ 1879 ∎ Anglo-Zulu War
See **Hlobane**

Inkerman ∎ 1854 ∎ Crimean War
Ten days after action near **Balaklava**, Russian Prince Alexander Menshikov made another attempt to cut off the Allied siege of **Sevastopol** and attacked at Inkerman. Following a desperate struggle in fog by outnumbered British infantry under General Fitzroy Somerset Lord Raglan, French General Pierre Bosquet arrived to seal victory and Menshikov withdrew (5 November 1854).

Inkovo ∎ 1812 ∎ Napoleonic Wars (Russian Campaign)
As Napoleon Bonaparte's invasion of Russia advanced along the Dnieper, cavalry on his left wing under General Francois Sébastiani were attacked by Cossacks led by General Matvei Platov at Inkovo, northwest of Smolensk. While the French suffered an unexpected check, this action failed to slow Bonaparte's continued advance to victory at **Smolensk** (8 August 1812).

Inönü (1st) ∎ 1921 ∎ 2nd Greco-Turkish War
A campaign to secure Anatolia for Greece saw General Anastasios Papoulas advance on **Eskisehir**, 150 miles west of Ankara. He was blocked just further west at Inönü, by Turkish forces under Ismet Pasha and the Greeks were checked in heavy fighting. Papoulas withdrew to regroup and reinforce his army before launching a second, much larger assault (10 January 1921).

Inönü (2nd) ∎ 1921 ∎ 2nd Greco-Turkish War
Greek General Anastasios Papoulas renewed his offensive in Turkish Anatolia with 150,000 men and drove Turkish General Refet Pasha out of Afyon. Once again, he was bravely blocked further north at Inönü by Ismet Pasha. Ismet was promoted to replace Refet (and later took the name Inönü), but he was unable to resist a subsequent Greek attack on nearby **Eskisehir** (28–30 March 1921).

In Rhar ∎ 1900 ∎ French Colonial Wars in North Africa
Sent to reinforce **In Salah**, in central Algeria, Colonel Clement d'Eu then marched west against In Rhar, where Captain Maurice Baumgarten had earlier failed for lack of artillery (24–26 January). With a large force and two guns, d'Eu inflicted heavy damage before storming the town. Tidikelt resistance was largely crushed and the French soon also took **Timimoun** (19 March 1900).

In Salah ∎ 1900 ∎ French Colonial Wars in North Africa
A week after securing the central Algerian town of In Salah after action at nearby **Ingosten**, French Captain Theodore Pein was attacked by a claimed 1,000 Arabs. Caught in heavy crossfire, the Tidikelt were driven off with over 150 dead for just one French spahi killed. Pein was soon reinforced by Captain Maurice Baumgarten, who led an abortive raid west against **In Rhar** (5 January 1900).

Intabanka-ka-Ndoda ∎ 1818 ∎ Xhosa Civil War
See **Amalinda**

Intibucá ∎ 1876 ∎ Central American National Wars
See **La Esperanza**

Inveraray ∎ 1644 ∎ British Civil Wars
James Graham Marquis of Montrose gathered his Royalist forces in the Highlands after sacking **Aberdeen** (13 September) and led a midwinter raid on Archibald Campbell Marquis of Argyll at Inveraray. Montrose's largely MacDonald force caused massive damage to their traditional Campbell enemies and Montrose defeated Argyll again two months later at **Inverlochy** (13 December 1644).

Invercarron ∎ 1650 ∎ British Civil Wars
See **Carbiesdale**

Invercullen I 961 I Later Viking Raids on Britain

The Scottish King Indulph, son of Constantine II, waged a constant war against Norse raids on the coast of Buchan and Banff. It is claimed Scottish King finally defeated the invaders on Moray Firth near Invercullen and was reputedly killed in the moment of victory (although this is still debated by historians). His son Cullen was defeated four years later at **Duncrub**.

Inverdovat I 877 I Viking Wars in Britain

During a reign of continuous warfare against Norwegian and Danish Vikings, Constantine I of Scotland marched to defend the coast of Fife against a fresh Viking landing, possibly by Olaf of Dublin and the Dane Ivar. At Inverdovat, in the Parish of Forgan on the Firth of Tay, Constantine is claimed to have repulsed the raiders, though he reputedly died at the moment of victory.

Inverkeithing I 1651 I British Civil Wars

Oliver Cromwell advanced into Scotland after his devastating victory at **Dunbar** (September 1650) and despatched General John Lambert along the northern shore of the Firth of Forth, where he routed a Royalist force under Sir John Browne at Inverkeithing. Although victory allowed Cromwell to occupy Perth, Charles II invaded England, leading to the decisive battle at **Worcester** (20 July 1651).

Inverlochy I 1431 I MacDonald Rebellion

With Alexander MacDonald Lord of the Isles defeated at **Lochaber** (June 1429) and imprisoned by James I, his cousin Donald Balloch of Ranald ravaged Lochaber before facing a Royal army at Inverlochy, near modern Fort William. Royalist commander Alexander Stewart Earl of Mar was defeated and fled. The King himself soon took command to restore peace in the Highlands.

Inverlochy I 1645 I British Civil Wars

Gathering Royalist forces in the Highlands after sacking **Aberdeen** (September 1644), James Graham Marquis of Montrose and General Alasdair MacDonald raided Archibald Campbell Marquis of Argyll at **Inveraray** in December, then attacked his large force of Campbell's and lowland Covenanters at Inverlochy. Argyll watched from a ship while his clan army was utterly destroyed (2 February 1645).

Invernahavon I 1370 I Scottish Clan Wars

After invading the Badenoch, 400 Camerons were met on the Spey at Invernahavon by a strong force of Mackintoshes, supported by MacPhersons and Davidsons. In a dispute over leadership, the MacPhersons allowed the Davidsons to be virtually destroyed before they rejoined the battle to help defeat the Camerons. The resulting MacPherson-Davidson feud was fought out at **North Inch** in 1396.

Inverness I 1646 I British Civil Wars

James Graham Marquis of Montrose withdrew to the Highlands following Royalist defeat at **Philiphaugh** (September 1645) and gathered fresh MacDonald and MacKenzie forces to besiege Inverness. However, Montrose was driven off by a large Parliamentary army under General John Middleton and he fled abroad when King Charles I surrendered three days later (26 April–5 May 1646).

Inverurie I 1308 I Rise of Robert the Bruce

Robert the Bruce defeated the English at **Loudon Hill** in May 1307, then secured his position in Scotland by marching against John Comyn Earl of Buchan, cousin of John Comyn the Younger who Bruce had murdered for the Scottish throne. At Inverurie, on the Don northwest of Aberdeen, Bruce routed Buchan and his English allies, then ravaged the whole of the Earldom (probably 22 May 1308).

Inverurie I 1745 I Jacobite Rebellion (The Forty-Five)

Sent to recover Aberdeen from Jacobite rebels, loyal Highlanders under MacLeod of MacLeod and Captain George Munro of Culcain occupied Inverurie, then faced a rebel offensive from Aberdeen under Lord Lewis Gordon. The government force was routed and driven out. Inverurie was later retaken by the Duke of Cumberland marching towards brutal victory at **Culloden** (23 December 1745).

Ionian Islands ∎ 1798 ∎ French Revolutionary Wars (1st Coalition)

In June 1797 France gained from Venice the Ionian Islands, off the coast of Greece, which came under attack in September 1798 by a combined Turkish-Russian fleet under Admirals Kadir Bey and Fedor Ushakov. The islands of Cerigo, Zante, Cephalonia and St Maure all fell quickly, though **Corfu** held out for four months. The islands were returned to France in 1807 (October 1798).

Ionian Islands ∎ 1810 ∎ Napoleonic Wars (5th Coalition)

With the Ionian Islands off Greece returned to France by Tsar Alexander of Russia in 1807, British General Sir John Oswald recaptured Zante, Cephalonia, Ithaca and Cerigo with little resistance in September 1809. However, there was heavy fighting at the fortress of Amaxichi on St Maura before General Louis Camus surrendered. Corfu was never retaken (22 March–16 April 1810).

Ioannina ∎ 1912–1913 ∎ 1st Balkan War
See **Jannina**

Ionkovo ∎ 1807 ∎ Napoleonic Wars (4th Coalition)
See **Bergfriede**

Ipsus ∎ 301 BC ∎ Wars of the Diadochi

In a decisive battle between the successors of Alexander the Great, Antigonus and his son Demetrius, who controlled Asia, were attacked by Lysimachus of Thrace and Seleucus of Babylon. The "Battle of the Kings" at Ipsus, in western Turkey northwest of modern Afyon, saw Antigonus defeated and killed. Demetrius fled, though he later secured Macedonia and his new dynasty ruled until **Pydna**.

Iquique ∎ 1879 ∎ War of the Pacific

While blockading Iquique, the obsolete Chilean ships *Esmerelda* and *Covadonga* were attacked by the Peruvian ironclads *Huascar* and *Independencia* under Captain Miguel Grau. Despite heroic defence, *Esmerelda* was sunk with heavy losses, including Captain Arturo Prat killed. *Independencia* was lured onto a reef and destroyed and *Huascar* was lost at **Angamos** in October (21 May 1879).

Iran ∎ 1941 ∎ World War II (Middle East)

When German forces advancing into Russia threatened the oilfields of Iran, British Generals Charles Harvey and William Slim launched a pre-emptive invasion from the south, while Russians attacked in the north. After a brief resistance, the Shah ordered a ceasefire and abdicated to his son, ensuring Iranian neutrality and securing the vital Allied supply route to Russia (25–28 August 1941).

Iraq ∎ 1941 ∎ World War II (Middle East)

After a pro-Axis coup under Rashi Ali seized power in Iraq, a British brigade landed at Basra and the Iraqi army attacked the British base at **Habbaniyah**. The siege was driven off and, following a further Iraqi defeat at **Fallujah**, Rashid Ali fled from Baghdad. The pro-British Regent Abd al-Ilah resumed government and the Allies turned against Vichy **Syria** and **Lebanon** (1 April–31 May 1941).

Iriba ∎ 1990 ∎ Chad Civil Wars

President Hissen Habré crushed an attempted coup in April 1989, but faced heavy attack in Biltine, when Libyan-backed coup leader Idriss Déby invaded from the Sudan and overwhelmed the border town of Iriba. After heavy losses on both sides, government forces retook Iriba and Déby was pursued into the Sudan. In November, he regrouped and attacked in **Ouaddai** (25 March–6 April 1990).

Iringa ∎ 1894 ∎ German Colonial Wars in Africa

With German East African forces massacred by Hehe rebels at **Lugalo**, new Commissioner

Friedrich von Schele slowly regrouped, then led a large force against Chief Mkwawa's massive fortress at Iringa (in modern Tanzania), which was taken by storm. While most of the Hehe soon surrendered, Mkwawa fought on until 1898 when he was cornered and took his own life (30 October 1894).

Iringa I 1916 I World War I
(African Colonial Theatre)

General Kurt Wahle withdrawing south from **Tabora** in German East Africa sent Major Georg Kraut and 2,000 men against Iringa, which had been seized by General Edward Northey advancing from Rhodesia. While the Germans cut off the town and defeated a relief column, a direct attack was repulsed. The British eventually secured the north of the colony (23–30 October 1916).

Irish Bend I 1863 I American Civil War
(Lower Seaboard)

On the offensive in western Louisiana, Union General Nathaniel P. Banks sent General Cuvier Grover to intercept the Confederates withdrawing upstream from **Fort Bisland,** on the Bayou Teche. The Union force was initially repulsed with costly losses in fierce fighting at Irish Bend, near Franklin, before reinforcements arrived and the Confederates abandoned the field (14 April 1863).

Iron Gates I 86 I Domitian's Dacian War
See **Tapae**

Iron Mountain, China I 630 I Tang
Imperial Wars

Taking advantage of war between Turkish tribes on the northern border, Tang general Li Jing led an expedition against Xieli of the Eastern Turks, who had previously raided deep into China. Driven out of his base at Danxiang, Xieli withdrew to Iron Mountain (Tieshan), where a one-sided slaughter cost perhaps 10,000 Turks killed. The Tang soon controlled the steppe north of the Gobi (27 March 630).

Iron Mountain, South Africa I 1852 I
8th Cape Frontier War

As war in Kaffraria drew to a close, British forces prevented reoccupation of the **Waterkloof** in the Amatolas, then Colonel John Michel led a bold assault on a strongly defended position at Iron Mountain. Despite costly initial British losses, the place was taken by storm and the Xhosa dispersed to the north. The great Chiefs Sandile and Macomo surrendered in March 1853 (15 March 1852).

Iron Triangle I 1967 I Vietnam War

Following success northwest of Saigon around **Dau Tieng**, 30,000 Americans and South Vietnamese attacked Viet Cong bases in the Iron Triangle, even closer to the capital (Operation Cedar Falls). While most Viet Cong escaped into Cambodia, the Allies bombed and bulldozed the bases, killing up to 700. The Viet Cong later reoccupied the area to launch the **Tet Offensive** (8–26 January 1967).

Irriwaddy I 1945 I World War II
(Burma-India)

With the Japanese "March to Delhi" stopped at **Imphal**, commander Hoyotaro Kimura fell back into Burma to hold the Irriwaddy. While he expected the main British advance north of Mandalay, General Sir William Slim atacked in the south and seized the key city of **Meiktila**. Soon afterwards **Mandalay** also fell, virtually ending the campaign in Burma (January–March 1945).

Irtysh I 1208 I Conquests of
Genghis Khan

In his final decisive battle for supremacy over the tribes of Mongolia, Genghis Khan attacked Khan Toqtoa Beki of the Merkit, supported by Kuchlug of the Naiman, who had escaped the defeat at **Khangai**. Toqtoa was defeated and killed in battle on the upper Irtysh, east of Lake Zaysan, while Kuchlug fled to the Kara Khitai. He was finally defeated 12 years later at **Kashgar**.

Irun ∎ 1837 ∎ 1st Carlist War

General Sir George de Lacy Evans recovered from defeat outside San Sebastian at **Oriamendi** (16 March) and led the British Legion east through **Hernani** (14 May) to storm the Carlist position at Irun. **Fuentarrabia**, where he had been bloodily repulsed in July 1836, quickly fell the next day. The British Legion was later disbanded and Evans was knighted for his services in Spain (17 May 1837).

Irurzun ∎ 1795 ∎ French Revolutionary Wars (1st Coalition)

See **Bilbao**

Irurzun ∎ 1813 ∎ Napoleonic Wars (Peninsular Campaign)

Withdrawing after French defeat at **Vitoria**, General Jean Baptiste d'Erlon's rearguard under General Jean Darmagnac was caught three days later by Lord Wellington's German Hussars as the French tried to cross the Araquil, northwest of Pamplona near Irurzun. During a sharp attack, Darmagnac lost about 100 men and one of only two guns reportedly brought off the battlefield at Vitoria (24 June 1813).

Isandhlwana ∎ 1879 ∎ Anglo-Zulu War

The British who invaded Zululand against King Cetshwayo set up camp at Isandhlwana then marched on, leaving the unprotected encampment under Colonel Anthony Durnford. Attacked by up to 20,000 warriors led by Matyana, over 600 European soldiers and 500 African irregulars were killed in one of Britain's worst military disasters. Zulus then attacked nearby **Rorke's Drift** (22 January 1879).

Isandula ∎ 1879 ∎ Anglo-Zulu War

See **Isandhlwana**

Isara ∎ 121 BC ∎ Rome's Gallic Wars

When Rome beat the Allobroges near **Avignon**, King Bituitus of the Arverni joined his Gallic allies in a powerful coalition. Later that year, Rome sent a fresh army under Consul Fabius Maximus, who crushed the Gauls at the Isara, possibly the Isère near its junction with the Rhone. Bituitis was later captured and the Allobroges made peace, effectively securing Southern Gaul (August 121 BC).

Isaszeg ∎ 1849 ∎ Hungarian Revolutionary War

Assuming the offensive at **Hatvan**, new commander General Artur Gorgey led 42,000 Hungarians against 27,000 Croats under Count Joseph Jellacic at Isaszeg, just east of Budapest. While Gyorgy Klapka's Hungarian Corps was driven from the field, General Gorgey secured victory and occupied Godollo next day. The Habsburgs soon lost again at **Waitzen** and **Nagy Sallo** (6 April 1849).

Isfahan ∎ 1050–1051 ∎ Seljuk Wars of Expansion

With Khorasan secured at **Dandanaqan** (1040), the Seljuk Toghril Beg determined to secure Isfahan in central Iran. In 1043 and 1046 he made Isfahan submit, but in face of renewed resistance laid siege to the city. After almost a year, Abu Mansur Framarz surrendered, ending the Kakuyid Dynasty, and was rewarded with Yadz. Toghril razed the walls of Isfahan and made it his capital (1050–May 1051).

Isfahan ∎ 1387 ∎ Conquests of Tamerlane

The Turko-Mongol Tamerlane marched south into Persia against the rebellious Shah Zayn al-Abidin, where he entered the Shah's capital at Isfahan in triumph. However, when some of Tamerlane's troops were killed, he stormed and sacked Isfahan, then ordered the entire population killed. It is claimed that 70,000 skulls were collected and cemented into towers as a warning to future rebels.

Isfahan ∎ 1722 ∎ Persian-Afghan Wars

After invading Persia, Mahmud Ghilzai of Kandahar routed a Persian army at **Gulnabad**, near Isfahan, then advanced to blockade the capital itself. Crown Prince Tahmasp fled to try and raise a relief army, but after eight months the starving city surrendered. Shah Sultan Hussein abdicated in favour of Mahmud, who ruled as Shah before he eventually went insane (February–12 October 1722).

Isfahan I 1726 I Turko-Persian War
    See **Kiemereh**

Ishibashiyama I 1180 I Gempei War
    Despite Minamoto disaster at **Ujigawa** in June, Minamoto Yoritomo gathered a force against Japan's ruling Taira clan, but was attacked west of Yokohama at Ishibashiyama, near Odawara, by troops of Taira Kiyomori under Oba Kagechika. Yoritomo was outnumbered and routed, escaping into the Hakone Mountains. He soon raised a fresh force to fight again at **Fujigawa** (15 September 1180).

Ishiyama Honganji I 1570 I Japan's Era of the Warring States
    After defeating his brother-in-law Asai Nagamasa at the **Anegawa** (30 July), Oda Nobunaga came under attack by 3,000 of the Ikko sect from Ishiyama Honganji (now Osaka Castle) and monks from Enryakuji. Nobunaga was beaten, but soon besieged Ishiyama Honganji. In 1571 he destroyed the Enryakuji monastery at Mount Heie and Ishiyama Honganji finally fell in 1580 (November 1570).

Island Number Ten I 1862 I American Civil War (Western Theatre)
    Union General John Pope and Flag-Officer Andrew H. Foote advanced down the Mississippi past Columbus, attacking the fortified Island Number Ten and nearby New Madrid, Missouri, held by Generals John P. McCown and William W. Mackall. New Madrid was abandoned (13 March) and Island Number Ten soon surrendered, leading to the fall of **Memphis** (28 February–8 April 1862).

Islas Formigues I 1285 I French-Aragonese War
    See **Las Hormigas**

Isly I 1844 I French Conquest of Algeria
    Determined to complete the conquest of Algeria after victory at **Smala** in May 1843, France forced Abd-el-Kader to withdraw into Morocco, where he linked up with the Sultan Abd-el-Rahman. In the war's decisive battle, Marshal Thomas Bugeaud routed a superior combined Arab force at the Isly and was created Duke of Isly. Kader escaped and fought on until November 1847 (14 August 1844).

Ismail I 1790 I Catherine the Great's 2nd Turkish War
    See **Izmail**

Ismailia I 1915 I World War I (Middle East)
    See **Suez Canal**

Isola del Giglio I 1646 I Thirty Years War (Franco-Habsburg War)
    In support of the French-Savoyard siege of **Orbetello**, on Italy's west coast, Admiral Jean-Armande de Maillé-Brézé attacked a Spanish relief force under Admiral Francisco Diaz Pimienta off Isola del Giglio. With the 27-year-old French leader killed by a cannon ball his deputy, General Louis Foucault Comte de Daugnon, prematurely broke off the attack and the siege was lifted (14 June 1646).

Isola di Ponza I 1435 I Aragon's Conquest of Naples
    See **Gaeta**

Isonzo I 489 I Goth Invasion of Italy
    See **Sontius**

Isonzo I 1915 I World War I (Italian Front)
    When Italy entered the war against Austro-Hungary, General Luigi Cadorna attacked Austrian Marshal Conrad von Hotzendorf along the Isonzo, north of Trieste. Four successive attacks were repulsed for little gain at the cost of about 280,000 Italian and 160,000 Austrian casualties (23 June–7 July, 18 July–3 August, 18 October–3 November & 10 November–2 December 1915).

Isonzo (1st) ∎ 1916 ∎ World War I (Italian Front)

Following four failed attacks along the Isonzo in 1915, Italian commander Luigi Cadorna launched a fifth attack in heavy snow, rain and fog against General Svetozar Boroevic. As before, Cadorna's forces were repulsed by the Austrians, notably around Tolmino and the action had to be called off to meet the Austrian offensive further north around **Asiago** (9–17 March 1916).

Isonzo (2nd) ∎ 1916 ∎ World War I (Italian Front)

Italian commander Luigi Cadorna repulsed an Austrian offensive around **Asiago** (25 June), then returned to the Isonzo front and launched four more attacks against General Svetozar Boroevic. After early success to seize Gorizio (9 August) the so-called Sixth to Ninth battles achieved little and each side lost about 100,000 men (4–17 August, 14–17 September, 10–12 October & 1–4 November 1916).

Isonzo (1st) ∎ 1917 ∎ World War I (Italian Front)

In the so-called Tenth Battle of Isonzo, reinforced Italian forces under General Luigi Cadorna launched a fresh offensive, which secured some early gains. However, Austrian General Svetozar Boroevic led a powerful counter-offensive and drove the Italians back to their starting point at the cost of perhaps 160,000 Italian and 75,000 Austrian casualties (12 May–8 June 1917).

Isonzo (2nd) ∎ 1917 ∎ World War I (Italian Front)

Determined on a fresh offensive on the Isonzo, Italian commander Luigi Cadorna sent General Luigi Capello north from Gorizio, while Emanuele Filibert Duke of Aosta attacked south towards Trieste. The so-called Eleventh Battle of Isonzo saw Capello seize the strategic Bainsizza plateau and Austria had to seek German aid, leading to Italian disaster at **Caporetto** (19 August–12 September 1917).

Issus ∎ 333 BC ∎ Conquests of Alexander the Great

Alexander the Great secured Asia Minor at **Granicus** and **Halicarnassus,** then soon marched east across Turkey to meet a much larger Persian army at Issus, on the Gulf of Iskenderun in Cilicia. Persian King Darius III lost perhaps 50,000 men in a terrible and decisive rout and fled, abandoning his family. Alexander then marched south through Syria to **Tyre** and **Gaza** (November 333 BC).

Issus ∎ 194 ∎ Wars of Emperor Severus

Emperor Septimius Severus beat his rival Pescennius Niger at **Cyzicus** and **Nicaea** in Asia Minor, then pursued him into Syria later that year for the final, decisive battle. On the Plain of Issus, on the Gulf of Iskenderun, Niger had assembled a much larger army, but his local levies broke and fled in the face of overwhelming casualties. Niger escaped, but was pursued and killed outside Antioch.

Istabulat ∎ 1917 ∎ World War I (Mesopotamia)

Driving north from **Baghdad**, Anglo-Indian commander Sir Frederick Maude secured **Mushahida**, then sent General Sir William Marshall against more than 7,000 Turks around Istabulat. Severe fighting cost over 2,000 casualties on either side before the Turks withdrew. Nearby Samarra fell next day and the northern front stabilised until the final advance on **Sharqat** (21–22 March 1917).

Itagüí ∎ 1841 ∎ Colombian War of Supreme Commanders

Amid continued campaigning in Antioquia, government forces under General Eusebio Borrero fought an inconclusive action at Itagüí, just southwest of Medellín, against rebel Colonel Salvador Córdoba. Soon afterwards, Borrera was defeated and captured at **Garcia**. Later the same year (8 July), Córdoba was executed by General Tomás de Mosquera at Cartago (2 February 1841).

Itala ∎ 1901 ∎ 2nd Anglo-Boer War
See **Fort Itala**

Italeni ∎ 1838 ∎ Boer-Zulu War
See **Ethaleni**

Italica ∎ 75 BC ∎ Sertorian War
A year after disaster in Spain at **Lauron**, Roman Quintus Metellus Pius attacked Lucius Hirtuleius, a lieutenant of the rebel commander Quintus Sertorius, at Italica, just northwest of Seville. Unwisely accepting a pitched battle, Hirtuleius was heavily defeated and was subsequently beaten again and killed near Segovia. Later that year, Metellus joined Gnaeus Pompey advancing towards the **Turia**.

Itamaraca ∎ 1640 ∎ Dutch-Portuguese Colonial Wars
Another attempt to recover Pernambuco in Portuguese Brazil saw a large Spanish-Portuguese fleet assembled in Bahia under Fernando Mascarenhas Conde de la Torre. In a four-day running battle north of Recife off Itamaraca, an outnumbered Dutch fleet under Admirals Willem Loos and Jacob Huygens defeated the Spaniards and the Dutch retained **Recife** until 1654 (12–15 January 1640).

Itapirú ∎ 1866 ∎ War of the Triple Alliance
See **Redencão, Ilha de**

Ita Ybate ∎ 1868 ∎ War of the Triple Alliance
In a fresh offensive in central Paraguay against President Francisco Solano López, Marshal Luíz Aldes Marquis of Caxias led Argentine, Brazilian and Uruguayan forces through **Avaí** against Ita Ybate, southeast of Asunción. Despite heavy Allied losses, the Paraguayans were massively defeated. President López fled the battlefield and died in March 1870 at **Cerro Corá** (21–27 December 1868).

Itororó ∎ 1868 ∎ War of the Triple Alliance
See **Ytororó**

Itsukushima ∎ 1555 ∎ Japan's Era of the Warring States
See **Miyajima**

Ituzaingó ∎ 1827 ∎ Argentine-Brazilian War
After Juan Antonio Lavalleja of Uruguay repudiated annexation by Brazil and secured victory at **Sarandi** in 1825, he sought aid from Argentina, which declared war and sent a force led by General Carlos de Alvear. They routed the Brazilians under Feliberto Marques de Barbacena in a decisive action at Ituzaingó in northeast Argentina and Uruguay soon secured independence (20 February 1827).

Iuka ∎ 1862 ∎ American Civil War (Western Theatre)
While General Braxton Bragg's Confederate army invaded Kentucky through **Munfordville**, he sent General Sterling Price west to capture Iuka, Mississippi. Attacked by a Union force under General William S. Rosecrans, Price had to withdraw. However the hesitant Rosecrans failed to secure a decisive victory and Price was able to fight again a few weeks later at **Corinth, Mississippi** (19 September 1862).

Ivangorod ∎ 1914 ∎ World War I (Eastern Front)
Russian commander Nikolai Ivanov opened his invasion of Silesia by sending Generals Pavel Plehve and Aleksei Evert to storm the Vistula near Ivangorod. Checked by Count Franz Conrad and Victor Dankl, the Russians were reinforced and attacked again. The Austro-German army was forced back through **Radom** but checked the Russians in December at **Limanowa** (11–26 October 1914).

Ivanovatz ∎ 1805 ∎ 1st Serbian Rising
When Serbs led by Kara George seized **Belgrade**, a Turkish relief force advancing from Nish under Hafiz Pasha was blocked by a tiny Serb force at the village of Ivanovatz, near Cuprija. When Kara George arrived with guns and reinforcements, the Turks were driven back to Nish, where the Pasha died of wounds. Twelve

months later they suffered a more serious defeat at **Misar** (18 August 1805).

Ivantelly ∎ 1813 ∎ Napoleonic Wars (Peninsular Campaign)

See **Echalar**

Ivrea ∎ 1800 ∎ French Revolutionary Wars (2nd Coalition)

As he crossed the Alps into northern Italy, Napoleon Bonaparte was delayed by the stubborn little fortress of **Bard**, guarding the St Bernard Pass. While some of his force drove forward to attack the town of Ivrea on the Dora, General Jean Lannes took the fortress by bayonet charge, seizing massive Austrian supplies, as the main French army prepared to advance into the Piedmont (23 May 1800).

Ivry ∎ 1590 ∎ 9th French War of Religion

Henry of Navarre claimed the French throne as Henry IV and mounted a final decisive campaign against the Catholic Holy League, led by Charles, Duke of Mayenne. The two large armies met at Ivry (modern Ivry-La-Battaille) near Evreux, where Huguenot artillery destroyed the Catholics with massive losses, except for Swiss mercenaries who negotiated surrender (14 March 1590).

Ivuna ∎ 1888 ∎ Zulu Rebellion

Facing rebellion by uSuthu Chief Dinuzulu, British under Colonel Henry Stabb moved forward to garrison Ivuna, with Mandlazaki ally Zibhebhu in camp at nearby Nduna. Advancing with perhaps 3,000 men, Dinuzulu routed Zibhebhu (who he had beaten in 1884 at **Tshaneni**). Following a previous government loss at **Ceza**, the troops abandoned Ivuna and withdrew to Nkonjeni (23 June 1888).

Ivy Mountain ∎ 1861 ∎ American Civil War (Western Theatre)

Confederate General John S. Williams was withdrawing towards Virginia after campaigning in eastern Kentucky, when he was met at Ivy Mountain, northeast of Pikeville, by Union forces under General William Nelson and Colonel Joshua W. Sill. Williams lost over 200 casualties in a confused action, though he was able to continue southeast into Virginia (8–9 November 1861).

Iwo Jima ∎ 1945 ∎ World War II (Pacific)

Advancing north from the **Mariana Islands**, General Harry Schmidt landed over 100,000 men on Iwo Jima, just 650 miles from Tokyo. Brutal action saw the garrison of 23,000 under General Tadamichi Kuribayashi annihilated at a cost of almost 7,000 Americans killed and 18,000 wounded. The island provided vital airfields to support the bombing of Japan (19 February–10 March 1945).

Izmail ∎ 1790 ∎ Catherine the Great's 2nd Turkish War

Driving deep into Turkish territory after **Focsani** and **Rimnik**, Russian General Paul Potemkin besieged the fortress of Izmail at the mouth of the Danube. After months of inaction, General Alexander Suvorov arrived and took the city by storm. The bloody fall of Izmail and the massacre which followed are said to have cost over 50,000 Turkish dead (March–22 December 1790).

Izmir ∎ 1344 ∎ Later Crusader-Muslim Wars

See **Smyrna**

Izmir ∎ 1402 ∎ Conquests of Tamerlane

See **Smyrna**

Izmir ∎ 1922 ∎ 2nd Greco-Turkish War

See **Smyrna**

Izúcar de Matamoros ∎ 1847 ∎ American-Mexican War

American General Joseph Lane relieved the siege of **Puebla**, then beat General Joaquin Rea at **Atlixco** (19 October) and pursued his guerrillas through defeat at Tlaxcala to Izúcar de Matamoros, 35 miles southwest of Puebla. Rea was defeated again, with heavy losses in supplies and ammunition and, by early the next year, the Mexican guerrilla campaign was effectively over (23 November 1847).

J

Jabani ▮ 1500 ▮ Persian-Turkoman Wars

Leading a fresh campaign against Shirvan (modern Azerbaijan), Sheikh Ismail of Ardabil in northern Iran attacked Shah Farrukh Yasar, who had killed Ismail's father in battle at **Dartanat** 12 years earlier. At Jabani, near Shemakha, 70 miles west of Baku, Ismail defeated and killed Farrukh Yasar, then defeated the Shirvan-Shah's Turkoman allies at **Sharur** and **Hamadan** (December 1500).

Jackson, Mississippi ▮ 1863 ▮ American Civil War (Western Theatre)

In support of the siege of **Vicksburg**, on the Mississippi, Union commander Ulysses S. Grant, with Generals William T. Sherman and James B. McPherson, attacked to the east at Jackson, defended by Generals Josiah E. Johnston and John Gregg. Fighting a rearguard action, the Confederates were forced to evacuate. Sherman soon won again further west at **Champion Hill** (14 May 1863).

Jackson, Tennessee ▮ 1862 ▮ American Civil War (Western Theatre)

On campaign in western Tennessee, Confederate General Nathan Bedford Forrest defeated Union cavalry Colonel Robert G. Ingersoll at Lexington, then next day met Colonel Adolph Englemann further west at Jackson. Although Englemann drove off the Confederates, Forrest continued operating to the north before withdrawing through **Parker's Cross Roads** (19 December 1862).

Jacobovo ▮ 1812 ▮ Napoleonic Wars (Russian Campaign)

As Napoleon Bonaparte advanced into Russia, his left wing led by Marshal Nicolas Oudinot was unexpectedly attacked by Russians under Prince Ludwig Wittgenstein close to Jacobovo, on the Nischtscha near Polotsk. Oudinot made a fighting withdrawal to **Polotsk**, where he was reinforced for a renewed action against Wittgenstein three weeks later (30 July–1 August 1812).

Jacob's Ford ▮ 1157 ▮ Crusader-Muslim Wars

See **Mallaha**

Jadar ▮ 1914 ▮ World War I (Balkan Front)

See **Cer**

Jaen ▮ 1810 ▮ Napoleonic Wars (Peninsular Campaign)

King Joseph Napoleon won at **Ocaña** in late 1809, then invaded Andalusia and defeated Spanish General Carlos Areizaga in the mountains north of the Guadalquivir around **La Carolina**. Pursuing the survivors across the river, General Francois Sébastiani finally dispersed them in a sharp action at Jaen in northern Granada, then marched west to take Cordova next day (23 February 1810).

Jaffa ▮ 1192 ▮ 3rd Crusade

See **Joppa**

Jaffa ▮ 1772–1773 ▮ Mamluk-Ottoman Wars

Driven out of **Cairo** by his former lieutenant Abu'l-Dhahab, the Great Mamluk Ali Bey fled to his ally Shayk Zahir al-Umar of Acre and supported his siege of Ottoman Jaffa, which held out despite a Russian naval bombardment (6 August). While Abu'l Dhahab sent four ships with supplies, the city was finally starved into surrender. It was retaken two years later (July 1772–17 February 1773).

Jaffa ▮ 1775 ▮ Mamluk Wars

Having defeated his former commander Ali Bey in Egypt at **Salihiyya** (1 May 1773), the Mamluk Abu'l-Dhahab, with Ottoman support, marched against one-time ally Shayk Zahir al-Umar in Palestine. Abu'l Dhahab besieged and captured Jaffa, followed by a terrible massacre. He then died while besieging Acre (8 June) and his lieutenant Murad Bey led the army home (29 May 1775).

Jaffa ▮ 1799 ▮ French Revolutionary Wars (Middle East)

Napoleon Bonaparte marched from Egypt into Syria, where he defeated Mamluks and Albanians at **El Arish** in February before besieging Jaffa. Bonaparte took the coastal city by storm, though a subsequent massacre of about 3,000 prisoners was a notorious stain on his record. He then went north to besiege **Acre** but was repulsed by disease and heavy battle losses (4–7 March 1799).

Jaffa ▮ 1948 ▮ Israeli War of Independence

With **Haifa** secured, Zionist forces moved against Jaffa, the port for Tel Aviv, the largest city in Palestine at that time. British General Sir Gordon MacMillan attempted to position troops to halt the advance, but the Arab population fled. After some sharp fighting and a tense confrontation, Jaffa surrendered the day before the creation of the State of Israel (25 April–13 May 1948).

Jaffna ▮ 1619 ▮ Later Portuguese Colonial Wars

Following the death of Portuguese puppet King Ethirimanna Cinkam of Jaffna in northern Ceylon—established after victory at **Mannar** in 1591—his nephew Cankili Kumara seized power and secured aid from Calicut. A Portuguese expedition from Colombo under Filipe de Oliveira drove off a fleet from Calicut, then defeated and captured Cankili, ending the Kingdom of Jaffna.

Jagaraga ▮ 1848 ▮ Dutch Conquest of Bali

Facing renewed resistance in northern Bali, previously put down in 1846 at **Singaraja**, a fresh Dutch expedition was launched against the young Prince Gusti Ketut Jelantik of Belelung. Lured into pursuing the Balinese to an inland fort at Jagaraga, the over-confident Dutch lost more than 200 men killed and withdrew. They returned to **Jagaraga** a year later with a much larger force (June 1848).

Jagaraga ▮ 1849 ▮ Dutch Conquest of Bali

To avenge a humiliating defeat by Balinese troops at **Jagaraga**, Dutch administrators in Java gathered a force of over 8,000 men and returned to the Kingdom of Buleleng, where Prince Gusti Ketut Jelantik was killed in the defeat of his army at Jagaraga, southeast of **Singaraja**. The Raja of Buleleng again sued for peace, giving the Netherlands control of the northern coast of Bali (16 August 1849).

Jagdalak (1st) ▮ 1842 ▮ 1st British-Afghan War

With Amir Dost Muhammad of Afghanistan deposed following defeat at **Ghazni** in 1839, his son Akbar Khan later besieged the British in **Kabul**, forcing their surrender in return for free passage. Passing through the Khurd-Kabul Pass to Jagdalak and Gandamak, General William Elphinstone's commander and its followers were massacred. Only one survivor reached **Jalalabad** (12–13 January 1842).

Jagdalak (2nd) ▮ 1842 ▮ 1st British-Afghan War

Marching back into Afghanistan to punish Akbar Khan for his massacre of British soldiers and civilians from **Kabul**, General Sir George Pollock's Army of Retribution captured Gandamak, then advanced against about 4,000 Ghilzais above Jagdalak, east of the Khyber Pass. A disciplined attack defeated and scattered the Afghans and Pollock marched towards **Tezin** (8 September 1842).

Jagdispur ▮ 1857 ▮ Indian Mutiny

Rebel leader Kunwar Singh withdrew southwest from defeat at **Arrah** (3 August) to his hereditary stronghold at Jagdispur, west of Patna, where he attempted to block the pursuing forces of Major Vincent Eyre. Taking a defensive position with 3,000 men just outside Jagdispur near the village of Dullaur, Kunwar Singh was defeated and fled and Eyre took the town (12 August 1857).

Jagdispur (1st) ▮ 1858 ▮ Indian Mutiny

Defeated at **Azamgarh** and **Maniar**, rebel leader Kunwar Singh reached Jagdispur, east of Patna, to join his brother Amar. A British force which advanced from Arrah under Captain Arthur Le Grand to intercept the rebel was defeated in a confused jungle action, with 130 killed, including Le Grand. Kunwar died three days later of wounds, apparently suffered at Maniar (23 April 1858).

Jagdispur (2nd) ▮ 1858 ▮ Indian Mutiny

When rebel leader Kunwar Singh died of wounds after the victory at Jagdispur, his brother Amar Singh advancing towards Arrah was intercepted near Jagdispur by General Sir Edward Lugard. Amar Singh was defeated and driven off and Lugard occupied Jagdispur next day. He then drove the defeated rebels from the jungle to the west and south with victory at **Dalippur** (9 May 1858).

Jahazi ▮ 1889 ▮ German Colonial Wars in Africa

See **Bagamoyo**

Jahrah ▮ 1920 ▮ Saudi-Kuwait War

During border war between Abd al-Aziz (Ibn Saud) of Riyadh and Salim ibn Mubarak of Kuwait, Faisal al-Dawish and his Ikhwan warriors won at **Hamad**, then advanced north on Jahrah, 20 miles west of Kuwait town. In a famous defence, Salim held the town despite heavy losses. After British intervention, Aziz made peace and turned on his old Rashidi foes at **Hail** (October 1920).

Jaitak ▮ 1814–1815 ▮ British-Gurkha War

British forces north of Chandigarh were repulsed by Gurkha General Amar Singh Thapa at **Mangu**, while further east near Nahan his son Ranjor Singh held the fortress of Jaitak against General Gabriel Martindell. After costly assaults and failing to secure the blockade, Martindell was dismissed. However, defeat at **Malaon** finally led Ranjor Singh to surrender (26 December 1814–21 May 1815).

Jaitpur ▮ 1729 ▮ Later Mughal-Maratha Wars

While Maratha forces were seizing Malwa after **Amjhera** (November 1728), Peshwa Baji Rao I marched to aid King Chhatrasal of Bundelkhand against Mughal General Muhammad Khan Bangash of Allahabad. Near Jaitpur, east of Jhansi, Muhammad Khan was defeated, along with his son Qaim Khan arriving with reinforcements, which secured Bundelkhand against the empire (18 April 1729).

Jajau ▮ 1707 ▮ Mughal Wars of Succession

As the Mughal Empire declined following the death of Aurangzeb, his eldest son Muazim (known as Shah Alam) returned from Afghanistan to claim the throne. At Jajau near Agra, he defeated and killed the second son, Prince Azam and took the throne as Emperor Bahadur Shah. Eighteen months later he defeated and killed his other brother Kambakhsh at **Hyderabad** (12 June 1707).

Jajce ▮ 1464 ▮ Turkish-Hungarian Wars

On a fresh offensive into Bosnia, Ottoman Sultan Mehmed II took 30,000 men and a huge siege train against Emrich of Zapolya defending the strategic fortress of Jajce (Yaytse), south of Banyaluka. Despite massive mining and bombardment, the final Turkish assault was heavily repulsed. With King Mathias of Hungary approaching, Mehmed then abandoned the siege (10 July–24 August 1464).

Jakarta I 1619 I Early Dutch Wars in the East Indies

Driven off by the British at **Bantam** in western Java, Dutch Governor Jan Pieterszoon Coen withdrew to the Moluccas, then returned with 16 ships and 1,200 men to attack the Prince of Jakarta, who was besieging the Dutch fortress east of Bantam, near Jakarta. Following a bloody assault and massacre, Jakarta was destroyed and the Dutch built the new city of **Batavia** (28–30 May 1619).

Jalalabad I 1710 I Mughal-Sikh Wars

Banda Singh Bahadur resolved to recover a large number of Sikh prisoners and marched against Jalalabad, south of Sarahanpur, held by local Mughal ruler Jalal Khan and a Pathan army. After a terrible four-day battle, the Pathans withdrew into the city. Facing strong walls and the onset of the rains, Banda raised his siege. Soon afterwards the Sikh prisoners were all killed (July 1710).

Jalalabad I 1841–1842 I 1st British-Afghan War

After capturing Jalalabad, east of the Khyber, General Sir Robert Sale held off up to 6,000 Afghans under Akbar Khan, son of deposed Amir Dost Muhammad. A brilliant counterattack against Akbar Khan's camp finally defeated and repulsed the Afghans, though Brigadier William Dennie was killed. General Sir George Pollock's force arrived a week later (13 November 1841–7 April 1842).

Jalalabad I 1989 I Afghan Civil War

Soon after the withdrawal of Soviet ground troops from Afghanistan, Mujahaden forces under Gulbuddin Hekmatyar attacked Jalalabad, held for the Russian-backed Kabul government by Chief of Staff General Assef Delawar. After a ten-week siege, Russian air attack forced the Mujahaden to withdraw. Jalalabad was not captured until **Kabul** fell in April 1992 (March–April 1989).

Jalandhar I 1298 I Mongol Invasions of India

A claimed 100,000 Mongols under the leader Kadar invaded northern India, where they marched against Ala-ud-dun, Sultan of Dehli. Southeast of Lahore at Jalandhar (modern Jullundur), the Mongols were heavily defeated by the Sultan's Generals Ulugh Khan and Zafar Khan and withdrew. An even larger Mongol invasion was defeated a year later at **Kili** (5 February 1298).

Jalna I 1679 I Mughal-Maratha Wars

See **Samgamner**

Jalula I 637 I Muslim Conquest of Iraq

After Persian disaster at **Qadisiyya** and **Madain**, Khurrazad and Mihran determined to hold Jalula, near modern Baghdad, against a large Muslim siege by Hashim ibn Utbah. With Persia routed in terrible defeat, conquest of Mesopotamian Iraq was virtually complete. Caliph Omar then regrouped before advancing into the Persian highlands for victory at **Nehavend** in 641(April–October 637).

Jamaica I 1655 I Anglo-Spanish Wars

English Admiral Sir William Penn failed in an assault on Spain's West Indian colony of **Santo Domingo** in April, then took his fleet and troops under Colonel Robert Venables against Jamaica, where they landed after a brief bombardment. The main fortress surrendered next day and the island was soon conquered, remaining a British possession until independence in 1962 (10–17 May 1655).

James Island I 1862 I American Civil War (Lower Seaboard)

See **Secessionville**

Jameson Raid I 1896 I Jameson's Raid
  See **Krugersdorp**

Jamestown I 1622 I Powhatan Indian Wars
  When white settlers in Virginia executed an Indian accused of murder, Opechancanough, leader of the Algonquin confederation founded by his later brother Powhatan, led a surprise attack on Jamestown. The raid killed 347, including 68 women and children, representing almost one in ten of the population of the young colony. The settlers struck back in 1625 at **Pamunkey** (22 March 1622).

Jamestown I 1676 I Bacon's Rebellion
  Amid virtual civil war in colonial Virginia, Nathaniel Bacon was declared a rebel after an unauthorised attack on Indians at **Occaneechee Island**. Marching with 500 men against Jamestown, Bacon defeated the forces of Governor Sir William Berkeley, then burned the Virginian capital. He died soon afterwards and Berkeley was later recalled after hanging many rebels (18 September 1676).

Jamestown Ford I 1781 I War of the American Revolution
  Withdrawing through Virginia, British commander General Charles Earl Cornwallis ambushed part of Marquis Marie de Lafayette's army under General Anthony Wayne at Jamestown Ford on the James near Green Spring. Very hard fighting cost heavy casualties before Wayne eventually counter-attacked and withdrew. Earl Cornwallis marched on to New York and later **Yorktown** (6 July 1781).

Jamkhed I 1560 I Wars of the Deccan Sultanates
  When Husain Nizam Shah of Ahmadnagar invaded Bijapur, Ali Adil Shah of Bijapur fled to Hindu Vijayanagar, where King Rama Raya joined forces with Ibrahim Qutb Shah of Golconda. The allies advanced on Ahmadnagar and to the southeast at Jamkhed, Nizam Shah was defeated and sued for peace. Ibrahim later supported a fresh offensive by Husain and was defeated at **Kondavidu**.

Jammu I 1712 I Mughal-Sikh Wars
  After Banda Singh Bahadur ambushed and killed the Mughal leader Shams Khan (June 1711), he was defeated at Parsur near Sialkot by Mughal General Muhammad Amin Khan who pursued the Sikh north to Jammu. Banda was heavily defeated in a large-scale attack (with a reported 500 Sikh heads sent to Lahore), though he later counter-attacked to besiege Sadhaura (22 January 1712).

Jamrud I 1738 I Persian Invasion of India
  At the peak of Persian expansion, Emperor Nadir Shah captured Afghanistan and took 50,000 men into India via the Tsatsobi Pass, bypassing a Mughal Governor of **Kabul** at the Khyber Pass. Taking the Indians in the rear near Jamrud, the Persians inflicted a costly defeat, then took Peshawar and Lahore before advancing on Delhi for decisive battle at **Karnal** in February (26 November 1738).

Jamrud I 1837 I Afghan-Sikh Wars
  Following Sikh annexation of **Peshawar** in 1834, General Hari Singh built a strong fortress at the mouth of the Khyber Pass at Jamrud. Attempting to recover Peshawar, Dost Muhammad of Kabul sent his son Muhammad Akbar Khan, who was defeated outside Jamrud. Though Hari Singh was killed, the Sikh garrison held out and Akbar raised the siege and withdrew (30 April 1837).

Jand I 1218 I Conquests of Genghis Khan
  As the Mongol Genghis Khan prepared his offensive against the Khwarezmian Empire, his son Juchi and General Subetai pursued their old rivals the Merkit into Kazakhstan. East of the Aral Sea, they met Sultan Muhammad II of Khwarezm advancing from Jand (near modern Kzyl-Ordu) on the Syr Darya. Following a bloody but indecisive action, Muhammad withdrew to **Samarkand**.

Jankau I 1645 I Thirty Years War (Franco-Habsburg War)

Swedish Marshal Lennart Torstensson advancing from the Elbe was intercepted southwest of Prague at Jankau, near Tabor, by a Bavarian-Austrian army under Generals Melchior Hatzfeld and Johann van Werth. In a brilliant Swedish victory—with Hatzfeld captured and Count Johann von Gotz killed—the Bavarian army was routed and Torstensson briefly threatened Vienna itself (5 March 1645).

Jannina I 1912–1913 I 1st Balkan War

With Thessalonica in Turkish Macedonia secured, Greek General Constantine Sapountzakis advanced to besiege Jannina, where he lost many men in costly assaults on surrounding forts, including **Bizani**. Prince Constantine then arrived to rebuild his force. A massive bombardment and assault finally forced Essad Pasha to surrender the city (12 December 1912–5 March 1913).

Jannitsa I 1912 I 1st Balkan War

Turkish forces withdrawing from defeat at **Sarandáporon** made a stand at Jannista (modern Yenitsá) to block Prince Constantine of **Greece**, northwest of Thessalonica. His advance units were checked, but a major assault next day threw the Turks back. A week later, Hassan Taksin Pasha surrendered Thessalonica, along with 25,000 men, 70 guns and munitions (1–2 November 1912).

Janos Massacre I 1851 I Apache Indian Wars

Mexican Colonel José Maria Carrasco and 400 soldiers crossed from Sonora into Chihuahua in northern Mexico, where they attacked the Chiricahua Apache camp of Mangas Coloradas at Janos on the Rio de Casas, while the warriors were away hunting. About 30 Indians were killed with others kidnapped and enslaved. The Apache were avenged a year later in an attack further west at **Arizpe** (5 March 1851).

Janowiec I 1606 I Zebrzydowski's Rebellion

When Sigismund III of Poland tried to increase Royal power, he was opposed by nobles led by Mikolaj Zebrzydowski, Palatine of Cracow. Facing civil war, the King sent his army against the rebels and after a confrontation at Janowiec, on the Vistula west of Lublin, the insurrectionists were pardoned on condition of allegiance. They renewed rebellion next year and were routed at **Guzów** (October 1606).

Janvilliers I 1814 I Napoleonic Wars (French Campaign)

See **Vauchamps**

Jaomodo I 1696 I Chinese-Mongol Wars

Following action against the Qing at **Ulan Butong** (1690), Galdan of the Zunghar Mongols again moved east and the Kangxi Emperor led a massive converging offensive across the Gobi. North of the Kerulen at Jaomodo, Galdan suffered a terrible defeat and died the following year. Victory stabilised China's northern border until a fresh Chinese offensive ended in 1731 at **Hoton Nor** (12 June 1696).

Japan Sea I 1904 I Russo-Japanese War

See **Ulsan**

Jarama I 1937 I Spanish Civil War

Stalemated north of Madrid at **Corunna Road**, Nationalist Generals Luis Orgaz and José Varela tried a fresh attack southeast of the capital in the Jarama Valley. Republicans under General Sebastián Pozas and later General José Miaja fell back after heavy losses on both sides, but finally held the line. In March they checked the Nationalists again at **Guadalajara** (6–27 February 1937).

Jarbuiyah I 1920 I Iraqi Revolt

Smarting from defeat at **Rustumiyah** (24 July), British General Frank Coningham was ordered to evacuate Diwaniyah and withdraw north to **Hillah**, south of Baghdad. Repairing the railway as he went, Coningham met a strong Arab force attempting to hold the bridge at Jarbuiyah. They were driven off with heavy losses and his large rail convoy reached Hillah two days later (5 August 1920).

Jargeau I 1429 I Hundred Years War

William de la Pole Earl of Suffolk was defeated and driven off from the long English siege of **Orleans** and withdrew east to nearby Jargeau, captured the previous October by his brother Sir John de la Pole. However, Suffolk was forced to surrender the city to besieging French forces under Jeanne d'Arc and Jean Duke of Alencon. He and his brother were taken prisoner (12 June 1429).

Jarnac I 1569 I 3rd French War of Religion

When Catherine de Medici attempted to arrest Huguenot leaders Louis I de Bourbon Prince of Condé and Admiral Gaspard de Coligny, the flimsy peace failed and Henry of Anjou led a large Catholic army into the field. At Jarnac, near the Charente, Henry and Marshal Gaspard de Tavannes surprised and defeated the Protestants. Condé was taken prisoner and murdered (13 March 1569).

Jarrab I 1915 I Saudi-Rashidi Wars
See **Jirab**

Jarville I 1477 I Burgundian-Swiss War
See **Nancy**

Jasini I 1915 I World War I (African Colonial Theatre)

Following British disaster at **Tanga**, General Michael Tighe in Mombasa sent a force, which occupied Jasini, just inside German East Africa (25 December 1914). The Anglo-Indian garrison later repulsed German Colonel Paul von Lettow-Vorbeck, but had to surrender after a second determined German assault. A relief column arrived just hours too late and was driven off (12–19 January 1915).

Jask I 1620 I Anglo-Portuguese Colonial Wars

To help protect trade in the Persian Gulf, four British ships met Portuguese Admiral Rui Freire de Andrade near Jask, east of Hormuz. The Portuguese withdrew after an indecisive first action, but in a second battle Andrade was badly defeated (though British commander Andrew Shilling was fatally wounded). Two years later, British and Persian forces attacked **Hormuz** (17 & 28 December 1620).

Jasmund I 1676 I Scania War

When Christian V of Denmark sided with the Netherlands against France and her ally Sweden, the brilliant Danish Admiral Niels Juel sailed against a 30-strong Swedish fleet off Jasmund, near Rügen, where the inexperienced Swedish Admiral Lorenz Creutz was defeated. Despite Danish defeats on land, within a year Juel achieved further naval victories at **Oland** and **Koge** (25 May 1676).

Jasna Gora I 1655 I 1st Northern War

After Charles X of Sweden captured **Warsaw** and **Cracow**, General Burkhardt Müller was blocked further west at the Pauline monastery of Jasna Gora at Czestochowa, held by Prior Augustin Kordecki, with Stefan Zamoiski and Pyotr Czarniecki. Charles withdrew after a brave defence, which rallied Polish resistance, but in 1657 he returned to retake Warsaw (18 November–24 December 1655).

Jassy I 1620 I Polish-Turkish Wars

Intervening to support a revolt by Gaspar Graziani of Moldavia, Poland sent veteran Hetman Stanislas Zolkiewski and Polish regulars to join Cossacks and Moldavians to defeat a Turk-Tatar force on the Pruth at Jassy (modern Iasi, Romania). Zolkiewski's allies abandoned him after the victory and an Ottoman army under Osman II pursued the Poles north to defeat at **Cecora** (20 September 1620).

Jassy-Kishinev I 1944 I World War II (Eastern Front)

Russian Generals Rodion Malinovksy and Fedor Tolbukhin cleared the southern Ukraine, then advanced on Romania, attacking Germans and Romanians under General Johannes Freissner along the Dniester between Jassy and Kishinev. When the Russians broke through, Romania changed sides and German forces began to withdraw from the **Balkans** (20–30 August 1944).

Játiva I 1707 I War of the Spanish Succession

Franco-Spanish commander Marshal James Duke of Berwick advanced from victory at **Almanza** and sent Claude-Francois Bidal Chevalier d'Asfeld to besiege Játiva, southwest of Valencia. When the town fell by storm, the English garrison held out in the citadel before capitulating. Játiva was sacked and razed, its destruction symbolising suppression of rebellion in Valencia (5–24 May 1707).

Jaunpur I 1858 I Indian Mutiny

Marching southeast from Lucknow to relieve besieged **Azamgarh**, General Sir Edward Lugard was blocked just northwest of Jaunpur at the village of Tigra by 3,000 rebels under Ghulaum Husain. Despite exhaustion from marching in intense heat, the British attacked at once. The rebels were routed and fled, leaving 80 dead, while Lugard continued on to relieve **Azamgarh** (10 April 1858).

Java I 1293 I Mongol Wars of Kubilai Khan

See **Singhasari**

Java I 1941–1942 I World War II (Pacific)

See **East Indies**

Java Sea I 1942 I World War II (Pacific)

After the Japanese victory in **Lombok Strait** in the **East Indies**, a large invasion force for Java under Admiral Takeo Takagi was met in the Java Sea by an Australian, British, Dutch and American force under Admiral Karel Doorman. Two Allied cruisers and four destroyers were sunk, with Doorman lost. Just days later, the surviving cruisers were sunk in the **Sunda Strait** (27 February 1942).

Jawra Alipur I 1858 I Indian Mutiny

The same day as the capture of **Gwalior** by General Sir Hugh Rose, General Robert Napier and 600 men marched west to nearby Jawra Alipur, where he intercepted Tantia Topi, with the remains of his army defeated at **Morar** and survivors from Gwalior. Enfiladed by artillery, the rebels broke and fled before Napier's cavalry charge, abandoning 25 guns and massive military stores (20 June 1858).

Jaxartes I 329 BC I Conquests of Alexander the Great

Alexander the Great defeated Persia at **Gaugamela** (331 BC), then invaded Turkestan and advanced east to the Jaxartes (Sir Darya), where he founded Alexandria/Khojent (modern Leninabad). Threatened by Turkoman Scythians, Alexander stormed over the river and inflicted a heavy defeat. He then returned to Samarkand to repulse Spitamenes of Sogdia and in 327 BC captured the **Sogdian Rock**.

Jazmin I 1876 I Diaz Revolt in Mexico

Early in a new rising against President Sebastián Lerdo de Tejada, 4,000 rebels in **Oaxaca** led by General Fidencio Hernandez attacked 1,000 Federal troops under General Ignacio Alatorre at Cerro del Jazmin, south of Puebla. Alatorre withdrew to nearby Yanhuitlan, where the rebels were routed with losses for the day of about 900. He won again in May at **San Juan Epatlán** (18 February 1876).

Jebel Akhdar I 1958 I Imam Revolt

Omani rebel Talib ibn Ali recovered from defeat at **Rustaq** in 1955 and returned from exile to help his brother Imam Ghalib renew rebellion against Sultan Said ibn Taymur. Responding to an appeal for military aid, a British SAS battalion arrived to attack the rebels cornered on the Jebel Akhdar plateau, southwest of Muscat. After fierce fighting, the stronghold fell and the rebels fled (January 1959).

Jebel Akhdar I 1971 I Dhofar War

After prolonged leftist rebellion in southern Oman's Dhofar, new Sultan Qabus ibn Said sought additional British aid and an SAS battalion and local forces under Colonel Johnny Watts advanced onto the precipitous Jebel Akhdar plateau. Attacking against very well-armed guerrillas, the Allies finally took the Jebel after costly losses on both sides and the rebels withdrew (October 1971).

Jebel Libni ∎ 1967 ∎ Arab-Israeli Six Day War

As Israelis on the coast attacked **Rafa**, further inland, General Avraham Yoffe led his tanks through supposedly impassable soft sand dunes to surprise and defeat Egypt at Bir Lahfan, then advanced on one of the main forward bases in the Sinai at Jebel Libni. A bold night attack routed General Osman Nasser's Egyptians and Yoffe raced southwest to **Mitla Pass** (6 June 1967).

Jeddah ∎ 1916 ∎ World War I (Middle East)

Soon after Sharif Hussein, Emir of Mecca, proclaimed the Arab Revolt against Turkey in the **Hejaz**, he attacked the key Red Sea port of Jeddah. Following a six-day bombardment by British warships offshore, a land assault forced the Turkish garrison to surrender. Jeddah was the first major centre in the Hejaz to fall to Sharifi forces and the port became a major Arab supply base (17 June 1916).

Jeddah ∎ 1925 ∎ Saudi-Hashemite Wars
See **Medina**

Jehol ∎ 1933 ∎ Manchuria Incident
See **Great Wall**

Jemappes ∎ 1792 ∎ French Revolutionary Wars (1st Coalition)

When Archduke Charles of Austria failed at the siege of **Lille** (6 October) he withdrew to winter quarters at Jemappes, west of Mons in the Austrian Netherlands. Defending entrenched positions, his outnumbered Austrians were soon routed by French General Charles-Francois Dumouriez, who marched into Brussels a week later to gain Belgium for the Republic (6 November 1792).

Jemmingen ∎ 1568 ∎ Netherlands War of Independence

Soon after Spanish defeat at **Heiligerlee** at the start of the Netherlands War, Don Fernando Alvarez, Duke of Alva marched into the northern Netherlands and drew Louis of Nassau, brother of William of Orange, into combat at Jemmingen (modern Jemgum) near Emden. The Dutch were utterly routed in a one-sided disaster and Spain crushed the rebellion in Friesland (21 July 1568).

Jena ∎ 1806 ∎ Napoleonic Wars (4th Coalition)

As Napoleon Bonaparte's army converged on Prussia, King Frederick William III divided his force and the greater part was defeated by Marshal Louis Davout at **Auerstadt**. The same day, Bonaparte heavily defeated the smaller Prussian force under Prince Friedrich-Ludwig of Hohenloe, 15 miles south at Jena. The twin defeats virtually knocked Prussia out of the war (14 October 1806).

Jenar ∎ 1751 ∎ Later Dutch Wars in the East Indies

Intervening in a Javanese war of succession, Dutch commander Johan von Hohendorff sent Major Hendrik de Clerq against rebel leader Mangkubumi. Attacked at the Bogowonto River near Jenar, de Clerq's Javanese allies fled and he was killed, with his column virtually destroyed. The Dutch eventually recognised Mangkubumi and gained territory in northern Java (12 December 1751).

Jenin ∎ 1948 ∎ Israeli War of Independence

After failing near **Gesher** (22 May), Iraqi forces regrouped and advanced strongly further south across the Jordan towards Jenin. Met by Israeli Colonel Moshe Carmel, victor of **Haifa**, a major battle developed and the Iraqis brought up reinforcements and aircraft. They were eventually forced to withdraw, though they held positions outside Jenin until the First Truce (28 May–9 June 1948).

Jenin I 1967 I Arab-Israeli Six Day War

On the offensive in the north, Israeli General Elad Peled and tank commander Colonel Moshe Bar-Kochva attacked Jenin, defended by Jordanian Colonel Awad el Khalid and armour led by General Runkun al-Ghazi. Some of the heaviest fighting of the war took place in the southwest around Kabatiya before Jenin fell. The Jews then turned south towards **Nablus** (5–7 June 1967).

Jenipapo I 1823 I Brazilian War of Independence

Facing insurgents in northern Brazil in Piauí, Portuguese Governor, Major João José de Cunha Fidié, marched against rebels at Jenipapo, near Campo Maior, and secured a hard-fought victory. However, Fidié suffered losses he could not replace and had to withdraw west across the Parnaiba to siege at Caixas. He later capitulated (31 July 1823) after the fall of **Salvador** (March 1823).

Jenkins' Ferry I 1864 I American Civil War (Trans-Mississippi)

Union General Frederick Steele marched across Arkansas to capture Camden, then lost men and supplies at **Poison Spring** and **Marks' Mills** and began retreating north through Princeton. On the Saline at Jenkins' Ferry, he drove off repeated Confederate attacks under General E. Kirby Smith, then crossed the River and took his failed expedition back to Little Rock (30 April 1864).

Jerba I 1560 I Turkish-Habsburg Wars
See **Djerba**

Jericho I 1918 I World War I (Middle East)

With **Jerusalem** secured (December 1917), Sir Edmund Allenby sent Australian and New Zealand cavalry under General Charles Cox northeast against Jericho. After storming advanced positions, the horsemen outflanked the entrenchments and attacked from the rear. Jericho quickly fell and a major Turkish counter-offensive in July was repulsed at **Abu Tellul** (19–21 February 1918).

Jericho Mills I 1864 I American Civil War (Eastern Theatre)
See **North Anna**

Jerusalem I 597 BC I Babylon's Wars of Conquest

After driving Egypt from Judah at **Carchemish**, King Nebuchadrezzar of Babylon faced revolt by King Jehoiakim and attacked Jerusalem. When the king died during the siege, his son Jehoiachin surrendered and was deported to Babylon. Nebuchadrezzar appointed Zedekiah as King, but when Zedekiah revolted ten years later, Nebuchadrezzar returned and destroyed Jerusalem (16 March 597 BC).

Jerusalem I 587–586 BC I Babylon's Wars of Conquest

King Zedekiah of Judah revolted against his overlord, Nebuchadrezzar of Babylon who returned to finally settle with Jerusalem. During a long siege Zedekiah escaped, but was captured and blinded. A month later Babylonian General Nebuzaradan stormed the city, which was sacked and burned. The citizens were then deported to Babylon, ending the Kingdom of Judah.

Jerusalem I 70 I Jewish Rising against Rome

As Rome moved to crush rebellion in Judea, General Vespasian was proclaimed Emperor and he left his son, Titus Flavius Vespasianus to lay siege to Jerusalem, which suffered extreme losses through assault and starvation. Titus finally stormed Jersualem, destroying much of the city and massacring its population. Two years later Roman forces besieged **Masada** (May–September 70).

Jerusalem I 614 I Byzantine-Persian Wars

Three years after capturing **Antioch**, Persians under General Shahbaraz advanced along the coast from Ceasarea and besieged Jerusalem. After failed negotiations the city was taken by storm and sacked, with claims of up to 50,000 killed. Patriarch Zacharias and thousands of prisoners were taken to Persia, along with

Rome's most precious relic, a supposed fragment of the True Cross (April–May 614).

Jerusalem ▌ 638 ▌ Muslim Conquest of Syria

With **Damascus** recaptured after his second great victory at the **Yarmuk** in 636, Muslim conqueror Khalid ibn al-Walid, supported by veteran General Abu Obaidah, turned against Jerusalem, the remaining key city. A severe four-month siege, with continuous attacks and counter-attacks, made the Patriarch Sophonius finally surrender the city. Khalid then marched north against **Aleppo**.

Jerusalem ▌ 1098 ▌ 1st Crusade

Fatimid Egyptian Vizier al-Afdal took advantage of a Turkish loss to Crusaders at **Antioch** (December 1097) to move against Suqman ibn Artuq, Amir of Jerusalem, who held out for six weeks against a large-scale siege before yielding the city. Despite defeating the Turks, the Egyptians held Jerusalem for less than a year before losing it to the forces of the First Crusade (July–August 1098).

Jerusalem ▌ 1099 ▌ 1st Crusade

The Crusader army under Godfrey of Bouillon and Raymond of Toulouse advanced from the capture of **Antioch** through Syria to attack Jerusalem, which was defended by a Fatimid garrison under Ala-al-adin. When Jerusalem was taken by storm after a bloody month-long siege, the city's Muslims and Jews were butchered and Godfrey was elected Guardian (7 June–15 July 1099).

Jerusalem ▌ 1187 ▌ 3rd Crusade

Two months after Crusader disaster at **Hattin**, Kurdish-Muslim conqueror Saladin besieged Jerusalem, held by a scratch garrison under Balian of Ibelin. The city surrendered after a two-week siege, but unlike the massacre which followed the Crusader victory in 1099, Saladin accepted ransom for the Christian populace and permitted them to leave (20 September–2 October 1187).

Jerusalem ▌ 1244 ▌ Later Crusader-Muslim Wars

When Emperor Frederick II and his Sixth Crusade returned to Europe, the Kingdom of Jerusalem was weakened by years of civil war and the city was attacked by the Khwarezmian army, previously driven out of Persia by the Mongols. The garrison surrendered after a violent assault and it was not until 1917 that Jerusalem was again captured by a Christian army (11 July–23 August 1244).

Jerusalem ▌ 1917 ▌ World War I (Middle East)

British commander Sir Edmund Allenby drove north along the coast from **Gaza** to seize Jaffa after victory at **Junction Station**, then wheeled northeast to outflank Jerusalem. General Philip Chetwode secured a bloody victory just west of the city on the heights of Nebi-Samweil and Jersualem fell after two days. A Turkish counter-attack two weeks later failed at **Tel el Ful** (9 December 1917).

Jerusalem (1st) ▌ 1948 ▌ Israeli War of Independence

As the British left Jerusalem, Jews under Colonel David Shaltiel seized most of the new city, then attempted to take the old walled city, now reinforced by the Arab Legion under Sir John Glubb. With Jerusalem itself effectively under Arab siege, Jewish troops in the Old Quarter were driven back in fierce house-to-house fighting and were finally forced to surrender (16–28 May 1948).

Jerusalem (2nd) ▌ 1948 ▌ Israeli War of Independence

During the so-called Ten Days Offensive, Jews under Colonel David Shaltiel launched a fresh offensive to regain the Old City on the supposed 2,500th anniversary of the breaching of the walls of Jerusalem by Nebuchadrezzar's Babylonians. Very heavy fighting saw the Jews repulsed by the Arab Legion and Jerusalem remained divided until the Six Day War of 1967 (9–18 July 1948).

Jerusalem ▌ 1967 ▌ Arab-Israeli Six Day War

Opening Jordan's attack on Israel, Brigadier Sherif Zeid Ben Shaker advanced on Jerusalem, where the old city was held by Jordanian Brigadier Ata Ali. Intense fighting developed as Israeli General Uzi Narkiss and Colonel Mordechai Gurr counter-attacked in force. With approaching Arab tanks destroyed by Israeli jets, the Jews stormed and reoccupied the city (5–7 June 1967).

Jerusalem Plank Road ▌ 1864 ▌ American Civil War (Eastern Theatre)

On an offensive against the Weldon Railroad, south of besieged **Petersburg**, Virginia, Union Generals Horatio G. Wright and David B. Birney were met in a counter-attack on the Jerusalem Plank Road by Confederate Generals Ambrose P. Hill and William Mahone. The Union advance was driven off, but fighting on the railroad resumed at **Sappony Church** and **Reams Station** (21–24 June 1864).

Jetersville ▌ 1865 ▌ American Civil War (Eastern Theatre)

See **Amelia Springs**

Jhansi ▌ 1858 ▌ Indian Mutiny

General Sir Hugh Rose marched north from **Sagar** through **Madanpur** to besiege and bombard the mountain fortress city of Jhansi, held by 12,000 rebels under the Rani of Jhansi. Two days after turning to defeat a relief force at the **Betwa**, Rose took the fortress by assault, followed by deadly retribution for an earlier massacre. The Rani escaped to **Kalpi** (21 March–3 April).

Jhelum ▌ 326 BC ▌ Conquests of Alexander the Great

See **Hydaspes**

Jiangkou ▌ 1851 ▌ Taiping Rebellion

On the offensive in Guangxi after losing at **Jintian** (1 January), new Imperial Commissioner Li Xingyuan sent Generals Xiang Rong and Zhou Fengqi against rebel Taiping headquarters at Jiangkou (Chiang-kou), west of Pingnan. The Imperial attack was repulsed with over 1,000 killed. When the rebels later withdrew west, the enraged Xiang Rong sacked and burned the town (February 1851).

Jiangling ▌ 1236 ▌ Mongol Conquest of China

Following the Mongol conquest of northern China, their former Song allies began seizing territory and the Mongol brothers Koten and Kochu, grandsons of Genghis Khan, took a large army into Hubei. On the Yangzi near Jiangling (modern Jingzhou), they were defeated by Song General Meng Hong (who helped capture **Kaifeng** in 1233). The Southern Song were later destroyed by Kubilai.

Jiangsu ▌ 1946 ▌ 3rd Chinese Revolutionary Civil War

Nationalist commander Chiang Kai-shek ended an American-brokered truce by launching the massive Jiangsu (Kiangsu) offensive in northern China against Communist General Chen Yi. With huge superiority in men and equipment, Chiang took major cities including Chengde and Zhangjiakou plus parts of Manchuria, then announced a unilateral ceasefire (10 July–8 November 1946).

Jiankang ▌ 548–549 ▌ Wars of the Six Dynasties

Following the death of Gao Huan of Eastern Wei, General Hou Jing rebelled and handed **Yingchuan** to Western Wei, then turned south across the Yangzi to besiege Jiankang (Chienk'ang, modern Nanjing), capital of Emperor Wudi of Southern Liang. Despite a brave, prolonged defence by Yang Kan, the city finally fell. Hou Jing later made himself Emperor, but was soon driven out and killed.

Jiankang ▌ 589 ▌ Wars of the Six Dynasties

With northern China reunited after the fall of **Taiyuan** (577), the throne was taken by Yangjiang who established the Sui Dynasty, then turned against the ailing Chen Dynasty in the south. A bold land and river offensive converged on the Chen capital Jiankang (Chien-k'ang, modern Nanjing), which fell after heavy fighting. The Sui then reunited north and south after almost four centuries of fragmentation.

Jicaral ∎ 1839 ∎ Central American National Wars

In the break-up of the Central American Federation, Conservative forces from Honduras under Francisco Ferrera, aided by Nicaragua, invaded eastern El Salvador against Liberal President Francisco Morazán. The Allies defeated Morazán at Jicaral, just east of San Miguel. However, the following month to the northwest at **Espiritu Santo** they were defeated and driven out (19 March 1839).

Jicin ∎ 1866 ∎ Seven Weeks War
See **Gitschin**

Jidballi ∎ 1904 ∎ Wars of the Mad Mullah

Capping victory at **Daratoleh** (April 1903), Britain sent a fourth expedition under General Charles Egerton to Somaliland, the largest so far against Muhammad Abdullah Hassan. Decisive action east of Olesan at Jidballi saw the Dervishes driven off then pursued and killed by Somali levies. After a small force stormed his fortress at **Illig** (21 April) the absent Mullah sued for peace (10 January 1904).

Jidda ∎ 1925 ∎ Saudi-Hashemite Wars
See **Medina**

Jieqiao ∎ 191 ∎ Wars of the Three Kingdoms

Amid civil war which led to the fall of the Han, the northern warlord Gongsun Zan advanced to meet his rival Yuan Shao south of the Jie Bridge (Jieqiao) on the Qing River in modern Hebei. Yuan's disciplined vanguard under Qu Yi repulsed Gongsun's cavalry and Yuan won a decisive victory. Gongsun was eventually defeated and committed suicide (199) and in 200 Yuan Shao was stopped at **Guandu**.

Jijelli ∎ 1664 ∎ North African War of Louis XIV

In the war against Barbary pirates, a French squadron led by Francois de Vendome Duke of Beaufort landed and captured the small Algerian port of Jijelli (modern Jijel), on the Gulf of Bougie. Turkish and Arab forces in Algiers made Beaufort beat a hasty withdrawal, though defeats at sea the following year persuaded the Dey of Algiers to make peace with France (22 July 1664).

Jijiga ∎ 1977 ∎ Ogaden War

Somali forces supporting separatist rebels in southeast Ethiopia, crossed into the Ogaden from Hargeisa and advanced on Jijiga, where their initial assault was driven off with heavy losses in men and tanks. Reinforced from **Dire Dawa** they attacked again and the Ethiopian army mutinied and withdrew. The Somalis then advanced west through **Marda** towards **Harer** (August–10 September 1977).

Jijiga ∎ 1978 ∎ Ogaden War

With Somali forces advancing deep into the northern Ogaden, Ethiopia secured a massive airlift of Soviet armour and Cuban troops then relieved **Harer** and **Dire Dawa**, before converging on Jijiga. Attacked on all sides, the Somalis lost perhaps 3,000 killed in severe fighting. Within days President Siad Barre ordered his army withdrawn from Ethiopia, effectively ending the war (3–5 March 1978).

Jilin ∎ 1900 ∎ Russo-Chinese War

Having stormed **Qiqihar** on the Eastern Railway in Manchuria, Russian General Pavel K. Rennenkamp advanced south from Harbin towards Jilin. With just a small force of Cossacks, Rennenkampf took the city, capturing 69 guns and large quantities of arms and ammunition. Resistance in Jilin Province effectively ended and General Chang Shun sued for peace (23 September 1900).

Jiliste ∎ 1574 ∎ Moldavian Rebellion

John the Brave, Prince of Moldavia, refused to pay tribute to Ottoman Constantinople and soon faced an invasion by a local Turkish-Wallachian army. Supported by Cossack troops he surprised and defeated the invaders near Focsani at Jiliste. However, Sultan Selim II then sent a large army which crushed the Moldavian rebellion in June near the mouth of the Danube at **Kagul Lagoon** (April 1574).

Jiluo Mountain | 90 | Wars of the Later Han

With the Northern Xiongnu threatening China's border, Han General Dou Xian took a large Imperial army into Mongolia, supported by his allies, the Southern Xiongnu. In a decisive battle at Jiluo Mountain, southwest of modern Ulaanbaatar, the Northern Xiongnu were routed, with the survivors fleeing west across the Altai Mountains. As a result they virtually ceased to exist as a military power.

Jimo | 279 BC | China's Era of the Warring States

Eastern states led by Yen defeated Qi (Ch'i) to curb its expansion (285 BC) and Yen occupied most of the country except two cities, including Jimo, which held out under virtual siege for six years. Garrison commander Tian Dan led a brilliant counter-attack, using stampeding cattle bearing flames and spears, and the army of Yen was routed and withdrew. The Kingdom of Qi was restored but weakened.

Jinan | 1928 | 2nd Chinese Revolutionary Civil War

As Nationalist forces overcame the warlords of northern China, Japan occupied Jinan (Tsinan) to protect national interests just as the Northerners withdrew. Following Japanese clashes with Chinese troops, Chiang Kai-shek secured order. However, when Chiang withdrew, General Hikouke Fukuda destroyed the remaining garrison and killed many civilians. Japan held Jinan for a year (3–11 May 1928).

Jinan | 1948 | 3rd Chinese Revolutionary Civil War

General Chen Yi continued the Communist offensive in northern China, converging with aid from Liu Bocheng, Chen Geng and Li Xiannian on Jinan (Tsinan) in Shandong, held by General Wang Yaowu. After key Nationalist forces changed sides, the city was taken by bloody assault with 80,000 men captured or defected, leading to the Communist offensive at **Huaihai** (14–24 September 1948).

Jing Luzhen | 1410 | Ming Imperial Wars

A month after destroying Mongol Prince Bunyashiri at the **Onon**, Ming Emperor Yongle pursued the Eastern Mongol Chancellor Arughtai east into the Khingan mountains between Mongolia and Manchuria. Arughtai was defeated in battle near the Chaor River at Jing Luzhen, but he later became a Ming ally. The Emperor returned to Beijing claiming victory over the Mongols (July 1410).

Jingxing | 205 BC | Chu-Han War

Recovering from defeat at **Pengcheng**, Han warlord Liu Bang sent Han Xin against Zhao, where General Chen Yu assembled a large force to defend the strategic gorge at Jingxing (Ching-Hsing). Lured out of their fortified position by a feigned Han withdrawal, the Zhao army suffered a devastating defeat, with King Zhao Xie captured and Chen Yu executed. Liu Bang was later defeated at **Chenggao**.

Jinji | 1648 | Bijapur-Maratha Wars
See **Gingee**

Jinji | 1689–1698 | Mughal-Maratha Wars
See **Gingee**

Jinji | 1750 | 2nd Carnatic War
See **Gingee**

Jintian | 1851 | Taiping Rebellion

Following defeat at Guangxi Province at **Huazhou** (November 1850), Imperial commander Zhou Fengqi sent General Yikebudan against massive Taiping forces gathered at Jintian, near Giuping, where he was killed in the war's first major action. When General Zhou arrived the Taiping withdrew with little loss.

Their leader Hong Xuiquan was then created Heavenly King (1 January 1851).

Jinzhou ▮ 1948 ▮ 3rd Chinese Revolutionary Civil War

Communist General Lin Biao opened the **Liaoshen** offensive in Manchuria by unexpectedly launching his main attack in the south against Jinzhou. A belated relief attempt west from **Mukden** (modern Shenyang) was destroyed and, after weeks of terrible artillery bombardment, General Fan Hanjie surrendered the city and its massive store of supplies (12 September–17 October 1948).

Jirab ▮ 1915 ▮ Saudi-Rashidi Wars

During the struggle for central Arabia, Emir Abd al-Aziz (Ibn Saud) of Riyadh led a claimed 6,000 men against the pro-Turkish Rashid at Jirab, near al-Artawiyah. When their Ajman allies defected, the Saudis suffered a terrible defeat with massive losses, including British observer Captain William Shakespear killed. Later that year Aziz met the Rashid again at **Kinzan** (24 January 1915).

Jiran ▮ 1857 ▮ Indian Mutiny

Marching south from Nimach against Mandasur rebels under Firoz Shah, 400 native troops of Captain Nathaniel B. Tucker's Bombay Light Cavalry attacked Jiran. While Tucker was killed in an early assault, Jiran fell after heavy fighting, although the British were too few to hold it and withdrew. Within a month Firoz Shah failed besieging **Nimach** and was defeated at **Goraria** (23 October 1857).

Jiron ▮ 1829 ▮ Peruvian-Colombian War
See **Tarqui**

Jisr Benat Yakub ▮ 1918 ▮ World War I (Middle East)

As part of the broad Allied offensive after **Megiddo**, the Australian Mounted Division under General Sir Henry Hodgson advanced north around the Sea of Galilee to cross the Upper Jordan near Jisr Benat Yakub. After some bloody resistance, the Turks were driven back.

Engineers repaired the partly demolished bridge and, within days, the Australians were in **Damascus** (28 September 1918).

Jitgargh ▮ 1815 ▮ British-Gurkha War

While British forces attempting to invade southern Nepal were crushed at **Parsa** and Samanpur, further west beyond Kathmandu General John Sullivan Wood advanced towards Palpa. But he was blocked at the mountain pass at Jitgargh, near Butwal, by General Vazir Singh. Although very heavy fighting saw the Gurkhas suffer greater losses, Wood was forced to withdraw (14 January 1815).

Jitra ▮ 1941 ▮ World War II (Pacific)

While Japanese invaders secured **Kota Bharu** in northeast Malaya, General Takuro Matsui advanced in the west towards the key airfields at Alor Star and Sangei Patania. General David Murray-Lyon was ordered to hold a defensive line at Jitra, but after two days of heavy Japanese attacks the British withdrew across the Perak towards **Kampar** (11–13 December 1941).

Jiujiang ▮ 1855 ▮ Taiping Rebellion

Zeng Guofan's Xiang army advanced down the Yangzi through Wuchang to attack Taiping Jiujiang (Kiukiang) held by Lin Qirong, later reinforced by Shi Dakai. Part of Zeng's navy was isolated and destroyed on nearby Lake Poyang and, after Zeng himself was routed in another naval defeat on the river, much of his force withdrew towards **Wuchang** (29 January & 11 February 1855).

Jobito ▮ 1895 ▮ 2nd Cuban War of Independence

Cuban insurgent José Maceo and his brother Antonio continued fighting northwest of Guantánamo, attacking a Spanish column at Jobito. Desperately short of ammunition, José waited until the Spanish had expended their cartridges, then attacked with machetes, killing commander Colonel Joaquin Bosch and many of his men. Antonio Maceo won again in July at **Peralejo** (13 May 1895).

**Jodoigne I 1568 I Netherlands War
of Independence**

Three months after disastrous Dutch defeat at **Jemmingen**, William of Orange withdrew southeast pursued by Spanish forces under Don Fernando Alvarez Duke of Alva. Crossing the Geete near Jodoigne, east of Brussels, William's rearguard suffered a sharp defeat, with Antonius de Lalaing Count Hoogstraaten killed. The Dutch Prince then continued south into France (20 October 1568).

**Jogjakarta I 1948 I Indonesian War
of Independence**

Dutch administrators established a provisional government for Indonesia, then launched a "police action" against Nationalists who had proclaimed independence in western Java. Heavy fighting saw Dutch paratroopers take the rebel capital Jogjakarta, but in the face of international condemnation the Netherlands accepted a ceasefire. Within a year they granted full sovereignty (19 December 1948).

**Johannesburg I 1900 I 2nd Anglo-
Boer War**

See **Doornkop**

**Johnsonville I 1864 I American Civil
War (Western Theatre)**

While Confederate commander John B. Hood prepared to invade Tennessee, cavalry under General Nathan B. Forrest attacked the Union supply depot on the Tennessee at Johnsonville, west of **Nashville**. Despite a courageous defence by Colonel Charles R. Thompson's garrison, Forrest caused massive damage before withdrawing and Hood advanced through **Columbia** (4–5 November 1864).

**Jonesborough I 1864 I American Civil
War (Western Theatre)**

With **Atlanta**, Georgia, virtually besieged, Union commander William T. Sherman took a large force against railroads south of the city, where he was met at Jonesborough by Confederate General William J. Hardee. Heavily outnumbered, Hardee suffered a decisive defeat and, the following night, Confederate commander John B. Hood evacuated Atlanta (31 August–1 September 1864).

**Jones Creek I 1824 I Karankawa
Indian War**

When Texas settlers on the Lower Brazos River were attacked by Karankawa Indians, Captain Randal Jones led a local militia force and attacked their camp near modern Freeport at what later became known as Jones Creek. In a sharp action, supported by the eccentric Captain James Bailey, the Indians lost 15 killed and withdrew across the San Bernard (22 June 1824).

**Jonkowo I 1807 I Napoleonic Wars
(4th Coalition)**

See **Bergfriede**

Joppa I 1102 I Crusader-Muslim Wars

Days after escaping the Crusader disaster at **Ramleh**, Baldwin I of Jerusalem rallied support against Fatimid commander Sharaf al-Maali, who was now besieging Joppa (modern Jaffa). Reinforced by European Crusaders, who arrived through the Egyptian naval blockade, the King led a major offensive against the Egyptian and Sudanese army and drove it back towards Ascalon (27 May 1102).

Joppa I 1192 I 3rd Crusade

Richard I of England withdrew from his failed advance on Jerusalem and took a small force by sea to relieve Saladin's siege of Joppa (modern Jaffa). Landing against powerful opposition, Richard held off the Muslims until reinforcements overland from Acre helped regain the city. Sultan Saladin then agreed to a five-year truce allowing pilgrims access to Jerusalem (August 1192).

Joppa I 1198 I 4th Crusade

Regrouping a year after defeat at **Sidon**, Sultan al-Adil Saif al-Din attacked the German garrison at Joppa (modern Jaffa) and Henry

Duke of Saxony was killed repulsing the first attack. A fresh Muslim assault during the Feast of St Martin stormed the city and massacred the inhabitants. However, when Emperor Henry V died in Germany, the "German Crusade" returned home (11 November 1198).

Jotapata I 67 I Jewish Rising against Rome

Faced by a Jewish rising in Judea, which destroyed a Roman Legion at **Beth Horon**, General Vespasian besieged the steep mountain city of Jotapata, north of Sepphoris. Vespasian stormed the fortress after a bloody 47-day siege and massacred the inhabitants. Most survivors committed suicide, though rebel leader Josephus (the future historian) escaped and later supported the Roman cause.

Jucar I 75 BC I Sertorian War
See **Sucro**

Jugdespore I 1857 I Indian Mutiny
See **Jagdispur**

Jugdulluk I 1842 I 1st British-Afghan War
See **Jagdalak**

Jujuy I 1821 I Argentine War of Independence

Spanish General Pedro Antonio Olañeta resolved to regain the initiative and advanced into northwestern Argentina, where the Royalist vanguard under his brother-in-law Guilllermo Marquigui marched against Jujuy, defended by Governor Ignacio Gorriti of Salta. In the so-called "Great Day of Jujuy," Marquigui was surprised and routed. Olañeta was killed in 1825 at **Tumusla** (27 April 1821).

Julesburg I 1865 I Cheyenne-Arapaho Indian War

Responding to the **Sand Creek Massacre** in November, about 1,000 Cheyenne and Arapaho marched on Julesburg on the South Platte in northern Colorado. Captain Nick O'Brien from nearby Camp Rankin was ambushed with 14

killed and the town was sacked. Eluding General Robert Mitchell, the Indians attacked again and burned Julesburg before withdrawing north (7 January & 2 February 1865).

Julian's Defeat I 363 I Later Roman-Persian Wars
See **Ctesiphon**

Jullundur I 1710 I Mughal-Sikh Wars
See **Rahon**

Julu I 207 BC I Fall of the Qin Dynasty

As rebel forces weakened the Qin (Ch'in) Dynasty, Qin General Zhang Han was sent to recover lost territory in the east. Stalled at the siege of rebel-held Julu (Chü-lu) in Zhao, he was attacked by the commanding warlord Xiang Yu. The Imperial army suffered a terrible and decisive defeat and Xiang Yu later executed thousands of prisoners. The fall of the capital **Xianyang** ended the brief Qin Dynasty.

Juncal I 1827 I Argentine-Brazilian War

When Argentina declared war on Brazil in support of Uruguay, Brazil's attempt to blockade the Rio de la Plata was driven off at **Quilmes** (July 1826). Captain Jacinto Roque de Sena Pereira later renewed the attempt and was met at Juncal, near Martín García, by Patriot Admiral William Brown. The Imperial ships were heavily defeated and later incorporated into Brown's fleet (8–9 February 1827).

Junction City I 1967 I Vietnam War
See **Suoi Tre**

Junction Station I 1917 I World War I (Middle East)
See **El Mughar**

Jungfernhof I 1700 I 2nd "Great" Northern War

At the start of the war Augustus II, Elector of Saxony, sent General George von Carlowitz into Swedish Livonia to besiege Riga. However, at nearby Jungfernhof, Carlowitz was killed and his Saxons were driven back across the Dvina by veteran Swedish commander Count Erik Dahlberg. The siege of **Riga** was later renewed with Russian support until driven off by Charles XII (May 1700).

Junín ▌ 1824 ▌ Peruvian War of Independence

With Chile secured, Simón Bolívar sent forces into Peru against Viceroy José de la Serna, then joined General Antonio José de Sucre against Spanish General José Canterac at Junín, 100 miles northeast of Lima. A cavalry attack by General William Miller, reputedly without a shot fired, saw Canterac lose 360 killed by lance and sabre. He withdrew to fight again at **Ayacucho** (6 August 1824).

Juno Beach ▌ 1944 ▌ World War II (Western Europe)
See **D-Day**

Jupiter Inlet ▌ 1838 ▌ 2nd Seminole Indian War

Following an Indian ambush on a patrol at the **Loxahatchee** in eastern Florida, near modern Palm Breach, General Thomas Jesup took his main force of regulars and Tennessee volunteers against the Seminole near the Jupiter River. The Indians were driven off in a sharp action, though Jesup was wounded in the face and later yielded command to Colonel Zachary Taylor (24 January 1838).

Juterbog ▌ 1644 ▌ Thirty Years War (Franco-Habsburg War)

The incompetent Count Matthias Gallas was sent to aid Denmark against Sweden, but was outmanoeuvred by Swedish Marshal Lennart Torstensson, who attacked him at Juterbog, 20 miles northeast of Wittenberg. With the Imperial army and its Danish allies overwhelmed, Gallas retreated into Bohemia. Torstensson won again the following year at **Jankau** (23 November 1644).

Juterbog ▌ 1813 ▌ Napoleonic Wars (War of Liberation)
See **Dennewitz**

Juthas ▌ 1808 ▌ Napoleonic Wars (Russo-Swedish War)

Despite a successful offensive against the Russian invasion of Finland, Sweden's army was driven to the coast, where Russian General Kiril Fedorovich Kazatchovski tried to cut off their route north. A courageous victory at Juthas saw Swedish General Georg von Dobeln repulse the Russians and secure the road for the Swedish retreat following battle next day at **Oravais** (13 September 1808).

Jutiapa ▌ 1844 ▌ Central American National Wars

When Guatemala supported the ageing Manuel José Arces in a failed invasion of El Salvador against President Francisco Malespín, the Salvadoran President invaded Guatemala and seized the town of Jutiapa, 45 miles southeast of Guatemala City. Terrible losses to disease eventually forced Malespín to withdraw and a peace treaty restored Guatemalan property (20 May–17 June 1844).

Jutland ▌ 1916 ▌ World War I (War at Sea)

Admiral Reinhard Scheer led the German High Seas Fleet out to challenge the Grand Fleet of Admiral John Jellicoe and they met off Jutland in the greatest naval battle of the war. The British lost six capital ships and eight destroyers before the Germans escaped with eleven older and smaller ships sunk. However, the German Fleet never again ventured out to sea (31 May–1 June 1916).

K

Kabatiya ▌ 1967 ▌ Arab-Israeli Six Day War
   See **Jenin**

Kabul ▌ 1504 ▌ Mughal Dynastic War
   Following the death of the Timurid Prince Ulugh Beg of Kabul, his son-in-law Muhammad Mukim Khan of the Arghunid Dynasty of Kandahar seized the throne. But Mukim was attacked in Kabul by the great Timurid Mughal Babur and withdrew to **Kandahar** after a brief struggle. Babur then used Kabul as his base to conquer India and establish the Mughal Dynasty (October 1504).

Kabul ▌ 1546–1549 ▌ Mughal Wars of Succession
   Kamran Mirza, second son of the great Babur, was driven out of **Kandahar** in 1545 by his brother Humayun, yet captured Kabul in 1546. However, in 1547 he was defeated and driven out by Humayun. Kamran was pardoned, but in 1549 again advanced on Kabul, where he defeated and wounded Humayun. With fresh forces, Humayun retook Kabul and eventually captured and blinded his brother.

Kabul ▌ 1738 ▌ Persian-Afghan Wars
   Nadir Shah of Persia recaptured **Kandahar** (24 March) and Ghazni, then attacked Kabul in eastern Afghanistan, defended by the Mughal commander Shir Khan. While the city quickly fell, there was severe fighting before the citadel finally surrendered, after which most of the garrison was slaughtered. Nadir then invaded Mughal India and sacked Delhi after a great victory at **Karnal** (21–29 June 1738).

Kabul ▌ 1800 ▌ Afghan Wars of Succession
   A well-planned coup saw Afghan ruler Zaman Shah attacked and defeated at Kabul by his brother Mahmud Shah, who was supported by Vizier Fath Khan, son of the former Sirdar Payanda Khan (who had been executed by Zaman). Mahmud blinded his brother and seized the throne, though he was in turn defeated and overthrown three years later by another brother, Shah Shuja.

Kabul ▌ 1818 ▌ Afghan Wars of Succession
   When Prince Kamran of Herat jealously blinded and executed Afghan Vizier Fath Khan after victory at **Kafir Qala**, he triggered the downfall of his own father Mahmud Shah of Kabul. Within months, the Vizier's brother Dost Muhammad Barakzai raised forces in Kashmir to defeat and overthrow Mahmud at Kabul, ending the Durrani Dynasty. Dost Muhammad himself became Amir in 1826.

Kabul ▌ 1841–1842 ▌ 1st British-Afghan War
   More than two years after Amir Dost Muhammad of Afghanistan was deposed following defeat at **Ghazni**, his son Akbar Khan besieged the British in Kabul and routed a sortie at nearby **Bemaru**. The unfortunate General William Elphinstone eventually surrendered Kabul in return for safe passage to **Jalalabad**. However, the British force was massacred at **Jagdalak (1st)** (November 1841–6 January 1842).

Kabul ▌ 1842 ▌ 1st British-Afghan War
 See **Maidan**

Kabul ▌ 1866 ▌ Later Afghan War of Succession
 In a war of succession after the death of Dost Muhammad, Amir Sher Ali won at **Khujbaz** (June 1865), but his brother Azim Khan and nephew Abdur Rahman (son of Afzal Khan) marched on Kabul, held by the son of the Amir. Muhammad Ibrahim Khan was defeated and forced to surrender, while his father's attempt to recover Kabul was repulsed in May at **Sheikhabad** (24 February 1866).

Kabul ▌ 1879 ▌ 2nd British-Afghan War
 During renewed hostilities following British victory at **Peiwar Kotal** (December 1878), a force of 2,000 Afghans from Herat attacked the British Residency at Kabul, defended by about 80 Guides. When envoy Sir Louis Cavagnari was shot, Lieutenant Walter Hamilton VC led a heroic defence before his entire detachment was killed. Britain was avenged a month later at **Charasia** (3 September 1879).

Kabul ▌ 1929 ▌ Afghan Reformist War
 Habibullah Kalakani rose against reformist King Amanullah and seized Kabul. Though the King fled into exile, a bloody counter-offensive by his cousin Muhammad Nadir Khan and his brother Shah Wali Khan retook Kabul. The usurper and ten others were executed and Nadir Khan became King. He introduced constitutional government, but was assassinated in 1933 (14 January–14 October 1929).

Kabul ▌ 1978 ▌ Afghan Civil War
 Soon after a rising in **Herat** was crushed by the increasingly repressive government of President Muhammad Daoud, a Marxist-led revolution saw dissident army and airforce officers attack Kabul with tanks and jet fighters. Despite a bloody defence by loyalist Presidential Guards, Daoud was overthrown and executed, then replaced by Nur Muhammad Taraki (27–28 April 1978).

Kabul ▌ 1979 ▌ Afghan Civil War
 When Afghanistan's Marxist President Nur Muhammad Taraki was killed by his former ally Hafizullah Amin (14 September), Russian General Sergei Sokolov invaded to support Soviet candidate Babrak Karmal. Fierce fighting in Kabul saw Amin killed and Karmal installed as puppet President. Russia then faced a brutal war until withdrawal in February 1989 (24–27 December 1979).

Kabul ▌ 1992 ▌ Afghan Civil War
 Despite the withdrawal of Soviet troops in 1989, President Mohammad Najibullah held out with continued Russian aid against resurgent Mujahaden forces, which had already captured **Khost**. However, Kabul finally fell to a hard-fought rebel advance, ending the last Communist government of Afghanistan. Najibullah was executed four years later by the Taliban when they took Kabul (15 April 1992).

Kabul ▌ 1996 ▌ Afghan Civil War
 With Afghanistan wracked by rival Mujahaden factions, Pakistani-backed Taliban Islamists took Kandahar late in 1995, then advanced on Kabul, defeating both warlord Gulbuddin Hekmatyar and Defence Minister Ahmad Shah Massud. The Taliban held the devastated city until they were driven out by the Northern Alliance and their British and American allies in November 2001 (September 1996).

Kabul ▌ 2001 ▌ Afghanistan War
 The coalition of warlords known as the Northern Alliance captured **Mazar-i-Sharif** and other key centres in northern Afghanistan, then raced towards Kabul where the Taliban government had vowed to defend the capital at all cost. However, after losses in action outside the city, the Taliban abandoned Kabul and moved south towards their last remaining stronghold at **Kandahar** (12–13 November 2001).

Kabylie ▌ 1959 ▌ Algerian War
 Having choked the flow of men and arms from Tunisia at the **Frontier** by mid-1958, General Maurice Challe launched 20,000 men on a

massive offensive into the forbidding Kabylie Mountains, east of Algiers. The French destroyed the ALN strongholds, killing or capturing over 3,700 insurgents to secure a crushing military victory. However, the political war was ultimately lost (July–October 1959).

Kacanik I 1915 I World War I (Balkan Front)
See **Kossovo**

Kadasiya I 636 I Muslim Conquest of Iraq
See **Qadisiyya**

Kadesh I 1275 BC I Egyptian-Hittite Wars
Ramses II of Egypt took a major expedition into northern Syria, where he ordered a large force against Hittites under Muwatalis at Kadesh, on the Orontes southwest of Hims. After an initial repulse for his advance guard, Ramses arrived to secure a decisive victory. Although the Hittites withdrew under siege into the city. Ramses eventually had to make peace and withdraw (trad date 1275 BC).

Kadesiah I 636 I Muslim Conquest of Iraq
See **Qadisiyya**

Kadir I 1751 I Later Dutch Wars in the East Indies
See **Jenar**

Kadirganj I 1751 I Pathan War
See **Qadirganj**

Kaffa I 1296 I Venetian-Genoese Wars
Two years after Venice had taken the Genoese colony at Galata on the Bosphorus, Venetian Giovanni Soranza advanced into the Black Sea against the Genoese at Kaffa (modern Feodosiya), controlling the rich Crimean grain trade. Attacking with 25 galleys, Soranza seized the port and captured massive plunder. Kaffa was eventually returned by treaty to Genoese control.

Kaffa I 1475 I Genoese-Turkish War
While Turkey was attacking Venetian colonial territories in Greece and the Adriatic, Sultan Mehmed II sent Vizier Ahmad Gedik Pasha against the powerful Genoese colony at Kaffa (modern Feodosiya) in the eastern Crimea. A large Turkish fleet attacked the port and forced its surrender, followed by the fall of Azov, which ended the Genoese presence in the Black Sea (2–5 June 1475).

Kafir Qala I 1818 I Persian-Afghan Wars
A large Persian army under Husayn Ali Mirza, son of Shah Fath Ali, approaching Herat was defeated by Afghan Vizier Fath Khan to the northwest at Kafir Qala (modern Kafir Islam). Shortly afterwards, however, Prince Kamran of Herat jealously blinded and killed the Vizier, whose brother Dost Muhammad soon drove Kamran's father Mahmud Shah out of **Kabul** and later seized the throne.

Kafr I 1925 I Druze Rebellion
After the Druze leader al-Atrash seized the town of Salkhad in the southeast of French Syria, a column of almost 200 Algerian and Syrian troops under Captain Normand set out from nearby Suwayda to rescue a downed aircrew. Ambushed just to the southeast at Kafr, Normand lost more than half his column killed and the survivors withdrew under siege to **Suwayda** (21 July 1925).

Kagera I 1978 I Tanzanian-Ugandan War
Ugandan President Idi Amin alleged Tanzanian interference in his country and sent forces into northwest Tanzania, where they seized the 700-square-mile Kagera Salient. Tanzanian troops quickly counter-attacked and sharp fighting expelled the Ugandans with costly civilian losses. Tanzania later invaded Uganda and drove Amin out of **Kampala** (31 October–27 November 1978).

Kagoshima I 1587 I Japan's Era of the Warring States
Japanese ruler Toyotomi Hideyoshi invaded Kyushu against Satsuma and advanced across the **Sendaigawa** towards Kagoshima, while other forces landed by sea to attack from the south. Kagoshima fell by storm and Shimazu

Yoshihisa and his brother Yoshihiro surrendered. Hideyoshi also secured Kyushu before returning to Honshu in 1590 to conquer the Hojo at **Odawara** (July 1587).

Kagoshima I 1863 I British-Satsuma War

When the merchant Charles Richardson was killed at Kagoshima, Kyushu, British chargé Colonel Edward Neale demanded redress from Prince Shimazu Hisamitsu of Satsuma, then ordered Admiral Augustus Kuper to bombard Kagoshima. Kuper destroyed much of the city, but suffered heavy battle damage and withdrew to Yokohama, allowing Satsuma to claim victory (15 August 1863).

Kagoshima I 1877 I Satsuma Rebellion

Driven off from a costly siege of **Kumamoto** in central Kyushu in April, rebel Japanese Marshal Saigo Takamori faced a massive Imperial counter-offensive by Prince Arisugawa Taruhito and gradually fell back on Kagoshima, where he fought his way in to retake the city. However, he was soon forced to withdraw to nearby **Shiroyama**, where he made a bloody final stand (18 August 1877).

Kagul I 1770 I Catherine the Great's 1st Turkish War

General Pyotr Rumyantsev advanced deep into Turkish Moldavia along the **Pruth** and found himself between Turk and Tatar armies near Kagul, north of Galati. Moving rapidly forward he routed Ottoman Grand Vizier Halil Pasha, capturing his guns and baggage and forcing him back towards the Danube. Rumyantsev then turned to defeat the Tatars, driving them back to the **Crimea** (21 July 1770).

Kagul Lagoon I 1574 I Moldavian Rebellion

Determined to punish John the Brave of Moldavia, who had defeated an Ottoman force in April at **Jiliste**, Sultan Selim II sent a massive force under the Beyleyby of Rumelia, who beat the rebels near the mouth of the Danube at Kagul Lagoon, southeast of Reni. Deserted by his cavalry, John surrendered after three days.

However, agreed terms were ignored and he was quartered (10–13 June 1574).

Kahan I 1840 I 1st British-Afghan War

Sir John Keane took **Ghazni** (July 1839), then sent Captain Lewis Brown to secure the southern pass at Kahan, where he was besieged by Dodah Khan. A column sent back to Quetta under Lieutenant Walpole Clarke was massacred and, when Major Thomas Clibborn's relief column was repulsed at the Nufoosk Pass (31 August), Brown negotiated his safe passage (11 May–12 September 1840).

Kahlenberg I 1683 I Later Turkish-Habsburg Wars

See **Vienna**

Kaifeng I 1126–1127 I Jin-Song Wars

When the Jurchen secured Manchuria at the **Songhua** (1114), new Jin (Chin) Emperor Wanyan Wuqimai sent his nephew Wo Li Bu against the Song capital, Kaifeng. Emperor Qin Zong offered a massive indemnity and the siege was lifted. But it soon resumed and Kaifeng fell by storm, effectively ending the Northern Song Dynasty. Resistance then moved to **Nanjing** (January 1126–9 January 1127).

Kaifeng I 1232–1233 I Mongol Conquest of China

Renewed invasion of north China saw the Mongols Ogedai and Tolui (sons of Genghis Khan) defeat the Jin at **Yuxian**, then leave General Subetai to besiege the capital Kaifeng. When the Southern Song sent General Meng Hong to aid the Mongols, Emperor Ai Zong fled and later committed suicide. After the city was taken, the victors soon fell out and fought at **Jiangling** (8 April 1232–29 May 1233).

Kaifeng I 1642 I Manchu Conquest of China

With the Ming under assault on all sides, rebel leader Li Zicheng in the north took Nanyang (1641), then attacked Kaifeng. Twice repulsed, he launched a third massive siege. After diverting the Yellow River to isolate Kaifeng, dikes were cut and the city was inundated. Several hundred thousand starved or drowned and Li Zicheng withdrew. In 1644 he captured **Beijing** (May–October 1642).

Kaifeng I 1948 I 3rd Chinese Revolutionary Civil War
One of the war's largest open battles to date saw more than 200,000 men under Communist General Chen Yi converge on Kaifeng, held by 250,000 Nationalists under Qiu Qingquan and Huang Bodao. Chen took Kaifeng (19 June), but when Chiang Kai-shek arrived with reinforcements, Chen had to withdraw. Chiang claimed victory, despite losing over 90,000 men (30 May–8 July 1948).

Kai-hsia I 202 BC I Chu-Han War
See **Gaixia**

Kaiping I 1895 I Sino-Japanese War
Determined to ease pressure on Japanese forces holding **Haicheng** in southern Manchuria, General Maresuke Nogi led a fresh offensive further west, advancing on 4,000 Chinese in well-built redoubts at Kaiping, west of Gai Xian. With a brilliant attack across a frozen river, Nogi seized the city in little more than two hours and the Chinese retreated north towards **Yingkou** (10 January 1895).

Kaiserslautern I 1793 I French Revolutionary Wars (1st Coalition)
The Prussians of Karl Wilhelm Ferdinand Duke of Brunswick fell back before an advance by French General Louis Lazare Hoche and established themselves in a strong defensive position at Kaiserslautern, west of the Rhine. Hoche attacked with the Moselle army and was beaten back with heavy losses after three days (28–30 November 1793).

Kaiserslautern I 1794 I French Revolutionary Wars (1st Coalition)
In a fresh initiative on the Rhine, French General Jean Victor Moreau's new army met with some success until repulsed at Kaiserslautern by Prussian Marshal Richard von Mollendorf. However, Mollendorf failed to follow up and after French success at nearby **Platzberg** and **Trippstadt**, the city fell to a two-month siege. Moreau then went on to besiege **Mainz** (23 May–17 July 1794).

Kaitake I 1864 I 2nd New Zealand War
Campaigning just south of New Plymouth, Patara Ruatakauri of the religio-military Hauhau built a strong fortified pa at Kaitake, near Oakura, which was shelled in December 1863 by Colonel Henry J. Warre. A few months later, with 420 regulars and militia, Warre bombarded and stormed the position. Another victory at **Sentry Hill** soon eased the threat to New Plymouth (25 March 1864).

Kaithal I 1240 I Wars of the Delhi Sultanate
Sultana Raziya succeeded her father Iltutmish as the only woman to occupy the throne of Delhi, but soon offended her nobles by favouritism for the Abyssinian slave, Yaqut. Despite marrying the rebel leader Altuniya to try and stem the revolt, she and her husband of just 12 days were defeated in battle at Kaithal, northwest of Karnal. Both were then executed (13 October 1240).

Kajwa I 1659 I War of the Mughal Princes
See **Khajwa**

Kajwa I 1857 I Indian Mutiny
See **Khajwa**

Kalanga I 1814 I British-Gurkha War
With British northern India threatened by Gurkha expansion west of Nepal, General Robert Gillespie (later Colonel Sebright Mawby) besieged the fortress of Kalanga, near Dehra Dun. Balbhadra Singh Thapa's garrison repulsed repeated assaults, inflicting heavy losses including Gillespie killed. However, after a month of bombardment the Gurkhas withdrew (31 October–30 November 1814).

Kalat I 1839 I 1st British-Afghan War

After Amir Shah Shuja of Afghanistan was restored following British victory at **Ghazni**, General Thomas Willshire and a small force marched against the Baluchi Mehrab Khan, who had hindered the British expedition. Willshire bombarded then stormed the powerful fortress of Kalat, in Baluchistan southwest of Quetta, killing the Khan and taking many prisoners (13 November 1839).

Kalighatta I 972 I Later Indian Dynastic Wars

Siyaka II of Malwa refused to pay allegiance to Khotigga of Rashtrakuta, who marched against the rebel and his kinsman Vamka of Vagada. Heavy fighting on the Narmada at Kalighatta saw Vamka killed before Siyaka won and plundered the capital Manyakheta (modern Malkhed). Rashtrakuta troops fought on nearby and Siyaka had to withdraw, but he had won independence for his Paramara Dynasty.

Kali Nadi I 1858 I Indian Mutiny
See **Fategarh**

Kaliningrad I 1807 I Napoleonic Wars (4th Coalition)
See **Königsberg**

Kalinjar I 1631 I Mughal-Ahmadnagar Wars

When Mughal commander Khan Jahan Lodi threatened to ally himself with Nizam Shah II of Ahmadnagar, Imperial forces defeated his rearguard at **Sironj**. In three days of battles near Kalinjar, south of Banda, Generals Abdallah Khan and Sayyid Muzaffar Khan defeated and killed the rebel and his sons. Ahmadnagar was destroyed two years later at **Daulatabad** (1–3 February 1631).

Kalisch I 1706 I 2nd "Great" Northern War

Augustus II—Elector of Saxony and deposed King of Poland—joined Russian Prince Alexander Menshikov in a fresh offensive against Charles XII of Sweden, defeating a small Swedish force under General Arvid Marderfeld in western Poland at Kalisch (modern Kalisz). Despite victory, Augustus was forced to make peace and recognise Stanislaus Leszcsynski as King (29 October 1706).

Kalisch I 1813 I Napoleonic Wars (Russian Campaign)

As Napoleon Bonaparte's army withdrew west after the disastrous retreat from Moscow, Saxons under General Jean-Louis Reynier found themselves isolated in southern Poland following the withdrawal of their Prussian allies. Near Kalisch (modern Kalisz), west of Lodz, Reynier was defeated by Russian Baron Ferdinand von Winzeingerode and retired on Glogau (13 February 1813).

Kalka I 1223 I Conquests of Genghis Khan

The Mongols Subetai and Jebei invaded Georgia for victory at the **Kuban**, then advanced to the Ukraine to meet a Russian–Kipchaq army under Princes Mstislav Romanovitch of Kiev and Mstislav Sviatoslavitch of Chernigov. At the Kalka (modern Kalmius) on the Sea of Azov, the Russians were destroyed with Mstislav of Kiev executed. Subetai later withdrew east after Jebei died (16 June 1223).

Kalka I 1380 I Russian-Mongol Wars

Faced by rebellious Russian Princes, the Mongol leader Mamai was defeated at **Kulikovo**, then was immediately challenged by his dynastic rival Toktamish, Khan of the White Horde. In battle at the Kalka (modern Kalmius) on the Sea of Azov, Mamai was defeated and Toktasmish, as Khan of the united Golden Horde, went on to suppress the Russian rebellion and burn **Moscow**.

Kalpi I 1858 I Indian Mutiny

With **Jhansi** captured (3 April), General Sir Hugh Rose defeated Tantia Topi at **Kunch**, then continued northeast towards the Rani of Jhansi at Kalpi. After an initial bombardment, a bold counter-offensive by the Rani's allies Rao Sahib and the Nawab of Banda surprised the British.

However, the rebels were defeated in heavy fighting and withdrew west towards **Gwalior** (19–23 May 1858).

Kalunga I 1814 I British-Gurkha War
See **Kalanga**

Kalyan I 1682–1683 I Mughal-Maratha Wars
As he advanced into western India, Mughal General Bahadur Khan defeated a Maratha army (28 November 1682) and seized Kalyan, on the Uhlas northeast of Bombay. A large Maratha counter-attack was repulsed in December, with commander Tukoji killed. The heaviest fighting (27 February 1683) saw the Marathas driven off with heavy losses, though the fort remained under blockade.

Kalyan I 1780 I 1st British-Maratha War
General Thomas Goddard marched northeast from Bombay, sending Captain Richard Campbell to surprise and capture Kalyan, which he held against a powerful Maratha counter-attack by Bajipant Joshi and Sakharampant Panase. At nearby Vithalwadi (24 May) a relief force under Colonel James Hartley routed the Marathas, who withdrew towards **Malang-gad** (10–15 May 1780).

Kamakura I 1333 I Genko War
Nitta Yoshisada secured victory for the Imperial cause at **Kyoto** (10 June), then switched sides to support Emperor Go-Daigo and marched on Kamakura, capital of Japanese Dictator Hojo Takatoki. Yoshisada seized the city in a brilliant attack and Takatoki and his followers committed mass seppuku. Go-Daigo regained his throne, but Ashikaga forces later recaptured Kamakura (5 July 1333).

Kamakura I 1335 I Ashikaga Rebellion
Following the restoration of Emperor Go-Daigo, Hojo forces rose in revolt in Kamakura and were suppressed by Ashikaga Takauji (March 1335). Hojo Tokiyuki (son of the later dictator Takatoki) then took the city by storm, expelling Ashikaga Tadayoshi (August 1335).

Returning in force, Takauji defeated and killed Tokiyuki, but soon turned against the Emperor and seized **Kyoto** (September 1335).

Kamarej I 1754 I Persian Wars of Succession
Amid the struggle for control of Persia, Azad Khan Afghan of Azerbaijan captured Shiraz after defeating Regent Karim Khan Zand at **Qomsheh**, then drove him further southwest. In a defile at Kamarej, near Kazerun, Karim and Rostam Soltan of Khost ambushed and routed Azad's army under Fath Ali Khan Afshar. Azad had to abandon Shiraz and Karim also recaptured Isfahan (October 1754).

Kamenets Podolsk I 1944 I World War II (Eastern Front)
Soon after the great Russian victory at **Korsun**, Marshals Georgi Zhukov and Ivan Konev tried another encirclement further west at Kamenets Podolsk, southeast of Lvov, where General Hans Hübe commanded 300,000 men of the First Panzer Army. Hübe broke out to the west and fought a brilliant defensive withdrawal to save his army, but died in an air crash (10 March–10 April 1944).

Kamieniec I 1633 I Polish-Tatar Wars
Despite defeat in the Ukraine at **Sasowy Rog** in July, Tatars under Abaza Mehmed Pasha advanced again and attacked Hetman Stanislas Koniecpolski in a strong position at Panowce, near Kamieniec. When his Moldavian and Walachian levees fled, Abaza Mehmed was defeated and withdrew. The following year Sultan Murad IV had him executed and sued for peace (22 October 1633).

Kamieniec I 1672 I Turkish Invasion of the Ukraine
Sultan Mehmed IV invaded the Polish Ukraine to support Cossack rebels and sent Grand Vizier Ahmed Fazil Koprulu against Kamieniec (modern Kamenetz). Aided by Cossacks and Tatars, Ahmed seized the key fortress and weak King Michael Wisniowiecki agreed to a humiliating peace. In late 1673 Hetman John Sobieski

rallied Poland to a great victory at **Khotin** (18–26 August 1672).

Kamina ∎ 1914 ∎ World War I (African Colonial Theatre)

At the start of the war, Captain Frederick Bryant of the West African Frontier Force secured French aid from Dahomey and invaded Togo to seize the naval wireless station at Kamina. A sharp action at the Chra River, near Nuatja, cost the Allies 23 killed and 50 wounded before the Germans blew up the radio station and Governor Hans Von Döring surrendered Togoland (22–26 August 1914).

Kampala ∎ 1979 ∎ Tanzanian-Ugandan War

After Tanzania repulsed Ugandan aggression in the **Kagera** Salient, about 5,000 Tanzanians and 3,000 anti-Amin exiles invaded Uganda to overthrow President Idi Amin. As they advanced on Kampala, Libyan troops sent to assist Uganda were used to meet the heaviest attack and suffered costly losses just outside the capital. Kampala fell and Amin fled into exile (February–11 April 1979).

Kampar ∎ 1941–1942 ∎ World War II (Pacific)

Driven back from **Jitra** in western Malaya, the Indian 11th Division abandoned Ipoh (27 December) and retreated to Kampar under new commander Brigadier Archie Paris. Facing frontal attack by General Saburo Kawamura, and threatened in the flank by a fresh coastal landing, the British withdrew to **Slim River**, the last natural defence north of Johore (29 December 1941–2 January 1942).

Kanauj ∎ 648 ∎ Sino-Indian War

Following the death of Harsha Vardhana of Kanauj, his minister Arjuna usurped the throne of the North Indian kingdom and later attacked a Chinese delegation sent by Tang Emperor Taizong. Ambassador Wang Xuanze escaped, then returned with Nepalese and Tibetan troops, supported by Chinese cavalry. They besieged

Kanauj, where Arjuna was defeated then taken in captivity to Chang'an.

Kanauj ∎ 916 ∎ Later Indian Dynastic Wars

In a remarkable military achievement by Rashtrakuta, Indra III took an army against Kanauj, the northern Imperial capital of the Pratiharas, where Mahipala I was defeated and the city was captured and plundered. While Kanauj was later recovered by Mahipala, aided by Chandella and other allies, the Pratihara Dynasty had begun its decline and eventually dwindled to no more than Kanauj itself.

Kanauj ∎ 1540 ∎ Mughal Conquest of Northern India

Afghan rebel Sher Khan, leading Indian-Muslim forces against the Mughal Humayun, beat Imperial forces at **Chausa**. He then pursued the Mughals up the Ganges Valley, where Humayun was again heavily defeated at Kanauj, southeast of modern Farrukhabad. Humayun fled to Persia for 15 years, leaving Sher Khan (later Sher Shah) to become Sultan of Delhi and effective ruler of the empire (17 May 1540).

Kanazawa ∎ 1087 ∎ Later Three Years War

Minamoto Yoshiie renewed war in northeast Japan, where he was repulsed by Kiyohara Iehira at **Numa** (1087). Reinforced by his brother Yoshimitsu, he then besieged Iehira and his uncle Takehira further north, at Kanazawa Stockade (modern Yokote in southern Akita). Iehira was eventually defeated and killed after a stubborn defence, ending the war and giving the Minamoto power in the east.

Kanchatzu ∎ 1937 ∎ Russo-Japanese Border Wars

Local Soviet forces occupied Kanchatzu Island in the Amur along the Manchurian border and Japan's Kwantung forces in puppet Manchukuo later bombarded and sank a Russian gunboat, killing 37 crew. While the Russians eventually agreed to withdraw, the so-called Amur Incident convinced them not to back down a year later at **Changfukeng** (19 June–3 July 1937).

Kanchi I 610 I Indian Dynastic Wars
See **Pullalur**

Kanchi I 655 I Indian Dynastic Wars
Following the death of Pulakesin II of Chalukya at **Vatapi** (642), the victorious Pallava occupied his capital until his bold young son Vikramaditya reasserted sovereignty and ousted the occupiers. He then invaded Pallava itself and in a remarkable military achievement, he defeated Narasimhavarman of Pallava and captured his strongly fortified capital, Kanchi (modern Kanchipuram).

Kanchi I 731 I Indian Dynastic Wars
See **Vilande**

Kanchi I 740 I Indian Dynastic Wars
Following up victory at **Kanchi** (731), Vikramaditya II of Chalukya again joined with Sripurusha of Ganga and invaded Pallava. The new King Nandivarman and his general Udaichandra suffered a decisive defeat. Vikramaditya then occupied and sacked Kanchi. He eventually withdrew and the declining Chalukya Empire was overthrown by the Rashtrakuta 12 years later at **Khandesh**.

Kanchi I 1692 I Mughal-Maratha Wars
During the siege of the Maratha fortress at **Gingee**, northwest of Pondicherry, Mughal General Zulfiqar Khan's Lieutenant Ali Mardan Khan was attacked by Santaji Ghorpade at Kanchi (modern Kanchipuram). When Ali Mardan led a bold counter-attack to protect Zulfiqar's rear, he was defeated and captured by Santaji's Marathas and was taken to Gingee for ransom (13 December 1692).

Kandahar I 1508 I Mughal-Uzbek Wars
When the Uzbek conqueror, Muhammad Shaybani Khan, seized Kandahar after victory at **Maruchak** (1507), he granted the city to Mukim Khan, son of the defeated Arghun Mughal Governor. However, Mukim was driven out by his Timurid rival, Babur of **Kabul**, who gave it to his brother Nasir Mirza. Shaybani returned to defeat Nasir and Babur did not recapture Kandahar until 1522.

Kandahar I 1520–1522 I Mughal Dynastic War
Determined to recover Kandahar in Afghanistan, on the vital southern trade route from India, the Mughal ruler Babur finally retook the city after a lengthy siege from Shah Beg of the Arghun Dynasty, who retired to Quetta. Babur's son Kamran held Kandahar against the Persians (1534–1536) before he finally lost it in 1545 to his brother Humayun and his Persian allies.

Kandahar I 1558 I Persian-Mughal Wars
Shah Tahmasp of Persia took advantage of the weak teenage Mughal Emperor Akbar, sending an army to besiege Kandahar, held by Shah Muhammad, an appointee of the Mughal Regent Bairam Khan. With Emperor Akbar unable to send aid, the strategic city of southern Afghanistan was forced to surrender to Persia and was not regained by the Mughals for almost 40 years.

Kandahar I 1622 I Persian-Mughal Wars
On campaign into southern Afghanistan, Shah Abbas of Persia laid siege to Kandahar, held for the Mughal Emperor Jahangir, who ill-advisedly prevented his son Shahjahan marching to relieve the city. Kandahar fell to Shah Abbas after a three-week siege and mining of the city walls. It was not recovered from the Persians for 15 years.

Kandahar I 1637 I Persian-Mughal Wars
During political unrest in Persia following the death of Shah Abbas, Ali Mardan Khan, Persian Governor of Kandahar, feared for his life and surrendered the southern Afghan city to the Mughals. A Persian army sent to retake Kandahar was defeated by Mughal forces of the Emperor Shahjahan. The city fell to Persia 12 years later and was never again ruled from the Mughal Empire.

Kandahar I 1649 I Persian-Mughal Wars

In response to a fresh Persian offensive in Afghanistan led personally by Shah Abbas, the Mughal Emperor Shahjahan sent his son Aurangzeb to relieve Kandahar. However, it fell before he arrived (11 February 1649). Supported by Chief Minister Sadullah Khan, Aurangzeb besieged the city, but lacked adequate artillery and had to withdraw in disgrace (May–5 September 1649).

Kandahar I 1652 I Persian-Mughal Wars

Having failed to recapture Kandahar from the Persian invaders in 1649, the Mughal Prince Aurangzeb and Chief Minister Sadullah Khan returned to Afghanistan to undertake a second siege. Although better equipped with heavy guns, Aurangzeb failed once more and was again forced to abandon his siege and withdraw (May–July 1652).

Kandahar I 1653 I Persian-Mughal Wars

The Mughal Prince Aurangzeb twice failed to recapture Kandahar from the Persian invaders and Emperor Shahjahan then sent his elder son Dara Shikoh to retake the key Afghan city. Like his brother before him, Dara Shikoh also failed in his father's military designs, withdrawing after an abortive five-month siege. The Mughals never again ruled in Kandahar (May–September 1653).

Kandahar I 1711 I Persian-Afghan Wars

Determined to recover Kandahar from the Afghan rebel Mir Weis, Shah Husain of Persia sent Khosru Khan, Governor of Georgia, who defeated Weis and besieged Kandahar. The Georgian general insisted on unconditional surrender, but when the besiegers ran short of food, Weis counter-attacked to defeat and kill Khosru, along with almost his entire army.

Kandahar I 1714 I Persian-Afghan Wars

In a second attempt to recover Kandahar from the Afghan rebel Mir Weis, Shah Husain of Persia sent a fresh army under General Mohammad Rustam. Once again, Weis was defeated in the field, but when the Persians be-sieged Kandahar, Weis attacked and destroyed the besieging army. The Afghan leader remained as virtual ruler of Kandahar Province until he died a year later.

Kandahar I 1737–1738 I Persian-Afghan Wars

Nadir Shah recaptured Herat to secure his position as Shah of Persia, then marched on Kandahar, defended by Mir Husayn Khan, brother of Mahmud. After a long siege, supported by the Abdalis, the town fell by storm and Mir Husayn became a leading general in Nadir's army. Nadir went on to capture **Kabul**, giving Persia effective control of Afghanistan (February 1737–24 March 1738).

Kandahar I 1834 I Afghan Wars of Succession

With Afghanistan threatened by Persian invasion, deposed Amir Shah Shujar attempted to recover his kingdom from Dost Muhammad. He attacked the key city of Kandahar, but was heavily defeated by Dost Muhammad's General Kohandil Khan and was driven off after a 54-day siege. Shah Shujar was not restored until five years later after British victory at **Ghazni** (May–29 June 1834).

Kandahar I 1841–1842 I 1st British-Afghan War

While Akbar Khan (son of deposed Amir Dost Muhammad) besieged **Kabul**, other Afghans besieged Kandahar, defended by British General William Nott. The Afghans suffered heavy losses in sorties at **Babi Wali Kotal**, then withdrew after further losses in a large-scale assault on the fort. Nott later evacuated Kandahar and marched to Kabul (September 1841–8 August 1842).

Kandahar I 1880 I 2nd British-Afghan War

When Britain proclaimed Abdur Rahman as Amir of Afghanistan, his cousin Ayub Khan beat the British at **Maiwand**, then besieged General James Primrose at Kandahar. Following a march from Kabul, General Sir Frederick

Roberts destroyed Ayub Khan's army outside Kandahar at Mazra, near Babi Wali Kotal, and Britain withdrew from Afghanistan (6 August–1 September 1880).

Kandahar | 1881 | Afghan Civil Wars

Following British withdrawal from Afghanistan in 1880, the rebel Ayub Khan made a renewed attempt to overthrow his cousin, Amir Abdur Rahman, and besieged Kandahar, where he had been routed a year earlier. Outside the walls of Kandahar the Amir personally defeated the rebel, who fled to Persia. Abdur Rahman then ruled for 20 years (27 July–22 September 1881).

Kandahar | 2001 | Afghanistan War

When **Kabul** fell, Taliban forces and the remnants of their government withdrew south to Kandahar, their last major stronghold and spiritual birthplace. Bombed from the air and besieged between Northern Alliance troops in the north and American and Allied forces to the south, Kandahar was forced to surrender, effectively ending the Taliban regime (25 November–7 December 2001).

Kandurcha | 1391 | Conquests of Tamerlane
See **Kunduzcha**

Kandy | 1803 | 1st British-Kandyan War

British Major-General Hay Macdowall invaded the Kingdom of Kandy, in central Ceylon (modern Sri Lanka), where he captured the capital and installed Muttusamy after King Sri Wikrama fled. Major Adam Davie's garrison was later attacked by Pilima Talauva. After Muttusamy was handed over then executed, the British force was destroyed and Davie died in captivity (January–June 1803).

Kandy | 1815 | 2nd British-Kandyan War

On a fresh invasion of Kandy, in central Ceylon, British General Sir Robert Brownrigg led a well-organised force against Molliguda, commanding the Sinhalese Royal troops. A brief campaign without any British battle losses then saw Brownrigg entered the deserted capital. King Sri Wikrama died in exile and the ancient Kingdom of Kandy came to an end (11 January–8 February 1815).

Kandy | 1818 | 3rd British-Kandyan War

Rebels attempting to restore the Kingdom of Kandy, in central Ceylon, led a successful guerrilla campaign, but suffered a major defeat in open battle while crossing the Mahivelli (16 July) and the rebellion collapsed. Rebels Keppitipola and Madugalla were executed and Kandyan Regent Pilimi Talauva was exiled. The successful British commander Sir Robert Brownrigg was created a Baronet.

Kangju | 36 BC | Wars of the Former Han

Xiongnu forces in northwest China split into two hordes (51 BC) and the Western horde under Zhizhi Chanyu attacked Han interests, then eventually withdrew to Kangju (Sogdiana). Han army officer Cheng Tang took a force to besiege Kangju, where Zhizhi was defeated and killed, bringing a period of stability in Central Asia. His claimed descendants were later known as the Kirghiz.

Kangwachai | 1894 | Sino-Japanese War

While defending strategic **Haicheng** in southern Manchuria, Japanese General Taro Katsura sent inadequate forces under General Naotoshi Oseko against Chinese General Song Qing at nearby Kangwachai. Song was eventually forced to withdraw when Oseko was reinforced, though the Japanese suffered about 400 casualties or 10 percent—their highest ratio of losses in the war (19 December 1894).

Kankar | 1858 | Indian Mutiny

As British forces advanced on **Lucknow**, Colonel Thomas Seaton determined to attack gathering rebel forces threatening the Doab. A night march northwest from Fategarh with 1,000 infantry and 300 cavalry saw Seaton surprise mutineers under Tej Singh near Aliganj at Kankar. The dawn attack caused over 250 rebel casualties and dispersed the planned invasion (7 April 1858).

Kankrauli I 1858 I Indian Mutiny

One week after defeat at **Sanganer**, the exhausted Gwalior rebels under Tantia Topi attempted to make a stand behind the Banas River, north of Udaipur at Kankrauli. Fording the river under fire, British forces led by General Henry Gee Roberts routed the rebels. However, Brigadier William Parke pursued weakly and the rebels escaped across the swollen Chambal into Jhalwar (14 August 1858).

Kankroli I 1858 I Indian Mutiny
See **Kankrauli**

Kano I 1903 I British Conquest of Northern Nigeria

When British Resident Captain C. W. Moloney was murdered in the north at Keffi (3 October 1902), Commissioner Frederick Lugard sent Colonel William Morland with 40 white officers and 800 African troops against the Emirate of Kano. Fulani forces tried to defend Kano, but heavy shelling smashed its gates and the city fell. The British then marched via **Rawiya** to **Sokoto** (3 February 1903).

Kanpur I 1857 I Indian Mutiny
See **Cawnpore**

Kanwah I 1527 I Mughal Conquest of Northern India
See **Khanua**

Kao-p'ing I 954 I Wars of the Five Dynasties
See **Gaoping**

Kapain I 1837 I Boer-Matabele War

On a second expedition to avenge Boer defeat at **Vegkop** in late 1836, Andries Potgieter and Piet Uys led over 300 men against Mzilikazi of the Matabele, who had escaped defeat at **Mosega** (January 1837). An assault on his camp to the north at Kapain, near Zeerust, saw the Matabele defeated with 400 killed. Mzilikazi and Mkhalipi dispersed north across the Limpopo (4–12 November 1837).

Kapolna I 1849 I Hungarian Revolutionary War

After defeating the Hungarians at **Schwechat** and **Mór** in late 1848, Austrian Field Marshal Alfred Windischgratz captured Budapest, then faced advancing Nationalists further east under General Henry Dembinski. An indecisive action at Kapolna, near Eger, saw General Franz von Schlick force the rebels to withdraw. Dembinski was then replaced by General Artur Gorgey (26–27 February 1849).

Kapotai I 1845 I 1st New Zealand War

Repulsed at **Puketutu** in New Zealand's far north (8 May), Colonel William Hulme withdrew to Auckland, leaving command to Major Cyprian Bridge, who took 200 regular troops and 100 friendly Maoris to attack a pa (fortified village) at Kapotai, on the Waikare just south of **Kororareka**. After fierce fighting, with two friendlies killed, the pa was abandoned and burned (15 May 1845).

Kappel I 1531 I Swiss Religious Wars

Amid open warfare between Catholics and Protestants in Switzerland, a large Catholic army marched on Zurich. Ten miles to the south at Kappel, a heavily outnumbered Protestant force was routed, the dead including the great Reformation leader Ulrich Zwingli. Following a further Protestant loss at **Zug** (24 October) Switzerland was permanently divided along religious lines (11 October 1531).

Kapyong I 1951 I Korean War

As part of their Spring Offensive, Chinese troops attacked south across the Imjin towards Seoul and further east towards Kapyong. While Commonwealth and South Korean forces had to withdraw in the face of massive assaults, the Communists failed to break through. A subsequent failed assault further east at the **No Name Line** ended the last major Chinese offensive (23–25 April 1951).

Karabagh I 1842 I 1st British-Afghan War
See **Ghoaine**

Karachi I 1971 I 3rd Indo-Pakistan War

At the start of the war, Indian missile boats under Commodore Babru Bahan Yadav attacked the Pakistani port of Karachi. The night assault saw a large Pakistani destroyer sunk with 200 men lost, and another badly damaged, as well as a minesweeper and a merchant ship sunk, plus massive devastation to the port and oil installations. A second attack four days later caused further destruction (4–5 December 1971).

Karakilise I 1915 I World War I (Caucasus Front)

Turkish General Abdul Kerim secured victory north of Lake Van at **Malazgirt** (26 July), then continued north and took Karakilise, southwest of **Sarikamish**, before Russian commander Nikolai Yudenich counter-attacked with 20,000 men under General Nikolai Baratov. Very heavy fighting saw the Turks defeated with about 10,000 casualties and another 6,000 captured (5–8 August 1915).

Karakorum I 1301 I Mongol Dynastic Wars

After Kubilai Khan conquered China and moved his capital to Beijing, his cousin Kaidu of Turkestan (grandson of Ogadei) claimed the Mongol throne and repeatedly attempted to capture Karakorum, in Mongolia. Kaidu was repulsed by Kubilai's General Bayan in 1277 and 1289 and finally (after Kubilai's death), Kaidu was defeated in September 1301 near Karakorum and was killed in flight.

Karakose I 1915 I World War I (Caucasus Front)

See **Karakilise**

Karala I 1898 I British-Sudan Wars

See **Omdurman**

Karama I 1968 I Arab-Israeli Border Wars

In response to Palestinian infiltration, Israeli troops and tanks crossed the Jordan to attack the Fatah base at Karama, northeast of Jericho. Palestinian forces suffered very heavy losses before the invaders were driven off by the Jordanian army. This highly mythologized action was claimed as a decisive Arab victory and led directly to Yasser Arafat becoming leader of Palestine (21 March 1968).

Karari I 1898 I British-Sudan Wars

See **Omdurman**

Karbala I 680 I Muslim Civil Wars

During the war of succession following the death of the first Umayyad Caliph Mu'awiya (May 680), a revolt was raised against his son and successor, Yazid I, by Hussain, grandson of the Prophet Mohammed and son of the former Caliph Ali. Hussain was defeated and killed at Karbala, on the Euphrates, where his tomb is still one of the most revered Shi'ite shrines (10 October 680).

Karbala I 749 I Muslim Civil Wars

In rebellion against the declining Umayyad Caliphs, supporters of Abdul Abbas (grandson of the Prophet's cousin al-Abbas) revolted under the leader Abu Muslim. On the Euphrates at Karbala, the rebel General Kahtaba defeated the army of Merwan II under General Hubaira, though Kahtaba was killed. Soon afterwards in Kufa, Abdul Abbas proclaimed himself Caliph (27–28 August 749).

Karditsa I 1948 I Greek Civil War

While insurgent forces attacked in northern Greece, further south on the Plain of Thessaly, Karagiorgis and about 6,000 troops, including many women, attacked and occupied Karditsa. Facing massive government reinforcements, Karagiorgis pulled out with huge quantities of loot, suffering badly under air attack as he withdrew. He attacked again a month later at **Karpenision** (11–14 December 1948).

Karee Siding I 1900 I 2nd Anglo-Boer War

With the Boers driven out of Bloemfontein after **Driefontein** (10 March), General Charles Tucker's infantry division attacked a position at Kareehalte, on the railway 18 miles to the northeast. Tucker lost over 180 casualties in a costly action before the Boers were forced to withdraw. However, two days later a Boer raid further east secured a decisive victory at **Sannah's Post** (29 March 1900).

Karelia ▌ 1941 ▌ World War II (Northern Europe)

The so-called Continuation War saw Finnish commander Carl Mannerheim take advantage of the German invasion of Russia to resume hostilities against the Soviets. Vyborg was recaptured (27 August) and, within two months, all territory in the Karelian Isthmus lost in the **Winter War** had been restored. Finnish forces then supported the German siege of **Leningrad** (25 June–2 September 1941).

Karelian Isthmus ▌ 1939 ▌ Russo-Finnish War

See **Mannerheim Line**

Karikal ▌ 1760 ▌ Seven Years War (India)

In the wake of British victory at **Wandewash**, in southeast India (22 January), Colonel Joseph Smith was sent south to join Major George Monson besieging Karikal, north of Negapatam. Several months later commander Pierre Renault was forced to surrender France's second most important local seaport. Renault was subsequently court-martialled and cashiered (February–5 April 1760).

Kariz ▌ 1719 ▌ Persian-Afghan Wars

See **Herat**

Karkal ▌ 1770 ▌ Catherine the Great's 1st Turkish War

See **Kagul**

Karkar ▌ 854 BC ▌ Early Assyrian Wars

See **Qarqar**

Karkuk ▌ 1733 ▌ Turko-Persian Wars of Nadir Shah

Regent Nadir Kuli (later Nadir Shah) resolved to recover land ceded to the Turks by former Shah Tahmasp II and won a victory outside **Baghdad**, then invested the city. However, a massive relief army of 80,000 men under Topal

Osman Pasha approached from the north and, near the Tigris at Karkuk, Nadir suffered a decisive defeat. Nadir had his revenge at **Leilan** in November (19 July 1733).

Karnal ▌ 1739 ▌ Persian Invasion of India

At the peak of Persian expansion, Emperor Nadir Shah invaded Mughal India and followed victory at **Jamrud** by crossing the Indus with a reported 100,000 men. West of Delhi at Karnal, Mughal Emperor Muhammed Shah was routed, with perhaps 20,000 killed, and cavalry commander Saadat Khan captured. Nadir restored Muhammed and returned to Persia with massive booty (13 February 1739).

Karo Pass ▌ 1904 ▌ British Invasion of Tibet

With British and Tibetan forces stalemated at **Gyantse**, Colonel Herbert Brander took a column 50 miles northeast against 3,000 Tibetans defending the narrow Karo Pass at 18,500 feet. In one of the highest actions ever fought, Brander's men climbed the steep walls and fired down on the Tibetans, who were driven out with heavy losses. Brander then returned to Gyantse (6 May 1904).

Karpenision ▌ 1823 ▌ Greek War of Independence

As Mustai Pasha led about 4,000 Turks and Catholic Albanians to reinforce the siege of **Missolonghi**, his vanguard under Djelaleddin Bey was surprised in mountains just north of Karpenision by Marcos Botzaris and just 350 Greeks. When Botzaris was killed, his brother Kosta completed the victory, inflicting heavy Turkish casualties, though Mustai continued on to **Anatoliko** (21 August 1823).

Karpenision ▌ 1949 ▌ Greek Civil War

Soon after rebel success in Thessaly at **Karditsa**, Karagiorgis turned south and stormed the mountain town of Karpenision. A counter-attack was driven off—the only time insurgents held a major town against government forces—and General Ketseas was relieved. Facing fresh attack by General Thrasyvoulos Tsakalotos, Karagiorgis withdrew with heavy losses (19 January–9 February 1949).

Kars I 1745 I Turko-Persian Wars of Nadir Shah

Determined on a fresh invasion of Persia, Sultan Murad IV assembled a reported 100,000 men at Kars in northeastern Turkey under Yeghen Mohammed Pasha. In a four-day battle nearby, Nadir Shah destroyed the Turks, who fled after murdering their commander. Murad finally made peace with Persia, but Nadir Shah was assassinated in June 1747 and his empire collapsed (11 August 1745).

Kars I 1828 I Russo-Turkish Wars

While the main Russian army crossed the Danube against Turkey in support of Greek independence, General Count Ivan Paskevich advanced into the Caucasus against Emin Pasha at Kars, in northeast Turkey. The fortress fell by storm after a heavy bombardment, yielding valuable military stores and cannon. Paskevich then immediately marched against **Akhaltsikhe** (5–6 July 1828).

Kars I 1854 I Crimean War

See **Kürük-Dar**

Kars I 1855 I Crimean War

Russian General Mikhail Muraviev marched into Armenia where he besieged Kars, defended by Turks under General Sir William Fenwick Williams. While a Russian assault was repulsed with very heavy losses (29 September), a Turkish relief force marching via the **Ingur** was sent too late and the starving fortress surrendered. However, Russia soon sued for peace (15 July–26 November 1855).

Kars I 1877 I Russo-Turkish Wars

As he advanced in the Caucasus, Russian Grand Duke Michael gained a valuable victory at **Aladja Dagh** over the Turks, who then withdrew under siege to the nearby fortress of Kars. General Mikhail Loris-Melikov stormed the fortress in a brilliant night-time assault and next day Hussein Pasha surrendered about 15,000 prisoners and 300 guns (17–18 November 1877).

Kartarpur I 1635 I Early Mughal-Sikh Wars

On campaign against the Sikhs of Guru Hargobind, a Mughal force under Painde Khan laid siege to Kartarpur, north of Jullundar, defended by Bhai Bidhi Chand, supported by the Guru and his son Baba Gurdita. The Mughals were heavily repulsed, with the dead including the leading commanders Qutab Khan of Jullundar and Kale Khan, brother of Mukhli Khan, killed just a year earlier at **Amritsar**.

Kartosuro I 1705 I Dutch Wars in the East Indies

Dutch Councillor Herman de Wilde intervened in a Javanese war of succession, leading a large force of Europeans and Javanese to support Pangeran Pugar against his nephew, Amangkurat III. Near Kartosuro, west of Surakarta, Amangkurat was defeated and fled to **Bangil**, in eastern Java. Pugar was enthroned as Pakubuwana, ceding the Dutch enormous trade and territorial gains (August 1705).

Karuse I 1270 I Early Wars of the Teutonic Knights

After a disputed succession in Lithuania and the murder of Mindaugus (who beat the Livonian knights at **Durbe** in 1260), Duke Traidenis of Lithuania sent a large force against the knights in modern western Estonia. In battle near Karuse, northeast of Virtsu, Livonian Master Otto Von Lutterberg was among more than 50 knights killed. Traidenis won again in 1279 at **Aizkraulke** (16 February 1270).

Kasama I 1918 I World War I (African Colonial Theatre)

Just weeks after inconclusive action in Mozambique after **Mahiwa**, Colonel Paul von Lettow-Vorbeck re-entered German East Africa and skirted Lake Nyasa to seize Kasama in Northern Rhodesia. In the reputed last action of the war, the German fought a sharp skirmish with British Major Edward Hawkins the day after Armistice in Europe. He surrendered two weeks later (12 November 1918).

Kasegaum ❘ 1774 ❘ Maratha Wars of Succession

At war with Raghunath Rao, who had murdered his nephew Narayan Rao, the Maratha Ministers at Poona sent General Trimbak Rao Pethe to protect Narayan Rao's widow at Purandar. In a surprise attack near Kasegaum, south of Pandharpur, Raghunath utterly routed Pethe, who died of wounds. The usurper was deposed a year later after defeat at **Adas** (26 March 1774).

Kasemark ❘ 1627 ❘ 2nd Polish-Swedish War

In a fresh offensive to support his siege of **Danzig** in Polish Prussia, Gustavus Adolphus of Sweden attacked Polish commander Stanislas Koniecpolski 15 miles to the southeast, on the Vistula at Kasemark (Keizmark). Wounded in a risky river crossing at night, Gustavus withdrew. A renewed attack six weeks later secured Kasemark and tightened the siege of Danzig (22–23 May & 4 July 1627).

Kasganj ❘ 1750 ❘ Pathan War

A massive offensive in northern India against Safdar Jang, the Mughal Wazir of Delhi, saw the Pathan leader Ahmad Khan Bangesh defeat the Wazir's army at **Farrukhabad**. He then meet the Wazir himself a month later to the northwest at Kasganj. With the Wazir severely wounded and his army completely defeated, the Pathans then sacked Lucknow and besieged Allahabad (12 September 1750).

Kasganj ❘ 1857 ❘ Indian Mutiny

Colonel Thomas Seaton heading a well-equipped advance against rebel forces, marched southeast from Delhi to Aligarh, where he left his convoy, then continued east towards Kasganj, joined by reinforcements from Bulandshahr. Northwest of Kasganj at Gangiri the rebels were heavily defeated and fled. Seaton seized Kasganj and pursued the mutineers north towards **Patiala** (14 December 1857).

Kashgar ❘ 1218 ❘ Conquests of Genghis Khan

In a prelude to his offensive in the west, Genghis Khan sent his son Jebei into Chinese Turkestan against Kuchlug of the Naiman, who had escaped to the Kara Khitai after defeat at the **Irtysh** and later usurped the throne. Pursued south of Lake Balkash, Kuchlug was defeated near the caravan city of Kashgar, then fled south towards the Pamir, where he was eventually captured and beheaded.

Kashgil ❘ 1883 ❘ British-Sudan Wars
See **El Obeid**

Kashlyk ❘ 1582 ❘ Russian Conquest of Siberia

To protect Russia's trade in western Siberia, Cossack leader Yermak Timofeyevich took fewer than 1,000 men against the Tatar Khanate of Sibir, where Khan Kuchum was defeated and driven out of his capital at Kashlyk (also called Sibir or Isker), near modern Tobolsk. Although Timofeyevich was killed a few years later in an ambush, the conquest of Siberia continued unabated (October 1582).

Kasos ❘ 1824 ❘ Greek War of Independence

After Ottoman forces secured Crete, Ismail Djebel Akhdar sailed east with 3,000 Albanian troops under Hussein Bey Djertili to attack the nearby pirate island of Kasos. In a terrible massacre, about 500 men of military age were killed and over 50 ships were seized, while 2,000 women and children were sold as slaves in Alexandria. Weeks later **Psara** was also devastated (19 June 1824).

Kassassin ❘ 1882 ❘ Arabi's Egyptian Rebellion

When War Minister Arabi Pasha attempted to assert Egyptian sovereignty, British General Sir Garnet Wolseley landed at the canal and marched west from Ismailia through **Tel-el-Maskhuta**. Advance units led by General Sir Gerald Graham and Colonel Sir Russell Baker beat the Egyptians at Kassassin Lock near Mahsama and Wolseley continued towards **Tel-el-Kebir** (28 August 1882).

Kassel I 1762 I Seven Years War (Europe)

Driving the French south towards the Rhine after victory at **Lutterberg** (23 July), Duke Ferdinand of Brunswick suffered a costly check at **Amoneburg** before returning to northern Hesse to besiege the key city of Kassel, which he had left under blockade. After two weeks the French garrison was forced to surrender and a few days later the war came to an end (16 October–1 November 1762).

Kasserine I 1943 I World War II (Northern Africa)

American General Lloyd Fredenhall landed in North Africa during Operation **Torch**, then advanced into southern Tunisia, where he was surprised and routed at the Kasserine Pass by German Panzer units under Field Marshal Erwin Rommel. Fredenhall suffered severe losses in men and tanks and was dismissed, but the Americans soon struck back at **El Guettar** (14–22 February 1943).

Kastel I 1948 I Israeli War of Independence

Jewish forces under Uzi Narkiss and Ytzak Rabin were determined to open the vital road to Tel Aviv and attacked the strategic town of Kastel, just five miles west of Jerusalem. A week of intense fighting saw the hilltop stronghold change hands several times before the charismatic Arab commander Abdul Khader Husseini was killed. His followers then withdrew (2–9 April 1948).

Kastoria I 1948 I Greek Civil War

With his army saved at **Grammos**, insurgent Markos Vaphiadis soon re-entered Greece from Albania and attacked Kastoria, where government forces fled then suffered continuing heavy losses. Taking command, Thrasyvoulos Tsakalotos bought up government reinforcements and finally secured the city. However, his army was too exhausted to take the offensive (29 August–14 November 1948).

Kastrikum I 1799 I French Revolutionary Wars (2nd Coalition)

See **Castricum**

Katalgarh I 1815 I British-Gurkha War

Determined to curb Gurkha expansion west of Nepal, Colonel William Gardner invaded the Kumaun and circled north towards **Almorah**, while Captain Hyder Hearsey in the south seized Champawat then besieged nearby Katalgarh. Just to the east at Khilpati, Gurkha commander Hasti Dal surprised and routed the British and Hearsey was captured wounded as his men fled (2 April 1815).

Katamanso I 1826 I 1st British-Ashanti War

See **Dodowa**

Katar I 1008 I Eastern Muslim Dynastic Wars

See **Balkh**

Katia (1st) I 1916 I World War I (Middle East)

In order to protect their position on the Suez Canal, British forces began to push a railway east into the Sinai and established a strong position at Katia (Qatia). A sudden Turkish attack drove the British out with costly losses, though reinforcements soon recovered the railhead. Katia was lost again three months later to a fresh Turkish advance, this time stopped further west at **Romani** (23 April 1916).

Katia (2nd) I 1916 I World War I (Middle East)

See **Romani**

Katikara I 1863 I 2nd New Zealand War

Resumed warfare around New Plymouth saw a nine-man military escort ambushed and killed to the southwest on the disputed Tataramaika block after which General Duncan Cameron led a large force, supported by artillery, to attack the fortified pa on the nearby Katikara. After heavy shelling the Maoris were driven out with the bayonet. The British won again in October at **Poutoko** (4 June 1863).

Katra I 1774 I Rohilla War
See **Miranpur Katra**

Katshanik I 1915 I World War I (Balkan Front)
See **Kossovo**

Katwa I 1742 I Later Mughal-Maratha Wars
Raghuji Bhonsle directed a Maratha invasion of Bengal, sending Bhaskar Pandit with 12,000 horsemen, who captured Katwa (modern Katoya) on the Bhagirathi north of Calcutta (May 1742) and also occupied Hooghly. However, Mughal Nawab Ali Vardi Khan eventually led a brilliant attack downriver on the Maratha camp at Katwa and drove them out of Bengal (17 September 1742).

Katwa I 1745 I Later Mughal-Maratha Wars
Three years after his failed invasion of Bengal, the Maratha Raghuji Bhonsle occupied Orissa and captured Cuttack, then led 20,000 horsemen into Bengal and sacked Murshidabad. But Mughal Nawab Ali Vardi Khan once again beat the Marathas and turned them back at Katwa (modern Katoya), on the Bhagirathi north of Calcutta. In 1747, Ali Vardi defeated yet another invasion at **Burdwan**.

Katwa I 1763 I Bengal War
When Nawab Mir Kasim of Bengal destroyed a British force at **Patna** (25 June) he faced a British column under Major Thomas Adams, who had been sent to restore rival Nawab Mir Jafar. Near the fortress of Katwa, on the Bhagirathi north of Calcutta, Adams defeated and killed Mir Kasim's General Mohammed Taki Shah. He then advanced against Mir Kasim himself at **Gheria** (19 July 1763).

Katzbach I 1813 I Napoleonic Wars (War of Liberation)
Following defeat at **Lützen** and **Bautzen** in May, Prussia and Russia determined to attack Napoleon Bonaparte's lieutenants. General Gebhard von Blucher turned on Marshal Jacques Macdonald, who had unwisely pursued him into Silesia. After a repulse at **Lowenberg**, the Prussians counter-attacked on the Katzbach at Bremberg, south of Liegnitz, to inflict a costly defeat (26 August 1813).

Kauhajoki I 1808 I Napoleonic Wars (Russo-Swedish War)
Continuing the offensive against Russia's invasion of central Finland, Swedish General Georg von Dobeln helped capture **Lapuu**, southeast of **Vasa** (14 July), then continued the advance towards Kauhajoki, where he met a greatly superior Russian force under General Vasily Schepeljeff. A decisive attack forced the Russians to withdraw, but they soon resumed the offensive (10 August 1808).

Kauthal I 1367 I Vijayanagar-Bahmani Wars
Muhammad Shah of Bahmani invaded Vijayanagar in southern India and marched on Adoni. At Kauthal on the Tungabhadra, in the claimed first battle in India to see artillery used, he defeated King Bukka Rai I and killed Hindu commander Mallinatha. Bukka fled to Vijayanagar and accepted a Muslim peace after Muhammad Shah reputedly massacred tens of thousands of Hindu civilians.

Kaveripak I 1752 I 2nd Carnatic War
Two months after taking **Conjeeveram** in eastern Madras, Britain's Robert Clive was ambushed at Kaveripak, on the River Palar, by Raza Sahib, son of French-appointed Nawab Chanda Sahib, marching to recover **Arcot**. In a moonlight counter-attack, Clive surprised and routed his enemy, killing 50 French and 300 sepoys and capturing nine guns and many prisoners (28 February 1752).

Kawasaki I 1058 I Earlier Nine Years War

Following victory over the rebellious Abe Clan at **Torinomi**, in northeast Japan (1057), Imperial Governor Minamoto Yoriyoshi attacked Abe Sadato at Kawasaki, in Iwate east of Ichinoseki. Yoriyoshi's undermanned force suffered a sharp defeat and had to withdraw. The war was suspended for four years until he was heavily reinforced and renewed his campaign at **Komatsu**.

Kawkareik I 1942 I World War II (Burma-India)

At the start of the Japanese invasion of **Burma**, General Hiroshi Takeuchi crossed the densely forested border from Thailand and attacked Anglo-Indian forces at Kawkareik. Amid a breakdown of communication and confused night fighting, Brigadier John "Jonah" Jones fell back to Martaban. The Japanese then advanced west towards **Moulmein** (20–22 January 1942).

Kay I 1759 I Seven Years War (Europe)

Count Pyotr Soltikov regrouped after Russia's defeat at **Zorndorf** (August 1758) and resumed the offensive on the Oder, where he was unwisely attacked at Kay, west of Zullichau, by a heavily outnumbered Prussian force under General Richard von Weddell. The Prussians lost over 6,000 men and Soltikov's Russians advanced on Frankfurt to join the Austrians at **Kunersdorf** (23 July 1759).

Kayseri I 1511 I Turko-Persian War in Anatolia

Encouraged by Shah Ismail I of Persia, the Safavid preacher Shah Kulu raised rebellion among the Turkomans of Anatolia against Ottoman Sultan Bayazid II, who sent a large army under Grand Vizier Hadim Ali and Prince Ahmed. At Kayseri, in central Anatolia, the rebels were crushed after Shah Kulu was killed. The Safavids were defeated again in 1514 at **Chaldiran** (August 1511).

Kayseri I 1624 I Anatolian Rebellion

When Governor Abaza Mehmed Pasha of Anatolia rebelled against Sultan Murad IV, he faced a large Ottoman army under Grand Vizier Cerkes Mehmed Pasha. In central Anatolia at Kayseri, Abaza Mehmed was defeated, though he was later restored. Despite further failed revolts in 1627 and 1628, the rebel was again pardoned and his men were absorbed into the army (5 September 1624).

Kazan I 1487 I Russia's Volga Wars

Duke Ivan III of Moscow intervened in a disputed succession in the Mongol Khanate of Kazan, despatching a large force under Daniil Dimitrievich Kholmsky to support Mehmet Amin against Ali Khan. After a failed sortie, Ali Khan withdrew under siege and later surrendered the city. Mehmet was installed as Khan and Moscow secured a virtual vassal in the Crimea (18 May–9 July 1487).

Kazan I 1552 I Russia's Volga Wars

Following three unsuccessful attacks on the middle Volga Khanate of Kazan, Russian Tsar Ivan IV took a large force against the Mongol capital. Kazan fell after two months siege by land and water, followed by the massacre of a reputed 60,000 inhabitants. Christianity was imposed and Russia advanced downriver towards **Astrakhan** (20 August–20 October 1552).

Kazan I 1774 I Pugachev Rebellion

Despite defeat at **Tatishchevo** in March, Cossack rebel Emelyan Pugachev stormed and burned the middle Volga city of Kazan, defended by Governor Yakov Illarionovich von Brandt. The same day, a small relief army under Colonel Ivan Michelson retook the city. When Pugachev attacked again two days later, his force was destroyed, with 2,000 casualties and 5,000 prisoners (12–14 July 1774).

Kazan I 1918 I Russian Civil War

Former Czech prisoners of war seized **Ekaterinburg** for the counter-revolution (25 July), then continued west towards Kazan. An important strategic victory saw troops under Russian Colonel Vladimir Kappel and Czech Colonel Svec capture the city, along with Russia's State gold reserve. Kazan was retaken a month later and the Czechs were soon routed at **Samara** (6 August 1918).

Kazanlik ∎ 1878 ∎ Russo-Turkish Wars
See **Senova**

Kazima ∎ 633 ∎ Muslim Conquest of Iraq
See **Hafir, Iraq**

Kazzaz ∎ 1756 ∎ Persian Wars of Succession
Amid struggle for control of Persia, Regent Karim Khan Zand faced a fresh offensive west of Isfahan by Mohammad Hasan Khan of Qajar. At Kazzaz, near Kashan, Karim's General Mohammad Khan Zand was decisively defeated and captured and Mohammad Hasan quickly occupied Isfahan. The great Zand general was later killed after escaping from captivity (27 March 1756).

Kearsage ∎ 1864 ∎ American Civil War (High Seas)
See **Cherbourg**

Keelung ∎ 1884 ∎ Sino-French War
See **Chilung**

Kehl ∎ 1796–1797 ∎ French Revolutionary Wars (1st Coalition)
Driven back to the Rhine by Archduke Charles Louis of Austria after defeat at **Emmendingen**, French General Jean Victor Moreau soon sent some of his force under General Louis Desaix across the river. Desaix then defended the Rhine town of Kehl for a remarkable three months before capitulating to Austrian General Maximilian Latour (28 October 1796–10 January 1797).

Kellogg's Grove ∎ 1832 ∎ Black Hawk Indian War
Following a futile advance on Apple River Fort, east of Galena in northwest Illinois, the Sauk Chief Black Hawk clashed next day at Kellogg's Grove with Major John Dement's Company. Unlike Major Isaiah Stillman at **Rock River**, Dement fought back bravely and after losses on both sides, including two of Black

Hawk's Chiefs killed, the Indians withdrew to their camp (25 June 1832).

Kelly's Ford (1st) ∎ 1863 ∎ American Civil War (Eastern Theatre)
Campaigning on the Rappahannock towards Culpeper, Virginia, Union General William Averell led almost 3,000 men across Kelly's Ford. In a largely cavalry action, heavily outnumbered Confederate General Fitzhugh Lee engineered a brilliant counter-attack and the Union forces fell back. A few weeks later Lee supported victory further south at **Chancellorsville** (17 March 1863).

Kelly's Ford (2nd) ∎ 1863 ∎ American Civil War (Eastern Theatre)
See **Rappahannock Station**

Kemmel ∎ 1918 ∎ World War I (Western Front)
German commander Erich von Ludendorff broke open the Allied front in Flanders on the **Lys**, but after retaking Messines Ridge his advance stalled and French reinforcements secured Kemmel Ridge, south of Ypres. While German Alpine troops then boldly stormed and seized the strategic ridge, further attacks failed and the German offensive was abandoned (17–19 & 25–29 April 1918).

Kemmendine ∎ 1824 ∎ 1st British-Burmese War
When Britain declared war on Burma, General Sir Archibald Campbell secured Rangoon then sent forces against the nearby fortress of Kemmendine. After an initial repulse, which cost 120 British dead, a second assault secured the fortress. It later came under attack in November and held out under siege against the all-out Burmese attack on **Rangoon** (3 & 10 June 1824).

Kempen ∎ 1642 ∎ Thirty Years War (Franco-Habsburg War)
French General Jean-Baptiste Guébriant supported the Swedish victory at **Wolfenbüttel** (29 June 1641), then started back towards the Rhine with the Army of Weimar. Just west of the Rhine

near Crefeld, between Kempen and Hulst, he defeated and captured Imperial General William von Lamboy. Soon afterwards Guébriant was created a Marshal of France (16 January 1642).

Kempten | 1525 | German Peasants' War

Weeks after destroying a rebel army at **Königshofen**, Georg Truchsess von Waldburg marched south against about 23,000 peasants around Kempten, southwest of Munich. Many rebel leaders surrendered after a massive bombardment and further fighting forced the remainder to also give up. About 20 leaders were executed, ending the war in Franconia and Swabia (19–25 July 1525).

Kéniéra | 1882 | Franco-Mandingo Wars

Mandingo leader Samory Touré besieging the French-allied city of Kéniéra, in Upper Guinea, faced a rash attack by hugely outnumbered force under Colonel Gustave Borgnis-Desbordes. In his first action against European troops, Samory was driven out by French artillery and Kéniéra was relieved. The following year Borgnis-Desbordes led a pre-emptive attack on **Bamako** (26 February 1882).

Kenilworth | 1265 | 2nd English Barons' War

After Henry III was beaten by Simon de Montfort Earl of Leicester at **Lewes** (14 May 1264), Prince Edward gathered a powerful army on the Severn, between the Earl and his son Simon the Younger advancing from London. Edward routed the younger de Montfort in a surprise attack near Coventry at Kenilworth and three days later he defeated and killed the Earl at **Evesham** (1 August 1265).

Kennesaw Mountain | 1864 | American Civil War (Western Theatre)

As Union commander William T. Sherman advanced through Georgia against General Joseph E. Johnston, he won at **Kolb's Farm** (22 June), then attacked the nearby main Confederate position on Kennesaw Mountain, northwest of **Marietta**. A rash frontal assault by Sherman was repulsed with over 2,000 men lost, but Johnston eventually withdrew to defend Atlanta at **Peachtree Creek** (27 June 1864).

Kentani | 1878 | 9th Cape Frontier War

The last major action of the war following Xhosa defeat at **Ibeka** and **N'Axama**, saw about 5,000 Xhosa under veteran leaders Kreili and Sandile attack Kentani, just north of the Great Kei. In the face of brave defence by Regulars, Colonials and Mfengu levies under Major Russell Upcher, the Xhosa were heavily defeated. The war soon ended with Britain securing the Transkei (17 February 1878).

Kentish Knock | 1652 | 1st Dutch War

Near Kentish Knock, off the mouth of the Thames, Dutch Admiral Cornelius Witte de With engaged English Admiral Robert Blake in a confused and indecisive action. Both sides had about 45 ships and, while the English were outmanoeuvred, de With was thwarted by his uncooperative subordinates. He was eventually driven off, yielding a narrow victory to Blake (8 October 1652).

Kenyermezo | 1479 | Transylvanian-Turkish Wars

Ottoman commander Ali Bey was returning from a large-scale raid into Transylvania, when he was intercepted by the Voivode Stephen Bathory on the Plain of Kenyermezo—"the Field of Bread"—near Orastie on the Mures. Badly wounded and almost defeated, Bathory was saved by the timely arrival of Paul Kinizsi of Temesvár and the Turks were driven back (13 October 1479).

Kepaniwai | 1790 | Hawaiian Wars

Eight years after securing the Big Island of Hawaii with victory at **Mokuohai**, the warrior Kamehameha took a large force against the island of Maui, held by Chief Kahekili. A decisive action at the Iao Valley saw the Chief's son Kalanikupulu routed with so many dead that the stream was renamed Kepaniwai—damming of the waters. Five years later, Kamehameha secured Oahu at **Nuuanu**.

Kerbela ∎ 680 ∎ Muslim Civil Wars
  See **Karbala**

**Kerch ∎ 1790 ∎ Catherine the Great's
2nd Turkish War**
  See **Yenikale Strait**

Kerch ∎ 1855 ∎ Crimean War
  In support of operations in the Crimean Pen-
insula, General Sir George Brown and Admiral
Sir Edmund Lyons took an Anglo-French-
Turkish force against the Straits of Kerch,
leading into the Sea of Azov. A powerful assault
destroyed the Russian base at Kerch and nearby
Yenikale was abandoned the same day, severing
Russian communications east of the Crimea (24
May 1855).

**Kerch ∎ 1942 ∎ World War II
(Eastern Front)**
  General Erich von Manstein left a covering
force at Sevastopol and took 15 divisions against
Kerch in eastern Crimea, where Russian General
Dmitri Kozlov had built up a large army under
siege. After a massive German assault, 80,000
Russians evacuated by sea though 175,000 men
were captured, along with all their equipment.
Manstein then returned to reduce **Sevastopol**
(8–20 May 1942).

**Kerch ∎ 1944 ∎ World War II
(Eastern Front)**
  While Russian forces broke into the Crimean
Peninsula at **Perekop**, General Andrei Yer-
emenko led an amphibious assault further east at
Kerch, aided at sea by Admiral Filip Oktyabrs-
ky's Black Sea Fleet, which struck German
communications and shipping. The Russians
rapidly cleared the Kerch Peninsula then raced
southwest towards **Sevastopol** (8–11 April
1944).

**Keren ∎ 1941 ∎ World War II
(Northern Africa)**
  British General William Platt left Sudan to
invade Eritrea, where he seized **Agordat**, then
advanced on General Luigi Frusci in the mountain stronghold at Keren. Some of the hardest

fighting of the campaign saw the Italians eventually driven out with very heavy losses. Platt
then seized the Eritrean capital Asmara, and then
Massawa, before turning south towards **Amba
Alagi** (2 February–27 March 1941).

**Keren ∎ 1977–1978 ∎ Eritrean War
of Independence**
  As part of their urban offensive, Eritrean forces attacked Keren using artillery taken at
Nakfa. Following heavy bombardment, the
rebels stormed the city and fort with perhaps
2,000 Ethiopians killed and 1,700 captured.
Keren was retaken by an Ethiopian counter-
offensive a year later and held out under siege
for many years against repeated fresh Eritrean
attacks (5–8 July 1977 & 26 November 1978).

**Kerensky Offensive ∎ 1917 ∎
World War I (Eastern Front)**
  Russia's renewed advance in the southwest
following the **Brusilov Offensive** was known as
the Second Brusilov or Kerensky Offensive (for
War Minister Aleksandr Kerensky). After initial
success around **Brzezany** and **Stanislau**, Germans counter-attacked through **Tarnopol** and
Russia's last offensive ended in terrible retreat,
with final defeat in the north around **Riga** (1–19
July 1917).

**Keresztes ∎ 1596 ∎ Turkish-
Habsburg Wars**
  Following Turkish defeats on the Danube,
Sultan Mehmed II personally led a fresh inva-
sion, supported by Grand Vizier Ibrahim Pasha.
In a bloody engagement near Erlau at Keresztes,
the Austro-Hungarians of Archduke Maxmilian
and Sigismund Bathory of Transylvania were
routed by a brilliant Ottoman cavalry charge.
However, the exhausted Turks then returned to
Belgrade (24–26 October 1596).

Kerman ∎ 1721 ∎ Persian-Afghan Wars
  Mahmud Ghilzai, son of Mir Weis of Kandahar, secured western Afghanistan after victory
at **Farah** (1719), then invaded Persia and captured the eastern city of Kerman. However, he
was heavily defeated by Persian General Lutf

Ali Khan (brother-in-law of the Grand Vizier) and driven back to Kandahar. A renewed offensive the following year won Mahmud the Persian crown at **Isfahan**.

Kerman I 1722 I Persian-Afghan Wars

Renewing his offensive against Persia, Mahmud Ghilzai of Kandahar again attacked the eastern city of Kerman, where he had been repulsed a year earlier. Mahmud took the city and eventually forced the citadel to surrender. He then marched northwest towards the capital at Isfahan and, despite a further repulse at Yazd, defeated the Persians at **Gulnabad** and **Isfahan**.

Kerman I 1794 I Persian Wars of Succession

Amid bitter struggle for Persia, the young Shah Lutf Ali marched into southeast Iran and seized the Kerman, where he was besieged by Aga Mohammad Khan of the Qajar. When the city fell by treachery it was utterly destroyed, with a reputed 20,000 males blinded and all the females enslaved. Lutf Ali was tortured to death in 1796, ending the tumultuous Zand Dynasty (July–24 October 1794).

Kermanshah I 1752–1753 I Persian Wars of Succession

In the fight for succession after the assassination of Nadir Shah, Regent Karim Khan sent his General Mohammad Khan Zand against Kermanshah fortress, southeast of Yadz, held for his rival Ali Mardan Khan by Abdul Ali Khan, who finally surrendered after two years. Ali Mardan himself was then attacked and defeated nearby (June 1753) and was later assassinated by Mohammad Khan.

Kernstown I 1862 I American Civil War (Eastern Theatre)

On the offensive in the northern Shenandoah, Confederate General Thomas "Stonewall" Jackson was met at Kernstown, Virginia, by an unexpectedly much larger Union force under General James Shields. With Shields wounded, Colonel Nathan Kimball led a brilliant assault and Jackson was repulsed with over 700 casu-

alties. Within weeks he recovered to win at **McDowell** (22–23 March 1862).

Kernstown I 1864 I American Civil War (Eastern Theatre)

Confederate General Jubal A. Early resumed the offensive in the Shenandoah Valley after a check at **Stephenson's Depot** (20 July) attacking General George Crook at Kernstown, just south of Winchester, Virginia. Defeated with about 1,200 casualties, the Union army fell back across the Potomac with Early in pursuit. The Confederates were turned back at **Cumberland** (24 July 1864).

Kerulen I 1203 I Conquests of Genghis Khan

Determined to secure supremacy in Mongolia, Temujin (later Genghis Khan) recovered from defeat at **Khalakhaljit** and returned to the Kerulen (modern Herelen) River in eastern Mongolia to attack his rival Ong Khan Toghril of the Kerait. After the Kerait were destroyed, with Toghril and his son Sanggum killed in flight, Temujin turned against the Naiman at **Khangai**.

Kerulen I 1409 I Ming Imperial Wars

Following victory at **Nanjing** (1356), Ming forces secured northern China (1368) then determined to invade Mongolia, where General Qiu Fu took a reported 100,000 men to the Kerulen River against Mongol Prince Bunyashiri and his chancellor Arughtai. Lured deep into the steppe, Qiu was defeated and killed west of Onohu. The Ming were soon avenged at the **Onon** (23 September 1409).

Kesseldorf I 1745 I War of the Austrian Succession

While Frederick II of Prussia met the Austrians at **Hennersdorf**, other Prussians under Leopold the Elder of Anhalt-Dessau marched up the Elbe towards Dresden against Austria's Saxon allies. At Kesseldorf, west of the capital, Saxon Marshal Friedrich August Rutowski suffered a decisive defeat and Dresden capitulated.

Empress Maria Theresa then sued for peace (15 December 1745).

Kessler's Cross Lanes | 1861 | American Civil War (Eastern Theatre)
See **Cross Lanes**

Kettle Creek | 1779 | War of the American Revolution
Encouraged by Britain's capture of **Savannah**, North Carolina Tory militia under Colonel James Boyd campaigned on the upper Savannah, but at Kettle Creek, Georgia, they were attacked in camp by a smaller pro-rebel militia force under Colonel Andrew Pickens. A decisive defeat saw Boyd among 40 killed and 70 others captured, five of them hanged for treason (14 February 1779).

Kettle Hill | 1898 | Spanish-American War
See **San Juan Hill**

Kettle Run | 1862 | American Civil War (Eastern Theatre)
Confederate General Thomas "Stonewall" Jackson outflanked General John Pope's Union army on the **Rappahannock**, reaching Bull Run Bridge, Virginia, where he defeated and killed General George W. Taylor. A larger action at nearby Kettle Run saw General Richard S. Ewell inflict heavy losses on Union General Joseph Hooker prior to the main battle at **Bull Run** (27 August 1862).

Keyes Raid | 1941 | World War II (Northern Africa)
On the eve of the British offensive at **Sidi Rezegh**, Colonel Geoffrey Keyes led a commando assault on Rommel's supposed headquarters near Appolonia in Tripolitania. Rommel was away in Italy and Keyes was killed in the failed assault on a minor administration building. All but two of 59 raiders were killed or captured and Keyes won a posthumous Victoria Cross (17–18 November 1941).

Khabar | 1107 | Crusader-Muslim Wars
Amid confused Muslim rivalry in Mesopotamia, Kilij Arslan, the powerful Sultan of Rum, extended his territory east to capture the city of Mosul, on the Tigris. In a battle of great significance to the Christian cause, Kilij Arslan, enemy of Byzantium and destroyer of three Crusades in Anatolia, was defeated and killed on the Khabar River by Ridwan of Aleppo (June 1107).

Khadima | 633 | Muslim Conquest of Iraq
See **Hafir, Iraq**

Khadki | 1817 | 3rd British-Maratha War
See **Kirkee**

Khafji | 1991 | 1st Gulf War
An apparent effort to capture prisoners as bargaining chips saw Iraq's only ground offensive of the war, when they entered Saudi Arabia and took Khafji. A counter-attack by American, Saudi and Qatari forces killed about 100 Iraqis and captured 430 as the survivors fled back across the border. The Allies had 44 killed, including 11 Americans and four Arabs lost to friendly fire (29–31 January 1991).

Khajwa | 1659 | War of the Mughal Princes
During bitter war between the sons of the ailing Mughal Emperor Shahjahan, the second son Shuja, after defeat at **Bahadurpur**, renewed rebellion against his brother Aurangzeb, who had seized the throne. Northwest of Fatehpur at Khajwa, Shuja was outnumbered and defeated by the Imperial army under Aurangzeb's command. He was beaten again three months later at **Maldah** (7 January 1659).

Khajwa | 1857 | Indian Mutiny
Preparing for Sir Colin Campbell's advance from **Fatehpur**, a small force under Colonel Thomas Powell attacked over 4,000 rebels blocking the road 20 miles to the northwest at Khajwa. After a gruelling forced march, Powell was killed in a bold assault. But Captain William

Peel of the Naval Brigade then secured a hard-fought victory and opened the road to **Cawnpore** (1 November 1857).

Khalakhaljit I 1203 I Conquests of Genghis Khan

Determined to secure supremacy in Mongolia, Temujin (later Genghis Khan) turned on Ong Khan Toghril of the Kerait, who was supported by Temujin's rival, Jamuqa. Outnumbered and defeated near the Kerulen at Khalakhaljit, Temujin withdrew when the Ong Khan's son Sanggum was wounded. Temujin fled to Lake Baljuna but returned later in the year to smash the Kerait at the **Kerulen**.

Khalkan Gol I 1939 I Russo-Japanese Border Wars

In the most serious clash between Russia and Japanese-occupied Manchukuo, fighting began near Nomonhan on the Mongolian border along the Khalkan Gol. After months of action, Russian General Georgy Zhukov launched a crushing air and land offensive. General Michitaro Komatsubara lost half his army before Tokyo sought a ceasefire (11 May–16 September 1939).

Khalule I 691 BC I Assyrian Wars

Assyrian King Sennacherib campaigning to reassert control over Babylon was confronted by the combined armies of King Mushezib-Marduk of Babylon and King Umman-Menanu of Elam in a huge battle at Khalule, in the Jordan Valley. After very heavy casualties both sides claimed victory. However, Sennacherib was able to seize Babylon the following year and destroyed much of the city.

Khambula I 1879 I Anglo-Zulu War

One day after repulsing the British at **Hlobane** in northern Zululand, a large Zulu army under Tshingwayo and Mnyamana attacked Colonel Henry Wood's camp further west at Khambula. A courageous defensive action saw the Zulus driven off with very heavy losses, dealing a decisive strategic blow to King Cetshwayo, who was finally defeated in July at **Ulundi** (29 March 1879).

Khan Baghdadi I 1918 I World War I (Mesopotamia)

After the fall of **Ramadi**, new Anglo-Indian commander Sir William Marshall sent Generals Harry Brooking and Robert Cassels west along the Euphrates from Baghdad. Supported by aircraft and armoured cars, they attacked and seized Khan Baghdadi. The campaign yielded over 5,000 Turkish prisoners and stabilised the front until the attack north on **Sharqat**, in October (26 March 1918).

Khandesh I 752 I Indian Dynastic Wars

Despite victory over Pallava at **Kanchi** (731), the south Indian Kingdom of Chalukya was in decline and, when Warrior King Vikramaditya died (747), his son Kirtivarman faced the rising power of his nominal feudatory, Dantidurga of Rashtrakuta. Dantidurga defeated Kirtivarman in Khandesh and Chalukya was overthrown. The new Rashtrakuta Dynasty dominated the Deccan for over 200 years.

Khandwa I 1720 I Mughal-Hyderabad War

See **Ratanpur**

Khangai I 1204 I Conquests of Genghis Khan

In one of the decisive battles of his rise to power, the Mongol Temujin (later Genghis Khan) met the Tayang-Khan Baibuqa of the Naiman in the mountains of Khangai (near future Karakorum), in central Mongolia. With Baibuqa fatally wounded, the Naiman were routed and died when they refused to surrender. The Tayang's son Kuchlug escaped and met Temujin in 1208 on the **Irtysh**.

Khania I 1645 I Venetian-Turkish Wars

After 400 years of Venetian occupation, Turkish forces landed on northern Crete to attack the fortified port of Khania. A brutal siege cost very heavy losses before Khania became the first Cretan centre to fall. The Turks later attacked further east at **Candia**. A Venetian attempt to retake Khania in 1666 failed and the port remained in Turkish hands until 1898 (24 June–August 1645).

Khania ▎1692 ▎Venetian-Turkish Wars

In an effort to recover Turkish Crete, Venice sent Domenico Mocenigo with a large fleet to besiege Khania. A relief effort was driven off (8 August), but on reports of a Turkish fleet approaching, Mocenigo over-ruled his Maltese and Papal allies and abandoned the siege. Venetian prestige suffered a terrible blow and Mocenigo was dismissed for incompetence (17 July–29 August 1692).

Khanigalbat ▎681 BC ▎Assyrian Wars

Near the end of his reign, the great King Sennacherib of Assyria established his favourite son Esarhaddon as co-ruler. While Esarhaddon was at war in Armenia, two other sons, Sharezer and Adarmalik, murdered Sennacherib and attempted to seize power. At Khanigalbat, near Nisibis west of the Tigris, Esarhaddon defeated the parricides and mounted the throne as King.

Khanikin ▎1916 ▎World War I (Mesopotamia)

Russian General Nikolai Baratov attempting to divert the Turks in Mesopotamia invaded northern Persia in late 1915 and took Hamadan and Kermanshah. Having captured **Kut-al-Amara**, General Ali Ihsan Pasha marched northeast from Baghdad to Khanikin, where he routed part of the Russian force. Baratov withdrew, but the Turks returned to defend **Baghdad** and fighting died down (1 June 1916).

Khanua ▎1527 ▎Mughal Conquest of Northern India

Opposing the Mughal conquest of northern India after Babur's great victory at **Panipat**, Rana Sanga, King of Mewar, took a massive Rajput force against the invaders southwest of Bharatpur at Khanua. Babur utterly destroyed the Rajputs, then advanced into Bihar and Bengal, culminating in his decisive victory at the **Gogra** in 1529 to establish the 300-year Mughal Empire (16 March 1527).

Khan Yaunis ▎1516 ▎Ottoman-Mamluk War

See **Yaunis Khan**

Kharda ▎1795 ▎Maratha Territorial Wars

Subadar Nizam Ali of Hyderabad took a reported 110,000 men to attack the Marathas of Daulat Rao Sindhia, who was supported by troops from Tukaji Holkar and Raghoji Bhonsle of Berar. While casualties in battle at Kharda, southeast of Ahmadnagar were light, Nizam suffered a humiliating defeat. In 1799 he fought alongside the British in the 4th British-Mysore War (11–12 March 1795).

Kharkov ▎1942 ▎World War II (Eastern Front)

Following Russia's winter offensive to save **Moscow**, Marshal Symeon Timoshenko sent his armour to recover Kharkov in the eastern Ukraine. The Russians penetrated deep before General Ewald von Kleist counter-attacked and cut off the Barvenkovo Salient. Timoshenko lost up to 250,000 men and 600 tanks, opening the way for the German offensive towards **Stalingrad** (12–22 May 1942).

Kharkov (1st) ▎1943 ▎World War II (Eastern Front)

Flushed with victory after **Stalingrad**, Russian General Filip Golikov stormed west and retook Kharkov (16 February). Despite being heavily outnumbered, Marshal Erich von Manstein launched a brilliant counter-attack and drove Golikov and General Nikolai Vatutin back to the Donetz with heavy losses. Manstein retook Kharkov and it was held until after **Kursk** in July (9–16 March 1943).

Kharkov (2nd) ▎1943 ▎World War II (Eastern Front)

As the German offensive at **Kursk** ground to a halt, Generals Nikolai Vatutin, Ivan Konev and Rodion Malinovsky launched a massive converging counter-offensive south towards Kharkov. Threatened with encirclement after the fall of Belgorod (5 August), General Herman Hoth abandoned Kharkov and Marshal Erich von

Manstein withdrew to the **Dnieper** (17 July–23 August 1943).

Khartoum I 1884–1885 I British-Sudan Wars

General Charles Gordon attempted to hold the Sudan against the Mahdi, Mohammed Ahmed, and found himself besieged at Khartoum on the Upper Nile. A relief force under General Sir Garnet Wolseley defeated the Dervishes at **Abu Kru**, but arrived too late. Wad el-Najumi had already stormed Khartoum and killed Gordon, so Wolseley returned down the Nile (March 1884–26 January 1885).

Khaybar I 628 I Campaigns of the Prophet Mohammed

A year after capturing **Medina**, the Prophet Mohammed took 1,800 men against Khaybar, where the Jews were accused of intriguing with his enemies. During a six-week campaign, he gradually captured the town's strong-points. One citadel held out under the Jewish Chief Kinana, who was killed along with most of his men. His teenage widow Safiyya became one of Mohammed's wives (September 628).

Khed I 1707 I Maratha Civil War

Returning to Ahmadnagar 17 years after he was captured at **Raigarh**, Shahu (son of former Maratha King Sambhaji) was opposed by his aunt Tarabai on behalf of her 12-year-old son, Shivaji. In battle south of Ahmadnagar at Khed, Tarabai's forces under Parashuram Pant Pratinidhi were routed when Dhanaji Jadhev deserted to Shahu, who was crowned a few months later (12 October 1707).

Khelat I 1839 I 1st British-Afghan War
See **Kalat**

Khelna I 1701–1702 I Mughal-Maratha Wars

Emperor Aurangzeb and General Asad Khan led a renewed offensive in western India, where they besieged the mountain fortress of Khelna, 35 miles northwest of Kolhapur. Over 6,000 Imperial troops were killed in months of attack by the field army of Dhanaji Jadhav, but Maratha commander Parashurampant finally surrendered in return for his life (26 December 1701–6 June 1702).

Khem Karan I 1965 I 2nd Indo-Pakistan War

As part of India's offensive towards **Lahore**, large forces from both sides met to the southeast in a massive armoured action around the key city of Khem Karan, just inside the Indian border. Almost 100 Pakistani tanks were destroyed or captured in an ambush to the north near Asal Uttar. However, India could not achieve a breakthrough and eventually had to accept a ceasefire (7–10 September 1965).

Khenifra I 1914 I French Colonial Wars in North Africa

Determined to suppress the Zaia of central Morocco after the costly action at **El Ksiba** (June 1913), Colonel Paul Henrÿs sent 14,000 men in three converging columns against Moha ou Hammou's capital at Khenifra. The French fought their way into the city after very heavy fighting, though Moha ou Hammou and his army had escaped. They struck back in November at **El Herri** (10–12 June 1914).

Kherla I 1428 I Malwa-Bahmani Wars

With Alp Khan (Hushang Shah) of Malwa occupied by war with Gujarat, Ahmad Shah I of the Bahmani Sultanate determined to recover his former feudatory Kherla. When Ahmad besieged the powerful fortress, on the headwaters of the Tapti east of Deogarh, Alp Khan advanced with a relief army, but suffered a crushing defeat. Renewed war in 1468 saw Malwa fail attempting to retake Kherla.

Khe Sanh I 1967 I Vietnam War

On a major offensive across the demilitarized zone, North Vietnamese regulars attacked the westernmost US marine base at Khe Sanh, close to Laos. While very heavy fighting for the surrounding hills cost the marines 155 killed, the Communists suffered over 900 killed and eventually withdrew to regroup for another offensive further east against the base at **Con Thien** (24 April–11 May 1967).

Khe Sanh ∎ 1968 ∎ Vietnam War

As part of the **Tet Offensive**, up to 30,000 North Vietnamese under General Vo Nguyen Giap besieged the US Marine base at Khe Sanh, inside the DMZ. Determined not to suffer a symbolic defeat, America responded with heavy reinforcements and some of the most intense bombing ever. Giap eventually abandoned the bloody siege but the Americans also withdrew (21 January–8 April 1968).

Khidrana ∎ 1705 ∎ Mughal-Sikh Wars

See **Muktsar**

Khios ∎ 412 BC ∎ Great Peloponnesian War

See **Chios**

Khios ∎ 357 BC ∎ 1st Greek Social War

See **Chios**

Khios ∎ 201 BC ∎ 2nd Macedonian War

See **Chios**

Khios ∎ 1694 ∎ Venetian-Turkish Wars

See **Chios**

Khios ∎ 1770 ∎ Catherine the Great's 1st Turkish War

See **Chios**

Khios ∎ 1822 ∎ Greek War of Independence

See **Chios**

Khiva ∎ 1740 ∎ Persian-Uzbek Wars

Determined to punish the Uzbeks for raiding his northern province of Khorasan, Nadir Shah of Persia defeated the Uzbeks of Bokhara at **Charjui**, then continued down the Oxus (Amu Darya) and defeated the local Uzbeks at Khiva. Ilbars Khan of Khiva was then forced to surrender at the nearby fortress of Jayuk and was

executed. The victories secured Nadir's northern borders (November 1740).

Khiva ∎ 1873 ∎ Russian Conquest of Central Asia

Russian General Konstantin von Kaufmann led a fresh offensive in Central Asia, where he captured the Khanate of **Bokhara** and five years later took a reported 10,000 men across the Karakum desert to besiege Khiva. After the city fell, Khan Sayid Muhammad Rahim II signed a peace treaty with von Kaufmann, who took his army against the remaining Khanate of **Khokand**, in 1875 (29 May 1873).

Khodynka ∎ 1608 ∎ Russian Time of Troubles

Gathering support after victory at **Bolkhov**, a pretender claiming to be Dimitri—murdered son of former Tsar Ivan IV—continued towards Moscow and, at Khodynka, again defeated Tsar Basil Shuiski. While the "Second False Dimitri" was unable to take the capital, he established a shadow government to the west at **Klushino** and was murdered in 1610 by one of his followers (25 June 1608).

Khoi ∎ 1584 ∎ Turko-Persian Wars

On a fresh invasion of Azerbaijan, Turkish commander Ferhad Pasha sent forces towards Tabriz. Eighty miles to the northwest near Khoi (modern Khvoy) his advance units were heavily defeated by Persian Crown Prince Hamza Mirza. After a second failure, Ferhad Pasha was succeeded in the command by Osman Pasha, whose renewed advance the following year captured **Tabriz**.

Khoi ∎ 1822 ∎ Turko-Persian War in Azerbaijan

After beating the Turks at **Erzurum** in 1821, Persian Prince Abbas Mirza captured Bayazid before being turned back by winter, but entered Azerbaijan again the following year. Near Khoi (modern Khvoy in northwest Iran) he routed an Ottoman army under former Grand Vizier Muhammad Emin Rauf Pasha. However, Abbas

Mirza's army was ravaged by cholera and he sued for peace (May 1822).

Khojend I 1220 I Conquests of Genghis Khan

When the Mongol Genghis Khan launched his western offensive against the Khwarezmian Empire, he besieged **Otrar**, on the Syr Darya, then sent a smaller force upstream against Khojend (Khudjand in Tajikistan), held for Muhammad II of Khwarezm by General Timur Malik. Withdrawing to the citadel on a mid-river island, Timur Malik led a brilliant defence then escaped as the fortress fell.

Khokand I 1875 I Russian Conquest of Central Asia

Russian General Konstanin von Kaufmann conquered **Bokhara** (1868) and **Khiva** (1873), then attacked Khokand, the last remaining independent Khanate. Following spirited fighting, commander Abd al-Rahman Avtobachi was decisively defeated at Makhram and nearby Khokand city fell a few days later. Amir Nasir al-Din surrendered, but rebel resistance continued at **Andizhan** (22 August 1875).

Khoosh-Ab I 1857 I Anglo-Persian War

In response to Persia's capture of **Herat** in Afghanistan, British forces in the Persian Gulf soon captured **Reshire** and **Bushire**, then marched inland towards Brazun. As General Sir James Outram returned he met a Persian army of 10,000 under Suja-ul-Mulk near Khoosh-Ab. The Persians were routed with about 700 killed and made peace. They soon lost again at **Mohammerah** (8 February 1857).

Khoraiba I 656 I Muslim Civil Wars
See **Camel, Iraq**

Khorramshahr I 1857 I Anglo-Persian War
See **Mohammerah**

Khorramshahr I 1980 I Iraq-Iran War

At the start of the war, an Iraqi armoured division advanced against Khorramshahr on the Karun River, but the tanks were repulsed when they attempted to enter the city unsupported. After heavy street fighting against regulars and militia, Khorramshahr was finally taken at severe cost to both sides. The delay enabled Iran to reinforce nearby **Abadan** (28 September–25 October 1980).

Khorramshahr I 1982 I Iraq-Iran War

Recovering from heavy losses relieving **Abadan**, Iran launched a broad offensive with up to 150,000 men against Iraqi forces in the south, then sent about 70,000 to recover Khorramshahr. Despite their strong defences, the Iraqis were overwhelmed with about 12,000 men captured. Within a month, President Saddam Hussein ordered most Iraqi forces withdrawn from Iran (30 April–23 May 1982).

Khost I 1985 I Afghan Civil War

On a large-scale guerrilla offensive against the Soviet-backed Kabul government, about 5,000 Mujahaden rebels besieged the city of Khost near the Pakistan border. Armed with rocket launchers they caused severe damage, threatening to close the airfield. Russian commando reinforcements were flown in and the city was saved until a fresh Mujahaden assault six years later (July 1985).

Khost I 1991 I Afghan Civil War

At the start of their final offensive, Mujahaden forces under Jalaluddin Haqqani attacked the city of Khost, held for the Russian-backed Kabul government by General Muhammad Zahir Solamal. After a massive rocket attack the city fell with over 2,000 prisoners, including General Solamal and other high-ranking officers. The next advance was against **Kabul** itself (13–30 March 1991).

Khosun I 1818 I Persian-Afghan Wars
See **Kafir Qala**

Khotin **I** 1600 **I** Balkan National Wars

Prince Michael the Brave of Wallachia seized Transylvania after **Selimbar** (October 1599) then led a surprise attack on Moldavia. He pursued the Voyevod Jeremiah Movila to Khotin on the Dniester, where Jeremiah was decisively beaten and expelled to Poland. By briefly uniting Transylvania, Wallachia and Moldavia, Michael is claimed today as the founder of future Romania (May 1600).

Khotin **I** 1621 **I** Polish-Turkish Wars

A year after defeating the Poles at **Cecora**, Sultan Osman II took a large army against the Polish fortified camp at Khotin near the Dniester in the Ukraine. Hetman Jan Karol Chodkiewicz led a brilliant defence and, when he was killed, Stanislas Lubomirski forced the Turks to withdraw. Osman blamed defeat on his Janissaries, who later mutinied and killed him (2 September–9 October 1621).

Khotin **I** 1673 **I** Turkish Invasion of the Ukraine

When he invaded the Polish Ukraine in aid of Cossack rebellion, Sultan Mehmed IV captured **Kamieniec** and humbled King Michael. Hetman John Sobieski then raised 40,000 men to inflict a terrible defeat on Turkish General Hussein Pasha on the Dniester at Khotin. Poland was saved and, after Michael died on the night of the victory, Sobieski was crowned as John III (11 November 1673).

Khotin **I** 1739 **I** Austro-Russian-Turkish War

See **Stavuchany**

Khotin **I** 1769 **I** Catherine the Great's 1st Turkish War

Russian Prince Alexander Golitsyn and General Pyotr Rumyantsev advancing against Turkey on the Dniester, were repulsed at Khotin by the Pole Ignatius Potocki. In a later assault, Golitsyn defeated Grand Vizier Emin Pasha (who was executed for failure) then beat new Vizier Moldovani. The Turks evacuated Khotin when the rising river destroyed their bridges (June–26 September 1769).

Khotin **I** 1788 **I** Catherine the Great's 2nd Turkish War

As Austrian Prince Friedrich Josias of Saxe-Coburg advanced into Turkish Moldavia from the west in support of Russia, he moved against Khotin, which held out heroically under siege before it fell after three months. The Moldavian capital Jassy also fell before the Austrians and their Russian allies went on to further victory the following year at **Focsani** and **Rimnik** (2 July–19 September 1788).

Khudaganj **I** 1858 **I** Indian Mutiny

See **Fategarh**

Khujbaz **I** 1865 **I** Later Afghan War of Succession

When Amir Dost Muhammad of Afghanistan died in June 1863, his son Sher Ali faced rebellion by his brothers Amin Khan and Sharif Khan. The rebels were defeated in battle at Khujbaz, near Kalat, though Sher Ali's son Muhammad Ali was killed by his uncle Amin Khan, who was in turn killed. By mid-1866 the Amir's forces had lost at **Kabul** and **Sheikhabad** (6 June 1865).

Khujbaz **I** 1867 **I** Later Afghan War of Succession

The war of succession following the death of Dost Muhammad saw usurper Azim Khan and his nephew Abdur Rahman (son of Afzal Khan) take their army south from Kabul against Sher Ali, who had been deposed following defeat at **Sheikhabad**. At Khujbaz, near Kalat, Sher Ali was defeated when his Kandahar levies deserted. He fled to Herat, held by his son Yakub Khan (17 January 1867).

Khurd-Kabul **I** 1581 **I** Mughal Wars of Succession

When Punjab nobles supported Muhammad Hakim of Kabul against his half-brother Akbar, the Emperor raised a massive army and drove the rebel back into Afghanistan. East of Kabul at the pass of Khurd-Kabul, Imperial forces under Prince Murad and General Man Singh heavily defeated Muhammad. Akbar entered Kabul three days later to pardon and reinstate his brother (August 1581).

Khurd-Kabul ∎ 1842 ∎ 1st British-Afghan War
See **Jagdalak**

Khyber Pass ∎ 1738 ∎ Persian Invasion of India
See **Jamrud**

Khyber Pass ∎ 1837 ∎ Afghan-Sikh Wars
See **Jamrud**

Kiangsu ∎ 1946 ∎ 3rd Chinese Revolutionary Civil War
See **Jiangsu**

Kickapoo Town ∎ 1838 ∎ Kickapoo Indian Wars
Soon after Indian attacks in eastern Texas at **Battle Creek** and the **Killough Massacre**, General Thomas J. Rusk led a dawn raid on Kickapoo Town, a group of Indian villages near Frankston. The Kickapoo's Mexican allies fled and after three days of very hard fighting, with 11 Indians dead, the elderly Chief Pecana sued for peace. However, Chief Benito withdrew to continue the war (15–18 October 1838).

Kidney Ridge ∎ 1942 ∎ World War II (Northern Africa)
Facing the British offensive at **El Alamein**, Field Marshal Erwin Rommel attempted to counter-attack around Kidney Ridge, 20 miles south of the coast. Brilliant defence by a small British unit without field artillery disabled up to 50 Axis tanks and the attack stalled. Commander Colonel Victor Turner was awarded the Victoria Cross. A week later the ridge saw the British breakout (27 October 1942).

Kiemereh ∎ 1726 ∎ Turko-Persian War
When Mahmud Ghilzai, the Afghan conqueror of Persia, went insane he was succeeded by his cousin Ashraf Shah, who faced a massive invasion by Turkish General Ahmad Rahman Pasha with 60,000 men and 70 guns. Outside Isfahan at Kiemereh the Turkish army was routed with a reported 12,000 killed. However, Ashraf made peace and Constantinople recognised him as Shah (November 1726).

Kiev ∎ 1069 ∎ Russian Dynastic Wars
Less than a year after being driven off the Kievan throne following defeat at the **Alta**, Prince Iziaslav returned with his brother-in-law, Boleslaw II of Poland. Just outside Kiev they met the army of Vseslav of Polotsk, who was defeated and fled. Kiev was then besieged and surrendered to Iziaslav, who regained the throne. Only four years later he was deposed by his brother Sviatoslav.

Kiev ∎ 1240 ∎ Mongol Conquest of Russia
After conquering northern Russia, the Mongol Batu (grandson of Genghis Khan) and his cousin Mongke crossed the frozen Dneiper and besieged Kiev, where Prince Michael of Kiev fled. When Governor Dmitri refused to surrender, the city was taken by storm and utterly destroyed before the Mongols marched west for their great victories at **Liegnitz** and on the **Sajo** (6 December 1240).

Kiev ∎ 1482 ∎ Polish-Crimean Tatar Wars
With the Mongols dispersed at the **Ugra** in November 1480, Crimean Tatars under Khan Mengil Girai, with encouragement from Duke Ivan III of Moscow, advanced into the Polish Ukraine and attacked Kiev. Military Governor Pan Ivan Khodkevich escaped but was captured, while many of those who remained were burned to death in the ensuing brutal sack of the city (1 September 1482).

Kiev ∎ 1658 ∎ Russo-Polish Wars
Cossack leader Ivan Vyhovksy claimed continued loyalty to Moscow despite burning **Poltava**, but weeks later sent his brother Danilo (supported by Tatar forces) against Kiev, garrisoned by Russian Colonel Fedor I. Sheremetev and Kievan Cossacks. Danilo Vyhovsky was

routed and his brother firmed his alliance with Poland. A year later they beat the Russians at **Konotop** (23 August 1658).

Kiev I 1920 I Russo-Polish War

Having reached the Berezina through **Minsk**, Polish commander Josef Pilsudski launched a massive offensive towards Kiev, supported by Ukrainian Hetman Semyon Petlyura. Soviet General Aleksandr Yegorov suffered terrible losses in men and equipment before withdrawing and Kiev itself fell without resistance (7 May). Russia soon counter-attacked on the **Berezina** (25–28 April 1920).

Kiev I 1941 I World War II (Eastern Front)

After the fall of **Smolensk**, Panzer General Heinz Guderian turned south into the Ukraine towards Kiev to join General Ewald von Kleist circling north after crushing the pocket at **Uman**. Stalin ordered Kiev held at all cost, but it fell with 665,000 prisoners, 900 tanks and 3,500 guns. While Kiev was Russia's worst defeat, the delay helped save **Moscow** (21 August–26 September 1941).

Kiev I 1943 I World War II (Eastern Front)

General Konstantin Rokossovksy spearheaded the Soviet offensive towards the **Dnieper**, driving west through Chernigov while further south General Nikolai Vatutin advanced on Kiev itself, held by General Herman Hoth's Fourth Panzer Army. Most of the German divisions escaped before Kiev fell. Hoth was dismissed and the Russians continued west to **Zhitomir** (3–6 November 1943).

Kila Alladad I 1867 I Later Afghan War of Succession

Defeated by his brother Azim Khan at **Sheikhabad** and **Khujbaz**, deposed Amir Sher Ali raised a fresh army, aided by Faiz Muhammad, Governor of Afghan Turkestan then marched towards Kabul. In battle to the north at Kila Alladad, near Charikar, Faiz Muhammad was

killed and Sher Ali was defeated. In early 1869, Sher Ali regained his kingdom at **Zurmat** (17 September 1867).

Kilblain I 1335 I Anglo-Scottish War of Succession

In the war between adherents of young David II of Scotland and English-backed Edward Baliol, Scottish Royalists Sir Andrew Moray, Patrick Dunbar Earl of March and Sir William Douglas of Liddesdale, surprised Earl David of Atholl, besieging Kildrummy, near Alford, Aberdeenshire. Atholl was defeated and killed at nearby Kilblain and his widow fled to **Lochindorb**.

Kilcommadan I 1691 I War of the Glorious Revolution
See **Aughrim**

Kilcullen I 1798 I Irish Rebellion

At the start of the rebellion in Ireland, Royalist General Sir Ralph Dundas with just 40 dragoons and 20 militia rashly attacked 300 rebels in a strong defensive position in the churchyard at Kilcullen. After losing about half his force, Dundas joined local Yeomanry to defeat the rebels in an ambush, but fell back to nearby **Naas** and left them to seize most of County Kildare (24 May 1798).

Kilcumney Hill I 1798 I Irish Rebellion

Father John Murphy and survivors of the disastrous rebel defeat at **Vinegar Hill** (21 June) trying to make their way back to Wexford were intercepted and beaten by General Sir Charles Asgill near the Wexford county border at Kilcumney Hill, in County Carlow. Father Murphy was later captured and beheaded, effectively ending the two-month rising (26 June 1798).

Kildrummy I 1335 I Anglo-Scottish War of Succession
See **Kilblain**

Kili I 1299 I Mongol Invasions of India

Despite a Mongol repulse in India at **Jalandhar**, Dawa Khan of Transoxonia (a descendant of

Genghis Khan) sent his son Qutlugh Khwaja with a force claimed to number 200,000 against Sultan Ala-ud-din of Delhi. Outside Delhi at Kili the Sultan's army under Ulugh Khan and Zafar Khan secured a great victory. The Mongols again withdrew, although Zafar Khan was killed.

Kilimanjaro I 1916 I World War I (African Colonial Theatre)
See **Morogoro**

Kilkis I 1913 I 2nd Balkan (Inter-ally) War
When Bulgaria suddenly attacked her former allies over Macedonia, the Serbs counter-attacked on the **Bregalnica**, while King Constantine of Greece met them north of Thessalonica. The Greeks suffered costly losses attacking near Kilkis, then advanced along the whole Lachanas-Nigrita front. The Bulgarians had to withdraw, soon trying to make a stand at **Kresna** (1–3 July 1913).

Killala (1st) I 1798 I French Revolutionary Wars (Irish Rising)
In an attempt to support Irish rebellion, three French frigates entered Killala Bay in northwest Ireland to land General Joseph Amable Humbert and 1,100 men, including Matthew Tone (brother of rebel leader Wolfe Tone) and considerable arms and guns. This advance party for the main invasion seized the small town, but French help was too little too late (23 August 1798).

Killala (2nd) I 1798 I French Revolutionary Wars (Irish Rising)
Two weeks after securing French-Irish surrender at **Ballinamuck**, the British turned their attention to the small force under French Colonel Armand Charost holding about 200 Loyalist prisoners in the port of Killala, County Mayo, where the invasion had first landed. The remaining garrison fled after a one-sided disaster, with about 400 killed, and the rebellion was over (23 September 1798).

Killdeer Mountain I 1864 I Sioux Indian Wars
General Alfred Sully beat the Sioux at **Whitestone Hill** (September 1863), then took 2,000 men towards the Badlands of North Dakota to secure a decisive victory. At Killdeer Mountain, between the Little Missouri and Knife Rivers, he attacked the camp of Chief Inkapduta and perhaps 5,000 warriors. Sully inflicted a terrible defeat, effectively ending organised Sioux resistance (28 July 1864).

Killiecrankie I 1689 I First Jacobite Rebellion
Scottish Catholic supporters of James II resisting the accession of William III attempted a Highland rising under John Graham Viscount Dundee. A Royalist army under General Hugh Mackay was ambushed and virtually destroyed at Killiecrankie, near Pitlochry. However, "Bonny Dundee" was killed in the battle and the rebellion petered out after defeat in August at **Dunkeld** (27 July 1689).

Killough Massacre I 1838 I Kickapoo Indian Wars
After killing a survey party at **Battle Creek**, Kickapoo Chief Benito was joined by Mexican insurrectionists under Vicente Cordova attacking a settlement just northwest of Jacksonville, Texas, where Isaac Killough and 17 of his family were killed or captured. The Indians were driven off next day by General Thomas J. Rusk and were defeated days later at **Kickapoo Town** (5 October 1838).

Kilmallock I 1922 I Irish Civil War
While government forces advanced on **Clonmel**, further west General Eoin O'Duffy marched south from **Limerick** against Kilmallock, held by Republicans since 14 July. Desperate fighting around the nearby villages of Bruff and Bruree saw the longest and hardest fought action of the war before Kilmallock fell. The survivors fled for Kerry (23 July–5 August 1922).

Kilsyth | 1645 | British Civil Wars

Six weeks after victory at **Alford**, James Graham Marquis of Montrose led his Scots and Irish Royalists south across the Forth to Kilsyth, where he destroyed the Covenanter army of Archibald Campbell Marquis of Argyll and Sir William Baillie. Glasgow and Edinburgh submitted to make Montrose master of Scotland, but he was defeated next month at **Philiphaugh** (16 August 1645).

Kilwa | 1505 | Portuguese Colonial Wars in East Africa

The island state of Kilwa Kisiwani, off East Africa, accepted tribute to Portugal (1502), but when Sultan Ibrahim ceased to make payments a large fleet arrived under Francisco d'Almeida. After sharp fighting, the Portuguese sacked the city then attacked **Mombasa**. Portugal built Fort Gereza in Kilwa, but lost the city to Arab mercenaries in 1512. They regained permanent control in 1597.

Kimberley | 1899–1900 | 2nd Anglo-Boer War

At the start of the war, with **Mafeking** besieged, further south Marthinus Wessels and later Piet Cronjé loosely besieged Kimberley, held by 4,000 men under Colonel Robert Kekewich. A relief force was repulsed at **Magersfontein**, but Kimberley was finally relieved by General John French. Cronjé was pursued east and captured a few days later at **Paardeberg** (15 October 1899–15 February 1900).

Kinairi | 1848 | 2nd British-Sikh War

See **Kineyre**

Kinburn | 1787 | Catherine the Great's 2nd Turkish War

Turkish forces resuming the war against Russia attempted a seaborne attack on the fortress at Kinburn, near the mouth of the Dnieper opposite **Ochakov**. Russian General Alexander Suvorov permitted 6,000–7,000 Turks to land before he counter-attacked with Cossack cavalry and infantry under his personal command and

the invaders were utterly annihilated (10 October 1787).

Kinburn | 1855 | Crimean War

In a fresh assault on the Russian coast, an Anglo-French expedition under Admirals Sir Edmund Lyons and Emile-Marius Bruat attacked Kinburn, east of Odessa, held by General Ivan Vasilevich Kokhanovich. A force of 10,000 landed under Generals Sir Augustus Spencer and Achille Bazaine and the town and fortress surrendered after a heavy bombardment (16–17 October 1855).

Kineyre | 1848 | 2nd British-Sikh War

When Britain renewed war against the Sikhs of the Punjab, Lieutenant Herbert Edwardes and a mixed Pathan-Baluchi force joined with Nawab Futteh Mohammed Khan of Bhawalpur at Kineyre, south of Multan, to attack the army of Dewan Mulraj of Multan under Rung Ram. Despite initial repulse, the Allies took the Sikh entrenchments and advanced to besiege **Multan** (18 June 1848).

King's Mountain | 1780 | War of the American Revolution

A few months after British victory at **Camden**, Loyalist militia under Major Patrick Ferguson pursued rebel militia under Colonels William Campbell and Isaac Shelby, but were forced to withdraw to King's Mountain, just inside the South Carolina border. In a decisive all-American action, the Tories were encircled, with Ferguson killed and virtually his entire force killed or captured (7 October 1780).

Kingston | 1758 | Seven Years War (North America)

See **Fort Frontenac**

Kinloss | 1009 | Later Viking Raids on Britain

See **Nairn**

Kinney's Farm | 1862 | American Civil War (Eastern Theatre)

See **Hanover Court House**

Kinsale I 1601 I Tyrone Rebellion

Following victory at **Blackwater** for Irish rebel Hugh O'Neill Earl of Tyrone (14 August 1598), 4,000 Spanish under Don Juan d'Aguila captured Kinsale, south of Cork, but were besieged by English forces under Charles Blount Lord Mountjoy and Sir George Carew. Attempting to relieve the siege, O'Neill and the Spaniards were heavily defeated and the rebellion was crushed (24 December 1601).

Kinston I 1862 I American Civil War (Eastern Theatre)

Union General John G. Foster resumed the offensive in North Carolina, advancing from **New Bern**, inland towards the strategic railway at **Goldsboro Bridge**. On the upper Neuse at Kinston, Foster met and defeated a Confederate brigade under General Nathan Evans. He then continued his march west through an inconclusive action two days later at **White Hall** (14 December 1862).

Kinston I 1865 I American Civil War (Western Theatre)

As Union commander William T. Sherman marched east across the Carolinas, Confederate General Braxton Bragg, attempting a flank attack up the Neuse from New Bern, was met by Union General John Schofield, marching north from Wilmington in support. Fierce fighting near Kinston, North Carolina, saw Bragg repulsed. Schofield then joined Sherman at **Bentonville** (7–10 March 1865).

Kinzan I 1915 I Saudi-Rashidi Wars

Defeated by the pro-Turkish Rashid at **Jirab** when his Ajman allies defected, Emir Abd al-Aziz (Ibn Saud) of Riyadh and his brother Sa'ad attacked the Ajman late in the year at Kinzan, just west of Hofuf. In the Saudis' worst defeat, Aziz was routed and wounded and Sa'ad was killed. Aziz was unable to support his British allies against Turkey, though by May 1919 he recovered for victory at **Turabah**.

Kip's Bay I 1776 I War of the American Revolution

Attacking General George Washington in New York City, British commander William Howe bombarded Kip's Bay, on Manhattan Island, held by Colonel William Douglas. General Israel Putnam ordered a withdrawal in order to avoid losses and General Henry Clinton landed his British and Hessian troops at Kip's Bay. Further action ensued next day at **Harlem Heights** (15 September 1776).

Kirchberg I 1797 I French Revolutionary Wars (1st Coalition)

In a renewed French offensive, General Louis Lazare Hoche crossed the Rhine to defeat the Austrians near **Neuwied** then sent General Michel Ney's cavalry after Field Marshal Franz Werneck. Ney repulsed the Austrians in a minor engagement next day near Kirchberg but was captured when he fell from his horse in a skirmish at Giessen. He was returned on parole on 6 May (19 April 1797).

Kirchdenkern I 1761 I Seven Years War (Europe)

See **Vellinghausen**

Kirin I 1900 I Russo-Chinese War

See **Jilin**

Kirina I 1235 I Wars of Sosso

Sumanguru of Kaniaga made the Sosso of West Africa into a major force, capturing the former Ghanaian Imperial capital of **Kumbi**. But the tyrannical rule of the warrior-ruler helped speed the fall of his short-lived Sosso Empire. At Kirina (near modern Koulikoro, Mali), Sumanguru was defeated and overthrown by the Mandingo leader Sundiata, marking the birth of the new Mali Empire.

Kirkeban I 1885 I British-Sudan Wars

General Sir Garnet Wolseley advanced up the Nile to relieve **Khartoum** and sent a column ahead under General Sir William Earle, who met a large Mahdist force entrenched at Kirkeban, 75 miles above Merowe. The Mahdists were routed, but Earle was killed at the head of his troops. News then arrived of the fall of Khartoum and Wolseley returned downstream (10 February 1885).

Kirkee ▮ 1817 ▮ 3rd British-Maratha War

With Pindari outlaws ravaging central India, Peshwa Baji Rao II of Poona renewed war against the British by burning the Residency in Poona, then attacked a British-Sepoy force under Colonel Charles Burr moving out from positions at nearby Kirkee (modern Khadki). Repulsed with over 500 casualties, the Peshwa withdrew until his offensive against **Koregaon** (5 November 1817).

Kirkenes ▮ 1944 ▮ World War II (Northern Europe)

German General Lothar Rendulic was driven out of **Petsamo** in northern Finland during the Lapland War and fell back west to Kirkenes in Norway, pursued by Finns and Soviet Marshal Kirill Meretskov. The Germans hoped to evacuate vital supplies out of the Arctic port, but were forced out in heavy fighting and withdrew into the mountains. Some held out until April 1945 (20–25 October 1944).

Kirkholm ▮ 1605 ▮ 1st Polish-Swedish War

On a fresh offensive in Livonia after Swedish defeat at **Weissenstein**, Charles IX took command and led his ill-trained army towards Riga. To the southeast at Kirkholm, he was met and heavily defeated by a much smaller Polish force under Hetman Jan Karol Chodkiewicz. The Swedes lost almost 10,000 casualties and Charles himself narrowly escaped capture (27 September 1605).

Kirkincliffe ▮ 1306 ▮ Rise of Robert the Bruce

Having defeated Robert the Bruce at **Methven** and **Dalry** in mid-1306, Edward II captured and executed Robert's brother, Nigel Bruce, then turned his vengeance against the last resistance of Sir Simon Fraser (hero of the Scots victory over Edward at **Roslin**). Attacked at Kirkincliffe, near Stirling, Fraser was defeated and captured. He was then taken in chains to London for execution.

Kirk Kilissa ▮ 1912 ▮ 1st Balkan War

Bulgarian General Radko Dimitriev opened the war by invading Thrace, where he met Turks under Abdullah Pasha at Kirk Kilissa (modern Kirklareli, Bulgarian Lozengrad) east of **Adrianople**. Bloody fighting routed the Turks and, on the same day as a Turkish disaster in Macedonia at **Kumanovo**, they abandoned the fort and fell back on **Lüleburgaz** (23–24 October 1912).

Kirksville ▮ 1862 ▮ American Civil War (Trans-Mississippi)

With southern Missouri secured for the Union at **Pea Ridge**, cavalry led by Colonel John McNeil marched into the northeast against about 2,500 Confederates under Colonel Joseph C. Porter at Kirksville, Adair County. Despite being heavily outnumbered, McNeil destroyed Porter's force. The Confederates were avenged within days in the west at **Independence** and **Lone Jack** (6 August 1862).

Kirovabad ▮ 1826 ▮ Russo-Persian Wars
See **Yelizavetpol**

Kirovograd ▮ 1944 ▮ World War II (Eastern Front)

After the **Zhitomir** offensive to the north, Russian General Ivan Konev sent 550,000 men west from the Dnieper towards Kirovograd under Generals Ivan Galanin and Pavel Rotmistrov. Smashing into part of the German Eighth Army under General Otto Wöhler, the Russians secured a decisive victory before turning north to encircle the pocket at **Korsun** (5–17 January 1944).

Kishm ▮ 1622 ▮ Anglo-Portuguese Colonial Wars
See **Hormuz**

Kislingbury ▮ 1645 ▮ British Civil Wars
See **Borough Hill**

Kissingen I 1866 I Seven Weeks War

Attacking Austria's German allies, Prussian General Edouard von Falckenstein invaded Bavaria and just days after victory at **Wiesenthal** and **Zella**, Prussian General August von Goeben attacked General Friedrich von Zoller at Kissingen. Following costly fighting, Prince Karl of Bavaria arrived with fresh troops but was forced to retire. Bavaria lost again the same day at **Hammelburg** (10 July 1866).

Kitakyushu I 1868 I War of the Meiji Restoration
See **Wakamatsu**

Kiukiang I 1855 I Taiping Rebellion
See **Jiujiang**

Kizil-Tepe I 1877 I Russo-Turkish Wars

Sent to relieve the Russian siege of **Kars**, the Turkish commander in the Caucasus, Ahmed Mukhtar Pasha, arrived with a much larger force and attacked General Mikhail Loris-Melikov at Kizil-Tepe, to the east near Subatan. While both sides lost about 1,000 casualties, the Russians were driven off. They later resumed the siege and took Kars by storm in November (25 August 1877).

Kjoge Bay I 1677 I Scania War
See **Koge Bay**

Kleck I 1506 I Polish-Crimean Tatar Wars

When Crimean Khan Mengli Girai sent his sons and 10,000 men into Lithuania, they raided up to Minsk and Novogrudok before Mikhail Glinski marched to aid the local Hetman Stanislas Kiska. Attacking unexpectedly across marshy ground, Glinski routed the Tatars at Kleck (near Nieswiez in modern Belorus) and the Khan switched allegiance to Alexander of Poland (5 August 1506).

Kleidion I 1014 I Byzantine Wars of Tsar Samuel
See **Balathista**

Kleinfontein I 1901 I 2nd Anglo-Boer War

Boer commander Jacobus de la Rey campaigning in the western Transvaal, recovered from a costly repulse at **Moedwil** (30 September) and attacked a large convoy under Colonel Stanley von Donop at Kleinfontein on the road to Zeerust. While the British lost 84 men in very heavy fighting, de la Rey lost 60 men before he managed to get away with just 12 wagons (24 October 1901).

Kliastitzy I 1812 I Napoleonic Wars (Russian Campaign)
See **Jacobovo**

Klissova I 1826 I Greek War of Independence

During the second Turkish siege of **Missolonghi**, 150 Greeks under Kitsos Tzavellas defended the harbour islet of Klissova against assault by Reshid Pasha and later by Hussein Bey Djertili, conqueror of **Sphakteria**. The Ottomans were driven off with 400 killed, including Hussein Bey, but this last Greek victory could not prevent the imminent fall of Missolonghi (6 April 1826).

Kliszow I 1702 I 2nd "Great" Northern War

Charles XII of Sweden defeated the Russians at **Narva** in late 1700 then marched into Poland, where he installed Stanislaus Leszczynski as King in Warsaw before advancing to Kliszow, near Katowice. There Charles destroyed a much larger Polish-Saxon army—though his brother-in-law, Frederick of Holstein-Gottorp was killed—and he went on to seize Cracow (9 July 1702).

Klokotnitsa I 1230 I Bulgarian Imperial Wars

Supporting Byzantine Nicaea against the Latin Emperors in Constantinople, Theodore Ducas of Epirus drove the Latins out of **Thessalonica**, then invaded Bulgaria against Tsar Ivan Asen II. On the Maritsa at Klokotnitsa, Theodore was routed, captured and blinded. Bulgaria replaced Epirus as the main Balkan power and Ivan switched to support Nicaea, attacking **Constantinople** in 1236 (April 1230).

Kloster-Kamp ▮ 1760 ▮ Seven Years War (Europe)

Allied commander Duke Ferdinand of Brunswick pursued the French west after victory at **Warburg** and sent his nephew Karl Wilhelm Ferdinand towards the Rhine. At Kloster-Kamp, north of the Eugenian Canal near Rheinberg, the Hereditary Prince's Prussian-British force was defeated by General Charles-Eugène Castries and he was forced to lift the siege of Wesel (16 October 1760).

Klushino ▮ 1610 ▮ Russian Time of Troubles

When King Sigismund III of Poland invaded Russia, Tsar Basil Shuiski obtained Swedish aid and sent a large force under his incompetent brother Dimitri Shuiski and Swedish commander Jakob de la Gardie to relieve the Polish siege of **Smolensk**. At Klushino, they were routed by a much smaller force of Poles under Hetman Stanislas Zolkiewski, who then captured **Moscow** (4 July 1610).

Kluszyn ▮ 1610 ▮ Russian Time of Troubles
See **Klushino**

Knin ▮ 1995 ▮ Croatian War

Four years after Serbian forces invaded western Croatia and created occupied Krajina, large Croatian forces, possibly with Western approval, launched a lightning offensive (Operation Storm). Amid shocking destruction and killing, the Croatians seized the key city of Knin and regained all their lost territory, displacing thousands of ethnic Serbs. War ended a few months later (4–7 August 1995).

Knockdoe ▮ 1504 ▮ Irish Barons' Wars

Nominally on behalf of the English crown, Gerald Fitzgerald Earl of Kildare led a large force from Dublin against his ambitious son-in-law, Ulich de Burgh of Clanrickard, and other rebellious nobles of Munster. Ulich was defeated and fled after terrible hand-to-hand fighting at Knockdoe, northeast of Galway town. Kildare then seized Galway and also Athenry (19 August 1504).

Knockfergus ▮ 1566 ▮ O'Neill Rebellion

Shane O'Neill Lord of Tyrone, campaigning against Anglo-Scots colonisation of Ulster, defeated the Protestant MacDonnells at **Ballycastle** then faced an English army under Sir Henry Sidney and Colonel Edward Randolph. Randolph was killed in battle at Knockfergus, near Lifford, but the English won. O'Neill was defeated again six months later at **Letterkenny** (12 November 1566).

Knoxville ▮ 1863 ▮ American Civil War (Western Theatre)
See **Fort Sanders**

Kobarid ▮ 1917 ▮ World War I (Italian Front)
See **Caporetto**

Kobryn ▮ 1812 ▮ Napoleonic Wars (Russian Campaign)

As Napoleon Bonaparte's army advanced into Russia, a Saxon brigade under General Heinrich von Klengel was surrounded by superior Russian forces under General Count Alexander Tormazov east of Brest-Litovsk at Kobryn. The Saxons were destroyed with 300 casualties and the remaining 2,000 men captured. Tormazov was defeated two weeks later at **Gorodeczno** (27 July 1812).

Kobylka ▮ 1794 ▮ War of the 2nd Polish Partition

With Polish commander Tadeusz Kosciuszko beaten and captured at **Maciejowice** (10 October), Russian Field Marshal Alexander Suvorov attacked the defeated Polish rearguard in swampy forest at Kobylka, just northeast of the capital. Bloody hand-to-hand fighting saw the heavily outnumbered Poles lose again and they withdrew to glorious defeat at **Warsaw** (26 October 1794).

Kochersberg ▮ 1677 ▮ 3rd Dutch War

Moving to stem the Imperial threat from the Rhineland, French Marshal Francois de Crequi (who had taken over command in Germany after the death of Turenne at **Sasbach**) was defeated in August 1675 at **Consarbruck**. But at Kochersberg, northwest of Strasbourg, he destroyed a large army under Duke Charles of Lorraine and drove the defeated Germans back to the Rhine (17 October 1677).

Koch's Plantation ▮ 1863 ▮ American Civil War (Lower Seaboard)

See **Cox's Plantation**

Kock ▮ 1939 ▮ World War II (Western Europe)

Despite the fall of **Warsaw**, Polish General Franciszek Kleeberg and Army Group Polesie held out for a few days southeast of the capital, around Kock. Heavy fighting along the Tysmienica against a Panzer Corps under General Gustav Von Wietersheim saw Kleeberg eventually forced to surrender his 17,000 men, ending the last organised resistance to the German invasion of **Poland** (2–5 October 1939).

Koge Bay ▮ 1677 ▮ Scania War

When Christian V of Denmark sided with the Netherlands against France and her ally Sweden, the brilliant Danish Admiral Niels Juel sailed against a large Swedish fleet in Koge Bay on the Oresund, southwest of Copenhagen. With Dutch support, the outnumbered Juel utterly routed Swedish Admiral Evert Horn, capturing or sinking 11 Swedish ships (30 June 1677).

Kogo ▮ 1944 ▮ World War II (China)

See **Central Henan**

Koheroa ▮ 1863 ▮ 2nd New Zealand War

As a large force under General Duncan Cameron invaded the Waikato to protect settlers and the new military road south from Auckland, he was blocked by a small Maori force near the Waikato River at the Koheroa Range. The Crimean war veteran drove the Maoris out at bayonet point, then advanced south along the river through Meremere to the bloody action at **Rangiriri** (17 July 1863).

Kohima ▮ 1944 ▮ World War II (Burma-India)

General Kotoku Sato led the Japanese offensive into India, crossing the Chindwin to advance on Kohima, held by a tiny garrison under Colonel Hugh Richards. Some of the bloodiest fighting of the war saw General John Grover eventually counter-attack to retake Kohima (18 April) and repulse Sato. The British then turned south to relieve besieged **Imphal** (5 April–3 June 1944).

Kojima ▮ 940 ▮ Masakado Uprising

When Japanese provincial Governor Taira Masakado seized the central Honshu Province of Kanto and declared himself "new Emperor," he was eventually surprised at Kojima, in Shimosa, by his cousin Taira Sadamori and Fujiwara Hidesato. Masakado was defeated and killed in a sharp action (Hidesato reputedly dealt the death blow) and the rebellion in Kanto was crushed (25 March 940).

Kokein ▮ 1824 ▮ 1st British-Burmese War

See **Rangoon**

Kokenhausen ▮ 1601 ▮ 1st Polish-Swedish War

After Swedish forces invaded and overran most of Livonia, almost 5,000 Swedes near Kokenhausen (Koknese in modern Latvia) were attacked by just 3,000 Poles led by Prince Krystof Radziwill, advancing from Vilna. With clever use of his cavalry, Radziwill won a brilliant victory. By 1605 Polish horsemen had been decisive again at **Weissenstein** and **Kirkholm** (10 March 1601).

Kokoda Trail ▮ 1942 ▮ World War II (Pacific)

Japanese General Tomitaro Horii, advancing across **Papua**, drove Australian defenders along the Kokoda Trail (or Track) over the steep Stanley Owen Range. The Japanese were finally halted at Imita Ridge, overlooking Port Moresby (28 September). They were then forced to withdraw in terrible jungle fighting back to the northern beaches at **Gona**, **Buna** and **Sanananda** (23 July–17 November 1942).

Kokonsaari ❙ 1808 ❙ Napoleonic Wars (Russo-Swedish War)

Withdrawing east from **Vasa** in western Finland, Russian invasion forces under General Jegor Wlastoff turned on the pursuing Swedish army at Kokonsaari. Reinforced by Russians from **Nykarleby** under General Ivan Fedorovich Jankovich, Wlastoff inflicted a sharp check on Swedish General Otto von Fieandt. However, the Swedes won handsomely a few days later at **Lapuu** (11 July 1808).

Kokumbona ❙ 1942–1943 ❙ World War II (Pacific)

Army General Alexander Patch took over command on **Guadalcanal** and launched a ground offensive west, taking Mount Austen, the hill positions known as Galloping Horse and Sea Horse, and the fort at Gifu. The key Japanese centre at Kokumbona then fell by storm and General Haruyoshi Hyakutake withdrew to evacuate from Cape Esperance (17 December 1942–23 January 1943).

Kolarovgrad ❙ 1774 ❙ Catherine the Great's 1st Turkish War

See **Kozludzha**

Kolberg ❙ 1760 ❙ Seven Years War (Europe)

An abortive attack on the coast of Prussian Pomerania saw the Russian Kronstadt fleet under Admiral Zakhar Danilovich Mishukov bombard Kolberg (modern Kolobrzeg), then land troops and guns. However, the assault was repulsed and the Russians withdrew with the loss of 600 men. Kolberg did not fall to Russian forces until after a lengthy siege the following year (5 September 1760).

Kolberg ❙ 1761 ❙ Seven Years War (Europe)

A renewed Russian offensive into Prussian Pomerania saw General Pyotr Rumyantsev lay siege to the port and fortress at Kolberg (modern Kolobrzeg), which was finally forced to surrender after six months. The capture of Kolberg gave Russia a vital strategic port on the Prussian flank, but the death of Empress Elizabeth a few weeks later took Russia out of the war (July–16 December 1761).

Kolberg Heath ❙ 1644 ❙ Thirty Years War (Franco-Habsburg War)

Swedish Admiral Klas Fleming launched a pre-emptive attack on Denmark and took Fehmarn, before being heavily defeated on nearby Kolberg Heath by Danish ships under command of 67-year-old King Christian IV. Fleming was killed when his ships were blockaded near Kiel, though Karl Gustav Wrangel led the fleet's escape. In October he beat a Danish squadron off **Lolland** (1 July 1644).

Kolb's Farm ❙ 1864 ❙ American Civil War (Western Theatre)

Pursuing General Joseph E. Johnston through Georgia, Union commander William T. Sherman was blocked by Johnston at **Marietta** and sent Generals John M. Schofield and Joseph Hooker circling to the southwest. A Confederate counter-attack by General John B. Hood was repulsed at Kolb's Farm and Sherman soon attacked to the north at **Kennesaw Mountain** (22 June 1864).

Kolin ❙ 1756 ❙ Seven Years War (Europe)

When Austrian Marshal Leopold von Daun advanced to relieve the Prussian siege of **Prague**, Frederick II of Prussia took as many men as he could spare to attack the Austrian camp at Kolin on the Elbe, east of the city. A bloody action saw Frederick's outnumbered force repulsed with heavy losses. He was forced to lift the siege of Prague and evacuate Bohemia (18 June 1757).

Kollum ❙ 1581 ❙ Netherlands War of Independence

Turning against William of Orange, Georges Lalaing Count Rennenberg declared for Spain and, after a check at **Steenwijk**, his army fled east into Groningen following heavy defeat near Kollum by loyal Dutch forces under Diederik Sonoy and Sir John Norris. Rennenberg, who had been too ill to take command, died four days later. His successor soon attacked again at **Noordhorn** (19 July 1581).

Kolombangara I 1943 I World War II (Pacific)

Admiral Shunji Izaki again attempted to reinforce the Japanese garrison on Kolombangara, west of **New Georgia**, and was met off Kolombangara in the **Kula Gulf** by Admiral Walden Ainsworth. A second deadly night action saw three American cruisers damaged and a destroyer sunk, while Izaki died when his cruiser sank. Meanwhile, the reinforcements got through to Vila (12–13 July 1943).

Kolomna I 1238 I Mongol Conquest of Russia

On campaign against the Princes of Russia, the Mongol Batu (grandson of Genghis Khan) and General Subetai killed Prince Yuri Igorevich at his capital, **Ryazan** (December 1237). They then besieged and captured Kolomna, southeast of **Moscow**, held by Yuri's brother Roman, who died in the fighting. The Mongols then systematically destroyed the towns in the Princedom of Ryazan (January 1238).

Kolubara I 1914 I World War I (Balkan Front)

Despite checking Austria at the **Drina**, Serbian Marshal Radomir Putnik fell back before a third invasion by Generals Oskar Potiorek and Liborius von Frank, who broke through and occupied Belgrade (1 December). A counteroffensive towards the Kolubara by Putnik and Zivojin Misic routed the invaders to retake Belgrade. Potiorek and Frank were both dismissed (3–16 December 1914).

Kolwezi I 1978 I Shaba War

After a previous failed attempt (March 1977), about 4,000 rebels under Nathaniel Mbumba entered Shaba Province (Katanga) in southeast Zaire and seized Kolwezi, where 50 whites and many

locals were killed. French Foreign Legion paratroops led by Colonel Philippe Erulin landed and there was fierce fighting before the rebels withdrew with perhaps 100 killed (19–21 May 1978).

Komaki I 1584 I Japan's Era of the Warring States
See **Nagakute**

Komandorski Islands I 1943 I World War II (Pacific)

Japanese Admiral Boshiro Hosogaya attempting to reinforce **Attu**, in the **Aleutians**, was intercepted near the Komandorski Islands by a cruiser squadron under Admiral Charles McMorris. A confused action saw either side suffer one cruiser damaged, but Hosogaya turned away when threatened by a destroyer torpedo attack and was later relieved of command (26 March 1943).

Komárno I 1594 I Turkish-Habsburg Wars
See **Komárom**

Komárom I 1594 I Turkish-Habsburg Wars

Responding to Austrian invasion of northern Hungary, Ottoman Grand Vizier Sinan Pasha drove off a siege of Gran by Archduke Matthias and captured Raab after three days. However, despite his huge army, he was frustrated by the stubborn Danube fortress of Komárom (modern Komárno), northwest of Budapest. After a long siege, he was forced to withdraw his expedition with little achieved.

Komárom I 1849 I Hungarian Revolutionary War

When Russia intervened in Hungary to help Austria crush revolution, Hungarian General Artur Gorgey was repulsed at **Acs**, northwest of Budapest, then surrendered the army following defeat at **Temesvár**. General Gyorgy Klapka continued to hold nearby Komárom (Komárno) fortress against besieging Russian and Austrian forces and finally capitulated a month later (27 September 1849).

Komárow ∎ 1914 ∎ World War I
(Eastern Front)

As Austrian commander Franz Conrad von Hotzendorf invaded eastern Poland, his northern flank secured **Krasnik**, while the centre under General Moritz von Auffenberg attacked the Russian Fifth Army around Komárow. The Russians were defeated and fell back to avoid encirclement. Further south, they quickly counter-attacked across the **Gnila Lipa** towards **Lemberg** (26–31 August 1914).

Komarów ∎ 1920 ∎ Russo-Polish War
See **Zamosc**

Komatsu ∎ 1062 ∎ Earlier Nine Years War

Renewing war against the rebel Abe Sadato of Mutsu in northeast Japan after his check at **Kawasaki** (1058), Imperial Governor Minamoto Yoriyoshi was massively reinforced by Kiyohara Takenori of Dewa and attacked his rival's fortified camp at Komatsu (near modern Ichinoseki in Iwate), where Sadato was defeated and driven out. He was soon routed at **Kuriyagawa** (5 September 1062).

Komorn ∎ 1849 ∎ Hungarian
Revolutionary War
See **Komárom**

Kondavidu ∎ 1515 ∎ Vijayanagar-
Gajapati War

At war with the Gajapati kingdom of Orissa, Krishnadeva Raya of Vijayanagar took **Udayagiri** (June 1514) and next season laid siege to Kondavidu, near Guntur, held by Prince Virabhadra, son of King Pratapudra. Krishnadeva defeated Pratapudra in battle and captured Kondavidu after a two-month siege. He then advanced north, taking other fortresses, and Pratapudra sued for peace (23 June 1515).

Kondavidu ∎ 1563 ∎ Wars of the
Deccan Sultanates

Following defeat for Husain Nizam Shah of Ahmadnagar at **Jamkhed** (1560), former rival Ibrahim Qutb Shah of Golconda joined him to attack Bijapur. Rama Raya of Hindu Vijayana-

gar again intervened and, when Ibrahim launched a diversionary attack in the east at Kondavidu, Golconda was routed and he sued for peace. In 1565 the Sultanates joined forces against Rama Raya at **Talikota**.

Koniah ∎ 1832 ∎ 1st Turko-Egyptian War
See **Konya**

Königgratz ∎ 1866 ∎ Seven Weeks War

Prussian Prince Friedrich Karl invaded Bohemia and won at **Münchengratz** and **Gitschin**, while Austrian Field Marshal Ludwig von Benedek concentrated east of Prague, between Sadowa and Königgratz (modern Hradec Kralove). Although Friedrich Karl attacked prematurely, Prussian Crown Prince Friedrich Wilhelm arrived with reinforcements and Austria was decisively defeated (3 July 1866).

Königsberg ∎ 1807 ∎ Napoleonic Wars
(4th Coalition)

With Russia falling back from disastrous defeat at **Friedland**, Napoleon Bonaparte advanced towards the Nieman and next day, Marshal Nicolas Soult bombarded Königsberg (modern Kaliningrad), defended by Prussian General Anton Lestocq. Soult occupied the Baltic port city when Lestocq evacuated overnight and the Emperors of France and Russia met to make peace (15 June 1807).

Königsberg ∎ 1945 ∎ World War II
(Eastern Front)

As part of the **Vistula-Oder** offensive, Generals Ivan Bagramyan and Ivan Chernyakovsky swept into East Prussia, but stalled outside Königsberg. With Chernyakovsky killed, Marshal Aleksandr Vasilevksy took command and led a massive assault, with 42,000 Germans killed and 92,000 captured when General Otto Lasch surrendered. Vasilevksy then reduced Samland at **Pillau** (6–9 April 1945).

Königshofen ∎ 1525 ∎ German
Peasants' War

Georg Truchsess von Waldburg driving into Franconia soon after victory at **Böblingen**, routed a peasant force at Krautheim, then advanced on the main force of 8,000 men and 32 cannon on the Tauber, southwest of Würzburg, at Königshofen. Attacking with artillery fire and lance, Truchsess destroyed the peasant army then marched to recover Würzburg and relieve **Frauenberg** (2 June 1525).

Königswartha I 1813 I Napoleonic Wars (War of Liberation)

As Napoleon Bonaparte marched east towards **Dresden** after victory at **Lützen** (2 May), Russian General Mikhail Barclay de Tolly attacked an Italian division under General Louis de Peyri at Königswartha, northeast of Kamenz. Bonaparte's Italian allies lost 3,000 men, including 750 prisoners, before the Russians were driven off by Marshal Michel Ney's cavalry (19 May 1813).

Konitsa I 1947–1948 I Greek Civil War

Defeated in northern Greece at **Florina**, Communist commander Markos Vaphiadis was then repulsed near the Albanian border at Konitsa. After insurgent action at **Grevena** and **Metsovo**, Vaphiadis attacked Florina again with 2,500 men. The garrison resisted strongly and he withdrew when US-equipped government troops arrived (13–15 July & 25 December 1947–7 January 1948).

Konitz I 1454 I Thirteen Years War
See **Chojnice**

Konotop I 1659 I Russo-Polish Wars

When Ukrainian Cossacks openly allied themselves with Poland, Prince Aleksei Trubetskoi led 150,000 Russians into the Ukraine, where he besieged Gregori Huliantski at Konotop, northeast of Kiev. Cossack leader Ivan Vyhovsky arrived with Polish and Tatar aid to rout the Russians and they withdrew. A fresh Russian offensive the following year was repulsed at **Liubar** (April–28 June 1659).

Kontum I 1972 I Vietnam War

During the **Eastertide Offensive**, four North Vietnamese Divisions with tanks invaded the central highlands to take Dak To (24 April), then attack Kontum. After overrunning fire-bases to the northwest, they surrounded and seized part of Kontum City. The offensive was finally halted, then repulsed by fierce South Vietnamese defence and massive US air support (14 May–19 June 1972).

Konya I 1832 I 1st Turko-Egyptian War

Ibrahim Pasha, son of Egyptian Viceroy Mohammed Ali, conquered Syria, then invaded Anatolia and occupied Konya (21 November). Turkish Grand Vizier Reshid Mehmed Pasha took a large force to cut off the Egyptian supplies, but near Konya the Ottoman army suffered a devastating defeat. Ibrahim eventually agreed to evacuate Anatolia in return for Adana and Syria (21 December 1832).

Konz I 1675 I 3rd Dutch War
See **Consarbruck**

Koppal I 1677 I Bijapur-Maratha Wars

On campaign in southern India, Maratha King Shivaji sent Hambir Rao Mohite and Dhanaji Jadhav against the fortress of Koppal, east of Gadag in Mysore, held by Pathan brothers, Husain Khan Miana and Abdul Rahman Khan in Bijapur service. Husain Khan was killed in severe fighting and his brother was captured and surrendered Koppal. Shivaji then attacked **Vellore** (January 1677).

Koppal I 1790–1791 I 3rd British-Mysore War

Nizam Ali of Hyderabad supported his British allies in renewed war against Tipu Sultan of Mysore by sending General Mahabat Jang against Koppal, near the Tungabhadra River, east of Gadag in northern Mysore. After a long siege, the town surrendered following Mysorean defeat at **Bangalore**. At the end of the war, Koppal was ceded to Hyderabad (18 April 1791).

Koppam I 1054 I Later Indian Dynastic Wars

Rajadhiraja of Chola, grandson of Rajaraja the Great of Chola, continued attacks on Chalukya territory, but in a decisive battle at Koppam, King Somesvara I (Ahavamalla) of Later Chalukya defeated and killed him. (Some Chola sources claim Rajadhiraja's brother Rajendra arrived late to secure victory.) Chola later won at **Kudalsangamam** (1063) but the dynasty was soon supplanted.

Koprukoy | 1916 | World War I (Caucasus Front)

Six months after checking the Turks at **Karakilise**, Russian commander Nikolai Yudenich prepared a massive advance southwest from Kars towards Koprukoy. Following intense fighting on the northern flank at Kara Dag, the main attack smashed the Turkish front. Abdul Kerim narrowly escaped encirclement and retreated to **Erzurum** with massive losses, many from frostbite (10–19 January 1916).

Kora | 1765 | Bengal War

After Britain's great victory in northern India at **Buxar** (October 1764), Major John Carnac pursued Mir Kassim of Bengal and Shujah-ud-Daula of Oudh into the Doab, where they joined up with Marathas under Mulhar Rao Holkar. On the Plain of Kora, south of Cawnpore, British artillery destroyed the Maratha army. Mulhar Rao fled to Kalpi and the Nawab made peace (3 May 1765).

Korbach | 1760 | Seven Years War (Europe)

Marshal Victor-Francois Broglie renewed France's offensive in Hesse following defeat at **Minden** the previous year, marching west from Kassel to Korbach, where Prince Karl Wilhelm Ferdinand of Brunswick was badly defeated. His uncle Duke Ferdinand of Brunswick arrived to stabilise the position and the Hereditary Prince was sent against the French days later at **Emsdorf** (10 July 1760).

Korcula | 1298 | Venetian-Genoese Wars
See **Curzola**

Koregaon | 1818 | 3rd British-Maratha War

In his first offensive since defeat at **Kirkee** (November 1817), Peshwa Baji Rao II of Poona took his Maratha army against a tiny British force northeast of Poona on the Bhima, at Koregaon. A remarkable defence by Captain Francis Staunton held off the Marathas all day until the approach of General Joseph Smith forced the Peshwa to withdraw with over 600 casualties (6 January 1818).

Korigaum | 1818 | 3rd British-Maratha War
See **Koregaon**

Korijan | 1731 | Turko-Persian War
See **Hamadan**

Kornspruit | 1900 | 2nd Anglo-Boer War
See **Sannah's Post**

Koromogawa | 1189 | Gempei War

After his great victory in 1185 at **Dannoura**, Minamoto Yoshitsune fell out with his powerful brother Yoritomo and fled to Fujiwara Hidehira in northeast Japan, who gave him Koromogawa fortress. When Hidehira died, his son Yasuhira, hoping to appease Yoritomo, besieged and defeated Yoshitsune, who committed seppuku. Yoritomo then marched north and conquered the Fujiwara.

Kororareka | 1845 | 1st New Zealand War

Resisting authority in the New Zealand's far north, Maori Chief Hone Heke thrice cut down the flagpole at Kororareka (modern Russell), then joined with Chief Kawiti to attack the town. About 250 inexperienced troops and militia were driven off, with 13 Europeans and 34 Maoris killed. Kororareka was plundered and burned, before Heke was attacked two months later at **Puketutu** (11 March 1845).

Korsun | 1630 | Cossack-Polish Wars
See **Pereiaslav**

Korsun I 1648 I Cossack-Polish Wars

The Polish Hetmen Marcin Kalinowski and Mikolaj Potocki sent to suppress rebellion in the Ukraine, lost their advance guard at **Zolte Wody** and were attacked at Korsun, southeast of Kiev, by Cossack leader Bogdan Chmielnicki and Crimean Tatars under Tuhai-Bei. The Poles were routed, with both leaders among 8,000 captured. Chmielnicki then marched west towards **Pilawce** (26 May 1648).

Korsun I 1944 I World War II (Eastern Front)

With the German Eighth Army trapped west of the Dneiper, General Nikolai Vatutin drove south from **Zhitomir** and General Ivan Konev moved north from **Kirovograd** to encircle the Korsun Pocket under General Wilhelm Stemmerman. While about 35,000 Germans escaped, perhaps 70,000 were killed or surrendered and the Russians advanced west to **Kamenets Podolsk** (24 January–17 February 1944).

Korupedion I 281 BC I Wars of the Diadochi

See **Corupedion**

Kos I 1943 I World War II (Southern Europe)

When the British seized some of the **Dodecanese Islands** after Italy's surrender, German forces launched an overwhelming parachute and seaborne assault on Kos. Colonel Lionel Kenyon's under-equipped garrison and their Italian allies had to surrender and Colonel Felice Leggio and 89 of his Italian officers were executed. The Germans then turned against **Leros** (5–6 October 1943).

Kose Dagh I 1243 I Mongol Conquest of Asia Minor

Marching into Asia Minor, the Mongol Baiju seized Erzurum then attacked the Seljuk Sultan Kaykhusraw at Kose Dagh, west of Sivas. Baiju decisively defeated the Sultan's mixed force, including Armenians, Greeks and western European mercenaries, opening Asia Minor to further Mongol conquest. The Sultanate of Rum later became a dependant of the Mongol regime in Persia (26 June 1243).

Kossovo I 1389 I Ottoman Conquest of the Balkans

Ottoman Sultan Murad I captured southern Bulgaria with victory at the **Maritza** (1371) and later marched against Lazar I of Serbia, who was aided by Bosnia and Albania. Murad was assassinated during battle at Kossovo, but his son Bayazid won a decisive victory, virtually securing the Balkans. Bayazid executed Lazar and defeated a Crusader army in 1396 at **Nicopolis** (15 June 1389).

Kossovo I 1448 I Turkish-Hungarian Wars

To avenge Christian defeat at **Varna** in November 1444, Hungarian Regent Janos Hunyadi invaded Serbia in the last major attempt to recover the Balkans from Sultan Murad II. Without waiting for support from George Kastriote Skanderbeg of Albania, Hunyadi was defeated in a bloody battle at Kossovo after his Wallachians deserted. **Constantinople** fell five years later (17–20 October 1448).

Kossovo I 1915 I World War I (Balkan Front)

Marshal Radomir Putnik attempting to defend central Serbia, made a stand on the Plain of Kossovo, north of Kacanik. Crushed between Bulgarians advancing north from Skopje and Austro-German forces driving south from **Belgrade**, the Serbians had to retreat west through a blizzard into Albania. The shattered survivors were evacuated and later fought at **Salonika** (24–29 November 1915).

Kossovo I 1999 I Kossovo War

After suppressing Kossovo separatists in southeast Serbia in 1998, Yugoslav troops and Serb militia renewed their offensive, causing heavy damage and huge displacement of mainly Muslim refugees. When NATO began an intensive campaign of air-strikes against Serbian targets, the Yugoslav government agreed to withdraw and international peacekeepers arrived (24 March–9 June 1999).

Kostalac ❙ 601 ❙ Byzantine-Balkan Wars
    See **Viminacium**

Kostliju ❙ 1774 ❙ Catherine the Great's 1st Turkish War
    See **Kozludzha**

Kosturino ❙ 1915 ❙ World War I (Balkan Front)
    As Anglo-French forces were driven back along the **Vardar** from a failed intervention to aid Serbia, British General Lewis Nicol attempted to hold the right flank in steep country at Kosturino, north of Lake Doiran. Attacked by a superior Bulgarian army under General Georgi Todorov, the British suffered costly losses and fell back to defend the line at **Salonika** (7–8 December 1915).

Koszeg ❙ 1532 ❙ Turkish-Habsburg Wars
    See **Guns**

Kota Bharu ❙ 1941 ❙ World War II (Pacific)
    Within hours of the attack on **Pearl Harbour**, Japanese forces landed unopposed at Singora and Patani in southern Thailand, while General Hiroshi Takumi stormed ashore at Kota Bharu in northeast Malaya. Stiff resistance by Indian troops under General "Billy" Key inflicted heavy Japanese losses. But when tanks landed the British withdrew south towards Kuala Lipis (8–9 December 1941).

Kotah ❙ 1804 ❙ 2nd British-Maratha War
    See **Monson's Retreat**

Kotah ❙ 1858 ❙ Indian Mutiny
    Lieutenant Frederick Roberts marched with 600 men and two guns from Nasirabad to Kotah on the Chambal, where troops of Rajah Ram Singh of Kotah had mutinied and besieged him in Kotah's citadel. After sending some troops to reinforce the Rajah, Roberts bombarded the town and took it by assault, capturing 50 guns. The Rajah's authority was then restored (27–30 March 1858).

Kotah-ki-Serai ❙ 1858 ❙ Indian Mutiny
    Marching west through intense heat in pursuit of defeated rebel forces from **Kalpi** (23 May), General Sir Hugh Rose secured victory at **Morar** then next day sent General Michael William Smith against rebels in a strong position at Kotah-ki-Serai, just five miles from Gwalior. The warrior-Queen, the Rhani of Jhansi, was killed in confused fighting and her disheartened followers fled (17 June 1858).

Kotelnikovo ❙ 1942 ❙ World War II (Eastern Front)
    In a desperate effort to relieve besieged **Stalingrad**, Marshal Erich von Manstein attacked from the southwest through Kotelnikovo. His German and Romanian divisions reached the Myshkova and Aksai Rivers where they were halted by bitter cold and stubborn defence. Von Manstein was forced to withdraw with over 16,000 casualties and Stalingrad was doomed (12–30 December 1942).

Kotlin Island ❙ 1705 ❙ 2nd "Great" Northern War
    Following the fall of **Narva** (August 1704), Swedish Admiral Cornelius Anckarstjerna sailed against Saint Petersburg and attempted to land forces. Off Kotlin Island, in the Gulf of Finland, he was met in a prolonged action by a much smaller Russian squadron under Admiral Kornely Kruys, aided by the Russian batteries, Kotlin and Kronstadt. The Swedes were finally driven off with heavy losses.

Kotor ❙ 1690 ❙ Venetian-Turkish Wars
    See **Cattaro**

Kotor ❙ 1813–1814 ❙ Napoleonic Wars (War of Liberation)
    See **Cattaro**

Koto-ri | 1950 | Korean War

After bitter fighting at **Chosin**, Marine General Oliver Smith famously "attacked in another direction" to break out through surrounding Chinese forces. A fighting retreat in extreme cold saw the Allies fall back through Hagaru-ri to Koto-ri, where a costly rearguard action secured the withdrawal to Hungnam. About 200,000 troops and civilians were evacuated by sea (5–10 December 1950).

Kouchanas | 1904 | German Colonial Wars in Africa

See **Freyer's Farm**

Kouno | 1899 | French Conquest of Chad

Emile Gentil determined to avenge the French disaster in July at **Niellim** and marched north from Fort Archambault along the Chari against Muslim leader Rabih az-Zubayr. At Kouno, southeast of Lake Chad, the "Black Sultan" was badly beaten. Early the following year, Gentil supported a combined French force which finally defeated and killed Rabih further north at **Kousséri** (October 1899).

Kousséri | 1900 | French Conquest of Chad

Six months after defeat at **Kouno**, Muslim leader Rabih az-Zubayr faced a massive converging assault south of Lake Chad under Emile Gentil from Congo, Francois Lamy and Fernand Foureau from Algeria and Jules Joalland from Niger. Battle on the Logone at Kousséri (just inside modern Cameroun) saw Rabih defeated and killed (Lamy also died) and France secured Chad (22 April 1900).

Kovel | 1916 | World War I (Eastern Front)

See **Stochod**

Kovno | 1812 | Napoleonic Wars (Russian Campaign)

To protect the tail end of Napoleon Bonaparte's retreat from Moscow, Marshal Joachim Murat stubbornly defended the bridgehead on the Nieman at Kovno (modern Kaunus, Lithua-

nia). The frozen river made the French position untenable, but he held off defeat until Marshal Michel Ney arrived with the last survivors. Ney was reputedly the last French soldier to leave Russia (13 December 1812).

Kovno | 1915 | World War I (Eastern Front)

On the northern flank of Germany's **Triple Offensive**, General Hermann von Eichhorn advanced on Kovno (Kaunas). Russia's Northwest commander Mikhail Alexeyev believed the fortress would hold out, but its garrison was weak and ill-disciplined. Kovno was taken by storm, yielding 1,300 guns and over 800,000 shells, opening the way to **Vilna** and **Dvinsk** (7–15 August 1915).

Kowloon | 1839 | 1st Opium War

Manchu Commissioner Lin Zexu drove the British out of Macao and sent war junks to prevent British Superintendent Captain Charles Elliot securing food for the British ships off Hong Kong. The frigates *Volage* and *Hyacinth* (Captain Henry Smith) shelled the junks off Kowloon to secure Elliot's supplies in an incident, which helped precipitate war with China (4 September 1839).

Kowloon | 1941 | World War II (China)

Just four hours after **Pearl Harbour**, Japanese General Tadayoshi Sano led 20,000 men against the Chinese border defences of Hong Kong. With the fall of the Shing Mun Redoubt, the so-called Gindrinkers Line collapsed and the invaders swarmed into Kowloon. The British Mainland Brigade under Brigadier Cedric Wallis then withdrew to **Hong Kong** Island (8–10 December 1941).

Kozludzha | 1774 | Catherine the Great's 1st Turkish War

With Russia and Turkey almost exhausted by war, an offensive by Generals Alexander Suvorov and Mikhail Kamenski defeated Ottoman forces under Abdul Rezak on the Danube at Kozludzha (modern Kozloduy) and drove the Turks into blockade at Shumla (Kolarovgrad).

Sultan Abdul-Hamid soon made peace, giving Russia effective command of the Black Sea (9 June 1774).

Kozuki ∎ 1577–1578 ∎ Japan's Era of the Warring States

Having secured **Nagashino**, Toyotomi Hideyoshi marched west and starved the Mori castle of Kozuki in Harima into surrender, assigning it to Amako Katsuhisa and Yamanka Shikanosuke. Besieged by Mori commanders Kikkawa Motoharu and Kobayakawa Takakage, Amako committed seppuku and Yamanka was captured and killed. In 1582 Hideyoshi attacked the Mori at **Takamatsu**.

Krajina ∎ 1995 ∎ Croatian War
See **Knin**

Krak de Chevaliers ∎ 1271 ∎ Later Crusader-Muslim Wars

Mamluk Sultan Baibars completed his capture of the major inland Crusader cities and fortresses by marching on the massive Hospitallier castle of Krak de Chevaliers in central Syria. As one of the most powerful fortifications of its day, it had never been captured. But during an intensive month-long assault its outer wall was breached and the castle was forced to capitulate (3 March–8 April 1271).

Krasnik ∎ 1914 ∎ World War I (Eastern Front)

As Austrian commander Count Franz Conrad von Hotzendorf invaded eastern Poland, his northern force under General Victor von Dankl smashed into Generals Aleksei Evert and Pavel Plehve, southwest of Lublin, at Krasnik. The Russian armies were driven back with heavy losses and a few days later other Austrians further east repulsed the Russians around **Komárow** (23–24 August 1914).

Krasnodar ∎ 1918 ∎ Russian Civil War
See **Ekaterinodar**

Krasnoi ∎ 1812 ∎ Napoleonic Wars (Russian Campaign)
See **Krasnoye**

Krasnoye (1st) ∎ 1812 ∎ Napoleonic Wars (Russian Campaign)

Napoleon Bonaparte's army advancing into Russia towards **Smolensk** crossed the Dnieper and found the road blocked at Krasnoye by a force of about 9,000 Russians under General Dmitri Sergeevich Neverovski. After some sharp fighting led by Marshals Joachim Murat and Michel Ney, the Russians withdrew to Smolensk, losing about 1,500 casualties and 800 prisoners (14 August 1812).

Krasnoye (2nd) ∎ 1812 ∎ Napoleonic Wars (Russian Campaign)

In order to cut off Napoleon Bonaparte's retreat from Moscow, Prince Mikhail Kutuzov's Russians attempted to ambush the French west of Smolensk at Krasnoye. A courageous but costly counter-attack by Marshals Louis Davout and Michel Ney drove off General Mikhail Miloradovich and the French retreat continued to the disastrous passage of the **Berezina** (17 November 1812).

Krefeld ∎ 1758 ∎ Seven Years War (Europe)
See **Crefeld**

Kresna ∎ 1913 ∎ 2nd Balkan (Inter-ally) War

When Bulgaria suddenly attacked her former allies over Macedonia, King Constantine of Greece checked their advance near **Kilkis** then pursued them through hard fighting to a defensive position in the Pass at Kresna, near the Struma. A bitter action cost heavy losses on both sides before Constantine broke through to secure Simitli. The war ended a week later (21–24 July 1913).

Kressenbrunn ∎ 1260 ∎ Bohemian Wars

In the breakup of the Babenberg inheritance, Ottokar II of Bohemia secured Austria by agreement, then determined to also grab Styria, which had been granted to Bela IV of Hungary. With victory at Kressenbrunn, on the March northeast of Vienna, Ottokar seized Styria and continued to aggressively expand his Bohemian Kingdom until killed by the Habsburgs at **Marchfeld**.

Krimiskop | 1901 | 2nd Anglo-Boer War
See **Tweefontein**

Kringen | 1612 | War of Kalmar
With Sweden and Denmark at war over Lapland, 300 Scottish mercenaries under Colonel Alexander Ramsay landed in Danish-ruled Norway on their way to aid Sweden at **Alvsborg** and were ambushed by Norwegian militia at Kringen, near Gudbrandsdalen. In an action much-celebrated in Norwegian legend, most of the Scots were killed in battle or executed afterwards (26 August 1612).

Krishna | 1398 | Vijayanagar-Bahmani Wars
Thirty years after Hindu Vijayanagar was routed at **Kauthal**, King Harihara II of Vijayanagar renewed the war against the Muslim Bahmanid Dynasty, leading a huge force against Sultan Firuz Shah. Harihara was surprised and defeated at the Krishna River by a much smaller force of Bahmani cavalry and his son was killed. The Hindu army dispersed back to Vijayanagar and a peace was agreed.

Krithia (1st) | 1915 | World War I (Gallipoli)
British General Aylmer Hunter-Weston landed at the tip of the Gallipoli Peninsula around **Helles** (25 April) and advanced inland towards Krithia, on the heights of Achi Baba. His disorganised attack stalled against reinforced Turkish defences and the Anglo-French Allies were driven off with more than 3,000 casualties. The Turks soon counter-attacked at **Eski Hissarlik** (28 April 1915).

Krithia (2nd) | 1915 | World War I (Gallipoli)
British commander Sir Ian Hamilton halted a Turkish counter-attack around **Eski Hissarlik** then determined on a fresh attack towards Krithia. The frontal assault was a disaster, with over 6,000 Allied casualties, including many Australians and New Zealanders transferred from **Anzac** after surviving **Baby 700**. Both sides then dug in for trench warfare (6–8 May 1915).

Krithia (3rd) | 1915 | World War I (Gallipoli)
Despite previous losses attacking towards Krithia, British General Aylmer Hunter-Weston, now heavily reinforced and supported by new French commander Albert Gouraud, determined on a fresh assault. Advancing out of trenches against powerful Turkish defences, the Allies suffered terrible losses for no gain and had to pin their hopes on a landing in the north at **Suvla Bay** (4 June 1915).

Krivoy Rog | 1944 | World War II (Eastern Front)
While the Russians took **Kirovograd**, further south Generals Rodion Malinovsky and Fedor Tolbukhin launched a massive offensive against German and Romanian divisions in the Dnieper Bend. The Nikopol bridgehead was lost, then the key city of Krivoy Rog, as Marshal Ewald von Kleist withdrew to escape encirclement falling back towards **Odessa** (10 January–22 February 1944).

Kroissenbrunn | 1260 | Bohemian Wars
See **Kressenbrunn**

Kromeriz | 1423 | Hussite Wars
Hussite nobles led by Divis Borek of Miletinek campaigned against Sigismund of Hungary, attacking Moravia, held by Sigismund's son-in-law Albert of Austria. Outside Kromeriz (German Kremsier), Borek defeated a Royalist force under Bishop John of Olomouc and Duke Premek of Opava then returned to Bohemia to

fight Hussite leader John Zizka in August at **Strachuv** (July 1423).

Krommydi I 1825 I Greek War of Independence

With **Navarino** besieged by Egyptian commander Ibrahim Pasha, Greeks under sea Captain Skourti tried to disrupt communication between Navarino and Methone. At Krommydi, up to 7,000 Greeks and irregulars were routed with about 600 killed by Ibrahim's much smaller, yet disciplined Egyptian force. Navarino soon fell and Ibrahim joined the siege of **Missolonghi** (19 April 1825).

Kronstadt I 1919 I Russian Civil War

In support of the White cause in the Baltic, British Admiral Walter Cowan bombed the key Bolshevik fortress of Kronstadt, outside **Petrograd**, then sent eight coastal motorboats against the Red Fleet. The battleships *Andrei Pervozvanni* and *Petropavlovsk* and the depot ship *Pamyut Azova* were sunk in shallow water in a bold assault, which saw two Victoria Crosses won (18 August 1919).

Kronstadt I 1921 I Kronstadt Rebellion

When sailors at the island fortress of Kronstadt, off Petrograd (St Petersburg), mutinied over post-war civilian famine, Leon Trotsky led Red infantry in a night assault over the ice and stormed the fortress amid heavy losses. About 800 mutineers escaped to Finland and the rest were executed or imprisoned, but the rising led to introduction of the New Economic Policy (17–18 March 1921).

Kronstadt Bay I 1790 I 2nd Russo-Swedish War

With the Swedish army repulsed at **Fredrikshamn** (18 May), Duke Charles of Sodermanland (brother of Gustav III) sailed into Kronstadt Bay, at the head of the Gulf of Finland, where he met Russian Admiral Alexander Kruse off Cape Styrsudden. Action over two days proved inconclusive and, when the Russian Reval Squadron arrived, Duke Charles withdrew into **Vyborg Bay** (3–4 June 1790).

Kroszka I 1739 I Austro-Russian-Turkish War

Supporting Russia against Turkey in the Balkans, Austrian Marshal Count Georg Oliver von Wallis faced a massive Turkish advance southeast of Belgrade at Kroszka (modern Grocka). Grand Vizier Al-Haji Mohammed inflicted a heavy defeat then advanced to besiege **Belgrade**, which was later given up when Austria made a separate peace (22 July 1739).

Krugersdorp I 1896 I Jameson's Raid

Encouraged by Cecil Rhodes, Dr Leandar Starr Jameson led 600 mounted police and volunteers from Rhodesia to raise rebellion in the Boer Transvaal. Defeated at Krugersdorp, west of Johannesburg, Jameson lost 17 killed and 55 wounded before surrendering to Pieter Cronjé at nearby Doornkop. He was then handed over and taken to England for trial and prison (1–2 January 1896).

Krujë, Albania I 1448 I Albanian-Turkish Wars

Ottoman Sultan Murad II invading Albania against George Kastriote Skanderbeg besieged **Svetigrad**, then left a covering force and continued on to besiege the strategic fortress of Krujë, on a mountain spur north of Tirana. However, after Skanderbeg defeated the Turks at **Dibra**, Murad had to withdraw to oppose a Hungarian invasion of Serbia, which he soon crushed at **Kossovo**.

Krujë, Albania I 1450 I Albanian-Turkish Wars

After decisive victory at **Kossovo** in 1448, Sultan Murad II again besieged the mountain fortress of Krujë in central Albania, held by Count Uran. With George Kastriote Skanderbeg harrying him from the hills and winter approaching, Murad withdrew after four months with up to 20,000 casualties. Skanderbeg later handed Krujë to Alfonso V of Naples (14 May–September 1450).

Krujë, Albania ∎ 1466–1467 ∎ Venetian-Turkish Wars

In a fresh Turkish invasion of central Albania, Ottoman Sultan Mehmed II and Balaban Pasha besieged Krujë, north of Tirana, held by Venetian troops. When the Sultan withdrew, George Kastriote Skanderbeg defeated and killed Balaban to relieve the siege. Mehmed returned with a great army but did not press the siege. Skanderbeg shortly died and Albania was soon conquered.

Krujë, Albania ∎ 1478 ∎ Venetian-Turkish Wars

Three years after a failed campaign against Scutari in Venetian Albania, Sultan Mehmed II launched a fresh assault and besieged the nearby fortress city of Krujë. The starving Venetian garrison surrendered after a year on a promise of safe conduct, but most were executed. Mehmed was then able to concentrate his army on the renewed siege of **Scutari** itself.

Krujë, Montenegro ∎ 1796 ∎ Montenegran-Scutari War
See **Krusi**

Kruptchitsa ∎ 1794 ∎ War of the 2nd Polish Partition

Polish Nationalist General Karol Sierakovski facing a Russian counter-offensive established about 15,000 men in a strong position east of the Bug near Kubrin at Kruptchitsa. Heavy bombardment by Russian Field Marshal Alexander Suvorov drove the Poles out with costly losses. They managed to withdraw with their guns and fought again three days later at **Brest-Litovsk** (16 September 1794).

Krusevac ∎ 1454 ∎ Turkish-Hungarian Wars

When Ottoman Sultan Mehmed II invaded Serbia, Hungarian Regent Janos Hunyadi marched to Belgrade, then advanced southeast to Krusevac on the Rasina, defended by a large contingent under Firuz Bey. Hunyadi destroyed the Ottoman force in a surprise dawn attack, capturing Firuz Bey and a large number of Turks, who were later exchanged for Serbian prisoners (September 1454).

Krusi ∎ 1796 ∎ Montenegran-Scutari War

On campaign against Peter I of Montenegro, Mahmud Pasha Bustalija of Shkoder (Scutari) was routed near Spuz at **Martinici** and two months later, with his invasion army reinforced to a reported 30,000 Turks, he was attacked again a few miles to the southwest at Krusi. The Pasha was decisively defeated and killed and Peter secured the Brda highlands (22 September 1796).

Kuangchang ∎ 1934 ∎ 2nd Chinese Revolutionary Civil War
See **Guangchang**

Kuan-tu ∎ 200 ∎ Wars of the Three Kingdoms
See **Guandu**

Kuba ∎ 1262 ∎ Mongol Dynastic Wars

Two years after a Mongol loss in Syria at **Ain Jalut**, Hulegu, the Il-Khan of Iran and grandson of Genghis Khan, came under attack in Georgia by his Muslim cousin Berke, Kipchak Khan of the Golden Horde. Marching north of the Caucasus, Hulegu beat Berke in Azerbaijan near modern Kuba. His son Abaqa then rashly pursued Berke and was soon defeated at the **Terek** (14 November 1262).

Kuban ∎ 1222 ∎ Conquests of Genghis Khan

With the Khwarezmian Empire destroyed after its final defeat at the **Indus**, the Mongol conqueror Genghis Khan sent General Subetai north into Christian Georgia, ruled by Queen Russudan. At the Kuban River the Georgian army was heavily defeated by Subetai and Jebei, who marched north into the Ukraine for victory the following year over the Russians at the **Kalka**.

Kuban ∎ 1920 ∎ Russian Civil War

White commander Pyotr Wrangel in the Crimea launched a late offensive, sending an amphibious expedition under General Sergei Ulugai east into the Kuban to threaten Ekaterinodar (modern Krasnodar). Despite little initial resistance, Ulugai faced massive Red Army reinforcements and was forced to withdraw with terrible losses. Wrangel was soon beaten at the **Perekop** (August 1920).

Kudalsangaman ∎ 1063 ∎ Later Indian Dynastic Wars

Rajadhiraja of Chola died at **Koppam** (1054) and his brother Virarajendra later faced attack by Somesvara (Ahavamalla) of Later Chalukya, who sent a large force under Dandanayaka and the Princes, Vikkalan and Singanan. Near the confluence of the Krishna and Tungabhadra at Kudalsangamam, Virarajendra won a great victory. However, within a few years Chalukya seized the throne of Chola.

Kudarangan ∎ 1904 ∎ American-Moro Wars

At war against the Americans on Mindanao in the southern Philippines, the Muslim Moro Datu Ali faced counter-attack by General Leonard Wood and withdrew to the huge fortress at Kudarangan, inland from Coabato. After heavy bombardment, Datu Ali slipped away overnight, along with about 5,000 men, women and children, and fought on until killed near **Buluan** (March 1904).

Kuei-ling ∎ 353 BC ∎ China's Era of the Warring States
See **Guiling**

Kufah ∎ 1060 ∎ Seljuk Wars of Expansion

With Toghril Beg occupied elsewhere, General Arslan al-Muzaffar al-Basasiri and Quraysh ibn Badran retook **Baghdad** (December 1058) and recognised Fatimid Egypt. But, al-Basasiri's sponsors soon abandoned him and he had to escape the city. Pursued by Seljuk cavalry to Saqy al-Furat, near Kufah, his brother-in-law Dubays fled and al-Basasiri was defeated and executed (15 January 1060).

Kufah ∎ 1920 ∎ Iraqi Revolt

On the offensive against Arab insurgents south of Baghdad, British General Henry Walker advanced southwest from **Hillah** to relieve Captain Dermot M. Dowling at Kufah. While another column struck west to seize Tuwairij, and other British forces further south advanced on **Samawah**, Walker fought his way into Kufah, effectively ending the war (21 July–17 October 1920).

Kufit ∎ 1885 ∎ Sudanese-Ethiopian War

Mahdist General Osman Digna was besieging Kassala on the Mareb when Abyssinian commander Ras Alula led a 10,000-strong relief force west from Asmara and inflicted a heavy defeat on the Dervishes at Kufit. The Mahdists lost at least 3,000 dead, including many killed after the battle. However, Kassala had already surrendered and Ras Alula returned to Asmara (23 September 1885).

Kula Gulf ∎ 1943 ∎ World War II (Pacific)

When Japanese forces tried to reinforce **Kolombangara**, west of **New Georgia**, ten destroyers under Admiral Teruo Akiyama were met in the nearby Kula Gulf by Admiral Walden Ainsworth's cruiser squadron. The Japanese lost two destroyers and Akiyama was killed, and an American cruiser was sunk. However, the Japanese troops were successfully landed (5–6 July 1943).

Kulevcha ∎ 1829 ∎ Russo-Turkish Wars

As he advanced through the Balkans after victory at **Varna** (October 1828), Russian General Count Hans von Diebitsch marched against Grand Vizier Reshid Mehmed Pasha 40 miles west at Kulevcha. Trapped in a deep valley, the Turks lost 5,000 men before they managed to withdraw. Diebitsch then took his army across the steep Balkan Mountains towards **Adrianople** (11 June 1829).

Kulikovo ∎ 1380 ∎ Russian-Mongol Wars

Encouraged by victory over the Mongols at the **Vozha**, Russian Princes under Dimitri of Moscow took a reputed 150,000 men to Kulikovo on the

Upper Don. Without his former Lithuanian allies, General Mamai's Mongol army was destroyed and Dimitri was named "Donskoi." Mamai was soon overthrown at the **Kalka** and Mongol forces captured **Moscow** in 1382 (8 September 1380).

Kul-i-Malik ∎ 1512 ∎ Mughal-Uzbek Wars

Uzbek conqueror Muhammad Shaybani Khan died at **Merv** (1510) and the Mughal Babur of Kabul seized Samarkand for the third time after **Pul-i-Sanghin**. Without his Persian allies he was defeated near Bokhara at Kul-i-Malik by new Uzbek leader Ubaid Khan. Babur was defeated again at **Ghujduwan** and abandoned hope of recovering the capital of his ancester Tamerlane (May 1512).

Kulm ∎ 1794 ∎ War of the 2nd Polish Partition
See **Chelmno**

Kulm ∎ 1813 ∎ Napoleonic Wars (War of Liberation)

Just days after massive defeat at **Dresden**, the Allies resumed their policy of attacking Napoleon Bonaparte's lieutenants and French General Dominique Vandamme found himself outnumbered by a huge Austrian-Prussian-Russian army under Prince Karl Philipp Schwarzenberg at Kulm in Bohemia. Vandamme was captured and his force was virtually destroyed (29–30 August 1813).

Kum ∎ 1950 ∎ Korean War

As North Korean forces advanced south from **Seoul** through **Osan** and **Chochiwon**, American commander William Walker tried to establish a defensive line on the Kum River. North Korean General Lee Kwon Mu stormed across on a broad front and threatened to envelop the defenders. As a result the Americans had to abandon the Kum and fell back 20 miles to the city of **Taejon** (14–16 July 1950).

Kumamoto ∎ 1877 ∎ Satsuma Rebellion

Despite supporting the Meiji Restoration, Japanese Marshal Saigo Takamori eventually led a rebellion in Satsuma, marching 30,000 men towards Kumamoto, in central Kyushu. Saigo defeated General Tani Tanjo (Tateki), who defended the town for 50 days until Prince Arisugawa Taruhito arrived with an Imperial army. The rebels then withdrew to **Kagoshima** (22 February–14 April 1877).

Kumanovo ∎ 1912 ∎ 1st Balkan War

As the war started, Prince Alexander of Serbia invaded Macedonia and met Turkish General Zekki Pasha northeast of Skopje at Kumanovo. A bloody action cost each side over 4,000 men before the Turks fled towards **Monastir** and Skopje fell more than 500 years after Ottoman conquest at **Kossovo**. Turkey was routed the same day in Thrace at **Kirk Kilissa** (23–24 October 1912).

Kumasi ∎ 1874 ∎ 2nd British-Ashanti War
See **Odasu**

Kumbakonam ∎ 1782 ∎ 2nd British-Mysore War

Aided by French Major Henri Lally, Tipu Sultan, heir to the ruler of Mysóre, surrounded British Colonel John Brathwaite in southeast India near Kumbakonam on the Coleroon River (modern Kollidam). With fewer than 2,000 men, Brathwaite was overwhelmed and surrendered after terrible slaughter. Tipu then marched north to capture the port of **Cuddalore** (18 February 1782).

Kumbi ∎ 1076 ∎ Fall of Ghana

Determined to spread Islam into the great West African Empire of Ghana (modern Mali and Mauretania), Almoravid Berbers under Abu Bakr ibn Umar took Audaghost (1054) and eventually seized the capital Kumbi (north of modern Bamako). While the invaders soon left, the empire entered a slow decline. Kumbi fell again to the Sosso in 1203 and was absorbed by Sundiata of Mali in 1240.

Kumbi ∎ 1203 ∎ Wars of Sosso

Amid the decline of the Empire of Ghana, the warrior-ruler Sumanguru of Kaniaga led a campaign of expansion for the Sosso people of

West Africa. After subsuming several neighbouring states, Sumanguru attacked and captured the former Ghanaian capital of Kumbi.
However, Kumbi's role in the strategic trans-
Saharan trade declined and the Sosso Empire
was soon overthrown at **Kirina**.

Kumeiky I 1637 I Cossack-Polish Wars

When Pavlo Pavliuk led a revolt by anti-Polish
Cossacks in the Ukraine, he captured Korsun
(August 1637). He was then badly defeated at
Kumeiky by a Polish army under Hetman Mikolaj
Potocki and withdrew under siege to nearby
Borovitsa (near Chigirin). During negotiations,
Pavliuk was handed over on condition of safe
conduct but he was taken to Warsaw and executed
(16 December 1637).

Kum Kale I 1915 I World War I
(Gallipoli)

In support of Allied landings on Gallipoli
Peninsula at **Helles** and **Anzac** Cove, 3,000
French under General Albert d'Amade landed
near Kum Kale, on the Asiatic side of the entrance to the Dardanelles. A Turkish counter-
attack cost about 1,700 French casualties before
the costly diversion was withdrawn to support
the main Allied offensives against **Krithia** (25–
27 April 1915).

Kumsong I 1953 I Korean War

Two days after victory at **Pork Chop Hill**,
about 150,000 Chinese with massive artillery
support assaulted the Kumsong Salient, east of
Pyongyang. The last Chinese offensive fell
mainly on South Korean troops, who suffered
costly losses. The Allies had to withdraw about
six miles to the Kumsong River, straightening
the line just a week before armistice ended the
war (13–20 July 1953).

Kunch I 1858 I Indian Mutiny

General Sir Hugh Rose captured the strategic
stronghold at **Jhansi** (3 April), then advanced
northeast towards Kalpi and was blocked at the
town of Kunch by a large force under the great
rebel leader Tantia Topi. With a brilliant flank
attack—in terrible heat, which caused many

British deaths from sunstroke—the rebels were
defeated and driven out. Rose then pressed on
towards **Kalpi** (6 May 1858).

Kunduz I 2001 I Afghanistan War

Having taken **Mazar-i-Sharif**, the Northern
Alliance turned east to besiege perhaps 10,000
Taliban at Kunduz, including 3,000 Arabs and
Chechens determined to fight to the death.
Massive American bombing and fierce ground
attack saw the last Taliban stronghold in the
north surrender to General Rashid Dostam.
Many prisoners died in transports or at **Qala-i-
Jangi** (14–26 November 2001).

Kunduzcha I 1391 I Conquests
of Tamerlane

The Turko-Mongol Tamerlane repulsed Toktamish, Khan of the Golden Horde, at the **Syr
Darya**, then marched north into Russia and
heavily defeated his former protégé in a three-day
battle at Kunduzcha, east of the Volga. Tamerlane
sacked the Khan's capital at Sarai before withdrawing to deal with rebellion in Persia. Four
years later he returned to destroy Toktamish at the
Terek (18 June 1391).

Kunersdorf I 1759 I Seven Years War
(Europe)

Frederick II of Prussia advanced across the
Oder to avenge the defeat at **Kay** (23 July) and
attacked a massively superior Austro-Russian
force under General Gideon von Loudon and
Count Pyotr Soltikov, just east of Frankfurt at
Kunersdorf. Frederick lost over 20,000 men and
almost 170 guns in his worst defeat, though
Allied losses and Russian dissent enabled him to
withdraw (12 August 1759).

Kunjpura I 1760 I Indian Campaigns
of Ahmad Shah

Recovering from defeat at **Sikandarabad** in
March, Marathas under Bhau Saheb captured
Delhi then marched north against Afghan invader
Ahmad Shah Durrani. In victory at Kunjpura, east
of Karnal, the Marathas inflicted nearly 10,000
Afghan casualties, including Abusammad Khan
killed and Qutb Shah executed. Within months

the Afghans were victorious at **Panipat** (17 October 1760).

Kunlun Guan I 1939 I Sino-Japanese War
See **Nanning**

Kunovica I 1444 I Turkish-Hungarian Wars (Long Campaign)
Ladislas of Hungary and General Janos Hunyadi were turned back from invading Bulgaria at **Zlatitsa** and withdrew across the Balkans in extreme winter conditions, repulsing the pursuing Turks at **Melshtitsa**. The Christians were then ambushed near Kunovica, between Pirot and Nish in Serbia, inflicting another heavy defeat on the Turks before continuing home to Hungary (4 January 1444).

Kunyang I 23 I Fall of the Xin Dynasty
When Wang Mang usurped the Former (Western) Han throne, he faced insurrection by Liu Xuan and his cousin Liu Xiu, whose forces were eventually besieged at Kunyang. Reinforcements arrived to win a decisive victory, then captured Chang'an and killed Wang Mang. Liu Xiu was proclaimed Emperor Guangwu and his new Later (Eastern) Han Dynasty ruled for 200 years (7 July 23).

Kup I 1762 I Indian Campaigns of Ahmad Shah
In a fresh Afghan invasion of the upper Punjab, Ahmad Shah Durrani reached Malerkotla, west of Sirhind, then attacked a 50,000-strong Sikh army just to the north at Kup. In one of their worst defeats—known as Ghallaghurga (Bloody Carnage)—the Sikhs lost perhaps 20,000 killed in a decisive battle of movement. The Afghans then marched north to sack Amritsar (5 February 1761).

Kurchukai I 1774 I Catherine the Great's 1st Turkish War
One month after the Turkish defeat on the Danube at **Kozludzha**, a Russian advanced detachment marched across the Balkan hills and along the Luda-Kamchia Valley to attack Kurchukai, about 50 miles south of Shumla.

While the Russians were repulsed, their presence south of the Balkans hastened the treaty signed 11 days later, which ended the war (10 July 1774).

Kurdlah I 1795 I Maratha Territorial Wars
See **Kharda**

Kurikara I 1183 I Gempei War
Taira Komemori marched north from Kyoto against the Minamoto rebel Yoshinaka to secure the fortress at **Hiuchi**, then met the full Minamoto army in the mountains at Kurikara, near Tsubata in Toyama, below the ridge at Tonamiyama. The Taira were routed in a comprehensive disaster, with perhaps 7,000 killed, and fled back towards Kyoto through further defeat at **Shinowara** (2 June 1183).

Kuriyagawa I 1062 I Earlier Nine Years War
Renewing war against Abe Sadato in northeast Japan, Governor Minamoto Yoriyoshi, aided by Kiyohara Takenori, beat the rebel at **Komatsu** and later Koromogawa, then attacked his last stronghold at Kuriyagawa (modern Morioka in Iwate). Sadato was defeated and killed and his brother Muneto surrendered, ending the war. The Kiyohara ruled the northeast until defeat at **Kanazawa** in 1087.

Kurna I 1914 I World War I (Mesopotamia)
See **Qurna**

Kursk I 1943 I World War II (Eastern Front)
Marshal Erich von Manstein retook Kharkov, then joined Marshal Gunther von Kluge in a massive assault on the Russian salient at Kursk, commanded by Marshal Georgi Zhukov. The huge battle of attrition involved two million men in World War II's largest tank action before the Germans were halted at **Prokhorovka**. The Soviets then struck back at **Orel** and **Kharkov** (5–16 July 1943).

Kürük-Dar ∎ 1854 ∎ Crimean War

When Russian Prince Vassily Bebutov invaded Armenia and won at **Bayazid**, Turkish commander Zarif Mustapha Pasha unwisely marched out of Kars with about 40,000 men. About 20 miles east at Kürük-Dar, Zarif Mustapha was heavily defeated, losing about 3,000 dead and 2,000 prisoners. However, the Russians were not yet strong enough to attack **Kars** (5 August 1854).

Kushliki ∎ 1661 ∎ Russo-Polish Wars

A year after victory in the Ukraine at **Chudnov**, Polish Hetman Stefan Czarniecki returned north to Lithuania against Russian commander Ivan Khovanski, previously defeated at **Polonka**. At Kushliki, west of Polotsk in modern Belarus, the Russians were crushed, losing up to 9,000 men. Vilna was retaken and by year's end Lithuania was largely cleared of the invaders (4 November 1661).

Kusseri ∎ 1900 ∎ French Conquest of Chad
See **Kousséri**

Kustendil ∎ 1330 ∎ Serbian Imperial Wars
See **Velbuzhde**

Kut-al-Amara ∎ 1915 ∎ World War I (Mesopotamia)

Anglo-Indian General Charles Townshend advanced up the Tigris from **Basra** through **Amara** and met Turkish commander Nur-ud-Din well-entrenched at the key city of Kut-al-Amara (modern Al Kut in Iraq). The Turks were badly beaten, losing over 5,000 men and all their guns before retreating upriver, pursued by Townshend towards **Ctesiphon** (28 September 1915).

Kut-al-Amara ∎ 1915–1916 ∎
World War I (Mesopotamia)

Repulsed outside Baghdad at **Ctesiphon**, Anglo-Indian General Charles Townshend rashly determined to hold Kut-al-Amara against siege by Turkish General Nur-ud-Din and Colmar von de Goltz. When relief efforts failed at **Sheik Sa'ad**, **Wadi**, **Hanna**, **Dujaila** and **San-naiyat**, Townshend surrendered 10,000 men. About 4,000 of them died in captivity (7 December 1915–29 April 1916).

Kut-al-Amara ∎ 1917 ∎ World War I (Mesopotamia)

New Anglo-Indian commander Sir Frederick Maude determined to regain the initiative in Mesopotamia and took a large force up the Tigris, advancing on General Kara Bekir Bey at Kut-al-Amara, scene of the British Army's worst surrender up to that time. Heavy fighting forced the outnumbered Turks to abandon the city and withdraw upriver to **Baghdad** (17–26 February 1917).

Kutna Hora ∎ 1421 ∎ Hussite Wars

Despite Imperial losses at **Vitkov Hill** and **Zatec** earlier in the year, Sigismund of Hungary led a third expedition into eastern Bohemia and attacked Hussite Jan Zizka outside Kutna Hora, southeast of Prague. When Germans in the city rose in support of Imperial General Pipo Spano (Count Filippe de Scolari), Zizka was forced to break out. He was soon avenged at **Nebovidy** (21 December 1421).

Kuttenberg ∎ 1421 ∎ Hussite Wars
See **Kutna Hora**

Kuwait ∎ 1990 ∎ 1st Gulf War

After an orchestrated campaign of aggression, Iraqi troops and tanks invaded and rapidly overwhelmed Kuwait, forcing Emir Sheik Jabir Al Sabah to flee. Despite Superpower military threats and United Nations economic sanctions, President Saddam Hussein of Iraq annexed Kuwait a week later, setting the stage for the coalition **Desert Storm** offensive in January 1991 (2 August 1990).

Kuwait ∎ 1991 ∎ 1st Gulf War

Following massive bombardment by warships in the Persian Gulf, Marine General Walter Boomer stormed through Iraqi southern defences into Kuwait towards the Al Wafra oil field and further west towards Al Jaber air base. The reputed largest tank battle in US Marine

Corps history saw the Iraqis routed and the Americans raced north to help liberate Kuwait City (24–28 February 1991).

Kuzeik ▎ 1942 ▎ World War II (Burma-India)

Japanese forces seized **Moulmein**, while further north General Shozo Sakurai took Pa-an then crossed the Salween downstream of Kuzeik and circled behind a small force under Colonel Jerry Dyer. Attempting to hold well-prepared positions, the British were overwhelmed with 300 killed (including Dyer) and 200 captured. The survivors fled west towards the **Bilin** (11–12 February 1942).

Kwajalein ▎ 1944 ▎ World War II (Pacific)

While marines attacked **Roi-Namur**, on the northern Kwajalein Atoll in the **Marshall Islands**, General Charles Corbett landed on Kwajalein Island in the south, defended by 5,000 Japanese under Admiral Monzo Akiyama. Although Corbett lost 177 dead and 1,000 wounded, virtually the entire garrison was killed, including Akiyama. The airfield was back in use within days (1–4 February 1944).

Kweilin ▎ 1852 ▎ Taiping Rebellion
See **Guilin**

Kweilin-Liuchow ▎ 1944 ▎ World War II (China)
See **Guilin-Liuzhou**

Kyo Chong ▎ 1597 ▎ Japanese Invasion of Korea

Japanese commander Konishi Yukinga renewed the war against Korea and sailed west from Pusan, supported by troops under Shimazu Yoshihiro on Koje Island, to surprise Korean Admiral Won Kyun near Kyo Chong. Won Kyun and Yo Ok-ki were utterly defeated and killed, losing perhaps 200 ships. Yi Sun-shin was soon recalled to restore Korean prestige at **Myongyang** (27 August 1597).

Kyoto ▎ 1221 ▎ Jokyo Disturbance

Concerned by the growing power of the Hojo clan in Kamakura, retired Japanese Emperor Go-Toba opposed the Kamakura Shogunate and rallied allies against Regent Hojo Yoshitoki. Marching on Kyoto with 100,000 men, Yoshitoki's son Yasutoki crushed the rising. Executions and confiscations then secured Hojo hegemony in Japan until the fall of **Kamakura** in 1333 (June 1221).

Kyoto ▎ 1333 ▎ Genko War

With his forces stalled at the siege of **Chihaya**, Japanese Dictator Hojo Takatoki in Kamakura sent a large force under Ashikaga Takauji against Emperor Go-Daigo. However, Takauji immediately declared for the Emperor and stormed the Hojo city of Kyoto, where the Shogun's representative was defeated and killed. Another Imperialist army soon attacked **Kamakura** itself (10 June 1333).

Kyoto ▎ 1336 ▎ Ashikaga Rebellion

Ashikaga Takauji supported the restoration of Japan's Emperor Go-Daigo (1319) and suppressed a Hojo rebellion in **Kamakura** (1333) then turned against the Emperor, marching west to seize Kyoto. Attacked by Imperial troops under Kitabatake Akiie, the rebel and his brother Tadayoshi were routed and fled to Kyushu, where they soon won a great victory at **Tatarahama** (February 1336).

Kyoto ▎ 1863 ▎ War of the Meiji Restoration

When anti-western forces in Choshu secured dominance in Japan's court at Kyoto and persuaded Emperor Komei to expel foreigners, the leaders of Satsuma and Aizu determined to stage a coup d'etat. Heavy fighting saw the moderates seize the gates of the palace and the Choshu Samurai were driven out. A year later, Choshu failed in an attempt to recapture **Kyoto** (30 September 1863).

**Kyoto ∎ 1864 ∎ War of the
Meiji Restoration**

In an attempt to retake the Imperial Palace, Choshu and its allies marched on Kyoto, defended by Aizu Katamori and Hitotsubashi Keiki. Much of Kyoto was burned in a fierce action, but Kusaka Genzui of Choshu was killed and the attack repulsed. The survivors fled to nearby Yamazaki, where Maki Izumi and his followers were defeated and committed suicide (20 August 1864).

Ky Phu ∎ 1965 ∎ Vietnam War
  See **Phuoc Ha**

**Kyrenia ∎ 1974 ∎ Turkish Invasion
of Cyprus**

After Greek army officers staged a coup in Cyprus, about 6,000 Turks landed near Kyrenia and 1,000 paratroops dropped north of Nicosia to protect the Turkish Cypriots. Facing heavy resistance, more Turks landed through the Kyrenia bridgehead and held one third of the island by the 16 August ceasefire. The invasion cost about 6,000 Greek Cypriot and 3,500 Turkish casualties (20 July 1974).

**Kyritz ∎ 1635 ∎ Thirty Years War
(Franco-Habsburg War)**

Elector John George of Saxony declared war on Sweden and was defeated in Mecklenberg at **Domitz** and **Goldberg**, before being driven back into Brandenberg, where a Swedish army under General Lennart Torstensson marched south to threaten Berlin itelf. To the northwest at Kyritz, near Rathenow, the Swedes were victorious again and swept into Saxony (17 December 1635).

**Kyunnairyang ∎ 1592 ∎ Japanese Invasion
of Korea**
  See **Hansan**

**Kyushu ∎ 1281 ∎ Mongol Wars of
Kubilai Khan**
  See **Hakata Bay**

L

La Amarilla ❙ 1899 ❙ Colombian War of the Thousand Days
 See **Peralonso**

La Arada ❙ 1851 ❙ Central American National Wars
 Attempting to support Liberal leader Jose Dolores Nufio in Guatemala, President Doroteo Vasconcelos of Salvador, aided by Honduras, led an Allied army into Guatemala. Meeting the invaders near the border at La Arada in Chiquimula, Guatemalan President Jose Rafael Carrera won a decisive victory. He soon imposed conservative regimes in Salvador and later Honduras (2 February 1851).

Labadieville ❙ 1862 ❙ American Civil War (Lower Seaboard)
 See **Georgia Landing**

La Bahía ❙ 1812–1813 ❙ Gutiérrez-Magee Expedition
 When American Filibusters under Lieutenant Augustus W. Magee invaded Spanish Texas to support Republican Bernardo Gutiérrez, they captured **Nacogdoches** then took La Bahía on the San Antonio near Goliad. A siege by Governor Manuel de Salcedo and Simón de Herrera failed and a month later the withdrawing Royalists were defeated at the **Rosillo** (7 November 1812–19 February 1813).

La Bassée ❙ 1914 ❙ World War I (Western Front)
 British under Sir John French sent north from the **Aisne** attempted to turn the German flank and General Horace Smith-Dorrien attacked near La Bassée, east of Bethune. Heavy fighting spread north through **Armentières** and **Messines** to merge into actions around **Ypres**, but the British were driven back to Neuve Chappelle and the Germans kept La Bassée (10 October–2 November 1914).

La Bicocca ❙ 1522 ❙ 1st Habsburg-Valois War
 See **Bicocca**

La Bisbal ❙ 1810 ❙ Napoleonic Wars (Peninsular Campaign)
 In order to divert French forces around **Tortosa**, Spanish commander General Henry O'Donnell concentrated about 6,000 men in northern Catalonia and attacked a brigade under General Francois-Xavier Schwarz at La Bisbal, just east of Gerona. Schwarz and about 1,000 men surrendered after heavy casualties while O'Donnell was later created Duke of La Bisbal (14 September 1810).

La Bourgonce ❙ 1870 ❙ Franco-Prussian War
 See **Etival**

Labuan ❙ 1945 ❙ World War II (Pacific)
 See **Brunei Bay**

La Cañada | 1847 | American-Mexican War

Facing a rising against America's annexation of New Mexico, Colonel Sterling Price marched north from Albuquerque and attacked over 1,000 Mexicans at La Cañada near Santa Cruz. The insurgents fled with 36 killed and Price advanced through **Embudo Pass** towards **Pueblo de Taos**. A separate American force was defeated the same day further east at **Mora** (24 January 1847).

La Cañada de Cepeda | 1820 | Argentine Civil Wars

See **Cepeda**

Lácar | 1875 | 2nd Carlist War

Carlist commander Torcuato Mendíri recovering from defeat at **Oteiza** secured a brilliant victory when he surprised and routed a government force under General Enrique Bargés at Lácar, east of Estella, nearly capturing newly crowned King Alfonso XII. However, the tide had turned against the Carlists and defeats at **Treviño** and **Estella** made Don Carlos VII leave Spain forever (3 February 1875).

La Carbonera | 1866 | Mexican-French War

An Austrian column sent to relieve Imperial commander General Carlos Oroñoz besieged at **Oaxaca** by Republican General Porfirio Diaz, was intercepted by Diaz about 30 miles to the northeast at La Carbonera. The Austrians were forced to withdraw after a day-long action and Diaz returned to the siege of Oaxaca, which surrendered two weeks later (18 October 1866).

La Carolina | 1810 | Napoleonic Wars (Peninsular Campaign)

Buoyed by victory at **Ocaña**, King Joseph Napoleon invaded Andalusia and met Spanish General Carlos Areizaga in the mountains north of the Guadalquivir. In related actions around La Carolina and at Linares, Despenaperros and Montison, French Generals Édouard Mortier, Jean-Baptiste Gérard and Francois Sébastiani drove the defeated Spaniards across the river (19 February 1810).

Lachanas | 1913 | 2nd Balkan (Inter-ally) War

See **Kilkis**

La Chanca | 1841 | Colombian War of Supreme Commanders

Rebel leader General José María Obando won at **Garcia** (12 March), then was met at La Chanca, in the Cauca Valley near Cali, by a large government force under Colonel Joaquín Barriga. Obando was routed and his force was dispersed in a decisive and bloody action which effectively ended the rebellion in the south. The war in the north was soon decided at **Ocaña** (11 July 1841).

Lachine | 1689 | King William's War

With England and France at war in Europe, 1,500 pro-British Iroquois crossed Lake St Louis and attacked Lachine, just west of Montreal, where they killed 24, burned most of the houses and took prisoners, many later killed. Reinforcements under Lieutenant de Rabeyre approaching to support nearby Fort Roland were intercepted and destroyed. The Indians then withdrew (5 August 1689).

La Ciudadela | 1831 | Argentine Civil Wars

After victory in March at **Rodeo de Chacón**, in western Argentina, Federalist leader Juan Facundo Quiroga marched north on Tucumán and at nearby La Ciudadela fortress decisively defeated Unitarist General Gregoria Araoz de Lamadrid, who fled to Bolivia. The Unitarist cause effectively collapsed, leading to a temporary ceasefire and the rise of Juan Manuel de Rosas (4 November 1831).

La Cluse | 1871 | Franco-Prussian War

See **Pontarlier**

La Coimas | 1817 | Chilean War of Independence

See **Putaendo**

Lacolle Mill ▮ 1814 ▮ War of 1812

American General James Wilkinson was beaten on the St Lawrence at **Chrysler's Farm** in late 1813 and tried to approach Montreal from Lake Champlain in the south. Advancing down the Lacolle River he was blocked at a stone mill held by a small garrison under Major Richard Handcock. After losing 150 casualties Wilkinson retreated across the border and was later dismissed (30 March 1814).

La Corona ▮ 1797 ▮ French Revolutionary Wars (1st Coalition)

Two days after an Austrian attempt to relieve the siege of **Mantua** was repulsed at **Rivoli**, French General Barthélemy Joubert pursued the defeated Baron Josef Alvinzi north along the Adige to La Corona, where he lost again and thousands surrendered. Another Austrian relief force was defeated the same day at **La Favorita** and Mantua fell two weeks later (16 January 1797).

La Coronilla ▮ 1866 ▮ Mexican-French War

As Imperial forces left eastern Mexico, Republican Commander Ramon Corona sent Colonel Eulogia Parra to intercept General Ignacio Gutiérrez withdrawing east of Guadalajara. The Imperial column was heavily defeated at La Coronilla—Parra claimed to have inflicted 450 casualties—and Gutiérrez then evacuated Guadalajara and took his troops towards **Querétaro** (18 December 1866).

Lade ▮ 494 BC ▮ Greco-Persian Wars

Resuming war against the Greek cities of Asia Minor a few years after victory off **Ephesus** and **Salamis**, Darius I of Persia took a large fleet to besiege Miletus. Off the nearby island of Lade the Chian ships fought bravely, but the Ionian fleet suffered a terrible defeat, when the Samians deserted. Miletus fell and the Ionian revolt collapsed. Four years later Darius invaded Greece and lost at **Marathon**.

Lade ▮ 201 BC ▮ 2nd Macedonian War

Philip V of Macedon was campaigning in Asia Minor when he fought an indecisive action at Chios and pursued the fleet of Rhodes further south, where they took up a defensive position near Lade, off Miletus. The Rhodian fleet was defeated and forced to withdraw, although it did not suffer heavy losses. Philip then moved north to the Dardanelles to attack the free city of **Abydos**.

La Decena Trágica ▮ 1913 ▮ Mexican Revolution
　　See **Mexico City**

Ladoceia ▮ 227 BC ▮ Cleomenic War

Determined to recover Mantinea in Arcadia, lost despite recent victory at **Mount Lyceum**, Cleomones III of Sparta attacked Aratus of Sicyon at Ladoceia, near Megalopolis. Sparta's advance forces were defeated, but Lydiades and the Achaean cavalry advanced alone against orders and were routed, with Lydiades killed. The Achaean infantry fled and was beaten next year at **Hecatombaeum**.

La Donjuana ▮ 1877 ▮ Colombian Civil Wars

Colombia's Liberal government resumed war against Conservative rebels and sent General Sergio Camargo, fresh from victory at **Garrapata**, into Norte de Santander. In battle at La Donjuana, south of Cúcuta, Camargo secured a bloody victory over a rebel force led by General Alejandro Posada. Decisive victory for the government followed three months later at **Manizales** (27 January 1877).

Ladysmith ▮ 1899–1900 ▮ 2nd Anglo-Boer War

As Boers under Petrus Joubert advanced deep into Natal, British commander Sir George White failed in a blocking move at **Nicholson's Nek** and fell back under siege at Ladysmith. While a major assault was repulsed at **Wagon Hill**, General Sir Redvers Buller's advance finally succeeded at **Tugela Heights** and Ladysmith was relieved after 119 days (2 November 1899–28 February 1900).

Lae ▮ 1943 ▮ World War II (Pacific)
　　See **Salamaua**

La Esperanza ∎ 1876 ∎ Central American National Wars

Determined to regain power in Honduras, former President José María Medina and General Indalecio Miranda defeated the forces of President Ponciano Levía under War Minister Juan López in a five-day battle at La Esperanza, north of Concepción near Intibucá. While Medina's victory enabled him to seize the Presidency, he was soon defeated by Levía at **San Marcos** River (January 1876).

La Estancia ∎ 1859 ∎ Mexican War of the Reform

Reactionary President Miguel Miramón marched northwest from Mexico City to intercept General Santos Degollado advancing on Querétaro and inflicted a decisive defeat on the Liberal army near Querétaro at La Estancia de las Vacas, on the Celaya Road, capturing huge quantities of arms and supplies. Degollado fled to San Luis Potosi and Miramón won again at **Colima** (13 November 1859).

La Favorita ∎ 1797 ∎ French Revolutionary Wars (1st Coalition)

Two days after an Austrian attempt to relieve the French siege of **Mantua** was defeated at **Rivoli**, a separate Austrian relief force under General Giovanni Provera almost reached Mantua but was routed by General Jean Sururier just to the north at La Favorita. A major sortie by besieged General Dagobert Wurmser was also routed and Mantua surrendered two weeks later (16 January 1797).

La Fère-Champenoise ∎ 1814 ∎ Napoleonic Wars (French Campaign)

While Napoleon Bonaparte campaigned southeast of Paris, the advancing Allies under Prince Karl Philipp Schwarzenberg crashed into Marshals Auguste Marmont and Édouard Mortier at La Fère-Champenoise, southwest of Chalons. The heavily outnumbered French were badly defeated and Schwarzenberg was joined by General Gebhard von Blucher in the advance on **Paris** (25 March 1814).

La Forbie ∎ 1244 ∎ Later Crusader-Muslim Wars

After Khwarezmian Turks captured Jerusalem, local Crusaders allied themselves with the Ayyubid Sultan of Damascus against the new invaders. At La Forbie, near Gaza, the Turks, supported by rival Ayyubid Sultan al-Salih of Egypt, inflicted one of the worst defeats suffered by a Crusader army. This defeat, and the loss of **Jerusalem**, led directly to the French 7th Crusade (17 October 1244).

Lafourche Crossing ∎ 1863 ∎ American Civil War (Lower Seaboard)

Despite the surrender of Confederate **Port Hudson** on the Mississippi in Louisiana, further south Confederate General James P. Major led an offensive east from Brashear City. Met at Lafourche Crossing by Union Colonel Albert Stickney, Major was eventually forced to withdraw north through Thibodeaux. He joined the attack a week later to the north at **Donaldsonville** (20–21 June 1863).

Lagos Bay ∎ 1693 ∎ War of the Grand Alliance

French Marshal Anne Comte de Tourville avenging defeat at **La Hogue** in May attacked a large merchant convoy approaching Gibraltar, bound for Smyrna, after the main Allied escort had turned back. De Tourville drove off the inadequate Anglo-Dutch squadron of Admiral Sir George Rooke in Lagos Bay, near Cape St Vincent, then destroyed or captured almost 100 ships (17–18 June 1693).

Lagos Bay ∎ 1759 ∎ Seven Years War (Europe)

Sailing from Toulon to Brest for a planned invasion of Britain, Commodore Jean-Francois de la Clue Sabran was intercepted near Gibraltar by Admiral Sir Edward Boscawen. Some French ships escaped to Cadiz, but in a running battle two were captured and four were pursued into neutral Lagos Bay, Portugal to be captured or burned. De la Clue was fatally wounded (17–19 August 1759).

La Guaira I 1902 I Venezuelan Incident

While Venezuelan President Cipriano Castro fought a civil war at **La Victoria**, British and German warships under Admiral Archibald Douglas attacked La Guaria in support of unpaid debts. After seizing Venezuelan ships and bombarding the port, Italy joined the Allies in blockading the Pacific coast. The blockade was lifted (13 February 1903) after US intervention (9–13 December 1902).

La Gueule I 891 I Viking Raids on Germany

Danish Vikings led by King Godefrid advanced deep into Lorraine, where they defeated a German force at La Gueule, near Maastricht. The warrior-Archbishop Sunderold of Mainz died leading his troops on the battlefield and the Danes continued raiding down the Rhine until their disastrous defeat later in the year at the **Dyle** (26 June 891).

La Herradura I 1819 I Argentine Civil Wars

At war with rebel Chiefs in the northeast, government troops under Colonel Juan Bautista Bustos were attacked at La Herradura, southeast of Villa María, by Estanislao Lopez of Santa Fe, with Ricardo López Jordán of Entre Rios and Indians led by the Irish-born Pedro Campbell. López suffered a costly repulse in heavy fighting, though he won in May at **Barrancas** (18–19 February 1819).

Lahijan I 1757 I Persian Wars of Succession

Mohammad Hasan Khan of Qajar led a brilliant winter offensive south of the Caspian, where he suddenly assaulted his rival Azad Khan Afghan who had advanced into Persia from Azerbaijan. Attacking at Rudsar, Mohammad Hasan routed the garrison at nearby Lahijan, then took Rasht. Azad fled with terrible losses and was defeated again in the summer at **Urmiya** (10 February 1757).

Lahn I 1797 I French Revolutionary Wars (1st Coalition)

See **Neuwied**

La Hogaza I 1817 I Venezuelan War of Independence

As they advanced along the Orinoco from **Angostura**, part of Simón Bolívar's rebel force under Generals Pedro Zaraza and Pedro Léon Torres was surprised near the Rio Manapire at La Hogaza by Spanish General Miguel de La Torre. When Bolívar's cavalry was outflanked and fled, his infantry was destroyed and he returned to Angostura before advancing on **Calabozo** (2 December 1817).

La Hogue I 1692 I War of the Grand Alliance

In a final French attempt to re-establish James II of England, Admiral Anne Comte de Tourville sailed with a large fleet and was defeated off Barfleur, on the Contentin Peninsula, by the Anglo-Dutch fleet of Admiral Edward Russell. Three days later 12 French ships were destroyed at La Hogue Bay by Admiral George Rooke and the invasion was abandoned (19–24 May 1692).

Lahore I 1241 I Mongol Invasions of India

Tair Bahadur, the Mongol military commander in Afghanistan, invaded the Punjab, where he advanced on Lahore and bombarded the city. Lahore fell when the local Governor Malik Kara Kush fled and the city was subjected to massacre and destruction. Troops sent from Delhi by Sultan Muiz-al-din Bahram Shah arrived too late and the Mongols withdrew with their booty (22 December 1241).

Lahore I 1712 I Mughal Wars of Succession

Amid war between the sons of the late Emperor Bahadur Shah, Jahandar Shah, Rafi-al-Shan and Jahan Shah joined forces against the second son and favourite Azim-al-Shan. With Azim defeated and killed in battle outside Lahore, Jahandar Shah defeated and killed his other two brothers to claim the throne. However, Jahandar was himself killed a year later at **Agra** (14–17 & 26–28 March 1712).

Lahore I 1752 I Indian Campaigns of Ahmad Shah

Despite initial defeat at **Manupur** (March 1748), Afghan General Ahmad Shah Durrani invaded the Punjab in 1749 and was bought off, then appeared two years later and besieged Lahore. He captured the city after four months and Mughal Emperor Ahmad Shah made peace by ceding Lahore and Multan. The Afghan leader invaded again in 1757 to capture **Delhi** itself (5–6 March 1752).

Lahore | 1759 | Indian Campaigns of Ahmad Shah

On his fifth invasion of the decaying Mughal Empire, Afghan General Ahmad Shah Durrani was met near Lahore by Sikhs attempting alone to resist his advance. Afghan General Jahan Khan was defeated and wounded in a sharp check, but as Maratha General Sabaji fled from the Punjab, the Sikhs allowed the invaders to advance towards Delhi and victory in early 1761 at **Panipat** (September 1759).

Lahore | 1965 | 2nd Indo-Pakistan War

As Pakistani forces invaded southwestern Kashmir around **Chhamb**, India launched a large counter-offensive towards Lahore, west through Chhamb and from the southeast along the Ravi-Sutlej corridor. Pakistani armour was destroyed around **Khem Karan** and, after a further bloody Indian offensive north of Lahore towards **Sialkot**, both sides accepted a ceasefire (6–22 September 1965).

Laiazzo | 1294 | Venetian-Genoese Wars

War between Venice and Genoa resumed after the expiry of a truce, and a great naval battle was fought off Laiazzo (modern Ayas) on the Cilician coast of Anatolia. Genoese ships were lashed together in the harbour to form a powerful fighting platform and they successfully repulsed a disorganised attack, inflicting heavy losses on the Venetians.

Laing's Nek | 1881 | 1st Anglo-Boer War

When Boers in the Transvaal declared independence and destroyed a British column at **Bronkhorstspruit**, 1,000 men advancing under General Sir George Colley were blocked in the Drakensbergs at Laing's Nek by Boer General Petrus Joubert. Colley was repulsed in an utter rout with almost 200 men lost and he was soon defeated again at **Ingogo** and **Majuba Hill** (28 January 1881).

Lake Ashangi | 1936 | 2nd Italo-Ethiopian War

Emperor Haile Selassie retreated south after decisive defeat at **Maychew**, east of Sekota (31 March), leading his survivors past Lake Ashangi where they were pursued and brutally attacked by Italian-armed Oromo tribesmen while being bombed and strafed from the air. A virtual rout saw the Imperial army destroyed before the Emperor reached **Addis Ababa** and fled into exile (4–9 April 1936).

Lake Asunden | 1520 | Wars of the Kalmar Union

See **Bogesund**

Lake Balaton | 1945 | World War II (Eastern Front)

Despite the fall of **Budapest**, SS Generals "Sepp" Dietrich and Hermann Balck launched a last offensive towards the oil fields around Lake Balaton. After initial success, an early thaw saw them repulsed by a counter-offensive under Marshal Fedor Tolbukhin. The "Ardennes in the East" cost Germany 500 tanks and 40,000 men and the survivors withdrew towards **Vienna** (6–15 March 1945).

Lake Benacus | 268 | Roman-Alemannic Wars

During a disputed succession in Rome (resolved at **Mediolanum**) Alemanni tribesmen crossed the Alps into northern Italy. On the shores of Lake Benacus (modern Lake Garda) they were met and decisively defeated by new Emperor Claudius II, who then returned to the Balkans to meet the Goths at **Nish**. The Alemanni later invaded again and won a bloody victory in 271 at **Placentia**.

Lake Borgne | 1814 | War of 1812

In preparation for the attack on **New Orleans**, British Admiral Sir Alexander Cochrane sent

Commander Nicholas Lockyer with a force of marines in launches and longboats against American gunboats under Lieutenant Thomas ap Catesby Jones on Lake Borgne, at the mouth of the Mississippi. Fierce fighting saw all six American gunboats captured and a schooner destroyed (14 December 1814).

Lake Champlain I 1814 I War of 1812
British General Sir George Prevost led an offensive south from the St Lawrence, where he captured **Plattsburg** on Lake Champlain then sent naval Captain George Downie against American ships at anchor nearby under Captain Thomas Macdonough. Downie was defeated and killed, with all his four ships captured, and Prevost withdrew to Canada in disgrace (11 September 1814).

Lake Chicot I 1864 I American Civil War (Trans-Mississippi)
See **Old River Lake**

Lake Como I 196 BC I Gallic Wars in Italy
With the Insubre Gauls of northern Italy defeated on the **Mincio**, Consul Marcus Claudius Marcellus (whose father and namesake had beaten them at **Clastidium** 25 years earlier) attacked the survivors the following year near the city of Comum at the southern end of Lake Como. The Insubre suffered another very costly defeat and signed a treaty finally accepting submission to Rome.

Lake Erie I 1813 I War of 1812
In a bloody and decisive naval action at the western end of Lake Erie near Put-in Bay, American Commodore Oliver Perry defeated and captured the outnumbered British squadron of Captain Robert Barclay. This strategically significant defeat ended British control of Lake Erie and quickly led to their withdrawal from **Detroit** (10 September 1813).

Lake Garda I 268 I Roman-Alemannic Wars
See **Lake Benacus**

Lake Garda I 1439 I Venetian-Milanese Wars
See **Maderno**

Lake George I 1755 I Seven Years War (North America)
Colonial militia led by Colonel William Johnson of New York advanced north from Albany and met a French and Indian force from Crown Point under Baron Ludwig Dieskau. In hard fighting at the head of Lake George, Dieskau was captured but Johnson did not follow up his victory. He built **Fort William Henry** nearby and the French withdrew to **Ticonderoga** (8 September 1755).

Lake Goplo I 1666 I Lubomirski's Rebellion
See **Matwy**

Lake Janda I 711 I Muslim Conquest of Spain
See **Guadalete**

Lake Khasan I 1938 I Russo-Japanese Border Wars
See **Changfukeng**

Lake Koloe I 229 BC I Pergamum-Seleucid Wars
A year after defeating Gallic tribes at **Pergamum**, in western Anatolia, King Attalus I of Pergamum renewed his war against Antiochus Hierax, who ruled part of Asia Minor after defeating his brother Seleucus II at **Ancyra**. Marching south into Lydia, Attalus defeated Hierax at Lake Koloe, then defeated him again later that year in Caria at the **Harpasus**.

Lake Kurukowa I 1625 I Cossack-Polish Wars
See **Borovitsa**

Lake Naroch I 1916 I World War I (Eastern Front)
Russian Generals Aleksei Kuropatkin and Aleksei Evert, attempting to ease pressure on

Verdun, attacked around Lake Naroch, east of Vilna, against General Hermann von Eichhorn's Germans. After an ineffective bombardment the Russian offensive ground to a halt in heavy mud with over 100,000 men lost. A subsidiary attack towards **Riga** also failed (18 March–14 April 1916).

Lake Okeechobee I 1837 I 2nd Seminole Indian War

In one of the war's largest field actions, over 1,000 men under Colonel Zachary Taylor met Seminole Chiefs Sam Jones and Hallack Tustenuggee in Central Florida at Lake Okeechobee. In very heavy fighting, with Missouri militia sacrificed and their Colonel Richard Gentry killed, the Seminole were defeated, though at the cost of 26 American dead and 112 wounded (25 December 1837).

Lake Peipus I 1242 I Rise of Russia

Two years after repulsing a Swedish invasion at the **Neva**, Prince Alexander Nevski of Novgorod faced an even greater threat from Estonia by German knights of the Sword Brethren and their Danish allies. In the "Battle on the Ice" on frozen Lake Peipus (modern Chudskoye) Nevski utterly destroyed the invasion, establishing himself as one of Russia's greatest heroes (April 1242).

Lake Poyang I 1363 I Rise of the Ming Dynasty
See **Poyang Lake**

Lake Poyang I 1855 I Taiping Rebellion
See **Jiujiang**

Lake Prespa I 1917 I World War I (Balkan Front)

Franco-Serb forces under General Maurice Sarrail commenced a fresh offensive into southern Serbia, advancing along a line west from **Monastir**, towards Lake Prespa. The attack met powerful German-Bulgarian defences and was driven back to Monastir with costly losses. Meanwhile, a British advance further to the east was repulsed around **Doiran** (11–22 March 1917).

Lake Providence I 1863 I American Civil War (Western Theatre)
See **Goodrich's Landing**

Lake Regillus I 496 BC I Early Roman-Etruscan Wars

A last effort to restore Roman monarchy saw deposed King Lucius Tarquinius join with sons Sextus and Titus and son-in-law Octavius Mamilius of Tusculum. In a semi-legendary battle against Aulus Postumius at Lake Regillus, somewhere southeast of Rome, the King was wounded and his sons and son-in-law were killed. With the Latin army routed the King's cause was destroyed (trad date 496 BC).

Lake Seit I 1903 I American-Moro Wars

Soon after America defeated Philippine Moros on Mindanao at **Bacolod**, Panglima Hassan attacked American troops on Jolo, then faced a large counter-offensive under General Leonard Wood and Major Hugh Scott. The rebel stronghold near Lake Seit was stormed, with up to 500 Moros killed. Hassan was captured but escaped and was defeated at **Pangpang** in March 1904 (14 November 1903).

Lake Smolino I 1502 I 1st Muscovite-Lithuanian War

The Livonian Order recovered from disaster at **Helmed** (November 1501) and Master Walther von Plettenberg besieged Pskov, then withdrew south to meet approaching Russians under Prince Daniil Shchenya. A bloody action at Lake Smolino saw both sides withdraw exhausted. Meantime, Duke Ivan III of Moscow failed to seize **Smolensk**, but Alexander of Poland soon sued for peace (September 1502).

Lake Tana I 1543 I Adal-Ethiopian War
See **Wayna Daga**

Lake Trasimene I 217 BC I 2nd Punic War

After wintering in northern Italy, the Carthaginian Hannibal Barca marched south across the Apennines and by-passed Romans waiting at Arretium. General Gaius Flaminius pursued him south and, in a narrow defile leading around the northern shore of Lake Trasimene, the Roman army was ambushed and cut to pieces. Gaius Flaminius was among thousands killed in the slaughter (April 217 BC).

Lake Urmiya I 1605 I Turko-Persian Wars
See **Sufiyan**

Lake Vadimo I 310 BC I 2nd Samnite War
As Rome continued her conquest of Central Italy, war resumed against the Samnites, who found fresh allies among the Etruscans and were able to drive Rome onto the defensive. However, at Lake Vadimo on the River Tiber north of Rome, the Etruscan army was defeated by Quintus Fabius Maximus Rullianus and they were soon forced out of the war.

Lake Vadimo I 283 BC I Later Roman-Etruscan War
Soon after Roman forces were devastatingly defeated at **Arretium**, a combined army of Etruscans and Gallic Senones assembled and advanced towards Rome. At Lake Vadimo in Etruria, the invaders were virtually annihilated by Publius Cornelius Dolabella. Despite some continued Etruscan and Senone resistance, the decisive victory virtually completed Rome's conquest of central Italy.

Lakhairi I 1793 I Maratha Territorial Wars
Campaigning against Mahadji Sindhia, Maratha General Tukaji Holkar and Chevalier Dudrenec marched against Viceroy Gopal Rao Bhao, who was supported by Benoit de Boigne and veteran General Lakwa Dada. Hard fighting on wet ground in the pass at Lakhairi, near Ajmer, saw Holkar's army shattered and Mahadji was undisputed Maratha ruler of Hindustan (20 September 1793).

Laknta I 1900 I French Conquest of Chad
See **Kousséri**

La Ladera I 1828 I Colombian Civil Wars
Colonels José María Obando and José Hilario López led a rebellion in the Cauca Valley against the dictatorship of Simón Bolívar. They took up arms in Popayán and seized the city, then met and defeated the garrison in battle at nearby La Ladera to secure the area. Bolívar later pardoned the rebels and signed an armistice with them to restore peace (November 1828).

La Laja I 1899 I Colombian War of the Thousand Days
See **Peralonso**

Lalsot I 1787 I Mughal-Maratha War of Ismail Beg
Supported by the Rajput rulers of Jodhpur and Udaipur, Partab Singh of Jaipur took a massive force southeast against Marathas under Mahadji Sindhia. When his Mughal cavalry under Mohammad Beg and his nephew Ismail Beg Hamadani defected, Sindhia was defeated in a bloody three-day battle at Tunga, near Lalsot. He then made peace and pressed on to reinforce **Agra** (30 May–1 June 1787).

La Maddalena I 1793 I French Revolutionary Wars (1st Coalition)
An ill-advised and confused assault on northern Sardinia saw French Revolutionary troops under Colonel Pietro-Paulo Colonna-Cesari land at La Maddalena. However, they were insufficient for the task and, although artillery Captain Napoleon Bonaparte bombarded the town, the force withdrew after two days. Bonaparte had to spike and abandon his guns (23–25 February 1793).

La Marfée I 1641 I Thirty Years War (Franco-Habsburg War)
Louis de Bourbon Count of Soissons (brother of Louis XIII) opposed Cardinal Richelieu and invited Imperial General William von Lamboy to support him and Duke Henry of Bouillon at Sedan. At nearby La Marfée, Royalists under Marshal Gaspard de Chatillon were routed, but Soissons was killed—reputedly by accident

using his pistol to raise his visor—and the rebellion collapsed (6 July 1641).

La Mesa | 1847 | American-Mexican War
See **San Gabriel, California**

Lamghan | 989 | Muslim Conquest of Northern India

After cross-border raiding, Amir Sebuktigin of Bokhara attacked Raja Jaipal of Punjab, who gathered support from other Hindu Princes, including Dhanga of Chandella. At Lamghan, near Kabul, his confederacy suffered a decisive defeat. Jaipal was forced to concede Kabul and other territory in the west of his Kingdom. In 1001 he was defeated by Sebuktigin's son Mahmud at **Peshawar**.

Lamia | 323–322 BC | Lamian War

Athens and other Greek cities which rebelled following the death of Alexander the Great seized Thermopylae then besieged Antipater of Macedonia at Lamia, in the Sperchios Valley. The death of Leosthenes and the arrival of troops from Asia forced the Hellenic League to lift the siege after almost six months. Defeat at **Crannon** and **Amorgos** ended their effort to overthrow Macedonian hegemony.

La Motta | 1513 | War of the Holy League
See **Vicenza**

Lam Son | 1971 | Vietnam War

A disastrous test of "Vietnamization" saw about 16,000 South Vietnamese invade Laos to cut Communist supply routes. After claiming initial success, the invaders were routed by large North Vietnamese reinforcements and withdrew with half the force killed or wounded. About 200 Americans were also killed, mainly crew of over 100 US helicopters destroyed (8 February–24 March 1971).

Lancaster Hill | 1900 | 2nd Anglo-Boer War
See **Vryheid**

Landau | 1702 | War of the Spanish Succession

Prince Louis of Baden led an Austrian offensive across the Rhine, where he besieged French General Ezekiel de Mélac at Landau, northwest of Karlsruhe. When Marshal Nicolas Catinat could not send relief the town capitulated. After Bavaria joined the war Louis withdrew and lost at **Friedlingen**. Landau was recovered after victory at **Speyer** in November 1703 (29 July–12 September 1702).

Landau | 1713 | War of the Spanish Succession

When England and Holland made peace, Austria resumed war and French Marshal Claude Villars crossed the Rhine to seize Speyer and Kaiserslautern, then besieged Landau, held by Prince Eberhard Ludwig of Württemburg and 12,000 troops. When Imperial commander Prince Eugène of Savoy could not send aid, Landau surrendered and Villars turned against **Freiburg** (20 August 1713).

Landau | 1793 | French Revolutionary Wars (1st Coalition)
See **Pirmasens**

Landen | 1693 | War of the Grand Alliance
See **Neerwinden**

Landi Kotal | 1897 | Great Frontier Rising

Despite a rebuff for rebellious Pathans at **Shabkadr**, Afridi and Orakzai tribesmen attacked the Khyber Forts. Ali Masjid and Fort Maude quickly fell, but at Landi Kotal, west of Peshawar, there was fierce fighting before the sepoys of the British Khyber Rifles were overwhelmed. The forts were eventually regained by General Sir William Lockhart after the end of the campaign (24–25 August 1897).

Landrécies I 1794 I French Revolutionary Wars (1st Coalition)

Driving French General Charles Pichegru back into northern France, the English and Austrian Allies under Prince Frederick Augustus Duke of York besieged Landrécies on the Sambre River near Le Cateau. Inadequate French relief attempts from the west were repulsed at **Villers-en-Cauchies** and **Beaumont-en-Cambresis** and the garrison agreed to a premature surrender (17–30 April 1794).

Landriano I 1529 I 2nd Habsburg-Valois War

A French army under Francois de Bourbon Count of St Pol ravaged northern Italy before being driven back from a siege of **Naples**. Withdrawing north they were defeated at Landriano, south of Milan, by Spanish commander Antonio de Leyva, who captured St Pol and his senior officers. Charles V of Spain and Francis I of France soon signed a treaty to end the war (21 June 1529).

Landshut I 1634 I Thirty Years War (Swedish War)

With Ferdinand of Hungary advancing up the Danube from Bohemia to threaten **Regensberg**, Protestant commander Bernard of Saxe-Weimar joined Marshal Gustavus Horn in a diversionary attack south against Landshut on the Isar. Bernard seized Landshut with General Johann von Aldringer killed, but the Imperials meanwhile captured Regensberg then besieged **Nördlingen** (22 July 1634).

Landshut I 1760 I Seven Years War (Europe)

Prussian Baron Ernst Heinrich de la Motte-Fouqué was forced out of the fortress of Landshut, southwest of Breslau in Silesia, but was ordered by Frederick II of Prussia to retake it from Austrian Marshal Gideon von Loudon. De la Motte-Fouqué's outnumbered force was virtually destroyed and Frederick advanced into Silesia to meet von Loudon in August at **Liegnitz** (23 June 1760).

Landshut I 1809 I Napoleonic Wars (5th Coalition)

The Austrian army of Archduke Charles invaded Bavaria, where it was defeated and split in two by Napoleon Bonaparte at **Abensberg**, with the Austrian left wing under Baron Johann Hiller driven southeast towards Landshut. They were attacked there the following day and routed by a large French force under Marshal Jean Lannes, with heavy losses in men and equipment (21 April 1809).

Landskrona I 1677 I Scania War

When Denmark sided with the Netherlands against France and Sweden, Charles XI of Sweden suffered several heavy defeats at sea, but beat the Danes at **Lund** (December 1676) then met them again in a bloody encounter at Landskrona, northwest of Malmo. The Danes were defeated with over 3,000 killed, but the war dragged on while Charles continued campaigning in Germany (14 July 1677).

Landstuhl I 1523 I German Knights' War

Franconian knights under Franz von Sickingen and Ulrich von Hutten resolved to preserve their rights and attacked Catholic Trier. But they fell back to Landstuhl, near Kaiserslautern, besieged by Landgrave Philipp of Hesse, Elector Palatine Ludwig IV and Richard von Griefenklau, Archbishop of Trier. Fatally wounded, Sickingen was forced to surrender, effectively ending the war (6 May 1523).

Lang Bac I 42 I Wars of the Later Han

When the sisters Trung Trac and Trung Nhi raised rebellion in Vietnam and drove out the Chinese Governor, Han Emperor Guangwu sent an army under the veteran General Ma Yuan. The rebels were beaten in battle at Lang Bac (near modern Hanoi) and lost again at Hat Mon (now Son Tay). Unable to face defeat, the sisters killed themselves and Chinese Imperial control was restored.

Langemark I 1914 I World War I (Western Front)

Opening the First Battle of **Ypres** following action further south at **Messines** and **Armentières**, ill-trained German volunteers attacked Langemark, north of Ypres, where the Allied defence had been badly underestimated. The force of mainly university students and army cadets was destroyed, while the main attack went in further south through **Gheluvelt** (21–24 October 1914).

Langemark I 1917 I World War I (Western Front)

Despite terrible losses around **Pilkem Ridge** at the start of Third **Ypres**, General Hubert Gough soon attacked again northeast towards Langemark. The ruined town was taken at heavy cost before the advance ground to a halt in terrible mud for little gain. General Sir Douglas Haig's offensive from Ypres resumed a month later further south along the **Menin Road** (16–18 August 1917).

Langensalza I 1866 I Seven Weeks War

While Prussia invaded Austrian Bohemia, Prussian General Edouard Vogel von Falckenstein attacked Hanover, which had sided with Austria. At Langensalza, near Erfurt, George V of Hanover repulsed the Prussian vanguard, but two days later, was decisively defeated by the main force. Hanover was annexed to Prussia and Falckenstein invaded Bavaria for victory at **Würzburg** (27–29 June 1866).

Langfang I 1900 I Boxer Rebellion

When anti-foreign Boxers threatened the legations at **Beijing**, a 2,000-strong multi-national relief force set out from Tianjin under British Admiral Sir Edward Seymour. With the railway destroyed at Langfang, Seymour was cut off and soon faced a major assault by well-armed Imperial troops. His failed expedition retreated to **Tianjin** with almost 300 casualties (14–17 June 1900).

Langport I 1645 I British Civil Wars

In the wake of his great victory over Charles I at **Naseby** (14 June), Sir Thomas Fairfax marched into Somerset to relieve **Taunton**, held for Parliament by Colonel Robert Blake. Twelve miles east at Langport, Royalist General George Lord Goring was heavily defeated by Oliver Cromwell's cavalry and withdrew to Devon. Taunton was saved and **Bridgwater** fell two weeks later (10 July 1645).

Langside I 1568 I Uprising against Mary Queen of Scots

Mary Queen of Scots escaped from captivity after defeat at **Carberry Hill** (June 1567), raising a 6,000-strong army under Archibald Campbell Earl of Argyll to regain the throne from her son James VI. At Langside, near Glasgow, her army was routed by her half-brother, the Regent Lord James Stewart, and Sir William Kirkaldy. Mary fled to England, where she was beheaded in 1587 (13 May 1568).

Lang Son I 1885 I Sino-French War

A major offensive from **Bac Ninh** in northern Vietnam (Tonkin) saw General Louis Brière de l'Isle secure strategic Lang Son from Chinese Guangxi forces (13 February). However, a massive counter-attack at nearby Bang Bo saw General Oscar de Négrier routed and the French abandoned Lang Son in panic. Paris quickly sued for peace and the pre-war status quo was restored (28–29 March 1885).

Lang Son I 1979 I Sino-Vietnamese War

To punish Vietnam for invading Cambodia, China invaded northern Vietnam, where General Yang Dezhi captured four provincial capitals. Fiercest fighting developed around Lang Son, where the Vietnamese counter-attacked with plentiful modern equipment. With severe losses in men and armour, China withdrew, each side suffering about 20,000 casualties (17 February–5 March 1979).

Lanhozo I 1809 I Napoleonic Wars (Peninsular Campaign)

See **Braga**.

Lanneau's Ferry **I** 1780 **I** War of the American Revolution

Attacking American communications during Britain's siege of **Charleston**, South Carolina, Colonel Banastre Tarleton won at **Monck's Corner** and later met American Colonels Anthony White and Abraham Burford 40 miles from Charleston on the Santee, at Lanneau's Ferry. Tarleton surprised and routed the Americans, then beat Burford again a few weeks later at **Waxhaw** (6 May 1780).

Lansdown **I** 1643 **I** British Civil Wars

Sir Ralph Hopton's Royalists advancing into Somerset after victory at **Stratton** (16 May) were blocked at Lansdown Hill, near Bath, by Parliamentary General Sir William Waller. After heavy losses on both sides Cornish infantry under Sir Bevil Grenville took the hill, but Grenville was killed. Waller withdrew after dark and Hopton, who was accidentally wounded, retired on **Devizes** (5 July 1643).

Lanskroun **I** 1771 **I** Polish Rebellion

Polish Nationalists under French Colonel Charles Dumouriez defending themselves against a Russian advance, took up a defensive position along a ridge near the fortress of Lanskroun, south of Cracow. Attacking with his Cossacks, Russian General Alexander Suvorov routed the Poles, killing about 500. Dumouriez fled to France, leaving the Poles without a commander (10 May 1771).

Lantada **I** 1068 **I** War of Castilian Succession

In the war of succession between the sons of Ferdinand I of Castile, Sancho II of Castile met his brother Alfonso VI of Leon in battle at Lantada, near Carrion, between the two kingdoms. According to legend, the brothers agreed the loser would forfeit his kingdom. However, after Sancho defeated Alfonso and drove him from the field, the brothers managed to patch up the peace.

Laohekou **I** 1945 **I** World War II (China)

Japanese General Takashi Takamori resumed the offensive into Western Henan, leading a large force against Allied airfields north of the Yangzi. The major base at Laohekou in Hubei fell after a bitter ten-day siege (8 April), though a huge Chinese counter-offensive saved the base at Ankang and retook Laohekou. Further south the Japanese advanced on **Zhijiang** (21 March–28 April 1945).

Laon **I** 941 **I** Franco-Norman Wars

In the struggle for the throne of France, Hugh the Great—Duke of the Franks and brother of the late King Rudolf—campaigned against Louis IV d'Outremer, son of the deposed Charles III. Louis was besieged at Laon, north of the Aisne and, although the siege was driven off by the intervention of German Emperor Otto I, Louis lost much of his support and fled to Burgundy.

Laon **I** 1814 **I** Napoleonic Wars (French Campaign)

Three days after achieving a costly victory at **Craonne**, northeast of Paris, Napoleon Bonaparte attacked General Gebhard von Blucher's Prussian-Russian army at nearby Laon. Bonaparte was eventually driven off in a confused two-day action and withdrew towards Soissons with heavy losses. Blucher meanwhile was able to continue his advance towards **Paris** (9–10 March 1814).

Laon **I** 1940 **I** World War II (Western Europe)

As German forces invaded **France** through the **Ardennes** and swept towards the coast, a French armoured Division attempted a bold counter-attack just north of Laon, where tanks under General Charles de Gaulle struck the Germans around Montcornet. After heavy fighting he was driven off by dive-bombers and concentrated armour and the Germans took Laon (17–19 May 1940).

La Palma **I** 1855 **I** Peruvian Civil Wars

In a rising against brutal President José Rufino Echénique, former President Ramón Castilla, supported by Mariano Ignacio Prado and Miguel San Román, met the President's army under General Juan Crisóstomo Torrico southeast of Lima, at La Palma. With Torrico decisively defeated, he and Echénique fled into exile and

Castilla secured a second term in office (5 January 1855).

La Placilla | 1891 | Chilean Civil War
See **Placilla**

Lapland | 1944–1945 | World War II (Northern Europe)
Under the Armistice with Moscow signed after **Ilomantsi**, Finland attacked its former German Allies in Lapland. Aided by the Soviets at **Petsamo**, General Hjalmar Siilasvuo recovered most of northern Finland. General Lothar Rendulic's retreating Germans caused massive destruction and burned Rovaniemi before withdrawing to **Kirkenes** in Norway (20 September 1944–24 April 1945).

La Plata, Colombia | 1816 | Colombian War of Independence
As they withdrew east from Popayán after the disaster at **El Tambo**, 150 Patriots led by Colonels Liborio Mejía and Pedro Monsalve attempted to defend a bridge at La Plata against 400 pursuing Royalists under Colonel Carlos Tolrá. Mejía was defeated and later executed, along with many other leaders, effectively completing Spanish reconquest of the Cauca Valley (10 July 1816).

La Plata, Cuba | 1957 | Cuban Revolution
Fidel Castro and Ernesto Che Guevara regrouped after **Alegría del Pío** and soon led a modest force against the army post at the mouth of the La Plata River. After an hour of fighting the small garrison surrendered and the rebels captured much-needed arms. While a minor action, it was hailed as the first victory of the revolution. Further success followed in May at **El Uvero** (16 January 1957).

La Polonia | 1840 | Colombian War of Supreme Commanders
At the start of a widespread Federalist rebellion, Colonel Manuel Gonzáles in the north seized Velez. Supported by Generals Juan José Reyes Patria and Juan Gómez, he then attacked government troops under Colonel Manuel María Franco and Major Alfonso Acevedo at La Polonia in Santander. Gonzáles secured a decisive victory, but was defeated next month at **Culebrera** (29 September 1840).

La Prairie | 1691 | King William's War
On a reconnaissance in force towards Montreal, British Major Peter Schuyler with 120 militia and 150 Mohawks attacked La Prairie de la Magdaleine on the St Lawrence, recently reinforced by Governor Louis-Hector de Callière. Schuyler drove off a sortie by Jean Bouillet de la Chassaigne, then fought a brilliant defensive withdrawal, inflicting heavy French losses (1 August 1691).

La Puerta (1st) | 1814 | Venezuelan War of Independence
Spanish irregulars led by José Tomás Boves advanced north from victory at **San Marcos** and met a blocking force of 2,000 Republicans under General Vicente Campo Elías in battle at La Puerta. While Boves was seriously wounded his cavalry won a decisive victory. Patriot leader Simón Bolívar responded by executing about 800 Spanish prisoners at Caracas and La Guaria (3 February 1814).

La Puerta (2nd) | 1814 | Venezuelan War of Independence
With Royalist forces advancing in western Venezuela, Patriot leader Simón Bolívar secured defensive victories at **La Victoria**, **San Mateo** and **Carabobo**. At La Puerta, near San Juan de Los Morros, he was decisively defeated by the Spanish leader José Tomás Boves. Withdrawing through **Aragua**, Bolívar fled into exile and Venezuelan independence was again crushed (15 June 1814).

La Puerta | 1818 | Venezuelan War of Independence
See **Semen**

Lapuu | 1808 | Napoleonic Wars (Russo-Swedish War)
Russian forces withdrawing from the West Finland port of **Vasa**, checked the Swedes at

Kokonsaari, then fell back on a strong position at the Lapuu River, held by General Nikolai Rayevski. In hard fighting a few days later, Swedish Commander Karl Adlercreutz drove the Russians out of Lapuu village. Rayevski was relieved of command and was replaced by Nikolai Kamenski (14 July 1808).

L'Aquila I 1424 I Condottieri Wars
See **Aquila**

Larache I 1936 I Spanish Civil War
When the military Nationalist uprising began in Spanish Morocco at **Melilla,** key centres such as Tetuán and Ceuta quickly fell. However in the western Moroccan city of Larache on that night, rebel army officers met with sharp resistance from pro-government troops and unionists. The loyal opposition was bloodily crushed and by morning the city was under rebel control (18 July 1936).

Laramie I 1854 I Sioux Indian Wars
See **Fort Laramie**

Laredo I 1842 I Texan Wars of Independence
In retaliation for Mexican raids on **San Antonio** earlier in the year, President Sam Houston of Independent Texas sent about 700 volunteers under Alexander Somervell, southwest to the Rio Grande, where the so-called Somervell Expedition captured Laredo. They also took Guerrero before disbanding, though some continued downriver to disaster two weeks later at **Mier** (8 December 1842).

Larga I 1770 I Catherine the Great's 1st Turkish War
Russian Generals Pyotr Rumyantsev and Grigori Potemkin led a new offensive in the Balkans, crossing the Pruth with 37,000 men. After victory at **Ryabaya Mogila** (17 June) they advanced to the junction with the Larga against 80,000 Turks and Crimean Tatars under Abaza Pasha and Khan Kaplan Girai. Rumyantsev attacked without delay and his routed enemy fled towards **Kagul** (7 July 1770).

Largs I 1263 I Norwegian Invasion of Scotland
When Scotland attempted to regain her western isles, Haakon IV of Norway took a substantial force against Alexander III of Scotland. With his fleet badly damaged by a storm, Haakon landed near Largs on the Clyde in Ayrshire, where he suffered a decisive defeat. As a result Norway gave up the Hebrides and Isle of Man after more than 150 years of rule (2 October 1263).

Larissa I 171 BC I 3rd Macedonian War
See **Callicinus**

Larissa I 1084 I 1st Byzantine-Norman War
The year after defeating Byzantine Emperor Alexius I for a second time at **Dyrrhachium** in Albania, the Norman army of Bohemund advanced into Thessaly to besiege Larissa. But Alexius had raised yet another army—including 7,000 Turkish cavalry—and beat the invaders. When Bohemund's father Robert Guiscard died in Italy in 1085 the Normans withdrew from Byzantine territory.

La Roche-L'Abeille I 1569 I 3rd French War of Religion
In the aftermath of the Protestant rout at **Jarnac** (13 March), Huguenot leader Admiral Gaspard de Coligny received large-scale German Protestant reinforcements and inflicted a sharp check on the Catholics in western France near La Roche-L'Abeille, south of Limoges. However, he failed in a siege of **Poitiers** and was heavily defeated in October at **Moncontour** (June 1569).

La Rochelle I 1372 I Hundred Years War
In response to an English claim on his kingdom, Henry II of Castile supported Charles V of France by attacking the English fleet attempting to relieve the siege of La Rochelle. Castilian Admiral Ambrogio Boccanegra (a Genoese) destroyed the English, capturing commander John Hastings Earl of Pembroke, and La Rochelle soon fell, leading to England losing all of Poitou (22–23 June 1372).

La Rochelle ∎ 1572–1573 ∎ 4th French War of Religion

The principal military campaign of the War following the notorious Massacre of **St Bartholomew's Eve** saw Charles IX of France send his brother Henry of Anjou against the Protestant stronghold of La Rochelle, held by Francois de la Noue. After seven months and increasing Catholic casualties, Henry lifted the siege and accepted a negotiated truce (December 1572–June 1573).

La Rochelle ∎ 1625 ∎ 2nd Huguenot Rebellion

Benjamin Duke de Soubise renewed the Huguenot revolt against the French Crown, seizing Royalist ships at Blavet and taking the islands of Re and Oleron, guarding Protestant La Rochelle. Using borrowed ships with French crews, Duke Henry of Montmorency defeated Soubise off La Rochelle, recapturing the islands. Cardinal Richelieu signed a hasty peace (September 1625).

La Rochelle ∎ 1627–1628 ∎ 3rd Huguenot Rebellion

Attacking the heart of Huguenot rebellion, Armand du Plessis Cardinal Richelieu and Duke Henry of Guise led a brutal land and sea blockade of La Rochelle. With English relief fleets driven off in May (William Feilding Lord Denbigh) and September (Robert Bertie Earl of Lindsey), the city capitulated and the rebellion effectively came to an end (August 1627–29 October 1628).

La Rothière ∎ 1814 ∎ Napoleonic Wars (French Campaign)

Three days after being repulsed from **Brienne**, southeast of Paris, General Gebhard von Blucher led his force of Prussians and Russians against Napoleon Bonaparte to recover nearby La Rothière. After a bitterly fought action, the outnumbered French withdrew during a snowstorm, abandoning guns and prisoners, and the Allies continued towards Paris (1 February 1814).

Larrainzar ∎ 1835 ∎ 1st Carlist War

Determined to relieve the Carlist siege of **Villafranca de Oria**, Liberal commander in Navarre, General Jéronimo Valdés, sent Colonel Marcelino Oráa with 3,500 men. At Larrainzar, north of Pamplona, Oráa was surprised and routed by Carlist leader José Miguel Sagastibelza, losing perhaps 500 killed and 500 captured. A second relief force was repulsed days later at **Descarga** (29 May 1835).

Larrasoaña ∎ 1836 ∎ 1st Carlist War
See **Tirapegui**

Larremiar ∎ 1835 ∎ 1st Carlist War

Spanish Liberal General Francisco Espoz y Mina and 1,500 men marching to relieve Elizondo in northern Navarre—besieged by Carlists under José Miguel Sagastibelza—came under attack at Mount Larremiar by Carlist commander Tomás Zumalacárregui. Mina lost about 300 casualties in heavy fighting before he managed to reach Elizondo. He resigned a few weeks later (12 March 1835).

La Salud ∎ 1813 ∎ Napoleonic Wars (Peninsular Campaign)

After news of defeat at **Vitoria**, French General Charles Decaen called off a planned attack on Vich, north of Barcelona. However, his subordinate General Maximilien Lamarque unwittingly proceeded with the attack alone. Lamarque was routed by Spanish General Baron Jaime Eroles at nearby La Salud, losing over 400 men before Decaen rescued him and Vich was saved (23 June 1813).

Las Cruces Pass ∎ 1810 ∎ Mexican Wars of Independence
See **Monte de las Cruces**

Las Gradas ∎ 1862 ∎ Ecuador-Colombia War
See **Tulcán**

Las Guásimas ∎ 1898 ∎ Spanish-American War

At the start of the American land invasion of Cuba, Commander William R. Shafter secured Siboney, then moved west towards Santiago, pursuing the Spanish army of General Arsenio Linares. Facing a rearguard delaying action at Las

Guásimas, American Generals Henry W. Lawton and Joseph W. Wheeler suffered the greater losses, but continued on towards **San Juan Hill** (24 June 1898).

Lashio ∎ 1942 ∎ World War II (Burma-India)

General Yoshiro Takeuchi drove the Chinese out of **Toungoo**, then advanced with great speed into northeast Burma to the key city of Lashio, the start of the Burma Road into China, where the Chinese 55th Army under General Chen Mianwu was beaten at Mauchi (19 April). As resistance failed, Lashio fell and the Chinese dispersed across the border, pursued to the Salween (29 April 1942).

Las Hormigas ∎ 1285 ∎ French-Aragonese War

When Pedro III of Aragon claimed Sicily after the **Sicilian Vespers**, Philip III of France invaded Aragon and besieged **Gerona**, aided by a strong fleet. His ships suffered costly losses at Rosas before being attacked by Admiral Roger di Loria at the islands known as Las Hormigas. The French fleet was destroyed and Philip had to retreat, dying of fever on the way home (9 September 1285).

Las Navas de Tolosa ∎ 1212 ∎ Early Christian Reconquest of Spain

Facing a massive Almohade army under Caliph Muhammed an-Nasir, Alfonso VIII of Castile gathered a huge force supported by the Kings of Navarre, Aragon and Leon, and Crusaders from Portugal and southern France. Marching south through the Sierra Morena to the Plains of Tolosa, north of Jaen, the Christians inflicted a terrible defeat, which broke Muslim power in central Spain (16 July 1212).

La Souffel ∎ 1815 ∎ Napoleonic Wars (The Hundred Days)

In the aftermath of French defeat at **Waterloo**, General Jean Rapp and the Army of the Rhine were driven back by overwhelming numbers under Austrian Prince Karl Philipp Schwarzenberg. At La Souffel, west of the Rhine, Rapp and his heavily outnumbered force inflicted a costly defeat on the Allies before withdrawing to Strasbourg, where a ceasefire was soon agreed (28 June 1815).

Las Piedras ∎ 1811 ∎ Argentine War of Independence

Viceroy Franscisco Javier de Elio campaigned north from Montevideo into modern Uruguay, where he sent Captain José Posadas and 1,000 men against José Gervasio Artigas near Las Piedras. The Spanish lost 100 dead and almost 500 prisoners in a decisive defeat and Artigas besieged Montevideo itself. Elio brought in Portuguese reinforcements and by October had restored order (18 May 1811).

Lastaguanes ∎ 1813 ∎ Venezuelan War of Independence

See **Taguanes**

Las Trincheras ∎ 1813 ∎ Venezuelan War of Independence

See **Bárbula**

Laswari ∎ 1803 ∎ 2nd British-Maratha War

Soon after capturing **Delhi** and **Agra**, British General Sir Gerard Lake pursued the army of Daulat Rao Sindhia of Gwalior west towards Laswari, near Alwar, where the Maratha Ambaji Inglia was driven from a strong defensive position after one of the hardest fought battles in India. Lake captured massive stores and prisoners, his victory securing the province of Sindhia (1 November 1803).

La Tablada ∎ 1829 ∎ Argentine Civil Wars

In support of Unitarist Governor Juan Galo Lavalle, José Maria Paz defeated Federalist Juan Bautista Bustos in Córdoba at **San Roque** and two months later beat Bustos and Juan Facundo Quiroga at La Tablada, north of Córdoba. However next day in Buenos Aires, after defeat at **Puente deMárquez**, Lavalle signed a pact with General Juan Manuel Rosas and went into exile (23 June 1829).

Latakia I 1973 I Arab-Israeli Yom Kippur War

At the start of the war, six Israeli missile boats under Michael Barkai sank a Syrian torpedo boat with gunfire off the port of Latakia, then engaged two Syrian missile boats and a minesweeper. While both sides fired missiles, all three Arab craft were sunk without Israeli loss. It was claimed as history's first ship-to-ship missile action and the first to see electronic countermeasures (7 October 1973).

Latham I 1644 I British Civil Wars

When Parliamentary forces overran Lancashire, Charlotte Countess of Derby boldly defended her fortified manor at Latham against Sir Thomas Fairfax, his cousin Sir William and then Colonel Alexander Rigby. The siege was lifted when Prince Rupert advanced, but **Marston Moor** ended the Royalist offensive in the north. Latham surrendered six months later (28 February–26 May 1644).

La Trinidad I 1827 I Central American National Wars

Conservative President Manuel José Arce of the Central American Federation overthrew President Dionisio Herrera of Honduras at **Comayagua**, after which the deposed President's nephew Francisco Morazán attacked and defeated Federal General José Justo Milla at La Trinidad. Morazán secured the country, then invaded El Salvador in 1828 for victory at **Gualcho** (11 November 1827).

Latrun (1st) I 1948 I Israeli War of Independence

A major offensive on the Tel Aviv-Jerusalem road saw Jewish commander Shlomo Shamir attack the key town of Latrun, held by the Arab Legion under Colonel Habes Majali. After terrible Israeli losses in a frontal assault, three attacks failed and American Jewish leader Micky Marcus was killed by one of his own sentries just before a ceasefire came into force (25 & 30 May & 9 June 1948).

Latrun (2nd) I 1948 I Israeli War of Independence

During the so-called Ten Days Offensive, Jewish forces again attacked the Arab Legion at Latrun, blocking the Tel Aviv Road west of Jerusalem. Colonel Ygal Allon took surrounding villages, but suffered heavy losses in men and armour before the Second Truce put an end to his failed assault. Latrun remained in Arab hands until the Six Day War of 1967 (14–18 July 1948).

La Tunas I 1897 I 2nd Cuban War of Independence

See **Victoria de la Tunas**

Laufach I 1866 I Seven Weeks War

As Prussian General August von Goeben advanced against Austria's south German allies after victory at **Kissingen**, his forward units under General Karl von Wrangel attacked Hessian General Karl von Perglach at Laufach, east of Frankfurt. Perglach fell back after house-to-house fighting and the Prussians advanced west through **Aschaffenburg** to Frankfurt (13 July 1866).

Lauffeld I 1747 I War of the Austrian Succession

When English commander William Duke of Cumberland and Austrian Marshal Count Leopold von Daun tried to destroy an isolated French force in the Netherlands under Louis Comte de Clermont, they were attacked by the main French army of Marshal Maurice de Saxe at Lauffeld, west of **Maastricht**. Saxe secured a hard-fought victory then besieged **Bergen-op-Zoom** (2 July 1747).

Laugharne I 1644 I British Civil Wars

On the offensive in southern Wales, Parliamentary leader Rowland Laugharne took 2,000 men against Laugharne Castle, on the Taf Estuary, held by just 200 Royalists under Colonel William Russell. After heavy bombardment, the castle was taken by assault and destroyed. Laugharne gradually secured Pembrokeshire, ending with victory in July 1645 on **Colby Moor** (29 October–3 November 1644).

Launceston I 1643 I British Civil Wars

Parliamentary General James Chudleigh resumed the offensive in Cornwall after defeat at **Braddock Down** in January, advancing on Launceston where Royalists Sir Ralph Hopton and Sir Bevil Grenville held Beacon Hill. Despite reinforcements under Sir John Merrick, Chudleigh's Puritans were repulsed after a full day's fighting, but promptly beat Hopton on **Sourton Down** (23 April 1643).

Laupen I 1339 I Burgundian-Swiss Wars

Faced by the rising power of Bern, Swiss and Burgundian nobles under Gerhard of Valangin supported the rival city of Fribourg to besiege nearby Laupen. In a remarkable victory of disciplined infantry over cavalry, an outnumbered relief force of Bernese pikemen under Rudolf von Erlach repulsed the mounted knights then drove their infantry from the field (10–21 June 1339).

Lauron I 76 BC I Sertorian War

With much of Spain held by rebel General Quintus Sertorius after victory at the **Baetis** and **Anas**, Rome sent a massive force across the Alps under Gnaeus Pompey, who advanced to relieve Lauron (modern Liria) northwest of Valencia, besieged by Sertorius. Pompey was routed, losing a legion, and withdrew north of the Ebro for winter. Sertorius captured and burned Lauron.

Lautulae I 315 BC I 2nd Samnite War

Roman forces resuming their campaign in central Italy after disaster at the **Caudine Forks** (321 BC), met some success against the Samnites. In Campania at Lautulae, a pass between **Tarracina** and Fundi, commander Quintus Fabius Maximus Rullianus suffered a costly defeat. However, the Romans soon resumed the offensive and Fabius Maximus was avenged five years later at **Lake Vadimo**.

Lava Beds (1st) I 1873 I Modoc Indian War

When war broke out against the Modoc following **Lost River** (November 1872), Colonel Frank Wheaten led about 320 regulars and volunteers against Captain Jack (Kintpuash) in the Lava Beds near Tulelake, northern California. Attacking in heavy fog, Wheaten was driven off with costly losses. General Edward Canby took personal command but was later murdered at a parley (17 January 1873).

Lava Beds (2nd) I 1873 I Modoc Indian War

General Jeff Davis and Colonel Alvan Gillem led a renewed and better-equipped assault on the Modoc in the Lava Beds of northern California, south of Tulelake, forcing their way in with heavy gunfire. After a six-week campaign near Dry Lake, Captain Jack (Kintpuash) was cornered in a cave. He and three other Modoc leaders were hanged and the war ended (14 April–1 June 1873).

Laval I 1793 I French Revolutionary Wars (Vendée War)

A prelude to battle at Entrammes against the Royalist rebels of western France saw Republican General Francois-Joseph Westermann—the Butcher of the Vendée—impulsively attack the nearby city of Laval. Led into a rebel trap at night, Westermann suffered a sharp defeat. However, this was reversed next day by the great Republican victory a few miles south at **Entrammes** (25 October 1793).

La Victoria I 1814 I Venezuelan War of Independence

While Spanish irregulars led by José Tomás Boves besieged Patriot commander Simón Bolívar at **San Mateo**, southwest of Caracas, Spanish General Tomás Morales was attacked and defeated at nearby La Victoria by a separate Republican force under Colonel José Félix Ribas. Boves was also repulsed from San Mateo, but in December he and Morales defeated Ribas at **Urica** (12 February 1814).

La Victoria I 1902 I Venezuelan Civil Wars

Three years after seizing power after **Tocuyito**, President Cipriano Castro faced a "Liberating

Revolution" under General Manual Antonio Matos, who won several early victories. In a prolonged large-scale action at La Victoria, in Aragua, Castro and General Juan Gomez secured a decisive victory. Resistance was finally crushed in July 1903 at **Ciudad Bolívar** (12 October–2 November 1902).

La Virgen ▌ 1855 ▌ National (Filibuster) War

Defeated by Nicaraguan forces at **Rivas** (29 June) American Filibuster William Walker withdrew down the Nicaraguan Isthmus, where he was later attacked at La Virgen (Virgin Bay) by new Legitimist commander, the Honduran José Santos Guardiola. Fighting with his back to Lake Nicaragua, Walker secured a bloody victory, then advanced north to capture **Grenada** (3 September 1855).

Lavis ▌ 1796 ▌ French Revolutionary Wars (1st Coalition)

French Generals André Masséna and Claude-Henri Vaubois pursued Austrian General Paul Davidovich after his decisive defeat at **Calliano**, driving him out of Trent, in the Adige Valley of northeastern Italy, then caught up with him at the River Lavis. Davidovich suffered another sharp defeat before continuing his withdrawal north along the Adige towards Austria (6 September 1796).

Lawrence ▌ 1863 ▌ American Civil War (Trans-Mississippi)

On a deadly incursion into Kansas, Confederate guerrillas under Colonel William C. Quantrill attacked the defenceless town of Lawrence, east of Topeka. In one of the most notorious raids of the war, the Confederates killed about 150 men and boys and destroyed much of the town before withdrawing back into Missouri with a massive quantity of captured supplies (21 August 1863).

Lazikou Pass ▌ 1935 ▌ 2nd Chinese Revolutionary Civil War

As the Red Army of Zhou Enlai and Mao Zedong marched north from **Zunyi**, they crossed the Snowy Mountains and Grasslands before reach-

ing Kongdong Mountain, where Nationalists tried to block their entry into Gansu (Kansu). A much-mythologised action saw Yang Chengwu storm the strategic Lazikou Pass and the Long March to Yan'an was almost over (16 September 1935).

Lebanon ▌ 1941 ▌ World War II (Middle East)

With Germany on the offensive in North Africa, British General Henry Wilson and Free French commander Paul Legentilhomme invaded the Vichy French Levant, where the heaviest fighting in Lebanon was around Jezzine, Merdjayoun and the Litani. Following defeat in **Syria**, Vichy General Henri Dentz agreed to an Armistice and Beirut was occupied next day (8 June–14 July 1941).

Lebouirate ▌ 1979 ▌ Western Sahara Wars

Polisario guerrillas from Western Sahara continued their offensive in southern Morocco after **Tan-Tan** in January, turning east against the major army base at Lebouirate. Following several failed attacks and a virtual siege, the base was taken by storm with about 40 Russian-supplied tanks captured. A relief column to **Zag** was destroyed in March 1980, taking Moroccan losses to perhaps 500 killed (14 August 1979).

Le Bourget (1st) ▌ 1870 ▌ Franco-Prussian War

An unauthorised fighting reconnaissance northeast from besieged **Paris** saw General Adrien-Adolph Carrey de Bellemare capture Le Bourget, about four miles away. Paris commander Louis Jules Trochu was reluctantly forced to send reinforcements, but after three days the village was retaken by a German counter-attack. The rash sortie cost about 1,200 French casualties (27–30 October 1870).

Le Bourget (2nd) ▌ 1870 ▌ Franco-Prussian War

General Auguste Alexandre Ducrot led a fresh breakout from besieged **Paris** and marched northeast towards Le Bourget, site of a failed sortie two months earlier. Advancing across open ground in extreme winter conditions the French temporarily gained the village. However, they suffered heavy losses to gunfire and frostbite and were driven out by German reinforcements (21 December 1870).

Leburnion I 1091 I Byzantine-Pecheneg Wars
See **Mount Leburnion**

Le Cateau I 1914 I World War I (Western Front)
Driven out of **Mons** by German commander Alexander von Kluck, Sir John French's badly outnumbered British Expeditionary Force retreated west and General Horace Dorien-Smith made a bold stand at Le Cateau. The delaying action cost very heavy losses to both sides and a French attack to the south at **Guise** further aided the Allied withdrawal towards the **Marne** (26–27 August 1914).

Le Cateau I 1918 I World War I (Western Front)
After the initial success of the Allied offensive against the **Hindenburg Line** between **Cambrai** and **St Quentin**, Generals Sir Henry Rawlinson and Julian Byng, with French support, advanced on Le Cateau, 15 miles southeast of Cambrai. Very heavy fighting forced General Adolph von Carlowitz to withdraw and the Allies continued east to the **Selle** and **Sambre** (6–10 October 1918).

Lech I 1632 I Thirty Years War (Swedish War)
See **Rain**

Lechaeum I 390 BC I Corinthian War
Determined to detach **Corinth** from Athens, King Agesilaus of Sparta blockaded the city while his brother Teleutius captured the port of Lechaeum. But outside Lechaeum, 600 Spartans were surprised and virtually destroyed by javelin-armed mercenaries under the Athenian Iphicrates. The blockade of Corinth was broken

and Agesilaus withdrew. In 388 BC, Iphicrates won in Asia Minor at **Cremaste**.

Lechfeld I 955 I Magyar Invasion of Germany
Twenty years after their defeat at **Riade**, a massive army of Magyars invaded Bavaria and was met on the River Lech, south of Augsburg, by Emperor Otto I and Duke Conrad of Lorraine. The Magyars were completely defeated, although Conrad was also killed. Magyar King Pulzko was executed and his Hungarian horsemen never again threatened western Europe (10 August 955).

L'Ecluse I 1340 I Hundred Years War
See **Sluys**

L'Ecluse I 1794 I French Revolutionary Wars (1st Coalition)
French General Jean Victor Moreau advanced against the remaining Allied strongholds in the Netherlands where he took **Nieuport** by siege, then moved against the powerful fortress of L'Ecluse (Sluys). In a terrible siege, which cost over 7,000 casualties from fever, Moreau's force withstood shocking conditions and eventually captured the city (28 July–25 August 1794).

Legations, Siege of I 1900 I Boxer Rebellion
See **Beijing**

Leghorn I 1653 I 1st Dutch War
Attempting to break the Dutch blockade of Leghorn, on the west coast of Italy, English Commodore Henry Appleton sailed to join up with Admiral Richard Badiley, due to arrive from **Elba**. Before the squadrons could meet, Dutch Commodore Jan van Galen routed Appleton with three ships sunk and three captured. Galen was killed and Appleton taken prisoner (14 March 1653).

Legnano I 1176 I Wars of the Lombard League
On his fifth expedition to northern Italy, Emperor Frederick Barbarossa was repulsed from a

siege of **Alessandria** (April 1175) and, after failed truce negotiations, met a large army of the Lombard allies at Legnano, northwest of Milan. German cavalry was destroyed by Milanese infantry and Frederick fled the field, later accepting a humiliating truce, which virtually ended the war (29 May 1176).

Legnano ▌ 1799 ▌ French Revolutionary Wars (2nd Coalition)
See **Verona**

Leh ▌ 1948 ▌ 1st Indo-Pakistan War
Advancing into northern Kashmir along the Indus, Pakistani regulars and Pathan tribesmen seized Kargill and besieged Leh, where Indian Major Priti Chand led a courageous defence, aided by airlifted troops and guns. Despite the fall of **Skardu**, to the north, Leh withstood the siege and was finally relieved after an Indian breakthrough to the west at **Zojila** (February–November 1948).

Le Havre ▌ 1563 ▌ 1st French War of Religion
In return for English support at the siege of **Rouen**, Huguenot leader Louis I de Bourbon Prince of Condé permitted Ambrose Dudley Earl of Warwick to seize Le Havre (20 September 1562). Rouen eventually fell and, after Protestant defeat at **Dreux** and a peace treaty, French Catholics and Protestants joined forces to recapture Le Havre and drive the English out of France (28 July 1563).

Leicester ▌ 1645 ▌ British Civil Wars
King Charles I marched north from Oxford and attacked Leicester, held for Parliament by Sir Robert Pye. The city fell to a midnight assault by Prince Rupert and was put to the sack with many civilians killed. However, a relief force under Parliamentary commander Sir Thomas Fairfax intercepted the King's returning army two weeks later at **Naseby** and inflicted a decisive defeat (30–31 May 1645).

Leilan ▌ 1733 ▌ Turko-Persian Wars of Nadir Shah
Determined to recover Persian territory from Turkey, Regent Nadir Kuli (later Nadir Shah)

besieged **Baghdad** before he was driven off at **Karkuk** by a massive relief army under Topal Osman Pasha. However, Nadir rallied his forces and at nearby Leilan, Topal Osman was defeated and killed. Nadir then marched south to Baghdad and made peace with Governor Ahmad Pasha (9 November 1733).

Leipheim ▌ 1525 ▌ German Peasants' War
Near the start of the Peasants' War in Germany, about 5,000 rebels under Jacob Wehe advancing towards Ulm were attacked to the northeast on the Danube at Leipheim by a Catholic force under Georg Truchsess von Waldburg. The peasant army was routed, with Wehe captured and executed. The survivors fled to Württemburg, where they were defeated in May at **Böblingen** (4 April 1525).

Leipzig ▌ 1631 ▌ Thirty Years War (Swedish War)
See **Breitenfeld**

Leipzig ▌ 1642 ▌ Thirty Years War (Franco-Habsburg War)
See **Breitenfeld**

Leipzig ▌ 1813 ▌ Napoleonic Wars (War of Liberation)
Defending strong positions at Leipzig, Napoleon Bonaparte was heavily outnumbered by the combined Allied armies under General Gebhard von Blucher and Prince Karl Philipp Schwarzenberg. After a huge battle, involving perhaps 500,000 men, the Emperor began withdrawing towards the Rhine, leaving an estimated 50,000 casualties, 15,000 prisoners and 150 guns (16–19 October 1813).

Leith ▌ 1560 ▌ Anglo-Scottish Royal Wars
When France sent troops to aid Mary of Guise, Regent for Mary Queen of Scots, Admiral Sir William Winter and an Anglo-Scots army under Lord William Grey de Wilton besieged the invaders at Leith. Marshal Pietro Strozzi inflicted heavy losses in a fierce sally (14 April) and while repulsing a major attack (7 May). However, he

surrendered when France agreed to withdraw (March–7 July 1560).

Leitha I 1246 I Austro-Hungarian War

With Hungary ravaged by the Mongols following disastrous defeat at the **Sajo** (1241), Frederick II "the Warlike" of Austria (son of Duke Leopold VI) invaded the western provinces. In northwest Hungary on the Leitha River, a revitalised Hungarian army under King Bela IV defeated and killed Frederick. With him died the Babenberg Dynasty of Austria and Styria (15 June 1246).

Leitskau I 1813 I Napoleonic Wars (War of Liberation)

See **Hagelsberg**

Le Mans I 1793 I French Revolutionary Wars (Vendée War)

Just days after defeat at **Angers**, the weakened Royalist rebel army of 12,000 under Henri de la Rochejaquelein captured the city of Le Mans and were attacked by a large Republican force under General Francois Vachot at the nearby village of Pontlieu-sur-l'Huisne. The Vendéeans were crushed, with perhaps 1,000 prisoners executed, and the survivors fled across the Sarthe (12 December 1793).

Le Mans I 1871 I Franco-Prussian War

A month after his defeat at **Beaugency**, General Antoine Eugène Chanzy tried to counterattack near Le Mans with a largely militia army of about 150,000 against the heavily outnumbered German veterans of Prince Friedrich Karl of Prussia and Grand Duke Friedrich Franz of Mecklenburg. Fierce fighting cost Chanzy 10,000 casualties and 20,000 prisoners and he retreated west (10–12 January 1871).

Lemberg I 1914 I World War I (Eastern Front)

See **Rawa Russka**

Lemberg I 1915 I World War I (Eastern Front)

Austro-German commander August von Mackensen campaigning north from **Gorlice-**Tarnow in Galicia, retook **Przemysl** (22 March), then advanced on the key city of Lemberg (Lvov). Mackensen dislodged the Russians to the west at Gorodok, while Austrian General Eduard Böhm-Ermolli defeated the Russians further north at Rawa-Russka and took Lemberg itself (17–22 June 1915).

Lemberg Offensive I 1917 I World War I (Eastern Front)

See **Kerensky Offensive**

Lemnos I 73 BC I 3rd Mithridatic War

A year after defeat at **Chalcedon** (74 BC), which gave the Sea of Marmara to Mithridates VI of Pontus, Roman commander Lucius Licinius Lucullus beat a Pontic squadron off Tenedos, then met the main fleet off Lemnos. Pontic commander Marcus Varius was defeated and captured, opening the way for Lucullus to pass through the Dardanelles to attack Mithridates at **Cyzicus**.

Lemnos I 1770 I Catherine the Great's 1st Turkish War

Despite Russia's great naval victory in the Aegean off **Chesme** (7 July), Admiral Alexei Orlov passed up an opportunity to force the Dardanelles and instead besieged the island of Lemnos. Surprised by Turkish commander Hasan Bey and a small force of volunteers in boats, the Russians were defeated and dispersed. Hasan was named Ghazi and became Kapudan Pasha (21 July–25 September 1770).

Lemnos I 1807 I Russo-Turkish Wars

Shortly after a failed British attack on **Constantinople**, Russian Admiral Dimitri Siniavin blockaded the Dardanelles and captured several ships. Just as the condition of his flotilla forced him to withdraw he met a larger Turkish fleet off Lemnos and inflicted heavy losses in men and ships. An armistice followed between Russia and Turkey (30 June 1807).

Le Mort-Homme I 1916 I World War I (Western Front)

Crown Prince Wilhelm captured **Douaumont**, northeast of **Verdun**, then sent forces west across the Meuse against the strategic French position on Le Mort-Homme (Dead Man's Hill). Nearby Hill 304 was taken after very heavy fighting (4 May) and Le Mort-Homme was also taken before both sides fell back exhausted. The positions were not retaken until August 1917 (6 March–31 May 1916).

Leningrad I 1941–1944 I World War II (Eastern Front)

When German forces invaded Russia, Army Group North under Marshal Wilhelm von Leeb drove hard for Leningrad. After failure to take the city by assault, it was placed under siege, which lasted for 900 days. Up to one million civilians died from bombardment and starvation before a massive offensive by four Soviet armies broke the long siege (1 September 1941–27 January 1944).

Lenkoran I 1813 I Russo-Persian Wars

Two months after victory at **Aslanduz**, Russian General Pyotr Kotliarevski attacked Lenkoran, in modern Azerbaijan, supported by Caspian flotilla commander Yegor Veselago. Following massive bombardment by land and sea, the fortress was stormed with terrible losses on both sides (Kotliarevski was badly wounded). Persia sued for peace, ceding parts of Azerbaijan and Georgia (1 January 1813).

Lens I 431 I Roman-Frankish Wars
See **Helena, France**

Lens I 1648 I Thirty Years War (Franco-Habsburg War)

The final Imperial offensive saw Archduke Leopold William (brother of Ferdinand III) invade northeast France to capture Lens, near Arras. French commander Louis II Duke d'Enghien, now Prince of Condé, enticed the Archduke into an open engagement, where he was utterly routed, losing about 10,000 casualties. The Emperor soon sued for peace, though war continued in Spain (20 August 1648).

Lenud's Ferry I 1780 I War of the American Revolution
See **Lanneau's Ferry**

Lenzen I 929 I German Imperial Wars

After years of intermittent warfare with the Pagan Wends of northern Germany, Emperor Henry I sent the Counts Bernhard and Thietmar to finally suppress them. A large Saxon army besieged the Wend stronghold of Lenzen on the Elbe and, then destroyed a massive relief force. The city surrendered next day and the Wends were forced to accept Christianity (4 September 929).

Leon I 1845 I Central American National Wars

With Morazánista rebels repulsed at **Danli**, President Francisco Malespín of El Salvador, aided by Honduran General José Santos Guardiola, invaded Nicaragua, which had supported the rebellion and he seized Leon after a long siege. A week later, Malespín was deposed by Juan José Guzman and Honduran efforts to restore him were crushed in August at **Obrajuela** (26 November 1844–24 January 1845).

Leontini I 214 BC I 2nd Punic War

When Sicilian cities began to declare for Carthage, Rome sent Marcus Claudius Marcellus, who first attacked Leontini and took it by storm. Marcellus had 2,000 citizens executed, but local commander Hippocrates and his brother Epicydes escaped to lead the defence of **Syracuse**, 20 miles to the southeast. The carnage at Leontini is said to have motivated Syracuse to hold out for two years.

Lepanto I 1499 I Venetian-Turkish Wars

An early Ottoman naval victory saw Turkish Admiral Borrak Rais take his ships into the eastern Mediterranean against Venice, which had recently captured Cyprus. In two decisive actions off southern Greece at Zonchio and Lepanto, Admiral Antonio Grimani was heavily defeated. Lepanto then fell, marking a significant setback for Venetian naval supremacy (12 & 14 August 1499).

Lepanto I 1571 I Turkish-Habsburg Wars

A large Christian fleet under Don John of Austria arrived too late to prevent Ottoman conquest of Cyprus at **Famagusta**, but met Turkish Admiral Ali Pasha off Lepanto in southern Greece in one of history's most decisive naval battles. The last great action between oared galleys saw the Ottoman fleet virtually destroyed and Turkey never again dominated the Mediterranean (7 October 1571).

Leptis I 238 BC I Truceless War

Recovering from defeat at **Tunis**, Carthage recalled former General Hanno (dismissed after losing at **Utica**) to join his rival Hamilcar Barca against the rebellious former mercenaries. In the final decisive action at Leptis (exact location not known), the remaining rebel army was defeated and their leader Mathos was captured. With his execution, the brutal war effectively came to an end.

Lequeitio I 1812 I Napoleonic Wars (Peninsular Campaign)

An offensive on the northern coast of Spain to relieve pressure on the Allied campaign around **Salamanca** saw British Admiral Sir Home Popham and Spanish Guerrilla leader Don Gaspar attack and capture the fortress of Lequeitio, west of San Sebastian, defended by Chef du Battalion Gillort. They then marched east in a failed attack on the small town of **Guetaria** (22 June 1812).

Le Quesnoy I 1793 I French Revolutionary Wars (1st Coalition)

Weeks after Frederick Augustus Duke of York captured **Valenciennes**, southeast of Lille, an Allied force under Austrian Field Marshal Charles Clerfayt besieged Le Quesnoy, nine miles further southeast. The town held out for two weeks before it fell to the Allies. It was recovered by the French the following August (28 August–12 September 1793).

Lérida I 78 BC I Sertorian War

See **Ilerda**

Lérida I 49 BC I Wars of the First Triumvirate

See **Ilerda**

Lérida I 1642 I Thirty Years War (Franco-Habsburg War)

French commander Philippe de la Motte-Houdancourt on campaign in Catalonia met a large Spanish army under Diego Felipe de Guzmán Marquis of Leganés outside Lérida. Leganés was defeated and retired on Fraga, while de la Motte entered Barcelona as Viceroy for Louis XIII. Leganés temporarily lost command, but won at **Lérida** in another campaign four years later (7 October 1642).

Lérida I 1644 I Thirty Years War (Franco-Habsburg War)

With most of Catalonia in French hands, Marshal Philippe de la Motte-Houdancourt attempted to relieve the Spanish Imperial siege off the key city of Lérida. However, he was heavily defeated and driven off by General Philippe de Silvas. After later being forced to lift his siege of Tarragona, de la Motte was recalled and was replaced the following year by Henri Comte d'Harcourt.

Lérida I 1646 I Thirty Years War (Franco-Habsburg War)

After a six-month siege of Lérida, on the Segre in Catalonia, French forces under Henri Comte d'Harcourt came under attack by Spanish commander Diego Felipe de Guzmán Marquis of Leganés, who had been repulsed at Lérida four years earlier. Harcourt was defeated and driven off, abandoning his heavy guns, and was replaced by Louis II Duke d'Enghien (June–November 1646).

Lérida I 1647 I Thirty Years War (Franco-Habsburg War)

Louis II Duke d'Enghien, now Prince of Condé, led a final French attempt to capture the Catalonian city of Lérida, laying siege to the city on the Segre, defended by Don Jorge Britt. Threatened by a large Spanish relief army under Diego Felipe de Guzmán Marquis of Leganés, Condé withdrew and later resigned in favour of Marshal Charles de Schomberg (12 May–17 June 1647).

Lérida ▌ 1707 ▌ War of the Spanish Succession

Despite initial repulse in July, French troops under Marshal James Duke of Berwick and Philippe II Duke d'Orleans again besieged Lérida, held by Prince Henry of Hesse. When an Allied relief force under Henri de Massue de Ruvigny was driven off, the Spanish city fell at the beginning of October. The garrison in the citadel capitulated six weeks later (September–14 November 1707).

Lérida ▌ 1810 ▌ Napoleonic Wars (Peninsular Campaign)

French Marshal Louis Suchet advanced into Catalonia where he besieged Lérida, defended by Spanish General Garcia Conde. A Catalan relief force under General Henry O'Donnell was bloodily repulsed at **Margalef** and Lérida was heavily shelled and taken by storm. Nearby Mequinenza surrendered a month later with little resistance (15 April–14 May 1810).

Lerin ▌ 1813 ▌ Napoleonic Wars (Peninsular Campaign)

See **Lodosa**

Lerna ▌ 1825 ▌ Greek War of Independence

A month after defeating the Greeks at **Maniaki**, the Egyptian-Turkish army of Ibrahim Pasha took Tripolitza (22 June), then advanced to threaten Nauplia. Blocked at the Mills of Lerna by a small force under Yannis Makriyannis, Konstantinos Mavromichalis and Dimitrius Ipsilantis, the Ottomans withdrew with about 500 killed. In July they checked the Greeks at **Trikorpha** (25 June 1825).

Leros ▌ 1943 ▌ World War II (Southern Europe)

After seizing **Kos** in the **Dodecanese Islands** (6 October), German General Friedrich Müller sent a parachute and seaborne assault against Leros, held by Brigadier Robert Tilney. Four days' fighting saw heavy casualties on both sides, plus costly Royal Navy losses. While Samos was evacuated to aid Leros, the doomed campaign ended with 3,000 British and 5,000 Italians captured (12–16 November 1943).

Lesbos ▌ 1462 ▌ Venetian-Turkish Wars

See **Mytilene**

Les Espagnols sur Mer ▌ 1350 ▌ Hundred Years War

See **Winchelsea**

Lesnaya ▌ 1708 ▌ 2nd "Great" Northern War

As Charles XII of Sweden advanced into Russia after victory at **Holowczyn**, his supply train from Riga was overwhelmed on the Dneiper, south of Mogilev at Lesnaya, by Tsar Peter. Swedish General Adam Lewenhaupt lost perhaps 8,000 casualties as well as his guns and 2,000 wagons of supplies before fighting his way through to join King Charles in the Ukraine (9–10 October 1708).

Les Saintes ▌ 1782 ▌ War of the American Revolution

See **Saints**

Letterkenny ▌ 1567 ▌ O'Neill Rebellion

English commander Sir Henry Sidney defeated Irish Catholic rebel Shane O'Neill at **Knockfergus** (November 1566) and restored Hugh O'Donnell Lord of Tyrconnell. Sidney then supported the O'Connells against O'Neill at Letterkenny on Lough Swilly, where O'Neill lost over 1,000 men in a terrible rout. He was murdered, when he sought refuge with former enemies, the MacDonnells (8 May 1567).

Leucimne ▌ 435 BC ▌ Corinthian-Corcyrean War

In an attempt to deter Corinthian interference in the Corcyrean colony of Epidamnus (modern Durres, Albania), ships from Corcyra (modern Corfu) besieged the city, then faced a large Corinthian fleet sailing to break the siege. In the nearby Ambracian Gulf, off Leucimne, the

Corinthians were defeated and Epidamnus capitulated. Another major action was fought two years later off **Sybota**.

Leucopetra I 146 BC I Roman-Achaean War
See **Corinth, Greece**

Leuctra I 371 BC I Wars of the Greek City-States
When Thebes stalled truce talks between Athens and Sparta, King Cleombrotus of Sparta took 10,000 men into Boeotia and, ten miles from Thebes at Leuctra, met 6,000 Thebans under Epaminondas. Using the innovative oblique attack, Epaminondas secured a brilliant victory, with 2,000 Spartans killed including Cleombrotus, finally overthrowing the power of Sparta (July 371 BC).

Leuthen I 1757 I Seven Years War (Europe)
Frederick II of Prussia secured victory in Saxony at **Rossbach**, then marched east into Silesia to avenge the Prussian defeat at **Breslau**. At nearby Leuthen he met Prince Charles of Lorraine and Marshal Leopold von Daun. In his greatest tactical victory Frederick destroyed the Austrian army, inflicting over 6,000 casualties and taking 20,000 prisoners, then retook Breslau (5 December 1757).

Leuven I 891 I Viking Raids on Germany
See **Dyle**

Leuze I 1692 I War of the Grand Alliance
While manoeuvering in Flanders against Prince George Frederic of Waldeck, French Marshal Duke Francois Henri of Luxembourg sent his cavalry to attack the Prince's camp at Leuze, east of Tournai. As at **Walcourt** two years earlier, Waldeck was utterly defeated and William III of England and Holland assumed command of the Dutch-German-English Alliance army (20 September 1691).

Lewes I 1264 I 2nd English Barons' War
Facing rebellion by Simon de Montfort Earl of Leicester, Henry III of England and his son Prince Edward defeated the Barons at **Northampton** and **Rochester**. But advancing to relieve a renewed rebel siege of Rochester, they were heavily defeated on the Sussex Downs at Lewes. The King was held prisoner for over a year until Edward killed de Montfort at **Evesham** (14 May 1264).

Lewis's Farm I 1865 I American Civil War (Eastern Theatre)
Union Generals Gouvernor K. Warren and Charles Griffin renewed the offensive against the southwest defences of besieged **Petersburg**, Virginia, where they were met by Generals Richard Anderson and Bushrod Johnson at Lewis's Farm, near the Boydton and Quaker Roads. Stubborn fighting eventually forced the Confederates back towards the **White Oak Road** (29 March 1865).

Lexington, Massachusetts I 1775 I War of the American Revolution
Determined to seize arms held by American patriots, Major John Pitcairn marched from Boston to nearby Lexington. Roused by Paul Revere, about 70 militia under Captain John Parker met the approaching British and a confused action which triggered the war, saw the Americans dispersed with eight dead and ten wounded. Pitcairn then marched west to **Concord** (19 April 1775).

Lexington, Missouri I 1861 I American Civil War (Trans-Mississippi)
Following victory in southwest Missouri at **Wilson's Creek**, secessionist General Sterling Price marched north against Lexington, strongly defended by Union forces under Colonel James A. Mulligan. After repeated assaults, and defeat of a column at **Blue Mills Landing**, Mulligan gave up hope of aid from General John C. Frémont and surrendered over 3,000 men (13–20 September 1861).

Lexington, Missouri I 1864 I American Civil War (Trans-Mississippi)
Confederate General Sterling Price marched west across Missouri from **Fort Davidson** and

advanced on Lexington, east of Kansas City, defended by a scratch force of Plains militia under General James G. Blunt. Heavily outnumbered, Blunt slowed the Confederate advance but was forced to fall back across the **Little Blue River** to **Independence**, Missouri (19 October 1864).

Lexington, Tennessee I 1862 I American Civil War (Western Theatre)
See **Jackson, Tennessee**

Leyden I 1573–1574 I Netherlands War of Independence
Spanish Viceroy Luis de Requesens sent General Francisco Valdez against George Noyelles at Leyden, north of the Hague, but later suspended his offensive to fight at **Mookerheyde**. After the siege resumed, William of Orange ordered the dykes cut and Dutch Admiral Louis de Boisot finally broke through. Valdez then had to withdraw (31 October 1573–21 March 1574 & 26 May–3 October 1574).

Leyte I 1944 I World War II (Pacific)
Opening the land campaign in the central **Philippines**, General Walter Krueger landed on eastern Leyte and seized major airfields. However, General Sosaku Suzuki led a stubborn resistance and Krueger had to make a second landing in the west at Ormoc (7 December). Leyte was finally secured at a cost of 3,500 Americans and up to 60,000 Japanese killed (22 October–25 December 1944).

Leyte Gulf I 1944 I World War II (Pacific)
Determined to repel the invasion of the Philippines, three Japanese naval forces converged on two massive American fleets protecting the beachhead at Leyte Gulf. After an ambush in the **Palawan Passage**, actions in the **Sibuyan Sea**, **Surigao Strait**, **Cape Engaño** and **Samar** saw Japan decisively defeated in history's largest and most complex naval battle (23–25 October 1944).

Liangtian I 883 I Huang Chao Rebellion
With bandit warlords threatening the Tang Empire, Huang Chao captured Luoyang (De-

cember 880) and drove Emperor Xizong out of the capital, Chang'an (January 881). From exile in Sichuan, Xizong secured an army from the steppe under Li Keyong, who helped decisively defeat Huang at Liangtian Hill. Huang soon abandoned Chang'an and was later defeated again at **Chenzhou**.

Liao I 1287 I Mongol Wars of Kubilai Khan
The final campaign of the Mongol Kubilai Khan saw him lead a large force into southern Manchuria to suppress rebellion by the Nestorian Christian Nayan, a distant relative and descendant of Genghis Khan. Commanding the battle from an elephant-borne palanquin, the 72-year-old Khan defeated Nayan at the mouth of the Liao River, near the Korean border, and had him executed.

Liaoshen I 1948 I 3rd Chinese Revolutionary Civil War
Communist General Lin Biao broke through to secure the railway at **Siping** (Szepingkau), then launched about 600,000 men on the massive Liaoshen offensive against remaining isolated Manchurian cities. The fall of **Changchun**, **Jinzhou** and **Shenyang** (previously Mukden) cost the Nationalists about 350,000 men and decisively ended their presence in the northeast (12 September–2 November 1948).

Liaoshi I 1947–1948 I 3rd Chinese Revolutionary Civil War
Having crossed the **Songhua** to isolate key Manchurian cities, Communist General Lin Biao circled south to attack the Liaoshi Corridor and Peining railway linking Mukden (modern Shenyang) to the rest of China. Costly defence by Nationalist General Liao Yaoxiang and later Chen Cheng eventually held the corridor and Lin switched his effort north against **Siping** (September 1947– February 1948).

Liaoshi-Shenyang I 1948 I 3rd Chinese Revolutionary Civil War
See **Liaoshen**

Liaoyang I 1900 I Russo-Chinese War

In the aftermath of the Boxer rebellion, Russian General Deian Subotich advanced north into Manchuria through **Haicheng** and **Shaho** and next day attacked Chinese commander Zengji at Liaoyang. The Chinese suffered a decisive defeat and abandoned Mukden, virtually ending the war. Russia's continued occupation of Manchuria eventually led to war with Japan (28 September 1900).

Liaoyang I 1904 I Russo-Japanese War

Three Japanese armies under Marshal Iwao Oyama converged on Liaoyang, second largest city in Manchuria, and attacked Russian General Aleksei Kuropatkin on the Tang and Taizi Rivers. After severe fighting, Kuropatkin withdrew towards **Mukden**. Yet he claimed victory as the enemy suffered greater losses and his Russian army escaped to fight another day (25 August–3 September 1904).

Libertwolkwitz I 1813 I Napoleonic Wars (War of Liberation)

A prelude to the decisive battle of **Leipzig** saw Austrian Field Marshal Wenzeslaus von Klenau and Russian cavalry under Prince Ludwig Wittgenstein probe the French defences five miles to the south near Libertwolkwitz. Marshal Joachim Murat's cavalry drove off their opponents in a sharp action and helped secure the French position for the main contest two days later (14 October 1813).

Liberty I 1861 I American Civil War (Trans-Mississippi)

See **Blue Mills Landing**

Lichtenburg I 1901 I 2nd Anglo-Boer War

On the offensive in the western Transvaal, Boer commander Jacobus de la Rey determined to recapture his hometown, Lichtenburg, southeast of Mafeking, held by 600 British under Colonel Charles Money. Attacking at night with 1,200 men, de la Rey broke into the town, but was driven out and withdrew after a courageous defence, with about 50 casualties on either side (2–3 March 1901).

Lidzbark Warminski I 1807 I Napoleonic Wars (4th Coalition)

See **Heilsberg**

Liebenau I 1866 I Seven Weeks War

Invading Austrian Bohemia with Prussia's 1st Army against Count Edouard von Clam-Gallas, Prussian Prince Friedrich Karl sent General August von Horn south through Reichenberg towards the Iser. At Liebenau, near Turnau, in the first action of the war, von Horn defeated the Austrians to take Turnau (modern Turnov), then marched downstream towards **Podol** (26 June 1866).

Liebishau I 1577 I Gdansk War

See **Lubieszow**

Liège I 1468 I Franco-Burgundian Wars

When Louis XI of France met his great rival Charles Duke of Burgundy at Peronne, Charles effectively imprisoned him and Louis agreed to accompany the Duke against the rebellious Liègeois, routed a year earlier at **Brusthem**. With token support from Louis, Charles attacked Liège. After three days, with heavy losses on both sides, he stormed and burned the city (27–30 October 1468).

Liège I 1914 I World War I (Western Front)

The first major action of the war saw German commander Karl von Bulow invade Belgium and send Generals Otto von Emmich and Erich von Ludendorff against Liège, defended by General Gérard Leman. Despite unexpected losses, the Germans seized the city (7 August) and bombarded and took the surrounding forts. The Belgians then fell back northwest on **Antwerp** (4–16 August 1914).

Liegnitz I 1241 I Mongol Invasion of Europe

With **Kiev** conquered (1240), the Mongol Batu (grandson of Genghis Khan) sent his cousins Kaidu and Baidur into Poland, where they captured **Cracow** (3 March) before meeting a German and Polish army under Henry II the Pius of Silesia near Liegnitz at Wahlstadt. While

Henry was routed and killed in a decisive defeat, the Mongols did not pursue but turned south towards Hungary (9 April 1241).

Liegnitz I 1760 I Seven Years War (Europe)

Frederick II advanced into Silesia following Prussian defeat at **Landshut** (23 June) and reached Liegnitz (modern Legnica), where he found himself between Austrians under Marshals Leopold von Daun and Gideon von Loudon and approaching Russians. Frederick brilliantly cut his way through the Austrians at night, inflicting over 10,000 casualties, and withdrew towards Berlin (15 August 1760).

Liesna I 1708 I 2nd "Great" Northern War

See **Lesnaya**

Light Brigade, Charge I 1854 I Crimean War

See **Balaklava**

Ligny I 1815 I Napoleonic Wars (The Hundred Days)

In a preliminary to battle at **Waterloo**, south of Brussels, Napoleon Bonaparte took his centre and right wing against General Gebhard von Blucher's Prussians at Ligny, while Marshal Michel Ney led the left wing against **Quatre Bras**. At Ligny Blucher was defeated and wounded. However, Bonaparte failed to adequately follow up in pursuit northeast towards **Wavre** (16 June 1815).

Liguria I 204 BC I 2nd Punic War

After defeat in Spain at **Ilipa** (206 BC), the Carthaginian Mago marched into Italy with 30,000 men to support his brother Hannibal. Having destroyed Genoa, Mago was met in Liguria by four Roman legions under Marcus Cornelius Cethegus and Publius Quintilius Varus. The Romans were eventually driven back in fierce action before Mago fell wounded and withdrew. He died on route to Carthage.

Lille I 1667 I War of Devolution

Following the death of Philip IV of Spain, Louis XIV of France invaded the Spanish Netherlands claimed for his wife, Maria Theresa, daughter of Philip IV. Lille, one of the few cities which resisted, was besieged by French Marshals Henri de Turenne and Francois de Crequi and fell two weeks later after the defeat of a Spanish relief army (27 August 1667).

Lille I 1708 I War of the Spanish Succession

Prince Eugène of Savoy advanced southwest from **Oudenarde** to besiege Lille, while John Churchill Duke of Marlborough drove off French armies under Louis Duke de Vendôme and Marshal James Duke of Berwick. After an heroic defence, which stalled the Allied offensive, Marshal Louis de Boufflers surrendered the town (22 October) and then the citadel (12 August–9 December 1708).

Lille I 1792 I French Revolutionary Wars (1st Coalition)

Invading France from the Austrian Netherlands, Archduke Charles of Austria sent Duke Albert Casimir of Saxe-Teschen to besiege Lille, which held out for a week under severe artillery fire. French General Charles-Francois Dumouriez then started north from victory at **Valmy** and the Austrians withdrew, followed by defeat a month later at **Jemappes** (29 September–6 October 1792).

Lilybaeum I 368–367 BC I 4th Dionysian War

Despite defeat at **Cronium** (383 BC), Dionysius the Tyrant of Syracuse led a fresh offensive into Carthaginian western Sicily, where he blockaded the key fortress at Lilybaeum (modern Marsala). After a failed siege, Dionysius died of fever and his son, Dionysius II, made a peace with Carthage which endured more than 20 years until the invasion by Timoleon of Corinth at **Adranum**.

Lilybaeum I 277–275 BC I Pyrrhic War

Invited into Italy to aid Greek Tarentum against Rome, King Pyrrhus of Epirus secured costly victories at **Heraclea** and **Asculum**, then crossed to Carthaginian Sicily, where he seized key cities and besieged the powerful fortress in the west at Lilybeaum (modern Marsala). After further losses while failing to take Lilybeaum by storm, Pyrrhus returned to the mainland, where he lost at **Beneventum**.

Lilybaeum ∎ 250–241 BC ∎ 1st Punic War

The powerful Carthaginian fortress at Lilybaeum (modern Marsala) on the west coast of Sicily was besieged by Romans and held out for eight years under the leadership of Himilco against constant attack by land and sea. Carthage drove off the Romans at nearby **Drepanum** (249 BC), though a fresh fleet under Lutatius Catulus took Lilybaeum. After naval defeat at the **Aegates Islands**, Carthage sued for peace.

Lima ∎ 1881 ∎ War of the Pacific
See **Miraflores**

Liman ∎ 1788 ∎ Catherine the Great's 2nd Turkish War

Eight months after the Turks were beaten near the mouth of the Dnieper at **Kinburn**, Admiral Hassan el Ghazi clashed with Russian commander Charles Nassau-Siegen at sea off the Liman near **Ochakov**. He was forced to withdraw after the intervention of American John Paul Jones in Russian service. Ten days later the Russians surprised and destroyed the Turkish fleet (7 & 17 June 1788).

Limanowa ∎ 1914 ∎ World War I (Eastern Front)

As Russians stormed the Vistula near **Ivangorod**, General Radko Dmitriev raced southwest to besiege Cracow. At nearby Limanowa, Austrian General Svetozar Boroevic launched a bold counter-offensive against General Aleksei Brusilov. Although Boroevic suffered terrible losses, the Russians withdrew to the Dunajec and lost six months later at **Gorlice-Tarnow** (1–9 December 1914).

Limbang ∎ 1962 ∎ Brunei Rebellion

During a brief revolt in Brunei, rebel leader Salleh bin Sambas attacked Bangar, then took hostages at Limbang, on the strip of Sarawak between the two halves of Brunei. British Royal Marines under Captain Jeremy Moore landed at Limbang and retook the town after fierce fighting. Fifteen rebels and five Marines were killed and the rebellion was virtually over (12 December 1962).

Limerick ∎ 1651 ∎ British Civil Wars

Oliver Cromwell returned to England after destroying **Drogheda** and **Wexford**, leaving his son-in-law Henry Ireton to compete the subjugation of Catholic-Royalist Ireland. Ireton besieged the last stronghold at Limerick, defended by Hugh O'Neill (who had resisted Cromwell at **Clonmel**) and forced the town to surrender. However, he died soon afterwards of plague (11 June–27 October 1651).

Limerick ∎ 1690 ∎ War of the Glorious Revolution

William III secured victory over the Catholic army of James II on the **Boyne** in July and captured Dublin, then besieged the Irish port of Limerick, defended by Patrick Sarsfield Lord Lucan. After William's siege train was intercepted and destroyed (10 August) and a costly assault failed (27 August), the King raised the siege. The town was taken a year later (9–30 August 1690).

Limerick ∎ 1691 ∎ War of the Glorious Revolution

After resisting a powerful siege the previous year, the north Irish port of Limerick was again defended by Patrick Sarsfield Lord Lucan as the last remaining Jacobite stronghold. Fresh from success at **Aughrim**, the Protestant army of General Godert de Ginkel forced the surrender of Limerick, effectively ending Irish resistance against William III (25 August–13 October 1691).

Limerick ∎ 1922 ∎ Irish Civil War

Driven out of Dublin at **Four Courts** and **O'Connell Street**, Republican forces in the west under Liam Lynch attempted to hold Limerick against Generals Michael Brennan and Donncada Hannigan. When General Eoin Duffy arrived to take command with government reinforcements and more guns from Dublin, heavy fighting soon forced the IRA to evacuate the city (11–21 July 1922).

Limoges I 1370 I Hundred Years War

With Edward Prince of Wales campaigning in France, a number of cities previously under English rule declared for Charles V of France, most importantly the city of Limoges, led into this fateful decision by its Bishop. In a terrible retribution, Prince Edward sacked the city, destroying part of its defensive walls and putting a reported 3,000 men, women and children to the sword.

Lin'an I 1275–1276 I Mongol Wars of Kubilai Khan
See **Hangzhou**

Linares I 1810 I Napoleonic Wars (Peninsular Campaign)
See **La Carolina**

Lincelles I 1793 I French Revolutionary Wars (1st Coalition)

During the failed Allied siege of **Dunkirk**, British Major General Gerard Lake was detached to support Dutch forces led by William V, Prince of Orange, who had been driven out of forts they had captured near Lille. In a sharp action near Lincelles, troops from the British Guards Regiments defeated the French and recaptured the lost positions (18 August 1793).

Lincoln I 1141 I English Period of Anarchy

Amid anarchy following the death of Henry I, King Stephen of England found himself at war with the late King's daughter Matilda and her half-brother, Earl Robert of Gloucester. Besieging the Castle of Lincoln, held by Earl Ranulf of Chester, Stephen was defeated by Robert after his cavalry deserted. Matilda imprisoned Stephen and was elected Queen (2 February 1141).

Lincoln I 1217 I 1st English Barons' War

When King John of England died, some Barons continued fighting his son Henry III in favour of Prince Louis of France. In battle at

Lincoln (the "Fair of Lincoln"), rebel leaders Falke de Breaute and Thomas de Perche were decisively defeated by William Marshal Earl of Pembroke (de Perche was killed). Louis soon abandoned his siege of **Dover** and the rebellion waned (20 May 1217).

Lindenau I 1813 I Napoleonic Wars (War of Liberation)

At the start of the three-day Battle of **Leipzig**, a sharp action was fought to the west around Lindenau. Defending marshy ground near the River Pleisse, French General Count Henri Bertrand drove General Ignace Gyulai's Austrians and Russians out of Lindenau, which secured the line of retreat for Napoleon Bonaparte after his resounding defeat in the main battle (16 October 1813).

Lindisfarne I 590 I Anglo-Saxon Territorial Wars

The Angles of Bernicia led by Theodoric threatened to invade northern Northumberland and found themselves facing a Celtic alliance led by the semi-legendary Urien of Rheged, supported by Gwallawg of Elmet and Rhydderch of Strathclyde. Theodoric was driven back to an epic siege on Lindisfarne (modern Holy Island), but Urien was killed and the Britons were eventually defeated.

Lindisfarne I 793 I Viking Raids on Britain

Near the start of Viking raids on England, a powerful Danish force attacked the island of Lindisfarne (Holy Island) off the eastern coast of Northumberland, with its monastery founded by St Aidan in 635. While not a true battle, the attack came to exemplify the "Norse fury" and the Christian world was stunned by its brutality, with the church destroyed amid an orgy of murder and pillage.

Lindley I 1900 I 2nd Anglo-Boer War

As British forces advanced across the **Zand** River towards Pretoria, Boers under General Piet de Wet besieged 500 mounted Irish volunteers under Colonel Basil Spragge at Lindley, further to the east on the Valsch. Spragge was killed while waiting for help, which came too late. When the Boer guns were brought up, his force surrendered and 530 men were captured (23–27 May 1900).

Linduz ∎ 1813 ∎ Napoleonic Wars (Peninsular Campaign)
See **Roncesvalles**

Linkoping ∎ 1598 ∎ Swedish War of Succession
See **Stangebro**

Linlithgow Bridge ∎ 1526 ∎ Scottish Royalist War
Determined to free 14-year-old James V of Scotland from virtual imprisonment by Regent Archibald Douglas Earl of Angus, 10,000 men under James Stewart Earl of Lennox approached Edinburgh and were heavily defeated on the Avon at Linlithgow by James Hamilton Earl of Arran. Lennox was captured then murdered by Arran's natural son, James of Finnart (4 September 1526).

Linying ∎ 1927 ∎ 1st Chinese Revolutionary Civil War
While Chiang Kai-shek prepared to invade northern China, Wuhan Nationalist Tang Shengzhi campaigned north through **Zhumadian** to repulse warlord Chang Xueliang, most decisively at Linying, where Tang's General Zhang Fakui secured a bloody victory. However, the delay allowed his rival Feng Yuxiang to advance through **Luoyang** to capture Zhengzhou (28 May 1927).

Lipantitlán ∎ 1835 ∎ Texan Wars of Independence
With invading Mexican forces besieged at **San Antonio**, a small Texan force under Adjutant Ira J. Westover attacked the Mexicans near a fort on the Lipantitlán near San Patricio on the Gulf Coast. A brief action saw 28 Mexicans killed for no Texas loss, though Westover allowed the fort to be retaken. He defeated the

Mexicans again next day at the Nueces (4 November 1835).

Lipany ∎ 1434 ∎ Hussite Wars
Bohemian Hussites repulsed the final German crusade at **Domazlice** (1431) then resumed their doctrinal war. During the decisive battle at Lipany, east of Prague, with terrible losses on both sides, moderate Utraquists (Calixtines) and Catholic allies defeated and killed radical Taborite leader, Prokob the Bald. Sigismund of Hungary was then finally accepted as King of Bohemia (30 May 1434).

Lipara ∎ 260 BC ∎ 1st Punic War
Gathering strength after losing **Acragas** in southern Sicily (262 BC), Carthaginian naval commander Hannibal sent Admiral Boodes from Panormus to Lipara, in the Lipari Islands north of Sicily, to surprise a Roman fleet under Cornelius Scipio Asina. Badly outnumbered, Asina was defeated and fled ashore, where he was captured. Rome's navy was avenged later that year off **Mylae**.

Lipari Islands ∎ 1676 ∎ 3rd Dutch War
See **Stromboli**

Lipitsa ∎ 1216 ∎ Early Russian Dynastic Wars
When Yaroslav of Pereiaslav and his brothers Yuri of Vladimir and Konstanin of Rostov attempted to suborn Novgorod, they were attacked by Prince Mstislav of Novgorod, supported by Smolensk and Pskov. At the Lipitsa, near Yurev-Polski, Mstislav decisively defeated the Princes of Vladimir-Suzdal. Twenty years later Yuri was killed by the Mongols at the **Sit** (21–22 April 1216).

Lippa ∎ 1658 ∎ Transylvanian National Revolt
Prince George Rákóczi II of Transylvania suffered a disastrous defeat in Poland at **Trembowla** (July 1657), but overthrew his pro-Turkish successor Ferenc Rédei and routed the Turks at Lippa (modern Lipova) on the Mures, east of Arad.

Though a Turkish counter-offensive drove Rá-kóczi out, he returned and overthrew Prince Akos Barcsay before he was killed in 1660 at **Gilau** (May 1658).

Lippa ▮ 1695 ▮ Later Turkish-Habsburg Wars
    See **Lugos**

Lippe ▮ 11 BC ▮ Rome's Germanic Wars
    Drusus, stepson of Emperor Augustus, led his Legions across the Rhine to campaign against Germanic tribes before returning to the Lippe, where he was outnumbered and surrounded. In a brilliant victory, the Romans fought their way out and returned to Gaul. Drusus died two years later in a fall from his horse. Roman ambition beyond the Rhine was destroyed in 9 AD at **Teutoburgwald**.

Liptingen ▮ 1799 ▮ French Revolutionary Wars (2nd Coalition)
    See **Stockach**

Lircay ▮ 1829 ▮ Chilean Conservative Revolution
    See **Ochagavía**

Lircay ▮ 1830 ▮ Chilean Conservative Revolution
    Following the overthrow of Chilean Dictator Bernardo O'Higgins, rival factions met at **Ochagavía**, before General Ramón Freire broke with the rebels to support the government. Attacked by General Joaquín Prieto at the Lircay, near Talca, Freire's Liberal forces were cut off and virtually annihilated. The Conservatives then ruled Chile for the next 30 years (17 April 1830).

Liri Valley ▮ 1944 ▮ World War II (Southern Europe)
    Stalled south of Rome, the Allies launched a massive offensive into the Liri Valley. French General Alphonse Juin led a bold flank attack through the mountains while Anglo-American forces stormed the western end of the **Gustav**

Line and the Poles took **Monte Cassino**. The Allies broke out from **Anzio** and Rome fell (4 June) as the Germans withdrew to the **Gothic Line** (11–17 May 1944).

Lisaine ▮ 1871 ▮ Franco-Prussian War
    See **Héricourt**

Lisbon ▮ 1147 ▮ Christian Reconquest of Portugal
    Launching a renewed offensive against the Muslims of central Portugal, King Alfonso I seized **Santarem** (March 1147) then marched south against the well-fortified city of Lisbon. A fleet with about 12,000 English, Flemish and German Crusaders on their way to Palestine was enlisted and, after a five-month siege, Lisbon fell by assault, followed by a notorious massacre (June–25 October 1147).

Lissa ▮ 1811 ▮ Napoleonic Wars (5th Coalition)
    On an expedition against the British-held Adriatic island of Lissa, French Commodore Bernard Dubourdieu led six French and Venetian frigates, with five smaller ships and 500 occupation troops. In a remarkable action off Lissa, Captain Sir William Hoste and just four frigates defeated and killed Dubourdieu, sank his flagship, and took three prizes (13 March 1811).

Lissa ▮ 1866 ▮ 3rd Italian War of Independence
    Despite Italy's disastrous defeat on land at **Custozza**, Admiral Carlo di Persano continued the war at sea and soon met Austrian Admiral Wilhelm von Tegetthof in the Adriatic near Lissa (modern Vis). In the reputed first open sea battle involving iron-clads as well as wooden vessels, the Austrians were better handled and sank three Italian ships. Peace followed soon afterwards (20 July 1866).

Litokhoro ▮ 1946 ▮ Greek Civil War
    Communist leader Nikos Zachariadis recovered from defeat at **Athens** and sent a small band under Markos Vaphiadis against Litokhoro, east

of Mount Olympus. The police station was burned and eight gendarmes and National Guards killed. However, when British troops approached, the guerrillas withdrew. The action was later mythologised as marking the resumption of open war (30 March 1946).

Littafatchee | 1813 | Creek
Indian War

Near the start of the war, General Andrew Jackson detached Colonel Robert Dyer with 200 Tennessee militia to attack the Creek village of Littafatchee on Big Canoe Creek, above modern Ashville, Alabama. Dyer surprised and destroyed the village, capturing large supplies of food and 29 prisoners. Within days Jackson's forces destroyed **Tallaseehatchee** and **Talladega** (29 October 1813).

Little Balur | 747 | Tang Imperial Wars
See **Gilgit**

Little Belt | 1658 | 1st Northern War
See **Funen**

Little Big Horn | 1876 | Sioux
Indian Wars

Days after American defeat at the **Rosebud**, General Alfred Terry sent Colonel George Custer against Sitting Bull and Crazy Horse on the Little Big Horn River, in southeast Montana. Unwisely dividing his force, Custer was surrounded and all 211 men were killed. His other columns under Major Marcus Reno and Captain Frederick Benteen also suffered costly losses (25–26 June 1876).

Little Blue River | 1864 | American Civil War (Trans-Mississippi)

In an attempt to slow Confederate General Sterling Price's advance across Missouri, General James G. Blunt fell back west from **Lexington** to join Union commander Samuel R. Curtis in a defensive position behind the Little Blue River. The Union troops fought a courageous holding action, but were soon forced to continue withdrawing west towards **Independence** (21 October 1864).

Little Concho | 1862 | Kickapoo
Indian Wars

Discontented with the American Civil War, about 500 Kickapoo under Machemanet trekked south from Kansas and were intercepted on the Little Concho, in southwest Texas, by a Confederate force which attempted to seize their horses. The Texans withdrew after a sharp action with 16 killed, while the Kickapoo settled under Mexican protection at **Nacimiento** (December 1862).

Little Egg Harbour | 1778 | War of the
American Revolution

British Captain Patrick Ferguson raiding rebel privateers at Little Egg Harbour, north of modern Atlantic City, New Jersey, destroyed a number of ships and facilities, then met a rebel force under the Polish adventurer Casimir Pulaski. The Pulaski Legion were surprised in a dawn attack and heavily defeated, with about 50 killed, before Ferguson withdrew (15 October 1778).

Little Mountain | 1782 | War of the
American Revolution

At the start of a new offensive into Kentucky, Wyandot Indians (who had attacked **Ruddle's Station** in June 1780) began raiding south of modern Lexington. Imprudently pursuing with just 25 men, Captain James Estill and six others were ambushed and killed at Little Mountain, near modern Mount Sterling. Another Kentucky force lost a few months later at **Blue Licks** (22 March 1782).

Little Rock | 1863 | American Civil War
(Trans-Mississippi)
See **Bayou Fourche**

Little Wichita | 1870 | Kiowa Indian War

Captain Curwen McClellan pursued a Kiowa war party under Chief Kicking Bird, attacking the Indian camp on the Little Wichita River, northeast of modern Archer City, Texas. However, the outnumbered cavalry was badly defeated and withdrew to Fort Richardson with three dead and 11 wounded. It was Kicking

Bird's last battle, as he never again went on the warpath (12 July 1870).

Liubar ∎ 1660 ∎ Russo-Polish Wars

Recovering from disaster in Ukraine at **Konotop** (June 1659), Russia sent Vasili P. Sheremetev towards Lvov. To the east at Liubar, near Zhitomir, Sheremetev was badly defeated by Poles and Tatars under Jerzy Lubomirski and Stefan Czarniecki. The Russians withdrew northeast to **Chudnov** to await reinforcements, though their Cossack allies were soon defeated at **Slobodyszcze** (August 1660).

Liubech ∎ 1016 ∎ Russian Dynastic Wars

When Russian Prince Sviatopolk seized Kiev (15 July 1015), he was attacked by his stepbrother Yaroslav of Novgorod, at the head of a reported 40,000 Novgorodians and 1,000 Varangian (Viking) mercenaries. In battle at Liubech, on the Dnieper north of Kiev, Sviatapolk was defeated and fled to Poland. He returned with Polish aid two years later to defeat Yaroslav at the **Bug**.

Livorno ∎ 1653 ∎ 1st Dutch War
See **Leghorn**

Lizard ∎ 1707 ∎ War of the Spanish Succession

Following victory off **Beachy Head**, French Admiral Claude Chevalier de Forbin was joined by René Duguay-Trouin attacking a large British supply convoy to Portugal off the Lizard, Cornwall. The heavily outnumbered escort of Commodore Richard Edwards lost three ships captured and one blown up (with the loss of almost 900 lives), and many merchantmen were captured (10 October 1707).

Lizasso ∎ 1813 ∎ Napoleonic Wars (Peninsular Campaign)

Just days after victory at **Maya** during the weeklong "Battles of the Pyrenees," French General Jean Baptiste d'Erlon was blocked at Lizasso by General Sir Rowland Hill to prevent him joining Marshal Nicolas Soult's advance on **Pamplona**. While Hill's Anglo-Portuguese force was badly beaten, Soult was meantime

defeated at **Sorauren** and d'Erlon joined the retreat (30 July 1813).

Lizhe ∎ 478 BC ∎ Wars of China's Spring and Autumn Era

In war between rival states in eastern China, Goujian of Yeu recovered from defeat at **Fuqiao** (478 BC) and marched against Fuchai of Wu, facing his army across the Lizhe River. In a brilliant tactical move, Goujian launched two noisy night flank attacks across the river to disperse the enemy, then attacked in force in the centre. Fuchai was routed and Goujian later besieged his capital at **Suzhou**.

Lizy ∎ 1814 ∎ Napoleonic Wars (French Campaign)
See **Ourcq**

Llandudoch ∎ 1088 ∎ Welsh Dynastic War

Soon after killing his rival Cadifor following victory at **Llechryd**, Welsh King Rhys ap Tewdwr faced rebellion by Cadifor's sons Llewelyn and Einion, his own brother Einion (the Elder) and Gruffyth ap Maredudd. Rhys killed Cadifor's sons in battle near Cardigan at Llandudoch (St Dogmael) and executed Gruffyth. However, Einion the Elder escaped to lead the attack at **Aberdare** in 1093.

Llanos ∎ 1817 ∎ Mexican Wars of Independence
See **San Juan de los Llanos**

Llechryd ∎ 1088 ∎ Welsh Dynastic War

The Welsh King Rhys ap Tewdwr was forced into exile by Cadifor of Dyffed and Madog, Rhyrid and Cadwyan (sons of Bleddyn), but returned to Wales with a large Irish force and sailed into the Teifi. Madog and Rhyrid were killed in a decisive defeat at Llechryd, just southeast of Cardigan, and Rhys went on to kill Cadifor at Blaen-Cych Castle before securing further victory at **Llandudoch**.

Llera ∎ 1812 ∎ Napoleonic Wars (Peninsular Campaign)

After defeat at **Villagarcia** drove the French in Badajoz Province back on Llerena, French cavalry under General Henri-Dominique Lallemand met British cavalry led by Sir John Slade north of the city between Llera and Maguilla. Lured into a rash pursuit, the British were routed by the French reserve and fled, leaving over 100 prisoners. Slade was blamed for mismanagement (11 June 1812).

Llerena I 1812 I Napoleonic Wars (Peninsular Campaign)
See **Villagarcia**

Loano I 1795 I French Revolutionary Wars (1st Coalition)
A bold French offensive in Italy saw Commander General Barthélemy Schérer split the Piedmontese and Austrian allies by sending General André Masséna across the Apennines in deep winter conditions. Over three days Masséna drove General Michael Wallis out of defensive positions behind the Italian Riviera port of Loano, capturing valuable guns and stores (23–25 November 1795).

Lobositz I 1756 I Seven Years War (Europe)
When Frederick II of Prussia invaded Saxony and besieged the Saxon army at **Pirna**, Austria sent Marshal Maximilian von Browne and 50,000 men, who met the Prussians at Lobositz (modern Lovosice) in Bohemia, northwest of Prague. The Austrian relief army suffered a hard-fought defeat and Pirna was forced to surrender, giving Frederick control of Saxony and its army (1 October 1756).

Lochaber I 1429 I MacDonald Rebellion
Alexander MacDonald Lord of the Isles continued the rebellion led by his father at **Harlaw** , taking a reported 10,000 men to burn Inverness. King James I of Scotland then met the rebels in Lochaber, where MacDonald was heavily defeated in marshy ground after the Camerons and Mackintoshes deserted. Shortly afterwards he surrendered and was imprisoned (26 June 1429).

Lochgarry I 1654 I British Civil Wars
A last effort to revive the Royalist cause defeated in 1651 at **Worcester** saw Scottish nobles loyal to the exiled Charles II led by John Middleton, raise an army against the Commonwealth. Oliver Cromwell then sent General George Monck to Scotland and near Lochgarry, Perthshire, he crushed the Scots. The Earls Glencairn and Kenmure made peace and Middleton fled (19 July 1654).

Lochindorb I 1336 I Anglo-Scottish War of Succession
In the war between adherents of young David II of Scotland and English-backed Edward Baliol, Scottish Regent Sir Andrew Moray killed Earl David of Atholl at **Kilblain**, then besieged his widow, the Countess Katherine, in Lochindorb Castle, near Grantown in Moray. In an unexpected repulse, Moray was held off, then forced to withdraw by approaching English troops under Edward III.

Lochmaben I 1484 I Anglo-Scottish Royal Wars
Alexander Duke of Albany renewed the war against his brother James III of Scotland (which had been suspended after the capture of **Berwick** in 1482) and led a 500-strong English force across the border, supported by the banished James Earl of Douglas. At Lochmaben, near Dumfries, the raiding party was routed with Douglas captured. Albany fled to France and died a year later (22 July 1484).

Loch Ore I 83 I Roman Conquest of Britain
Governor Gnaeus Julius Agricola resolved to extend Roman control into Scotland and sent a force across the Firth of Forth, where the Ninth Legion were boldly attacked by Caledonian forces while in camp at Loch Ore, near Ballingry in Fife. The Legion was rescued by Agricola after severe losses and it was not until a year later at **Mons Graupius** that Romans finally defeated the Highlanders.

Lochrey's Defeat I 1781 I War of the American Revolution
Marching to join Americans under George Roger Clark campaigning in Illinois, Colonel Archibald Lochrey led Pennsylvania volunteers

down the Ohio. Attacked below the Big Miami by Iroquois and Mohawks under the British ally Chief Joseph Brant, the Americans were routed, with 40 dead and 60 captured. Several prisoners were later killed, including Lochrey (24 August 1781).

Lochryan ∎ 1307 ∎ Rise of Robert the Bruce

Thomas and Alexander Bruce (brothers of Robert the Bruce) returned from Ireland with fresh recruits and landed at Lochryan in Galloway, where they were defeated and captured by Duncan McDougal, who delivered them to Edward II of England for execution. While only a skirmish, it cost the lives of two Scottish Princes. Robert had his revenge seven years later at **Rushen** (February 1307).

Loc Ninh ∎ 1967 ∎ Vietnam War

After a North Vietnamese attack across the DMZ at **Con Thien**, Viet Cong crossed from Cambodia to attack weak local forces at Loc Ninh, north of Saigon. Americans and South Vietnamese arrived to drive them off with up to 850 killed, while another offensive in the central highlands around **Dak To** further diverted attention from the impending **Tet Offensive** (29 October–8 November 1967).

Locri ∎ 205 BC ∎ 2nd Punic War

When Quintus Pleminius attacked Locri on the "toe" of Italy, Carthaginian commander Hamilcar was driven back into one of the city's citadels. With Hannibal approaching from Caulon, Publius Scipio the Younger sailed from Messina and a decisive action saw Hannibal's attack and Hamilcar's sortie defeated. Both Carthaginians then withdrew and Pleminius held Locri.

Lod ∎ 1948 ∎ Israeli War of Independence
See **Lydda-Ramleh**

Lodge Trail Ridge ∎ 1866 ∎ Red Cloud's War

With Colonel Henry Carrington pursuing Ogala Sioux Indians under High Back Bone and

Yellow Eagle northwest of **Fort Phil Kearney**, Wyoming, part of his force under Lieutenant Horatio Bingham was lured into ambush on Lodge Trail Ridge. Bingham and a sergeant were killed with five others wounded in a foretaste of the **Fetterman Massacre** two weeks later (6 December 1866).

Lodi ∎ 1796 ∎ French Revolutionary Wars (1st Coalition)

Just two days after failing to halt the French advance into Lombardy near **Piacenza**, Austrian General Jean-Pierre de Beaulieu's retreating rearguard under General Karl Sebottendorf was attacked by Napoleon Bonaparte on the Adda River. Despite courageous Austrian resistance, Bonaparte won a bloody battle around the bridge at Lodi and five days later he marched into Milan (10 May 1796).

Lodosa ∎ 1808 ∎ Napoleonic Wars (Peninsular Campaign)

Marshal Michel Ney moving along the Ebro against the Spanish Army of the Centre, attacked Logrono, where the Spaniards fled without fighting, while further south at Lodosa French General Bon Adrien Moncey inflicted heavy casualties capturing a key bridge. General Francisco Castanos then regrouped to meet the main French offensive a month later at **Tudela** (25–26 October 1808).

Lodosa ∎ 1813 ∎ Napoleonic Wars (Peninsular Campaign)

When Spanish guerrilla Francisco Espoz y Mina defeated the French at **Tiebas** and siezed Tafalla (11 February), General Bertrand Clausel sent part of the Army of the North under General Marie Étienne Barbot against the rebel. On the Ega at Lerin, northeast of Lodosa, Mina routed Barbot, causing nearly 1,000 casualties, before escaping into the mountains (30 March 1813).

Lodz ∎ 1914 ∎ World War I (Eastern Front)

With an Austro-German offensive into Poland repulsed at **Warsaw (1st)** and **Ivangorod**,

Russia renewed the offensive into Silesia where General August von Mackensen smashed into General Pavel Plehve around Lodz. Very heavy fighting saw the Germans checked and their spearhead almost captured. However, the Russians later evacuated Lodz to defend **Warsaw (2nd)** (11–25 November 1914).

Lofoten (1st) | 1941 | World War II (Northern Europe)

Determined to harass the Germans in Norway, 500 British commandos under Brigadier Charles Haydon attacked fish oil factories on the Lofoten Islands, which produced glycerine for German munitions. The successful raid cost no losses while 11 factories and five ships were destroyed and many Germans were captured, giving British morale a much-needed boost (4 March 1941).

Lofoten (2nd) | 1941 | World War II (Northern Europe)

On a second raid against the Lofoten Islands, off Norway just below the Arctic Circle, 300 British commandos and a few Norwegian troops under Colonel Stewart Harrison landed unopposed and destroyed the German radio station. The raid itself was not significant, yet it provided a valuable diversion from the strongly opposed attack further south at **Vaagso** (26–27 December 1941).

Loftche | 1810–1811 | Russo-Turkish Wars

Two months after Turkish defeat on the Danube at **Batin**, a weak Turkish force sent into Bulgaria against Russian General Nikolai Kamenski was heavily defeated at Loftche (modern Lovech) losing 3,000 men. The Russians soon lost Loftche, but retook it a few months later before fresh Turkish forces drove them back across the Danube at **Ruschuk** (29 October 1810 & 9 February 1811).

Loftche | 1877 | Russo-Turkish Wars

During the Russian siege of **Plevna**, south of the Danube, Prince Alexander Konstantinovich Immeritinski was sent south against the powerful position at Loftche (modern Lovech) on the

Turkish communication lines with the Balkans. The Turks under Adil Pasha were driven out of Loftche with a reported 5,000 casualties, though Plevna held out another three months (3 September 1877).

Logan's Crossroads | 1862 | American Civil War (Western Theatre)
See **Mill Springs**

Logie | 844 | Scottish Dynastic Wars

On the death of the Pictish King Uven, King Kenneth I MacAlpin of the Dalriad Scots marched east to claim the throne through his grandmother. In battle at Logie, near Cambuskenneth in modern Stirling, Kenneth the Hardy achieved a sharp victory over the Picts, establishing himself as the first King of united Dalriada and southern Pictavia, the foundation of modern Scotland.

Logrono | 1808 | Napoleonic Wars (Peninsular Campaign)
See **Lodosa**

Lohgarh | 1710 | Mughal-Sikh Wars

Responding to Sikh victories in the Punjab, Mughal Emperor Bahadur Shah's army recaptured **Sirhind**, then advanced on the Sikh fortress of Lohgarh, near Sadhaura. Both sides lost heavily in assaults and sorties before the Emperor arrived with 60,000 troops. Banda Singh Bahadur soon fled and General Kanwar Khan then took the fortress by storm (13 October–10 December 1710).

Loigny | 1870 | Franco-Prussian War

French General Louis d'Aurelle followed French recapture of Orleans after **Coulmiers** by sending General Antoine Eugène Chanzy northwest against outnumbered Germans under Grand Duke Friedrich Franz II of Mecklenburg near Loigny. Facing a massive counter-attack by Prince Friedrich Karl of Prussia, the French withdrew with costly losses and abandoned **Orleans** (2–3 December 1870).

Loja ∎ 1482 ∎ Final Christian Reconquest of Spain

Continuing the recovery of Muslim Granada after his capture of **Alhama**, Ferdinand of Castile and Aragon besieged the city of Loja on the River Genil. In a brilliant defensive victory, Muslim General Ali Atar sortied from the city, lured the Spaniards into pursuit and destroyed them. Ferdinand's personal bravery enabled the survivors to escape and withdraw to Cordova (1 July 1482).

Lokhvitsa ∎ 1663 ∎ Russo-Polish Wars

John II Casimir of Poland intervened in Eastern Ukraine to storm Lokhvitsa, supported by Cossacks under Pavel Teteria and 5,000 Tatars. The bloody action cost him terrible losses and he withdrew after a check further north at Glukhov. Threatened by civil war at home, Casimir agreed to a truce. After defeat three years later at **Matwy** he made peace and divided the Ukraine with Russia.

Lolland ∎ 1644 ∎ Thirty Years War (Franco-Habsburg War)

After the Swedish fleet was defeated at **Kolberg Heath**, Swedish Admiral Karl Gustav Wrangel joined with Dutch ships against a heavily outnumbered Danish squadron under Admiral Pros Mund near the Baltic island of Lolland. Mund was killed in a decisive defeat and only three of 17 Danish ships returned home. Christian IV of Denmark quickly sued for peace (13 October 1644).

Loma del Gato ∎ 1896 ∎ 2nd Cuban War of Independence

With resistance continuing in eastern Cuba, 1,500 Spanish troops led by Colonel Joaquín Vara de Rey, serving under General Arsenio Linares, attacked a rebel position at Loma del Gato. In a six-hour action the rebels were defeated and driven out with the bayonet, leaving 59 killed, including their commander José Maceo, brother of the great insurgent General Antonio Maceo (5 July 1896).

Lomas Valentinas ∎ 1868 ∎ War of the Triple Alliance
See **Ita Ybate**

Lombok ∎ 1894 ∎ Dutch Conquest of Bali
See **Cakranegara**

Lombok Strait ∎ 1942 ∎ World War II (Pacific)

During the Japanese invasion of the **East Indies**, Allied ships led by Admiral Karel Doorman intercepted an invasion force under Admiral Takeo Takagi in the Lombok Strait off Bali. A confused night action saw a Dutch destroyer sunk and the cruiser *Tromp* badly damaged before Doorman was driven off. Bali fell and days later Doorman was defeated in the **Java Sea** (19–20 February 1942).

Lomitten ∎ 1807 ∎ Napoleonic Wars (4th Coalition)
See **Queetz**

Lonato (1st) ∎ 1796 ∎ French Revolutionary Wars (1st Coalition)

As a fresh Austrian army advanced into northern Italy, Napoleon Bonaparte lifted his siege of **Mantua** and marched northwest towards Brescia, which had been captured by General Peter von Quosdanovich. Near Lonato he heavily defeated an Austrian brigade under General Karl Ott and entered Brescia next day. He defeated the Austrians at **Lonato** again three days later (31 July 1796).

Lonato (2nd) ∎ 1796 ∎ French Revolutionary Wars (1st Coalition)

Austrian Commander Dagobert Wurmser marching into northern Italy to relieve **Mantua** sent General Peter von Quosdanovich towards Brescia. Napoleon Bonaparte lifted his siege and, a few days after defeating an Austrian brigade near **Lonato** to retake Brescia, he routed Quosdanovich and General Joseph von Oeskay near Lonato. He then returned east to beat Wurmser at **Castiglione** (3 August 1796).

Loncomilla ∎ 1851 ∎ 1st Chilean Liberal Revolt

When Liberals opposing Conservative President Manuel Montt Torres were crushed at **Petorca** (14 October), Pedro Félix Vicuña Aguirre led a rising in the south at Concepción and José María de Cruz y Prieto met government troops under General Manuel Bulnes Prieto to the northeast at the Loncomilla. Cruz y Prieto was defeated and surrendered a week later at Purapel (8 December 1851).

London Bridge **I** 1450 **I** Cade's Rebellion

Rebels under Jack Cade defeated Royalist forces at **Sevenoaks** and killed several officials in London before being forced to withdraw. A fresh advance was blocked with heavy losses at London Bridge by a large force under Thomas Lord Scales, Governor of the Tower (Scales' Lieutenant Sir Matthew Gough was killed). Cade and other ringleaders were hunted down and executed (5 July 1450).

Londonderry **I** 1600 **I** Tyrone Rebellion
See **Derry**

Londonderry **I** 1689 **I** War of the Glorious Revolution

Resisting the accession of William III, James II and Count Conrad de Rosen besieged Protestant Londonderry in northern Ireland, defended by Major Henry Blake. After 105 days and costly losses on both sides, Colonel Percy Kirke arrived across Lough Foyle to break the blockade. The Catholics withdrew to defeat a few days later at **Newtown Butler** (17 April–30 July 1689).

Lone Jack **I** 1862 **I** American Civil War (Trans-Mississippi)

Confederate Colonel Gideon W. Thompson renewed the offensive in western Missouri by helping take **Independence**, near Kansas City, then supported Colonel John T. Coffee against a Union force under Major Emory S. Foster to the southeast at Lone Jack. Wounded and defeated, Foster retreated to Lexington. However, threatened in the rear, Coffee later also withdrew (16 August 1862).

Lone Pine **I** 1915 **I** World War I (Gallipoli)

As a southern diversion from the offensive at **Sari Bair**, Australian General Harold Walker advanced inland from **Anzac** to Lone Pine Ridge. Heavy shelling failed to destroy the Turkish defences, but the Ridge was eventually taken, lost, then retaken again. Bloody fighting cost over 2,000 Australian and 5,000 Turkish casualties and seven Victoria Crosses were won (6–10 August 1915).

Long Bridge **I** 1775 **I** War of the American Revolution
See **Great Bridge**

Long Cheng **I** 1971–1972 **I** Laotian Civil War

After years of warfare in northern Laos, a large offensive by the Communist Pathet Lao, with North Vietnamese regulars, seized the Plain of Jars and attacked Long Cheng, the mountain base of Meo commander General Vang Pao. Aided by US air-strikes and Thai infantry the attack was repulsed. A few months later, as in Vietnam, a ceasefire ended the war (December 1971–January 1972).

Longcloth **I** 1943 **I** World War II (Burma-India)

Determined to prove the value of long-range penetration, British General Orde Wingate led Operation Longcloth into northern Burma, where his Chindits damaged the Mandalay–Myitkyina railway. However, the eccentric Wingate over-reached himself by crossing the Irriwaddy and was forced to withdraw, losing over 1,000 out of 3,000 men for little real gain (14 February–27 March 1943).

Longewala **I** 1971 **I** 3rd Indo-Pakistan War

In a bold offensive against India, 45 Pakistani tanks and a mobile infantry brigade advanced ten miles into Indian Rajasthan before being stalled at Longewala by courageous Indian artillery under Major Kuldip Singh Chandpuri. The invading column was then destroyed by Indian Hunter jets, with 34 tanks lost and more than 500 other vehicles. India then counter-attacked into Sind (5–6 December 1971).

Long Island ▌ 1776 ▌ War of the American Revolution

British General William Howe attacking New York City landed 20,000 men from Staten Island on western Long Island. In desperate fighting, the outnumbered Americans were driven back from Brooklyn Heights. Americans under General William Alexander surrendered after a brave delaying action, but General Israel Putnam crossed to **Harlem Heights** on Manhattan Island (27 August 1776).

Longling ▌ 1944 ▌ World War II (China)

As Chinese crossed the **Salween** in Yunnan, the southern force under General Sun Lianzhong seized part of Longling (modern Longshan), but were driven out by Japanese counter-attack. After the fall of **Songshan**, to the northeast, a fresh assault was launched (29 October) and the Japanese under Colonel Kurashiga had to withdraw to avoid annihilation (9 June–3 November 1944).

Longstop Hill ▌ 1942 ▌ World War II (Northern Africa)

Thrown out of **Tébourba**, in northern Tunisia, British and Americans tried to force the Germans off Longstop Hill (Djebel Rhar), commanding the strategic Medjerda Valley, southwest of Tunis before winter. Fighting in terrible conditions, the Allies took the summit before being driven off by a counter-attack. The hill was retaken with more costly losses in April 1943 (22–24 December 1942).

Longtan, China ▌ 1927 ▌ 2nd Chinese Revolutionary Civil War

Determined to recover **Nanjing**, warlord Sun Zhuanfang crossed the Yangzi further east at Longtan, then faced counter-attack by Nationalist General Bai Chongxi, supported by Admiral Yang Shu Zhang. After very heavy losses on both sides, 30,000 Northerners surrendered with their guns. Sun withdrew and in December he struck back at **Xuzhou** (26–31 August 1927).

Long Tan, Vietnam ▌ 1966 ▌ Vietnam War

While patrolling from Nui Dat, in Phuoc Tuy, Australian troops under Major Harry Smith were nearly over-run in a rubber plantation at Long Tan by about 2,000 Viet Cong, who were finally driven off by heavy artillery and machine-gun fire with perhaps 500 killed. The massively outnumbered Australians lost 18 killed and 24 wounded in their fiercest action of the entire war (18 August 1966).

Longueuil ▌ 1775 ▌ War of the American Revolution

In a final attempt to relieve besieged **St Johns**, southeast of Montreal, British General Guy Carleton assembled 800 men, supported by Colonel Allan MacLean. While attempting to cross the St Lawrence east of **Montreal** at Longueuil, they were heavily defeated by Colonel Seth Warner and his Green Mountain Boys. Three days later St Johns was forced to surrender (30 October 1775).

Longwood ▌ 1814 ▌ War of 1812

American Captain Andrew Holmes patrolled in force up the Thames River in Ontario and reached Longwood, where he established a well-prepared log breastwork. An unwise frontal assault by regulars and militia under Captain James Basden was heavily repulsed, though with over-stretched lines the Americans withdrew to Detroit. Basden was wounded and did not pursue (5 March 1814).

Longwy ▌ 1792 ▌ French Revolutionary Wars (1st Coalition)

At the start of their invasion of France, Prussians and Austrians under Karl Wilhelm Ferdinand, Duke of Brunswick, attacked the border fortress of Longwy, west of Luxembourg. It fell after two days of bombardment and **Verdun**, further south, capitulated soon afterwards. Longwy was abandoned by Brunswick (19 October) when he was forced to retreat after defeat at **Valmy** (23 August 1792).

Lookout Mountain ▌ 1863 ▌ American Civil War (Western Theatre)

See **Chattanooga (2nd)**

Loon Lake ▌ 1885 ▌ 2nd Riel Rebellion

The Cree Chief Big Bear (Mistahimaskwa) repulsed a pursuing Canadian army force at

Frenchman's Butte after defeat at **Batoche** (12 May), then withdrew north towards Loon Lake in northwest Saskatchewan, where he was attacked by a party of Mounted Police under Samuel Steele. Big Bear again escaped after a sharp action, but surrendered a few weeks later (3 June 1885).

Loos I 1915 I World War I (Western Front)

As part of the Allied offensive in **Artois**, British forces under General Douglas Haig attacked north of Lens towards Loos. Advancing behind their first use of poison gas, the British enjoyed early success before lack of reserves forced them back with 50,000 casualties. Commander-in-Chief Sir John French was dismissed and was replaced by Haig (25 September–15 October 1915).

L'Orient I 1795 I French Revolutionary Wars (1st Coalition)

See **Ile de Groix**

Loros I 1859 I 2nd Chilean Liberal Revolt

In a rising against Conservative Chilean President Manuel Montt Torres, Pedro León Gallo and 1,400 men faced Colonel José Maria Silva Chávez at Loros, southeast of Copiapo. Following a bloody hand-to-hand action, the government forces withdrew south towards Coquimbo after losing 160 casualties and 250 prisoners. Gallo's rising was crushed next month at **Cerro Grande** (14 March 1859).

Lorraine I 1914 I World War I (Western Front)

French Commander Joseph Joffre recovered from repulse at **Mulhouse** (10 August) and sent General Paul Pau into Lorraine southeast of Metz, with Auguste Dubail and Noel de Castelnau. As the French advanced on Sarrebourg and Morhange, German commanders Prince Rupprecht and Josias von Heeringen launched a devastating counter-attack and Pau fell back on **Nancy** (14–22 August 1914).

Los Angeles, California I 1847 I American-Mexican War

See **San Gabriel, California**

Los Angeles, Peru I 1880 I War of the Pacific

After landing on Peru's coast, Chilean General Manuel Baquedano marched inland with 10,000 men and attacked a smaller Peruvian force under Colonel Andrés Gamarra defending a defile near Questa de Los Angeles, northwest of Moquegua. While Baquedano lost the greater casualties, the outflanked Peruvians were defeated and withdrew to rejoin the main force at **Tacna** (22 March 1880).

Los Arcos I 1833 I 1st Carlist War

Early in the war against Spanish Regent Maria Cristina, Carlist Marshal Santo Ladron gathered Royalist volunteers in Logroño, then advanced into Navarre against a larger government force under General Manuel Lorenzo. Attempting to make a stand at Los Arcos, near Estella, Ladron was routed, then executed next day as a rebel. Lorenzo won again next month at **Peñacerrada** (11 October 1833).

Los Chancos I 1876 I Colombian Civil Wars

Amid disorder following Colombia's election of 1876, Conservatives in Antioquia and Tolima resorted to arms against the government. In a bloody battle at Los Chancos, southwest of Manizales, a heavily outnumbered Liberal government force under General Julián Trujillo defeated rebel General Joaquín M. Córdoba. The rebels were defeated again in November at **Garrapata** (31 August 1876).

Lose-Coat Field I 1470 I Wars of the Roses

Edward IV recovered after **Edgecote** (July 1469) and attacked Lancastrian rebels in the north, who were routed at Lose-Coat Field, near Empingham north of Stamford—shedding their distinctive coats in flight. Before execution, rebel leader Sir Robert Welles implicated the King's brother George Duke of Clarence and Richard Neville Earl of Warwick, who both fled to France (12 March 1470).

Los Gelves I 1510 I Spanish Colonial Wars in North Africa

After Spain secured **Tripoli** (26 July), Garcia de Toledo, son of the Duke of Alba, arrived with reinforcements to join Pedro Navarro on an expedition to nearby Los Gelves Island. Rashly marching inland in extreme heat, Toledo was attacked by a Moor force and died with most of his men. Navarro turned for home, meeting further destruction when his fleet was struck by a storm (28 August 1510).

Losheim Gap I 1944 I World War II (Western Europe)

See **Schnee Eifel**

Loshnitza I 1812 I Napoleonic Wars (Russian Campaign)

As Napoleon Bonaparte's retreat from Moscow approached the **Berezina**, Russian Admiral Paul Tchitchakov attempted to seize the river crossing at **Borisov**. On the nearby Plain of Loshnitza, Marshal Nicolas Oudinot drove off the attack, securing Borisov and capturing a large quantity of Russian stores. However, Tchitchakov was able to destroy the river bridges (23 November 1812).

Los Horcones I 1813 I Venezuelan War of Independence

Weeks after defeating a Royalist force in western Venezuela at **Niquitao**, Republican Colonel José Félix Ribas occupied El Tocuyo then set out northeast towards Barquisimeto in pursuit of Colonel Francisco Oberto. Intercepting the Royalists at Los Horcones, Ribas secured another decisive victory, then marched to join his commander Simón Bolívar in the great victory at **Taguanes** (22 July 1813).

Los Negros I 1944 I World War II (Pacific)

American General William Chase invaded the **Admiralty Islands**, west of **Rabaul**, and landed on Los Negros, where intense attacks on his beachhead saw over 100 Americans killed. The island was eventually secured with about 1,200 Japanese dead, many committing suicide to avoid surrender. The Americans then turned west against the larger island of **Manus** (29 February–8 March 1943).

Los Pozos I 1826 I Argentine-Brazilian War

A fresh attempt to enforce the blockade of Buenos Aires saw the Brazilian fleet attack part of Argentine commander William Brown's squadron at Los Pozos, just outside the capital. In a brief engagement, reportedly witnessed by 10,000 spectators ashore at Buenos Aires, the Brazilians were driven off by heavy gunfire. Action resumed six weeks later off **Quilmes** (11 June 1826).

Los Remedios I 1817–1818 I Mexican Wars of Independence

In pursuit of rebel Francisco Javier Mina, Royalist Marshal Pascual Liñan captured **Sombrero**, then besieged the remaining rebel stronghold at Los Remedios, southwest of Guanajuato. When Mina was captured at **Venadito** and executed (11 November), the starving garrison attempted a breakout and hundreds of men, women and children were killed or captured (31 August 1817–1 January 1818).

Lost River, California I 1872 I Modoc Indian War

When Modoc under Captain Jack (Kintpuash) refused to return to the Klamath Reservation, Captain James Jackson's cavalry troop was sent to return them by force. In a confrontation on the Lost River, just inside northern California, two soldiers and one Indian were killed. While only a skirmish, it triggered a bitter war and the Modoc withdrew south to the **Lava Beds** (29 November 1872).

Lost Valley, Texas I 1874 I Red River Indian War

Kiowa Chief Lone Wolf seeking revenge for his son and nephew killed at **Adobe Walls**, ambushed Major John B. Jones and 25 men of the Texas Rangers' Frontier Battalion at Lost Valley, near Jacksboro, Texas, close to the site of the **Salt Creek** Massacre. The green Rangers lost two killed and several wounded in a sharp action before the Indians withdrew at nightfall (12 July 1874).

Lostwithiel ∣ 1644 ∣ British Civil Wars

King Charles I won at **Cropredy Bridge** in June and pursued Robert Devereux Earl of Essex to siege at Lostwithiel in Cornwall. With the fall of nearby **Beacon Hill**, the Ironsides cavalry under Sir William Balfour escaped to Plymouth (31 August). When Essex fled, Philip Skippon surrendered the town with 6,000 men, 40 guns and 5,000 muskets (7 August–2 September 1644).

Loudon Hill ∣ 1307 ∣ Rise of Robert the Bruce

Resuming his struggle against England after defeat at **Methven** (June 1306), Robert the Bruce gathered a fresh Scots army and after a sharp victory at **Glentrool** over Aymer de Valence Earl of Pembroke, decisively beat the Earl again at Loudon Hill, near Ayr. When Edward I died soon after, his son Edward II withdrew to England and lost Scotland in 1314 at **Bannockburn** (10 May 1307).

Loudon Hill ∣ 1679 ∣ Scottish Covenanter Rebellion
See **Drumclog**

Loudoun ∣ 1760 ∣ Cherokee Indian Wars
See **Fort Loudoun**

Lough Swilly ∣ 1798 ∣ French Revolutionary Wars (Irish Rising)
See **Donegal Bay**

Louisbourg ∣ 1745 ∣ King George's War

A decisive offensive against France in North America saw 4,000 Maine militia under William Pepperell besieged the fortress port of Louisbourg on Cape Breton Island in Nova Scotia. Supported by naval gunfire from ships under Commodore Peter Warren, the Anglo-American expedition forced the fortress to capitulate. King George II later created Pepperell a Baronet (25 April–16 June 1745).

Louisbourg ∣ 1758 ∣ Seven Years War (North America)

In a large-scale siege of Louisbourg, on Cape Breton Island, British Generals Jeffrey Amherst and James Wolfe attacked by land while Admiral Edward Boscawen blockaded a French naval squadron in the harbour. After weeks of very heavy fighting, French Governor Auguste Drucour surrendered the fortress, reputedly the most powerful in North America (2 June–27 July 1758).

Loushan Pass ∣ 1935 ∣ 2nd Chinese Revolutionary Civil War

Recovering from disaster at the **Xiang** (December 1934), the Red Army of Zhou Enlai and Mao Zedong continued north, then doubled back to retake Zunyi. The claimed first victory of the Long March saw Peng Dehuai storm the Loushan Pass, then rout the Nationalists to seize nearby Zunyi. The March continued on to eventually cross the **Lazikou Pass** in September (26 February 1935).

Louvain ∣ 891 ∣ Viking Raids on Germany
See **Dyle**

Louvain ∣ 1793 ∣ French Revolutionary Wars (1st Coalition)

French General Charles-Francois Dumouriez was disastrously defeated at **Neerwinden** and was beaten again three days later by Friedrich Josias, Prince of Saxe-Coburg at Louvain, east of Brussels. When French Minister of War, Pierre Riel, came to relieve Dumouriez of his command, Dumouriez handed Riel over to the Austrians and defected to his former opponents (21 March 1793).

Louvement ∣ 1916 ∣ World War I (Western Front)

When French forces recaptured the Verdun fortresses of **Douaumont** and **Vaux**, General Charles Mangin launched a final major advance northeast through Louvement and Bezanvaux, taking 11,000 prisoners and over 100 guns in three days. German High Command finally had to accept defeat in the great struggle for **Verdun** and withdrew to their original lines (15–18 December 1916).

Lovejoy's Station ∎ 1864 ∎ American Civil War (Western Theatre)

In support of his campaign against **Atlanta**, Georgia, Union commander William T. Sherman sent General H. Judson Kilpatrick against Confederate railroads to the south of the city. Kilpatrick destroyed the line at **Jonesborough**, but further south at Lovejoy's Station he was attacked and driven off by Confederates under General William H. Jackson (20 August 1864).

Lovek ∎ 1587 ∎ Siamese-Cambodian Wars

Prince (later King) Naresuan of Siam turned against his former ally King Chetta I of Cambodia (who had previously supported him against Burma) and invaded Cambodia, campaigning right up to the walls of the capital Lovek (north of modern Phnom Penh). While lack of supplies finally forced the Siamese army to withdraw, Naresuan succeeded in a second attempt seven years later.

Lovek ∎ 1594 ∎ Siamese-Cambodian Wars

Having securing Siam from Burmese control at **Nong Sarai**, King Naresuan took 100,000 men on a renewed expedition against Cambodia and captured many towns. However, the capital Lovek (north of modern Phnom Penh) refused to capitulate and had to be taken by storm (although King Chetta I himself escaped). Siam ruled Cambodia as a vassal until it was overthrown in 1622 (July 1594).

Lowenberg ∎ 1813 ∎ Napoleonic Wars (War of Liberation)

Prior to the decisive battle at the Katzbach, Prussian General Gebhard von Blucher turned on Marshal Jacques Macdonald, who had pursued him into Silesia after victory at **Lützen** and **Bautzen**. On the Bober at Lowenberg, southwest of Leignitz, the Prussians attempted to make a stand but were driven back. The French then advanced to defeat a few days later on the **Katzbach** (21 August 1813).

Lowestoft ∎ 1665 ∎ 2nd Dutch War

While cruising off Lowestoft, Dutch Admiral Jacob Opdam van Wassenaer with over 100 ships met a larger English fleet under James Duke of York. Opdam was killed when his vessel blew up and the resulting rout saw the Dutch lose more than 30 ships before Cornelius van Tromp skillfully managed the withdrawal. York lost only two ships, though failure to pursue cost him his command (13 June 1665).

Loxahatchee ∎ 1838 ∎ 2nd Seminole Indian War

General Thomas Jesup was campaigning in eastern Florida, where he sent a navy boat party under Lieutenant Levin Powell against a Seminole village on the Loxahatchee, near modern Palm Beach. Led into an ambush, Powell was forced to retreat with five killed and 22 wounded. A week later Jesup himself took his main force against the Seminole at **Jupiter Inlet** (15 January 1838).

Lozengrad ∎ 1912 ∎ 1st Balkan War

See **Kirk Kilissa**

Loznitza ∎ 1810 ∎ 1st Serbian Rising

Despite defeat northwest of **Nish** at **Varvarin**, a Muslim-Bosnian army attacked Serbian patriot Kara George and Irish-born Russian General Joseph O'Rourke at Loznitza, near the Drina west of Belgrade and were badly beaten again. With Napoleon Bonaparte threatening in the west, Russia abandoned Serbia to make peace with Turkey and Kara George fled to Austria (17–19 October 1810).

Luanda ∎ 1648 ∎ Dutch-Portuguese Colonial Wars

With Portuguese troops absent on campaign against Kongo, 2,000 Dutch seized Luanda (1641) to capture part of the lucrative Angolan slave trade. Following a troubled occupation, Salvador Correia de Sá led a powerful force from Brazil against Luanda. A sharp siege forced the Dutch to surrender and the Portuguese soon imposed a humiliating peace on their ally King Garcia of Kongo (August 1648).

Lubar ∎ 1660 ∎ Russo-Polish Wars
See **Liubar**

**Lubeck ∎ 1806 ∎ Napoleonic Wars
(4th Coalition)**
Retreating north after the twin defeats at **Jena** and **Auerstadt** (14 October), Prussian General Gebhard von Blucher reached the free city of Lubeck where he turned to face French Marshals Nicolas Soult and Jean Baptiste Bernadotte, who stormed and sacked the Baltic port. Blucher escaped with part of his force but was captured next day, surrendering the once-proud Prussian army (7 November 1806).

Lubieszow ∎ 1577 ∎ Gdansk War
When Danzig (modern Gdansk) supported the Habsburg candidate for the throne of Poland, King Stephen Bathory marched against the city. To the southwest at Lubieszow his army under Jan Zborowski destroyed a much larger Danzig-mercenary force under Hans Winkelbruch of Cologne. The Poles then imposed a siege of **Danzig**, which eventually agreed to pay allegiance (17 April 1577).

**Lubina ∎ 1812 ∎ Napoleonic Wars
(Russian Campaign)**
See **Valutino**

**Lublin ∎ 1944 ∎ World War II
(Eastern Front)**
Just days after the fall of **Minsk**, Russian General Konstantin Rokossovsky launched a fresh offensive from Kovel, west across the Bug into Poland, where he advanced on Lublin, held by Army Group North Ukraine under Marshal Walther Model. The city fell after heavy fighting (Brest-Litovsk also fell a few days later) cutting off aid to **Lvov** and opening the way to **Warsaw** (18–24 July 1944).

**Lubnitz ∎ 1813 ∎ Napoleonic Wars
(War of Liberation)**
See **Hagelsberg**

Lubny ∎ 1596 ∎ Cossack-Polish Wars
Amid revolt against Poland, Ukrainian Cossacks under Severyn Nalyvaiko, Hryhori Lo-

boda and Matvii Shaula were besieged by Hetman Stanislas Zolkiewski at Solonitsa, near Lubny. Loboda was killed by mutineers and, when Nalyvaiko and Shaula were handed over during negotiations, Zolkiewski surprised and slaughtered the Cossacks. His two prisoners were later executed (26 May–7 July 1596).

Lucania ∎ 71 BC ∎ 3rd Servile War
See **Silarus**

Lucca ∎ 1341 ∎ Florentine-Pisan Wars
In dispute over possession of Lucca, the armies of Pisa and Florence met outside the walls of the city, where a great battle saw the Florentine cavalry destroyed by Pisan crossbowmen. The Pisans then invested Lucca and, after repeated attempts by Florentine General Malatesta to relieve the siege were driven off, Pisa eventually took possession of Lucca in July 1342 (2 October 1341).

**Lucena ∎ 1483 ∎ Final Christian
Reconquest of Spain**
Encouraged by victory at **Axarquia**, King Abu Abdallah (Boabdil) of Granada soon invaded Christian territory and besieged Lucena. South of Lucena at the Genil, the Muslims were routed by a relief army under Diego Fernández de Cordoba Count of Cabra. General Ali Atar was killed and the Muslim King was captured, then later ransomed as a tributary of Ferdinand of Aragon (21 April 1483).

Lucenec ∎ 1451 ∎ Polish-Bohemian War
Czech General Jan Jiskra of Brandyz campaigned in Upper Hungary on behalf of the infant-King Ladislav V (posthumous son of Albert of Hungary) against Regent Jan Hunyadi, most notably at Lucenec, in modern Slovakia. Jiskra's Bohemian mercenaries won decisively, though Jiskra was driven out two years later when Ladislav succeeded to the Hungarian throne (10 August 1451).

Luchana ∎ 1836 ∎ 1st Carlist War
See **Bilbao**

Lu-chou ∎ 1853–1854 ∎ Taiping Rebellion
See **Luzhou**

Luckau I 1813 I Napoleonic Wars (War of Liberation)

Napoleon Bonaparte advanced across the Spree after victory at **Bautzen** and sent Marshal Nicolas Oudinot's division north towards Berlin, where Prussian General Friedrich von Bulow was repulsed at **Hoyerswerda**. A week later, south of the capital at Luckau, von Bulow drove Oudinot back with heavy losses. In August he inflicted a decisive defeat at **Grossbeeren** (6 June 1813).

Lucknow (1st) I 1857 I Indian Mutiny

Indian mutineers under Nana Sahib swept aside a British force at **Chinhat** (30 June) and besieged the British Residency on the north of Lucknow, held by General Sir Henry Lawrence. Marching north through **Mangalwar** and **Alambagh**, Generals Sir Henry Havelock and Sir James Outram suffered heavy losses fighting their way into the Residency, but the siege continued (25 September 1857).

Lucknow (2nd) I 1857 I Indian Mutiny

Despite relief by General Sir Henry Havelock (25 September), the British Residency north of Lucknow had remained under siege by Nana Sahib since 1 July. A second relief force approached under Sir Colin Campbell and, following hard fighting at the **Sikander Bagh**, the Residency was relieved. Campbell evacuated the garrison and families to **Cawnpore** (19 November 1857).

Lucknow I 1858 I Indian Mutiny

Four months after evacuating **Lucknow** following victory at **Sikander Bagh**, General Sir Colin Campbell returned to retake the city from mutineers under Nana Sahib. Advancing with a large army and siege train through nearby **Alambagh**, Campbell and Sir James Outram took the city after more than a week of terrible street fighting. This was followed by massive looting (9–21 March 1858).

Lucon I 1793 I French Revolutionary Wars (Vendée War)

During the Royalist rebellion in western France, Maurice d'Elbée and 6,000 rebels were repulsed at Lucon by Republican General Claude Sandoz and a garrison of just 800. New commander Augustin Tuncq drove off a second attempt and, two weeks later, Tuncq and 5,000 men routed 30,000 rebels under the personal command of Francois-Athanese Charette (15 & 28 July & 14 August 1793).

Ludford Bridge I 1459 I Wars of the Roses

Six weeks after decisive victory at **Blore Heath**, the outnumbered army of Richard Duke of York and his father-in-law Richard Neville Earl of Salisbury was confronted at Ludford Bridge, near Ludlow, Shropshire, by Henry VI. Without waiting for battle, York fled to Ireland, while his son Edward Earl of March and Salisbury and his son Richard Earl of Warwick fled to Calais (12 October 1459).

Lugalo I 1891 I German Colonial Wars in Africa

A punitive column led by Lieutenant Emil von Zelewski was sent against rebellious Hehe tribesmen under Mkwawa in the south of German East Africa. Ambushed at Lugalo, east of Iringa in modern Tanzania, by Mkwawa's brother Mpangile, Zelewski was overwhelmed and killed, along with most of his 300 men. Mkwawa was eventually defeated in 1894 at **Iringa** (17 August 1891).

Lugdunum I 197 I Wars of Emperor Severus

Emperor Septimius Severus defeated Pescennius Niger in the east at **Issus** (194), then turned west and treacherously revoked his previous recognition of Decimus Clodius Albinus in Gaul. Severus crossed the Alps with a large army and a bitter mid-winter battle at Lugdunum (modern Lyon) saw Albinus defeated and take his own life, giving Severus control in the west (19 February 197).

Lugo I 1809 I Napoleonic Wars (Peninsular Campaign)

As Sir John Moore's British army retreated from **Benavente** towards Corunna in northwest Spain, he determined to make a stand on the Minho at

Lugo. Despite heavy losses of men and equipment, Moore still had a strong force and an attack by Marshal Nicolas Soult was sharply repulsed. Moore then retired during the night through Betanzos to **Corunna** (7–8 January 1809).

Lugos I 1695 I Later Turkish-Habsburg Wars

Sultan Mustafa II renewed Turkey's offensive in Romania where his invasion force captured Lippa then advanced south to Lugos (modern Lugoj), east of Timisoara, where Austrian Field Marshal Friedrich Veterani was defeated with heavy losses on both sides. Veterani was taken prisoner and beheaded and the offensive continued until Turkish defeat two years later at **Zenta** (22 September 1695).

Lugouqiao I 1937 I Sino-Japanese War
See **Marco Polo Bridge**

Luino I 1848 I 1st Italian War of Independence

Disregarding an armistice between Sardinia and Austria after Austrian victory in July at **Custozza**, Giuseppe Garibaldi continued fighting and was attacked near Luino on the eastern shore of Lake Maggiore by 700 Croats under Major Anton von Molinary. The Croats were defeated and withdrew, but days later a larger force was sent against Garibaldi at **Morazzone** (15 August 1848).

Lukouchiao I 1937 I Sino-Japanese War
See **Marco Polo Bridge**

Lüleburgaz I 1912 I 1st Balkan War

Turks under Abdullah Pasha withdrawing south days after defeat at **Kirk Kilissa**, tried to hold a line between Lüleburgaz and Bunahissar against General Radko Dimitriev's Bulgarians. A massive action—claimed to have decided Turkey's fate in Europe—saw the Turks crushed by artillery fire. They then fled to the defensive line outside Constantinople at **Chataldja** (28 October–3 November 1912).

Lumphanan I 1057 I Scottish War of Succession

Despite defeat at **Dunsinane** (July 1054), the usurper King Macbeth of Scotland retained power in the north and held out against Malcolm Canmore, son of the murdered Duncan I. Aided by Macduff, Thane of Fife, Malcolm defeated and killed Macbeth at Lumphanan, near Alford in Aberdeenshire. He became King in 1058 after victory over Macbeth's stepson at **Essie** (15 August 1057).

Luncarty I 980 I Later Viking Raids on Britain

Forced to wage continuous war against the Saxons of Northumberland and Viking raiders from the north, Kenneth II of Scotland secured a decisive victory against Danes, who had landed on the Tay, northwest of Perth. In one of their worst defeats, the Danish Vikings were utterly routed at Luncarty and their ships were sunk at the mouth of the Tay (trad date 980).

Lund I 1676 I Scania War

When Denmark sided with the Netherlands against France and her ally Sweden, Charles XI of Sweden invaded Danish territory, despite heavy Swedish losses at sea. Charles and General Simon Grundel Baron of Helmfelt attacked the Danes at Lund, near Horsens, where King Christian V of Denmark suffered a terrible defeat. He reputedly lost almost half his army (3 December 1676).

Lundy's Lane I 1814 I War of 1812

American Generals Jacob Brown and Winfield Scott, marching north along the Canadian shore of the Niagara River after victory at **Chippewa** (5 July), were met at Lundy's Lane near Niagara Falls by Generals Sir Gordon Drummond and Sir Phineas Riall. After a confused and bloody action, and short of water and ammunition, Brown and Scott both withdrew wounded to **Fort Erie** (25 July 1814).

Luneberg I 1813 I Napoleonic Wars (War of Liberation)

Following Prussia's defection from his alliance, Napoleon Bonaparte marched into Germany and

General Charles Morand crossed the Weser to occupy Luneberg, southeast of **Hamburg**, where he was heavily repulsed by Generals Wilhelm Dornberg and Alexander Tchernitcheff. Next day Marshal Louis Davout's French army appeared and the Allies were forced to withdraw (1 April 1813).

Lunga Point I 1942 I World War II (Pacific)
  See **Tassafaronga**

Lung-ling I 1944 I World War II (China)
  See **Longling**

Lungtan I 1927 I 2nd Chinese Revolutionary Civil War
  See **Longtan, China**

Luoyang I 311 I Wars of the Sixteen Kingdoms Era

As civil war wracked northern China, the Xiongnu leader Liu Yuan proclaimed himself King of Han and threatened the Jin Imperial capital at Luoyang. When he died (310), his son Liu Cong and Jie leader Shi Le stormed Luoyang and destroyed much of the city, virtually ending Jin rule in northern China. Emperor Huai was captured and later executed and the Jin capital moved to **Chang'an**.

Luoyang I 328 I Wars of the Sixteen Kingdoms Era

With the end of the Jin Dynasty in northern China at **Luoyang** (311) and **Chang'an** (316), Xiongnu leader Liu Yao and his Jie ally Shi Le fell out and established rival kingdoms. Liu Yao of Former Zhao seized Luoyang, then faced a massive counter-attack by Shi Le. Outside the city, Liu was defeated and captured. Shi Le's Kingdom of Later Zhao effectively came to rule most of northern China.

Luoyang I 620–621 I Rise of the Tang Dynasty

After securing northwest China at **Qianshuiyuan** (618), Li Shimin, son of Emperor Gaozu, turned east against the Sui loyalist Wang Shichong at Luoyang, who was defeated outside the city, then fell back under siege. When a Xia relief army under Dou Jiande was defeated at **Hulao** (28 May), Wang surrendered Luoyang and the Tang had eliminated their last major rival (September 620–4 June 621).

Luoyang I 755 I An Lushan Rebellion

Military Governor An Lushan led a revolt in China's northern provinces, where he captured modern Kaifeng then advanced on the Eastern capital at Luoyang. Tang commander Feng Chang Qing fought boldly to halt the rebels, but was heavily defeated and Luoyang was taken by storm. An Lushan then declared himself Emperor and the Tang fell back to defend **Tongguan** (December 755).

Luoyang I 762 I An Lushan Rebellion

After victory over an Imperial army at **Xiangzhou** (758), Shi Siming overthrew rebel leader An Qingxu and retook Luoyang (759) before he was murdered in 761 by his son Shi Chaoyi. Following three years of military deadlock, new Tang Emperor Daizong launched a fresh offensive. In battle outside Luoyang, Shi Chaoyi was decisively defeated, virtually ending the rebellion (November 762).

Luoyang I 1927 I 1st Chinese Revolutionary Civil War

As Wuhan Nationalist Tang Shengzhi advanced north into Henan through **Zhumadian** and **Linying**, his rival Feng Yuxiang converged from the west against Northern General Zhang Zhigong. Feng stormed Luoyang after heavy fighting, then easily took Zhengzhou and Kaifeng. He soon abandoned the Wuhan clique to support Chiang Kai-shek (10–28 May 1927).

Luoyang I 1948 I 3rd Chinese Revolutionary Civil War

On the offensive in northern China, Communist General Chen Geng seized Luoyang in Henan on the strategic Longhai Railway, but six days later was driven out by a Nationalist counter-attack. After further heavy fighting, Chen retook Luoyang and entered Shanxi to capture Linfen (17 May). He then led his army southeast to join the major offensive against **Kaifeng** in June (12 March–7 April 1948).

Lupia ∎ 11 BC ∎ Rome's Germanic Wars
See **Lippe**

Lupstein ∎ 1525 ∎ German Peasants' War
See **Zabern**

Lüshun ∎ 1894 ∎ Sino-Japanese War
See **Port Arthur**

Lüshun ∎ 1904–1905 ∎ Russo-Japanese War
See **Port Arthur**

Lutnyia ∎ 1757 ∎ Seven Years War (Europe)
See **Leuthen**

Lutsk ∎ 1915 ∎ World War I (Eastern Front)
In support of Germany's **Triple Offensive**, Austrian Franz Conrad von Hotzendorf launched the Black and Yellow Offensive into the Ukraine and seized Lutsk. When General Aleksei Brusilov counter-attacked and retook the city Germany had to send reinforcements. Brusilov withdrew from Lutsk, though the campaign had cost Conrad 300,000 men (31 August–28 September 1915).

Lutsk ∎ 1916 ∎ World War I (Eastern Front)
As part of the stunning **Brusilov Offensive** on the Eastern Front, Russian General Aleksei Kaledin led a major attack south of the Pripet Marshes around Lutsk. The Austrian Fourth Army of Archduke Josef Ferdinand was badly defeated and Lutsk was taken along with up to 40,000 prisoners. However, the offensive later stalled further north around **Kovel** and **Brzezany** (4–6 June 1916).

Lutter am Barenberg ∎ 1626 ∎ Thirty Years War (Saxon-Danish War)
Christian IV of Denmark intervened in Germany and marched south from Brunswick. After his ally Count Ernst von Mansfeld was defeated at **Dessau** (26 April), Christian withdrew in the face of a massive Catholic army under Johan Tserclaes Count Tilly. Christian tried to make a stand at Lutter, on the Barenberg near Wolfenbüttel, but he was routed and had to abandon Brunswick (27 August 1626).

Lutterberg ∎ 1758 ∎ Seven Years War (Europe)
Counter-attacking across the Rhine through Hesse, French Duke Charles of Soubise secured victory at **Sandershausen**, northeast of Kassel (23 July) and was later attacked at nearby Lutterberg by a Prussian-British force under General Christoph Ludwig von Oberg. Soubise won a decisive victory, but failed to follow up and was eventually replaced by Marquis Louis de Contades (10 October 1758).

Lutterberg ∎ 1762 ∎ Seven Years War (Europe)
A month after defeat in Hesse at **Wilhelmstahl**, French Marshals Charles Soubise and Louis d'Estrées fell back on the Fulda, northeast of Kassel, with the right wing around Lutterberg held by Prince Franz Xavier of Saxony. Duke Ferdinand of Brunswick attacked and routed the Saxons, forcing the French army to continue withdrawing through **Amoneburg** to the Rhine (23 July 1762).

Lutzelburg ∎ 1758 ∎ Seven Years War (Europe)
See **Lutterberg**

Lützen ∎ 1632 ∎ Thirty Years War (Swedish War)
Imperial commander Albrecht von Wallenstein checked Gustavus Adolphus of Sweden at **Furth**, then advanced into Saxony where he faced a Swedish counter-offensive southwest of Leipzig, at Lützen, where the Swedish King and Catholic leader Gottfried zu Pappenheim were killed. Bernard of Saxe-Weimar secured Protestant victory and Wallenstein withdrew into Bohemia (16 November 1632).

Lützen ∎ 1813 ∎ Napoleonic Wars (War of Liberation)

Napoleon Bonaparte followed Prussia's defection from his alliance by marching into Germany, where he captured Leipzig before meeting General Gebhard von Blucher's Prussians and Prince Ludwig Wittgenstein's Russians near Lützen at Gross-Gorschen. Both sides suffered heavy losses before the outnumbered Allies were forced back across the Elbe. Bonaparte then occupied Dresden (2 May 1813).

Luxembourg ∎ 1684 ∎ Franco-Spanish War

A brief renewal of war between Louis XIV and the Spanish Netherlands saw France seize Coutrai then lay siege to Luxembourg. Supported by the great siege-master Marshal Sebastien Vauban, French Marshal Francois de Crequi forced Luxembourg to surrender. In the peace which followed it was retained by France (April–6 June 1684).

Luxembourg ∎ 1794–1795 ∎ French Revolutionary Wars (1st Coalition)

As he drove the Allies from the left bank of the Rhine, French General Charles Pichegru besieged the stubborn fortress of Luxembourg, defended by Austrian Baron Blasius von Bender. The starving city surrendered to General Jacques-Maurice Hatry after eight months and Pichegru then joined General Jean-Baptiste Jourdan to cross into Germany (21 November 1794–25 June 1795).

Luzhou ∎ 1853–1854 ∎ Taiping Rebellion

As the Taiping campaigned west from **Nanjing** into Anhui, commander Shi Dakai sent Hu Yihuang west against Luzhou (modern Hefei) recently reinforced by Imperial Governor Zhiang Zhongyuan. Despite a brilliant defence, the city was taken by storm with Zhiang killed, followed by a terrible massacre. It was held by the rebels until November 1855 (12 December 1853–15 January 1854).

Luzon ∎ 1941–1942 ∎ World War II (Pacific)

See **Philippines**

Luzon ∎ 1945 ∎ World War II (Pacific)

Two weeks after seizing **Leyte** in the **Philippines**, General Walter Krueger moved north to Luzon, where over 200,000 Americans eventually landed to secure **Manila**, **Bataan** and **Corregidor**. Fierce fight on Luzon cost 8,000 Americans killed and perhaps 190,000 Japanese, but General Tomoyuki Yamashita held out with 50,000 men until the war ended (9 January–4 July 1945).

Luzzara ∎ 1702 ∎ War of the Spanish Succession

After losing cavalry at **Santa Vittoria** (26 July), Imperial commander Prince Eugène of Savoy raised his siege of Mantua and marched south to attack Louis Duke de Vendôme outside Imperial-held Luzzara. Though the French and Spanish were driven from their trenches with heavier losses, Eugène's Austrians withdrew. A stalemate ensued in Lombardy until **Cassano** in 1705 (15 August 1702).

Luzarra ∎ 1734 ∎ War of the Polish Succession

See **Guastalla**

Lvov ∎ 1655 ∎ Russo-Polish Wars

Having checked a Polish invasion at **Okhmatov**, the Cossack Bogdan Chmielnicki and Russian Vasili Buturlin besieged Lvov. When Stanislas Potocki's relief force was driven off by Grigori Romodanovsky at Slonihodrek, Lublin fell (20 October). The siege was lifted when a Crimean-Tatar army intervened and the Russians withdrew through **Ozernoe** (September–October 1655).

Lvov ∎ 1675 ∎ Turkish Invasion of the Ukraine

See **Zloczow**

Lvov ∎ 1915 ∎ World War I (Eastern Front)

See **Lemberg**

**Lvov ▌ 1917 ▌ World War I
(Eastern Front)**
See **Kerensky Offensive**

**Lvov ▌ 1944 ▌ World War II
(Eastern Front)**
The final great offensive in the Ukraine saw Marshal Ivan Konev launch 850,000 men on a broad front towards Lvov. Eight German divisions were annihilated northeast around Brody and, after a massive flanking attack west towards Sandomierz, General Josef Harpe was forced to evacuate Lvov. The operation cost severe German losses and opened the way to **Warsaw** (13–27 July 1944).

**Lycia ▌ 654 ▌ Early Byzantine-
Muslim Wars**
See **Mount Phoenix**

**Lycus ▌ 66 BC ▌ 3rd Mithridatic
War**
Despite defeat at **Tigranocerta** and **Artaxata** for Tigranes of Armenia, his father-in-law Mithridates VI of Pontus regained part of his kingdom at Zela and was attacked on the Lycus (Kelkit) in Armenia by new Roman commander Gnaeus Pompey. Mithridates was routed and Tigranes sued for peace. Mithridates later killed himself and Pompey built the city of Nicopolis to mark his victory.

**Lydda-Ramleh ▌ 1948 ▌ Israeli War
of Independence**
At the start of the so-called Ten Days Offensive, Palmach forces under Ygal Allon launched a large-scale assault southeast of Tel Aviv against Lydda (Lod) and Ramleh. Heavy fighting secured Lydda and its important airport and nearby Ramleh quickly surrendered. However, further along the Jerusalem road at **Latrun**, the Israelis were halted with costly losses (9–12 July 1948).

**Lyesna ▌ 1708 ▌ 2nd "Great"
Northern War**
See **Lesnaya**

**Lyman's Wagon Train ▌ 1874 ▌ Red River
Indian War**
As Captain Wyllys Lyman escorted a wagon train to re-supply Colonel Nelson A. Miles in western Oklahoma, he was besieged for five days just north of the Washita River by 400 Kiowas under Lone Wolf, Satanta and others. An approaching patrol was repulsed at **Buffalo Wallow**, but Lyman was eventually relieved by Major William R. Price from Fort Union, New Mexico (9–14 September 1874).

Lyme ▌ 1644 ▌ British Civil Wars
When Prince Maurice and 6,000 Royalists besieged Lyme in Dorsetshire, they were repulsed by Colonel Robert Blake and fewer than 1,000 men. The town came to symbolise Parliamentary resistance in the west and, after Robert Rich Earl of Warwick brought supplies by sea (23 May), Blake held out until Sir Thomas Fairfax approached. Maurice then had to withdraw (20 April–15 June 1644).

**Lynchburg ▌ 1864 ▌ American Civil War
(Eastern Theatre)**
Union General David Hunter advancing south along Virginia's Shenandoah Valley from victory at **Piedmont**, approached the key railway junction at Lynchburg, where he was met by new Confederate reinforcements under General Jubal A. Early. Unexpectedly outnumbered, Hunter was chased into West Virginia and Early invaded Maryland for victory at **Monocacy** (17–18 June 1864).

**Lynn Haven Bay ▌ 1781 ▌ War of the
American Revolution**
See **Chesapeake Capes (2nd)**

**Lyons ▌ 1793 ▌ French Revolutionary
Wars (1st Coalition)**
Faced by a Royalist insurrection in Lyons, the Convention sent General Francois Kellerman against the garrison of General Louis-Francois Précy. Lyons fell after a costly siege and Kellerman returned to the war, leaving General Francois Doppet and the Jacobins to exact a terrible revenge. They demolished much of the city

and executed thousands of civilians (8 August–
10 October 1793).

Lys 1918 World War I (Western Front)
    German commander Erich von Ludendorff
smashed the Allies on the **Somme**, then launched
his second offensive south of Ypres, where Generals Friedrich von Arnim and Ferdinand von
Quast attacked General Sir Herbert Plumer on the
Lys. The Germans advanced ten miles and retook
Messines before stalling at **Kemmel**. Ludendorff
then turned south to the **Aisne** (9–29 April 1918).

M

Maan I 1918 I World War I (Middle East)

Arab forces under Prince Feisal and Jafaar Pasha advanced northeast from **Aqaba** and, aided by British armoured cars, attacked Maan on the Hejaz Railway south of the Dead Sea. The Turkish garrison held out under siege and were heavily reinforced from **Amman**. Amid the final offensives of the war, some defenders fled north and the town fell to the Arabs (17 April–23 September 1918).

Maarat an-Numan I 1098 I 1st Crusade

In preparation for the main Crusader advance towards **Jerusalem**, Bohemund of Taranto and Raymond of Toulouse marched southeast from **Antioch** to attack the fortified town of Maarat an-Numan. The town fell by bloody assault after a frustrating two-week siege and most of the population were massacred or sold into slavery (27 November–12 December 1098).

Maastricht I 1579 I Netherlands War of Independence

A fresh offensive in the northern Netherlands saw Spanish Viceroy Alexander Farnese attack Maastricht, defended by soldiers and militia under Melchior van Schwartzenburg. After a hard-fought siege, with costly mining and counter-mining, the city fell by storm, followed by a terrible massacre. William of Orange was blamed for failing to relieve the city (12 March–29 June 1579).

Maastricht I 1632 I Netherlands War of Independence

Frederick Henry of Orange secured the south at **Hertogenbosch** in 1629 then took a large force, including English, Scots and French, east against Maastricht, held by Willem Bette Baron van Lede. Spanish under Gonzalo Fernández de Cordoba, reinforced by Imperial General Gottfried zu Pappenheim, were repulsed (18 August) before the fortress capitulated (10 June–31 August 1632).

Maastricht I 1673 I 3rd Dutch War

During the French campaign in the Dutch Republic, King Louis XIV himself led a large army against the city of Maastricht, defended by General Jacques de Fariaux Vicomte de Maulde. Brilliant tunnelling operations by the master of siege warfare, Marshal Sebastien Vauban, took only 12 days to undermine the city's defensive walls and Maastricht quickly capitulated (13–30 June 1673).

Maastricht I 1748 I War of the Austrian Succession

Having captured the Dutch fortress at **Bergen-op-Zoom** (September 1747) after victory at **Lauffeld**, French Marshal Maurice de Saxe marched against nearby Maastricht on the Meuse. Following a half-hearted winter siege, Saxe gathered his forces in spring and took the city by assault. The campaign then became stalemated as negotiations brought the war to an end (7 May 1748).

Maaten-as-Sarra I 1987 I Libyan-Chad War

With Libyan invaders routed in northern Chad at **Ouadi Doum**, 2,000 Chadians in armed Toyota pickups made a lighting raid on the military base at Maaten-as-Sarra, 60 miles inside Libya. Chad claimed to have killed 1,700 Libyans and destroyed 26 aircraft and 70 tanks before withdrawing across the border with just 65 killed. Libya quickly sued for peace to end the war (5–6 September 1987).

Macalo I 1427 I Venetian-Milanese Wars
See **Maclodio**

Macassar I 1660 I Dutch Wars in the East Indies

Dutch Commander Joan van Dam and a fleet of over 30 ships attacked Macassar, in eastern Indonesia's Celebes, where he destroyed six Portuguese vessels in the harbour and seized Fort Panakkukan. Sultan Hasanuddin had to accept peace, but when a wrecked Dutch ship was plundered in 1665 and an investigating official was killed, the Dutch sent a fresh expedition (June 1660).

Macassar I 1667–1668 I Dutch Wars in the East Indies

Determined to recapture Macassar, in the southwest Celebes, Dutch Admiral Cornelius Speelman attacked with 21 ships and defeated the Makasarese fleet off Butong. At the end of a bloody land campaign, supported by Prince Palakka of Bone, Speelman imposed Dutch sovereignty. When Sultan Hasanuddin resumed fighting the following year, he was defeated again and was finally deposed.

Macassar Strait I 1942 I World War II (Pacific)

A Japanese invasion force anchored off the burning oil port of Balikpapan in Borneo was surprised at night by four American destroyers under Admiral William A. Glassford, which sank a torpedo boat and four heavily loaded troopships before withdrawing without serious damage. Despite the American success however,

the invasion of Borneo proceeded on schedule (23–24 January 1942).

Machias I 1775 I War of the American Revolution

When a British schooner and two sloops entered Machias Bay, in eastern Maine, they were pursued by American volunteers under Jeremiah O'Brien, who captured the schooner *Margaretta* and the sloop *Unity*. This first naval action of the war became known as the "Lexington of the Sea." O'Brien later operated *Margaretta* as the renamed privateer *Machias Liberty* (11–12 June 1775).

Machiwara I 1560 I Mughal Wars of Succession

Former Regent Bairam Khan rebelled against the young Mughal Emperor Akbar and marched to the northern Punjab, where he was met by a large army under the loyal Governor Atjah Khan. After a heavy defeat at Machiwara near Jullundur, Bairam Khan fled to Tilwara on the Sutlej. He was later forgiven by Akbar, who sent him to Mecca, where he was killed by an Afghan assassin.

Maciejowice I 1794 I War of the 2nd Polish Partition

With Russian Field Marshal Alexander Suvorov advancing from the Ukraine, Polish commander Tadeusz Kosciuszko marched from **Warsaw** against General Ivan Fersen before the two Russian armies could join. On the Vistula at Maciejowice, 40 miles southeast of Warsaw, Kosciuszko was routed and taken prisoner and the spirit went out of the rising (10 October 1794).

Mackinac I 1814 I War of 1812
See **Michilimackinac**

Maclodio I 1427 I Venetian-Milanese Wars

Three months after taking **Brescia** and defeating the Milanese at **Casa-al-Secco**, Venetian Captain-General Francesco Bussone Count Carmagnola lured his enemy into battle at Maclodio, between Brescia and Crema. Making clever use of swampy terrain, Carmagnola routed the Milanese and took thousands of prisoners, including field commander Carlo Malatesta (11 October 1427).

Macon I 1862 I American Civil War (Eastern Theatre)
See **Fort Macon**

Macta I 1835 I French Conquest of Algeria
Following the capture of **Algiers**, France faced continued resistance in western Algeria by the Arab warrior Abd-el-Kader, who had his capital at Mascara. Campaigning south from Oran, General Camille Trézel was repulsed by Kader at Moulay Ishmael and lost heavily two days later near Macta, prompting Paris to send reinforcements for final victory in November at **Mascara** (26 & 28 June 1835).

Mactan I 1521 I Philippines Expedition
Portuguese explorer Ferdinand Magellan and his Spanish men-at-arms reached the distant islands later known as the Philippines where they joined Rajah Humabon of Cebu against his rival Lapu-Lapu, ruler of the nearby island of Mactan. In a sharp fight on the beach at Mactan, the Spanish and their allies were repulsed and Magellan was killed (27 April 1521).

Madagascar I 1942 I World War II (Indian Ocean)
Threatened by possible Japanese use of the Vichy French naval base in Madagascar at Diégo Suarez, General Robert Sturges and Admiral Neville Syfret took a large amphibious force and seized the port, with about 100 British and 200 French killed. Later landings by General Sir William Platt secured the island and Governor Armand Annet surrendered (5–7 May & 10 September–5 November 1942).

Madain I 637 I Muslim Conquest of Iraq
Following the great Muslim victory at **Qadisiyya** (636), Arab Governor Sa'ad ibn Abi

Waqqas sent his commander Zohra against the Sassanian Persian winter capital at Madain, the complex of cities around Ctesiphon on the Tigris 20 miles south of Baghdad. The Persians withdrew after a two-month siege, abandoning massive booty. Within months they were beaten to the northeast at **Jalula** (March 637).

Madanpur I 1858 I Indian Mutiny
General Sir Hugh Rose marched north from **Sagar** towards the rebel stronghold at Jhansi and faced well-defended passes onto the upper Plateau. In a hard-fought action, he stormed the pass at Madanpur, held by the Rajah of Shahgarh, then captured nearby Madanpur town. Rebel forces in nearby passes at Malthon and Narhat then had to withdraw as Rose continued towards **Jhansi** (4 March 1858).

Madeira I 1812 I War of 1812
In battle in the eastern Atlantic off Madeira, the American frigate *United States* (Captain Stephen Decatur) defeated and captured the outgunned British frigate *Macedonian* (Captain John Carden). The badly damaged British ship was taken into American service and Decatur went on to become one of his country's greatest naval heroes (25 October 1812).

Madeira I 1815 I War of 1812
Unaware that peace was signed in Europe, the large American frigate *Constitution* (Captain Charles Stewart) left Boston for the Atlantic and near Madeira, met the British frigate *Cyane* (Captain Gordon Falcon) and the sloop *Levant* (Captain the Hon. George Douglas). The heavily outgunned British ships attacked bravely before both were captured and taken as prizes (20 February 1815).

Maderno I 1439 I Venetian-Milanese Wars
Determined to attack Milan, Venetian forces under Niccolo Sorbolo and Francesco Sforza dragged their ships overland from the Adige to Lake Garda, but were defeated off Maderno by Milanese commander Niccolo Piccinino. However, when Piccinino later narrowly escaped

capture, Sforza retook Verona and Venice secured the lake. Piccinino lost the following June at **Anghiari** (29 September 1439).

Madoera Strait ▮ 1942 ▮ World War II (Pacific)

An Allied force under Dutch Admiral Karel Doorman sailing to intercept a convoy heading for Macassar was attacked by Japanese bombers in the Strait between Java and Madoera Island. The ships dispersed to fight back, but the US cruiser *Marblehead* was severely damaged and limped back home. Doorman withdrew and a similar interception failed ten days later off **Palembang** (4 February 1942).

Madonna del Olmo ▮ 1744 ▮ War of the Austrian Succession

Charles Emmanuel of Sardinia marched to relieve the Franco-Spanish siege of **Cuneo**, west of Turin, and reached as far as Madonna del Olmo on the outskirts of the town, where he was heavily repulsed by Louis-Francois de Bourbon, Prince of Conti, with the Infante Philip of Spain. The siege continued until casualties and losses to disease forced Conti to withdraw (30 September 1744).

Madras (1st) ▮ 1746 ▮ 1st Carnatic War

French Admiral Bertrand Mahé de la Bourdonnais repulsed the British off **Negapatam** in southeastern India in June, then besieged Governor Nicholas Morse at the British base at Madras. After a week—with no French and only six British casualties—Madras and Fort St George surrendered. They were returned to Britain after peace in Europe in 1749 ended the war (14–21 September 1746).

Madras (2nd) ▮ 1746 ▮ 1st Carnatic War
See **St Thomé**

Madras ▮ 1758–1759 ▮ Seven Years War (India)

After a failed siege of **Tanjore** in August, French Governor General Comte Thomas Lally attacked Madras, on the southeast coast, defended by about 4,000 British and Indian troops under Major Stringer Lawrence. Lally captured part of the city, though Fort St George held out for two months until Admiral Sir George Pocock arrived and Lally had to withdraw (13 December 1758–17 February 1759).

Madras ▮ 1782 ▮ War of the American Revolution
See **Sadras**

Madrid (1st) ▮ 1936 ▮ Spanish Civil War

When troops in Madrid rose against the Popular Front government, about 2,000 soldiers and 500 civilians held out at the Montana Barracks under Colonel Moisés Serra and later, General Joaquín Fanjul. After artillery bombardment, the barracks were stormed with several hundred killed, including Serra and Fanjul (who was executed). A subsequent Nationalist assault failed (18–19 July 1936).

Madrid (2nd) ▮ 1936 ▮ Spanish Civil War

Nationalist commander Francisco Franco sent Generals José Varela and Juan Yagüe on a bloody assault against Madrid, where General José Miaja led a brave defence, aided by International Brigades. The Nationalists withdrew with very costly losses, then tightened the siege at **Corunna Road**, **Jarama** and **Guadalajara**. Madrid held out until the end of the war (8–23 November 1936).

Madura ▮ 862 ▮ Later Indian Dynastic Wars

Following the defeat of Srimara of Pandya by Pallava at the **Arisil** (860), Sena II of Ceylon, who supported rebel Prince Varaguna of Pandya, sent an army under general Kutthaka, who besieged the Pandyan capital, Madura. After fierce fighting, Madura was taken and sacked and Srimara died of wounds. His son, who took the throne as Varaguna II, was in turn killed in 880 at **Sripurambiyan**.

Maeredun ▮ 871 ▮ Viking Wars in Britain
See **Merton**

Mafeking I 1899–1900 I 2nd Anglo-Boer War

As the war began, Colonel Robert Baden-Powell in Mafeking was besieged by General Piet Cronjé (and later General Jacobus "Koos" Snyman), while other Boers struck further south at **Kimberley**. The garrison of under 1,000 held out for 217 days, fighting off an assault at **Stadt**, until relieved by General Bryan Mahon. The siege entered Victorian heroic legend (13 October 1899–20 May 1900).

Magagua I 1812 I War of 1812

A few days after American defeat at **Brownstown**, forces under American Colonel James Miller made a further attempt to escort supplies to **Detroit**, on Lake St Clair. On the United States side of the Detroit River at Magagua, they were driven off by a British-Indian force under Captain Adam Muir and the Americans failed to break the British blockade of Detroit (9 August 1812).

Magango I 1840 I Zulu Wars of Succession

See **Maqonqo**

Magdala I 1868 I British Expedition to Ethiopia

General Sir Robert Napier led a punitive expedition against Emperor Theodore (Tewodros) of Ethiopia and his Anglo-Indian army marched 400 miles inland from the Red Sea. Three days after defeating the Ethiopian army at **Arogi**, they bombarded and stormed the Emperor's mountain fortress at Magdala. Theodore killed himself and Napier released the Emperor's British captives (13 April 1868).

Magdeburg I 1630–1631 I Thirty Years War (Swedish War)

On campaign in northern Germany against Gustavus Adolphus of Sweden, General Gottfried zu Pappenheim besieged Magdeburg, held by Swedes under Dietrich von Falkenburg. Reinforced by Imperial commander Johan Tserclaes Count Tilly, Pappenheim stormed the city, which then suffered a notorious orgy of destruction, with over 25,000 citizens killed (November 1630–20 May 1631).

Magdeburg I 1806 I Napoleonic Wars (4th Coalition)

As the Prussian army retreated north across Germany after the twin defeats at **Jena** and **Auerstadt**, the powerful Elbe fortress of Magdeburg resisted the tide of defeat. General Franz Kasimir von Kleist and 25,000 men held out against Marshal Michel Ney for six weeks before the city finally surrendered and the garrison went into captivity (20 October–11 November 1806).

Magdhaba I 1916 I World War I (Middle East)

Having blunted a Turkish advance into Egypt at **Romani** (5 August), General Charles Dobell crossed the Sinai to seize El Arish, then sent General Harry Chauvel against nearby Magdhaba with Australian and New Zealand cavalry and an Imperial Camel Corps. Heavy fighting forced the Turkish redoubt to surrender, leaving the only Turks remaining in Sinai at **Rafa** (23 December 1916).

Magenta I 1859 I 2nd Italian War of Independence

Napoleon III of France intervened in northern Italy to support King Victor Emmanuel II of Piedmont against Austria and Marshal Marie MacMahon led a powerful force against Austrian General Count Franz Gyulai at Magenta, 15 miles west of Milan. Gyulai withdrew after a mismanaged battle with costly losses on both sides and the Allies marched into Milan (4 June 1859).

Magersfontein I 1899 I 2nd Anglo-Boer War

Northwest of the British defeat at **Stormberg**, General Lord Paul Methuen attempted a frontal assault on General Piet Cronjé well entrenched at Magersfontein, near **Kimberley**. In the second disaster of "Black Week," Methuen was driven off with over 800 casualties (including

General Andrew Wauchope killed). Britain was soon defeated again at **Colenso** (10–11 December 1899).

Magnano ▌ 1799 ▌ French Revolutionary Wars (2nd Coalition)

Amid renewed fighting in northern Italy, Austrian General Paul Kray defeated the French army under General Barthélemy Schérer around **Verona**, then again to the south at Magnano. Schérer was driven back to the Adda, where he yielded command to General Jean Victor Moreau. However, the new French commander was unable to prevent a further defeat at **Cassano** (5 April 1799).

Magnesia ▌ 190 BC ▌ Roman-Syrian War

Soon after victory at **Myonnesus**, General Lucius Cornelius Scipio and his brother Scipio Africanus invaded Asia Minor and were joined by Eumenes II of Pergamum against Antiochus III of Syria. The decisive action at Magnesia Manisa, near Ismir, saw the larger Seleucid army routed after its elephants stampeded. The Romans then required Antiochus to abandon Asia Minor (December 190 BC).

Magruntein ▌ 1916 ▌ World War I (Middle East)

See **Rafa**

Maguilla ▌ 1812 ▌ Napoleonic Wars (Peninsular Campaign)

See **Llera**

Maharajpur, Gwalior ▌ 1843 ▌ British-Gwalior War

During a disputed succession of the Maharaja of Gwalior in central India, Governor General Edward Lord Ellenborough sent a large force under General Sir Hugh Gough. In battle south of Gwalior at Maharajpur, near Lashkar, Gough inflicted a terrible defeat on Maratha General Bhagerat Rao Scindhia. Another defeat the same day at **Panniar** brought the war to an end (29 December 1843).

Maharajpur, Uttar Pradesh ▌ 1857 ▌ Indian Mutiny

See **Cawnpore (2nd)**

Mahdiyya ▌ 1550 ▌ Turkish-Habsburg Wars

On a fresh offensive in North Africa, Emperor Charles V sent forces to recapture (al-)Madhiyya, south of Tunis, which had been lost to Ottoman Corsair Admiral Turgut Reis (Dragut). Venetian Admiral Andrea Doria retook the city by a brilliant assault, but it became untenable after the fall of **Tripoli** in 1551. Its fortifications were then destroyed and abandoned (8 September 1550).

Mahenge ▌ 1905 ▌ German Colonial Wars in Africa

During the most serious rising in German East Africa, about 4,000 Maji Maji rebels of the Mbunga and Pogoro attacked Mahenge (in modern Tanzania), defended by Captain L. L. von Hassel and 60 Askaris. After an initial failed assault, the rebels besieged Mahenge. Captain Ernst Nigmann then counter-attacked at **Namabengo** (30 August–23 September 1905).

Mahidpur ▌ 1817 ▌ 3rd British-Maratha War

See **Mehidpur**

Mahiwa ▌ 1916 ▌ World War I (African Colonial Theatre)

A month after defeat at **Tabora** in German East Africa, German forces withdrew southeast where they were attacked inland of Lindi at Mahiwa. A frontal assault cost South African General Gordon Beves shocking losses and Colonel Paul Lettow-Vorbeck claimed the victory. However, his own losses could not be replaced and he withdrew south into Portuguese Mozambique (17–18 October 1916).

Mahoetai ▌ 1860 ▌ 2nd New Zealand War

General Thomas Pratt assumed command in New Plymouth after the rout at **Puketakauere** and led 900 Regulars and two companies of militia to meet the hostile Ngati Haua west of Waitara. Pratt routed an advance party of about 150 in fierce fighting at Mahoetai, but did not achieve strategic victory until he completed a hard campaign in early 1861 on the Waitara River at **Te Arei** (6 November 1860).

Mahsama I 1882 I Arabi's Egyptian Rebellion
   See **Kassassin**

Mahungwe I 1684 I Later Portuguese Wars in East Africa
   Changmire Dombo seized the Kingdom of Butua on the Zimbabwe Plateau, then met a Portuguese force at Mahungwe. A fine victory of hand weapons over muskets forced the Portuguese off the Plateau and Changmire later seized Dambarare and Macequece. However, his death in 1694 allowed the Portuguese to remain on the lower Zambezi. The Changmire Dynasty built the Rozwi Empire.

Maicanesti I 1789 I Catherine the Great's 2nd Turkish War
   See **Rimnik**

Mai Ceu I 1936 I 2nd Italo-Ethiopian War
   See **Maychew**

Maida I 1806 I Napoleonic Wars (4th Coalition)
   When French Marshal André Masséna and General Jean-Louis Reynier invaded the Kingdom of Naples, Britain sent an expedition from Sicily to Calabaria under General Sir John Stuart, who heavily defeated Reynier at San Pietro di Maida, near Catanzaro. Stuart then captured Scylla Castle, but the expedition was not followed up and he withdrew back to Siciliy (4 July 1806).

Maidan I 1842 I 1st British-Afghan War
   British General William Nott advanced from Kandahar in southern Afghanistan towards Kabul against Akbar Khan, son of deposed Amir Dost Muhammad and defeated Afghan General Shems-ud-Din at **Ghoaine** (30 August). Nott met him again with 12,000 men outside Kabul at Maidan (modern Maydan Shah) and inflicted another heavy loss. He entered Kabul three days later (14 September 1842).

Maidstone I 1648 I British Civil Wars
   With war virtually over, Royalist rebels in Kent seized Rochester, Deptford and Dartford, and George Goring Earl of Norwich (father of Royalist Commander George Lord Goring) was elected leader. However, at Maidstone the disorderly rising was routed by disciplined Puritans under Sir Thomas Fairfax. Norwich then took his few Cavalier regulars to defend **Colchester** (1 June 1648).

Maine I 1898 I Spanish-American War
   In a notoriously contentious incident, the American warship *Maine* blew up in Havana Harbour, Cuba, killing 260 crew. While America blamed a Spanish mine and Spain blamed an explosion of coal gas, the incident triggered a war, which immortalised the slogan "Remember the Maine" and eventually gave the United States Cuba, Puerto Rico, the Philippines and Guam (15 February 1898).

Mainpuri I 1857 I Indian Mutiny
   On campaign east of Aligarh, Colonel Thomas Seaton defeated rebels at **Kasganj** and **Patiala**, then gathered his convoy and marched against new forces under Tej Singh, self-proclaimed Rajah of Mainpuri. The rebels fled with 250 killed after a brief action about a mile west of Mainpuri. Seaton established his camp in the town, clearing the road to **Fategarh** (27 December 1857).

Mainz I 1635 I Thirty Years War (Franco-Habsburg War)
   French under Louis de Nogaret (Cardinal de la Valette) and Bernard of Saxe-Weimar advanced to the Rhine to relieve Mainz, where they defeated Imperial commander Count Matthias Gallas and raised the siege. With insufficient food however, the French had to destroy their stores and retreat across the mountains towards Lorraine, fighting off an Imperial attack at **Boulay** (July–8 August 1635).

Mainz **|** 1792 **|** French Revolutionary Wars (1st Coalition)

While fighting in the Rhine Valley, French General Adam Philippe Custine learned that the garrison of the fortified city of Mainz was weak and believed there was a strong pro-French group in the city. He immediately besieged and captured Mainz after just three days. The city was eventually recovered by the Prussians in mid-1793 after a four-month siege (19–21 October 1792).

Mainz **|** 1793 **|** French Revolutionary Wars (1st Coalition)

One year after the French captured Mainz, the key Rhine city was besieged by a large Allied force under Karl Wilhelm Ferdinand Duke of Brunswick. After a courageous defence, led by General Francois-Ignace d'Oyse, the garrison were released after agreeing not to take arms against any foreign army. Many later supported the Republic against the Vendée Rebellion (6 April–23 July 1793).

Mainz **|** 1794–1795 **|** French Revolutionary Wars (1st Coalition)

As French forces campaigned on the Rhine, General Jean-Baptiste Kléber commenced a fresh siege of Mainz, later continued by General Charles Pichegru. Almost a year after, following French defeat at **Höchst**, Austrian Field Marshal Charles von Clerfayt advanced to the Rhine, where he defeated Pichegru at Mainz and the siege was lifted (14 December 1794–29 October 1795).

Maiozamalcha **|** 363 **|** Later Roman-Persian Wars

Emperor Julian advanced down the Euphrates against Sassanian Shah Shapur II of Persia, where he razed **Pirisabora**, then moved along the strategic canal to the Tigris against the powerful fortress city of Maiozamalcha, the last major defence before the capital. After a brutal siege, the Romans stormed the city, which was pillaged and destroyed, then advanced on **Ctesiphon** (10–13 May 363).

Maipú **|** 1818 **|** Chilean War of Independence

Resolved to restore Spanish authority after defeat at **Chacabuco** (February 1817), General Manuel Osorio and 6,000 men won at **Cancha Rayada**, then met 9,000 Patriots under General José de San Martin south of Santiago at the Maipú River. The Royalists were crushed, with 1,000 killed and over 2,000 captured. Osorio withdrew to Peru and Chilean independence was secured (5 April 1818).

Maisalun **|** 1920 **|** French Occupation of Syria

Prince Faisal of Hijaz had helped Britain drive the Turks out of **Damascus** (October 1918) and was declared King of Greater Syria (March 1920). However, the League of Nations had granted France a mandate over Syria and fighting broke out. The Arabs were defeated at Maisalun and the French occupied Damascus. Faisal fled to Iraq, where the British made him King (24 July 1920).

Maiwand **|** 1880 **|** 2nd British-Afghan War

When Britain proclaimed Abdur Rahman Amir of Afghanistan, his cousin Ayub Khan, brother of former Amir Yakub Khan, appeared from Herat to claim the throne and marched on Kandahar. General George Burrows was sent to meet him with a small British force, which was routed at Maiwand with over 1,000 men lost. The survivors fled east and were besieged at **Kandahar** (27 July 1880).

Maizières **|** 1870 **|** Franco-Prussian War
See **Bellevue**

Majadahonda **|** 1812 **|** Napoleonic Wars (Peninsular Campaign)

As Arthur Wellesley Lord Wellington marched on Madrid after his great victory at **Salamanca** (22 July), Anglo-Portuguese advance units under General Sir Benjamin D'Urban were attacked by French cavalry at Majadahonda, northwest of the capital. They suffered unexpected casualties until Wellington's main force drove off the attack. He entered Madrid next day (11 August 1812).

Majalahonda I 1812 I Napoleonic Wars (Peninsular Campaign)
See **Majadahonda**

Majorca I 1936 I Spanish Civil War
Majorca easily fell to Nationalist forces under General Manuel Goded (19 July), but Catalan Captain Alberto Bayo recaptured Ibiza (9 August) then landed to recover Majorca. With Nationalist resistance under Colonel Louis García Ruiz much stronger, a counter-attack forced Bayo to withdraw. Ibiza was also retaken and Majorca became a key air and naval base (16 August–3 September 1936).

Majuba Hill I 1881 I 1st Anglo-Boer War
After defeat at **Laing's Nek** and **Ingogo**, General Sir George Colley and about 600 men attempted to hold strategic Majuba Hill, south of Volksrust. A brilliant victory saw Boer General Petrus Joubert storm the hill and the British fled with 91 killed (including Colley), 134 wounded and 59 captured. War quickly ended with British recognition of independent Transvaal (27 February 1881).

Makale I 1895–1896 I 1st Italo-Ethiopian War
Buoyed by victory at **Amba Alagi**, Ethiopian commander Ras Makonnen advanced north to besiege the Italian invaders at Makale, heroically defended by a small garrison under Major Guiseppe Galliano. The Italians repulsed many heavy assaults, inflicting costly losses, but were starved into capitulation then permitted to withdraw northwest to **Adowa** (7 December 1895–20 January 1896).

Makaretu I 1868 I 2nd New Zealand War
The Hauhau rebel Te Kooti ravaged **Matawhero** then withdrew to the hills inland from Poverty Bay, pursued by militia under Lieutenants George Preece and Frederick Gascoigne with Maori allies under Ropata Wahawaka. Brought to action at Makaretu, near the Wharekopae Stream, Te Kooti lost about 20 killed before escaping wounded southwest to his stockade at **Ngatapa** (3 December 1868).

Makhram I 1875 I Russian Conquest of Central Asia
See **Khokand**

Makin I 1942 I World War II (Pacific)
As a diversion before the assault on **Guadalcanal**, Marines under Colonel Evans Carlson landed by two submarines on Makin, in the **Gilbert Islands**, killing about 70 Japanese and destroying the radio station and stores. The raid had little true value, costing 30 American lives and prompting the Japanese to fortify Makin and **Tarawa** before the real attack there a year later (17 August 1942).

Makin I 1943 I World War II (Pacific)
After heavy bombardment, Admiral Kelly Turner and General Ralph Smith attacked Makin in the **Gilbert Islands**, well fortified but with only about 500 troops under Lieutenant Seizo Ishikawa. Most of the Japanese were killed for the loss of just over 60 Americans dead, though a further 650 Americans were lost when the escort carrier *Liscombe Bay* was torpedoed offshore (20–23 November 1943).

Makry Plagi I 1264 I 3rd Latin-Byzantine Imperial War
In the aftermath of Byzantine restoration in **Constantinople** (1261), William of Villehardouin Prince of Achaea recovered from Latin defeat at **Pelagonia** to oppose Emperor Michael VIII. The Emperor's brother Constantine invaded Greece and seized Lacedaemonia. But after repulse at **Prinitza** (1263) he was routed at Markry Plagi (modern Yerani) northeast of Corinth and withdrew.

Makwanpur I 1816 I British-Gurkha War
General Sir David Ochterlony advanced into Nepal after Gurkha surrender in the west at **Malaon** (May 1815) and found his route to Kathmandu blocked at a mountain pass near Makwanpur. Despite heroic defence, the Nepa-

lese army was driven off with heavy losses and the war quickly came to an end. Gurkhas soon became an important element in the British army (27 February 1816).

Malacca I 1511 I Early Portuguese Colonial Wars in Asia

With Indian **Goa** secured in 1510, Portuguese commander Afonso de Albuquerque sailed with 800 men to attack Malacca in modern Malaysia. Despite an initial repulse, the Portuguese force seized Malacca by storm and Sultan Mahmud and his son Ahmad fled to Pahang. The settlement remained a key Portuguese trading port until it was taken by the Dutch in 1641 (25 July–24 August 1511).

Malacca I 1568 I Portuguese Colonial Wars in Asia

After Portugal seized Malacca in 1511, she faced constant attack by neighbouring states, most notably Acheh in northern Sumatra, which first attacked in 1537. In 1568 Sultan Ala al-Din of Acheh assembled a huge fleet, with 15,000 troops and Turkish mercenaries, and besieged Malacca. Aided by Johore, Dom Leonis Pereira drove off the siege, but Achinese attacks continued for many years.

Malacca I 1606 I Dutch-Portuguese Colonial Wars

A year after Dutch capture of Portuguese **Ambon**, Admiral Cornelius Matalief besieged the fortress port of Malacca, in modern Malaysia, but was finally driven off by Dom Martin Afonso de Castro, with two ships burned. He later returned and defeated Portuguese commander Dom Manuel Mascarenhas, who lost seven ships left to defend the port (30 April–17 August & 22 October 1606).

Malacca I 1640–1641 I Dutch-Portuguese Colonial Wars

Determined to secure Portuguese Malacca (modern Melaka, Malaysia) Dutch Admiral Willmsoon Cartekoe and ships from Johore besieged the powerful fortress, commanded by Governor Manuel de Sousa Coutinho. With no hope of aid from Goa, the city surrendered six months later after a bloody assault, effectively ceding control of the spice trade (June 1640–14 January 1641).

Malaga I 1487 I Final Christian Reconquest of Spain

Spanish forces under Ferdinand V of Castile and Aragon advancing into Granada captured **Loja** (where they had been defeated five years earlier) and besieged the key city of Malaga. Malaga fell after four months with many residents enslaved or exchanged for Christian prisoners. Ferdinand then moved on towards the Muslim capital at **Granada** (17 April–18 August 1487).

Malaga I 1704 I War of the Spanish Succession

French Admiral Louis de Bourbon Comte de Toulouse sailing to recover **Gibraltar** was attacked at nearby Malaga by an Anglo-Dutch fleet under Sir George Rooke and Admiral Gerard Callenburgh. Badly damaged and out of ammunition, Rooke withdrew and was later relieved of his command. However, Toulouse also withdrew badly damaged and Gibraltar was secured (13 August 1704).

Malaga I 1937 I Spanish Civil War

In command of a southern offensive in Andalusia, Nationalist commander Gonzalo Queipo de Llano, with General Mario Roatta's Italians, took Marbella (17 January), then advanced on Malaga, defended by Colonel José Villalba. The Republicans abandoned the Mediterranean port after taking heavy casualties and fighting shifted back to the Madrid front at **Jarama** (3–8 February 1937).

Malaghur I 1857 I Indian Mutiny
See **Bulandshahr**

Malakand I 1895 I Chitral Campaign

During a disputed succession in the Kashmir Kingdom of Chitral, tribesmen under Sher Afzul and Umra Khan besieged a small British-Sepoy garrison. A field force of 16,000 men was sent northeast from Peshawar under General Sir Robert Low and 12,000 Chitrali attempting to block the advance at the Malakand Pass were driven out with heavy losses. Low continued on towards **Chitral** (3 April 1895).

Malakand I 1897 I Great Frontier Rising

Two years after British forces secured the Kingdom of **Chitral**, Pathan tribesmen inspired by the Mullah Sadullah besieged the small garrison in the Malakand Pass (Colonel William Meiklejohn) and nearby Chadkara. A relief force under General Sir Bindon Blood drove off the rebels to secure the fortresses and, after action at **Shabkadr**, the campaign was virtually over (26 July–2 August 1897).

Malakov (1st) I 1855 I Crimean War

A poorly co-ordinated assault on the defences of the besieged Black Sea fortress of **Sevastopol** saw French forces under General Amiable Pélissier attack the position to the southeast known as the Malakov, while British troops attacked The **Redan**. The French were driven back with costly losses and, with the British also repulsed, the siege continued (17–18 June 1855).

Malakov (2nd) I 1855 I Crimean War

Three months after costly Anglo-French failure at the Malakov and The **Redan**, guarding besieged **Sevastopol**, French General Pierre Bosquet made a fresh assault, forcing his way into the Malakov, from where he was able to support the British assault on The Redan. Russian General Mikhail Gorchakov evacuated Sevastopol next day, effectively ending the war (8 September 1855).

Malala I 1905 I American-Moro Wars

The Muslim Moro hero Datu Ali was driven out of **Kudarangan**, on Mindanao in the southern Philippines, in early 1904 but continued resisting American occupation until cornered on the Malala River, near Buluan, by Captain Frank McCoy. One of the bloodiest actions of the early occupation saw American guns kill several hundred men, women and children, including Datu Ali (22 October 1905).

Malandarai Pass I 1586 I Mughal Conquest of Northern India

Facing insurrection following the death of Governor Muhammad Hakim Mirza of Kabul, Mughal Emperor Akbar sent General Zain Khan Kuka and court poet Raja Birbal against the Yusufzai tribesmen of Swat. In disaster at Malandarai Pass, near Peshawar, Birbal and 8,000 Imperial troops were killed. Mughal Generals Todar Mal and Man Singh eventually restored order (25 February 1586).

Malang-gad I 1780 I 1st British-Maratha War

After victory at **Kalyan** (15 May), Britain attacked the powerful mountain fortress of Malang-gad south of the Sharavati, held by Pandurang Sambhaji Ketkar. A Maratha relief force under Gangadhar Ram Karlekar was repulsed at the Sharavati by Colonel James Hartley, but repeated assaults failed. The British finally lifted the siege and moved against **Bassein, India** (4 August–November 1780).

Malaon I 1815 I British-Gurkha War

Despite British losses at **Mangu** and **Jaitak**, General David Ochterlony assaulted the Gurkha fortress at Malaon, south of Bilaspur, where 74-year-old Bhakti Thapa and several hundred of his men died in an heroic sortie at nearby Deothal. A month later General Amar Singh Thapa made terms and marched out with his arms and colours. Ochterlony won a knighthood (16 April–15 May 1815).

Malatya I 576 I Byzantine-Persian Wars
See **Melitene**

Malavalli I 1799 I 4th British-Mysore War

When Tipu Sultan of Mysore renewed war against Britain in southern India, General George Harris advanced towards **Seringapatam** and met the Mysorean army on the Maddur River at Malavalli. A brilliant cavalry charge by Colonel John Floyd and conspicuous bravery by

Colonel Arthur Wellesley saw the Indians forced to flee with over 1,000 casualties (27 March 1799).

Malaya ∎ 1941–1942 ∎ World War II (Pacific)

Within hours of **Pearl Harbour**, General Tomoyuki Yamashita and Admiral Jizaburo Ozawa began landing 60,000 men and advanced into Malaya through **Kota Bharu**, **Jitra** and **Slim River**. The warships *Prince of Wales* and *Repulse* were sunk off the coast while the British, with obsolete aircraft and no tanks, were overwhelmed and driven back to **Singapore** (8 December 1941–31 January 1942).

Malazgirt ∎ 1054 ∎ Seljuk Wars of Expansion
See **Manzikert**

Malazgirt ∎ 1071 ∎ Byzantine-Turkish Wars
See **Manzikert**

Malazgirt ∎ 1915 ∎ World War I (Caucasus Front)

As Turkish forces recovered from disaster at **Sarikamish**, new commander Abdul Kerim concentrated west of Lake Van, then marched north against Russian General Pyotr Ivanovitch Oganovski at Malazgirt. The Turks were initially driven from the nearby heights of Belican, but further costly fighting saw the Russians defeated and withdraw north towards **Karakilise** (10–26 July 1915).

Malborghetto ∎ 1797 ∎ French Revolutionary Wars (1st Coalition)

Napoleon Bonaparte smashed the Austrians in northern Italy and sent General André Masséna to cut off their withdrawal through the Carnic Alps. Masséna was repulsed at the Pass of **Tarvis**, on the Isonzo, but next day to the west at Malborghetto, Masséna routed Archduke Charles, seizing his guns and supply wagons. Within weeks Austria sued for peace (23 March 1797).

Maldah ∎ 1659 ∎ War of the Mughal Princes

Amid bitter war between the sons of the ailing Mughal Emperor Shahjahan, the second son Shuja, was defeated by his brother the Emperor Aurangzeb at **Khajwa**. Then north of the Ganges near Ingraj Bazar at Maldah, he was decisively defeated by Aurangzeb's General Mir Jumla. Shuja fled to the Arakan, where he and his family were murdered by King Sandathudamma (5 April 1659).

Maldon ∎ 991 ∎ Later Viking Raids on Britain

In a return of Vikings to the coast of England, Olaf Tryggvason (later King of Norway) raided near Sandwich with a fleet of almost 100 ships, then landed in Essex east of Chelmsford. When East Saxon Ealdorman Byrhtnoth was killed in a disastrous defeat at nearby Maldon, King Aethelred II paid a tribute to make the raiders leave. However, they eventually returned to conquer England (August 991).

Malegaon ∎ 1818 ∎ 3rd British-Maratha War

One of the final actions of the war saw the Maratha fortress of Malegaon, 150 miles northeast of Bombay, attacked by British forces under Lieutenant-Colonel Robert McDowell. Lack of heavy guns prolonged the siege and a premature assault was driven off. However, with the arrival of a British siege train from Bombay, the fortress fell and the war was effectively over (16 May–18 June 1818).

Malegnano ∎ 1859 ∎ 2nd Italian War of Independence
See **Melegnano**

Maleme ∎ 1941 ∎ World War II (Southern Europe)

A key battle in the German invasion of **Crete** was in the northwest at Maleme, where glider and parachute forces under General Karl Student were met by stubborn New Zealand resistance. The strategic airfield was captured after bloody fighting and Crete soon fell, but shocking losses among the German parachute troops helped ensure it was the last such major airborne action (20–22 May 1941).

Malerkotla ▮ 1762 ▮ Indian Campaigns of Ahmad Shah
See **Kup**

Malesov ▮ 1424 ▮ Hussite Wars
The Hussites of Bohemia defeated Imperialist invaders at **Nemecky Brod** (January 1422), then began a self-destructive doctrinal war. After several losses the moderate Utraquist (Calixtine) faction eventually joined Catholic nobles against the radical Taborites of the great Jan Zizka. At Malesov, near Kutna Hora, Zizka secured victory. He later took Prague but died soon after (7 June 1424).

Maling ▮ 341 BC ▮ China's Era of the Warring States
Despite suffering a terrible defeat at Guiling (353 BC), Wei again interfered in neighbouring Han and was once more attacked by the army of Qi under Generals Tian Ji and Sun Bin. At the mountain pass of Maling the army of Wei was virtually destroyed, with the inexperienced young Crown Prince Shen of Wei captured. This second defeat led directly to the decline of Wei as a state power.

Malinta ▮ 1899 ▮ Philippine-American War
See **Polo**

Mallaha ▮ 1157 ▮ Crusader-Muslim Wars
Baldwin III of Jerusalem recaptured the fortress of **Baniyas** in the upper Jordan Valley (previously besieged by Sultan Nur-ed-Din), then established himself further south towards Lake Tiberias at Mallaha. While crossing the Jordan at nearby Jacob's Ford the Crusaders were ambushed and suffered heavy casualties. Baldwin barely managed to escape with his life (19 June 1157).

Malloy ▮ 1941 ▮ World War II (Northern Europe)
See **Vaagso**

Malmaison ▮ 1870 ▮ Franco-Prussian War
Despite earlier failed sorties from besieged **Paris**, General Auguste Alexandre Ducrot tried a further breakout, leading about 8,000 men with 120 guns west through Mt Valerian between Rueil and Malmaison to reach Buzenval. Badly hit in open fields by Prussian shellfire, his force withdrew with losses of 400 killed, 100 wounded and 120 captured (21 October 1870).

Malmo ▮ 1523–1524 ▮ Wars of the Kalmar Union
See **Copenhagen**

Malmo ▮ 1535–1536 ▮ Danish Counts' War
See **Copenhagen**

Malnate ▮ 1859 ▮ 2nd Italian War of Independence
See **Varese**

Malolos ▮ 1899 ▮ Philippine-American War
American General Arthur MacArthur captured **Caloocan**, just north of **Manila** (10 February), then drove Philippine General Antonio Luna out of **Polo** and marched on the Revolutionary capital further northwest at Malolos. After a week of fighting, with over 530 American casualties, MacArthur captured Malolos. However, President Emilio Aguinaldo escaped to **San Isidro** (31 March 1899).

Maloyaroslavetz ▮ 1812 ▮ Napoleonic Wars (Russian Campaign)
Spearheading the French retreat southwest from Moscow, an advance unit under Prince Eugène de Beauharnais was blocked at Maloyaroslavetz on the Luhza by Prince Mikhail Kutuzov's Russians. The French took the town after a bloody engagement, though the action forced Bonaparte's main army to retreat along the more northerly "scorched" route via Smolensk (24–25 October 1812).

Malplaquet ❚ 1709 ❚ War of the Spanish Succession

French Marshal Claude Villars advancing to relieve **Mons**, southwest of Brussels, established himself just to the south at Malplaquet, where John Churchill Duke of Marlborough and Prince Eugène of Savoy frontally attacked French trenches. In the bloodiest battle of the war, both sides had heavy losses, including Villars wounded, before the French withdrew and Mons fell (11 September 1709).

Malpura ❚ 1800 ❚ Maratha Territorial Wars

When Partab Singh of Jaipur tried to throw off Maratha rule, General Pierre Perron sent the army of Sindhia under Lakwa Dada, who met the Raja and his allies from Jodhpur at Malpura, southwest of Jaipur. During terrible fighting, the Rajput cavalry was destroyed by Maratha gunfire. Partab Singh was forced into a humiliating peace and never regained his prestige (15 April 1800).

Malsch ❚ 1796 ❚ French Revolutionary Wars (1st Coalition)

Having crossed the Rhine at Strasbourg, French General Jean Victor Moreau defeated Archduke Charles Louis of Austria at **Rastatt** and five days later, they fought an indecisive engagement further east at Malsch. After unsuccessfully attempting to hold the advance at nearby Ettlingen, south of Karlsruhe, Charles continued to withdraw towards Swabia (9 July 1796).

Malta ❚ 1565 ❚ Turkish Imperial Wars

Forty years after relocating from the island of **Rhodes**, the Knights Hospitalier of St John faced a massive assault on Malta by a Turkish force under Mustafa Pasha. In one of history's epic sieges, Grandmaster Jean de la Valette's garrison held out for four months with terrible losses on both sides until the arrival of a Spanish fleet forced the Turks to withdraw (19 May–11 September 1565).

Malta ❚ 1798 ❚ French Revolutionary Wars (Middle East)

En route to invade Egypt, young General Napoleon Bonaparte—apparently on his own authority—landed on Malta and bombarded the fortress of **Valetta**. At the cost of just three French dead, the once-powerful Knights of Malta surrendered and Bonaparte sailed for Egypt a week later. Valetta remained in French hands until it was captured by the British in September 1800 (9–12 June 1798).

Malta ❚ 1940–1943 ❚ World War II (Southern Europe)

With Malta commanding vital sea-lanes to the desert war, the island was massively bombed and besieged by Axis naval and air forces. Bloody convoy battles included **Calabria, Cape Passaro, Matapan, Cape Bon, Sirte** and **Pedestal** before the starving population were effectively relieved in November 1942. Attacks continued until Allied victory in North Africa (June 1940–May 1943).

Maltepe ❚ 1328 ❚ Byzantine-Ottoman Wars

See **Pelacanon**

Malthan ❚ 1751 ❚ Later Mughal-Maratha Wars

During resumed war between Maharashtra and Hyderabad, Maratha Peshwa Balaji Rao marched towards Ahmadnagar. After losing a skirmish at Parner (21 November) he attacked the Nizam's army under Saiyad Lashkar Khan, south of Ahmadnagar. Near Malthan on the River Ghod, the Marathas secured a bloody victory and Nizam Salabat Jang soon made peace (27 November 1751).

Mal Tiempo ❚ 1895 ❚ 2nd Cuban War of Independence

With scant ammunition following **Iguará** and **Manacal**, insurgents Máximo Gómez and Antonio Maceo intercepted a Spanish column under Colonel Salvador Arizón at Mal Tiempo, southwest of Santa Clara near Cruces. Attacking with machete and bayonet, the rebels secured a bloody victory, capturing 200 rifles and 10,000 rounds, then marched on **Coliseo** in Matanzas (15 December 1895).

Maluna ▌ 1897 ▌ 1st Greco-Turkish War
See **Vigla**

Malvasia ▌ 1689–1690 ▌ Venetian-Turkish Wars
See **Monemvasia**

Malventum ▌ 275 BC ▌ Pyrrhic War
See **Beneventum**

Malvern Hill ▌ 1862 ▌ American Civil War (Eastern Theatre)
In the last of the **Seven Days' Battles**, south of Richmond, Virginia, Union commander George B. McClellan crossed the **White Oak Swamp** and took a defensive position north of the James at Malvern Hill. Confederate General Robert E. Lee withdrew after terrible fighting and over 5,000 casualties, but Richmond was saved and the Peninsula Campaign was over (1 July 1862).

Mams ▌ 688 ▌ Muslim Conquest of North Africa
Berber "King" Kusayla expelled the Muslim Arabs from Ifrikiya following his victory at **Biskra** (683), then faced a renewed Arab invasion led by the powerful General Zuhayr ibn Kays al-Balawi. The armies met at Mams, in mountains west of al-Kayrawan (Kairouan) in modern Tunisia, where Kusayla was defeated and killed. The Arabs steadily completed their conquest of the Maghrib.

Manacal ▌ 1895 ▌ 2nd Cuban War of Independence
After battle in western Cuba near **Iguará** (3 December), insurgent leaders Máximo Gómez and Antonio Maceo took a defensive position at Manacal, near Santa Clara, against a large pursuing Spanish force under General Fernando Oliver. They were finally driven out by Spanish artillery, but Oliver returned to La Siguanea. The Cubans soon struck back at **Mal Tiempo** (10–13 December 1895).

Manado ▌ 1958 ▌ Indonesian Civil Wars
Jakarta crushed dissident forces on Sumatra at **Bukittingi**, then turned its attention to Sulawesi, where the rebel capital had been moved to Manado under Colonel J. F. "Joop" Warouw. Manado fell after heavy fighting, though resistance continued in rural areas until a ceasefire in 1962. The revolt is claimed to have cost almost 10,000 government troops and 22,000 rebels killed (28 June 1958).

Manara ▌ 1948 ▌ Israeli War of Independence
Lebanese troops under Fawzi el Kaukji advanced on Manara, in Upper Galilee extending between Lebanon and Syria, to support Egypt's offensive in the south. The Arabs took nearby Sheikh Abad, but the Jews at Manara held out against fierce and sustained attack. The besieged village was eventually relieved after Arab defeat further south at Safad and **Tarshiha** (22 October 1948).

Manassas ▌ 1861 ▌ American Civil War (Eastern Theatre)
See **Bull Run**

Manassas ▌ 1862 ▌ American Civil War (Eastern Theatre)
See **Bull Run**

Manassas Gap ▌ 1863 ▌ American Civil War (Eastern Theatre)
Confederate commander Robert E. Lee withdrew from decisive defeat at **Gettysburg** and crossed the Potomac at **Williamsport**, pursued by General George G. Meade's Union army. Attempting a flanking attack at Manassas Gap, east of Front Royal, Union General William G. French was repulsed in an inconclusive action and Lee was able to continue south through Virginia (23 July 1863).

Manassas Station ∎ 1862 ∎ American Civil War (Eastern Theatre)
  See **Kettle Run**

Mancetter ∎ 61 ∎ Roman Conquest of Britain
  See **Boudicca**

Manchuria ∎ 1945 ∎ World War II (China)
  With war almost over, Russian Marshal Aleksandr Vasilevksy led a converging invasion of Japanese-occupied Manchuria—from Outer Mongolia towards Mukden (modern Shenyang), across the Amur towards the Songhua, and from Valdivostok towards Harbin. General Otozo Yamada's Guandong Army was crushed and, as the war ended, the Russians continued into Korea (8–22 August 1945).

Manchuria Incident ∎ 1931 ∎ Manchuria Incident
  See **Mukden**

Mandalay ∎ 1945 ∎ World War II (Burma-India)
  While heavy fighting continuing around the vital Japanese communication centre at **Meiktila**, General Sir William Slim pursued General Shihachi Katamura's army north to Mandalay, where they dug in for a hard-fought siege. After a month of fierce resistance, the Japanese evacuated and, with the capture of Rangoon in the south, the campaign was largely over (12 February–19 March 1945).

Mandali ∎ 1982 ∎ Iraq-Iran War
  Despite terrible losses against Iraq north of **Basra**, Iran launched a fresh offensive further north near Mandali, east of Baghdad. "Human wave" infantry assaults with little armoured support again cost Iran heavy casualties for some territory, yet negligible strategic advantage. A second assault, in support of action around **Musian**, also achieved little (1–6 October & 7–11 November 1982).

Mandasur ∎ 1857 ∎ Indian Mutiny
  See **Goraria**

Mandonium ∎ 338 BC ∎ Archidamian Wars
  In an attempt to support Tarentum against Lucania, Archidamus III of Sparta took a mercenary force into southern Italy. Three years' unsuccessful campaigning ended when he was defeated and killed, along with most of his troops, at Mandonium (modern Manduria) 20 miles southeast of Tarentum (modern Taranto). This was ostensibly on the same day as the Macedonian victory at **Chaeronea**.

Mandora ∎ 1801 ∎ French Revolutionary Wars (Middle East)
  As General Sir Ralph Abercromby marched from **Aboukir** towards **Alexandria**, his seaward column of marines and Scottish infantry, led by General Richard Lambart Earl of Cavan, came under heavy French attack at Mandora. Hard fighting cost 160 British killed and 2,000 wounded before the French were driven off and Abercromby's advance continued (13 March 1801).

Mandu ∎ 1535 ∎ Mughal Conquest of Northern India
  Emperor Humayun extended the Mughal Empire into central India, where he drove off Sultan Bahadur Shah of Gujarat besieging **Chitor** and pursued him to the great mountain fortress of Mandu, southwest of Indore. Bahabur Shah's Governor Mallu Kadir Khan attempted a defence, but Humayun's army forced their way in and took the fortress by storm as the Sultan fled to **Champaner**.

Manduri ∎ 1857 ∎ Indian Mutiny
  Nepalese troops under Dhir Shamsar Rana marching to support the British at **Azamgarh**, met a rebel force ten miles away at the village of Manduri. Advancing through fields of sugarcane the Gurkhas routed the rebels, inflicting over 200 casualties. This action, and a larger victory at **Chanda, Uttar Pradesh**, confirmed British

willingness to use Nepalese against the rebels (19 September 1857).

Mañeru **|** 1873 **|** 2nd Carlist War

During continued campaigning in Navarre, Spanish Republican General Domingo Moriones met a Carlist force under Nicolás Ollo at Mañeru, near Puente de la Reina. Both sides claimed victory in a hard-fought yet indecisive action, though the Carlists were said to have had the advantage. A month later Moriones was repulsed in a costly assault further west against **Estella** (6 October 1873).

Mangalore **|** 1783–1784 **|** 2nd British-Mysore War

When Tipu Sultan of Mysore continued his father's war against Britain, he captured **Bednur** (30 April 1783) then marched on the southwest Indian port of Mangalore, defended by Colonel John Campbell. Amid failed negotiations, Campbell was starved into surrender (he later died in captivity of exhaustion). A subsequent settlement brought the war to an end (20 May 1783–26 January 1784).

Mangalwar **|** 1857 **|** Indian Mutiny

As they marched northeast from Cawnpore to relieve besieged **Lucknow**, British Generals Sir James Outram and Sir Henry Havelock crossed the Ganges and were blocked five miles away at Mangalwar by a strong rebel force. A four-hour action saw them clear the rebels with a bold cavalry attack, killing over 100, before continuing north towards the fort of **Alambagh** (21 September 1857).

Mangapiko **|** 1864 **|** 2nd New Zealand War

British General Duncan Cameron advancing south into the Waikato secured **Rangiriri**, then besieged the Maori position at Paterangi. After a bloody ambush at nearby Mangapiko Creek, a large hand-to-hand action developed (with the first Victoria Cross won by a non-regular soldier) before the Maoris were repulsed. Paterangi was evacuated after defeat at **Rangiaowhia** (11 February 1864).

Mangrol **|** 1761 **|** Later Mughal-Maratha Wars

Encouraged by Maratha disaster at **Panipat** (14 January), the Rajput Principalities of northern India attempted to reassert their power under the leadership of Madho Singh of Jaipur. At Mangrol, northeast of Kota, Maratha General Mulhar Rao Holkar decisively defeated the Rajput allies. However, he then had to return to Maharashtra and Maratha power in the north declined (29–30 November 1761).

Mangshan **|** 543 **|** Wei Dynastic Wars

With an offensive by Western Wei defeated at **Heqiao** (538), war between the rival factions in northern China died down apart from a failed attack by Eastern Wei on Yubi (542). The following year, Yuwen Tai of Western Wei again advanced on Luoyang, but withdrew after a very heavy defeat by Gao Huan at nearby Mangshan. Fighting then eased until 546, when Gao made a fresh assault on **Yubi**.

Mangu **|** 1814 **|** British-Gurkha War

While General David Ochterlony checked Nepalese expansion into northern India at **Nalagarh**, further north Colonel William Thompson attacked the fortress of Mangu, near Ramgarh, held by Amar Singh Thapa. The British were repulsed in large-scale heavy fighting, but Amar Singh later abandoned the fort to intercept Ochterlony's advance towards **Malaon** (27–29 December 1814).

Maniaki **|** 1825 **|** Greek War of Independence

With **Navarino** about to fall, Bishop Gregorios Dikaios (Papaflesas) boldly led 3,000 Greeks towards the Egyptians and met a claimed 6,000 men under Ibrahim Pasha marching northeast from Navarino at Maniaki, on Mount Malia. A ferocious action cost 800 Greeks killed (including

Dikaios) as well as 400 Muslims before the Greeks finally had to withdraw (20 May 1825).

Maniar I 1858 I Indian Mutiny

Rebel leader Kunwar Singh lost at **Azamgarh** (15 April) and suffered further casualties at Naghai two days later before escaping to Maniar, just south of the Gaghara near Sikandarpur. Surprised at dawn by British forces under Brigadier Claude Douglas, the rebels fled with terrible losses. Kunwar was wounded, but escaped south across the Ganges at Bulliah to fight at **Jagdispur** (20 April 1858).

Manila I 1610 I Dutch-Spanish Colonial Wars

On an expedition against the Philippines, Dutch Admiral Francois Wittert was met off Manila by a much larger Spanish fleet under Governor Don Juan de Silva. In a decisive defeat, during which Wittert was killed, two Dutch ships were captured and one was burned. The two remaining Dutch vessels played no part in the battle and escaped safely to Palani in India (25 April 1610).

Manila I 1762 I Seven Years War (Philippines)

In response to Spain entering the war, British Admiral Sir Samuel Cornish and General Sir William Draper took a large force to the Philippines, where they besieged Manila, which surrendered after brief resistance. Britain captured the Acapulco galleon and levied a massive ransom (which was never honoured). After the war Manila was returned to Spain (23 September–6 October 1762).

Manila I 1898 I Spanish-American War

With the Spanish fleet destroyed at **Manila Bay**, American General Thomas M. Anderson landed troops at Cavite, followed by the main force under General Wesley Merritt, to besiege Manila, defended by Spanish General Fermín Jáudenes. Manila fell in an almost bloodless assault and the United States seized the Philippines, triggering a bloody war with the Filipinos (17 July–14 August 1898).

Manila I 1899 I Philippine-American War

After an incident outside Manila at San Juna del Monte, provoked by Colonel John Stotsenburg's Nebraskans against Colonel Luciano San Miguel, fighting broke out in Manila and part of the city was burned. The insurgents were repulsed at a cost of over 230 American and 500 Filipino casualties, opening a bitter war which continued with an attack on **Caloocan** (4–5 February 1899).

Manila I 1945 I World War II (Pacific)

When Americans landed on **Luzon**, General Oscar Griswold drove south towards Manila, with a fresh landing to the southwest by General Joseph Swing. Army and navy forces under Admiral Sanji Iwabuchi fought a ferocious defence of the Philippine capital, which fell after terrible destruction with 16,000 Japanese killed as well as a large number of Filipino civilians (4 February–3 March 1945).

Manila Bay I 1898 I Spanish-American War

At the start of war with Spain, American Admiral George Dewey took five cruisers and two gunboats to the Philippines and cornered Admiral Patricio Montojo's eight-ship squadron in Manila Bay. At the cost of just one American killed and eight wounded, Dewey destroyed the Spanish fleet, inflicting over 380 casualties. He then had to wait for land forces to capture **Manila** (1 May 1898).

Manizales I 1860 I Colombian Civil Wars

Former President Tomás Cipriano de Mosquera of Cauca rose against the government of Mariano Ospina and marched on Manizales against General Joaquín Posada Gutiérrez. An indecisive seven-hour action saw Mosquera withdraw and an armistice was agreed. However by mid-1861, Mosquera had won at **Subachoque** and **Bogotá** and regained the Presidency (28 August 1860).

Manizales I 1877 I Colombian Civil Wars

Resuming war against Conservative rebels after his previous victory at **Los Chancos** (August 1876), General Julián Trujillo for the Liberal government attacked General Marcelino Vélez, who had earlier secured armistice after defeat at **Garrapata**. Following a recent rebel defeat at **La Donjuana**, Vélez and the rebellion were crushed at Manizales and Trujillo later became President (3–5 April 1877).

Mannar I 1591 I Portuguese Colonial Wars in Asia

King Puvijara Pandaram of Jaffna besieged the Portuguese island colony of Mannar off the northwest coast of Ceylon (modern Sri Lanka), supported by the fleet of Samudri of Calicut. But in a bold attack, Portuguese commander Andre Furtado de Mendonca destroyed the Calicut fleet. He then defeated and killed Puvijara and installed Ethirimanna Cinkam as puppet King of **Jaffna**.

Mannerheim Line I 1939 I Russo-Finnish War

As the **Winter War** began, Soviet General Kirill Meretskov took 120,000 men and 1,000 tanks against Finland's Mannerheim Line across the Karelian Isthmus. However, outnumbered commander Hugo Östermann, with Generals Harold Öquist and Erik Heinrichs, achieved a courageous defensive victory. Meanwhile, the Russians were also repulsed further north at **Tolvajärvi** (1–20 December 1939).

Mannerheim Line I 1940 I Russo-Finnish War

New Russian commander Semyon Timoshenko recovered from terrible losses at **Tolvajärvi** and **Suomussalmi** and launched a massive fresh assault on the Mannerheim Line across the Karelian Isthmus. After one of the heaviest bombardments seen in Europe, the Russians broke through around Summa to capture Vyborg. Finland sued for peace to end the **Winter War** (1–15 February 1940).

Mannheim I 1622 I Thirty Years War (Palatinate War)

When defeat at **Höchst, Frankfurt**, drove the main Protestant army west across the Rhine, the victorious Johan Tserclaes Count Tilly captured **Heidelberg**, then besieged Mannheim, held by 1,400 English troops under Sir Horace Vere. Following stout resistance, Vere was permitted to withdraw with the honours of war. The last Rhine fortress at Frankenthal held out until early 1623 (5 November 1622).

Mannheim I 1794 I French Revolutionary Wars (1st Coalition)

Campaigning on the Rhine, French General Jean-Victor Moreau besieged Mannheim, garrisoned by over 15,000 Prussians. The fortress on the left bank capitulated two months later with agreement that the French would not bombard the right bank city unless their army crossed the Rhine—which came to pass in September of the following year (10 October–25 December 1794).

Mannheim I 1795 I French Revolutionary Wars (1st Coalition)

French troops invaded Germany and the major Rhine city of Mannheim quickly surrendered to General Charles Pichegru (20 September 1795). However, in the Austrian counter-offensive after their victory at nearby **Höchst, Frankfurt**, the large French garrison was forced to capitulate after holding out for a month against siege by General Dagobert Wurmser (10 October–22 November 1795).

Mannheim I 1799 I French Revolutionary Wars (2nd Coalition)

Archduke Charles of Austria defeated the French at **Zurich** (14 August), then marched from Switzerland to the Rhine and launched a massive attack against Mannheim, defended by Antoine Baron de Laroche-Dubouscat. The heavily outnumbered French garrison inflicted severe Austrian casualties in a bloody struggle before it was forced to withdraw from the city (18 September 1799).

Manresa I 1810 I Napoleonic Wars (Peninsular Campaign)

During the Spanish offensive in Catalonia by General Henry O'Donnell, General Juan Caro was wounded defeating the French at **Villafranca del Penedes** and a few days later, Luis Gonzalez Torres Marquis of Campoverde moved the force north against Manresa, northwest of Barcelona. General Francois-Xavier Schwarz's German Brigade lost 800 men before the town fell to the Spanish (5 April 1810).

Mansfield I 1864 I American Civil War (Trans-Mississippi)

As Union commander Nathaniel P. Banks advanced up Louisiana's Red River from **Fort de Russy**, Confederate General Richard Taylor determined to block Banks at Mansfield and moved out to meet him at nearby Sabine Cross Roads. In the decisive action of the campaign, Union assaults were driven off with heavy losses and Banks fell back to a defensive line at **Pleasant Hill** (8 April 1864).

Mansilla I 1808 I Napoleonic Wars (Peninsular Campaign)

Untrained Spanish levies under General Pedro La Romana, advancing to support the British army as it withdrew to the northwest of Spain, were routed by Marshal Nicolas Soult while attempting to cross the river at Mansilla, southeast of Leon. La Romana had arrived too late to support the British at **Benavente** and now joined their retreat towards **Corunna** (30 December 1808).

Mansura, Egypt I 1250 I 7th Crusade

King Louis IX of France advanced towards Cairo and was repulsed at the **Ashmoun Canal** where, after months of delay, his brother Robert of Artois stormed the town of Mansura, killing Ayyubid Egyptian commander Fakr-ed-din. In a violent counter-attack the Crusaders were driven out with severe losses, including Count Robert killed, and were forced back towards Damietta (8 February 1250).

Mansura, Louisiana I 1864 I American Civil War (Trans-Mississippi)

Withdrawing down Louisiana's Red River from **Mansfield** and **Pleasant Hill**, Union commander Nathaniel P. Banks repulsed an attack at **Monett's Ferry** (23 April) then continued to Mansura, south of Marksville, where he was met by Confederate General Richard Taylor. Taylor withdrew after a mainly artillery action and Banks marched east through **Yellow Bayou** (16 May 1864).

Mantapike Hill I 1864 I American Civil War (Eastern Theatre)
See **Walkerton**

Mantinea I 418 BC I Great Peloponnesian War

On a fresh offensive, Argis II of Sparta led a force into Tegea to secure his allies, then marched into Mantinea against a coalition of Argives, Athenians and Mantineans. In a classic hoplite action at Mantinea—reportedly involving 5,500 Spartans and 7,000 of the coalition forces—the brilliant discipline of the Spartans secured victory, boosting Spartan authority in the Peloponnese.

Mantinea I 362 BC I Wars of the Greek City-States

Determined to challenge Theban supremacy, established with victory at **Leuctra** (371 BC), Athens and Sparta combined against Epaminondas of Thebes, who was invading the Peloponnese. Despite very substantial forces deployed, action at Mantinea was indecisive. However, the death of Epaminondas in the pursuit and that of Pelopidas at **Cynoscephalae** ended Theban hegemony.

Mantinea I 207 BC I Spartan-Achaean Wars

When Machanidas of Sparta invaded northwest Peloponnesia, he was met by Achaean cavalry under Philopoemen of Megalopolis, near Mantinea. After his Tarantine mercenaries fled, Machanidas led a courageous counter-attack, but was defeated and killed, reputedly by Philopoemen himself. A temporary truce resulted and in 199 BC, Philopoemen met Machanidas' successor Nabis at **Scotitas**.

Mantua ❙ 1629–1630 ❙ Thirty Years War (Mantuan War)

In a disputed succession in Mantua and Montferrat, Imperial Commander Rambaldo Collalto besieged Mantua, held for the French-born heir Charles di Gonzaga Duke of Nevers. Cardinal Richelieu himself crossed the Alps, though could not prevent Mantua falling to Collalto. However, **Casale** held out and the ensuing peace secured Nevers his inheritance (13 October 1629–18 July 1630).

Mantua ❙ 1796–1797 ❙ French Revolutionary Wars (1st Coalition)

Napoleon Bonaparte captured most of northern Italy, where he besieged the powerful city of Mantua. He then withdrew to fight a fresh Austrian army under General Dagobert Wurmser. After Austrian defeats at **Lonato** and **Castiglione**, Wurmser was trapped in a renewed siege of Mantua and capitulated with terrible losses (4 June–30 July 1796; 24 August 1796–2 February 1797).

Manupur ❙ 1748 ❙ Indian Campaigns of Ahmad Shah

Following the death of Persian Emperor Nadir Shah, General Ahmad Shah Durrani seized Persian Afghanistan and launched the first of many invasions of India. At Manupur, in the Punjab northwest of Sirhind, he was heavily repulsed by Mughal Prince Ahmad after Vizier Qamruddin was killed. Durrani's later expeditions yielded him much of northern India (11 March 1748).

Manus ❙ 1944 ❙ World War II (Pacific)

Having taken **Los Negros**, in the **Admiralty Islands** west of **Rabaul**, American commander General Innis Swift sent General Verne Mudge west against the larger island of Manus, aided by massive artillery and bomber support. The small Japanese garrison held out for a week of heavy fighting before the island was secured and the survivors retreated into the jungle (12–25 March 1944).

Manzikert ❙ 1054 ❙ Seljuk Wars of Expansion

On a fresh Seljuk offensive into Byzantine Armenia after victory at **Hasankale** (September 1048), Kutalmish invested Kars while the Sultan Toghril Beg captured Arjish, then laid siege to Manzikert, north of Lake Van. When the Greeks counter-attacked to burn his siege machines, and heavy snow fell, Toghril withdrew to **Rayy**. His nephew and successor won a great victory here 15 years later.

Manzikert ❙ 1071 ❙ Byzantine-Turkish Wars

In a final effort against Turkish invasion of Anatolia and Armenia after his defeat at **Sebastia**, Byzantine Emperor Romanus IV led a large army—including many Western mercenaries—to Manzikert (modern Malazgirt) near Lake Van, against the Seljuk Alp Arslan. One of the medieval world's decisive battles saw Romanus defeated and captured, leading directly to the Crusades (19 August 1071).

Mao Khé ❙ 1951 ❙ French Indo-China War

Viet Minh commander Vo Nguyen Giap was heavily repulsed at **Vinh Yen** (17 January), but began a new attack in the **Red River Delta** at Mao Khé, northwest of Haiphong, where a small garrison held out. Next day bombardment by French warships broke up the advance before paratroops arrived. A final Viet Minh frontal assault cost 400 killed before Giap was forced to withdraw (23–28 March 1951).

Maqonqo ❙ 1840 ❙ Zulu Wars of Succession

A year after his terrible loss to the Boers at **Blood River**, Zulu King Dingane faced a coup by his brother Mpande. Dingane's army under Ndlela suffered a crushing defeat in battle at Maqonqo, near the Mkuzi River north of Nongoma, which cost both sides over 1,000 dead. The King fled to the north and a month later

Mpande was acknowledged as the new Zulu monarch (30 January 1840).

Marabout **|** 1801 **|** French Revolutionary Wars (Middle East)

See **Alexandria (2nd)**

Maracaibo **|** 1823 **|** Venezuelan War of Independence

Two years after victory at **Carabobo**, the ultimate battle for Independence was fought along the western shore of Lake Maracaibo between the Patriot navy of General José Padilla (with troops under General Manuel Manrique) and Royalists Admiral Angel Laborde and General Francisco Tomás Morales. After a decisive naval defeat Spain finally abandoned Venezuela (24 July 1823).

Maracesti **|** 1917 **|** World War I (Balkan Front)

In support of the **Kerensky Offensive** in Galicia, Russo-Romanian forces in Moldavia under Generals Andrei Zayonchovsky and Alexandru Averescu advanced north of Focsani around Maracesti against Bulgarian-German forces under August von Mackensen. Though Averescu eventually held the line, the Russians were forced to withdraw and Romania soon sued for peace (6–28 August 1917).

Maragheh **|** 1760 **|** Persian Wars of Succession

Azad Kahn of Azerbaijan recovered from his terrible defeat at **Urmiya** in July 1757, raising fresh forces in Kurdistan to advance towards Tabriz. Southeast of Tabriz at Maragheh, Azad met a confederation of his former allies led by Fath Ali Khan Afshar and Shahbaz Khan Donboli. The Azerbaijani leader was utterly defeated in a decisive battle and took refuge in Georgia (July 1760).

Marais des Cygnes **|** 1864 **|** American Civil War (Trans-Mississippi)

As he retreated south from defeat near Kansas City, Missouri, at **Westport**, Confederate General Sterling Price was attacked near Trading Post by Union General Alfred Pleasonton. At Marais des Cygnes his rearguard under Generals John S. Marmaduke and James F. Fagan fought a holding action before falling back to join Price in a better defensive position at **Mine Creek** (25 October 1864).

Maraita **|** 1907 **|** Nicaraguan-Honduran War

President José Santos Zelaya of Nicaragua invaded Honduras to win at **San Marcos de Colón** and **Namasigue**, while another invading force under José María Valladares advanced on Maraita, southeast of Tegucicalpa. Bloody fighting saw Honduran General Sotero Barahona defeated and killed and the capital fell. President Manuel Bonilla fled into exile, replaced by Miguel Dávila (22–23 March 1907).

Marakesh **|** 1912 **|** French Colonial Wars in North Africa

See **Sidi Ben Othman**

Marathon **|** 490 BC **|** Greco-Persian Wars

Darius I of Persia recovered Greek Ionia at **Lade**, then sent Artaphernes and Datis against Eretria and Athens, which had aided the rebels. The Persians landed at Marathon, northeast of Athens, and were routed by Callimachus and Miltiades. Losing 6,400 killed for just 192 Athenians (including Callimachus) the Persians withdrew, but returned in 480 BC at **Thermopylae** (12 September 490 BC).

Marauder **|** 1966 **|** Vietnam War

See **Plain of Reeds**

Marbella **|** 1705 **|** War of the Spanish Succession

Sent to relieve the Franco-Spanish siege of **Gibraltar**, Admiral Sir John Leake, reinforced by Sir Thomas Dilkes and Dutch and Portuguese ships, pursued French commander Jean-Bernard Desjeans Baron de Pointis east through the Strait of Gibraltar to Marbella. With three French ships taken and two burned to avoid capture, de Pointis withdrew and the siege was raised (10 March 1705).

Marcellae ∎ 759 ∎ Byzantine-Bulgarian Wars

Emperor Constantine V repulsed Bulgar raids on Byzantine territory, then personally led an army into Bulgaria and met his enemy northwest of Burgas at Marcellae (near modern Karnobad). Constantine won a bloody battle, though both sides suffered costly losses and agreed on a truce. The Bulgars later renewed the war and were defeated in June 763 at **Anchialus**.

Marcellae ∎ 792 ∎ Byzantine-Bulgarian Wars

Determined to assert his authority, the 21-year-old Byzantine Emperor Constantine VI overthrew his mother, the Regent Irene, then unwisely marched into Bulgaria, where he came under attack by the Khan Kardam at Marcellae (near modern Karnobad). Constantine suffered a humiliating defeat and fled. He then restored his mother as Empress, but she later deposed and blinded him.

Marchfeld ∎ 1278 ∎ Bohemian Wars

Two years after the Habsburg King Rudolf of Germany captured Vienna from Ottokar II of Bohemia, his powerful rival returned with a large army. On the Plain of Marchfeld, north of Vienna, the Bohemian King was defeated and killed by a massive force under Rudolf and his ally Ladislav IV of Hungary. Victory established Habsburg dominance in Austria (26 August 1278).

Marchfeld ∎ 1809 ∎ Napoleonic Wars (5th Coalition)

See **Aspern-Essling**

Marciano ∎ 1554 ∎ 5th Habsburg-Valois War

During the 15-month siege of **Siena** by Imperial forces under Gian Medecino Marquis of Marignano, a French army led by Pietro Strozzi approached to try and relieve the Republic. Strozzi's relief army was utterly defeated east of Siena at Marciano. Medecino then returned to the siege of Siena, which held out until April

1555 before starvation forced surrender (2 August 1554).

Marcianopolis ∎ 377 ∎ 5th Gothic War

Goths under Fritigern and Alvivus crossed the Danube with the permission of Emperor Valens (376), but war soon broke out against Governor Lupicinus, who had failed in an attempt to assassinate the Goth chiefs. Outside Marcianopolis (modern Preslav, Bulgaria), the local Roman army was annihilated. Valens himself then marched to Thrace and died in a disastrous defeat at **Adrianople**.

Marco Polo Bridge ∎ 1937 ∎ Sino-Japanese War

Under pretext of conducting a military exercise, Japanese troops clashed with Chinese at Marco Polo Bridge (Lugouqiao) just outside Beijing, triggering an undeclared war. Colonel Ji Xingwen was driven off and Chinese commander Song Zheyuan negotiated a truce. A few days later, the Japanese were reinforced and began their attack on Tianjin and **Beijing** (7 July 1937).

Marda ∎ 1977 ∎ Ogaden War

Somali forces invaded the Ogaden in southeastern Ethiopia, then advanced through **Jijiga** to the strategic pass at Marda (Karamarda) in the Ahmar Mountains. Overwhelmed by tanks and air-strikes, the Ethiopian army suffered a decisive defeat, opening the way to **Harer**. Somalis later dug in to defend Marda, but were bypassed by the Ethiopian counter-offensive of February 1978 (29 September 1977).

Mardia ∎ 317 ∎ Roman Wars of Succession

See **Campus Ardiensis**

Mardon ∎ 871 ∎ Viking Wars in Britain

See **Merton**

Mared ∎ 1563 ∎ Nordic Seven Years War

After invading Danish Halland and failing in an attempt on **Halmstad**, the defeated Swedes came under attack by Frederick II of Denmark while withdrawing at nearby Mared. The Swedes were beaten when their cavalry fled, though a courageous defensive action under Klas Kristersson Horn and Charles de Mornay saved the withdrawing army from complete destruction (9 November 1563).

Marengo I 1799 I French Revolutionary Wars (2nd Coalition)
See **Alessandria**

Marengo I 1800 I French Revolutionary Wars (2nd Coalition)
At Marengo, near the Lombard city of Alessandria, Austrian Baron Michael von Melas attacked the unprepared French and defeated General Claude Victor. However, a counter-attack by General Louis Desaix and a fine cavalry charge by General Francois Kellerman routed the Austrians, though Desaix was killed. A further defeat at **Höchstädt** made Austria sue for peace (14 June 1800).

Mareth Line I 1943 I World War II (Northern Africa)
British General Sir Bernard Montgomery brushed aside an Axis spoiling attack at **Médenine** (6 March), then launched a major assault on the Mareth Line in southern Tunisia, held by General Giovanni Messe. After initial failure, a flanking attack across the Matmata Hills by New Zealand General Bernard Freyberg broke through the Tebaga Gap and Messe fell back to **Wadi Akarit** (20–27 March 1943).

Marga I 1946 I Indonesian War of Independence
Determined to restore order, Dutch forces attacked the stubborn nationalist I Gusti Ngurah Rai on Bali. Surrounded and massively outnumbered, the 29-year-old Colonel and 94 guerrillas refused to surrender and died to a man in a suicidal stand reminiscent of the puputan at **Denpasar** 40 years earlier. Although Balinese resistance was crushed, the Dutch left three years later (20 November 1946).

Margalef I 1810 I Napoleonic Wars (Peninsular Campaign)
Catalan General Henry O'Donnell was advancing to relieve the siege of **Lérida**, when his vanguard led by General Miguel de Ibarrola was surprised six miles from Lérida at Margalef by a large French force under General Louis Musnier. By the time O'Donnell arrived, the French cuirassiers had killed 500 and taken more than 2,000 Spanish prisoners and he hastily withdrew (23 April 1810).

Margate I 1387 I Hundred Years War
In a short-lived period of French authority at sea after victory at **La Rochelle**, Duke Louis of Anjou, Regent for Charles VI, sent his fleet on an ill-prepared invasion of England. Off Margate, Kent, the French-Castilian fleet was destroyed by English ships under Richard Fitzalan Earl of Arundel and Thomas Mowbray Earl of Nottingham, ending the threat of invasion (24 March 1387).

Margus I 285 I Roman Military Civil Wars
When Aurelius Carinus, commander in the East, became Emperor, he was soon opposed by Diocletian, who was elevated by the Army of Asia. Setting out from Gaul with a large, well-disciplined force, Carinus defeated the usurper on the Margus (modern Morava) in Serbia. However, he was killed in the moment of victory by dissident officers and Diocletian was proclaimed Emperor.

Margus I 505 I Gothic War in Italy
See **Horreum Margi**

Maria I 1809 I Napoleonic Wars (Peninsular Campaign)
Spanish General Joachim Blake repulsed new French commander General Louis Suchet at **Alcaniz** in May, then led his Army of the Right northwest to threaten the key city of Saragossa, on the Ebro. Near the small town of Maria, in the Huebra Valley south of Saragossa, Blake was defeated by Suchet with heavy losses in men and

guns and withdrew east towards **Belchite** (15 June 1809).

Maria de la Cabeza I 1936–1937 I Spanish Civil War

With the loss of **Oveida**, the monastery of Maria de la Cabeza, north of Andujar, was the last rebel outpost in the north, held by 2,000 Civil Guards and civilians under Captain Santiago Cortés. In a determined assault to crush the stubborn resistance, about 20,000 Republicans under Colonel Carlos García Vallejo finally took it by storm. Cortés died of his wounds (22 August 1936–1 May 1937).

Mariana Islands I 1944 I World War II (Pacific)

American forces in the central Pacific under General Holland Smith and Admiral Kelly Turner advanced north from the **Marshall Islands** into the Mariana Islands, defended by Admiral Chuichi Nagumo and General Hideyoshi Obata. Bloody fighting secured **Saipan**, **Guam** and **Tinian**, and with them the vital airfields for B-29 bombers to attack the Japanese homeland (June–August 1944).

Marias I 1870 I Piegan Indian Expedition

Colonel Eugene Baker was sent to the Marias River in northern Montana against hostile Piegan under Mountain Chief, but instead he attacked the nearby camp of the friendly Chief Heavy Runner. In a dawn massacre in extreme cold, Heavy Runner and 172 other Piegan were killed, including many women and children. About 140 more were captured, along with over 300 horses (23 January 1870).

Maria Zell I 1805 I Napoleonic Wars (3rd Coalition)

As Napoleon Bonaparte advanced towards Vienna after victory at **Ulm**, French Marshal Louis Davout caught up with a retreating Austrian force under Count Maximilian von Merveldt at Maria Zell, east of **Durrenstein**. The Austrians suffered a sharp defeat with a heavy loss of prisoners and Bonaparte continued on to capture Vienna, a week later (8 November 1805).

Marienthal I 1645 I Thirty Years War (Franco-Habsburg War)

See **Mergentheim**

Marienwerder I 1629 I 2nd Polish-Swedish War

See **Sztum**

Marietta I 1864 I American Civil War (Western Theatre)

While General William T. Sherman's Union army advanced through Georgia, Confederate commander Joseph E. Johnston was forced out of Allatoona following defeat at **Dallas** and withdrew east to defensive positions around Marietta. After three weeks of inconclusive action Johnson secured victory at nearby **Kennesaw Mountain**, then slowly fell back on **Atlanta** (10 June–3 July 1864).

Marignano I 1515 I War of the Holy League

When Francis I of France invaded Lombardy, where the Swiss held a virtual protectorate in alliance with the Pope, a two-day battle at Marignano, south of Milan, saw the hitherto invincible Swiss pikemen defeated by artillery combined with ferocious cavalry. The Swiss withdrew across the Alps and the Pope sued for peace, leaving the French in Milan (13–14 September 1515).

Marignano I 1859 I 2nd Italian War of Independence

See **Melegnano**

Marigüeñu I 1554 I Spanish Conquest of Chile

Following the execution of Pedro de Valdivia after defeat at **Tucapel**, new Spanish Governor Francisco de Villagrán assembled an army in Concepción and marched south across the Bio Bio, where he was attacked at Marigüeñu by up to 8,000 Araucanian Indians under Lautaro. Villagrán suffered a terrible defeat and abandoned Concepción, which was twice sacked by Lautaro (23 February 1554).

Marion | 1864 | American Civil War (Western Theatre)

On a second Union raid into southwest Virginia against the vital saltworks at Saltville, General George Stoneman advanced from Knoxville and led a feint against the leadworks at nearby Marion. Confederate General John C. Breckinridge moved east to try and protect Marion, but after a brief skirmish, Stoneman eluded pursuit and marched west to attack **Saltville** (17–18 December 1864).

Maritza | 1363 | Ottoman Conquest of the Balkans

During the first united Christian campaign against growing Ottoman power, Serbian and Bosnian forces joined Louis the Great of Hungary advancing to the Maritza in southern Bulgaria against Lala Shahin Pasha. Hadji Ilbeki completely destroyed the Christians in a brilliant unauthorised attack and Louis only just escaped with his life. Ilbeki was later allegedly poisoned by his jealous commander.

Maritza | 1371 | Ottoman Conquest of the Balkans

When the Despot Vukashin Mernitchevitch and his brother Ugliecha secured southern Serbia, they were threatened by Sultan Murad I who retook **Adrianople**. Their attempted counter-offensive was defeated on the Maritza near Cernomen, where both brothers were killed. Murad seized much of southern Bulgaria and the remainder fell after victory at **Samokov** and **Kossovo** (26 September 1371).

Marjal-Saffar | 635 | Muslim Conquest of Syria

See **Marj as-Suffar**

Marj as-Suffar | 635 | Muslim Conquest of Syria

Continuing his advance towards Damascus, the great Muslim commander Khalid ibn al-Walid drove back the Byzantine General Baanes at **Fihl**, then a month later faced a last-ditch Byzantine stand at Marj as-Suffar, 20 miles south of Damascus, northeast of the Sea of Galilee. Baanes was again defeated and the Arabs moved forward to lay siege to **Damascus** (25 February 635).

Marj-Dabik | 1516 | Ottoman-Mamluk War

Sultan Selim I defeated Persia at **Chaldiran** and **Turna Dag**, then turned to meet a flank attack from Persia's Mamluk allies in the south in Syria. Using disciplined infantry and newly introduced mass artillery, Selim overcame and killed Mamluk Sultan Kansu al-Gauri north of Aleppo at Marj-Dabik. Victory at **Yaunis Khan** in October completed Selim's conquest of Syria (24 August 1516).

Marj Rahit | 634 | Muslim Conquest of Syria

The Muslim commander Khalid ibn al-Walid was recalled from Mesopotamia after victory at **Firadz** in January to support the conquest of Byzantine Syria, marching west through the desert to inflict a sharp defeat on a Byzantine force at Marj Rahit, east of Damascus, traditionally on Easter Sunday. He then joined the main Muslim forces in Palestine for victory at **Ajnadin** and at the **Yarmuk**.

Marj Rahit | 684 | Muslim Civil Wars

Following the death of the Umayyad Caliph Yazid I and his short-lived and feeble son Mu'awiya II, the former Regent Merwan ibn al-Hakam was appointed Caliph in Damascus, while the rebel Abdullah ibn Zubair continued to be recognised as Caliph in Arabia and Egypt. Near Damascus, at Marj Rahit, the Zubair faction was decisively defeated and Merwan reclaimed Syria.

Marks' Mills I 1864 I American Civil War (Trans-Mississippi)

After capturing Camden, Arkansas, Union General Frederick Steele lost a foraging party to the west at **Poison Spring**, then sent Colonel Francis Drake with a supply train northeast to Pine Bluff. Attacked by General James B. Fagan at Marks' Mills, west of the Saline, Drake lost the wagons and was captured with most of his men. Steele soon retreated through **Jenkins' Ferry** (25 April 1864).

Marmiton I 1864 I American Civil War (Trans-Mississippi)

Confederate General Sterling Price retreating south from defeat at **Westport**, Missouri, suffered terrible losses at **Mine Creek**, then attempted to make a stand at the Marmiton River, east of Fort Scott. Defeated by General John H. McNeil, Price destroyed an estimated 400 wagons to prevent their capture. His shattered force then continued south through Carthage to **Newtonia** (25 October 1864).

Marne I 1914 I World War I (Western Front)

As German commander Helmuth von Moltke swept into France through Belgium, his army was struck in the flank east of Paris along the Marne by the Anglo-French Allies under Marshal Joseph Joffre. One of history's decisive actions saw the German offensive halted and Paris was saved. The Germans had to withdraw to the **Aisne** and von Moltke was replaced (5–9 September 1914).

Marne I 1918 I World War I (Western Front)

When German commander Erich von Ludendorff launched his fifth and final offensive on the Marne around Rheims, Generals Bruno von Mudra and Karl von Einem enjoyed initial success, then faced a massive Allied counteroffensive under Marshal Ferdinand Foch. Threatened in the flank, the Germans withdrew and the Allies soon won again at **Amiens** and **Arras** (15 July –5 August 1918).

Marqab I 1285 I Later Crusader-Muslim Wars

Mamluk Sultan Qalawun led a renewed campaign against the Crusader States and laid siege to the Hospitaller fortress near the Syrian coast at Marqab. Attacking with siege machines from Damascus, he eventually forced the knights to surrender. They were permitted to leave without their arms and possessions and the Sultan marched south to capture **Tripoli** (17 April–25 May 1285).

Marsaglia I 1693 I War of the Grand Alliance

Victory at **Staffarda** in 1690 gave France Savoy and Piedmont. However, the defeated Duke Victor Amadeus of Savoy obtained Austrian and English reinforcements and invaded Dauphiné. French Marshal Nicolas Catinat once more crossed the Alps and, at Marsaglia southwest of Turin near Staffarda, Catinat again defeated the Duke, who eventually made a separate peace (4 October 1693).

Marseilles I 49 BC I Wars of the First Triumvirate
See **Massilia**

Marseilles I 413 I Goth Invasion of the Roman Empire
See **Massilia**

Marseilles I 1524 I 1st Habsburg-Valois War

After repulsing a French invasion of Lombardy, Imperial commanders Charles Duke of Bourbon and Fernando d'Avalos Marquis of Pescara invaded France and besieged Marseilles. With the Imperial navy defeated at sea off Marseilles, the garrison under Renzo da Ceri held out until Francis I aproached with a relief army. The invaders then had to withdraw (19 August–29 September 1524).

Marseilles I 1536 I 3rd Habsburg-Valois War

With Emperor Charles V occupied in **Tunis**, Francis I of France invaded northern Italy and

Charles returned to attack in the south of France. Notwithstanding the costly Imperial repulse at Marseilles in 1524, Charles personally led a large force against the city. After two months of siege, disease and lack of ammunition forced his withdrawal and Pope Paul III negotiated a ten-year truce.

Marseilles ❙ 1793 ❙ French Revolutionary Wars (1st Coalition)

General Jean-Baptiste-Francois Carteaux was sent against Royalist insurrection in the south of France where he took 2,500 men down the Rhone and defeated the rebels at Orange and Cadenet, then continued south and forced his way into Marseilles. He soon marched east to join the siege of **Toulon**, but his military competence was called into question and he was relieved of command (25 August 1793).

Marseilles ❙ 1944 ❙ World War II (Western Europe)

When Allied forces invaded southern France along the **Riviera**, Free French Commander Jean de Lattre de Tassigny ordered General Joseph Goislard de Monsabert against Marseilles, France's largest port. Severe fighting, including a Resistance uprising in the city, forced the German garrison of 11,000 to surrender. Marseilles and **Toulon** became key Allied supply ports (22–28 August 1944).

Marshall Islands ❙ 1944 ❙ World War II (Pacific)

With the **Gilbert Islands** won, American Admiral Ray Spruance and General Holland Smith continued 500 miles north into the Marshalls. The key Kwajalein Atoll was secured at **Roi-Namur** and **Kwajalein**, followed by the **Eniwetok** Atoll 350 miles to the west (supported by a massive attack on **Truk**), opening the way for the next offensive north into the **Mariana Islands** (1–20 February 1944).

Mars-la-Tour ❙ 1870 ❙ Franco-Prussian War

Prince Friedrich Karl of Prussia attempting to intercept the French west of the Moselle after

Colombey defeated Marshal Francois-Achille Bazaine's left flank at Mars-la-Tour, while General Konstantin von Alvensleben secured nearby Vionville. But at Rezonville the Prussians were checked by Marshal Francois-Antoine Canrobert, while Bazaine retired through **Gravelotte** (16 August 1870).

Marston Moor ❙ 1644 ❙ British Civil Wars

Defending the Parliamentary siege of **York, England**, Prince Rupert and William Cavendish Earl of Newcastle were met on nearby Marston Moor by Ferdinando Lord Fairfax, Edward Montagu Earl of Manchester and Scots under Alexander Leslie Earl of Leven. More than 3,000 Royalists died in a bloody rout and the fall of York meant the north was effectively lost (2 July 1644).

Martaban ❙ 1824 ❙ 1st British-Burmese War

When Burma conquered Arakan and attacked British India, General Sir Archibald Campbell secured Rangoon (May 1824), then sent Colonel (later General) Henry Godwin and naval Lieutenant Charles Keele 100 miles east against the fortress at Martaban, on the Salween opposite Moulmien. They stormed the stockade after three days, capturing a massive store of arms and ammunition (30 October 1824).

Martaban ❙ 1852 ❙ 2nd British-Burmese War

Britain resumed war with Burma for commercial gain and General Henry Godwin and Admiral Charles Austen attacked Martaban, at the mouth of the Salween opposite Moulmein, held by 5,000 experienced Burmese troops. The city fell by storm and a few days later Godwin secured **Rangoon** before advancing northwest against **Bassein, Burma** (5 April 1852).

Martinesti ❙ 1789 ❙ Catherine the Great's 2nd Turkish War

See **Rimnik**.

Martín García I 1814 I Argentine War of Independence

During an attack on the Spanish fleet block-ading Buenos Aires, Argentine Commodore William Brown was repulsed near the island of Martín García, with American-born Captain Benjamin Franklin Seaver killed. A second at-tack five days later saw Spanish commander Jacinto de Romarate defeated and he withdrew up the Uruguay River towards **Arroyo de la China** (11 & 16 March 1814).

Martinici I 1796 I Montenegran-Scutari War

Mahmud Pasha Bustalija of Shkoder (Scutari) and 18,000 Turks who invaded Montenegro were met in the Zeta Valley north of Podgorica at Martinici, near the fortress of Spuz, by a claimed 3,000 men under Peter I of Montenegro. Bustalija was wounded and badly defeated and his reinforced army suffered an even more de-cisive defeat two months later at **Krusi** (11 July 1796).

Martinique I 1667 I 2nd Dutch War

Shortly after arriving in the West Indies, new English Admiral Sir John Harman was repulsed attempting to recapture St Christopher, then took his large force against more than twenty French warships at Martinique following their defeat at **Nevis**. In a one-sided action, Admiral Joseph de La Barre suffered a major disaster, with just two or three ships escaping destruction (25 June 1667).

Martinique I 1759 I Seven Years War (Caribbean)

British General Sir Peregrine Hopson and Commodore John Moore led an attempted of-fensive in the French West Indies, where they successfully landed on Martinique at Fort Royal. However, when heavy surf prevented unloading of their guns the ineffectual Hopson withdrew with over 100 casualties. The expedition then turned its attention instead to **Guadeloupe** (16–18 January 1759).

Martinique I 1762 I Seven Years War (Caribbean)

Following the conquest of French Canada, Britain captured **Dominica** and Admiral George Rodney and General Sir Robert Monckton lan-ded on Martinique. Reinforced by General An-drew Lord Rollo, Monckton captured Port Royal and Martinique soon surrendered. Nearby St Lucia was taken without fighting and both were returned to France after the war (16 January–12 February 1762).

Martinique I 1780 I War of the American Revolution

When Admiral Luc-Urbain Comte de Guichen sailed from Martinique to attack Barbados, fleet and troop convoys were intercepted near Marti-nique by British Admiral George Rodney. After a confused drawn action, with heavy casualties on both sides, the French abandoned their expedition and withdrew to Guadeloupe. Rodney blamed his subordinates for the failure (17 April 1780).

Martinique I 1781 I War of the American Revolution

British commander George Rodney took **St Eustatius** in the West Indies (3 February), then sent Admiral Sir Samuel Hood (1724–1816) with an inadequate force to intercept a large con-voy from France, escorted by Admiral Francois-Joseph de Grasse. In battle off Martinique, Hood's outnumbered squadron was driven off with heavy damage and the French convoy ar-rived safely in Port Royal (29 April 1781).

Martinique I 1793 I French Revolutionary Wars (1st Coalition)

While campaigning against French territory in the West Indies, Admiral Sir Alan Gardner sailed from Barbados against Martinique with French Royalist troops and 3,000 British regu-lars. The troops under General Thomas Bruce landed but were repulsed after five days. Marti-nique remained under French Republican rule until a further attack the following February (16–21 June 1793).

Martinique ▌ 1794 ▌ French Revolutionary Wars (1st Coalition)

A British expedition from Barbados under Admiral Sir John Jervis and General Sir Charles Grey renewed the attack on France in the West Indies, where they landed on Martinique and quickly captured St Pierre. With the fall of the strongpoints Fort Royal and Fort Louis, Governor Donatien Rochambeau surrendered. Jervis and Grey went on to capture **St Lucia** (5 February–23 March 1794).

Martinique ▌ 1809 ▌ Napoleonic Wars (5th Coalition)

The West Indian island of Martinique was returned to France in 1802, but the resumption of war saw Britain mount a fresh expedition to recover the colony. Captain Sir Thomas Cochrane and General Sir George Beckwith landed with their force and, after sharp fighting, French Governor Admiral Louis Villaret de Joyeuse was forced to surrender (30 January–24 February 1809).

Martinsbruch ▌ 1799 ▌ French Revolutionary Wars (2nd Coalition)

Determined to prevent the union in Switzerland of the French Army of the Rhine and General Jean-Joseph Dessoles advancing from Italy, Austrian Field Marshal Johann Loudon turned first against General Claude-Jacques Lecourbe approaching from the north. At Martinsbruch (modern Martina), the Austrian repulsed Lecourbe, but he was beaten by Desoles a week later at **Tauffes** (17 March 1799).

Martin's Point ▌ 1840 ▌ 2nd Seminole Indian War

Marching towards Wacahoota from Fort Micanopy, south of Gainesville, Florida, Lieutenant Walter Sherwood and a small patrol were ambushed by Seminole under Halleck Tustenuggee at Martin's Point, close to a previous ambush site at **Bridgewater, Florida**. Before aid could be sent from the fort, Sherwood, four soldiers and an officer's wife under escort had been killed (28 December 1840).

Martin's Station ▌ 1780 ▌ War of the American Revolution
    See **Ruddle's Station**

Marton ▌ 871 ▌ Viking Wars in Britain
    See **Merton**

Martynow ▌ 1624 ▌ Polish-Tatar Wars

Stanislas Koniecpolski was ransomed from captivity after **Cecora** (1620) and led a Polish force against Tatars at Martynow, in the southern Ukraine northeast of Ivano-Frankovsk. Koniecpolski won a decisive victory and was created Palatine of Sandomierz by a grateful Sigismund III. Over the next 20 years he defeated the Tatars again at **Sasowy Rog**, **Kamieniec** and **Okhmatov** (20 June 1624).

Martyropolis ▌ 588 ▌ Byzantine-Persian Wars

Despite mutiny in the east against army pay reforms, Germanus invaded Persia, where he was checked by Sassanian General Marouzas and fell back to the frontier city of Martyropolis (modern Silvan in Armenia). Germanus killed Marouzas and took 3,000 prisoners, but the next year the city was betrayed to the Persians. It was later recovered for helping restore Chosroes II after **Ganzak** in 591.

Maruchak ▌ 1507 ▌ Mughal-Uzbek Wars

Uzbek conqueror Muhammad Shaybani Khan drove the Mughal Babur from **Samarkand** (1501), then marched southwest into the Khorasan, where he was met by Dhu'l-Nun, the Arghunid Mughal Governor of Kandahar. Dhu'l-Nun was defeated and killed in battle at Maruchak, on the Murghab River near Bala Morghab. His son Shah Beg retained **Kandahar** as an Uzbek vassal.

Masada ▌ 72–73 ▌ Jewish Rising against Rome

Facing rebellion in Judea, Roman forces stormed **Jerusalem** (70) then systematically crushed resistance, besieging the last Jewish stronghold near the Dead Sea at Masada, held by Zealots under Eleazor ben Yair. Threatened by perhaps 15,000 men under Flavius Silva, the entire garrison of over 900 men, women and children finally killed themselves rather than be captured (72 AD–15 April 73).

Masaguara ❙ 1856 ❙ Central American National Wars

Guatemala and Honduras agreed a truce following action at **Omoa** in 1853 to meet the threat of American Filibusters, later resuming their border war. In southwest Honduras at Masaguara, Honduran President José Trinidad Cabañas was defeated by Guatemalans under Juan López. Cabañas was soon overthrown and the combatants united again to meet the Filibusters at **Granada, Nicaragua** (6 October 1856).

Masaya ❙ 1856 ❙ National (Filibuster) War

With American Filibuster William Walker defeated in southwest Nicaragua at **Rivas**, the Central America allies took Masaya, 50 miles to the north. An attempt by Colonel John Waters to retake Masaya was repulsed by José Victor Zavala of Guatemala and Jose Maria Estrada of Nicaragua. After a second costly failure, Walker fell back on **Granada** (13 October & 15–17 November 1856).

Mascara ❙ 1835 ❙ French Conquest of Algeria

In the campaign to complete the conquest of western Algeria, France faced the Arab warrior Abd-el-Kader, who established his capital at Mascara, southeast of Oran. Following defeat at Moulay Ishmael and **Macta**, France sent fresh forces under Marshal Bertrand Clausel, who defeated Kader and took Mascara. However, the Arab fought on until eventual defeat at **Smala** and **Isly** (November 1835).

Maserfield ❙ 641 ❙ Anglo-Saxon Territorial Wars

Threatened by the growing power of Northumbria, Penda of Mercia challenged King Oswald at Maserfield (probably Oswestry) in Shropshire. In a repeat of his victory over Edwin of Northumbria at **Heathfield**, Penda now defeated and killed Oswald, who was Edwin's ne-

phew and successor. Northumbrian supremacy was restored in 655 at **Winwaed** (5 August 641).

Masindi ❙ 1872 ❙ Egyptian Wars of Expansion

Sir Samuel Baker, Viceroy of the Egyptian Khedive, advanced south into the Nile basin, where he annexed Bunyoro in northern Uganda, then came under attack by King Kabarega. At Masindi, east of Lake Albert, Baker's 200-strong force repulsed the Bunyoro with heavy losses. However, continued skirmishing forced Baker to burn his stores and endure a costly retreat to the Nile (8 June 1872).

Maskat ❙ 1507 ❙ Portuguese Colonial Wars in Arabia
See **Muscat**

Maskat ❙ 1650 ❙ Later Portuguese Colonial Wars in Arabia
See **Muscat**

Maskin ❙ 701 ❙ Muslim Civil Wars

When Ibn al-Ash'ath in the east rebelled against the Umayyad Caliph, he was defeated near Kufa at **Dayr al-Jamajim** by Governor al-Hajjaj of Iraq and retreated north to Maskin on the Shatt al-Dujayl. There, al-Hajjaj inflicted a terrible defeat, with many drowned in the river trying to escape. Ibn al-Ash'ath fled and bloody retribution against his supporters ended the insurrection (October 701).

Massacre Canyon ❙ 1873 ❙ Sioux Indian Wars

While hunting buffalo in southwest Nebraska under the protection of Fort McPherson, about 350 peaceful Pawnee were unexpectedly attacked near modern Trenton by a large war party of Brulé and Oglala Sioux under Chief Snow Flake. Army help arrived too late and up to 100 Pawnee were slaughtered, including Sky Chief. The site was later known as Massacre Canyon (5 August 1873).

Massacre Hill ❙ 1866 ❙ Red Cloud's War
See **Fetterman Massacre**

Massawa ▮ 1941 ▮ World War II (Northern Africa)

After British forces in Eritrea captured **Keren** and Asmara, General Lewis Heath was sent east against Massawa. Italian Admiral Mario Bonetti demolished much of the Red Sea port before the British and Free French stormed in with tanks to seize the last Italian stronghold in Eritrea. Bonetti surrendered almost 10,000 men and the Allies turned south towards **Amba Alagi** (8 April 1941).

Massawa ▮ 1977 ▮ Eritrean War of Independence

At the high-water mark of their urban offensive, Eritrean forces attacked the port of Massawa and seized most of the city. However, a frontal assault on the nearby naval base was driven off, with 200 killed and 400 wounded, by Ethiopian tanks supported by shelling from Ethiopian and Soviet warships. The rebels tried to maintain a siege but were later forced to withdraw (21–31 December 1977).

Massawa ▮ 1990 ▮ Eritrean War of Independence

With rebel forces on the offensive throughout Eritrea, a land and sea attack was launched against Massawa, where speedboats sank most of the Ethiopian warships in the harbour. The city and naval base were taken with very heavy losses on both sides. After the surrender Ethiopian aircraft bombed the city for ten days, causing massive damage and civilian losses (8–16 February 1990).

Massilia ▮ 49 BC ▮ Wars of the First Triumvirate

Julius Caesar marched into Gaul and besieged Massilia (modern Marseilles) held for his rival Pompey by Lucius Domitius Ahenobarbus. He then departed for Spain, leaving Gaius Trebonius to maintain the siege, aided at sea by Decimus Brutus. Ships sent by Pompey were repulsed and, when Caesar returned from victory at **Ilerda**, Domitius fled and the city fell (March–6 September 49 BC).

Massilia ▮ 413 ▮ Goth Invasion of the Roman Empire

On campaign in southern Gaul, the Visigoth Ataulf took Toulouse and Narbonne, then besieged the key Roman city of Massilia (modern Marseilles) defended by the powerful Roman General John Bonifacius. However, Ataulf failed to take Massilia and later made peace with Emperor Honorius, marrying the Emperor's sister Placidia. He was later sent to recover Spain for the empire.

Masterby ▮ 1361 ▮ Wars of the Hanseatic League
See **Visby**

Masts ▮ 654 ▮ Early Byzantine-Muslim Wars
See **Mount Phoenix**

Mastung ▮ 1758 ▮ Baluchi Rebellion

After defeats in the Punjab for the Afghan ruler Ahmad Shah Durrani, his former General, Baluchi Chief Nasir Khan, declared independence. Ahmad sent his vizier to attack the rebel at Kalat, but further north near Mastung the Afghan army was badly beaten. Ahmad Shah himself then arrived to besiege Kalat. After failed assaults he made peace and accepted homage from Nasir Khan.

Masulipatam ▮ 1759 ▮ Seven Years War (India)

To take pressure off the British in **Madras**, Governor Robert Clive of Bengal sent Colonel Francis Forde south from Calcutta to support Raja Ananda Raj against the French under Herbert de Brienne Comte de Conflans. After victory at **Condore**, Forde besieged then stormed the key coastal town of Masulipatam. Conflans surrendered with almost 3,000 men (6 March–8 April 1759).

Masumpur ▮ 1760 ▮ Seven Years War (India)

Renewing the Mughal invasion of Bengal following defeat at **Patna** (April 1759), Emperor Shah Alam II and General Kamgar Khan marched on Patna, defended by Raja Ramnarain who met them at Masumpur, east of Futwar. Ramnarain was heavily defeated when three of his divisional commanders deserted on the battlefield, but the Imperials were beaten two weeks later at **Sherpur** (9 February 1760).

Masurian Lakes ▮ 1914 ▮ World War I (Eastern Front)

German General Paul von Hindenberg destroyed a Russian army at **Tannenberg** (31 August), then turned north against the First Army of Pavel Rennenkampf. Heavy fighting around the Masurian Lakes cost 125,000 Russian and 40,000 German casualties before Rennenkampf eluded envelopment and abandoned East Prussia. Russia soon counter-attacked at **Augustovo** (9–14 September 1914).

Masurian Lakes ▮ 1915 ▮ World War I (Eastern Front)

A massive mid-winter offensive from East Prussia saw Marshal Paul von Hindenberg attack north of the Masurian Lakes, with Generals Otto von Below and Hermann von Eichhorn. A Russian Corps was sacrificed holding Augustovo, costing General Thadeus Sievers 56,000 casualties and perhaps 100,000 captured. A counter-attack finally halted the German advance (7–21 February 1915).

Mata Carmelera ▮ 1898 ▮ Venezuelan Civil Wars

When President Joaquín Crespo fraudently secured election of his successor, Ignacio Andrade, General Jose Manuel Hernandez began the "Revolution of Queipa." In action at Mata Carmelera, in Cojedes, Crespo was shot and killed, though Hernandez was later defeated and captured by General Ramóin Guerra (12 June). Andrade was overthrown the following year after **Tocuyito** (16 April 1898).

Matamaros ▮ 1866 ▮ Mexican-French War

Days after destroying an Imperial convoy at **Santa Gertrudis**, Liberal commander Mariano Escobedo marched west against Matamaros, held by just 300 men under General Tomás Mejía, who was forced to capitulate. Although Mejía was controversially permitted to withdraw with all his arms except 43 cannon, the loss of the city was a severe blow to the Imperial cause (23–24 June 1866).

Matanikau ▮ 1942 ▮ World War II (Pacific)

With Japanese forces on **Guadalcanal** reinforced after **Cape Esperance**, General Masao Maruyama launched a large-scale attack across the Matanikau River, west of General Alexander Vandergrift's Americans at Henderson Field. Two badly co-ordinated assaults were repulsed, with up to 3,500 Japanese casualties, ending the last major Japanese ground offensive (23–25 October 1942).

Matanzas ▮ 1628 ▮ Dutch-Spanish Colonial Wars

Dutch Admiral Piet Heyn returned to the West Indies the year after his victory at **Salvador** and led a large fleet to capture the King of Spain's annual silver shipment from America. Off Matanzas Bay, in western Cuba, Heyn intercepted and seized the galleons, securing a massive treasure for the West India Company and earning the title Lieutenant Admiral of Holland (8 September 1628).

Matapan ▮ 1941 ▮ World War II (War at Sea)

See **Cape Matapan**

Mataquito ▮ 1557 ▮ Spanish Conquest of Chile

On a fresh offensive against the Araucanian Indians of southern Chile, Governor Francisco de Villagrán took a large army against Lautaro, who had defeated him at **Marigüeñu** (1554). In battle at Mataquito, Lautaro was decisively defeated and killed, along with perhaps 600 of his guerrillas. Within a year, Chief Caupolicán was also defeated and killed and resistance was suppressed (29 April 1557).

Matará I 1815 I Peruvian War of Independence

In the rising by Indian leader Mateo Pumacahua against Peru's Spanish rulers, rebel leaders Manuel Hurtado de Mendoza and José Gabriel Bejar rebuilt their forces in Anadahuaylas after defeat at **Huanta**. They were beaten again by the Royalists at Matará and escaped east towards Cuzco. Both men were eventually executed after the rising was crushed in March at **Umachiri** (4 February 1815).

Mataram I 1894 I Dutch Conquest of Bali

Determined to avenge his defeat on Lombok, Dutch General Jacobus Vetter returned three months later with a much larger force to burn **Cakranegara**, then met the Balinese army just outside the capital Mataram on a hill called Gunung Sari. Crown Prince Anak Agung Nengah was killed in a terrible ritual defeat (puputan) and the elderly Raja went into exile in Batavia (22 November 1894).

Matarikoriko I 1861 I 2nd New Zealand War
See **Te Arei**

Matawhero I 1868 I 2nd New Zealand War

Hauhau rebel Te Kooti returned to New Zealand's east coast after escaping from the Chatham Islands and descended on the remote settlement at Matawhero, west of Turanganui (modern Gisborne). In one bloody night, his followers killed 37 friendly Maoris and 33 Europeans, including Major Reginald Biggs and his family. They were soon checked further inland at **Makaretu** (9–10 November 1868).

Matchevitz I 1794 I War of the 2nd Polish Partition
See **Maciejowice**

Matchin I 1791 I Catherine the Great's 2nd Turkish War

Advancing up the Danube after taking **Izmail** (December 1790), 40,000 Russians under General Prince Nikolai Repnin approached Vizier Yusuf Pasha with 100,000 men at Matchin (modern Macin). Without waiting for reinforcements from Prince Grigory Potemkin, Repnin and General Mikhail Kutuzov won a massive victory, ending the war with Russian gains on the Black Sea (28 June 1791).

Matehuala I 1864 I Mexican-French War

Five months after winning at **San Luis Potosi**, General Tomás Mejía and French under Colonel Alphonse-Édouard Aymard cornered Liberal commander Manuel Doblada further north at Matehuala, where he was supported by Florencio Antillón and Antonio Carbajal. Following heavy losses on both sides, Doblada fled to the United States. He died in New York in June 1865 (17 May 1864).

Mati I 1897 I 1st Greco-Turkish War

Despite checks at **Nezeros** and **Vigla** as he advanced into Thessaly, days later Edhem Pasha assembled a large Ottoman force near Mati against Greek Crown Prince Constantine, supported by Colonels Mastrapas and Mavromichalis. After action north from Tyrnavos, the Turks launched a bloody assault and the Greeks fled south through Larissa to **Velestino** and **Pharsalus** (22–23 April 1897).

Matmata Hills I 1943 I World War II (Northern Africa)
See **Mareth Line**

Mato Grosso I 1864 I War of the Triple Alliance
See **Coimbra, Brazil**

Matwy I 1666 I Lubomirski's Rebellion

Bitterly opposed to Royal reforms, former Polish Marshal Jerzy Lubomirski led a rebellion against John II Casimir, whose army under John Sobieski (later King) was routed at Matwy on Lake Goplo. Though Lubomirski later yielded and left for Silesia, the weakened Polish King was forced to cede the Eastern Ukraine, Kiev and Smolensk to Moscow. He abdicated in 1668 (13 July 1666).

Maubeuge I 1793 I French Revolutionary Wars (1st Coalition)
See **Wattignies**

Maubeuge I 1814 I Napoleonic Wars (French Campaign)
As the Allies advanced from Brussels, Courtrai and Oudenarde were taken before Karl August Duke of Weimer sent General Karl-Christian von Lecocq against Maubeuge. Facing a stout defence by Colonel Jean-Baptiste Schouller, Lecocq's Saxons were checked and withdrew after five days. However, the broad advance could not be stopped and the Allies drove on towards **Paris** (19–24 March 1814).

Mauku I 1863 I 2nd New Zealand War
Maori warriors campaigning against settlements south of Auckland were repulsed at **Pukekohe East**, then attempted to seize cattle further west near Mauku. Boldly counter-attacking in dense bush, 50 militia under Lieutenant Daniel Lusk met the raiders at nearby Titi Hill. In close quarters action, 20 Maoris and eight British were killed before the Maoris withdrew (23 October 1863).

Maumee I 1813 I War of 1812
See **Dudley's Defeat**

Maupertuis I 1356 I Hundred Years War
See **Poitiers**

Mauriacus I 451 I Hun Invasion of the Roman Empire
See **Chalons**

Mauritius I 1810 I Napoleonic Wars (5th Coalition)
After British failure at **Grand Port** (23 August), Admiral Albemarle Bertie and General John Abercomby with over 10,000 men attacked the Indian Ocean island of Mauritius (French Ile de France). Surrendered by General Charles Decaen, the island was confirmed as British at war's end and resumed its earlier name. Nearby **Réunion** had already been captured (24 September–3 December 1810).

Mauron I 1352 I Hundred Years War
French Marshal Guy de Nesle was ransomed after his capture at **Saintes** in April 1351 and seized Rennes. Then advancing west towards Brest he was intercepted at Mauron by Sir William Bentley. In perhaps the most decisive French defeat since **Crecy** (1346) the outnumbered English archers destroyed the French knights. Nesle was among up to 2,000 claimed killed (14 August 1352).

Maxen I 1759 I Seven Years War (Europe)
Following his disastrous defeat at **Kunersdorf** (12 August), Frederick II of Prussia sent an inadequate force under General Frederick von Finck against Marshal Leopold von Daun's Austrians at Maxen, south of Dresden. The massively outnumbered Prussians were overwhelmed and the entire army of 12,000 men surrendered. Finck was later court-martialled and imprisoned (20 November 1759).

Maya I 1813 I Napoleonic Wars (Peninsular Campaign)
During the weeklong "Battles of the Pyrenees," French Marshal Nicolas Soult sent General Jean Baptiste d'Erlon to relieve besieged **Pamplona**, but he was blocked at the Pass of Maya by British General Sir William Stewart. As at **Roncesvalles** the same day, the outnumbered British fell back with heavy losses. However, they had successfully delayed the French advance (25 July 1813).

Mayals I 1834 I 1st Carlist War
Determined to spread the Carlist insurrection to Catalonia, Commander Manuel Carnicer crossed the Ebro and was met at Mayals, southwest of Lerida, by General José Carratalá, commanding in Tarragona, and Governor Manuel Breton of Tortosa. Despite a courageous attack by Colonel Ramón Cabrera, Carnicer was defeated and the Carlists suffered a major setback (10 April 1834).

Maychew I 1936 I 2nd Italo-Ethiopian War

Although his armies in the north were destroyed at **Amba Aradam**, **Tembien** and **Shire**, Emperor Haile Selassie personally led 35,000 men to meet Marshal Pietro Badoglio at Maychew, east of Sekota. Haile Selassie was badly defeated in the battle, which decided the fate of his country. He fell back through disaster at **Lake Ashangi** to **Addis Ababa**, then fled into exile (31 March 1936).

May-en-Multien I 1814 I Napoleonic Wars (French Campaign)
See **Ourcq**

Mazar I 633 I Muslim Conquest of Iraq

Muslim General Khalid ibn al-Walid routed a Persian army at **Hafir, Iraq** before another Sassanian Persian force under Qarin ibn Quryana crossed the Tigris later the same year and attempted to block his advance into Mesopotamia at Mazar. Qarin was killed in a bloody action and his desperate army was destroyed. The Persian Emperor soon sent a fresh army, which met the invaders at **Walaja** (April 633).

Mazar-i-Sharif I 2001 I Afghanistan War

After widespread British and American bombing of Taliban and al-Qaeda targets in Afghanistan, the Northern Alliance ground offensive began towards the strategic northern city of Mazar-i-Sharif. Carpet bombing destroyed nearby defensive positions and the Taliban were forced to withdraw as the city fell. The main effort then turned east against **Kunduz** (9–10 November 2001).

Mazinan I 1755 I Persian-Afghan Wars
See **Sabzavar**

Mazra I 1880 I 2nd British-Afghan War
See **Kandahar**

Mazraa I 1925 I Druze Rebellion

With Syria in revolt against French rule, General Roger Michaud left Azra with 3,000 French, Syrian and Madagascan troops to relieve **Suwayda**, besieged by Druze leader al-Atrash. A few miles northwest at Mazraa, he was ambushed and lost about 800 men killed or wounded and 2,000 rifles. Michaud was recalled and another column was stopped six weeks later at **Museifré** (3 August 1925).

Mbutuy I 1865 I War of the Triple Alliance

In a sharp encounter at Mbutuy, northeast of Asunción near San Estanislao, a force of 400 Paraguayans led by Major José López met about 2,300 Brazilians under Colonels Antonio Fernandez Lima and Sezefredo Mesquita. The Brazilians lost about 100 casualties, but the Paraguayans, caught between two attacks, were forced to withdraw with 116 dead and 120 wounded (26 June 1865).

Mbwila I 1665 I Portuguese Colonial Wars in West Africa
See **Ambuila**

McClellan Creek I 1872 I Red River Indian War

Colonel Ranald Mackenzie pursued Comanche forces across Western Texas and attacked Kotsoteka Chief Mow-way near McClellan Creek, on the north fork of the Red River near Lefors. At least 50 Indians were killed, with 124 women and children captured, the camp destroyed and 1,000 horses seized then recovered. The ensuing conflict was named for the Red River (29 September 1872).

McDowell I 1862 I American Civil War (Eastern Theatre)

Two weeks after defeat at **Kernstown**, Confederate General Thomas "Stonewall" Jackson resumed the offensive in Virginia's Shenandoah Valley and intercepted Union troops under Generals Robert H. Milroy and Robert C. Schenck at McDowell, northwest of Staunton. Heavy fighting drove the Union force back into West Virginia and Jackson marched northeast to **Front Royal** (8 May 1862).

McNeill's Zareba I 1885 I British-Sudan Wars
    See **Tofrek**

Mearcredesburn I 485 I Anglo-Saxon Conquest of Britain
    With victory on the west Sussex coast secured near **Selsey** (477), the Saxon adventurer Aella and his son Cissa faced an alliance of British and Welsh forces at the frontier on the banks of the Mearcredesburn. The battle was inconclusive and Aella received Saxon reinforcements before the decisive battle at **Anderida** (491). He eventually became King of the South Saxons.

Meaux I 1421–1422 I Hundred Years War
    Henry V of England was recognised by Charles VI of France as his heir and moved to secure his heritage by besieging the town of Meaux, east of Paris, held by Jean de Gast, the Bastard of Vaurus. The mid-winter siege saw disease break out and the King fell seriously ill. Meaux finally surrendered and de Gast was hanged. Three months later Henry was dead (6 October 1421–10 May 1422).

Mecca I 630 I Campaigns of the Prophet Mohammed
    Following repeated defeats by the Prophet Mohammed of Medina, the Koreish Arabs of Mecca signed a treaty permitting the Muslims to pray at the Ka'bah. When some Koreish breached the treaty their leader, Abu Sufyan, attempted to restore peace, but Mohammed took the opportunity to attack. Mecca fell with minimal losses and the local Arabs converted to Islam (11 January 630).

Mecca I 683 I Muslim Civil Wars
    After the death of the Umayyad Caliph Mu'awiya (May 683), his son Yazid I faced a revolt in Arabia by Abdullah ibn Zubair, son of the conqueror of Egypt. An Umayyad army captured **Medina, Saudi Arabia**, but Zubair soon defended a brutal monthlong siege of Mecca by Syrian General Hosein ibn Numair. The siege was lifted when Yazid died and Zubair was recognised as Caliph in Arabia and Egypt.

Mecca I 692 I Muslim Civil Wars
    Caliph Abdul-Malik resolved to end the rival Caliphate in the south and sent the brilliant General Hajjaj ibn Yusuf from Damascus with a large Umayyad army to recapture Mecca. The Arabian rebel, Abdullah ibn Zubair, now in his seventies, held out for six months against a brutal and destructive siege. However, he was killed in the final assault and the Umayyad Caliphate reclaimed Arabia.

Mecca I 930 I Sack of Mecca
    As a climax to years of campaigning in Syria and Iraq, the radical Shi'ite Carmathians of Bahrain attacked and sacked the Holy City of Mecca. Thousands of Meccans and pilgrims were reported killed in a brutal assault and the raiders seized the Black Stone of the Ka'bah, one of Islam's holiest relics. The stone was eventually ransomed and returned about 20 years later (12 December 930).

Mecca I 1924 I Saudi-Hashemite Wars
    See **Taif**

Mechanicsville I 1862 I American Civil War (Eastern Theatre)
    See **Beaver Dam Creek**

Mechili I 1941 I World War II (Northern Africa)
    Days after taking **Tobruk**, General Richard O'Connor headed into the desert against Italian armour at Mechili. Both sides suffered costly losses in one of the first tank battles of the desert war before General Valentino Babini broke off and eluded pursuit. O'Connor then gathered his forces to strike west through Msus to intercept the Italians south of Benghazi at **Beda Fomm** (24 January 1941).

Medak I 1993 I Croatian War
    On a brutal offensive into the Medak Pocket in Serb-occupied Krajina, Croatian troops shelled and destroyed villages and executed Serb soldiers and civilians. Canadian UN peacekeepers eventually had to open fire to restore order before the Croats finally withdrew with 27 killed.

Croatian commander General Mirko Norac was later indicted and imprisoned for war crimes (9–17 September 1993).

Medellin I 1809 I Napoleonic Wars (Peninsular Campaign)

Turning south from his victory at **Uclés** (13 January), French Marshal Claude Victor advanced towards Portugal and at Medellin, on the Guadiana, met the large Spanish force of General Gregorio Cuesta. Striking against the overextended Spanish lines, Victor inflicted a crushing defeat and General Marie Latour-Mauberge's cavalry drove the survivors south in a bloody pursuit (28 March 1809).

Médenine I 1943 I World War II (Northern Africa)

Field Marshal Erwin Rommel routed the Americans in southern Tunisia at **Kasserine** (22 February) and returned to his defences at Mareth, then launched a spoiling attack at Médenine against British General Sir Bernard Montgomery. A costly defeat saw 52 Axis tanks lost and Rommel, ill and tired, returned to Germany. Two weeks later Montgomery stormed the **Mareth Line** (6 March 1942).

Medina, Saudi Arabia I 627 I Campaigns of the Prophet Mohammed

The Arabs of Mecca were repulsed at **Ohud** in 625, but regrouped and joined local Jews to attack Mohammed in Medina. With insufficient men for another open battle, the Prophet defended a strong trench around the city. The Meccans abandoned the siege after five weeks in the face of costly losses. The Muslims then killed many of the Jews of Medina and expelled the rest (24 February 627).

Medina, Saudi Arabia I 683 I Muslim Civil Wars

Faced by a revolt in Arabia following the death of the Ommayad Caliph Mu'awiya (May 683), his son and successor Yazid I sent an army from Damascus under the elderly General Muslim. The city of Medina was taken by storm after a short siege and was then put to a violent and destructive sack. General Muslim subsequently died while marching his army further south to attack **Mecca**.

Medina, Saudi Arabia I 762 I Muslim Civil Wars

When Muhammad ibn Abd'Allah and his brother Ibrahim raised Shi'ite rebellion against Caliph al-Mansur, Muhammad won over the people of Medina and Mecca before the Caliph sent 4,000 men under Isa ibn Musa. The Abbasid General won back some of the rebels before he defeated and killed Muhammad at Medina. He then turned east to defeat Ibrahim at **Bakhamra** (6 December 762).

Medina, Saudi Arabia I 1916–1919 I World War I (Middle East)

With support from Britain and France, Sharif Hussein proclaimed the Arab Revolt against Turkey in the **Hejaz**. However, he was repulsed at the key Ottoman city of Medina, which held out under commander Fakhri en din Pasha against a loose three-year siege. After Turkey ended the war (October 1918), Fakhri refused to surrender until ordered by the Sultan himself (June 1916–10 January 1919).

Medina, Saudi Arabia I 1925 I Saudi-Hashemite Wars

Sultan Abd al-Aziz (Ibn Saud) of Nejd secured Mecca at **Taif** (September 1924), then besieged the Hashemite Sharif Ali in Jeddah for a year, while his Ikhwan ally Faisal al-Dawish besieged Medina. Forced to surrender, the Holy City of Medina was occupied by Aziz's son Muhammad. Two weeks later Sharif Ali fled Jeddah and Aziz became the new King of Hejaz (5 December 1925).

Medina, Texas I 1813 I Gutiérrez-Magee Expedition

After seizing San Antonio in Spanish Texas with victory at **Rosillo** (29 March), Republican forces under José Álvarez Toledo marched out to prevent a junction between Royalist General Joaquin de Arredondo and Colonel Ignacio Elizondo. Near the Medina River, Toledo and his

American Filibuster allies were routed with over 1,000 killed and they fled back to Louisiana (18 August 1813).

Medina del Rio Seco ∎ 1808 ∎ Napoleonic Wars (Peninsular Campaign)

An ill-advised decision to challenge Marshal Jean-Baptiste Bessières on the open plain of Old Castile saw Spanish Generals Gregorio de la Cuesta and Joachim Blake meet the out-numbered French north of Valladolid, at Medina del Rio Seco. The Spaniards were routed in a one-sided disaster and newly crowned King Joseph Bonaparte marched into Madrid (14 July 1808).

Mediolanum ∎ 268 ∎ Roman Military Civil Wars

While Emperor Gallienus fought the Goths in the east at the **Nestus**, his General Aureolus mutinied in Italy and Gallienus returned to Mediolanum (modern Milan), where the usurper was defeated and withdrew under siege. When Gallienus was murdered by his deputy Claudius, Aureolus surrendered. New Emperor Claudius II put him to death then returned to meet the Goths at **Nish**.

Medole ∎ 1796 ∎ French Revolutionary Wars (1st Coalition)
See **Castiglione**

Medway ∎ 43 ∎ Roman Conquest of Britain

When Emperor Claudius ordered the conquest of Britain, Aulus Plautius landed in Kent with 50,000 men and at the Medway between Aylesford and Rochester, defeated Togodumnus and Caratacus, sons of late King Cunobellin of the Catuvellauni (Togodumnus was killed). After the Romans seized Camulodunum (Colchester), Caratacus fled to Wales where he was defeated in 50 AD at **Caer Caradoc**.

Medway ∎ 1667 ∎ 2nd Dutch War

When peace attempts failed, Dutch Admiral Mihiel de Ruyter broke into the Medway and led a remarkable raid up the Thames almost to London and took Sheerness. After burning six warships at Chatham, the Dutch withdrew with the former flagship *Royal Charles* as a prize. With London recently ravaged by plague and the Great Fire, the raid convinced England to seek peace (20–23 June 1667).

Meeanee ∎ 1843 ∎ British Conquest of Sind
See **Miani**

Meeker Massacre ∎ 1879 ∎ Ute Indian Wars
See **White River**

Meerut ∎ 1399 ∎ Conquests of Tamerlane

The Turko-Mongol Tamerlane concluded his devastating campaign in northern India and, with his plunder from the destruction of **Delhi**, marched northeast into the Himalayan foothills against the powerful fortress city of Meerut. Tamerlane's troops took the city by storm and massacred the garrison. The Mongols then deliberately destroyed Meerut before returning north to Samarkand.

Meerut ∎ 1857 ∎ Indian Mutiny

In a culmination to months of unrest among native troops in the Indian Army, troops at Meerut, northeast of Delhi, rose in mutiny after men were court-martialled for refusing to use greased cartridges. British officers and civilians were killed in confused fighting at Meerut and the mutineers marched on **Delhi**, triggering the bloody war which followed (10 May 1857).

Megalopolis ∎ 331 BC ∎ Macedonian Conquests

With Alexander the Great absent on campaign against Persia, King Agis III of Sparta raised revolution in Greece against Macedonian rule and besieged Megalopolis, on the Helisson on Arcadia. Attacked by Antipater—Alexander's Regent in Macedonia—Agis was defeated and killed. Revolt in Greece was effectively suppressed until after Alexander's death eight years later.

Megara I 424 BC I Great Peloponnesian War

On a fresh two-pronged Athenian offensive into Boeotia, General Demosthenes advanced west from Athens against Megara and seized its nearby port of Nisaea. Before he could force Megara to surrender, a large army approached under the Spartan Brasidas and Demosthenes retired, leaving a garrison at Nisaea. Another Athenian force was repulsed to the northeast at **Delium** (August 424 BC).

Megiddo I 1468 BC I Egyptian-Syrian Wars

When Tuthmosis III of Egypt marched into Palestine to put down a revolt, he routed a Syrian-Palestinian force led by the King of Megiddo and Kadesh outside Megiddo, southeast of Haifa in modern Israel. The local force then withdrew into Megiddo, which fell after a seven-month siege. The battle is claimed to be the first for which there is a written record (trad date 1468 BC).

Megiddo I 609 BC I Egyptian Conquest of Judah

Marching into Judah to support the collapsing Assyrian Empire, Necho II of Egypt met King Josiah of Judah at Megiddo (Biblical Armageddon), southeast of Haifa in modern Israel. Josiah was defeated and killed and Necho seized Judah, then occupied **Carchemish**, where he was attacked and defeated by Babylon. Josiah's son Jehoiakim died in the Babylonian siege of **Jerusalem** in 597 BC.

Megiddo I 1918 I World War I (Middle East)

General Sir Edmund Allenby rebuilt his army after the capture of **Jerusalem**, then launched his great offensive north through Megiddo. Attacking along a 65-mile front from Jaffa to the Jordan, he destroyed the Turkish army under General Liman von Sanders. Allenby's brilliant victories secured over 70,000 prisoners and opened the way to **Damascus** (19 September–30 October 1918).

Megray Hill I 1639 I 1st Bishops' War

When Covenanters under James Graham Earl of Montrose opposed King Charles I's attempt to impose a new prayer book on Scotland, James Gordon Viscount Aboyne and the incompetent Colonel William Burr attempted an offensive from Aberdeen. At nearby Megray Hill, the Royalists were heavily repulsed by Montrose. They lost again days later at the Bridge of **Dee** (15 June 1639).

Mehidpur I 1817 I 3rd British-Maratha War

Peshwa Baji Rao II of Poona and his ally Mulhar Rao Holkar of Indore renewed war against the British in central India and Holkar soon faced General Sir Thomas Hislop on the Sipra at Mehidpur. Hislop dispersed the Marathas with a frontal attack under heavy fire, inflicting heavy losses, and seized treasure and stores. Three weeks later the Marathas lost again at **Rampura** (21 December 1817).

Mehlsack I 1807 I Napoleonic Wars (4th Coalition)

See **Queetz**

Mehmandost I 1729 I Persian-Afghan Wars

Shah Tahmasp II resolved to recover Persia from its Afghan conquerors, capturing **Meshed** and **Herat** before the Afghan usurper Ashraf Shah led a large army against Persian General Nadir Kuli (later Nadir Shah). On the Mehmandost, east of Damghan in northeastern Persia, Ashraf suffered a massive defeat. He retired to Isfahan and soon lost again at **Murchakhar** (29 September 1729).

Mehran I 1983 I Iraq-Iran War

Recovering from losses at **Amara** in February, Iran launched a large force further north against the border town of Mehran, southwest of Ilam. Despite shocking casualties in the face of fierce Iraqi fire, the Iranians secured the nearby strategic heights, then attacked in the north towards **Haj Omran**. Mehran was finally taken by a new Iranian offensive in October 1984 (31 July–10 August 1983).

Mehran ▮ 1986 ▮ Iraq-Iran War

Determined to strike back after defeat in the south at **Al Faw** (14 February), about 25,000 Iraqi troops seized the lightly garrisoned border town of Mehran, 100 miles east of Baghdad. They claimed a symbolic victory though failed to consolidate the area. Iran later counter-attacked in force, inflicting costly Iraqi losses, to recapture the town and advance into Iraq (14–17 May & 20 June–3 July 1986).

Mehran ▮ 1988 ▮ Iraq-Iran War

After decisive victories in the south at **Al Faw** and **Salamcheh**, Iraqi forces on the central front, supported by anti-Khomeini Iranians, began a final offensive to retake the ruined border town of Mehran. The Iranians were rapidly and disastrously defeated and, with further losses to the south around Majnoon, Iran accepted a ceasefire to end the twentieth century's longest war (18–21 June 1988).

Meiktila ▮ 1945 ▮ World War II (Burma-India)

General Sir William Slim deceived the Japanese that he would cross the **Irriwaddy** north of Mandalay and attacked in the south towards the vital command centre at Meiktila, held by General Tomekichi Kasuya. When Meiktila fell (9 March), General Shihachi Katamura counter-attacked in force, but he was finally forced to withdraw after the fall of **Mandalay** (12 February–30 March 1945).

Mejicanos ▮ 1823 ▮ Central American National Wars

When El Salvador resisted annexation by Emperor Agustin Iturbide of Mexico, Spanish General Vicente Filísola invaded to defeat Salvadoran forces under Jose Manuel Arce at Mejicanos, just north of San Salvador. Filísola occupied the capital but had to withdraw after the fall of Iturbide (March 1823). Independent El Salvador joined the Central America Federation (3 February 1823).

Melanthius ▮ 559 ▮ Byzantine-Balkan Wars

When Zabergan of the Kutrigur Huns crossed the frozen Danube from Bulgaria to invade Macedonia and Thrace, threatening Constantinople itself, the great Byzantine General Belisarius was brought out of retirement. With a hastily assembled small force, he defeated the Bulgar horsemen and their Slav allies at Melanthius, west of the capital, forcing them to withdraw.

Meldorf ▮ 1500 ▮ Wars of the Kalmar Union

See **Hemmingstedt**

Melegnano ▮ 1515 ▮ War of the Holy League

See **Marignano**

Melegnano ▮ 1859 ▮ 2nd Italian War of Independence

French Marshal Achille d'Hilliers advancing east from victory at **Magenta**, soon sent General Achille Bazaine towards Melegnano (Marignano), southeast of Milan, where he attacked the Austrian rearguard under General Ludwig von Benedek. In a strategically pointless action, the French suffered costly casualties before Benedek withdrew behind the Mincio. Milan fell the same day (8 June 1859).

Melilla ▮ 1774–1775 ▮ Spanish-Moroccan Wars

The Spanish Moroccan enclave of Melilla had already withstood several sieges when Sultan Sidi Mohammed determined on a large-scale assault and sent 13,000 men against the town, held by Marshal Juan Sherlock. The Moors reportedly fired 9,000 shells during the siege, but eventually had to withdraw. Peace was concluded in early 1780 at Aranjuez (9 December 1774–6 March 1775).

Melilla ▮ 1893–1894 ▮ War of Melilla

When Rif tribesman in Morocco besieged the Spanish enclave of Melilla, killing General Juan García Margallo, General Arsenio Martínez

Campos despatched a large relief force. After naval shelling and a sharp action, the siege was lifted and the Sultan of Morocco paid a war indemnity. A more serious Rif War began with Spanish disaster in 1921 at **Anual** (29 September 1893–5 March 1894).

Melilla ∎ 1936 ∎ Spanish Civil War

At the start of the military rebellion against the Popular Front government, forces in Spanish Morocco under Colonels Juan Segui and Dario Gazapo seized the city of Melilla, where local commander General Manuel Romerales was shot. Tetuán and Ceuta then quickly fell, largely without fighting, though there was sharp resistance in Morocco that same night at **Larache** (17 July 1936).

Melitene ∎ 576 ∎ Byzantine-Persian Wars

Three years after victory in Mesopotamia at **Dara**, Chosroes II of Sassanid Persia led a fresh invasion of Roman Armenia before withdrawing under pressure to Melitene in the northwest, where he was confronted by General Justinian. Facing encirclement on the Upper Euphrates at Melitene (modern Malatya), Chosroes and his army abandoned their baggage and fled across the river with heavy losses.

Melitene ∎ 1100 ∎ Crusader-Muslim Wars

Responding to an appeal from the Armenian Gabriel of Melitene, Crusader Prince Bohemund of Antioch took a small force of knights and infantry to combat Malik Ghazi, Danishmend Emir of Sebastea (Sivas). Near Melitene (modern Malatya on the Upper Euphrates), the Crusaders were ambushed and virtually destroyed. Bohemund was captured and held prisoner for three years.

Melitopol ∎ 1920 ∎ Russian Civil War

After Poland took **Kiev** in April, new White commander Pyotr Wrangel began a bold offensive from the Crimea. General Iakov Slashev seized Melitopol and General Aleksandr Kutepov advanced even further north. When the Poles made peace, Red Commander Mikhail Frunze stormed into the Northern Taurida and in November, he drove the Whites back through **Perekop** (6–15 June 1920).

Melitopol ∎ 1943 ∎ World War II (Eastern Front)

At the southern end of the Soviet offensive towards the **Dnieper**, General Fedor Tolbukhin's Fourth Ukrainian Front advanced west through Taganrog (30 August) and along the Sea of Azov to take the key city of Melitopol after heavy fighting. Tolbukhin then reached the Dnieper and joined the offensive towards **Krivoy Rog** before invading the Crimea at **Perekop** (14–23 October 1943).

Melloone ∎ 1826 ∎ 1st British-Burmese War

General Sir Archibald Campbell advanced up the Irriwaddy from **Rangoon** in late 1824 and beat the Burmese at **Danubyu** and **Wattee-Goung**. However, King Bagyipaw declined to stop fighting. When hostilities resumed, Campbell stormed Melloone (later Minhla), the last major fortress outside the ancient capital at Ava. Following further loss at **Pagahm-mew** the king made peace (19 January 1826).

Meloria ∎ 1241 ∎ Imperial-Papal Wars

A Genoese fleet carrying Prelates to Rome to help Pope Gregory IX resolve his dispute with Emperor Frederick II was attacked off northwest Italy, between Meloria and Montecristo, by Sicilian Admiral Ansaldo de Mari and Fredrick's illegitimate son, King Enzo of Sardinia. The English, French and Spanish Prelates were captured and the Papacy soon sued for peace (3 May 1241).

Meloria ∎ 1284 ∎ Genoese-Pisan War

The decisive battle between Pisa and Genoa saw a powerful fleet of 72 Pisan galleys under Mayor Alberto Morosini meet Genoese Admirals Oberta Doria and Benedetto Zaccaria off the island of Meloria, near Livorno (Leghorn). In a bitter clash, with Morosini captured, half the

Pisan ships were sunk or captured and the rest were badly damaged, ending the maritime power of Pisa (6 August 1284).

Melrose I 1526 I Scottish Royalist War

Attempting to free 14-year-old James V of Scotland from virtual imprisonment by his stepfather Archibald Douglas Earl of Angus, Borderer Chieftain Sir Walter Scott of Buccleuch attacked the Regent at Melrose, on the Tweed southeast of Edinburgh, returning from an expedition on the border. Scott was heavily defeated and another attempt was soon defeated at **Linlithgow Bridge** (25 July 1526).

Melshtitsa I 1443 I Turkish-Hungarian Wars (Long Campaign)

After invading Turkish Bulgaria, King Ladislas of Hungary and General Janos Hunyadi were turned back at **Zlatitsa** but two weeks later on Christmas Eve repulsed the pursuing Turks at Melshtitsa, near Sofia. Withdrawing across the Balkans in extreme winter conditions, the Christians defeated the Turks again at **Kunovica** in early January 1444 before finally reaching Hungary (24 December 1443).

Melun I 1420 I Hundred Years War

Charles VI of France recognised Henry V of England as his heir and together with Duke Philip of Burgundy they campaigned against the disinherited son—the Dauphin Charles VII. Having captured Sens and Montereau, the allies then besieged Melun, southeast of Paris, held for the Dauphin by Arnaud Guillaume Signeur de Barbazan, who was starved into submission (9 July–18 November 1420).

Membrillo I 1811 I Napoleonic Wars (Peninsular Campaign)

See **Navas de Membrillo**

Memel I 1923 I Lithuanian War of Independence

Lithuania had lost **Vilna** to Poland in 1920 and determined to regain the mainly German Baltic city and district of Memel (Lithuanian Klaipeda), which had been under French mandate since 1919. Lithuanian forces invaded Memel, forcing the French garrison to withdraw. The Allies reluctantly accepted Memel becoming an autonomous region within Lithuania (10–15 January 1923).

Memphis, Egypt I 456–454 BC I Greco-Persian Wars

See **Prosopitis**

Memphis, Egypt I 321 BC I Wars of the Diadochi

As war began between the successors of Alexander the Great, Perdiccas (accompanied by Alexander's widow Roxanne and her infant son) took a large army into Egypt against Ptolemy. Blocked on the Nile at Pelusium, Perdiccas marched south and attempted to cross near Memphis, where he was heavily repulsed, with many of his soldiers drowned. When his troops mutinied, he was killed by his officers.

Memphis, Tennessee I 1862 I American Civil War (Western Theatre)

Two months after capturing the Confederate fort on the Mississippi at **Island Number Ten**, Union naval forces led by Flag-Officer Charles H. Davis and Colonel Charles Ellet moved downstream to Memphis, Tennessee, where they destroyed seven out of eight Confederate gunboats under Captain James E. Montgomery. Memphis surrendered, opening the river to **Vicksburg** (6 June 1862).

Memphis, Tennessee I 1864 I American Civil War (Western Theatre)

Regrouping just weeks after defeat at **Tupelo**, Confederate General Nathan B. Forrest led a daring raid northwest from Oxford against Memphis, Tennessee, heavily occupied by Union General Cadwallader C. Washburn. Forrest's cavalry caused little damage, but withdrew with many prisoners and a large quantity of supplies, diverting Union troops from northern Mississippi (21 August 1864).

Menai Strait ∎ 1282 ∎ English Conquest of Wales
  See **Bangor**

Menbij ∎ 1108 ∎ Crusader-Muslim Wars
  Amid confused Muslim and Crusader alliances on the Upper Euphrates, Baldwin of le Bourg and Joscelin of Edessa allied themselves with Jawali Saqawa, Turkish Governor of Mosul, against the Muslim Ridwan of Aleppo and the Crusader Tancred of Antioch. At Menbij, northeast of Aleppo, Baldwin and Joscelin were routed but later regained the city of Edessa (October 1108).

Mendaza ∎ 1834 ∎ 1st Carlist War
  Pursued through Navarre by the Spanish Liberal army, Carlist commander Tomás Zumalacárregui with 10,000 men unwisely accepted open battle against 14,000 troops of General Luis Fernández de Córdova and Colonel Marcelino Oráa. The Carlists were forced to withdraw after a bloody five-hour action at Mendaza, then made a stand at nearby **Arquijas** (12 December 1834).

Mendigorría ∎ 1835 ∎ 1st Carlist War
  New Carlist commander Vicente González Moreno recovered from a costly repulse at **Bilbao** (1 July) and resolved to meet the Liberals in pitched battle. At Mendigorría, southeast of Estella, Liberal General Luis Fernández de Córdova lost perhaps 1,000 casualties in bloody fighting. However, Moreno lost 2,000 and this was followed a year later by disastrous Carlist defeat at **Luchana** (16 July 1835).

Mengibar ∎ 1808 ∎ Napoleonic Wars (Peninsular Campaign)
  In a prelude to **Baylen**, Spanish General Francisco Castanos began his offensive on the Guadalquivir by sending General Teodoro Reding against part of General Pierre Dupont de L'Etang's army at Mengibar. Overcoming a stubborn French defence under General Dominique Vedel, Reding won a valuable victory and crossed the river towards Baylen (14–16 July 1808).

Mengshan ∎ 1851 ∎ Taiping Rebellion
  See **Yung'an**

Menin ∎ 1793 ∎ French Revolutionary Wars (1st Coalition)
  Days after victory over Frederick Augustus Duke of York at **Hondschoote**, French commander General Jean Nicolas Houchard took his poorly trained recruits against the Dutch army of William V Prince of Orange at Menin, seven miles west of Courtrai. Houchard defeated the Dutch force, but lost heavy casualties in subsequent manoeuvring and was guillotined for his failure (13 September 1793).

Menin Road ∎ 1917 ∎ World War I (Western Front)
  Recovering from terrible losses around **Pilkem Ridge** and **Langemark**, British forces resumed the Third Battle of **Ypres** with General Sir Herbert Plumer's Second Army attacking east along the Menin Road. Advancing after heavy bombardment, he seized the Menin Road Ridge and followed up with fresh attacks northeast towards **Polygon Wood** and **Broodseinde** (20–25 September 1917).

Mentana ∎ 1867 ∎ Garibaldi's Second March on Rome
  Giuseppe Garibaldi took advantage of war between Italy and Austria to renew his own invasion in support of insurgency in Rome. After defeating Papal troops at **Monterotondo**, his advance towards Rome was blocked a week after at Mentana, just 12 miles from the capital. French reinforcements had arrived just in time and Garibaldi's force was routed (3 November 1867).

Mequelle ∎ 1895–1896 ∎ 1st Italo-Ethiopian War
  See **Makale**

Mequinenza ∎ 1810 ∎ Napoleonic Wars (Peninsular Campaign)
  See **Lérida**

Mereton I 871 I Viking Wars in Britain
See **Merton**

Mergentheim I 1645 I Thirty Years War (Franco-Habsburg War)
Encouraged by a decisive Bavarian defeat at **Jankau** in March, Marshal Henri de Turenne led a Franco-Weimar army into Bavaria. At the village of Herbsthausen, near Bad Mergentheim south of Würzburg, he was surprised by Imperial Baron Franz von Mercy and General Johann von Werth and withdrew with heavy losses. In August he invaded Bavaria again and won at **Nördlingen** (5 May 1645).

Merida I 428 I Vandal-Suevic War
As Vandal King Gaiseric prepared to invade North Africa after capturing southern Spain, he was attacked by the Suevi, the Germanic tribe who invaded Galicia and were spreading into Lusitania. At Merida, their King Hermigarius suffered a decisive defeat and drowned while fleeing in the nearby Guadiana. Gaiseric then crossed into Africa and succeeded in 431 at **Hippo Regius**.

Merida I 713 I Muslim Conquest of Spain
When the brilliant Muslim General Musa ibn Nusair took command from Tarik ibn Ziyad, he continued the advance into Visigothic Spain and captured Seville before meeting strong resistance at Merida on the Guadiana River in western Spain. After a lengthy siege, with heavy losses on both sides, the city was starved into surrender. In September Musa won decisively at **Segoyuela** (30 June 713).

Merida I 1936 I Spanish Civil War
When the Nationalist Army of Africa crossed from Morocco to Seville, advance units under Colonel Carlos Asenio dashed north towards Merida. They were halted at nearby Almendralejo until Colonel Juan Yagüe arrived and took Merida against heavy odds. Yagüe then led the main force north against **Badajoz** and Colonel Heli Tella repulsed a heavy counter-attack (11 August 1936).

Meridian I 1864 I American Civil War (Western Theatre)
Union General William T. Sherman marching east from Vicksburg, pursued the retreating forces of General Leonidas Polk, who was forced to abandon the key transport junction at Meridian, Mississippi. Sherman destroyed railroads and much of the town, but did not wait to link up with forces advancing from the north through **Okolona** and retired to Vicksburg (14–20 February 1864).

Mersa Brega I 1942 I World War II (Northern Africa)
Just days after withdrawing from **Sidi Rezegh** to El Agheila, German commander Erwin Rommel launched a second offensive into western Cyrenaica. The under-strength British were defeated at Mersa Brega and Saunnu, then lost Benghazi with its stores of fuel. General Neil Ritchie ceded most of his gains and was driven back to the lines at **Gazala** (21 January–4 February 1942).

Mersah Matruh I 1942 I World War II (Northern Africa)
After driving the British out of Libya at **Gazala** and taking **Tobruk**, newly created Field Marshal Erwin Rommel raced along the coast into Egypt and slammed into an attempted delaying action at Mersah Matruh. General William Gott's poorly organised defence was overwhelmed and the British fell back on **El Alamein** after losing 6,000 men and 40 tanks captured (26–29 June 1942).

Merseburg I 933 I Magyar Invasion of Germany
See **Riade**

Merseburg I 1080 I German Civil Wars
Amid civil war against Henry IV, Duke Rudolf of Swabia was elected rival King and joined nobles, including Berthold of Zahringen, in a bitter and costly campaign. At Merseburg, west of Leipzig, Rudolf was defeated and killed and the Emperor gave Swabia to his son-in-law, Frederick of Hohenstaufen. This in turn

triggered war against Rudolf's son, Berthold of Rheinfelden.

Mers el Kebir I 1505 I Spanish Colonial Wars in North Africa

After King Ferdinand V completed the Reconquest of Spain at **Granada** (1492), Cardinal Francisco Jimenes de Cisneros equipped a crusade against Muslim Mers el Kebir, in northwest Algeria on the Gulf of Oran. The city was taken by storm and was held by Spain until 1792. In 1509 the Cardinal personally led a larger expedition against the great port of **Oran** (23 October 1505).

Mers el Kebir I 1940 I World War II (Northern Africa)

In a controversial action to prevent Germany securing French warships, British Admiral James Somerville led a large force to Mers el Kebir, near Oran in Algeria, where Admiral Marcel Gensoul refused to yield his ships. A brief bombardment then saw three battleships lost and 1,297 French sailors killed. A fourth battleship escaped to Toulon, where the fleet was later scuttled (3 July 1940).

Mersivan I 1101 I Crusader-Muslim Wars

An attempt to rescue Bohemund of Antioch, captured at **Melitene** (1100), saw a mixed French-German-Lombard army march east under Raymond of Toulouse, Stephen of Blois and Conrad, Constable of Germany. Reaching Mersivan, east of the Halys in northeast Anatolia, the so-called "Lombard Crusade" was destroyed by Malik Ghazi, Danishmend Turkish Emir of Sebastea (July 1101).

Merta I 1790 I Mughal-Maratha War of Ismail Beg

Mahadji Sindhia beat Ismail Beg's Mughals at **Patan** (20 June) and sent General Benoit de Boigne to besiege Ajmer in central Rajasthan, then attacked a large Rajput force under Bijai Singh of Jodhpur northeast at Merta. In a hard-fought battle, Rajput cavalry drove the Marathas from the field, but they were then destroyed by

artillery fire. Bijai Singh soon made peace (10 September 1790).

Merton I 871 I Viking Wars in Britain

Within weeks of defeat at **Ashdown**, Danish Vikings struck back at the West Saxon army at **Basing**. With reinforcements from the Baltic they then attacked again further west at Merton (Maeredun), near the Savernake Forest in Wiltshire. The Saxons were disastrously defeated, with King Aethelred fatally wounded. His brother Alfred soon lost again at **Wilton** (April 871).

Merv I 999 I Eastern Muslim Dynastic Wars

When the Samanid Amir Abdul Harith Mansur of Bokhara was deposed and blinded, Mahmud of Ghazni marched north and forced the nobles Faiq and Begtuzun to give him Herat and Balkh. Mahmud then attacked and defeated the rebels and their nominee Amir Abdul Malik at Merv (modern Mary in Turkmenistan). The usurper fled and Mahmud seized the Khorasan (16 May 999).

Merv I 1221 I Conquests of Genghis Khan

Genghis Khan attacked the Khwarezmian Empire (broadly Afghanistan and most of Iran), where he destroyed the capital **Samarkand** (1220) then sent his youngest son Tolui against the great city of Merv (modern Mary). When the inhabitants surrendered in return for mercy, the Mongols massacred them and destroyed Merv. Tolui took Balkh and in April destroyed **Nishapur** (25 February 1221).

Merv I 1510 I Persian-Uzbek Wars

Marching north to the Khorasan, Shah Ismail Safawi of Persia met a large army under Uzbek conqueror Muhammad Shaybani Khan, who attacked near Merv (modern Mary, Turkmenistan) without waiting for reinforcements. Shaybani was decisively defeated and killed. His Mongol mercenaries plundered the defeated Uzbeks as they withdrew into Transoxonia (2 December 1510).

**Merxem I 1814 I Napoleonic Wars
(French Campaign)**

With the European allies crumbling before the French east of Paris, British General Sir Thomas Graham led a dawn attack on the village of Merxem (modern Merksem) just outside Antwerp. General Jean-Jacques Ambert initially repulsed the attack, but with Prussian aid Graham penetrated Merxem under cover of a snowstorm and the French withdrew to Antwerp (2 February 1814).

Mesa I 1847 I American-Mexican War
See **San Gabriel, California**

Meshed I 1726 I Persian-Afghan Wars

In the campaign to recover Persia from its Afghan conquerors, Shah Tahmasp II and his General Nadir Kuli (later Nadir Shah) besieged Meshed (modern Mashad) held by the independent Afghan chief Malik Mahmud. The city was eventually betrayed by Malik Mahmud's commander Pir Mohammad, whose leader was captured and subsequently killed (29 September–11 December 1726).

**Meshed I 1754 I Persian-
Afghan Wars**

Afghan ruler Ahmad Shah Durrani advanced into northeast Persia, where he besieged Meshed (modern Mashad), which was held by the independent chieftain Sharokh Shah Afshar. Sharokh was starved into surrender after a long siege, though he was then reinstated to rule the Khorasan as an Afghan vassal. Ahmad Shah was defeated a year later near **Sabzavar** (July–November 1754).

Meshik I 244 I Roman-Persian Wars
See **Misiche**

**Mesolóngion I 1822–1823 I Greek War
of Independence**
See **Missolonghi**

Messana I 264 BC I 1st Punic War

When Carthage supported Mamertine mercenaries in Messana (modern Messina) against Hiero of Syracuse, they secured the city but were later driven out by Roman Consul Appius Claudius. The Carthaginians then joined Hiero to besiege Messana. However, Hiero was defeated and driven back to Syracuse. Outside Messana the Carthaginians were defeated and subsequently lost at **Acragas**.

**Messana I 48 BC I Wars of the First
Triumvirate**

With Julius Caesar and Pompey preparing for the showdown at **Pharsalus**, Pompeian Admiral Gaius Cassius Longinus surprised Caesar's galleys under Marcus Pomponius at Messana (modern Messina, Sicily). Attacked by fireships, Caesar's entire fleet of 35 ships was burned, though the city itself was protected by a strong Legion. Another attack by Cassius that year was repulsed at **Vibo**.

Messifré I 1925 I Druze Rebellion
See **Museifré**

**Messina I 843 I Byzantine-
Muslim Wars**

As Muslim forces slowly conquered Byzantine Sicily, securing the city of **Palermo** in 831, the Arab General al Fadl ibn Djafar, with aid from Christian Naples, laid siege by land and sea to Messina in the northeast. Feigning a withdrawal on land, he launched a massive diversionary assault by sea then rushed the landward walls. The city capitulated and the next great objective was **Castrogiovanni**.

**Messina I 1061 I Norman Conquest of
Southern Italy**

At the start of the 30-year Norman conquest of Muslim Sicily, Roger d'Hauteville, in support of his brother Duke Robert Guiscard, landed with 2,000 foot-soldiers and knights to attack Messina in the northeast. Despite initial repulse in February, the city was captured at the second attempt. In 1063 Roger marched inland to meet the Muslims in the mountains at **Cerami** (May 1061).

Messina I 1283 I War of the Sicilian Vespers

When the uprising of the **Sicilian Vespers** in 1282 overthrew Charles I of Anjou, the newly established King Pedro III of Aragon fought a lengthy war to secure Sicily. Aragonese and Catalan ships under Admiral Roger di Loria defeated the Angevin fleet in a great naval battle off Messina. However, the French navy recovered for the decisive clash the following year off **Naples** (July 1283).

Messina I 1676 I 3rd Dutch War

With Sicily in rebellion against Spanish rule, Louis XIV of France sent troops to help seize and garrison Messina. After a Dutch-Spanish naval attack was driven off near **Stromboli**, French Marshal Louis Victor de Vivonne defeated the Spanish army on land near Messina. Further Spanish defeats at sea later that year off **Augusta, Sicily** and **Palermo** secured the island for France (25 March 1676).

Messina I 1719 I War of the Quadruple Alliance

Determined to regain losses from the War of the Spanish Succession, Spain's Jean de Bette Marquis de Lede reoccupied Sicily and besieged the citadel at Messina, where he was attacked by Austrian General Franz Wetzel, with English Admiral Sir George Byng (fresh from **Cape Passaro**). Despite heavy Austrian losses, the city capitulated and Austria gained Sicily (July– 7 October 1719).

Messina I 1860–1861 I 2nd Italian War of Independence

Giuseppe Garibaldi beat Neapolitan troops in northeastern Sicily at **Milazzo** (20 July) then pursued the survivors to nearby Messina, which immediately opened its gates. But Messina's citadel stubbornly held out long after Francis II of Naples abdicated following defeat at **Gaeta**. The garrison finally surrendered after bombardment by General Enrico Cialdini (25 July 1860– 12 March 1861).

Messina I 1943 I World War II (Southern Europe)

The Allies broke through the Etna Line, from **Troina** to **Catania**, and Axis commanders Alfredo Guzzoni and Hans Hube fell back to northeast Sicily. While American General George Patton's self-defined "race" beat Sir Bernard Montgomery to Messina, 100,000 Axis troops and 10,000 vehicles escaped to the mainland, where they helped resist the advance on **Salerno** (16 August 1943).

Messines I 1914 I World War I (Western Front)

As British forces in Flanders attacked through **La Bassée** and **Armentières**, just to the north General Edmund Allenby's Cavalry Corps led an advance through Messines towards Comines on the Lys. The attack was blunted by a massive counter-offensive, which retook Messines. The Germans then tried to drive a wedge south of the salient at **Ypres** (12 October–2 November 1914).

Messines I 1917 I World War I (Western Front)

British commander Sir Herbert Plumer was determined to seize the strategic Messines Ridge and ordered a prolonged bombardment, followed by detonation of 19 massive mines. General Friedrich von Arnim was driven off with very heavy losses and British and French troops exploited the break-through to prepare the way for the planned July offensive further north at **Ypres** (7–14 June 1917).

Metaurus I 207 BC I 2nd Punic War

When the Carthaginian Hasdrubal invaded Italy to support his brother Hannibal, Gaius Claudius Nero checked Hannibal at **Grumentum**, then left a holding force and marched north to join Marcus Livinius Salinator against Hasdrubal at the Metaurus River. The fresh invaders were utterly destroyed and Nero returned south to catapult Hasdrubal's severed head into his brother's camp.

Metaurus I 271 I Roman-Alemannic Wars
See **Fano**

Metemma I 1889 I Sudanese-Ethiopian War
See **Gallabat**

Methone I 431 BC I Great Peloponnesian War

Shortly after the outbreak of war between Athens and Sparta, a large Athenian fleet was sent to ravage the western Peloponnesian coastline. At the small town of Methone (Modon), Brasidas inspired his outnumbered garrison to such a defence that the invaders were driven back to their ships. Brasidas was honoured as a hero and became one of Sparta's greatest generals (July 431 BC).

Methone I 355–354 BC I 3rd Sacred War

A year after capturing the colony of **Potidaea**, Philip II of Macedon attacked Methone, the last Athenian stronghold on the Thermaic Gulf. After a long and bitter siege (the King lost his right eye to an arrow) the citizens were eventually forced to surrender, reputedly allowed to leave with just a single garment. The fall of Methone opened the way for Philip to invade Thessaly two years later at **Pagasae**.

Methone I 31 BC I Wars of the Second Triumvirate

As he prepared to attack his rival Mark Antony at **Actium**, Octavian sent Marcus Vipsanius Agrippa and half the fleet against Methone (Modon) in southwestern Greece, held by Bogud of Mauretania, who had been driven out by his brother Bocchus, an ally of Octavian. The town was taken by storm and Bogud executed, providing Octavian an important naval base on Antony's flank.

Methven I 1306 I Rise of Robert the Bruce

Robert the Bruce Earl of Carrick had himself crowned King of Scotland then took a force towards Perth. Surprised just to the west at Methven by an English army under Aymer de Valence Earl of Pembroke, the Scots were routed and scattered. Bruce was driven into hiding until he raised a fresh army in 1307 and met Pembroke again at **Glentrool** and **Loudon Hill** (19 June 1306).

Metsovo I 1947 I Greek Civil War

Three months after their costly repulse at **Grevena**, Communist forces (now equipped with Yugoslav artillery) continued their offensive in northwest Greece and attacked further south at Metsovo. The insurgents failed to secure the heights before assaulting the town and were eventually driven off. However, it is claimed by some as the first large-scale open battle of the war (18–25 October 1947).

Metulum I 34 BC I Wars of the Second Triumvirate

On campaign in the Balkans, Octavian progressively subdued the warlike Iapudae, before besieging their capital at Metulum (probably modern Metlika) on the Kupa in Slovenia, southwest of Zagreb. In a ferocious assault, supported by Marcus Agrippa, Octavian took the town by storm, though he was badly wounded. Metulum was razed and later that year Octavian marched east against **Siscia**.

Metz I 1552 I 5th Habsburg-Valois War

Henry II of France invaded Lorraine where he seized Metz, Toul and Verdun, then faced a major counter-offensive by Emperor Charles V of Spain. Investing Metz with over 100,000 men, Charles inflicted heavy damage. However, the defence under Francis Duke of Guise held firm and, after enduring massive casualties, the Emperor lifted the siege (19 October–26 December 1552).

Metz I 1870 I Franco-Prussian War

Driven east from **Mars-la-Tour** and **Gravelotte**, French Marshal Achille Bazaine meekly led about 180,000 men into siege at Metz on the Moselle. After a costly sortie towards **Noiseville** and the French disaster at **Sedan** (1 September), Bazaine disgracefully surrendered his entire army, freeing Prince Friedrich Karl's Prussians to reinforce the siege of **Paris** (19 August–27 October 1870).

**Metz I 1918 I World War I
(Western Front)**
    See **Noyon-Montdidier**

**Metz I 1944 I World War II
(Western Europe)**
    Soon after the fall of **Nancy** in Lorraine, American General Walton Walker attacked the fortified city of Metz. Following costly failure at nearby **Fort Driant**, heavy losses and lack of supplies halted the assault until a new attack in shocking weather later surprised and captured Metz. American commander George Patton then turned north to help in the **Ardennes** (27 September–21 November 1944).

Meuse I 900 I German Imperial Wars
    In order to defend against Vikings and the rival rulers of Burgundy, German King Arnulf established his illegitimate son Zventibold on the throne of Lorraine. However, the arrogant young ruler quickly alienated the people, who rebelled against him. Zventibold was defeated and killed in battle at the River Meuse and Arnulf was forced into a more lenient policy in Lorraine (13 August 900).

**Meuse-Argonne I 1918 I World War I
(Western Front)**
    American commander John Pershing and French General Henri Gourard eliminated the German salient south of Verdun at **St Mihiel** and days later attacked north of Verdun through the Argonne to the Meuse. General Max von Gallwitz and Prince Friedrich Wilhelm were defeated in heavy fighting and the Allies took Sedan before Armistice ended the war (26 September–11 November 1918).

**Mewe I 1626 I 2nd Polish-
Swedish War**
    While Sweden besieged **Danzig**, Sigismund III of Poland advanced to besiege Mewe (modern Gniew) on the Vistula, 35 miles to the southeast. Gustavus Adolphus was repulsed

from an early probing expedition but succeeded in a second attack a week later. Sigismund was forced to withdraw, though Gustavus Adolphus soon abandoned Mewe for winter quarters (12 & 21 September 1626).

**Mexico City I 1847 I American-
Mexican War**
    See **Chapultepec**

**Mexico City I 1867 I Mexican-
French War**
    As Liberal forces regained Mexico after French withdrawal, General Porfirio Diaz captured **Puebla** then besieged Mexico City, held by General Leonardo Márquez and an Austrian-Hungarian garrison under Count Carlos Khevenhuller. The city eventually surrendered (the day after Emperor Maximilian was shot at **Querétaro**) and the Republic was re-established (13 April–20 June 1867).

Mexico City I 1913 I Mexican Revolution
    In a bloody coup against Mexican President Francisco Madero, General Félix Diaz (nephew of the former dictator) fought Federal troops in Mexico City led by General Victoriano Huerta. About 500 soldiers and civilians were killed in ten days of shelling (La Decena Trágica) before Huerta went over to the rebels. Madero was arrested and killed and Huerta became President (9–19 February 1913).

**Meza de Ibor I 1809 I Napoleonic Wars
(Peninsular Campaign)**
    When French Marshal Claude Victor turned south from victory at **Uclés**, Spanish General Gregorio Cuesta ordered Lorenzo Duke del Parque to hold the steep ravine at Meza de Ibor, between Almaraz and Arzobispo. Although General Jean Francois Leval suffered heavy losses storming the heights, La Parque dumped his guns in the ravine and withdrew towards Deleytosa (17 March 1809).

**Mezo Keresztes I 1596 I Turkish-
Habsburg Wars**
    See **Keresztes**

Mhlatuze I 1819 I Rise of Shaka Zulu

The young Zulu King Shaka was flushed with victory at **Gqokli** (April 1818) and led a fresh offensive against his rival Zwide of the Ndwandwe. Zwide was routed in a decisive, bloody action on the Mhlatuze, northwest of Bulawayo. Shaka then destroyed the Ndwandwe capital at Emgazeni, slaughtering the population and consolidating his dominance over the Zulu nation.

Miahuatlán I 1866 I Mexican-French War

With the war turning in his favour, Republican commander General Porfirio Diaz marched against Miahuatlán, held by 3,000 Mexican and French Imperialists under General Carlos Oroñoz. When Oroñoz was forced to withdraw after bloody fighting and heavy losses on both sides, abandoning his guns and baggage, Diaz advanced south against the key city of **Oaxaca** (3 October 1866).

Miajadas I 1809 I Napoleonic Wars (Peninsular Campaign)

Spanish General Gregorio Cuesta was falling back before the French advance in the southwest when his rearguard under Colonel Juan Henestrosa ambushed General Antoine Lasalle at Miajadas, north of Don Benito. The French vanguard of Colonel Jacques-Gervais Subervie was driven off with costly losses. Cuesta withdrew to **Medellin**, where he was lost heavily a week later (21 March 1809).

Miami I 1781 I War of the American Revolution
See **Lochrey's Defeat**

Miani I 1843 I British Conquest of Sind

In an opportunistic war against the Baluchi Amirs of Sind (in Pakistan), British General Sir Charles Napier advanced to relieve the besieged Residency at Hyderabad and met a massive Baluchi force under Sher Muhammad six miles north at the Fulailee River, near Miani. The elderly British General personally led a brilliant victory then continued towards **Hyderabad, Pakistan** (17 February 1843).

Micanopy I 1840 I 2nd Seminole Indian War
See **Bridgewater, Florida**

Michelberg Heights I 1805 I Napoleonic Wars (3rd Coalition)
See **Haslach**

Michilimackinac I 1763 I Pontiac's War

Encouraged by Pontiac's ongoing siege of **Detroit**, Ojibwa Chief Minweweh (Minavavana) surprised Fort Michilimackinac (modern Mackinaw) between Lakes Huron and Michigan. About 20 of the British garrison were killed, including Lieutenant John Jamet, and the fort was destroyed. Captain George Etherington and 12 others taken prisoner were eventually released (2 June 1763).

Michilimackinac I 1814 I War of 1812

American Colonel George Croghan attempting to open the route from Lake Huron into Lake Michigan took five ships and 700 men against the fortress of Michilimackinac on Mackinac Island, seized by the British in July 1812. Croghan was heavily repulsed by Captain Robert McDouall and two armed schooners left to blockade the island were subsequently captured (26 July–4 August 1814).

Michmash I 1013 BC I Philistine-Israel Wars

As Philistines and Israelites fought to secure central Israel, Saul of Judah advanced northeast of Jerusalem against a large Philistine force in a powerful position near Geba at Michmash (modern Mukmas). A brutal frontal attack by Saul and his son Jonathan secured a brilliant victory and the Philistines fled northwest to Bethel. They were later avenged at **Mount Gilboa** (trad date 1013 BC).

Middelburg, Netherlands I 1572–1574 I Netherlands War of Independence

In the face of early Dutch success in the war against Spain in the Netherlands, the Spanish garrison of Middelburg on Walcheren Island held out for 15 months under the veteran

Christoforo de Mondragón. Eventually, a Spanish relief fleet sent from Bergen-op-Zoom was destroyed off **Walcheren** and Middleburg surrendered less than a month later (November 1572–18 February 1574).

Middleburg, Virginia I 1863 I American Civil War (Eastern Theatre)

Confederate commander Robert E. Lee advanced north towards **Gettysburg** and part of his cavalry screen led by General James "Jeb" Stuart came under attack near Middleburg, southwest of Leesburg, Virginia, by Union General David M. Gregg. While Stuart was eventually forced back, he managed to hold the key passes and soon repulsed another attack at **Upperville** (17–19 June 1863).

Middle Creek I 1862 I American Civil War (Western Theatre)

Despite a check in eastern Kentucky at **Ivy Mountain** (November 1861), a fresh Confederate advance by General Humphrey Marshall was met at Middle Creek, north of Prestonburg, by Union Colonel James Garfield. Marshall withdrew south after an indecisive engagement. A much larger action a week later at **Mill Springs** drove the Confederates back to Virginia (10 January 1862).

Middleton I 1864 I American Civil War (Eastern Theatre)

See **Cedar Creek**

Midea I 368 BC I Wars of the Greek City-States

With Sparta at war against her neighbours, led by Thebes, Persia intervened and provided Sparta with Spanish and Syracusan mercenaries. At the pass of Midea in Laconia, Archidamus, son of King Agesilaus of Sparta, ambushed and routed a force from Argos, Arcadia and Messenia. The Spartans claimed to have suffered no casualties and called it the "Tearless Battle."

Midway I 1942 I World War II (Pacific)

While a diversionary force attacked the **Aleutians**, Japanese Admiral Isoruku Yama-

mato led a massive armada against Midway, where American Admiral Ray Spruance secured a great, decisive victory, sinking six aircraft carriers for one American carrier lost. With the previous check in the **Coral Sea**, Japanese expansion was halted. The Allies soon struck back at **Guadalcanal** (4–6 June 1942).

Mier I 1842 I Texan Wars of Independence

In reponse to Mexican raids on **San Antonio**, Texan volunteers captured **Laredo** then William S. Fisher marched down the Rio Grande and occupied Mier. Attacked by General Pedro de Ampudia, 176 Texans surrendered after heavy fighting. Three months later, 17 were selected by lottery for execution—the Black Bean Incident. The survivors were eventually released (25 December 1842).

Mikata ga hara I 1572 I Japan's Era of the Warring States

Advancing to attack Oda Nobunaga in Kyoto, Takeda Shingen of Kai was blocked southeast of Nagoya at Hamamatsu Castle, held for Nobunaga by Tokugawa Ieyasu. At nearby Mikata ga hara, Ieyasu was badly defeated, though when he fell back to Hamamatsu the Takeda withdrew. Shingen was killed in a minor siege the next year and his clan was routed in 1575 at **Nagashino** (November 1572).

Milan I 268 I Roman Military Civil Wars

See **Mediolanum**

Milan I 1158 I Frederick's 2nd Expedition to Italy

Emperor Frederick Barbarossa on campaign in northern Italy, defeated the Milanese at **Cassano** and soon laid siege to Milan. Lacking sufficient equipment to storm such a large city, he ravaged the countryside to destroy food and forced a surrender in little over a month. His unexpectedly lenient terms required acknowledgement of his Imperial authority (August–September 1158).

Milan I 1161–1162 I Frederick's 3rd Expedition to Italy

Having surrendered to Emperor Frederick Barbarossa in 1158, Milan began to reassert its independence. Following over a year of renewed warfare, Milan was once more besieged by the German army and its Italian allies and was again starved into surrender after nine months. This time Frederick was less lenient and much of the city was razed to the ground (June 1161–6 March 1162).

Milan I 1449–1450 I Milanese War of Succession

Amid confusion following the death of Filippo Visconti Duke of Milan, his son-in-law Francesco Sforza beat Venice at **Caravaggio** (1448) and his allies held **Borgomanero** against Savoy. When Milan itself made a separate peace with Venice, Sforza turned on the city and placed it under siege. The starving city finally capitulated and he became Duke of Milan (1449–25 February 1450).

Milazzo I 1860 I 2nd Italian War of Independence

After invading Sicily for victory at **Calatafimi** and **Palermo**, Giuseppe Garibaldi advanced against Neapolitan Colonel Ferdinando del Bosco at Milazzo, west of Messina. Although Garibaldi suffered greater losses, the demoralised Neapolitians were driven out and fell back on **Messina**. Garibaldi later crossed to the mainland and marched through Naples to the **Volturno** (20 July 1860).

Miletopolis I 85 BC I 1st Mithridatic War

While Roman General Lucius Sulla repulsed a Pontic invasion of Greece at **Orchomenus**, his rival Flavius Fimbria in Asia Minor attacked Mithridates the younger, son of the King. On the Rhyndacus, near Miletopolis (modern Karacabey, Turkey) the Pontic army was routed, with up to 6,000 killed. Following a subsequent naval defeat off **Tenedos**, King Mithridates VI sued for peace.

Miletus I 494 BC I Greco-Persian Wars
See **Lade**

Miletus I 412 BC I Great Peloponnesian War

Spartan General Chalcideus and the Athenian Alcibiades captured **Chios**, then seized the powerful Athenian ally Miletus, on the Greek coast of Asia Minor, and faced a fresh Athenian fleet under Phrynicus. A Spartan and local army was defeated, but before Phrynicus could assault the walled city, Spartan reinforcements approached and the outnumbered Athenian ships withdrew to Samos.

Miletus I 334 BC I Conquests of Alexander the Great

Crossing the Dardanelles into Asia Minor, Alexander the Great advanced through **Granicus** to besiege Miletus, on the Latmian Gulf. Pledging to defeat Persia on land (he later disbanded his navy), Alexander declined a battle at sea with the blockading Persian fleet and instead took Miletus by assault. The Persian fleet then withdrew south to **Halicarnassus**, which soon came under siege.

Miletus I 201 BC I 2nd Macedonian War
See **Lade**

Milingo I 1827 I Central American National Wars

Two months after repulsing Salvadoran Liberals in Guatemala at **Arrazola**, President Manuel José Arce of the Central American Federation invaded El Salvador. However, Arce withdrew after his decisive defeat outside the capital San Salvador at Milingo. Within two years, Liberal forces routed the Federal army in El Salvador at **Gualcho** and overthrew Arce at **Guatemala City** (18 May 1827).

Milk River I 1879 I Ute Indian Wars
See **Red Canyon**

Mill Creek | 1839 | Texan Wars of Independence

The so-called "Córdova Rebellion" saw Mexican Loyalists and Indians under Captain Vicente Córdova attack settlers in eastern Texas. Returning to Mexico they were intercepted on Mill Creek, north of modern Austin near Seguin, by Colorado Volunteeers under Colonel Ed Burleson. Córdova lost 25 killed—about a third of his force—and he died in September at the **Salado** (29 March 1839).

Millesimo | 1796 | French Revolutionary Wars (1st Coalition)

The day after Austrian defeat at **Montenotte**, west of Genoa, French General Pierre Augereau turned west against the Piedmontese. Despite stubborn resistance by General Giovanni Provera at nearby **Cosseria**, Austrian Baron Michael Colli was cut off at nearby Millesimo from the main Austrian force and driven back. He was finally defeated a week later at **Mondovi** (13–14 April 1796).

Milliken's Bend | 1863 | American Civil War (Western Theatre)

In support of the Union siege of **Vicksburg** on the Mississippi, Union Colonel Hermann Lieb attempted a reconnaisance from further upstream towards Richmond, Louisiana. Driven back to the river at Milliken's Bend by Confederate General Henry E. McCulloch, Lieb suffered heavy losses before two Union gunboats arrived in support and the Confederates were forced to withdraw (7 June 1863).

Mill Springs | 1862 | American Civil War (Western Theatre)

Days after a Confederate advance in eastern Kentucky was checked at **Middle Creek**, a larger action occurred at Mill Springs, near Somerset, where Confederate General George B. Crittenden met General George H. Thomas. Crittenden was routed in heavy fighting and fled across the Cumberland, securing eastern Kentucky. Fresh fighting soon started further west at **Fort Henry** (19 January 1862).

Milne Bay | 1942 | World War II (Pacific)

As Japanese forces in Papua fought across the **Kokoda Trail** towards Port Moresby, about 2,400 others landed further east at Milne Bay, defended by Australian General Cyril Clowes. Very heavy fighting saw costly losses on both sides before the invaders were forced to withdraw, yielding the claimed first Allied victory on land against the Japanese (25 August–9 September 1942).

Milvian Bridge | 312 | Roman Wars of Succession

When Constantine invaded Italy from Gaul, he defeated his rival Maxentius at **Turin** and **Verona**, then met him in final battle that year at the Milvian Bridge, outside Rome. With very heavy casualties in both armies, Maxentius tried to withdraw across the Tiber and was among many drowned when the bridge collapsed. Constantine went on to seize the Roman Capital (27 October 312).

Mimikawa | 1578 | Japan's Era of the Warring States

While the Shimazu of Satsuma expanded their territory in southern Kyushu, rival Otomo Sorin of Bungo in the northeast sent Tawara Chikakata to besiege Takajo in Hyuga. The Shimazu brothers Yoshihiro and Ieshira led a large relief force and at the nearby Mimikawa, the Otomo army was routed. The Shimazu occupied Hyuga and marched west in 1581 to attack **Minamata** (10 December 1578).

Minamata | 1581 | Japan's Era of the Warring States

Rapidly expanding their territory in Kyushu, the Shimazu of Satsuma secured Hyuga in the east with victory at the **Mimikawa** (1578) then later attacked Higo in the west, laying siege to Minamata. The massive Shimazu army forced the garrison to surrender, securing the whole of southern Kyushu for the Shimazu, who subsequently conquered the northwest in 1584 at **Okita Nawate** (17 September 1581).

Minarica I 1835 I Ecuadorian Civil Wars

As General José Félix Valdivieso extended his faction's influence south from Quito, José Vicente Rocafuerte in Guayaquil sent a small army under General Juan José Flores, who met and crushed the Quito force at Minarica, near Ambato. Valdivieso fled to Colombia and Flores governed in Quito for several months before Rocafuerte assumed the Presidency of the Republic (20 January 1835).

Minatogawa I 1336 I Ashikaga Rebellion

Ashikaga Takauji secured victory in Kyushu at **Tatarahama** in April, then returned east along the Inland Sea to meet Japan's Imperial army at the Minatogawa, near Kobe, led by Nitta Yoshisada and the great Kusunoki Masashige. The Imperial troops were routed in a famous action. The badly wounded Kusunoki committed seppuku and Takauji captured Kyoto, establishing a rival Emperor (5 July 1336).

Mincio I 197 BC I Gallic Wars in Italy

Three years after the Gauls were defeated at **Cremona**, Consul Gaius Cornelius Cethegus launched a fresh offensive in northern Italy and met the Insubres on the Mincio. When their Cenomani allies changed sides, the Insubres were routed, with perhaps 35,000 killed and 5,000 captured, including Carthaginian General Hamilcar. The survivors were beaten again the following year at **Lake Como**.

Mincio I 1800 I French Revolutionary Wars (2nd Coalition)

French General Guillaume Brune launched an offensive against Austria in northern Italy just weeks after the disastrous Austrian defeat in Bavaria at **Hohenlinden**. In a poorly managed action to force passage of the Mincio, Brune succeeded only through the timely arrival of General Louis Suchet. However, this further defeat helped convince Austria to sue for peace (25–27 December 1800).

Mincio I 1814 I Napoleonic Wars (French Campaign)

See **Borghetto**

Mindanao I 1945 I World War II (Pacific)

While American forces struggled to secure **Luzon**, General Robert Eichelberger attacked the southern Philippines, where many islands fell quickly. However, there was fierce resistance on Mindanao led by General Sosaku Suzuki. The southern campaign cost about 2,500 Americans killed and 50,000 Japanese dead. Last pockets on Mindanao held out to the end of the war (17 April–15 July 1945).

Mindelheim I 1796 I French Revolutionary Wars (1st Coalition)

As General Jean Victor Moreau pursued Archduke Charles Louis of Austria across southern Germany, the French right wing under General Pierre-Marie Ferino advanced on Memmingen. At nearby Mindelheim, Ferino's forward units under General Charles Abbatucci routed the Austrians under Prince Louis-Joseph Condé and hastened the withdrawal towards **Augsburg** (13 August 1796).

Minden I 16 I Rome's Germanic Wars

See **Weser**

Minden I 1759 I Seven Years War (Europe)

Despite defeat at **Bergen, Hesse** (13 April) Prussians, Brunswickers and British led by Duke Ferdinand of Brunswick attacked French Marquis Louis de Contades near Minden, on the Weser southwest of Hanover. De Contades was badly defeated in hard fighting though he was able to withdraw when British Cavalry commander George Lord Sackville refused to advance (1 August 1759).

Mine Creek I 1864 I American Civil War (Trans-Mississippi)

As he retreated south from defeat at **Westport**, Missouri, Confederate General Sterling Price was pursued by Union General Alfred Pleasonton through **Marais des Cygnes** to Mine Creek, east of Mound City, Kansas. Generals John S. Marmaduke and William L. Cabell were among about 600 captured in a rearguard disaster and Price continued south towards the **Marmiton** (25 October 1864).

Mine Run ∎ 1863 ∎ American Civil War (Eastern Theatre)

Union commander George G. Meade pursued General Robert E. Lee south of the Rapidan after victory at **Rappahannock Station**, where he advanced on Lee in a strongly fortified position along Mine Run, northeast of Orange. Following some preliminary skirmishing, Meade prudently pulled back before a full battle and withdrew northwest to Culpeper (27 November–2 December 1863).

Mingolsheim ∎ 1622 ∎ Thirty Years War (Palatinate War)

See **Wiesloch**

Minhla ∎ 1826 ∎ 1st British-Burmese War

See **Melloone**

Minhla ∎ 1885 ∎ 3rd British-Burmese War

King Thebaw of Burma began to threaten British trading interests and Britain determined to invade and overthrow the monarch. General Sir Harry Prendergast and a large land and naval force advanced up the Irriwaddy from Thayet-myo to bombard then storm the fortress at Minhla. The King surrendered and was exiled in India, losing Burma her independence until 1948 (17 November 1885).

Minisink ∎ 1779 ∎ War of the American Revolution

When the Mohawk Chief Joseph Brant and Loyalist allies raided and destroyed the settlement of Minisink, west of Goshen New York (19 July) 150 local militia under Colonel Benjamin Tusten set out in pursuit and were ambushed at the Minisink Ford on the Lackawack. A four-hour action cost the militia 44 killed, including Tusten, and the raiders escaped with their booty (22 July 1779).

Minorca ∎ 1708 ∎ War of the Spanish Succession

A combined assault on Spanish Minorca saw British Admiral Sir Edward Whitaker seize forts at Fornelle and Ciudadella, while General Sir James Stanhope besieged Fort St Philip, guarding Port Mahon. Although the commander's brother Captain Philip Stanhope was killed during a costly assault by General George Wade, Fort St Philip surrendered next day and Minorca was secured (3–18 September 1708).

Minorca ∎ 1756 ∎ Seven Years War (Europe)

Attempting to relieve the French siege of **Port Mahon** on the Mediterranean island of Minorca, British Admiral John Byng was heavily repulsed by Admiral Marquis Augustine de la Galissonière and withdrew to Gibraltar without landing his reinforcements. Byng was shot for dereliction of duty "to encourage the others" and Port Mahon later surrendered (20 May 1756).

Minorca ∎ 1781–1782 ∎ War of the American Revolution

A Franco-Spanish force under Louis Duc de Crillon attacked the Mediterranean island of Minorca and occupied it all except Port Mahon, boldly defended by a British garrison under General James Murray. After a six-month siege, Murray was forced to surrender with heavy losses to disease and casualties. At war's end the island was ceded to Spain (July 1781–5 February 1782).

Minorca ∎ 1798 ∎ French Revolutionary Wars (1st Coalition)

Three months after victory at the Battle of the **Nile**, a British force under General Sir Charles Stuart attacked the Spanish-held island of Minorca. Supported by Commodore John Duckworth, Stuart captured most of the island before Governor Juan Quesada surrendered, giving the British a key naval base in the Mediterranean, reputedly without the loss of a man (7–15 November 1798).

Minsk | 1919 | Russo-Polish War

Polish General Stanislaw Szeptycki helped secure **Vilna** (19 April), then led 15,000 men further south against Minsk, where Russians were outflanked by cavalry Colonel Wladislaw Anders. Following a last stand just north of Minsk at Radoszkowice, the Russians withdrew east and Poland established a line on the Berezina until the following year's offensive towards **Kiev** (1–8 August 1919).

Minsk | 1941 | World War II (Eastern Front)

When Germany invaded Russia, Panzer Generals Heinz Guderian and Herman Hoth circled behind Minsk, where they trapped 15 Soviet divisions. The double encirclement of Minsk and **Bialystok** yielded 320,000 prisoners, 2,500 tanks and 1,400 guns, and Russian Commander Dmitri Pavlov was arrested and shot. The Germans continued east towards **Smolensk** (22 June–9 July 1941).

Minsk | 1944 | World War II (Eastern Front)

As Soviet forces raced into **Belorussia**, General Ivan Chernyakovsky from **Vitebsk** and Konstantin Rokossovsky from **Bobruysk** encircled a large German force at Minsk. The Belorussian capital fell after heavy fighting (3 July) with survivors trapped east of the city. The pocket was crushed with up to 70,000 killed and 30,000 captured, opening the way to **Vilna** (29 June–11 July 1944).

Mir | 1812 | Napoleonic Wars (Russian Campaign)

At the beginning of Napoleon Bonaparte's advance into Russia, French light cavalry under Alexander Roznicki were attacked at Mir, near Stolsty southwest of Minsk, by Cossacks led by General Matvei Platov. The Russians were driven off with heavy casualties and had to withdraw. Platov attacked the invaders again a few days later at **Romanov** (10 July 1812).

Miraflores | 1881 | War of the Pacific

Chilean General Manuel Baquedano resumed the offensive against Peru, advancing on Lima to take the defensive line at **Chorrillos**. After a failed armistice, Baquedano attacked again two days later at Miraflores, defended by General Andrés Avelino Cáceres, who suffered a crushing defeat. Lima was quickly occupied, though Cáceres fought on until defeat at **Huamachuco** in 1883 (15 January 1881).

Miraj | 1762–1763 | Maratha Wars of Succession

Having defeated his nephew Peshwar Madhav Rao at **Alegaon** in November 1762, ambitious Maratha Regent Raghunath Rao moved against the Patwardhans in western India at Miraj, defended by veteran General Govind Hari. Two months' fighting saw Govind Hari surrender, but the Marathas soon patched up an alliance to meet a fresh invasion by Hyderabad (29 December 1762–3 February 1763).

Miranda | 1808 | Napoleonic Wars (Peninsular Campaign)

See **Pancorbo**

Mirandola | 1511 | War of the Holy League

In the wake of breakup of the League of Cambrai, Pope Julius II formed a new alliance with Venice against France in Italy. The Papal army repulsed a French attack on Bologna, then marched north and stalled besieging Mirandola. The Pope himself rose from his sickbed to take field command in heavy snow and captured the castle. It was lost again a few months later (January 1511).

Miranpur Katra | 1774 | Rohilla War

When Afghan Rohillas joined Marathas against Nawab Shuja-ud-Daula of Oudh, Bengal Governor Warren Hastings loaned the Nawab East India Company troops under Colonel Alexander Champion. On St George's Day at Miranpur Katra, near Bareilly, Champion defeated and killed Hafiz Rahmat Khan and secured a massive booty. However, Hastings was later impeached (23 April 1774).

Mirbat I 1972 I Dhofar War

Despite defeat at **Jebel Akhdar**, about 250 leftist rebels in southern Oman attacked a small post east of Salalah at Mirbat, held by nine British SAS and about 40 local militia under Captain Mike Kealy. Heroic defence saw two SAS and two militia killed before Mirbat was relieved by air-strikes and reinforcements. The rebels lost about 70 killed and the back of the rebellion was broken (19 July 1972).

Mire I 1365 I Conquests of Tamerlane
See **Tashkent**

Mirischlau I 1600 I Balkan National Wars

German Emperor Rudolf II encouraged rebellion in Transylvania, sending General George Basta against Prince Michael of Wallachia, who had seized the principality after victory at **Selimbar**. A year later near Mirischlau, north of Alba Iulia, Michael was defeated and Sigismund Bathory was put on the throne of Transylvania. Michael soon also lost Wallachia after defeat at **Bucov** (18 September 1600).

Misar I 1806 I 1st Serbian Rising

A year after repulsing a Turkish force at **Ivanovatz**, Serbian forces under Kara George took a strong entrenched position on the Sava at Misar, near Shabatz west of Belgrade, where they faced two days of costly assault by a Turkish army and its Bosnian allies. The Turks were routed by Serbian cavalry on the third day and the citadels at Shabatz and **Belgrade** soon fell (13 August 1806).

Mishmar Hayarden I 1948 I Israeli War of Independence

Defeated south of the Sea of Galilee around **Deganiya** in May, Syrian General Husni el Zaim moved north and stormed Mishmar Hayarden on the Upper Jordan after costly fighting. In the Ten Days Offensive, a converging Jewish counter-attack under General Moshe Carmel was very sharply repulsed and the Arabs held their beachhead into the Second Truce (6–10 June & 9–14 July 1948).

Misiche I 244 I Roman-Persian Wars

After Roman victory in Iraq at **Resaena** in 243, the teenage Emperor Gordian III attempted to march on the Persian capital at Ctesiphon. West of Baghdad at Misiche (modern Fallujah), he suffered a decisive defeat and was killed by his troops at the instigation of Philip the Arab. The usurper promptly bought peace with Shapur I of Persia, who invaded Syria in 260 for victory at **Edessa**.

Misilmeri I 1068 I Norman Conquest of Southern Italy

The Norman Roger d'Hauteville secured eastern Sicily after victory at **Cerami** in 1063 and gradually conquered towards the northwest, where he met a strong Arab force under the Emir Ayub just southeast of Palermo at Misilmeri (Menzil el emir). The Muslims were brutally defeated in a rout, which was said to have broken the back of their resistance. **Palermo** itself fell after a brutal siege in 1072.

Miskolc I 1919 I Hungarian-Czech War
See **Salgótarján**

Missionary Ridge I 1863 I American Civil War (Western Theatre)
See **Chattanooga (2nd)**

Mississinewa I 1812 I War of 1812

Attacking Britain's Indian allies, Colonel John Campbell took 600 men northwest from Greenville, Ohio against the Miami village at Mississinewa, near modern Marion, Indiana. The Miami were driven out and their village burned, before they counter-attacked fiercely. Harrison withdrew, with 60 casualties and 300 cases of frostbite, but the Miami had been neutralised (17–18 December 1812).

Missolonghi I 1822–1823 I Greek War of Independence

Omer Vironi and Kurshid Pasha leading a fresh Turkish advance into western Greece were stopped before Missolonghi, held by 600 Greeks under Alexandros Mavrocordatos and Marcos Botzaris. When his final assault was repulsed with very heavy losses, Vrioni abandoned the siege (Kurshid Pasha killed himself) and the town was soon refortified (6 November 1822–6 January 1823).

Missolonghi ∎ 1825–1826 ∎ Greek War of Independence

A renewed Ottoman offensive in western Greece saw Reshid Pasha (later joined by Ibrahim Pasha) again besiege Missolonghi, now better fortified and boldly held by 4,000 men under Notaris Botzaris. After a year of bloody defence, the starving garrison sortied and were routed. Missolonghi fell by storm and Reshid Pasha advanced on Athens and the **Acropolis** (7 May 1825–23 April 1826).

Mitau ∎ 1621–1622 ∎ 2nd Polish-Swedish War

Gustavus Adolphus of Sweden renewed war against Poland in Livonia where he captured **Riga** (September 1621), then seized Mitau (modern Jelgava) 25 miles to the southwest. The town was soon retaken by Polish General Christopher Radziwill (December), but the citadel under Anders Hastehufvud held out six months before capitulating. A truce was quickly signed (3 October 1621–25 June 1622).

Mitau ∎ 1917 ∎ World War I (Eastern Front)

See **Aa River**

Mitla Pass ∎ 1956 ∎ Arab-Israeli Sinai War

Determined to regain her blocked access to the Red Sea, Israel attacked Egypt in the Sinai, sending paratroops and then tanks under Colonel Ariel Sharon against Mitla Pass, guarding the route to Suez. A rash frontal assault cost heavy Israeli losses and failed to take the pass, though the Egyptians eventually withdrew. Sharon then turned south to the disputed **Straits of Tiran** (29–31 October 1956).

Mitla Pass ∎ 1967 ∎ Arab-Israeli Six Day War

Israeli General Avraham Yoffe drove from **Jebel Libni** deep into the Sinai, where he took

Bir el-Hassne and Bir-Tamade while Colonel Yiska Shadmi raced ahead to Mitla Pass. Out of fuel and ammunition, Shadmi was almost overwhelmed. However, he blocked the withdrawing Egyptians tanks, which were then destroyed by Yoffe, aided by Ariel Sharon arriving from **Abu Ageila** (7 June 1967).

Miyajima ∎ 1555 ∎ Japan's Era of the Warring States

In order to avenge his master Ouchi Yoshitaka, overthrown by former ally Sue Harukata, Mori Motonari built a fortress on Miyajima, an island off Hiroshima, and allowed Sue to capture it. Motonari then besieged the fortress and took it by a brilliant assault. Harukata and his defeated troops committed mass sepukku and the Mori secured virtual control of western Japan (1 October 1555).

Mizushima ∎ 1183 ∎ Gempei War

Minamoto Yoshinaka seized Kyoto after victory at **Shinowara** (12 June), then advanced west into Taira territory. At Mizushima Bay, near modern Kurashiki, Yoshinaka was soon heavily defeated by Taira cavalry. Another initiative under his uncle Yukiie was soon repulsed at Muroyami in Harima. Yoshinaka then turned against former Emperor Go-Shirakawa at **Hojuji** (17 November 1183).

Mobile ∎ 1780 ∎ War of the American Revolution

Six months after taking **Baton Rouge**, Spanish Governor Don Bernardo de Galvez of Lousiana landed 1,400 men in British West Florida outside Mobile, where Fort Charlotte was held by 300 men under Governor Elias Durnford. With relief under General John Campbell approaching from Pensacola, Galvez stormed the fort. Campbell turned back and a year later lost **Pensacola** (14 March 1780).

Mobile Bay ∎ 1864 ∎ American Civil War (Western Theatre)

In a combined attack on Mobile Bay, Alabama, Union Admiral David G. Farragut, supported by General Gordon Granger, led four monitors and 14 gunboats against the small Confederate squadron. Admiral Franklin Buchanan surrendered his ships after a bloody action and General Richard L. Page lost Forts Morgan and Gaines. However, Mobile itself was not captured (2–23 August 1864).

Mobile Point ▌ 1814 ▌ War of 1812
See **Fort Bowyer**

Mockern (1st) ▌ 1813 ▌ Napoleonic Wars (War of Liberation)
The Allies under Prince Ludwig Wittgenstein marched west across Germany and Napoleon Bonaparte sent Prince Eugène de Beauharnais across the Elbe near Mockern, south of Magdeburg, to stem the advance. After a widespread action against General Hans Yorck, Eugène withdrew over the river. However, Yorck's battered force was unable to press any pursuit (3–5 April 1813).

Mockern (2nd) ▌ 1813 ▌ Napoleonic Wars (War of Liberation)
At the start of the three-day Battle of **Leipzig**, General Gebhard von Blucher's advancing Prussians were blocked on the Elster, just to the northwest at Mockern, by French General Auguste Marmont. In a brutal struggle vital to the overall battle, Prussian General Hans Yorck drove Marmont's veterans back to Leipzig (16 October 1813).

Modder ▌ 1899 ▌ 2nd Anglo-Boer War
As British General Lord Paul Methuen advanced to relieve besieged **Kimberley**, he drove the Boers out of **Belmont, South Africa** and **Graspan**, then faced Piet Cronjé and Jacobus de le Rey dug in at the Modder near its junction with the Riet. In very heavy fighting, with about 500 casualties on either side, the Boers were outflanked and Cronjé withdrew northeast to **Magersfontein** (28 November 1899).

Modderspruit ▌ 1899 ▌ 2nd Anglo-Boer War
See **Nicholson's Nek**

Modena ▌ 193 BC ▌ Gallic Wars in Italy
See **Mutina**

Modena ▌ 1799 ▌ French Revolutionary Wars (2nd Coalition)
French General Jacques Macdonald marched north through the Apennines and attacked Austrian advance units under Prince Herman Hohenzollern at Modena, northwest of Bologna. The Austrians were defeated and Macdonald sent General Joseph Montrichard in pursuit northeast towards Ferrara, while he himself advanced to the decisive battle on the **Trebbia** (12 June 1799).

Modon ▌ 431 BC ▌ Great Peloponnesian War
See **Methone**

Modon ▌ 355–354 BC ▌ 3rd Sacred War
See **Methone**

Modon ▌ 31 BC ▌ Wars of the Second Triumvirate
See **Methone**

Moedwil ▌ 1901 ▌ 2nd Anglo-Boer War
Boer commanders Jacobus de la Rey and Jan Kemp campaigning in the western Transvaal attacked Colonel Robert Kekewich and about 1,300 men in camp at Moedwil, on the Selons Rivers west of Rustenberg. Kekewich lost 214 casualties and over 300 horses in a courageous defence, while the Boers lost 60 irreplaceable experienced troops and were forced to withdraw (30 September 1901).

Möerskirch ▌ 1800 ▌ French Revolutionary Wars (2nd Coalition)
See **Mosskirch**

Moesia ▌ 86 ▌ Domitian's Dacian War
See **Tapae**

Mogadishu ▌ 1990–1991 ▌ Somalian Civil War
Despite crushing rebellion in the north at **Hargeisa**, the military government of President

Siad Barre of Somalia faced renewed attack by rebel movements which combined to advance on Mogadishu. Bloody fighting in the capital is claimed to have cost up to 5,000 lives before Barre fled into exile. Somalia then entered a decade of clan-based warlord rivalry and famine (December 1990–2 January 1991).

Mogadishu ▌ 1993 ▌ Somalian Civil War

With Somalia starving and torn by rival warlords, when Mohammed Farah Aidid was blamed for killing 24 Pakistani peacekeepers, 160 US Rangers under General William Garrison went to arrest Aidid. The heliborne raid on Mogadishu was ambushed, with 18 Americans killed and 84 wounded. Hundreds of Somalis also died. Within six months all UN and US forces were withdrawn (3 October 1993).

Mogaung ▌ 1944 ▌ World War II (Burma-India)

On campaign in northern Burma, General Joseph Stilwell's Chinese divisions advanced down the **Hukawng** towards Mogaung, while British Chindits under Brigadier Mike Calvert advanced northeast from **Indaw**. The small Japanese garrison from General Masaki Honda's division fought a courageous defence before withdrawing. The Allies then turned east to **Myitkyina** (6–26 June 1944).

Mogilev ▌ 1620 ▌ Polish-Turkish Wars
See **Cecora**

Mogilev ▌ 1812 ▌ Napoleonic Wars (Russian Campaign)

As Napoleon Bonaparte advanced into Russia, he tried to prevent the junction of two Russian armies under Prince Pyotr Bagration and General Mikhail Barclay de Tolly. On the Dnieper in the south, Marshal Louis Davout repulsed Bagration at Mogilev with massive losses, forcing his continued retreat until the two Russian forces were eventually able to unite at **Smolensk** (23 July 1812).

Mogilev ▌ 1944 ▌ World War II (Eastern Front)

At the centre of the Russian offensive into **Belorussia**, General Georgi Zakharov's Second Belorussian Front broke through German defences on the first day to encircle Mogilev (modern Mahilyow) on the Dnieper. Mogilev fell by storm, along with **Vitebsk** to the north and **Bobruysk** to the southwest. Zakharov then fought his way across the Berezina towards **Minsk** (26–28 June 1944).

Mohacs ▌ 1526 ▌ Turkish-Hungarian Wars

On a fresh invasion of Hungary through **Peterwardein**, Sultan Suleiman I and Grand Vizier Ibrahim Pasha led a large force to Mohacs, on the Danube south of Buda, against a Christian force under Louis II of Hungary. A disastrous defeat saw the King and half his army killed, including the flower of Hungarian nobility, and Suleiman occupied Budapest (29 August 1526).

Mohacs ▌ 1687 ▌ Later Turkish-Habsburg Wars
See **Harkany**

Mohaka ▌ 1869 ▌ 2nd New Zealand War

Hauhau rebel Te Kooti recovered from defeat at **Ngatapa** and continued ravaging the East Coast, where he attacked the river-mouth settlement at Mohaka. Residents at Te Huke stockade were murdered under a flag of truce and Constable George Hill bravely defended the Hiruharama stockade until relieved. The raid cost 60 lives before Te Kooti withdrew inland to **Te Porere** (10 April 1869).

Mohammerah ▌ 1857 ▌ Anglo-Persian War

Following defeat in the Persian Gulf at **Khoosh-Ab** (8 February), Persia signed a peace in Paris agreeing to evacuate Afghanistan. However, the news did not reach British General Sir James Outram, who took 5,000 men and stormed Mohammerah (modern Khorramshahr) at the mouth of the Euphrates. The Shah's army under Prince Khanzler Mirza fled and peace was ratified at Tehran (26 March 1857).

Mohi ▮ 1241 ▮ Mongol Invasion of Europe
See **Sajo**

Mohilev ▮ 1812 ▮ Napoleonic Wars (Russian Campaign)
See **Mogilev**

Mohilow ▮ 1812 ▮ Napoleonic Wars (Russian Campaign)
See **Mogilev**

Mohrungen ▮ 1807 ▮ Napoleonic Wars (4th Coalition)
At the start of Russia's mid-winter offensive against Napoleon Bonaparte in eastern Prussia, an advance force under General Evgenii Markov met French Marshal Jean Baptiste Bernadotte in a sharp action southeast of Danzig at Mohrungen (modern Morag). Bernadotte is credited with victory, though he withdrew south while Bonaparte advanced from Warsaw to battle at **Eylau** (25 January 1807).

Mojkovac ▮ 1916 ▮ World War I (Balkan Front)
Austrian General Herman Kovess von Kovesshaza captured **Belgrade** in October 1915, then invaded Montenegro and tried to intercept the Serbians retreating to the sea from **Kossovo**. While Montenegran commander Janko Vukotic fought a brilliant delaying action at Mojkovac near Brskovo, his country was occupied. After the war, Montenegro was absorbed into Serbia (6–7 January 1916).

Mokundra Pass ▮ 1804 ▮ 2nd British-Maratha War
See **Monson's Retreat**

Mokuohai ▮ 1782 ▮ Hawaiian Wars
On the death of King Kalanipu of Hawaii, the Big Island was divided between his son Kiwalao and his nephew Kamehameha, soon leading to war between the cousins. At Mokuohai, on the west coast of the Big Island, Kiwalao was defeated and killed. By 1795 Kamehameha had gradually conquered the entire island group, in-cluding victories at **Kepaniwai** and **Nuuanu** (July 1782).

Molino del Rey ▮ 1847 ▮ American-Mexican War
With expiry of a brief truce after victory at **Contreras** and **Churubusco**, American General Winfield Scott advanced on Mexico City and sent General William Worth on a major diver-sionary attack against Generals Antonio Léon and Joaquin Rangel at nearby Molino del Rey. Worth withdrew after very heavy fighting and days later Scott attacked through **Chapultepec** (8 September 1847).

Molins de Rey ▮ 1808 ▮ Napoleonic Wars (Peninsular Campaign)
Barcelona fell after **Cardedeu** and days later French General Laurent Gouvion Saint-Cyr sent General Louis-Francois Chabot west against Spanish forces on the Llobregat River under Generals Francois Vives and Teodoro Reding. Attacking at the Bridge of Molins de Rey, Chabot drove off the blockade, capturing over 1,200 prisoners and 30,000 English muskets (21 December 1808).

Mollerusa ▮ 1102 ▮ Early Christian Reconquest of Spain
In the years following the great Muslim vic-tory at **Zallaka** (1086), the Muslim offensive in northern Spain continued with the fall of **Valencia** in March 1102 and a threat to Barcelona itself. Count Armengol V of Urgel attempted a Christian counter-offensive, but at Mollerusa, 14 miles east of Lerida, he was routed with terrible losses (14 September 1102).

Molln ▮ 1225 ▮ Danish Wars of Expansion
Six years after conquering Estonia with vic-tory at **Reval**, Waldemar II of Denmark was treacherously seized by former vassal Heinrich of Schwerin. The King's nephew, Albert of Orlamunde, led a substantial rescue force, but at Molln, south of Lubeck, Albert was defeated by Heinrich and Adolf of Schauenberg (later Hol-stein). Waldemar was later ransomed, then lost in 1227 at **Bornhoved**.

Mollwitz I 1741 I War of the Austrian Succession

The first major battle of the European war saw Austrian Marshal Count Wilhelm von Neipperg sent to meet the invasion of Silesia by Fredrick II of Prussia. Southeast of Breslau at Mollwitz, the Prussian cavalry were repulsed and Frederick left the field. However, his disciplined infantry under Count Kurt von Schwerin secured victory, bringing the other powers into the war (10 April 1741).

Molodi I 1572 I Russian-Tatar Wars

A year after burning part of **Moscow**, Khan Devlet Girai of Crimea returned with a reported 120,000 men in a further attack. South of Moscow at Molodi, Prince Mihkail Ivanovitch Vorotinski secured a brilliant defensive victory and the invaders were forced to withdraw. Vorotinski was later executed after being accused of negotiating with the Tatars (26 July–3 August 1572).

Mombasa I 1505 I Portuguese Colonial Wars in East Africa

Soon after the first Portuguese expedition to East Africa by Vasco da Gama (1498), 21 ships under Francisco d'Almeida (later Viceroy of India) sacked **Kilwa** then arrived in Mombasa, where they met resistance by the King's troops. The royal army was routed, with over 1,000 reported killed. The Portuguese sacked the city and burned it to the ground, then sailed away and did not return for 15 years.

Mombasa I 1528 I Portuguese Colonial Wars in East Africa

The East African city of Mombasa, burned by Portuguese adventurers in 1505, was largely rebuilt within a relatively short period. A fresh Portuguese fleet then arrived under Nuno de Cunha (Viceroy of India 1529–1328). After sharp fighting, Mombasa was once more looted and sacked. Parts of the city were again burned to the ground and the Portuguese sailed away.

Mombasa I 1589 I Portuguese Colonial Wars in East Africa

With Turkish adventurers active off East Africa, Portuguese Governor in India Manuel de Sousa Coutinho sent a large force under his brother Tomé to support their ally, the King of Malinde. Bloody fighting saw the King of Mombasa killed and Turkish commander Mir Ali Beque captured. Portugal finally secured Mombasa and built the powerful Fort Jesus (7 March–15 April 1589).

Mombasa I 1631–1633 I Later Portuguese Wars in East Africa

Rising against the Portuguese in Mombasa, Don Jerónimo, Christian son of the murdered Sultan of Malindi, resumed the Islamic faith as Yusuf ibn al-Hasan and seized Fort Jesus, slaughtering commander Pedro Leitao de Gamboa, along with his garrison and many civilians. A relief force under Francisco de Moura was bloodily repulsed before Yusuf later razed Mombasa and withdrew.

Mombasa I 1696–1698 I Later Portuguese Wars in East Africa

With Portugal driven out of **Muscat**, Sayf ibn Sultan, Imam of Oman, besieged Fort Jesus, outside Mombasa, Portugal's greatest stronghold in East Africa. General Luís de Mello de Sampaio brought a relief force from Goa, but starvation and plague forced the surrender. Mombasa was briefly regained (1728–1729) before the Portuguese finally withdrew (13 March 1696–13 December 1698).

Mombasa I 1728–1729 I Later Portuguese Wars in East Africa

Aided by the King of Pate, Portuguese forces from Goa made a last attempt to regain Mombasa and General Sampoya seized the city. However, Patean support soon waned and Mombasa townsmen attacked outlying posts. When the Omani Arabs returned in force to besiege Fort Jesus, the Portuguese had to surrender and finally abandoned Mombasa (12 March 1728–29 November 1729).

Mome I 1906 I Bambatha Rebellion

With rebel forces concentrating in northern Natal, Colonel Duncan McKenzie launched a converging dawn assault, which trapped Zulus in the Mome Gorge. Facing artillery and Maxim guns the rebels were slaughtered, with leaders Bambatha and Mehlokazulu killed. Chief Sigananda surrendered a few days later and, apart from some minor skirmishing, the rebellion was over (10 June 1906).

Monacacy | 1864 | American Civil War (Eastern Theatre)
See **Monocacy**

Monash Valley | 1915 | World War I (Gallipoli)
See **Baby 700**

Monastir | 1912 | 1st Balkan War
Invading Serbs routed Turkey's Western Army in Macedonia at **Kumanovo** (24 October) and seized Skopje, then detached forces to help Bulgaria besiege **Adrianople** before advancing south on Monastir (modern Bitola). Three days' heavy fighting north of the city saw the Turks routed and they fled, abandoning their guns. Monastir itself fell the following day (16–18 November 1912).

Monastir | 1916 | World War I (Balkan Front)
After a failed offensive from **Salonika** towards **Florina**, Allied commander Maurice Sarrail attempted another advance against Bulgarian General Nikola Zhekov. While a British attack stalled near Lake Doiran, Franco-Serb forces in the west seized Monastir (modern Bitola) before winter halted the offensive. Sarrail later attacked again towards **Lake Prespa** (13 September–18 November 1916).

Moncada | 1953 | Cuban Revolution
Fidel Castro and about 160 young militants opened the revolution against President Fulgencio Batista with a much-celebrated attack on the Moncada Barracks in Santiago. However, over 1,000 regular troops easily repulsed the attackers with about half killed or subsequently murdered. Castro was imprisoned, but was freed

in an amnesty after two years and resumed the revolution (26 July 1953).

Monck's Corner | 1780 | War of the American Revolution
To disrupt American communications during the British siege of **Charleston, South Carolina**, Colonels Banastre Tarleton and James Webster attacked rebel cavalry 30 miles north at Monck's Corner, near Lake Moultrie. American General Isaac Huger was routed attempting to use mounted troops in defence and Tarleton struck again a few weeks later at **Lanneau's Ferry** (14 April 1780).

Moncontour | 1569 | 3rd French War of Religion
Following defeat at **Jarnac** in March, French Huguenots rallied behind 15-year-old Henry of Beárnais (later Henry IV), son of Anthony of Navarre (killed at **Rouen** in 1562 fighting for the Catholics). Marshal Gaspard de Tavennes—with Spanish, Italian and Swiss support—surprised and slaughtered the Protestants at Moncountour, near Loudon, leading to peace (3 October 1569).

Mondovi | 1796 | French Revolutionary Wars (1st Coalition)
When defeat at **Dego** split the Austrian and Piedmontese armies in northwest Italy, Napoleon Bonaparte pursued the Piedmontese under Baron Michael Colli, who withdrew towards their capital at Turin. Colli lost at **Millesimo**, then attempted to make a stand at Mondovi, 14 miles east of Cuneo. He was routed and two days later sued for peace, taking Piedmont out of the war (21 April 1796).

Monemvasia | 1689–1690 | Venetian-Turkish Wars
With his reputation established at the capture of **Castelnuovo, Albania** in 1687, Venetian Captain-General at Sea Girolamo Cornaro attacked the great fortress of Monemvasia, the last Turkish possession in southeastern Greece. The 1,200-strong Turkish garrison surrendered after a hard-fought siege and Cornaro captured 78

cannon. He died just a few weeks later (April 1680–12 August 1690).

Monemvasia I 1821 I Greek War of Independence

Demitrius Ipsilantis attacked Ottoman positions in Peloponnesia, where he first besieged the powerful fortress at Monemvasia in the far southeast. Cut off at sea by Greek ships, the starving garrison finally surrendered to Ipsilantis on promise of safe passage to Asia Minor. However, his irregulars attacked and slaughtered the prisoners. He then marched west to attack **Navarino** (April–5 August 1821).

Monett's Ferry I 1864 I American Civil War (Trans-Mississippi)

Union commander Nathaniel P. Banks withdrew down Louisiana's Red River from the costly actions at **Mansfield** and **Pleasant Hill** and was intercepted at Monett's Ferry, above Grand Ecore, by Confederate cavalry under General Hamilton P. Bee. Attacked in front and flank, Bee was forced to withdraw. Another attempt to slow the Union army was driven off at **Mansura, Louisiana** (23 April 1864).

Monghyr I 800 I Later Indian Dynastic Wars

Nagabhata II of Pratihara secured much of northern India, but when he seized Kanauj, his great rival Dharmapala of Pala counter-attacked. In battle at Monghyr, Nagabhata and his feudatory allies Kakka of Jodhpur, Vahukadhavala Chalukya and Sankaragana of Dhod routed Dharmapala and Chakrayudha of Kanauj. Nagabhata himself soon lost in the **Bundelkhand** (disputed date c 800).

Mongkus I 1964 I Indonesian-Malaysian Confrontation

Patrolling close to Borneo's southwest border, a Gurkha platoon led by Sergeant Barmalal Limbu was ambushed at Mongkus by a greatly superior Indonesian force. In an action typical of this undeclared war, the Gurkhas fought off three assaults and were down to their last rounds

when failing light saw the invaders withdraw, carrying their casualties back into Indonesia (5 October 1964).

Monitor vs *Merrimac* I 1862 I American Civil War (Eastern Theatre)

See **Hampton Roads**

Monjuich I 1809 I Napoleonic Wars (Peninsular Campaign)

As part of the French siege of **Gerona** in Catalonia, General Jean-Antoine Verdier attacked the outlying strongpoint of Castle Monjuich, southeast of the city. After extreme French losses in a foolhardy frontal assault (7 July), Verdier reverted to traditional siege works. The Spanish garrison finally evacuated to Gerona with half killed and most others wounded (3 July–10 August 1809).

Monjuich I 1811 I Napoleonic Wars (Peninsular Campaign)

Spanish commander Luis Gonzalez Torres Marquis of Campoverde preparing a fresh offensive in Catalonia sent a force of 1,800 men against Monjuich, southeast of Gerona, which he believed was ready to surrender as a result of treachery. However, his force was intercepted outside the town by French forces under General Maurice Mathieu and was driven off with heavy losses (19 March 1811).

Monmouth I 1778 I War of the American Revolution

As he evacuated Philadelphia, British General Sir Henry Clinton was intercepted to the northeast at Monmouth, where General Charles Lee attempted a weak assault but withdrew prematurely. General George Washington then attacked. In extreme heat and with costly losses on both sides, Clinton eventually prevailed and reached New York. Lee was cashiered (28 June 1778).

Mono I 1943 I World War II (Pacific)

See **Treasury Islands**

Monocacy | 1864 | American Civil War (Eastern Theatre)

Confederate General Jubal A. Early marched north along the Shenandoah after victory at **Lynchburg** (18 June), crossing the Potomac into Maryland, where he was met on the Monocacy near Frederick by General Lew Wallace. In the "battle that saved Washington" Wallace was defeated, but the delay permitted reinforcement of the Capital, where Early was repulsed at **Fort Stevens** (9 July 1864).

Monongahela | 1755 | Seven Years War (North America)

British regulars and colonials led by General Edward Braddock advancing towards Fort Duquesne (modern Pittsburgh, Pennsylvania) were attacked at the Monongahela River by French and Indians under Captains Liénard de Beaujeu (killed) then Jean-Daniel Dumas. Braddock and over half his men were killed in a one-sided rout before Colonel George Washington evacuated the survivors (9 July 1755).

Monopoli | 1042 | Norman Conquest of Southern Italy

With Byzantine forces defeated by Normans and Lombards in 1041 at **Montemaggiore**, **Olivento** and **Monte Siricolo**, Constantinople sent a fresh force to southern Italy under the successful George Maniakes. A bloody assault recovered Monopoli, southeast of Bari, along with Matera. Maniakes then turned against Constantine IX and was killed in May 1043 at **Ostrovo**.

Monroe's Cross Roads | 1865 | American Civil War (Western Theatre)

As Union commander William T. Sherman crossed North Carolina, his left flank under General H. Judson Kilpatrick was attacked at Monroe's Cross Roads, near Fayetteville, by Confederate Generals Joseph Wheeler and Wade Hampton. After initial repulse, with Kilpatrick nearly captured, the Confederates were driven off and Sherman marched on towards **Averasborough** (10 March 1865).

Mons | 1572 | Netherlands War of Independence

Encouraged by victory at **Brielle** (1 April) Louis of Nassau captured Mons (23 May), where he was besieged by Spanish under Don Fadrique Alvarez, son of the Duke of Alva. With hope of French aid ended by the **St Bartholomew's Eve** massacre and the repulse of a relief army at **Havré**, the city surrendered, though Louis and his garrison escaped the ensuing butchery (3 June–19 September 1572).

Mons | 1678 | 3rd Dutch War

See **St Denis, France**

Mons | 1691 | War of the Grand Alliance

French Marshal Duke Francois Henri of Luxembourg followed his decisive victory at **Fleurus** (1 July 1690) by laying siege to the key city of Mons, in modern Belgium, assisted by his monarch Louis XIV. Although William III of Holland and England was at Brussels with a large army, he failed to intervene to relieve Mons, which fell by storm after just three weeks (15 March–8 April 1691).

Mons | 1709 | War of the Spanish Succession

Soon after capturing the French fortress of **Tournai**, John Churchill Duke of Marlborough and Prince Eugène of Savoy marched southeast and laid siege to Mons, on the Scheldt southwest of Brussels. Leaving enough men to sustain the siege, the Allies then turned south to defeat Marshal Claude Villars at nearby **Malplaquet**. Mons fell a few weeks after (4 September–26 October 1709).

Mons | 1914 | World War I (Western Front)

As German forces swept through Belgium, the British Expeditionary Force led by Sir John French found itself facing a massively superior army under Alexander von Kluck around Mons, west of **Namur**. The British fought a bold delaying action but, with the French defeated at **Charleroi**, they began the Retreat from Mons through **Le Cateau** towards the **Marne** (23–24 August 1914).

Mons I 1944 I World War II (Western Europe)

While the British seized **Antwerp**, American General Courtney Hodges drove across southern Belgium and sent General Joseph Collins against a German concentration around Mons. The Mons Pocket was eliminated with 25,000 prisoners taken. Within a week Hodges had liberated Namur, Liège and Luxembourg before crashing into the **Siegfried Line** at **Aachen** (3 September 1944).

Mons Badonicus I 497 I Anglo-Saxon Conquest of Britain

Cerdic of the West Saxons established the Kingdom of Wessex, fighting a series of encounters against Britons under the semi-mythical King Arthur. In the last and decisive battle at Badon or Mons Badonicus (possibly Caer Vadon near Bath), Cerdric was heavily defeated, leading to a long period of peace before the great Saxon victory in 577 at **Deorham** (trad date c 497).

Mons-en-Pevele I 1304 I Franco-Flemish Wars

Two years after the great victory of Flemish infantry over Philip IV's mounted French knights at **Courtrai**, Flanders was decisively defeated at Mons-en-Pevele, southeast of Lille. Lacking defensive cover, the Flemish infantry of Philip de Thiette, son of Guy of Dampierre, were destroyed and French reputation was restored. Peace followed and Philip IV gained parts of Flanders (18 August 1304).

Mons Graupius I 84 I Roman Conquest of Britain

In a brilliantly successful campaign, Governor Gnaeus Julius Agricola extended Roman control of Britain north to the Forth and defeated Caledonians under Calgacus at Mons Graupius (traditionally Bennachie northwest of Aberdeen). Agricola's army reputedly killed 10,000 Highlanders, though he lacked the men to conquer Scotland. Forty years later Hadrian's Wall was built to mark the border.

Monson's Retreat I 1804 I 2nd British-Maratha War

Sent into northwest India to support the Raja of Jaipur against Jaswant Rao Holkar of Indore, Colonel William Monson was ordered to defend Kotah on the Chambal River. But he advanced beyond and faced a massive Maratha army, which drove him back through the Mokundra Pass. Harried and pursued, Monson finally reached Agra with less than half his original force (8 July–30 August 1804).

Mons Seleucus I 353 I Later Roman Military Civil Wars

Despite victory at **Pavia** in 351 after his defeat at **Mursa**, the usurper Flavius Magnus Magnentius was pursued back to Gaul by Emperor Constantius II, who later took an army west from Milan to finally deal with his rival. In eastern France at Mons Seleucus (near modern Gap), Magnentius suffered a decisive defeat. He fled northwest to Lugdunum, where he took his own life (11 August 353).

Montagne-Noire I 1794 I French Revolutionary Wars (1st Coalition)

See **Figueras**

Montaigu I 1793 I French Revolutionary Wars (Vendée War)

Republican Generals Jean-Baptiste Kléber and Jean-Michel Beysser advancing south from victory over Royalist rebels at **Nantes** (29 June), defeated rebel leader Francois-Athanese Charette at Montaigu, driving him further east. Returning from success at nearby **Torfou**, Charette then drove Beysser out of Montaigu and seized a large amount of stores (16 & 22 September 1793).

Montana Barracks I 1936 I Spanish Civil War

See **Madrid (1st)**

Montaperti I 1260 I Guelf-Ghibelline Wars

In the continuing factional war in northern Italy, Ghibellines driven out of Florence by Guelfs were supported by Siena and Manfred, King of the Two Sicilies. In a massive battle at Montaperti, near Siena, the more numerous Guelfs were crushed by Farinata degli Uberti. His Ghibelline party then re-took Florence and formed a government loyal to Manfred (4 September 1260).

Montargis I 1427 I Hundred Years War

Having secured most of northern France, the English army led by Richard Beauchamp Earl of Warwick advanced towards the Loire and besieged Montargis, south of Paris. The Dauphin Charles VII sent a large relief army under his cousin, Jean Count of Dunois, who attacked and destroyed the camps of Sir John de la Pole and Henry Bassett, forcing Warwick to withdraw to Normandy.

Montauban I 1621 I 1st Huguenot Rebellion

Louis XIII's French army won at **St Jean d'Angely** (25 June) then marched against Huguenot Marshal Armand Nompar Duke de la Force at Montauban in Quercy. Duke Henry of Mayenne was killed in a Catholic assault and, after Duke Henry of Rohan broke in with Huguenot reinforcements, the King's Minister Alfred de Luynes lifted the siege and made peace (18 August–2 November 1621).

Montbéliard I 1871 I Franco-Prussian War

See **Héricourt**

Mont Cassel I 1677 I 3rd Dutch War

See **Cassel**

Montdidier I 1918 I World War I (Western Front)

See **Noyon-Montdidier**

Monte Aperto I 1260 I Guelf-Ghibelline Wars

See **Montaperti**

Monte Baldo I 1637 I Thirty Years War (Franco-Habsburg War)

While campaigning in northern Italy after victory at **Tornavento** (June 1636), a French-Savoyard army under Duke Victor Amadeus and Marshal Charles de Crequi reached Monte Baldo, near the Adige east of Lake Garda, where a force of Spanish cavalry was heavily defeated and put to flight. Just a month later the Duke of Savoy was dead of a mysterious illness (8 September 1637).

Monte Battaglia I 1944 I World War II (Southern Europe)

See **Apennines**

Montebello I 1800 I French Revolutionary Wars (2nd Coalition)

French General Jean Lannes advanced to relieve **Genoa**, which had fallen five days earlier, and met Austrian Generals Karl Ott and Andrew O'Reilly marching north after the siege. Saved by the timely arrival of General Claude Victor, Lannes drove off the Austrians at Montebello. The two sides withdrew to regroup for the decisive battle a week later at **Marengo** (9 June 1800).

Montebello I 1859 I 2nd Italian War of Independence

When King Victor Emmanuel II of Sardinia-Piedmont mobilised in support of independence, he faced an Austrian invasion under General Philipp Stadion von Thannhausen. Marching against the Austrians east of Verona at Montebello, a Franco-Piedmontese force under General Elie-Frederic Forey repulsed the Austrians with heavy losses and drove them back to Stradella (20 May 1859).

Monte Caseros I 1852 I Argentine Civil Wars

See **Caseros**

Monte Cassino ∎ 1944 ∎ World War II (Southern Europe)

Key to the German **Gustav Line** across Italy was Monte Cassino, where an American assault was thrown back followed by heavy bombing, then two costly failures by New Zealand General Bernard Freyberg. The strategic monastery was finally taken at terrible cost by Polish General Wladislaw Anders as part of the offensive into the **Liri Valley** (5 & 16 February, 15 March & 11–17 May 1944).

Montecatini ∎ 1315 ∎ Guelf-Ghibelline Wars

Following a defeat at Lucca, the pro-Papal Guelf forces of Florence were besieged in Montecatini, northeast of Florence, by the Ghibelline-Pisan army of Ugoccione da Faggiuola, supported by German cavalry and other Imperial allies. A relief force under Neapolitan Princes Philip of Taranto and Peter of Anjou was routed nearby. Philip later sought a truce (10–29 August 1315).

Monte Christi (1st) ∎ 1780 ∎ War of the American Revolution

The 64-gun British warship *Lion* (Captain William Cornwallis) with three other ships cruising north of Haiti intercepted a French convoy from Martinique to Cap Francois, escorted by Admiral Toussaint-Guillaume de La Motte-Picquet. Manoeuvring off Monte Christi in near calm, one British ship was badly damaged. However, reinforcements arrived and de le Motte withdrew (20–22 March 1780).

Monte Christi (2nd) ∎ 1780 ∎ War of the American Revolution

While escorting a convoy with 6,000 French troops for Rhode Island, Commodore Charles de Ternay was met north of Haiti off Monte Christi by a smaller force under Captain William Cornwallis. In an action of manoeuvre, Cornwallis rescued one of his ships which had become isolated, but the over-cautious French commander failed to use his superior numbers and withdrew (20 June 1780).

Montecristo ∎ 1241 ∎ Imperial-Papal Wars
See **Meloria**

Monte de las Cruces ∎ 1810 ∎ Mexican Wars of Independence

As they advanced through **Guanajuato** towards Mexico City, Miguel Hidalgo's peasant army was blocked west of the capital at Monte de las Cruces by Spanish Colonel Torcuato de Trujillo. The smaller yet well-equipped Spanish force was defeated and fled. However, scarce ammunition and heavy losses forced Hidalgo back towards Guadalajara and he was soon beaten at **Aculco** (30 October 1810).

Monte Grappa ∎ 1917 ∎ World War I (Italian Front)

Austro-German commander Otto von Below routed the Italians after **Caporetto** and attempted a further offensive on the **Piave** against Italian General Mario di Robilant. Heavy fighting around Monte Grappa halted the advance and Anglo-French reinforcements under Generals Herbert Plumer and Marie Fayolle helped check a fresh attack (14–26 November & 11–21 December 1917).

Monte Grappa ∎ 1918 ∎ World War I (Italian Front)

When Austrian forces renewed their offensive along the **Piave**, General Conrad von Hotzendorf in the north on the Upper Brenta attacked the Italian Fourth Army under General Gaetano Giardino around Monte Grappa. Aided by Anglo-French forces, the Italians halted the Austrian advance and later joined the broad offensive which routed the Austrians at **Vittorio Veneto** (15–16 June 1918).

Montejurra ∎ 1873 ∎ 2nd Carlist War

Determined to recapture the key city of Estella, in Navarre, Spanish Republican General Domingo Moriones advanced on the Carlists under General Joaquín Elío at nearby Montejurra. Both sides claimed victory after very heavy fighting, though Moriones withdrew. Estella remained in Carlist hands for almost two years until after a further action at **Montejurra** (7 November 1873).

Montejurra I 1876 I 2nd Carlist War

Near the end of war, new Republican commander General Fernando Primo de Rivera followed victory at **Treviño** (July 1875) by marching on the remaining Carlist stronghold at Estella. Despite a courageous and costly defence by about 1,600 men under General Carlos Calderón at nearby Montejurra, Calderón was forced to withdraw. **Estella** finally fell two days later (17 February 1876).

Monte Lacteria I 553 I Gothic War in Italy

See **Mount Lactarius**

Montélimar I 1944 I World War II (Western Europe)

American General Lucian Truscott invaded southern France through the **Riviera**, then pursued General Friedrich Weise's Nineteenth Army up the Rhone, where General Frederick Butler circled north to trap the Germans at Montélimar. Despite a brutal Panzer counterattack, Wiese suffered severe losses in men and equipment before eventually breaking through to escape (2–28 August 1944).

Montemaggiore I 1041 I Norman Conquest of Southern Italy

During a fresh offensive in southern Italy, Norman and Lombard forces beat a Byzantine army at the **Olivento** (17 March). The Norman William d'Hauteville then attacked again at Montemaggiore, on the Ofanto near **Cannae**. Byzantine Catapan Michael Doukeianus was defeated once more and was sent to Sicily. His successor was beaten later the same year at **Monte Siricolo** (May 1041).

Montemuro I 1874 I 2nd Carlist War

See **Estella**

Montenaeken I 1465 I Franco-Burgundian Wars

Encouraged by Louis XI of France in the months following battle at **Montlhéry**, the people of Liège revolted against Philip Duke of Burgundy, who sent a large force under his son Charles the Bold. Just north of Liège at Montenaeken the rebels suffered a costly defeat, but two years later the revolt was renewed. The rebels were finally crushed at **Brusthem** and **Liège** itself was burned (15 October 1465).

Montenotte I 1796 I French Revolutionary Wars (1st Coalition)

Facing Napoleon Bonaparte's advance from the Italian Riviera, Austrian commander Jean Pierre Beaulieu sent General Eugène von Argenteau to seize the Ligurian Alpine pass at Montenotte, 25 miles west of Genoa. Argenteau drove out General Jean-Baptiste Cervoni, though he was routed next day by the full French army. He was defeated again two days later at **Dego** (12 April 1796).

Montepulciano I 225 BC I Gallic Wars in Italy

See **Faesulae**

Montereau I 1814 I Napoleonic Wars (French Campaign)

Napoleon Bonaparte defeated Blucher's Army of Silesia east of Paris, then marched towards **Troyes** to meet the Austrians and Russians of Prince Karl Philipp Schwarzenberg. A sharp defeat at **Mortmant** forced Schwarzenberg to continue withdrawing southeast and at Montereau next day his rearguard under Prince Eugene of Württemberg was badly defeated (18 February 1814).

Monterey I 1846 I American-Mexican War

On the offensive against Spanish California, American Commodore John Sloat landed near Monterey, held by Spanish-Californian forces under Captain Mariano Silva. The port had to capitulate after a brief action and Sloat then claimed the annexation of California and captured nearby San Francisco. His successor Commodore Robert Stockton won next January at **San Gabriel, California** (7 July 1846).

Monterotondo I 1867 I Garibaldi's Second March on Rome

Giuseppe Garibaldi took advantage of war between Italy and Austria to renew his own offensive in support of insurgency in Rome. He met with early success, defeating Papal troops at Monterotondo, near the Tiber northeast of Rome. However, some of his men were killed in a futile raid at **Villa Glori** and just over a week later his army was routed at **Mentana** (25 October 1867).

Monterrey I 1846 I American-Mexican War

Crossing the Rio Grande into Mexico after victory at **Resaca de la Palma** (9 May), American General Zachary Taylor took 6,000 men against Monterrey, defended by a large force of regulars and militia under General Pedro de Ampudia. Ampudia capitulated after a three-day action, with costly losses on both sides, and surrendered the citadel known as the Black Fort (20–24 September 1846).

Monterroso I 982 I War of Leonese Succession

See **Portela**

Monte Santiago I 1827 I Argentine-Brazilian War

Just weeks after routing a Brazilian fleet near Buenos Aires at **Quilmes**, Argentine commander William Brown and four ships met a large Brazilian squadron off Monte Santiago, outside Ensenada. Scottish-born Francis Drummond in *Independencia* was killed and his ship captured by Brazil in a prolonged action. Brown returned to Buenos Aires, but Brazil soon made peace (23 March 1827).

Montes Claros I 1665 I Spanish-Portuguese Wars

Two years after Spain was routed at **Ameixial**, Luis Marquis of Caracena led a fresh attempt to reconquer independent Portugal. Advancing towards Villaviciosa, Caracena was badly beaten at nearby Montes Claros by Franco-Portuguese forces under Antonio de Marialva and Frederick Herman Schomberg. Spain eventually recognised Portuguese independence (17 June 1665).

Monte Siricolo I 1041 I Norman Conquest of Southern Italy

Soon after Byzantine defeats in the field at **Olivento** and **Montemaggiore**, Catapan Boioannes (kinsman of Emperor Basil) tried to besiege Melfi. The Normans and Lombards counter-attacked against his camp at Monte Siricolo, near Montepeloso, where Boioannes was routed and captured. Constantinople sent George Maniakes who was avenged in 1042 at **Monopoli** (3 September 1041).

Monte Suella I 1866 I 3rd Italian War of Independence

Despite Italy's disastrous defeat at **Custozza** (24 June) Giuseppe Garibaldi and his volunteers took the offensive in the Tyrol, marching north from Salò on Lake Garda against Austrian General Franz Kuhn at Monte Suella. On the same day as Prussia's great victory over Austria at **Königgratz**, Garibaldi was wounded and repulsed. Within weeks his forces advanced again at **Bezzecca** (3 July 1866).

Montevideo I 1807 I Napoleonic Wars (4th Coalition)

British General Sir Samuel Auchmuty was sent to retake Buenos Aires (recently recovered by the Spanish), but had insufficient forces and instead attacked the smaller city of Montevideo, defended by French General Jacques Liniers Bremont. While Auchmuty took the city after losing about 400 men, it was abandoned in July after the disastrous British expedition against **Buenos Aires** (3 February 1807).

Montevideo I 1811 I Argentine War of Independence

See **Las Piedras**

Montevideo I 1814 I Argentine War of Independence

Despite defeat on the Uruguay River at **Arroyo de la China** in March, the Argentine

Patriot fleet under Irish-born Admiral William Brown blockaded Montevideo, later supported on land by General Carlos de Alvear. Following victory for Brown off Montevideo near Lobos Island (16 May) Gaspar Vigodet, the last Spanish Viceroy of La Plata, surrendered the city (April–20 June 1814).

Montevideo ∎ 1823–1824 ∎ Brazilian War of Independence

With Portugal under attack in northern Brazil at **Salvador**, forces loyal to Brazilian Regent Pedro led by General Carlos Frederico Lecor besieged Montevideo, in recently occupied Uruguay. Portuguese commander Don Alvaro Da Costa de Sousa Macedo was eventually forced to evacuate to Lisbon and Brazilian independence was assured (January 1823–28 February 1824).

Montevideo ∎ 1843–1851 ∎ Argentine-Uruguayan War

Argentine General Manuel Cerefino Oribe intervened in Uruguay to support the Conservative Blanco faction against Liberal Colorado leader José Fructuoso Rivera at **Arroyo Grande** (December 1842), then besieged him at Montevideo. Argentine rebel Justo José de Urquiza drove off Oribe after eight years and fighting continued until **Caseros** in early 1852 (16 February 1843–8 October 1851).

Montfaucon ∎ 886 ∎ Viking Raids on France

During the long Viking siege of **Paris**, Odo (Eudes), Marquess of Neustria and Count of Paris, took a force against the invaders in northeast France at Montfaucon, near Verdun. The Vikings were heavily defeated and, after being unable to capture Paris, were brought off by the Frankish King Charles III—the Fat. Charles was later deposed by Odo.

Montgisard ∎ 1177 ∎ Crusader-Muslim Wars

On a major campaign against Palestine, Saladin of Egypt besieged the coastal city of Ascalon before advancing towards Jerusalem. In a des-

perate counter-offensive, King Baldwin IV of Jersualem, supported by the Knights Templar, ambushed the Muslim army at Montgisard, near Ramleh. Saladin was badly defeated and withdrew to Egypt with heavy losses (25 November 1177).

Montgomery's Tavern ∎ 1837 ∎ Canadian Rebellion
See **Toronto**

Montiel ∎ 1369 ∎ Castilian War of Succession

Two years after Prince Edward of England—the Black Prince—restored Pedro IV to the throne of Castile following **Navarette**, Pedro faced renewed rebellion by his brother Henry of Trastamara and his French ally Bertrand du Guesclin. At the castle of Montiel, east of Valdepenas, Pedro was defeated and murdered by his brother, who took the throne as Henry II of Castile (23 March 1369).

Montijo ∎ 1644 ∎ Spanish-Portuguese Wars

When Spain lost the throne of Portugal in 1640, she continued her attempts to reassert control and John IV of Portugal sent General Mathias de Albuquerque against the former rulers. At Montijo, west of Badajoz, Albuquerque routed a Spanish army. War continued intermittently for another 20 years before Phillip II finally recognised Portuguese independence (26 May 1644).

Montison ∎ 1810 ∎ Napoleonic Wars (Peninsular Campaign)
See **La Carolina**

Montjuich ∎ 1705 ∎ War of the Spanish Succession
See **Barcelona, Spain (1st)**

Montlhéry ∎ 1465 ∎ Franco-Burgundian Wars

Faced by the rebellious "League of the Public Weal," the autocratic Louis XI of France took the field at Montlhéry, south of Paris, against dissident nobles led by his own brother, Charles Duke of Berry and Charles the Bold, son of Philip of Burgundy. After suffering a narrow cavalry defeat, Louis was forced to surrender land in Normandy to his brother and in Burgundy to Charles (13 July 1465).

Montmartre I 1814 I Napoleonic Wars (French Campaign)
See **Paris**

Montmirail I 1814 I Napoleonic Wars (French Campaign)
Napoleon Bonaparte led a brilliant campaign against General Gebhard von Blucher east of Paris, where he destroyed part of Blucher's Prussian-Russian army at **Champaubert**, then turned next day against a separate Corps under General Dimitri Osten-Sacken. At Montmirail, Sacken's Corps was also destroyed and Bonaparte moved against a third force at **Chateau-Thierry** (11 February 1814).

Montmorency Gorge I 1759 I Seven Years War (North America)
During the British siege of **Quebec**, General James Wolfe sent General George Townshend against the French camp at the nearby Gorge of Montmorency, defended by Marquis Louis de Montcalm. Advancing without waiting for Brigadier Robert Monckton, the British grenadiers suffered over 400 casualties and were forced to withdraw. However, Quebec fell six weeks later (31 July 1759).

Montreal I 1760 I Seven Years War (North America)
Following a failed French attempt to recover **Quebec** (27 April), British forces converged on Montreal, where a siege was established by General Jeffrey Amherst, supported by Generals James Murray from Quebec and William Haviland from Lake Champlain. French Governor Pierre Rigaud, Marquis de Vaudreuil, capitulated after two days and Canada became British (6–8 September 1760).

Montreal I 1775 I War of the American Revolution
American commander Richard Montgomery was investing **St Johns** when he sent Major Ethan Allen northwest against Montreal, defended by General Guy Carleton. Allen was captured (25 September) in a failed assault with Colonel John Brown. After victory at **Longueuil** and St Johns, Montgomery attacked and captured Montreal. Carleton escaped to **Quebec** (13 November 1775).

Montréjeau I 1799 I French Revolutionary Wars (2nd Coalition)
When Royalists in southwestern France were routed at **Toulouse** (9 August), Republican forces pursued the survivors 60 miles down the River Garonne to Montréjeau. Just west of Montréjeau, on the road to Cuguron, the Royalists were completely shattered, losing perhaps 2,000 killed and 1,000 captured out of 4,000, effectively ending the counter-revolution (20 August 1799).

Montrevel I 1944 I World War II (Western Europe)
With Germans in southern France withdrawing along the Rhone, further east Colonel Charles Hodge tried to hold Montrevel, near Bourg, to block a secondary escape route. Attacked by General Wend von Wietersheim's Panzer Division, which had broken through at **Montélimar**, the Americans were overwhelmed and surrendered and German withdrawal continued (3 September 1944).

Montserrat I 1811 I Napoleonic Wars (Peninsular Campaign)
While French forces besieged **Figueras** in Catalonia, newly created Marshal Louis Suchet took 10,000 men against the hilltop monastery of Montserrat, overlooking the Llobregat, northwest of Barcelona. Although General Jean-Francois Abbé took the monastery by storm in a brilliant assault, most of the garrison of Spanish irregulars managed to escape down the mountain (25 July 1811).

Mont St Jean I 1815 I Napoleonic Wars (The Hundred Days)
  See **Waterloo**

Mont Valerian I 1871 I Franco-Prussian War

On the day the last outside attempt to relieve besieged **Paris** was defeated at **St Quentin**, General Louis Jules Trochu reluctantly agreed to a sortie from the capital with nearly 90,000 men, advancing west through Mont Valerian to Buzenval and Malmaison. Lacking proper coordination, the French were driven back with over 4,000 casualties. Paris capitulated a week later (19 January 1871).

Monzon I 1809 I Napoleonic Wars (Peninsular Campaign)

Advancing along the Cinca Valley in northeast Spain, French General Pierre Habert sent a force across the river near the Spanish-held town of Monzon, southeast of Huesca, where they were trapped by rising water. Habert's rescue attempt was driven back from the bridge at Monzon and, after almost 1,000 of his men surrendered, Habert withdrew to Villafranca (16–19 March 1809).

Moodkee I 1845 I 1st British-Sikh War
  See **Mudki**

Mookerheyde I 1574 I Netherlands War of Independence

Spanish Viceroy Don Luis de Zuniga y Requesens withdrew troops from the siege of **Leyden** and sent a large force under Sancho d'Avila to the Mookerheyde, near Mook on the Meuse, held by Counts Louis and Henry of Nassau, younger brothers of William of Orange. The Dutch were utterly crushed, with both Louis and Henry killed, and the siege of Leyden resumed (14 April 1574).

Moonlight Battle I 1780 I War of the American Revolution
  See **Cape St Vincent**

Moonlight Raid I 1808 I Napoleonic Wars (Russo-Swedish War)
  See **Virta bro**

Moorefield I 1864 I American Civil War (Eastern Theatre)

On return from a raid into Maryland, Confederate General John McCausland was ambushed at **Cumberland**. Then a week later he was attacked at Moorefield, on the south branch of the Potomac in West Virginia by pursuing Union cavalry under General William W. Averell. McCausland was badly defeated, but commander Jubal A. Early soon struck back at **Summit Point** (7 August 1864).

Moore's Creek Bridge I 1776 I War of the American Revolution

Facing revolution in North Carolina, British commander Thomas Gage sent General Donald McDonald to lead Scottish and other local Loyalists against rebel Colonel James Moore. Marching to support the British at Wilmington, the Tories were routed to the northwest at Moore's Creek Bridge. About 50 were killed with another 800 captured, including General McDonald (27 February 1776).

Moorosi's Mountain I 1879 I Baputhi War

Baputhi Chief Moorosi in Lesotho threatened increasing resistance and about 500 Cape colonial troops tried to assault his steep mountain stronghold along the Orange near Qthing in Lesotho. Despite modern arms, the whites were bloodily repulsed. However, after a long siege, reinforcements arrived and the fortress fell by storm. Moorosi died in the final assault (17 March–20 November 1879).

Mopsuestia I 1152 I 2nd Crusade

With Constantinople distracted by the Second Crusade, the Armenian leader Thoros gradually seized Cilicia and Emperor Manuel I sent an army under his cousin Andronicus. The Greeks retook Tarsus, but near Mopsuestia (Crusader Mamista) Thoros routed the invaders with over 3,000 killed. In 1159 Cilicia was recovered by

Manuel, who later ceded control to Armenian vassal Princes.

Mór | 1848 | Hungarian Revolutionary War

As Habsburg Field Marshal Alfred Windischgratz advanced into Hungary, nationalist General Moritz Perczel attempted to hold Mór, 50 miles west of Budapest. Attacked by Croat commander Joseph Jellacic, Perczel withdrew south towards Stuhlweissenberg with over 1,000 prisoners lost. Windischgratz captured Budapest, then continued east to **Kapolna** (30 December 1848).

Mora, Cameroon | 1915–1916 | World War I (African Colonial Theatre)

Despite the loss of **Garua** in upper German Cameroon (June 1915), a small force under Hauptmann von Raben held out further north in the small fortress of Mora. With little ammunition, and the fall of the German "capital" in the south at Yaunde (1 January 1916), the Germans surrendered to General Charles Dobell and withdrew north into Spanish territory (October 1915–18 February 1916).

Mora, New Mexico | 1847 | American-Mexican War

Threatened by resistance to American annexation of New Mexico, Captain Israel Hendley occupied Las Vegas (NM) then marched north against about 200 insurgents at nearby Mora. Hendley and four others were killed in a sharp action and the survivors withdrew to Santa Fe. Other Mexican rebels were beaten the same day at **La Cañada** and a week later at **Pueblo de Taos** (24 January 1847).

Morales | 1813 | Napoleonic Wars (Peninsular Campaign)

As Arthur Wellesley Lord Wellington advanced across the Duoro towards his great victory at **Vitoria**, British Hussars under Colonel Colquhoun Grant caught up with French regiments led by General Alexandre Digeon. Grant smashed the French rearguard in a one-sided action at Morales, east of Toro, and the Allied advance continued (2 June 1813).

Moramanga | 1947 | Madagascan Insurrection

Malagasy nationalists who rose against French rule in Madagascar, attacked a military camp in the railway junction city of Moramanga, where Senegalese troops repulsed the insurgents then exacted brutal reprisals. As insurrection spread, French reinforcements crushed the 21-month rising at terrible cost. The attack is commemorated in independent Madagascar as Insurrection Day (29 March 1947).

Morar | 1858 | Indian Mutiny

General Sir Hugh Rose advanced west from **Kalpi** to reach Morar, just east of Gwalior, where he was blocked by a rebel force twice as large under Tantia Topi. A hard-fought hand-to-hand action, with costly losses on both sides, forced the rebels to flee. Rose then joined the siege of **Gwalior** and sent General William Smith against the Rhani of Jhansi at **Kotah-ki-Serai** (16 June 1858).

Morat | 1476 | Burgundian-Swiss War

Three months after defeat at **Grandson**, Charles the Bold of Burgundy returned to Switzerland with a large force and besieged Morat (modern Murten) on Lake Murten west of Bern. Attacking in heavy rain, a Swiss army under Hans Waldmann and Adrian von Bubenberg routed the Burgundians. Thousands were killed trapped against the lake and Duke Charles fled to Lorraine (22 June 1476).

Morava | 285 | Roman Military Civil Wars

See **Margus**

Morava | 1190 | Byzantine-Serbian War

When Stephen Numanja of Serbia overthrew Byzantine rule and seized territory in coastal Dalmatia, Emperor Isaac II marched into Serbia and defeated him in battle on the Morava. Isaac then pardoned Numanja, who accepted the Byzantine title Sebastocrator and married his son to the Emperor's niece. However, Isaac's new prestige was soon destroyed by the Bulgarians at **Berroea**.

Moraviantown ▮ 1813 ▮ War of 1812
See **Thames**

Morazzone ▮ 1848 ▮ 1st Italian War of Independence

Despite an armistice after **Custozza**, Giuseppe Garibaldi continued the war against Austria and repulsed an attack near Lake Maggiore at **Luino** (15 August), then faced a much larger force sent by Baron Konstantin d'Aspre further south at Morazzone. Heavily bombarded by General Ferdinand von Simbschen, Garibaldi had to withdraw and retreated into Switzerland (26 August 1848).

Morbihan Gulf ▮ 56 BC ▮ Rome's Later Gallic Wars

Soon after subjugating the Belgae at **Aduatuca**, Julius Caesar turned on the seafaring Veneti people of Brittany and had a fleet built at the mouth of the Loire. Watched by Caesar from the land, Decimus Brutus took his hastily built ships close to the opposing fleet and, after slashing their rigging, boarded and burned the Veneti ships. The Veneti and the rest of Brittany quickly sued for peace.

Morella ▮ 1837–1838 ▮ 1st Carlist War

While Carlist forces were defeated in north and northwest Spain, Carlist leader Ramón Cabrera took the offensive in Catalonia, where he besieged Morella. With insufficient resources to take the city by assault, the siege was close to being called off when Catalan Lieutenant Pablo Alió and about 80 men scaled the walls by night. The Cristino garrison surrendered (9 December 1837–26 January 1838).

Morella ▮ 1838 ▮ 1st Carlist War

With Carlist forces defeated in north and northwest Spain, Liberal General Marcelino Oráa marched on the key stronghold city of Morella in Catalonia. After an incompetent siege, and under persistent attack in the field by Carlist leader Ramón Cabrera, Oráa withdrew to avoid further losses. He was dismissed while Carlos V named Cabrera as Count of Morella (24 July–18 August 1838).

Morella ▮ 1840 ▮ 1st Carlist War

Despite Carlist Commander Rafael Maroto signing the peace (August 1839), Ramón Cabrera fought on in Catalonia, where Liberal General Baldomero Espartero besieged Morella. With the capture of outlying positions, the emblematic Carlist city was doomed and a nighttime break out was repulsed with heavy losses. Morella surrendered and Cabrera fled into exile, ending the war (19–23 May 1840).

Morgarten ▮ 1315 ▮ Habsburg Wars of Succession

In the struggle for the German throne between the Habsburg Frederick of Austria and the Wittelsbach candidate Louis of Bavaria, Frederick's brother Leopold took an army to punish the Swiss for supporting Louis. In Morgarten Pass southeast of Zug, the invading Habsburg army was utterly destroyed, though war continued until the decisive battle in 1322 at **Mühldorf** (15 November 1315).

Morhange ▮ 1914 ▮ World War I (Western Front)
See **Lorraine**

Morlaix ▮ 1342 ▮ Hundred Years War

William Bohun Earl of Northampton relieved **Brest** in August then joined Robert of Artois to besiege Morlaix 30 miles to the northeast. Facing the approaching army of Charles of Blois at nearby Lanmeur, English longbowmen secured a decisive victory over French knights. However, Northampton chose to retire. Edward III of England soon arrived and secured a truce in Brittany (30 September 1342).

Morogoro ▮ 1916 ▮ World War I (African Colonial Theatre)

Regrouping after defeat at **Salaita** (12 February), new British commander in German East Africa, Jan Smuts, attacked east of Kilimanjaro, aided by British from Rhodesia and Belgians advancing from the Congo. The so-called Morogoro Offensive secured Dar Es Salaam and the key railways of East Africa. The Germans were soon driven out at **Tabora** and **Mahiwa** (March–September 1916).

Morpeth I 629 I Anglo-Saxon Territorial Wars

Reportedly to avenge British defeat at **Chester** (615), Caedwalla of Gwynned (North Wales) invaded the territory of his foster-brother, King Edwin of Northumbria. But at Morpeth, on the Wansbeck River north of Newscastle, Caedwalla and his son Cadfan were heavily defeated and fled to Ireland. The Welsh King returned in 633 to help defeat Edwin at **Heathfield**.

Morro Castle I 1762 I Seven Years War (Caribbean)

See **Havana**

Mortain I 1944 I World War II (Western Europe)

Determined to cut off the Allied breakout from **Normandy**, commander Marshal Günther von Kluge counter-attacked towards **Avranches**, where he was blocked at Mortain by infantry of General George Patton's Third Army. Fighting around the town developed into the largest tank action in Normandy before Mortain was relieved. The Germans then withdrew towards **Falaise** (6–12 August 1944).

Mortara I 1849 I 1st Italian War of Independence

Resuming his campaign for Italian independence after **Custozza** (July 1848), King Charles Albert of Sardinia sent his son Victor Emmanuel and General Giacomo Durando to challenge Marshal Josef Radetzky's Austrians at Mortara, south of **Novara**. The town was stormed by General Baron Konstantin d'Aspre and the Italians withdrew to Novara with heavy losses (21 March 1849).

Mortemer I 1054 I Rise of William of Normandy

Henry I of France helped William of Normandy beat rebellious nobles at **Val-ès-Dunes** (1047)

then turned against the Normans. Defending a two-pronged invasion of Normandy, Duke William (later William I of England) routed Henry's brother Odo (Eudes) at Mortemer near Neufchatel. Henry and his ally Charles Martel Count of Anjou withdrew, but invaded again four years later through **Varaville**.

Mortimer's Cross I 1461 I Wars of the Roses

Just days after the death of Richard Duke of York at **Wakefield**, his son Edward intercepted a Lancastrian army marching from Wales under Jasper Tudor Earl of Pembroke and James Butler Earl of Wiltshire. At Mortimer's Cross, north of Hereford, Edward secured a decisive victory, then executed several Lancastrian captives, including Pembroke's father Owen Tudor (2 February 1461).

Mortlack I 1010 I Later Viking Raids on Britain

A renewed Viking invasion of Scotland saw King Sweyn Forkbeard (Svend I) of Denmark defeat Malcolm II at **Nairn**. The following year he returned to meet the Scots at Mortlack, northwest of Aberdeen. Malcolm defeated the Danes after a desperate struggle, driving them back to their ships. Sweyn then turned his attention instead to the conquest of England.

Mortmant I 1814 I Napoleonic Wars (French Campaign)

Napoleon Bonaparte defeated Blucher's Army of Silesia four times in five days east of Paris, then marched south to meet the Austrians and Russians of Prince Karl Philipp Schwarzenberg. At Mortmant, Russian advance units under General Count Pyotr Pahlen were beaten by Marshal Étienne Gérard and fell back through Nangis and Valjouan to **Montereau** (17 February 1814).

Morton's Ford I 1864 I American Civil War (Eastern Theatre)

On a diversionary offensive against the Confederates in northern Virginia, Union General John C. Caldwell, with General Alexander Hays, advanced across the Rapidan against General Richard Ewell. In the heaviest fighting, at Morton's Ford, the Union forces met unexpected resistance and withdrew during the night after being held down by Confederate fire all day (6–7 February 1864).

Morval ▮ 1916 ▮ World War I (Western Front)

General Sir Henry Rawlinson quickly regrouped after losses around **Flers-Courcelette** during the Battle of the **Somme** and renewed the offensive east towards Morval. The British secured Morval and Lesboeufs and the following day took Combles, while further west the offensive secured **Thiepval**. The advance then continued further east against the **Transloy Ridges** (25–28 September 1916).

Moscow ▮ 1238 ▮ Mongol Conquest of Russia

While campaigning in Russia, the Mongol Batu (grandson of Genghis Khan) and his General Subetai destroyed **Ryazan**, then marched into the Princedom of Vladimir-Suzdal and attacked newly established Moscow. The young city fell after a brief siege and was plundered and destroyed by fire before the Mongols marched east against the city of **Vladimir**.

Moscow ▮ 1382 ▮ Russian-Mongol Wars

Two years after Grand Prince Dimitri of Moscow defeated Mongol Chief Mamai at **Kulikovo**, Mamai was in turn overthrown at the **Kalka** by his rival Toktamish, who then led a fresh Mongol offensive to crush the Russian rebellion. Toktamish captured Moscow after Dimitri fled. The city then suffered a terrible massacre and destruction as Mongol overlordship was reimposed (23 August 1382).

Moscow ▮ 1571 ▮ Russian-Tatar Wars

On campaign deep in Russia, Khan Devlet Girai of Crimea led 100,000 men to Moscow, where Princes Ivan Mstislavsky, Ivan Belsky, Mikhail Vorotinski and others were unable to defend the city. The Tatars burned part of Moscow—with a claimed 60,000 killed—before withdrawing with thousands of prisoners. Another attack a year later was repulsed at **Molodi** (24–26 May 1571).

Moscow ▮ 1611–1612 ▮ Russian Time of Troubles

Sigismund III of Poland captured Moscow with his victory at **Klushino** (July 1610), but Russians then besieged the city and the Polish garrison under Jan Karol Chodkiewicz was defeated by Prince Dimitri Pozharski (22–25 August 1612). The survivors led by Colonel Mikolaj Strus withdrew into the Kremlin, where they were starved into surrender and then massacred (27 October 1612).

Moscow ▮ 1618 ▮ Russian Time of Troubles

At the end of the Time of Troubles, 22-year-old Prince Ladislav of Poland, supported by Hetman Jan Karol Chodkiewicz and Cossacks under Pyotr Sahaidachny, marched on Moscow to claim the throne. Assaulting Moscow itself, he was repulsed by Prince Dimitri Pozharski. However, Russia soon sued for peace in which Poland kept its conquests, including **Smolensk** (1 October 1618).

Moscow ▮ 1941–1942 ▮ World War II (Eastern Front)

Soon after victory at **Bryansk** and **Vyazma**, German forces reached 25 miles from Moscow before being stalled by bloody defence and extreme cold. General Georgi Zhukov then launched a massive counter-offensive west of the capital. The Germans fell back with heavy losses, but soon stabilised the front. They later checked a Russian advance at **Kharkov** (4 December 1941–March 1942).

Mosega ▮ 1837 ▮ Boer-Matabele War

Determined to avenge Boer defeat at **Vegkop** (October 1836), Andreis Hendrik Potgieter and Gert Maritz led 100 whites and 100 Africans across the Vaal against Mzilikazi's Matabele at Mosega, near Zeerust, northeast of Mafeking. A surprise assault destroyed the camp and recovered over 7,000 cattle, but Mzilikazi was absent. In November Potgieter attacked again at **Kapain** (17 January 1837).

Moskva I 1812 I Napoleonic Wars (Russian Campaign)
See **Borodino**

Mosquiteros I 1813 I Venezuelan War of Independence
Spanish irregulars led by José Tomás Boves defeated a Patriot force at Santa Catalina in western Venezuela, then faced 2,500 Republicans under General Vicente Campo Elías at Mosquiteros, east of Calabozo. A disastrous rout saw Boves beaten with terrible slaughter, though Spanish Royalists advancing from the east turned the tables a month later near **Barquisimeto** (14 October 1813).

Mosskirch I 1800 I French Revolutionary Wars (2nd Coalition)
French General Jean Victor Moreau pursued the Austrians after their twin defeats at **Engen** and **Stockach**, continuing his offensive across the Rhine north of Lake Constance by chasing defeated General Paul Kray north towards the Danube. At Mosskirch two days later, Kray fought and lost a stubborn rearguard action. He soon counter-attacked at **Biberach** and **Erbach** (5 May 1800).

Mossy Creek I 1863 I American Civil War (Western Theatre)
On campaign east of Knoxville, Tennessee, after victory at **Fort Sanders**, Union General Samuel D. Sturgis advanced against Confederate forces under General William T. Martin. At Mossy Creek (modern Jefferson City), Martin attacked an isolated Union brigade under Colonel Archibald P. Campbell. But the main force soon arrived and the Confederates withdrew (29 December 1863).

Mostar I 1993–1994 I Bosnian War
After Bosnian Croats and Muslims ejected Serbs from Mostar (June 1992), Muslim refugees entered Herzegovina's capital and Croats west of the Neretva besieged Muslim east Mostar. Croat shelling caused massive damage (including the historic Ottoman bridge) and Muslims from Mostar and nearby villages were brutalised before a peace agreement ended the siege (9 May 1993–January 1994).

Mosul I 1743 I Turko-Persian Wars of Nadir Shah
Nadir Shah of Persia captured Karkuk in Mesopotamia then besieged Mosul on the Upper Tigris, defended by Husain Shah. Using 160 cannon and 230 mortars, Nadir inflicted a terrible bombardment on the city, though the Persian assaults were repulsed with heavy losses. Faced by a rising at home, Nadir negotiated a truce and withdrew (14 September–20 October 1743).

Mosynopolis I 1185 I 2nd Byzantine-Sicilian War
See **Strymon**

Mota I 629 I Muslim Conquest of Syria
See **Muta**

Motien Pass I 1904 I Russo-Japanese War
While Russians on the Liaodong Peninsula north of **Port Arthur** tried to halt Japanese forces in the south at **Delisi**, General Tamemoto Kuroki's First Army advanced from the east and captured the vital Motien Pass, on the Liaoyang-Dandong Road. Russian General Feodor Keller tried to recapture Motien, but was caught in artillery fire and withdrew with heavy losses to **Liaoyang** (17 July 1904).

Moti Talav I 1771 I Maratha-Mysore Wars
See **Chinkurli**

Moturoa I 1868 I 2nd New Zealand War
Colonel George Whitmore assumed command in Wanganui after disaster at **Te Ngutu-o-te-manu** and attacked the Hauhau chief Titokowaru at Moturoa. An unwise frontal assault saw his armed constabulary routed with 40

casualties, including Major William Hunter killed. They fell back to nearby Wairoa, but Whitmore later marched to attack the Hauhau at **Ngatapa** (7 November 1868).

Motya ▌ 397–396 BC ▌
1st Dionysian War

When Dionysius the Elder, Tyrant of Syracuse, attacked the island city of Moyta, just off the west coast of Sicily, the Carthaginian garrison cut the causeway. However, Dionysius eventually took the city by storm and massacred the residents. The following year the Carthaginian General Himilco easily recaptured Motya, re-establishing its residents at nearby Lilybeaum, then attacked **Syracuse**.

Moulay Ishmael ▌ 1835 ▌ French
Conquest of Algeria
See **Macta**

Moulmein ▌ 1942 ▌ World War II
(Burma-India)

General Hiroshi Takeuchi invaded **Burma** through **Kawkareik** (22 January) and attacked Moulmein, Burma's third largest city, held by units of General Thomas Hutton's army under Brigadier Roger Ekin. A fierce struggle ensued for the airfield with costly hand-to-hand fighting before the British withdrew across the Salween to Martaban, which was soon abandoned (30–31 January 1942).

Mountain Meadows ▌ 1857 ▌
Mormon War

With Federal government relations strained, Mormon fanatics led Paiute Indians against a wagon train from Arkansas passing through southern Utah to California. In a valley called Mountain Meadows, deceived by a ceasefire proposed by white men, about 120 emigrants were murdered. Twenty years later, John D. Lee was convicted for the crime and was executed on the site (7–11 September 1857).

Mount Badon ▌ 497 ▌ Anglo-Saxon
Conquest of Britain
See **Mons Badonicus**

Mount Barbosthene ▌ 192 BC ▌ Spartan-
Achaean Wars

On a renewed offensive against the Achaean League, Nabis of Sparta recovered the recently liberated port of **Gytheum**, then faced a counter-invasion by Achaeans under Philopoemen. Attempting to block Philopoemen in the Barbosthene Mountains, ten miles northeast of Sparta, Nabis was utterly crushed. Rome then intervened to enforce a truce and the Tyrant was assassinated soon afterwards.

Mount Gaurus ▌ 342 BC ▌ 1st
Samnite War

Rome went to war with the Samnites to win supremacy in central Italy and Marcus Valerius Corvus and Decius Mus secured a victory just west of Naples at Mount Gaurus (modern Barbaro). Unable to fully conquer the Sammites, Rome turned to crush the Latins at **Trifanum**, before resuming war with the Samnites and suffering a decisive defeat in 321 BC at the **Caudine Forks**.

Mount Gilboa ▌ 1010 BC ▌ Philistine-
Israel Wars

Despite victories against Philistines (including **Michmash** in 1013 BC), King Saul of Judah found himself under attack on Mount Gilboa, above the Plain of Jezreel east of Megiddo in the north of modern Israel. In a bloody and decisive defeat, Saul's three sons, including the outstanding commander Jonathan, were all killed. The King fell on his sword to avoid capture (trad date 1010 BC).

Mount Grammos ▌ 1948 ▌ Greek
Civil War
See **Grammos**

Mount Haemus ▌ 981 ▌ Byzantine Wars
of Tsar Samuel

Byzantine Emperor Basil marched into Bulgaria against the newly established Tsar Samuel and failed in a poorly managed siege of Sardica (modern Sofia). He then faced attack as he withdrew through the passes of Mount Haemus, south of the Danube. The Imperial army was heavily defeated, with substantial quantities of valuable baggage lost. Basil himself was lucky to escape with his life.

Mount Hermon I 1973 I Arab-Israeli Yom Kippur War

At the start of the Syrian offensive on the **Golan Heights**, helicopter-borne troops surprised the key fortified position in the north on Mount Hermon (6 October). When Israeli forces counter-attacked on the plain, paratroops under Colonel Hezi retook part of the strategic position. Commando forces finally secured the 8,200-foot peak just as a ceasefire ended the war (20–22 October 1973).

Mount Hope I 1676 I King Philip's War

With his allies destroyed at the **Great Swamp Fight** (December 1675), the Wampanoag Chief Metacomet—King Philip—returned to his tribal home at Mt Hope (Bristol, Rhode Island), where he was ambushed by colonial militia under Colonel Benjamin Church. Philip was shot by Alderman—a Wampanoag scout—ending resistance to white settlement in southern New England (12 August 1676).

Mount Kenya I 1955 I Mau Mau Revolt

Following his offensive against Mau Mau rebels north of Nairobi in the forest of **Aberdare, Kenya**, General Sir George Erskine sent his forces further east against guerrilla strongholds on Mount Kenya (Operation First Flute). While the big sweep saw fewer than 300 Mau Mau killed or captured, the tide had begun to turn. Erskine's successor soon attacked again at Aberdare (February–April 1955).

Mount Lactarius I 553 I Gothic War in Italy

A year after the disastrous defeat of Totila at **Taginae**, Goths in Italy and their newly elected leader Teias resolved to avenge the death of their great Chief. The hopeless last battle against Roman General Narses took place on Mount Lactarius, near the Sarnus (modern Sarno) River,

south of Vesuvius. Teias and thousands of his warriors died and the Goths submitted to Emperor Justinian.

Mount Leburnion I 1091 I Byzantine-Pecheneg Wars

Emperor Alexius I faced a fresh incursion from Bulgaria into Thrace by the Pechenegs and secured aid from the Pechenegs' former Kipchaq allies. When Alexius attacked at Mount Leburnion, at the mouth of the Maritza, the Pechenegs were routed and a subsequent massacre virtually destroyed their power. A final Pecheneg offensive was destroyed in 1122 at **Eski Zagra** (29 April 1091).

Mount Longdon I 1982 I Falklands War

British troops captured **San Carlos, Falklands**, then advanced towards **Stanley** and attacked to the northwest at Mount Longdon, with other actions at Two Sisters and Mount Harriet. Despite artillery support, Longdon was finally taken at bayonet-point, with 23 British killed and 47 wounded, and heavy Argentine losses. The final attack then went in at **Mount Tumbledown** (11–12 June 1982).

Mount Lyceum I 227 BC I Cleomenic War

As part of his ambition to bring the whole Peloponnese into the Achaean League, Aratus of Sicyon led a force into Elis in the northwestern Peloponnese, which sought aid from Cleomenes III of Sparta. Cleomenes defeated the Achaeans in battle at Mount Lycaeum, near Megalopolis. Aratus recovered to surprise and capture Mantinea and he soon fought Cleomenes again at **Ladoceia**.

Mount Oeta I 1821 I Greek War of Independence
See **Vasilika**

Mount Phoenix I 654 I Early Byzantine-Muslim Wars

At the head of an expedition against Constantinople, the Saracen General Mu'awiya was met by the Emperor Constans, personally in command at sea off Mount Phoenix, near Rhodes in Asia Minor. The Byzantines suffered heavy casualties in a great naval battle, but the victorious Muslim fleet was also badly damaged and withdrew to allow Mu'awiya to contest for the Caliphate.

Mount St Nicholas I 1877 I Russo-Turkish Wars

Turkish Commander Suleiman Pasha determined to clear Russians from the strategic **Shipka Pass** through the Balkan Mountains in Bulgaria to relieve besieged **Plevna** and attacked the nearby Mount St Nicholas. Suleiman was repulsed with over 3,000 casualties and the campaign settled into a three-month stalemate until the Russian attack on the Turkish camp at **Senova** (16–17 September 1877).

Mount Suribachi I 1945 I World War II (Pacific)

See **Iwo Jima**

Mount Tabor I 1799 I French Revolutionary Wars (Middle East)

During Napoleon Bonaparte's siege of **Acre**, a Turkish and Mamluk relief army from Damascus under Ahmed Pasha surrounded French General Jean-Baptiste Kléber at Mount Tabor, south of Tiberias near the Jordan. Bonaparte marched east in time to save Kléber and destroy the Muslims, though he was unable to capture Acre and was forced to withdraw to Egypt (16–17 April 1799).

Mount Talipao I 1913 I American-Moro Wars

Soon after the massacre of Philippine Muslims at **Bud Bagsak** on Jolo, the Moro leader Datu Sabtal and his supporters fortified themselves on nearby Mount Talipao, where they were routed by Major George Shaw, losing perhaps 100 killed. The Moro later returned and, in virtually the last action of the war, they were again defeated and forced to surrender (13 August–22 October 1913).

Mount Tifata I 83 BC I Sullan Civil War

General Lucius Cornelius Sulla returned from Asia Minor to support the Senate against Gaius Marius the Younger and landed with 40,000 men at Brundisium, then marched north gathering support. On the Volturno near Mount Tifata he met and destroyed the Marian General Gaius Norbanus, who fled under siege to Capua. Sulla soon defeated Marius himself further north near Rome at **Sacriportus**.

Mount Tumbledown I 1982 I Falklands War

As British forces advanced across East Falkland to **Stanley**, there was fierce fighting in the mountains to the west at **Mount Longdon**, then at Mount Tumbledown as Scots Guards attacked the most heavily defended Argentine position on the island. Despite their massive artillery fire, the British suffered costly losses storming entrenched troops before the final peak was taken (13–14 June 1982).

Mount Vesuvius I 339 BC I Latin War

See **Suessa**

Mount Vesuvius I 71 BC I 3rd Servile War

See **Silarus**

Mount Zion Church I 1861 I American Civil War (Trans-Mississippi)

In order to secure northeastern Missouri, Union General Benjamin M. Prentiss marched from Palmyra against secessionists near Sturgeon. After a check at nearby Hallsville, he defeated Colonel Caleb Dorsey near Mount Zion Church, inflicting over 200 casualties, then returned to Sturgeon. The rebels dispersed, but some fought again ten days later at **Roan's Tan Yard** (28 December 1861).

Mouquet Farm I 1916 I World War I (Western Front)

See **Pozières**

Mouscron I 1794 I French Revolutionary Wars (1st Coalition)

Prince Friedrich Josias of Saxe-Coburg resolved to stem a new French offensive in the north and sent Count Charles von Clerfayt towards Menin. However, Clerfayt was attacked and overwhelmed at Mouscron, just southwest of Courtrai, by the much larger force of General Joseph Souham. Further Allied defeats followed within weeks at **Courtrai** and **Tourcoing** (29 April 1794).

Moutoa I 1864 I 2nd New Zealand War

As they descended the North Island's Wanganui River, religio-military Hauhau led by Matene Rangi-Tauira were blocked at the mid-river island of Moutoa by loyal Ngati Hau under Tamehana te Aewa as well as Ngati Pamoana under Haimona Hiroti. A fierce semi-ritualistic action saw the lower river Maoris defeat the Hauhau, who lost 50 killed, including the prophet Matene (14 May 1864).

Moyry Pass I 1600 I Tyrone Rebellion

Two years after victory at **Blackwater** for Irish rebel Hugh O'Neill Earl of Tyrone, English commander Charles Blunt Lord Mountjoy attempted to march from Dundalk into Tyrone and was blocked by O'Neill at the Moyry Pass. Mountjoy captured some rebel entrenchments before being driven back with heavy losses. However, O'Neill was later bypassed and withdrew (2–5 October 1600).

Moys I 1757 I Seven Years War (Europe)

Withdrawing west across Saxony to meet the Allies after defeat at **Kolin** (18 June), Frederick II of Prussia left his brother Duke August-Wilhelm and General Hans Karl von Winterfeldt to hold an Austrian advance into Silesia. At Moys (modern Zgorzelec) near Gorlitz, Winterfeld was overwhelmed and killed. Duke August-Wilhelm was soon defeated near **Schweidnitz** (8 September 1757).

Mpukonyoni I 1906 I Bambatha Rebellion

In support of rebellion in Natal, the veteran Zulu leader Mehlokazulu (son of Chief Sihayo, killed at **Ondini** in 1883) gathered forces and marched towards the Nkandla, but was intercepted at Mpukonyoni by government troops marching north across the Tugela. Mehlokazulu suffered a costly defeat and withdrew to join up with Bambatha near the **Mome** Gorge (28 May 1906).

Msebe I 1883 I Zulu Civil War

After the British-restored Zulu King Cetshwayo returned to his kingdom following defeat at **Ulundi** (4 July 1879), about 5,000 of his uSuthu were ambushed in the Msebe Valley by the Mandlakazi faction under Zibebhu. Over 4,000 uSuthu were reported killed in the bloodiest ever Zulu battle. A few months later Zibebhu attacked Cetshwayo himself in his capital at **Ondini** (30 March 1883).

Mstislavl I 1501 I 1st Muscovite-Lithuanian War

Duke Ivan III of Moscow routed a Lithuanian army at the **Vedrosha** (July 1500) then sent a fresh force under Princes Vasily Shemyachich and Semen Mozhaysky against Alexander of Lithuania and Poland. At Mstislavl, south of Smolensk, Lithuanian commanders Astafy Dushkovich and Mikhail Zheslasky were routed with perhaps 7,000 killed but Ivan failed to take **Smolensk** (4 November 1501).

Muar I 1942 I World War II (Pacific)

While Australian forces tried to stall the Japanese in Malaya's northwest Johore at **Gemas**, further west Brigadier Herbert Duncan tried to hold the Muar River. Japanese Imperial Guards advancing under General Takumo Nishimura drove the allies back with heavy losses. Despite Australian reinforcements, nearby Bakri was also lost and the withdrawal continued to **Singapore** (15–20 January 1941).

Mucuritas I 1817 I Venezuelan War of Independence

Determined to crush Venezuelan insurrection, Spanish commander Pablo Morillo sent General Miguel de La Torre, who unexpectedly met 1,300 llaneros under General Antonio José Páez west of San Fernando near Apurito at Mucuritas. De La Torre's force withstood the rebel cavalry until Páez set fire to dry grass. The Spanish were defeated and withdrew to the Apure (28 January 1817).

Muddy Creek I 1877 I Sioux Indian Wars

In a final campaign against the Sioux following the **Little Big Horn**, General Nelson Miles routed Crazy Horse at **Wolf Mountain** then pursued a small Miniconjou band under Lame Deer. At Muddy Creek, an eastern tributary of the Rosebud in southern Montana, effectively the last action of the war saw 14 Indians killed, while the whites lost four killed and seven wounded (7 May 1877).

Mudgal I 1443 I Vijayanagar-Bahmani Wars

When Deva Raya II of Vijayanagar invaded Raichur Doab, Bahmani general Malik Tajjur relieved Raichur and Bankapur, while Sultan Ala-ud-din and a claimed 100,000 men drove the invaders back under siege at Mudgal, south of the Krishna. Three battles were fought over two months, the first won by Deva Raya, but Ala-ud-din then won twice. Deva Raya withdrew and agreed to pay tribute.

Mudki I 1845 I 1st British-Sikh War

A large Sikh army crossed the Sutlej into British East Punjab where they attacked a British force under General Sir Hugh Gough at Mudki, 20 miles southeast of Ferozepur. The Sikhs under Tej Singh were eventually repulsed after very hard fighting, losing heavy casualties and most of their guns. They suffered an even worse defeat three days later at **Ferozeshah** (18 December 1845).

Mughulmari I 1575 I Mughal Conquest of Northern India

See **Tukaroi**

Muhamdi I 1858 I Indian Mutiny

When Ahmadullah Shah, Maulvi of Faizabad, attacked Shahjahanpur, General Sir Colin Campbell sent Brigadier John Jones northeast from Fategarh to meet the Maulvi in a strong position just northeast of Shahjahanpur at Muhamdi. After cavalry reinforcements arrived Muhamdi fell by assault and the Maulvi fled to Oudh, virtually ending resistance in the Rohilkhand (18–24 May 1858).

Mühlberg I 1547 I War of the German Reformation

At war with the Schmalkaldic League of Protestant German states, Emperor Charles V and the Duke of Alva, supported by loyal Protestants under Maurice of Saxony, took a large army to Mühlberg, near Leipzig. In a massive blow to the Protestant cause, the Leader of the League, Elector John Frederick of Saxony (cousin of Maurice), was utterly defeated and captured (24 April 1547).

Mühldorf I 1322 I Habsburg Wars of Succession

Following the death of Henry VII, the Habsburg Frederick of Austria and the Wittelsbach candidate, Louis of Bavaria, fought a bitter civil war ending in battle at Mühldorf, east of Munich. Attacking rapidly before Frederick could be reinforced by his brother Leopold, Louis defeated and captured his rival and secured the German throne to reign as Louis IV (28 September 1322).

Mühlhausen I 58 BC I Rome's Later Gallic Wars

With the Helvetii repulsed at **Bibracte** (July 58 BC), Julius Caesar marched into Upper Alsace against another Germanic invasion, led by Ariovistus. At an uncertain site, between Belfort and Mühlhausen, Ariovistus was routed and died fleeing across the Rhine. With the Germans expelled from Gaul, Caesar turned on the Belgae the following year at the **Aisne** and **Sambre** (10 September 58 BC).

Mühlhausen ∎ 1674 ∎ 3rd Dutch War

After an apparent withdrawal, French Marshal Henri de Turenne made secret mid-winter marches from Lorraine and surprised the Imperial army by a sudden reappearance in southern Alsace. At Mühlhausen, west of the Rhine, Turenne routed a large force under Prince Alexandre de Bournonville. Within days, he drove on north towards Strasbourg and battle at **Turckheim** (29 December 1674).

Mühlhausen ∎ 1914 ∎ World War I (Western Front)

As German forces swept into Belgium through **Liège**, French Commander Joseph Joffre sent General Louis Bonneau into German-occupied Alsace where he captured Altkirch and Mühlhausen. General Josias von Heeringen then counter-attacked in force and Bonneau withdrew into France. He was replaced by General Paul Pau, who led a fresh advance a week later into **Lorraine** (7–10 August 1914).

Mukden ∎ 1621 ∎ Manchu Conquest of China

See **Shenyang**

Mukden ∎ 1905 ∎ Russo-Japanese War

In the final land battle of the war, Marshal Iwao Oyama launched a massive offensive against General Aleksei Kuropatkin, entrenched south of the Manchurian city of Mukden (modern Shenyang). Three weeks later—after the Japanese had lost about 75,000 casualties and the Russians 70,000 plus 20,000 captured—Kuropatkin withdrew north and Mukden fell (22 February–9 March 1905).

Mukden ∎ 1931 ∎ Manchuria Incident

Threatened in Manchuria by Chiang Kai-shek's unification of China, Japan's Guandong Army exploited an explosion on the railway to seize Mukden (modern Shenyang). Without authority from Tokyo, they proceeded to occupy Manchuria and create the puppet state of Man-chukuo. Jehol (Inner Mongolia) was later added after victory at the **Great Wall** in 1933 (18 September 1931).

Mukden ∎ 1946 ∎ 3rd Chinese Revolutionary Civil War

As Soviet forces withdrew from their post-war occupation of **Manchuria**, Communist Chinese General Lin Biao moved in and seized Mukden (modern Shenyang). When the Nationalist 25th Army, and later the 52nd, arrived in force, the Communists were driven out after very heavy fighting. They withdrew north to defend the important railway city of **Siping** (10–15 March 1946).

Mukden ∎ 1948 ∎ 3rd Chinese Revolutionary Civil War

Concluding the **Liaoshen** offensive in Manchuria, about 200,000 men under Communist General Lin Biao encircled Mukden. Commander Wei Lihuang sent General Liao Yaoxiang west to relieve Jinzhou, but Liao was killed and his force was destroyed near Heishan (26–28 October). Mukden fell after a ten-month siege and was renamed Shenyang (October–1 November 1948).

Mukden-Jinzhou ∎ 1948 ∎ 3rd Chinese Revolutionary Civil War

See **Liaoshen**

Muktsar ∎ 1705 ∎ Mughal-Sikh Wars

Sikh Guru Gobind Singh, relentlessly pursued by Mughal forces after battle in 1704 at **Anandpur** and **Chamkaur**, was attacked in a semi-desert area of the Punjab at Khidrana-ki-Dhab (modern Muktsar), south of Ferozepur. The Mughals were held off in this final battle, but 40 Sikhs of the Majha, who had deserted the Guru at Anandpur, died to a man and are revered as martyrs (8 May 1705).

Mulaydah ∎ 1891 ∎ Saudi-Rashidi Wars

Emir Abd al-Rahman overthrew Rashidi Governor Salim ibn Subhan and retook Riyadh, then he drove off a siege by Muhammad ibn

Rashid and raised revolt among his Qasim allies under Zamil. At Mulaydah, west of Buraydah, Zamil was routed and killed and Abd al-Rahman fled into exile. His son Abd al-Aziz eventually regained **Riyadh** by coup in 1902 (21 January 1891).

Mulbagal I 1768 I 1st British-Mysore War

When Haidar Ali of Mysore captured the British fort at Mulbagal, east of Kolar, Colonel Joseph Smith sent Colonel John Wood with a force of 5,000 European and Sepoy troops. Surrounded and heavily outnumbered, Wood lost over 200 men repulsing Mysorean attacks before Smith arrived with the main force and drove Haidar Ali off. The war ended early the next year (4 October 1768).

Mulheim I 1605 I Netherlands War of Independence

Forced back to the Rhine, Spanish commander in the Netherlands, Ambrogio de Spinola, took up position at Mulheim, near Duisberg, where he was attacked by Maurice of Orange and his brother Frederick Henry. The Dutch cavalry were repulsed in a hard-fought action, though infantry under Sir Horace Vere allowed Maurice to withdraw and save his army from destruction (9 October 1605).

Mulher I 1671–1672 I Mughal-Maratha Wars
See **Salher**

Mulhouse I 1674 I 3rd Dutch War
See **Mühlhausen**

Multan I 1398 I Conquests of Tamerlane

The Turko-Mongol conqueror Tamerlane began a huge invasion of northern India by sending his grandson Pir-Mohammed through the Hindu Kush into the southern Punjab against Multan on the Chenab. Local commander Sarang Khan surrendered after a bloody six-month siege and the Mongols continued east with Tamerlane to the decisive battle in December near **Delhi** (May–October 1398).

Multan I 1818 I Afghan-Sikh Wars

When Sikh leader Ranjit Singh sent Misr Dewan Chand against the great trading city of Multan, on the Chenab River near its junction with the ancient Ravi, Afghan Nawab Muzaffar Khan was defeated nearby and withdrew into the city under siege. He was killed in a last desperate sortie after three months and Multan fell, effectively ending Afghan presence in the Punjab (March–2 June 1818).

Multan I 1848–1849 I 2nd British-Sikh War

In renewed war against the Sikhs of the Punjab, Lieutenant Herbert Edwardes and a force of Indian irregulars won at **Kineyre** and **Sadusam**, and drove the rebels back to Multan. While Edwards was forced to lift his siege (July), it was renewed by General William Whish, who took the city by storm and forced Governor Dewan Mulraj to surrender the citadel (4 September 1848–22 January 1849).

Mulwagal I 1768 I 1st British-Mysore War
See **Mulbagal**

Münchengratz I 1866 I Seven Weeks War

Prussian Prince Friedrich Karl invaded Austrian Bohemia through **Liebenau** and **Podol**, and joined General Herwarth von Bittenfeld advancing through **Huhnerwasser**, to attack Münchengratz (Mnichovo Hradiste) northeast of Prague. Austrian commander Count Edouard von Clam-Gallas was heavily defeated then driven back to further loss within days at **Gitschin** and **Königgratz** (28 June 1866).

Munda, Solomon Islands I 1943 I World War II (Pacific)
See **New Georgia**

Munda, Spain I 45 BC I Wars of the First Triumvirate

With the sons of Pompey defeated in North Africa at **Thapsus** (46 BC), Julius Caesar marched against Pompey's son Gnaeus, who had fled to Spain. At Munda (an uncertain site south of Cordoba) Caesar secured a decisive victory. Pompeian commander Titus Labienus was killed, while Gnaeus was pursued and executed. Caesar went home in triumph but was soon assassinated (17 March 45 BC).

Munderkingen I 1703 I War of the Spanish Succession

On campaign in the upper Danube Valley, Imperial forces under Prince Louis Margrave of Baden advancing towards Augsburg were attacked by Marshal Claude Villars, in the service of Elector Maximilian Emanuel of Bavaria. Upstream of Ulm at Munderkingen, Villars defeated Prince Louis then marched northeast to defeat another Austrian force in September at **Höchstädt** (31 July 1703).

Munfordville I 1862 I American Civil War (Western Theatre)

Confederate commander Braxton Bragg led a invasion of Kentucky from Tennessee and attacked Munfordville, southwest of previous victory at **Richmond, Kentucky**, where General James R. Chalmers was initially repulsed. When the main Confederate army arrived, Colonel John T. Wilder surrendered the garrison of over 4,000 men. Bragg then continued northeast to **Perryville** (14–17 September 1862).

Munger I 800 I Later Indian Dynastic Wars

See **Monghyr**

Munster I 1534–1535 I German Religious Wars

When Anabaptists took over Munster in Westphalia it was besieged by Catholic Bishop Franz von Waldeck. Anabaptist commander Jan Matthys died in a sortie (5 April 1534) and the communalist city was eventually betrayed by a deserter. Jan van Leyden, Bernhard Knipperdolling and other leaders were tortured and executed and Anabaptism was brutally suppressed (February 1534–June 1535).

Munychia I 403 BC I Great Peloponnesian War

In the aftermath of the Peloponnesian War, Lysander of Sparta established the oligarchy of the Thirty Tyrants in **Athens, Greece**. However, the Athenian Thrasybulus raised a Theban force, which captured Phyle and Piraeus, while a Spartan relief force was repulsed at nearby Munychia, with the Tyrant Critias killed. King Pausanius withdrew Spartan troops, Lysander was deposed and democracy was restored.

Muong-Khoua I 1953 I French Indo-China War

When Viet Minh commander Vo Nguyen Giap launched a large-scale spring offensive into Laos, local Lao-French forces were utterly overwhelmed. Ordered to make a stand at Muong-Khoua Captain Teullier's Lao Battalion fought a brilliant defence before being virtually wiped out. Only late reinforcements and the monsoon saved the royal capital at Luang-Prabang (12 April–18 May 1953).

Muottothal I 1799 I French Revolutionary Wars (2nd Coalition)

General Alexander Suvorov defeated General Claude Lecourbe at **Airolo** (23 September), but arrived from Italy too late to prevent Russian disaster at **Zurich** and advanced into the Muottothal Valley between Altdorf and Shwyz, east of Lake Lucerne. Lecourbe was joined by General André Masséna yet Suvorov again drove off the French and managed to reach the Rhine (30 September 1799).

Murchakhar I 1729 I Persian-Afghan Wars

Advancing to reover Persia from its Afghan conquerors, General Nadir Kuli (later Nadir Shah) routed the usurper Ashraf Shah on the **Mehmandost** (29 September). Ashraf withdrew to Isfahan to regroup and took a defensive position to the north at Murchakhar (modern Murcheh Khvort). However, he was again routed and fled south to Shiraz and to further defeat at **Zarghan** (6 November 1729).

Muret ❙ 1213 ❙ Albigensian Crusade

When Pope Innocent III proclaimed a Crusade against Albigensian heretics in southern France, Anglo-Norman knight Simon de Montfort led the campaign. Concluding years of warfare, Raymond IV of Toulouse and his Spanish brother-in-law, Peter of Aragon, besieged de Montfort's garrison at Muret, south of Toulouse. However, they were routed and Peter was killed (12 September 1213).

Murfreesboro (1st) ❙ 1862 ❙ American Civil War (Western Theatre)

As Union General Don Carlos Buell advanced east towards Chattanooga, Tennessee, Confederate cavalry under General Nathan Bedford Forrest raided the Union rear to the northwest at Murfreesboro. Surprised by a brilliant dawn attack, General Thomas T. Crittenden and his garrison of over 1,000 surrendered and Buell's advance was diverted north towards Nashville (13 July 1862).

Murfreesboro (2nd) ❙ 1862–1863 ❙ American Civil War (Western Theatre)
See **Stones River**

Murfreesboro ❙ 1864 ❙ American Civil War (Western Theatre)

Despite defeat at **Franklin** (30 November), Confederate commander John B. Hood continued towards Nashville, Tennessee, sending General Nathan B. Forrest northeast against General Lovell H. Rousseau at Murfreesboro. After inconclusive fighting, a counter-attack by General Robert Milroy forced Forrest to withdraw. A week later Hood was routed at **Nashville** (5–7 December 1864).

Mursa ❙ 260 ❙ Roman Military Civil Wars

When Valerian was captured at **Edessa**, Ingenuus, Roman commander on the Danube, rose in revolt against the new Emperor Gallienus, who led a force into Pannonia. At Mursa (modern Osijek, Croatia), Ingenuus was defeated and killed by Roman cavalry under Aureolus, who then defeated another usurper, Macrianus, in Illyricum before turning against Gallienus himself in 268 at **Mediolanum**.

Mursa ❙ 351 ❙ Later Roman Military Civil Wars

Roman General Flavius Magnus Magnentius in Gaul murdered Constans, brother of the Emperor Constantius, and rose in rebellion, taking a large army to Lower Pannonia. On the Drava River at Mursa (modern Osijek, Croatia), Constantius skillfully used his cavalry to defeat the usurper in the "bloodiest battle of the century." Magnentius then fled to **Pavia** (28 September 351).

Murviedro ❙ 75 BC ❙ Sertorian War

Soon after defeat at the **Sucro**, Rome's commanders in Spain, Gnaeus Pompey and Quintus Metellus Pius, were attacked in camp north of Valencia at Murviedro (modern Sagunto) by the combined rebel armies of Quintus Sertorius and Marcus Perpenna. While Metellus defeated Perpenna in a complex action, Pompey was badly beaten by Sertorius and both sides dispersed for the winter.

Murviedro ❙ 1811 ❙ Napoleonic Wars (Peninsular Campaign)
See **Sagunto**

Mus ❙ 1916 ❙ World War I (Caucasus Front)
See **Bitlis**

Musa Bagh ❙ 1858 ❙ Indian Mutiny

General Sir Colin Campbell advancing on **Lucknow** sent General Sir James Outram against the Musa Bagh, a fortified palace about four miles to the northeast held by an estimated 9,000 rebels said to be under Hazrat Mahal, Begum of Oudh. Supported by artillery fire across the Gumti, Outram secured the position in a brilliant action. Lucknow itself fell two days later (19 March 1858).

Muscat ❙ 1507 ❙ Portuguese Colonial Wars in Arabia

The great Portuguese commander Afonso de Albuquerque resolved to protect the sea-route to

India, taking seven ships and a reported 500 men against the port of Muscat, on the southeastern shore of the Gulf of Oman. Muscat fell by bloody assault, followed by a terrible sack and massacre. The Portuguese then sailed northwest across the mouth of the Persian Gulf to attack **Hormuz**.

Muscat I 1650 I Later Portuguese Colonial Wars in Arabia

Following Portugal's expulsion from **Hormuz** (1622), Imam Sultan ibn Sayf of Oman attacked Muscat, across the Persian Gulf. After a siege in 1648 forced the Portuguese to yield neighbouring fortresses, the Imam led a fresh assault on Muscat itself. The garrison finally surrendered, ending Portugal's presence in the Gulf. In 1652 Oman turned south against **Zanzibar** (January 1650).

Museifré I 1925 I Druze Rebellion

After a French column nearing **Suwayda** in southeast Syria was destroyed at **Mazraa**, Foreign Legion Captain René Landriau reached Museifré, to the southwest, and built rough defences against Druze rebels. An heroic defence inflicted terrible Bedouin losses before Landriau was relieved just as ammunition was running out. Suwayda was relieved a week later (17 September 1925).

Mushahida I 1917 I World War I (Mesopotamia)

Anglo-Indian commander Sir Frederick Maude secured the prized city of **Baghdad**, then quickly sent General Sir Alexander Cobbe in pursuit to Mushahida, on the railway 20 miles to the north, strongly defended by about 5,000 Turks. A frontal assault by General Vere Fane cost over 500 British casualties before the Turks withdrew north through **Istabulat** towards Samarra (14 March 1917).

Musian I 1982 I Iraq-Iran War

Despite terrible losses advancing on **Basra** in July, Iran launched a fresh offensive towards Basra in the area southwest of Musian. Renewed fighting further north towards **Mandali** was in-tended to provide support and the Iranians managed to take Abu Ghurab. However, seasonal rains and strong Iraqi resistance ended Iran's offensive with heavy losses and Basra little closer (1–11 November 1982).

Musjidiah I 1858 I Indian Mutiny

General Sir Colin Campbell pursuing Nana Sahib across the Gaghara, drove the rebels from **Burgidiah** to Musjidiah, northeast of Nanpara, said to be the strongest fortress in Oudh. After bombardment with guns and mortars Campbell stormed Musjidiah to find it abandoned. The fortress was demolished and within days the rebels were defeated near the Rapti at **Banki** (27 December 1858).

Muta I 629 I Muslim Conquest of Syria

In the first clash between the Byzantine Empire and the spreading power of Islam, a raid into Syria was repulsed at Muta, east of the Dead Sea, by Byzantine and Christian Arab troops of Emperor Heraclius. When Muslim leaders Zaid and Jafar (the Prophet's adopted son and cousin) were killed, their army was saved by Khalid ibn al-Walid, who became Islam's greatest warrior (September 629).

Muthul I 108 BC I Jugurthine War

Rome's new commander in North Africa Caecilius Metellus was determined to avenge Roman defeat the previous year at **Suthul** and led a large army against King Jugurtha of Numidia. On the Muthul, an unidentified river inside modern Tunisia near the Bagradas, Metellus and Gaius Marius secured a brilliant decisive victory. Jugurtha then withdrew to his desert stronghold at **Thala**.

Mutina I 193 BC I Gallic Wars in Italy

In the years after crushing the Insubre Gauls at the **Mincio** and **Lake Como**, Rome continued to campaign against the Boii, established around Bologna. In battle at Mutina (modern Modena) Consul Lucius Cornelius Merula inflicted a decisive defeat, with perhaps 15,000 Gauls killed, although up to 5,000 Romans and their allies also died. Eventually the Boii too submitted to Rome.

Mutina ∎ 44–43 BC ∎ Wars of the Second Triumvirate

Amid civil war after the murder of Julius Caesar, Decimus Brutus was besieged by Mark Antony at Mutina (modern Modena) and a relief army repulsed at nearby **Forum Gallorum**. However, Mark Antony was then defeated outside Mutina by Aulus Hirtius and Caesar's nephew Octavian, though Hirtius was killed at the moment of victory. Antony was forced to flee (December 44–21 April 43 BC).

Muye ∎ 1045 BC ∎ Wars of the Western Zhou

The Zhou people expanded into the Wei River Valley and King Wu led a large force across the Yellow River to threaten the ruling Shang Dynasty at Anyang. About 30 miles south at Muye, in modern Henan, the Shang army was decisively defeated. Di Xing, the last Shang King, killed himself and Wu established the Western Zhou Dynasty, which ruled until 771 BC at **Zongzhou** (trad date 1045 BC).

Muysers Bay ∎ 1625 ∎ Dutch-Spanish Colonial Wars

Despite Dutch defeat off **Manila** in 1609, a second fleet comprising six vessels was sent to the Philippines under Commander Carel Lievensz. Governor Jeronimo de Silva sailed out with seven ships to meet the Dutch and action between Bolinea and Los Dos Irmanos, known as Muysers Bay, saw one small Dutch ship abandoned. However, Lievensz eventually secured a decisive victory.

Mycale ∎ 479 BC ∎ Greco-Persian Wars

At the same time as Persian defeat at **Plataea**, the Greek fleet under Leotychidas trapped a Persian force at Mycale, on the mainland of Asia Minor. The Persians beached their ships to join an army under Tigranes and at first held off the Greeks. However, their Ionian allies changed sides and in the ensuing rout, Tigranes was killed and Persian naval commander Artayntes fled (August 479 BC).

Myer's Drift ∎ 1879 ∎ Anglo-Zulu War

Sent to escort an incoming wagon train in northern Zululand, British Captain David Moriarty and 103 men left Luneburg, northwest of Paulpietersburg, and were ambushed at Myer's Drift on the flooded Ntombe by about 1,000 Zulus under Mbilini. A terrible rout saw Moriarty, 62 soldiers and 18 wagon-crew killed before reinforcements arrived under Major Charles Tucker (12 March 1879).

Myitkyina ∎ 1944 ∎ World War II (Burma-India)

General Joseph Stilwell's Chinese divisions and Merrill's Marauders advanced down the **Hukawng** and secured the vital airfield at Myitkyina. However they had to besiege Myitkyina city itself, bravely defended by 3,000 Japanese under General Genzu Mizukami. With the fall of **Mogaung** to the west, Mizukami committed suicide and about 800 survivors withdrew north (17 May–3 August 1944).

Mylae ∎ 260 BC ∎ 1st Punic War

Two years after escaping Carthaginian defeat in southern Sicily at **Acragas** (later Agrigentum), Carthaginian naval commander Hannibal, contemptuous of Roman naval experience, led his small fleet against Roman ships off Mylae (modern Milazzo) in northeast Sicily. Hannibal was decisively defeated and fled to Carthage, while Consul Gaius Duilius was awarded a victory column in the Forum.

Mylae ∎ 36 BC ∎ Wars of the Second Triumvirate

In the first of three naval battles off Sicily, Octavian's Admiral Marcus Vipsanius Agrippa cruised west while Octavian guarded the Straits of Messina. Agrippa encountered Sextus Pompeius (Pompey the Younger) off Mylae in northeast Sicily. However, an indecisive engagement saw Sextus elude Agrippa's heavier ships and he withdrew until two days later at **Tauromenium** (13 August 36 BC).

My Lai ▌ 1968 ▌ Vietnam War

On a search and destroy mission in Quang Ngai, US infantry under Lieutenant William Calley stormed the supposedly Viet Cong village of My Lai, where they killed more than 200 unarmed old men, women and children. When revealed a year later, news of the massacre caused unprecedented political and public outcry. Calley was eventually imprisoned, but only briefly (16 March 1968).

Mylapore ▌ 1746 ▌ 1st Carnatic War
See **St Thomé**

Mynydd Carn ▌ 1081 ▌ Welsh Dynastic War

Gruffydd ap Cynan was driven from the throne of Gwynnedd (North Wales) by Trahaiarn ap Caradog after defeat at **Bron yr Erw** (1075). He later joined Rhys ap Tewdwr of Deheubarth (South Wales) against Trahaiarn and the Princes Caradog ap Gruffydd and Meilyr ap Rhiwallon. In battle at Mynydd Carn, in the Pencelly Mountains, Trahaiarn was killed and Gruffydd regained the throne.

Myongyang ▌ 1597 ▌ Japanese Invasion of Korea

Admiral Yi Sun-shin was recalled to command after Korean naval disaster at **Kyo Chong** (27 August) and surprised the Japanese fleet in the narrow strait of Myongyang near the island of Chido, off southwestern Korea. The "miracle of Myongyang" saw the hugely outnumbered Koreans secure a brilliant victory with Japanese Admiral Kurushima Michifusa routed and killed (26 October 1597).

Myonnesus ▌ 190 BC ▌ Roman-Syrian War

In naval war against the Seleucid Antiochus, Rome's Rhodian allies secured victory in July off **Eurymedon** before the main Seleucid fleet under Polyxenidas attacked Lucius Aemilius Regillus outside Ephesus off Myonnesus, in Ionia. Polyxenidas was routed in a large-scale action, losing 42 ships, allowing Rome to soon invade Asia Minor for victory at **Magnesia** (September 190 BC).

Myriocephalum ▌ 1176 ▌ Byzantine-Turkish Wars

Emperor Manuel I Comnenus renewed his offensive against the Turks and took a large army into Anatolia, supported by his Crusader brother-in-law Baldwin of Antioch. Seljuk Sultan Kilij Arslan II destroyed the allies at Myriocephalum (southeast of modern Ankara) where Baldwin was killed. After the worst Byzantine defeat in over 100 years since **Manzikert** Manuel sued for peace (17 September 1176).

Mystic ▌ 1637 ▌ Pequot Indian War

When Pequot in Connecticut attacked **Wethersfield** and threatened Fort Saybrook, commander Lion Gardiner was reinforced by Captain John Mason, who led militia (supported by Mohegans under Uncas) against the Indian stronghold at Mystic, near modern Stonington. A decisive action saw the Pequot virtually annihilated, with perhaps 600 killed, which effectively ended the war (26 May 1637).

Mytilene ▌ 428–427 BC ▌ Great Peloponnesian War

With Athens diverted by the siege of **Plataea**, five cities on Lesbos attempted an insurrection and Athens sent a fleet under Paches to besiege the city of Mytilene (modern Mitilini). Spartan Admiral Alcidas was sent to relieve their ally, but the Spartan fleet was intimidated and driven off. The garrison of Mytilene was forced to surrender and the rebel leaders were executed (September 428–June 427 BC).

Mytilene ▌ 406 BC ▌ Great Peloponnesian War
See **Arginusae**

Mytilene ▌ 1462 ▌ Venetian-Turkish Wars

Vizier Mahmud Pasha was determined to capture the Aegean island of Lesbos and took a large fleet against the capital Mytilene, held by Niccolo Gattilusio. Two weeks of bombardment, watched by Sultan Mehmed II from the Asian shore, destroyed city walls and Gattilusio surrendered the city and the island. A Venetian siege two years later failed to recover Lesbos (19 September 1462).

Myton ▌ 1319 ▌ Rise of Robert the Bruce

As Edward II of England besieged **Berwick**, Robert the Bruce sent Sir James "Black" Douglas and Thomas Randolph Earl of Moray into Yorkshire. On the Swale near Myton they routed a local force raised by William Melton Archbishop of York and Chancellor John Hotham. With the Scots now threatening his rear, Edward abandoned his siege of Berwick and withdrew (12 September 1319).

N

Naarden ❘ 1572 ❘ Netherlands War of Independence

Advancing into Holland from the capture of **Mons** (19 September), Don Fadrique Alvarez (son of the Duke of Parma) reached the fortress city of Naarden, east of Amsterdam. While the city surrendered with little resistance, its loss was significant as the citizens were butchered and the defences demolished. As a result other Dutch cities resolved to fight to the death (1 December 1572).

Naas ❘ 1798 ❘ Irish Rebellion

At the start of the rising in Ireland, about 1,000 rebels under Michael Reynolds attacked the garrison at Naas, 20 miles southwest of Dublin, comprising 150 Armargh Militia and dragoons under Colonel Arthur Acheson Lord Gosford. In the early morning the rebels penetrated into the town, where they were mown down by intense rifle fire and fell back with heavy losses (24 May 1798).

Nabdura ❘ 741 ❘ Berber Rebellion
See **Bakdura**

Nablus ❘ 1918 ❘ World War I (Middle East)
See **Megiddo**

Nablus ❘ 1967 ❘ Arab-Israeli Six Day War

On the offensive in the north, Israeli tank commander Uri Ram circled behind the key city of Nablus while Colonel Moshe Bar-Kochva's tanks turned south from **Jenin**. With other Jewish forces advancing north from **Jerusalem**, Jordanian General Runkun al-Ghazi suffered further severe losses before the Jews entered Nablus and soon effectively secured the West Bank (6–7 June 1967).

Nacaome (1st) ❘ 1844 ❘ Central American National Wars

Honduran General Joaquín Rivera went into exile with Francisco Morazán following defeat at **Guatemala City**. After Morazán was executed in **Cartago** (1842), Rivera invaded from Nicaragua against President Francisco Ferrera of Honduras. He raised Morazánista insurrection in the east at Texiguat, but was routed by government forces at Nacaome and lost again at **Danli** (24 October 1844).

Nacaome (2nd) ❘ 1845 ❘ Central American National Wars
See **Comayagua**

Nacaome ❘ 1903 ❘ Honduran Civil War

During a disputed election in Honduras, former President Terencio Sierra tried to annul the result and install his nominee Juan Angel Arías. However, American-born commander Lee Christmas changed sides to support Presidential claimant Manuel Bonilla and Sierra was heavily defeated at Nacaome. He and Arías fled into exile and Bonilla was declared elected (22 February 1903).

Nachod I 1866 I Seven Weeks War

While the Prussian Army of Silesia invaded Austrian Bohemia through **Trautenau**, further east Prussian Crown Prince Friedrich Wilhelm sent advance units under General Karl Friedrich von Steinmetz against the Vysokov Plateau, just west of Nachod. Austrian forces led by General Wilhelm Ramming were sharply repulsed and withdrew west to battle next day at **Skalitz** (27 June 1866).

Nacimiento I 1873 I Kickapoo Indian Wars

Colonel Ranald Mackenzie retaliated for attacks on the Texas border by taking 400 men into northern Mexico against the Kickapoo villages at Nacimiento, near the Remolina. Attacking while the men were away hunting, Mackenzie killed 19 and captured 40, mainly old men, women and children. Over 300 Kickapoo later voluntarily joined the hostages in Indian Territory (18 May 1873).

Naco I 1914–1915 I Mexican Revolution

A brave action on Mexico's northern border saw badly outnumbered forces loyal to President Venustiano Carranza defend Naco against Governor José María Maytoreno, a supporter of Francisco (Pancho) Villa. Colonels Plutarco Elías Calles and Benjamín Hill held out for over three months until Maytoreno withdrew. In November 1915 Calles defended **Agua Prieta** (October 1914–January 1915).

Nacogdoches I 1812 I Gutiérrez-Magee Expedition

In support of the revolutionary cause in Spanish Texas, American Filibuster forces under Lieutenant Augustus W. Magee invaded from Louisiana with Bernardo Gutiérrez against Royalist Governor Manuel Maria de Salcedo. The self-styled Republican Army of the North quickly seized Nagocdoches, then towards year's end marched inland against **La Bahía** (2 August 1812).

Nacogdoches I 1832 I Texan Wars of Independence

Just weeks after success at the east Texas town of **Anahuac**, Texan Patriots under Captain James Bullock opposed Mexican commander Colonel José de las Piedras at Nagocdoches. After a brief fierce action—with three Texans and more than 40 Mexicans killed—Piedras surrendered command to his Federalist deputy, Don Francisco Medina. He was then escorted to San Antonio (2 August 1832).

Nacori I 1886 I Apache Indian Wars

See **Aros**

Nadaun I 1691 I Mughal-Sikh Wars

When the Mughal commander in the northern Punjab, Mian Khan, sent his son Alif Khan to levy tribute from the hill Rajas, some Rajas under Bhim Chand of Kahlur joined their former enemy, the Sikh Guru Gobind Singh, while others supported the Imperial troops. Alif Khan was defeated and driven back in battle at Nadaun, on the Beas south of Kangra, though the rebel Rajas soon made peace.

Ñaembé I 1871 I Argentine Civil Wars

Federalist General Ricardo López Jordán seized power in Entre Rios and a government force under General Ignacio Rivas beat him at **Santa Rosa**. They met again three months later at Ñaembé, just east of Goya, where López Jordán was even more decisively defeated and fled to Brazil. He eventually returned after six years and was repulsed at Don Gonzalo (26 January 1871).

Nafels I 1352 I Habsburg-Swiss Wars

When troops from Zurich occupied the Upper Linth Valley attempting to extend the newly founded Swiss confederacy to include Habsburg Glarus, Duke Albert of Austria sent Walter de Stadion, who was defeated and killed near Nafels. Glarus then joined the Confederacy, but was soon restored to the Habsburgs until the more famous battle at **Nafels** 36 years later (2 February 1352).

Nafels I 1388 I Habsburg-Swiss Wars

Two years after the rout at **Sempach**, a fresh force under Albert III of Austria invaded Glarus in Switzerland and was ambushed in a steep mountain pass above Nafels. As at **Morgarten** 75 years earlier, the outnumbered Swiss rolled boulders down on the invaders before attacking and destroying them. A subsequent truce recognised Swiss independence within the German Empire (9 April 1388).

Nagakute I 1584 I Japan's Era of the Warring States

Determined to secure power after the death of Oda Nobunaga, Toyotomi Hideyoshi defeated the son Oda Nobutaka at **Shizugatake**, then attacked Oda Nobuo, who had joined Tokugawa Ieyasu. In a complex battle at Nagakute, east of Nagoya, Ieyasu defeated and killed Hideyoshi's Generals Ikeda Nobuteru and Mori Nagakazu. He later submitted and fought alongside Hideyoshi (18 May 1584).

Nagal I 1858 I Indian Mutiny

Brigadier John Jones marched from Roorkee across the Ganges into the Rohilkund, where he met a rebel force just four miles beyond the river near Nagal. A brilliant assault across a dry canal, supported by Colonel John Coke, routed the mutineers. They fled into the jungle, while Jones advanced southeast through Najibabad towards a larger rebel concentration at **Nagina** (17 April 1858).

Nagapatam I 1746 I 1st Carnatic War
See **Negapatam**

Nagapatam I 1758 I Seven Years War (India)
See **Negapatam**

Nagapatam I 1781 I 2nd British-Mysore War
See **Negapatam**

Nagapatam I 1782 I War of the American Revolution
See **Negapatam**

Nagashino I 1575 I Japan's Era of the Warring States

A renewed offensive against Oda Nobunaga after the action at **Mikata ga hara**, southeast of Nagoya (1572), saw new Takeda leader Katsuyori besiege nearby Nagashino Castle. Determined to crush his enemy, Nobunaga took a massive relief force supported by Tokugawa Ieyasu and Toyotomi Hideyoshi. Using effective musketry they secured a bloody and decisive victory (29 June 1575).

Nagina I 1858 I Indian Mutiny

Crossing the Ganges into the Rohilkund, Brigadier John Jones defeated rebels near **Nagal** and days later continued southeast through Najibabad against a much larger concentration at Nagina, said to comprise 10,000 infantry, 2,000 cavalry and 15 guns. After a bold assault, bravely supported by Colonel Charles Cureton's Multanis, the rebels fled and Bijnor was reoccupied (21 April 1858).

Nagpur I 1817 I 3rd British-Maratha War

Raja Appa Sahib of Nagpur took advantage of renewed war in central India between the British and Peshwa Baji Rao II to beat his local British garrison, but was checked at **Sitibaldi** (26 November). He then faced a large British force under General Sir John Doveton (1768–1847) and was routed outside Nagpur. The Marathas surrendered the city after a brief siege and heavy assault (16–24 December 1817).

Nagy Sallo I 1849 I Hungarian Revolutionary War

As Austrian Imperial forces were driven out of Hungary after defeat at **Hatvan**, **Isaszeg** and **Waitzen**, a 10,000-strong rearguard tried to hold Nagy Sallo, north of Gran (Esztergom). Hungarian General Artur Gorgey and 25,000 Nationalists won decisively to secure the strategic crossing on the Gran before returning southeast to besiege the isolated Imperial garrison at **Buda** (19 April 1849).

Nagyszollos I 1662 I Transylvanian National Revolt

George Rákóczi II of Transylvania died after **Gilau** (May 1660) and Janos Kemény was elected Prince. However, in battle against Mehmed Kucuk in the Ukraine near Mukachevo at Nagyszollos (modern Vinogradov) Kemény too was defeated and killed. The defeat effectively ended Romania's struggle against the Turks, who appointed Mihaly Apafi as vassal Prince (22 January 1662).

Nagyvarad ┃ 1660 ┃ Transylvanian National Revolt

Just after George Rákóczi II of Transylvania died of wounds following **Gilau**, a Turkish army which had invaded Transylvania under the Sirdar Kose Ali Pasha laid siege to Nagyvarad (modern Oradea) on the Koros near the Hungarian border. Having resisted more than a month until gunpowder ran out, the siege ended when a mere 300 men marched out to surrender (14 July –17 August 1660).

Nahavand ┃ 641 ┃ Muslim Conquest of Iran

See **Nehavend**

Nahawand ┃ 641 ┃ Muslim Conquest of Iran

See **Nehavend**

Naic ┃ 1897 ┃ Philippines War of Independence

On a fresh offensive south of Manila after victory in March at **Imus**, new Spanish Governor Fernando Primo de Rivera led a massive assault on Revolutionary leader Emilio Aguinaldo at Naic, southwest of Cavite. Following very heavy fighting, with costly rebel losses, Aguinaldo was forced to retreat northeast towards Montalban, where he made a stand in the mountains at **Puray** (3 May 1897).

Nairn ┃ 1009 ┃ Later Viking Raids on Britain

King Sweyn Forkbeard of Denmark led a renewed Viking invasion of Scotland, landing on the Moray Firth to besiege Nairn. To the east between Forres and Kinloss, Malcolm II of Scotland was wounded and defeated trying to drive off the siege. However, the Danes eventually withdrew for the winter. They returned the following year to meet Malcolm again at **Mortlack**.

Naissus ┃ 269 ┃ 3rd Gothic War

See **Nish**

Najaf ┃ 2003 ┃ 2nd Gulf War

American forces advancing north from **Nasiriya** met unexpectedly strong resistance by Iraqi Republican Guards at the strategic city of Najaf, where fierce fighting saw perhaps 500 Iraqis killed. Further heavy fighting ensued when Iraq counter-attacked against Americans attempting to break out to the north towards **Baghdad** and Najaf was finally secured (25 March–2 April 2003).

Najafghar ┃ 1857 ┃ Indian Mutiny

While British forces besieged **Delhi**, a new siege train under General John Nicholson, fresh from success at **Trimmu Ghat**, was intercepted by 7,000 rebels just west of Delhi at Najafghar. Nicholson routed the rebels, who lost 800 killed in a 24-hour action. However, a month later the 35-year-old "Lion of the Punjab" was killed taking Delhi. He was posthumously knighted (25 August 1857).

Najera ┃ 1367 ┃ Hundred Years War

See **Navarette**

Nakfa ┃ 1977–1988 ┃ Eritrean War of Independence

On the offensive in northern Eritrea, Liberation forces besieged then seized the highland city of Nakfa (23 March 1977). Despite rebel withdrawal from most cities in 1978, the mountain stronghold resisted years of Ethiopian siege, including the massive Red Star offensive of February 1982. Nakfa held out as a symbol of resistance until rebel victory at **Afabet** (March 1988) secured the north of the country.

Nakheila ┃ 1898 ┃ British-Sudan Wars

See **Atbara**

Naklo ┃ 1109 ┃ Polish-German Wars

Boleslaw III of Poland overthrew his brother Zbigniew (1107), then faced an offensive in the north by Pomeranians in support of the former King. In battle at Naklo, near Bydgoszcz,

Boleslaw secured a decisive victory over Pomerania, which was later incorporated into Poland. He then returned south to meet an invading
Imperial army later that year at Glogow and **Psie
Pole** (August 1109).

Naktong Bulge (1st) ▐ 1950 ▐
Korean War

With American and South Korean forces driven southeast into the **Pusan Perimeter**, North
Koreans launched the first major offensive
across a u-shaped bend in the Naktong River
southwest of Taegu. The invaders were finally
halted by desperate defence in the Naktong
Bulge, and further north in the valley known as
the Bowling Alley, but only after severe losses
on both sides (5–19 August 1950).

Naktong Bulge (2nd) ▐ 1950 ▐
Korean War

North Korean forces recovered from losses
while attempting to breach the **Pusan Perimeter**, then launched a renewed assault towards
Taegu, Korea's third largest city. After brutal
fighting at the Naktong Bulge and further east
around **Yongchon**, the invaders were driven
back. The American and South Korean Allies
were soon able to counter-attack towards **Seoul**
(2–16 September 1950).

Nalagarh ▐ 1814 ▐ British-Gurkha War

General David Ochterlony responded to Nepalese expansion into northern India, advancing
from the Punjab to attack the fortress at Nalagarh, north of Chandigarh, held by troops of
Amar Singh Thapa's army. Unlike the costly
resistance further east at **Kalanga**, the Gurkhas
surrendered after 30 hours bombardment. Ochterlony continued north through **Mangu** to
Malaon (2–5 November 1814).

Nalapani ▐ 1814 ▐ British-Gurkha War

See **Kalanga**

Namabengo ▐ 1905 ▐ German Colonial
Wars in Africa

One month after raising a siege by Maji Maji
rebels at **Mahenge** in German East Africa, a

well-armed column under Captain Ernst Nigmann marched on Namabengo (near Songea in
Tanzania), which was threatened by over 5,000
Ngoni tribesmen. The rebels were destroyed by
machine-gun fire, ending faith in the protection
of Maji Maji magic, and the rebellion was soon
crushed (21 October 1905).

Namasigue ▐ 1907 ▐ Nicaraguan-
Honduran War

As President José Santos Zelaya of Nicaragua
invaded Honduras, **San Marcos** fell and further
south General Roberto González was met at
Namasigue, southeast of Choluteca, by Salva-
doran-Honduran troops under General José
Preza. When General Nicasio Vázquez arrived
with the main Nicaraguan force Preza was routed. Hondurans lost again days later at **Maraita**
(18–20 March 1907).

Nam Dinh ▐ 1883 ▐ French Conquest
of Indo-China

Captain Henri Rivière on campaign in northern Vietnam (Tonkin) captured **Hanoi** and later
attacked Nam Dinh, to the southeast on the Red
River, strongly defended by Prince Hoang supported by 500 Chinese mercenaries. The French
and some Vietnamese levies took the port by
storm after a heavy naval bombardment. Rivière
was killed a few weeks later near **Hanoi** (27
March 1883).

Nam Dong ▐ 1964 ▐ Vietnam War

Following heavy mortar bombardment, a reported 900 Viet Cong attacked the remote camp
at Nam Dong in northwest Vietnam near the
Laotian border, manned by 300 Vietnamese
troops, Nung irregulars and Allied Special Forces, who drove them off in fierce fighting. US
Captain Roger Donlon won the first Congres-
sional Medal of Honour of the war and Australia
had its first fatality (6 July 1964).

Namka Chu ▐ 1962 ▐ Sino-Indian War

After weeks of skirmishing in the border dispute in northeast India, Chinese forces began
their assault across the Namka Chu River, north
of Tawang. Suffering from lack of artillery and

political interference, the Indians under General Brij Mohan Kaul were driven off with heavy losses. Tawang fell three days later and the Indians withdrew south to **Se La** and **Bomdila** (20 October 1962).

Namozine Church ▌ 1865 ▌ American Civil War (Eastern Theatre)

On the day that Confederate **Petersburg**, Virginia, formally surrendered, Union forces under General George A. Custer attacked the rearguard of the withdrawing Confederates to the west at Namozine Church. Following inconclusive action, General Fitzhugh Lee's Confederate cavalry eluded pursuit and withdrew further west towards **Amelia Springs** (3 April 1865).

Namsi ▌ 1951 ▌ Korean War

Nine B-29 bombers set out from Okinawa on a daylight raid against Namsi Airfield in North Korea. Despite heavy fighter escort, Soviet-manned MiG jets shot down three of the veteran bombers and four were damaged beyond repair. With 28 American aircrew killed, "Black Tuesday" was one of the bloodiest air actions of the war and B-29s were restricted to night operations (23 October 1951).

Namsos ▌ 1940 ▌ World War II (Northern Europe)

See **Andalsnes**

Nam Tha ▌ 1962 ▌ Laotian Civil War

Rightist General Phoumi Nosavan secured **Vientiane** then resolved to combat the Communist Pathet Lao in northern Laos, sending heavy reinforcements to besieged Nam Tha. When a government column was ambushed and routed nearby, the 5,000 strong garrison panicked and fled, alarming US President John F. Kennedy who deployed troops to northeast Thailand (May 1962).

Namur ▌ 1692 ▌ War of the Grand Alliance

A decisive siege saw French Marshal Duke Francois Henri of Luxembourg invest Namur, the most powerful fortress in the Netherlands. Supported by the great engineer, Marshal Sebastien Vauban, Luxembourg drove off a relief attempt by William III of England and Holland. Garrison commander Baron Menno von Coehoorn was then forced to capitulate (25 May–5 June 1692).

Namur ▌ 1695 ▌ War of the Grand Alliance

The powerful Netherlands fortress of Namur, taken by French siege in 1692, was later besieged by William III of England and Holland and Dutch engineer Baron Manno von Coehoorn, who had built its defences. French commander Francois de Neufville Marshal Villeroi was unable to relieve Namur and Louis Duke de Boufflers had no choice but to surrender the town (1 July–1 September 1695).

Namur ▌ 1815 ▌ Napoleonic Wars (The Hundred Days)

In the pursuit following **Waterloo**, Prussian Generals Georg von Pirch and Johann Adolf Thielmann were sent to cut off Marshal Emmanuel de Grouchy from the French frontier. Grouchy inflicted a sharp repulse on Thielmann's advance guard at Namur, though when Pirch's main army arrived he skilfully escaped across the Meuse and retired on Laon (20 June 1815).

Namur ▌ 1914 ▌ World War I (Western Front)

General Karl von Bulow led over 100,000 Germans sweeping through Belgium to attack the supposedly impregnable fortress at Namur, defended by about 37,000 Belgians under General Augustin Michel. Following bombardment by heavy artillery used at **Liège**, Namur fell with thousands captured, just two days after French defeat at nearby **Charleroi** (21–25 August 1914).

Namwon ∎ 1597 ∎ Japanese Invasion of Korea

Renewing the war in Korea, Japanese forces under Konishi Yukinaga, Kato Kiyomasa and Kobayakawa Hideaki besieged the strategic fortress of Namwon, northeast of Kwangju, held by Chinese cavalry and Koreans under Yi Boknam. The garrison was routed and slaughtered in a bloody night assault. The Japanese advance on Seoul was blocked next month at **Chiksan** (September 1597).

Nanawa ∎ 1933 ∎ Chaco War

Four months after losing **Boquerón** in the Chaco Boreal to Paraguayan forces, Bolivians under German General Hans Kundt attacked the heavily entrenched fortress at nearby Nanawa—the "Verdun of America"—defended by Colonel Luís Irrázabal. Despite air, tank and artillery support, assaults in January and July failed and Kundt withdrew northwest to attack **Gondra** (20 January–14 July 1933).

Nanchang ∎ 1363 ∎ Rise of the Ming Dynasty

Amid bitter fighting for the Yangzi Valley, Han commander Chen Yuliang took a large armada to besiege Nanchang, held by Zhu Wenzheng for his uncle, the great Zhu Yuanzhang. After very costly losses on both sides, Zhu Yuanzhang sailed upriver with the Ming fleet to relieve Nanchang. Chen broke off the siege and the two forces met in a decisive battle on **Poyang Lake** (5 June–28 August 1363).

Nanchang ∎ 1853 ∎ Taiping Rebellion

With **Nanjing** captured in March to become Taiping capital, their Western Expedition under Shi Dakai secured Anqing, then besieged Nanchang, defended by Governor Zhangfei and General Zhiang Zhongyuan. The Taiping eventually withdrew after repeated failed assaults and a 90-day siege. They later seized Hankou and Hanyang before attacking **Wuchang** (24 June–24 September 1853).

Nanchang ∎ 1913 ∎ 2nd Chinese Revolution

President Yuan Shikai of Republican China seized arbitrary power and cracked down on the Kuomintang, provoking a military response, which was strongest in Jiangxi under Governor Li Liejun. Heavy fighting saw government forces capture the provincial capital Nanchang before the fall of **Nanjing** in September ended the so-called Second Revolution (1 August 1913).

Nanchang ∎ 1926 ∎ 1st Chinese Revolutionary Civil War

While General Chiang Kai-shek took **Wuchang**, he sent Zheng Qian east to seize Nanchang. He was driven out by Lu Xiangting for warlord Sun Zhuanfang and Chiang suffered heavy losses failing to retake the city. When a new offensive took Sun's base at Kuikiang, Nanchang fell and the Nationalists continued downstream towards **Hangzhou** (19 September–8 November 1926).

Nanchang ∎ 1939 ∎ Sino-Japanese War

When Japan had secured **Wuhan**, General Yasuji Okamura led a major force south against Nanchang. The strategic city fell by storm and Chiang Kai-shek ordered a massive counteroffensive under General Luo Zhuoyin. The Chinese reached Nanchang, where they were eventually repulsed. In September Okamura advanced on **Changsha** (18–27 March & 21 April–8 May 1939).

Nancy ∎ 1477 ∎ Burgundian-Swiss War

Swiss forces twice routed Charles the Bold of Burgundy in Switzerland in early 1476—at **Grandson** and **Morat**—then invaded Lorraine to support Rene of Lorraine against Burgundian occupation. Attempting to recapture Nancy, west of Strasbourg, Charles was killed in a heavy defeat at nearby Jarville, finally curbing the ambition of the Duchy of Burgundy (5 January 1477).

Nancy ❙ 1914 ❙ World War I
(Western Front)

Following defeat in **Lorraine**, French forces fell back on Nancy and Lunéville, where the Germans soon began a fresh offensive. Very heavy fighting in the nearby Grand-Couronné hills eventually checked the German advance. Despite regular bombardment by air and artillery, the French bravely held the line east of Nancy for the rest of the war (31 August–11 September 1914).

Nancy ❙ 1944 ❙ World War II
(Western Europe)

American General George Patton was driving deep into Lorraine, when General Manton Eddy attacking the city of Nancy met unexpectedly stiff resistance from newly arrived Panzers. The city finally fell by storm, after which Eddy had to repulse severe German counter-attacks with both sides suffering heavy losses in tanks. The Americans then turned north against **Metz** (11–16 September 1944).

Nandi Drug ❙ 1791 ❙ 3rd British-Mysore War

When Tipu Sultan of Mysore renewed war against Britain, Governor-General Charles Earl Cornwallis captured **Bangalore** in March, then sent General William Medows north against the mountain fortress of Nandi Drug, near Chik Ballapur. The reputedly impregnable position fell to a courageous assault and Earl Cornwallis marched on **Seringapatam** (22 September–17 October 1791).

Nangis ❙ 1814 ❙ Napoleonic Wars
(French Campaign)

See **Mortmant**

Nanjing ❙ 1129 ❙ Jin-Song Wars

With Emperor Qin Zong captured by Jin invaders in defeat at **Kaifeng** (1127), his brother Gao Zong fled to Nanjing and established the Southern Song Dynasty. However, Nanjing fell by storm and Gao Zong withdrew further south. The great General Yue Fei later checked the invaders and established a boundary between Jin and Song China. In 1161, the Jin were repulsed at **Chenjia** and **Caishi**.

Nanjing ❙ 1356 ❙ Rise of the Ming Dynasty

During widespread uprising against China's ailing Mongol Yuan Dynasty, the former monk Zhu Yuanzhang led a force across the Yangzi, where repeated assaults secured the key city of Nanjing. In a prolonged and bloody war, he defeated rivals including the Han at **Poyang Lake** and the Wu at **Suzhou**, to secure China and establish the Ming Dynasty as Hong Wu. The Ming ruled until 1644 (10 April 1356).

Nanjing ❙ 1659 ❙ Manchu Conquest of China

Despite the Manchu taking **Beijing** in 1644, remnants of the Ming Dynasty fought on in the east until Ming General Zheng Chenggong (Koxinga) and a reported 200,000 men attempted to retake Nanjing. The over-confident Ming army suffered a terrible defeat, effectively ending resistance on the mainland. Zheng soon crossed to Taiwan and seized **Fort Zeelandia** (24 August–9 September 1659).

Nanjing ❙ 1853 ❙ Taiping Rebellion

Taiping commander Shi Dakai advancing down the Yangzi through **Anqing** with perhaps 100,000 men reached Nanjing, held by disgraced Comissioner Lu Jianying with Generals Fuzhu Hang'a and Xiang Hou. When explosives breached the walls, Nanjing was taken by storm with all three Imperial leaders killed. After a shocking massacre it became the Taiping capital (6–20 March 1853).

Nanjing ❙ 1856 ❙ Taiping Rebellion

Determined to relieve the Imperial siege of Nanjing, Shi Dakai (from victory at **Changshu**) and Qin Rigang (from victory at **Zhenjiang**) led a massive attack on the Southern Imperial Barracks, outside the capital. Imperial Generals Xiang Rong and Zhang Guoliang were routed in a humiliating defeat and fled. However, the Taiping were then wracked by fratricidal war (17–20 June 1856).

Nanjing I 1860 I Taiping Rebellion

After years of costly fighting in the provinces, new Taiping commander Hong Rengan and Li Xuicheng feinted towards nearby Zhenjiang, then led a huge converging attack on the Southern Imperial Barracks outside besieged Nanjing. Imperial Commissioner He Zhou and General Zhang Guoliang suffered a terrible defeat and the capital was again saved from siege (1–6 May 1860).

Nanjing I 1862–1864 I Taiping Rebellion

As Imperial forces converged on Nanjing, the siege began at **Yuhuatai** and by late 1863 Zeng Guoquan had encircled the Taiping capital, defended by Li Xuicheng. Soon after Taiping King Hong Xiuquan died (1 June) the city was taken by storm, followed by widespread massacre. Li was captured and executed and China's greatest civil war was virtually over (30 May 1862–19 July 1864).

Nanjing I 1911 I 1st Chinese Revolution

When **Hankou** was lost to a Manchu counter-attack (30 October) Republican forces marched on the Imperial capital Nanjing, where advance units were routed at nearby Yuhuatai by General Zhang Xun (9 November). However, Nanjing fell by storm and boy-Emperor Puyi (Xuan Tong) abdicated. President Yuan Shikai then moved the capital to Beijing (28 November–2 December 1911).

Nanjing I 1913 I 2nd Chinese Revolution

President Yuan Shikai of Republican China seized arbitrary power, then crushed the Kuomintang in Jiangxi at **Nanchang** and KMT leader Huang Xing was forced to abandon Nanjing. But local commander He Haiming held out against the government army of Zhang Xun, who finally stormed and sacked the city, ending the so-called Second Revolution (29 July–1 September 1913).

Nanjing I 1927 I 1st Chinese Revolutionary Civil War

While his Nationalist army attacked **Shanghai**, Chiang Kai-shek's General Zheng Qian at-tacked and stormed Nanjing. In the so-called "Nanjing Incident" troops then looted foreign embassies, killing and destroying, and a British cruiser used shellfire to protect foreigners before Zheng restored order. In August Northern forces counter-attacked to the east at **Longtan** (23–24 March 1927).

Nanjing I 1937 I Sino-Japanese War

Japanese forces captured **Shanghai** (11 November) then marched inland against Nanjing, where Chiang Kai-shek moved his capital to Chonqing. General Tang Shengzhi led a courageous defence before the city fell by storm, followed by the notorious "Rape of Nanjing," which reportedly cost over 100,000 lives. The Japanese then advanced northwest against **Xuzhou** (6–16 December 1937).

Nanjing I 1949 I 3rd Chinese Revolutionary Civil War

After decisive victory at **Huaihai** in January, Communist Generals Chen Yi and Liu Bocheng advanced south to the Yangzi and converged on Nanjing, held by General Zhang Yaoming for commander Tang Enbai. The Nationalist capital fell by storm, quickly followed by other major cities including Shanghai, effectively ending the Kuomintang government (20–23 April 1949).

Nanking I 1129 I Jin-Song Wars
See **Nanjing**

Nanking I 1356 I Rise of the Ming Dynasty
See **Nanjing**

Nanking I 1659 I Manchu Conquest of China
See **Nanjing**

Nanking I 1853 I Taiping Rebellion
See **Nanjing**

Nanking I 1856 I Taiping Rebellion
See **Nanjing**

Nanking I 1860 I Taiping Rebellion
See **Nanjing**

Nanking I 1862–1864 I Taiping Rebellion
See **Nanjing**

Nanking I 1911 I 1st Chinese Revolution
See **Nanjing**

Nanking I 1913 I 2nd Chinese Revolution
See **Nanjing**

Nanking I 1927 I 1st Chinese Revolutionary Civil War
See **Nanjing**

Nanking I 1937 I Sino-Japanese War
See **Nanjing**

Nanking I 1949 I 3rd Chinese Revolutionary Civil War
See **Nanjing**

Nanning I 1939 I Sino-Japanese War

Japanese forces frustrated at **Changsha** in Hunan in October, opened a new front in Guangxi, where General Kinichi Imamura landed near Qinzhou and advanced to take Nanning. He then captured nearby Kunlun Guan and Binyang (modern Binzhou), though lost them both to a Chinese counter-attack under Bai Chongxi. Japan eventually evacuated Nanning in October 1940 (15–23 November 1939).

Nanshan I 1904 I Russo-Japanese War

An attempt to seal off the Liaodong Peninsula saw General Yasukata Oku land on the isthmus at Jinzhou, where Colonel Nikolai Tretyakov tried to defend the town but was refused reinforcements. In the face of suicidal Japanese attacks and naval bombardment, Tretyakov had to abandon the nearby fortress of Nanshan and **Port Arthur** (modern Lüshun) was cut off (25–26 May 1904).

Nantes I 1793 I French Revolutionary Wars (Vendée War)

Three weeks after victory at **Saumur** for the Royalists in western France, 30,000 rebels under Jacques Cathelineau, supported by Francois-Athanese Charette in the south, advanced down the Loire against Nantes, defended by the Marquis de Canclaux. In a turning point for the whole rebellion, the Vendéeans were crushed attempting a frontal attack, with Cathelineau fatally wounded (29 June 1793).

Nantwich I 1644 I British Civil Wars

Anglo-Irish Royalist troops under Sir John Byron were recalled from Ireland and besieged the Parliamentary stronghold at Nantwich, Cheshire, where they were in turn attacked by a relief force under Sir Thomas Fairfax. A bitter midwinter defeat saw the Royalists lose 500 killed as well as 1,500 prisoners. More than half of the captives switched sides to join the victors (25 January 1644).

Naoussa I 1946 I Greek Civil War

At the start of a large-scale guerrilla offensive in Macedonia, insurgent forces besieged Naoussa and were driven off by Liberal and government forces. Following a major action further south at **Deskarti**, the rebels attacked again and overwhelmed the small National Guard garrison. Naoussa was held briefly until fresh government forces arrived (6–8 August & 1 October 1946).

Naoussa I 1948–1949 I Greek Civil War

Insurgent forces attempting to regain the initiative in northern Greece were badly repulsed at Serres (1 December 1948) then at the key industrial city of Naoussa. Attacking again three weeks later, they overpowered the garrison. So-called economic warfare saw Nouassa's factories and shops destroyed before new government forces drove them out (21 December 1948 & 12–16 January 1949).

Napata I 593 BC I Egyptian-Nubian War

Determined to punish the Nubian kingdom of Kush, which continued to claim the Egyptian throne, Psammetichus (Psamthek) II of Egypt led a large force, comprising Egyptians and Greek mercenaries, up the Nile. After defeating the Nubian army he sacked and burned the city of Napata, near the Fourth Cataract. King Aspelta of Kush withdrew his capital further south to Meroe.

Napata I 23 BC I Roman-Nubian War

When Nubian Meroe on the Upper Nile raided into Roman Egypt, Governor Petronius marched south with 10,000 men and 800 horses. Petronius defeated the Meroite army near Primis (Qasr Ibrim) then attacked Napata, burned it to the ground and sold several thousand prisoners into slavery. Queen Candace Amanirenas fled Napata and made peace. Rome soon pulled back to Hiera Sykaminos.

Naples I 1284 I War of the Sicilian Vespers

In war for Sicily between Pedro III of Aragon and Charles I of Anjou, the Anjevin fleet was beaten off **Messina** (July 1283), then virtually destroyed off Naples by Aragonese Admiral Roger di Loria. The King's son Charles was captured and forced to acknowledge the separate throne of Sicily. Charles later revoked the treaty and war raged for 20 years until Aragon won the island (5 June 1284).

Naples I 1442 I Aragon's Conquest of Naples

René of Anjou was finally released from captivity after defeat at **Bulgnéville** (1431) and went to Italy to claim the disputed Kingdom of Naples. At the end of four years' war against Alfonso V of Aragon, René was beaten at Naples and had to withdraw. René returned to France, abandoning his claim on the kingdom. His son Jean was beaten 20 years later in Appulia at **Troia** (2 June 1442).

Naples I 1528 I 2nd Habsburg-Valois War

Genoese Admiral Filippino Doria supporting a French siege of Naples, intercepted Spanish galleys off Naples bringing supplies from Sicily. Imperial commander Ugo de Moncada was kil-

led and his fleet destroyed. However, Doria and his uncle Andrea soon switched sides to the Imperial cause and the French had to withdraw. Further defeat followed in June 1529 at **Landriano** (28 April 1528).

Naples I 1647 I Masaniello's Insurrection

Taxes imposed by Spanish Viceroy Rodrigo Ponce de Léon Duke of Arcos provoked people in Naples to rebel under Masaniello (Tommaso Aniello), seizing armouries and opening the prisons. However, Masaniello was soon murdered by his disillusioned followers. Spain suppressed a similar rising in **Palermo** then retook Naples in 1648 and executed the remaining rebel leaders (7–16 July 1647).

Naples I 1799 I French Revolutionary Wars (1st Coalition)

When the Neapolitan army was crushed at **Civita Castelana** by French General Jean-Étienne Championnet (December 1798), Admiral Horatio Nelson took King Ferdinand IV and his family to Palermo. Championnet then advanced on Naples itself, which fell after hard fighting. Although Championnet was recalled, Naples was held by French forces until the following June (23 January 1799).

Naples I 1943 I World War II (Southern Europe)

Soon after breaking out from the hard-won bridgehead at **Salerno**, Anglo-American forces led by General Mark Clark drove 50 miles north towards Naples against a brutal fighting withdrawal under General Heinrich von Vietinghoff. The Germans demolished bridges to slow the advance, then destroyed much of Naples and its port before falling back to defend the **Volturno** (1 October 1943).

Narbonne I 436–437 I Goth Invasion of the Roman Empire

Theodoric the Visigoth broke the peace with Rome and was again repulsed at **Arles** (435) before taking heavy siege machines against Narbonne. With the Mediterranean city virtually starving, Roman General Litorius broke in to raise the siege. Theodoric was then defeated by a largely Hun army under the Roman General Flavius Aetius and withdrew to his capital at **Toulouse**.

Naris | 1904 | German Colonial Wars in Africa

With Herero rebels fighting in the north of German Southwest Africa, Nama tribesmen in the south joined in, led by the 80-year-old Hendrik Witbooi. At Naris, northwest of Marienthal, Colonel Berthold von Deimling surprised the Nama camp and more than 50 rebels were killed. Witbooi escaped and continued guerrilla war until killed in late 1905 near **Vaalgras** (4 December 1904).

Narmada | 620 | Indian Dynastic Wars

Harsha Vardhana of Kanauj conquered all of northern India, but when he attempted to invade the Deccan he was halted in a decisive battle at the Narmada by the warrior-King Pulakesin II of Chalukya. After further fighting, the Narmada was accepted as the boundary between the two empires and Harsha made no further attempt to expand southwards (disputed date c 620).

Narnaul | 1857 | Indian Mutiny

Colonel John Gerrard led 2,500 men southwest from Delhi and met rebels under Sanand Khan, who had seized the fort at Narnaul then lost it to Gerrard through incompetence. Attempting to recover the position, the Erinpuram mutineers were defeated in very heavy fighting and fled, abandoning the fort and their camp. Gerrard was killed in the pursuit (16 November 1857).

Naroch | 1916 | World War I (Eastern Front)

See **Lake Naroch**

Narrow Seas | 1602 | Netherlands War of Independence

English Admiral Sir Robert Mansell was sent to intercept six Spanish galleys under Frederigo Spinola sailing to the Netherlands from Lisbon and began the attack off Dungeness. Action continued across the Narrow Seas towards Dunkirk, where Dutch Admiral Jan van Cant and a violent gale completed the destruction. Two galleys were sunk and three were driven ashore (23–24 September 1602).

Narungombe | 1917 | World War I (African Colonial Theatre)

During a relative lull in fighting in German East Africa, General Louis van Deventer sent British and South African forces against Hauptmann Eberhard van Lieberman at Narungombe, on the Lukuledi 40 miles upstream from Kilwa. Very heavy fighting caused unexpectedly high losses on both sides before the Germans were forced to withdraw (19 July 1917).

Narva | 1558 | Livonian War

Determined to conquer Livonia, Ivan IV of Russia sent a large army under the Tatar Segelei and Grandmaster Wilhelm Furstenberg of the Livonian Order soon negotiated a ceasefire. However, Livonians at Narva (in modern Estonia) attacked the nearby Russian fort at Ivangorod and Narva was taken by storm. Dorpat and other cities also fell before an armistice in May 1559 (11 May 1558).

Narva | 1581 | Livonian War

In support of Poland fighting Moscow over Livonia, Swedish forces under French-born Pontus de la Gardie (son-in-law of King John III) launched an offensive against Russian cities in Karelia and Estonia. In his greatest victory, de la Gardie captured the key port of Narva. This action, along with the continuing Polish siege of **Pskov**, soon persuaded the Tsar to sue for peace (6 September 1581).

Narva | 1700 | 2nd "Great" Northern War

Charles XII of Sweden defeated Denmark at **Copenhagen** in August, then moved against Russian Tsar Peter I and Field Marshal Fedor Golovin besieging the Estonian city of Narva. Attacking during a snowstorm with only one-fifth as many troops, Charles utterly destroyed the huge Russian army and Peter fled, leaving Charles to attack the Saxons at **Riga** (4 October–20 November 1700).

Narva ▌ 1704 ▌ 2nd "Great" Northern War

A spring offensive saw Tsar Peter I of Russia besiege the powerful Baltic fortress of Narva, held by Swedish Count Arvid Horn against Scottish-born Russian Field Marshal George Ogilvie. With the fall of **Dorpat** (24 July), the Tsar and Marshal Boris Sheremetev reinforced the siege to 45,000 men. Narva was then bombarded and fell by storm, followed by a terrible massacre (June–20 August 1704).

Narva ▌ 1919 ▌ Estonian War of Independence

With a White Russian and Estonian offensive repulsed at **Petrograd** (12 November), Red forces advanced on the Narva against Estonian General Jaan Tönnisson, later reinforced by General Johan Laidoner. Outnumbered Estonians withstood six weeks of heavy assault before the Bolsheviks accepted an armistice. They soon recognised Estonian Independence (16 November–30 December 1919).

Narvik (1st) ▌ 1940 ▌ World War II (Northern Europe)

At the start of the German invasion of Norway, naval forces seized the vital northern port of Narvik, where they were attacked by Royal Navy destroyers under Captain Bernard Warburton-Lee. Two German destroyers and seven transports were sunk, though the British lost two destroyers and Warburton-Lee was killed. He was awarded a posthumous Victoria Cross (10 April 1940).

Narvik (2nd) ▌ 1940 ▌ World War II (Northern Europe)

In a renewed assault on German ships at Narvik, in northern Norway, Admiral William Whitworth in the British battleship *Warspite* led a second destroyer raid into Ofot Fjord, where the remaining eight large German destroyers

were sunk or scuttled. The two actions effectively halved Germany's destroyer fleet and helped the brief Allied recapture of Narvik (13 April 1940).

Narvik (3rd) ▌ 1940 ▌ World War II (Northern Europe)

Although the German destroyer flotilla at Narvik was destroyed, continued fighting for the vital northern port was the hardest of any in the Norwegian campaign. Anglo-British forces under General Pierse Mackesy eventually retook Narvik from General Eduard Dietl (28 May). However, Britain had decided to evacuate Norway and the Allies abandoned their hard-fought gain (14 April–8 June 1940).

Naseby ▌ 1645 ▌ British Civil Wars

Charles I captured **Leicester** (31 May) then turned against a Parliamentary relief force under Sir Thomas Fairfax. Southwest of Market Harborough at Naseby, while Prince Rupert recklessly pursued Parliamentary cavalry, the Royalist infantry was destroyed with 1,000 killed and 4,000 prisoners. Apart from some minor actions, the defeat virtually ended the King's war (14 June 1645).

Nashville ▌ 1864 ▌ American Civil War (Western Theatre)

Despite a terrible defeat at **Franklin**, Tennessee, Confederate commander John B. Hood continued north against Nashville, defended by General George H. Thomas, supported by General James Steedman. Outnumbered two to one, Hood suffered another decisive defeat, losing over 4,000 prisoners. The Army of Tennessee was virtually destroyed and Hood soon resigned (15–16 December 1864).

Nasiriya ▌ 1915 ▌ World War I (Mesopotamia)

While commander Charles Townshend sailed up the Tigris towards **Kut-al-Amara**, General George Gorringe followed success at **Ahwaz** by marching northwest from Basra along the Euphrates to protect the other British flank. After a very difficult advance, supported by naval guns,

Gorringe stormed Nasiriya, where the Turks lost 1,000 captured and 2,000 killed or wounded (22–24 July 1915).

Nasiriya I 2003 I 2nd Gulf War

Bypassing the southern Iraqi city of **Basra**, American forces raced northwest towards Nasiriya, where they met stiff resistance. While the main American thrust continued north through **Najaf**, hard fighting continued to secure the city and its strategic crossing of the Euphrates. Nasiriya was finally taken and a subsequent Iraqi counter-attack was later repulsed (22–23 March 2003).

Nasratpur I 1858 I Indian Mutiny

See **Chanda, Uttar Pradesh**

Nassau I 1776 I War of the American Revolution

See **New Providence**

Nations I 1813 I Napoleonic Wars (War of Liberation)

See **Leipzig**

Natural Bridge I 1865 I American Civil War (Lower Seaboard)

Union General John Newton took the offensive in northwest Florida near the end of the war, landing with a mainly black force south of Tallahassee to advance up the St Mark's River. While attempting to cross at Natural Bridge, eight miles northeast of Newport, Newton was heavily defeated by Confederate General Sam Jones and had to withdraw to his ships (6 March 1865).

Naukluf I 1894 I German Colonial Wars in Africa

With his camp destroyed at **Hornkranz** in German Southwest Africa (April 1893), Nama leader Hendrik Witbooi fought a guerrilla war until cornered in the Naukluf Mountains by new German commander Theodor Leutwein. Witbooi was decisively beaten and submitted after a two-week action. He rose in rebellion again ten years later but was defeated at **Naris** (27 August–9 September 1894).

Naulochus I 36 BC I Wars of the Second Triumvirate

Two weeks after defeating Octavian off **Tauromenium**, Sextus Pompeius—Pompey the Younger—was forced into battle with Octavian's remaining fleet under Marcus Vipsanius Agrippa. Off Naulochus, in the Straits of Messina, most of Pompey's ships were destroyed, virtually ending the war. Sextus was pursued to Asia Minor, where he was captured and executed (3 September 36 BC).

Naupactus I 429 BC I Great Peloponnesian War

When Sparta sent a large fleet under Admiral Cnemus to attack Acarnania, the Athenian Phormio routed a supply convoy off **Patras**, then sailed out from Naupactus (modern Navpaktos) in the Gulf of Cornith to attack the main fleet. With just 20 ships against 77, Phormio lost some ships captured before recovering through superior seamanship. Cnemus was forced to retire (September 429 BC).

Nauplia I 1770 I Catherine the Great's 1st Turkish War

At the head of Russia's Baltic fleet in the Mediterranean, Scots-born Admiral John Elphinston attacked Turkish ships in the Gulf of Argolis in southeast Greece using newly invented explosive shells. The Turks withdrew to anchor at Nauplia, where Elphinston's squadron continued the attack. However, he could not force a decisive outcome until six weeks later at **Chesme** (27–28 May 1770).

Nauplia I 1821–1822 I Greek War of Independence

Governor Ali Pasha of Nauplia, in eastern Greece, had been under siege since the start of the war when an Ottoman relief army under Dramali (Mohamet Ali Pasha) approached. While some advance units reached the city, Dramali withdrew through disaster at **Devernaki**. The garrison finally surrendered, saved from massacre by the presence of a British ship (April 1821–22 December 1822).

Naushera I 1823 I Afghan-Sikh Wars
See **Nowshera**

Navalcarnero I 1936 I Spanish Civil War

As the Nationalist army advanced on Madrid through **Chapinería** and **Ilescas**, Republican forces determined to hold the well-entrenched positions southwest of the capital at Navalcarnero. Nationalist General Juan Yagüe, with veterans from Africa and supported by Italian tanks, smashed through the defences in heavy fighting and the Republicans fell back on **Madrid** (21 October 1936).

Navarette I 1367 I Hundred Years War

Crossing the Pyrenees to restore Pedro IV of Castile, Edward the Black Prince led an English army against Pedro's brother Henry of Trastamara and French allies under Bertrand du Guesclin. In a one-sided victory near the Ebro River between Najera and Navarette, Edward's archers routed the French and Spanish army. Pedro was restored, but was overthrown in 1369 at **Montiel** (3 April 1367).

**Navarino I 425 BC I Great
Peloponnesian War**
See **Pylos-Sphacteria**

**Navarino I 1821 I Greek War
of Independence**

After the bloody surrender of **Monemvasia**, in southeast Peloponnesia in early August, Greek commander Dimitrius Ipsilantis marched west to the siege of Navarino. Ipsilantis offered honourable terms, agreeing to transport the Turks to Egypt, though his irregulars again slaughtered the prisoners. The Greeks then advanced northeast towards the wealth of **Tripolitza** (29 March–19 August 1821).

**Navarino I 1825 I Greek War
of Independence**

Egyptian commander Ibrahim Pasha invaded southwestern Greece from Crete and besieged Navarino and neighbouring Pylos, defended by Alexandros Mavrocordatos and Georgios Sachtouris. With Greek defeat at **Krommydi**, and the

fall of nearby **Sphakteria**, Pylos surrendered. Navarino fell soon afterwards while Ibrahim defeated a Greek force at **Maniaki** (21 March–21 May 1825).

**Navarino I 1827 I Greek War
of Independence**

With Turkey again controlling Greece after **Missolonghi** and **Navarino**, British Admiral Sir Edward Codrington, French Henri Comte de Rigny, and Count Lodewijk Heiden's Russians attacked and destroyed the Egyptian-Turkish fleet under Tahir Pasha at Navarino. The Turks lost 60 out of 89 ships and 8,000 men, effectively ending the war and securing Greek independence (20 October 1827).

Navarro I 1828 I Argentine Civil Wars

General Juan Galo Lavalle opposed Argentina's peace with Brazil after victory at **Ituzaingó** (February 1827) and led a revolt against Governor Manuel Dorrego of Buenos Aires and General Juan Manuel de Rosas. Southwest of the capital at Navarro, Lavalle's veterans won a decisive victory. While Rosas escaped, Dorrego was seized and executed. Lavalle made himself Governor (9 December 1828).

**Navas de Membrillo I 1811 I Napoleonic
Wars (Peninsular Campaign)**

General Sir Rowland Hill advanced into southwest Spain to relieve **Tarifa** and sent cavalry to attack 300 French infantry on patrol from Merida under Captain Neveux. Forming a square in wooded country, Neveux's men courageously drove off the cavalry, inflicting about 40 British casualties. The French abandoned Merida that night and marched south to Almendralejo (29 December 1811).

**Navas de Tolosa I 1212 I Early Christian
Reconquest of Spain**
See **Las Navas de Tolosa**

Navsari I 738 I Muslim Conquest of Sind

Arab forces seized Sind after victory at **Raor** (712) and the next 20 years saw expansion into Malwa and Broach before Governor Tamim attempted to invade Gujarat. His forces were decisively defeated at Navsari by the Chalukya Prince Avanijanasraya Pulakesin, checking Muslim expansion. The Arabs had to abandon parts of Sind until control was restored by the new Governor Hakam.

Nawabganj ❙ 1858 ❙ Indian Mutiny

On campaign northeast from Lucknow, Colonel Sir Hope Grant attacked a reported 15,000 rebels under Beni Madhav in a strong defensive position 20 miles away at Nawabganj. At the end of an overnight march in terrible heat, Hope Grant inflicted a decisive defeat with a surprise dawn assault. About 600 rebels were killed and the disheartened survivors withdrew east (13 June 1858).

N'Axama ❙ 1878 ❙ 9th Cape Frontier War

As war continued in the Transkei after Xhosa defeat at **Ibeka** (September 1877), the Galekas of Krieli were joined by the veteran warrior Sandile and their large combined force attacked Regulars and Frontier Armed Police at N'Axama. The Xhosa were driven off with about 150 men killed for no European loss. The final action was fought a month later at **Kentani** (12 January 1878).

Naxos ❙ 376 BC ❙ Wars of the Greek City-States

Determined to support Thebes against Sparta, Athens sent Admiral Chabrias against the Spartan fleet under Pollio, which was based at Aegina to intercept Athenian grain supplies. During a decisive action near Naxos, in the Cyclades, the outnumbered Spartans reportedly lost 49 out of 63 triremes and Athens secured mastery of the Aegean for the next decade (September 376 BC).

Nazareth ❙ 1948 ❙ Israeli War of Independence

During the so-called Ten Days Offensive, Israeli General Moshe Carmel moved northeast from **Haifa** to secure the Valley of Zebulon, then launched his main attack southeast towards Nazareth against a mixed Palestinian and Leba-

nese army under Fawzi el Kaukji. A brilliant advance through defended Arab villages saw Kaukji forced to flee and Nazareth fell before the Second Truce (12–16 July 1948).

Ncome River ❙ 1838 ❙ Boer-Zulu War
See **Blood River**

N'Djamena ❙ 1979 ❙ Chad Civil Wars

With Chad descending into chaos, Defence Minister Hissen Habré broke with President Félix Malloum and heavy fighting broke out in the streets of N'Djamena. Malloum was overthrown and rebel leader Goukouni Oueddei was named President, with Habré in support. The allies soon fell out and next year Goukouni used Libyan aid to defeat Habré and retake the capital by force (March 1979).

N'Djamena ❙ 1980 ❙ Chad Civil Wars

Supported by about 5,000 Libyan troops and 100 tanks, nominal President Goukouni Oueddei began a broad offensive towards N'Djamena, where Libyan air-strikes caused heavy damage. Although severe fighting outside the capital cost perhaps 50 Libyan tanks, former Defence Minister Hissen Habré was forced to withdraw. In 1982 Habré ousted Goukouni to become President (15 December 1980).

Ndondakusuka ❙ 1856 ❙ Zulu Wars of Succession

In the violent struggle to succeed Zulu King Mpande, his sons Mbulazi and Cetshwayo eventually went to war and met at Ndondakusuka near the mouth of the Tugela. Outnumbered, and with his back to the river, Mbulazi and five of his brothers were killed in a bloody rout. Cetshwayo became undisputed heir and later virtual Regent until Mpande's death in 1872 (3 December 1856).

Neaje ❙ 1016 ❙ Scandinavian National Wars
See **Nesjar**

Nebi-Samweil I 1917 I World War I (Middle East)

See **Jerusalem**

Nebovidy I 1422 I Hussite Wars

Despite Imperial defeats at **Vitkov Hill** and **Zatec**, Sigismund of Hungary led a third expedition into eastern Bohemia and drove the Hussite Jan Zizka out of **Kutna Hora**, southeast of Prague. In a brilliant counter-offensive, Zizka soon attacked and routed the Imperial army at Nebovidy, three miles to the northwest. Sigismund then retreated southeast through **Habry** to **Nemecky Brod** (6 January 1422).

Neches I 1839 I Cherokee Indian Wars

Commander Kelsey H. Douglass led Texan troops against local Cherokees, sending Generals Thomas J. Rusk and Ed Burleson against 700 Indians along the Neches River, west of modern Tyler. A two-day battle and pursuit saw the Cherokee routed, with the veteran Chief Bowle killed. While most survivors fled to Oklahoma, a few fought again in December at the **San Saba** (15–16 July 1839).

Nechtanesmere I 685 I Anglo-Saxon Territorial Wars

See **Dunnichen Moss**

Nedao I 454 I Hun-Ostrogoth Wars

In the struggle for power following the death of Attila the Hun (453), his former ally Ardaric of the Gepids attacked and defeated Attila's sons in Pannonia at the Nedao (Netad), probably a tributary of the Sava. Attila's eldest son Ellac was killed and his brothers fled towards the Black Sea. Thereafter, apart from a few minor incursions, the Huns virtually disappeared from European history.

Neerwinden I 1693 I War of the Grand Alliance

The Anglo-Dutch army of William III of England and Holland defended a strongly entrenched position at Neerwinden, west of Liège near Landen, and appeared well protected.

However, they were utterly routed by French veterans under Marshal Duke Francois Henri of Luxembourg. The French also suffered high casualties and the Marshal did not pursue his defeated enemy (29 July 1693).

Neerwinden I 1793 I French Revolutionary Wars (1st Coalition)

French General Charles-Francois Dumouriez, driven back after invading Holland, was defeated at Neerwinden, northwest of Liège, by Austrians under Friedrich Josias Prince of Saxe-Coburg. When he lost again three days later at **Louvain**, Dumouriez was accused of treason and went over to the Allies, who reoccupied Belgium, which had been lost in late 1792 with defeat at **Jemappes** (18 March 1793).

Negapatam I 1746 I 1st Carnatic War

After the British fleet established itself on the southeastern coast of India, French Admiral Bertrand Mahé de la Bourdonnais arrived from Mauritius with eight ships and attacked the British squadron of Commodore Edward Peyton, cruising between Negapatam and **Fort St David**. Peyton withdrew after a long-range battle leaving Bourdonnais to besiege **Madras** (25 June 1746).

Negapatam I 1758 I Seven Years's War (India)

In resumed warfare against Britain in India, French Admiral Ann-Antoine d'Aché arrived on the southeast coast in support of new Governor General Comte Thomas Lally. After a previous clash off **Cuddalore**, d'Aché and Admiral Sir George Pocock fought another indecisive action off Negapatam, with heavy French casualties. They met again in September 1759 off **Pondicherry** (3 August 1758).

Negapatam I 1781 I 2nd British-Mysore War

At the outbreak of war in Europe, Haidar Ali of Mysore allied himself with the Dutch in southern India, prompting a British expedition to Dutch-held Nagore. Advancing towards

Negapatam, General Sir Hector Munro gradually captured the outlying Mysorean redoubts and trenches until Haidar Ali withdrew. The garrison then surrendered (21 October–12 November 1781).

Negapatam | 1782 | War of the American Revolution

The third of five indecisive naval actions off the east coast of India saw British Admiral Edward Hughes intercept French Admiral Pierre André Suffren supporting an attempt from **Cuddalore** to capture Negapatam. Suffren withdrew with two ships heavily damaged after a bloody engagement. The fleets met again three months later off **Trincomalee** (6 July 1782).

Negro Fort | 1816 | 1st Seminole Indian War

Colonel Duncan Clinch was determined to protect American trade on the Apalachicola River, through Spanish West Florida, and took a force, including Creek warriors, against Negro Fort, held by Seminole harbouring escaped slaves. Clinch destroyed the fort in a bloody assault with 270 Negroes and Seminole killed. In the ensuing war, General Andrew Jackson seized **Pensacola** (27 July 1816).

Negroponte | 1470 | Venetian-Turkish Wars

After years of campaigning against Venice's Greek and Adriatic colonies, Sultan Mehmed II sent Vizier Mahmud Pasha with a massive fleet against the city of Negroponte (modern Khalkis) on the Greek island of Euboea. Venetian Admiral Niccolo Canale failed to drive off the attack and the Turks took the city, massacring the population. Canale was exiled for life (15 June–12 July 1470).

Nehavend | 641 | Muslim Conquest of Iran

In four years after conquering Iraq at **Qadisiyya** and **Jalula**, Caliph Omar consolidated before sending his army into the Iranian highlands against Sassanian commander Firuzan. At Nehavend, near ancient Ecbatana in western Iran, General Nohman's bloody victory ended organised Persian resistance, though both commanders were killed. Arabs called it the "Victory of Victories."

Nekujyal | 1612 | Mughal Conquest of Northern India

Thirty years after the Mughals completed their conquest of Bengal at **Rajmahal**, the local Afghan leader Usman Khan Lodi, son of Isa Khan, took advantage of a change of Governors to rebel against Mughal Emperor Janhagir. However, Usman was defeated and killed in battle at Nekujyal by the new Governor Islam Khan, ending Afghan influence in Bengal (12 March 1612).

Nemea | 394 BC | Corinthian War

After the Spartan victory at **Haliartus** (395 BC), the four-power alliance of Thebes, Argos, Corinth and Athens challenged the Spartans at the Nemea, southwest of Corinth. A classic hoplite action proved indecisive, though Sparta inflicted heavy casualties as their opponents withdrew. King Agesilaus of Sparta soon returned from Asia Minor to win at **Coronea** and lay siege to **Corinth**.

Nemecky Brod | 1422 | Hussite Wars

Sigismund of Hungary was driven out of **Kutna Hora**, southeast of Prague, by Hussite General Jan Zizka and retreated southeast through **Habry** to Nemecky Brod (modern Havlickuv Brod) on the Sásava, held by Polish Baron Zawiza of Garbow. Zizka's outnumbered force destroyed almost half the Imperial army of 23,000 and Sigismund was forced to withdraw from Bohemia (9–10 January 1422).

Nemiga | 1067 | Russian Dynastic Wars

Kievan Princes Iziaslav, Sviatoslav and Vsevolod (sons of Yaroslav the Wise) were determined to punish Vseslav of Polotsk for raiding Novgorod and attacked him at the Nemiga River, outside Minsk. Vseslav was beaten in a bloody action and Minsk was destroyed. Vseslav was taken captive to Kiev, where he was elected to rule after the brothers' defeat a year later at the **Alta** (10 March 1067).

Neoheroka | 1713 | Tuscarora Indian War
See **Nohoroco**

Neon | 354 BC | 3rd Sacred War
In the war between Greek city-states, Philomelus of Phocia, supported by Achaean allies, invaded Locria and was met at Neon, north of Mount Parnassus, by 13,000 Thebans and Locrians. The badly wounded Philomelus killed himself after a terrible defeat and his successor Onomarchus led the withdrawal. Onomarchus himself was killed two years later at **Pagasae** (August 354 BC).

Neresheim | 1796 | French Revolutionary Wars (1st Coalition)
French General Jean Victor Moreau pursued Archduke Charles Louis of Austria into Germany, where he sent General Laurent Gouvion Saint-Cyr against the Austrians at Neresheim, southwest of Nördlingen. After an indecisive battle, with heavy losses on both sides, Moreau showed no sign of action next day and Charles drew off undisturbed towards Donauwörth (11 August 1796).

Néry | 1914 | World War I (Western Front)
During the Retreat from **Mons**, British forces under General Charles Briggs were attacked by German cavalry and artillery at Néry, south of Compiègne. The bloody rearguard action included an heroic stand by the Royal Horse Artillery—which saw three Victoria Crosses won—before the British had to withdraw with over 500 men lost then continued south towards the **Marne** (1 September 1914).

Nesbit | 1355 | Anglo-Scottish Border Wars
Despite a decisive Scottish defeat at **Neville's Cross** (1346), Scottish forces under Gilbert de Umfraville Earl of Angus and Patrick Dunbar Earl of March advanced towards Berwick and at nearby Nesbit defeated and captured English commander Sir Thomas Gray. While the Scots then took Berwick by surprise, Edward III later returned from France and easily recaptured the town (August 1355).

Nesbit | 1402 | Anglo-Scottish Border Wars
When Sir Patrick Hepburn of Hailes led Scottish horsemen raiding into Northumberland, he was defeated and killed on his return at Nesbit, near Berwick, by a large force under Henry Percy Earl of Northumberland and George Dunbar Earl of March. While only a minor action, Hepburn's defeat led directly to a large-scale Scottish attack and disaster in September at **Homildon Hill** (22 June 1402).

Nesjar | 1016 | Scandinavian National Wars
Olaf II Haraldsson was determined to regain Norwegian independence, lost at **Svolde** in 1000, and seized Danish parts of the country. He then attacked and defeated Swedish Earls under Sweyn Hakonsson in a great naval battle at Nesjar, near Larvik. Olaf was soon recognised as King of Christian Norway, but lost his crown ten years later at **Helgeaa** and died in 1030 at **Stiklestad** (25 March 1016).

Nesri | 1674 | Bijapur-Maratha Wars
In order to allow Pratap Rao Gujar to atone for having let General Bahlol Khan escape at **Umrani** (April 1673), Maratha commander Shivaji sent his disgraced general against the Bijapur army at Nesri, 45 miles south of Kolhapur, near Belgaum. Pratap Rao was killed in a suicidal charge and the Muslim forces of Bijapur destroyed his disheartened army (24 February 1674).

Nestus | 267 | 2nd Gothic War
When the Heruls overran Moesia, Emperor Gallienus marched to attack the invaders, who met him at the Nestus, on the border of Macedonia and Thrace. A bloody action saw a reported 3,000 tribesmen killed, before the Herul Chief Naulobatus surrendered. Gallienus had to go home Italy to face a rebellion at **Mediolanum**.

His successor Claudius later returned to defeat the Goths at **Nish**.

Netad I 454 I Hun-Ostrogoth Wars
See **Nedao**

Netherlands I 1940 I World War II (Western Europe)
See **Rotterdam**

Nether Wroughton I 825 I Later Wars of Wessex
See **Ellandun**

Neubrandenburg I 1631 I Thirty Years War (Swedish War)
Imperial commander Johan Tserclaes Count Tilly attempting to isolate Gustavus Adolphus of Sweden in northern Germany, advanced against Neubrandenburg, in Mecklenberg, held by Marshal Dodo von Knyphausen. The city fell by storm with the garrison of about 3,000 slaughtered, triggering further outrages at **Frankfort** and **Magdeburg** (February–19 March 1631).

Neu-Breisach I 1870 I Franco-Prussian War
With **Schlettstadt** taken, German General Hermann von Schmeling took his siege train further south along the Rhine against Neu-Breisach fortress. Following the fall of nearby Fort Mortier (6 November), Neu-Breisach capitulated, yielding a reported 5,000 prisoners and 100 guns. Schmeling then moved his heavy artillery southwest to the siege of **Belfort** (27 October–10 November 1870).

Neubrunn I 1866 I Seven Weeks War
See **Helmstadt**

Neuhausel I 1663 I Later Turkish-Habsburg Wars
Turkish Grand Vizier Ahmed Fazil Koprulu crossed the Danube with 120,000 men, then stalled at the fortress of Neuhausel (modern Nove Zamky) in Slovakia, defended by Adám Forgách, who held out for six weeks before capitulating. The siege delayed the advance on

Vienna and the Imperial army was able to rally against the invaders in August 1664 at **St Gotthard** (August–October 1663).

Neuhausel I 1685 I Later Turkish-Habsburg Wars
Two years after the decisive Turkish repulse at **Vienna**, Austrian Field Marshal Aeneas Caprara advanced to besiege the powerful fortress of Neuhausel (modern Nove Zamky) in Slovakia, defended by Bohemian troops converted to Islam. Charles V of Lorraine defeated a relief army at Gran and three days later took Neuhausel by storm, killing most of the garrison (19 August 1685).

Neumarkt I 1796 I French Revolutionary Wars (1st Coalition)
As French General Jean-Baptise Jourdan advanced across the Rhine into Germany, Archduke Charles Louis of Austria counter-attacked from the Danube and repulsed General Jean Baptiste Bernadotte at **Deining**, southeast of Nuremberg. Bernadotte suffered another sharp repulse next day further north at Neumarkt, but had managed to protect Jourdan's retreat (23 August 1796).

Neumarkt-St-Viet I 1809 I Napoleonic Wars (5th Coalition)
After the failed Austrian invasion of Bavaria, Baron Johann Hiller was driven south following defeat at **Landshut** (21 April), then turned on the pursuing Franco-Bavarian army of Marshal Jean-Baptiste Bessières at Neumarkt-St-Viet, north of Mühldorf. Hiller inflicted over 1,000 casualties in a tactical victory, but had to continue withdrawing through **Ebelsberg** towards **Vienna** (24 April 1809).

Neuss I 1474–1475 I Franco-Burgundian Wars
Charles the Bold of Burgundy interfered in a dispute involving the Archbishop of Cologne and besieged the Archbishop's fortified town of Neuss, close to Dusseldorf. Emperor Frederick III arrived with German forces though full-scale battle was avoided. Frederick agreed to with-

draw, while Louis XI of France made peace and allowed Charles to conquer Lorraine (June 1474–March 1475).

Neuve Chappelle ∎ 1915 ∎ World War I (Western Front)

Determined to demonstrate offensive action to aid the French in **Champagne**, General Sir Henry Rawlinson attacked the German salient, southwest of Lille. Initial success secured strategic Neuve Chappelle before Prince Rupprecht sent reinforcements and battle ended with about 12,000 casualties on either side. Two months later the British attacked again towards **Aubers** (10–13 March 1915).

Neuwarp ∎ 1759 ∎ Seven Years War (Europe)

Swedish galleys campaigning against Prussian shipping off Pomerania attacked a Prussian flotilla at Neuwarp (modern Nowe Warpno), 25 miles northwest of Stettin. A four-hour fight saw the Swedes capture all the larger vessels, taking 600 prisoners. However, Prussia's flotilla was quickly rebuilt and Swedish involvement remained peripheral to the war in Europe (10 September 1759).

Neuwied ∎ 1796 ∎ French Revolutionary Wars (1st Coalition)

While Archduke Charles Louis of Austria was pursuing General Jean Victor Moreau along the Upper Rhine, further north near Coblenz other Austrian forces made a determined attack on the French rearguard at Neuwied. General Jean-Baptiste Kléber drove the Austrians off with heavy losses but, shortly afterwards he withdrew west across the Rhine (20–21 October 1796).

Neuwied ∎ 1797 ∎ French Revolutionary Wars (1st Coalition)

General Louis Lazare Hoche led a renewed French offensive across the Rhine north of Coblenz and, east of Neuwied near the Lahn, he routed an Austrian army under General Paul Kray, who suffered massive losses in men and guns. After French victory the same day at **Altenkirchen**, then on the Upper Rhine at **Dier-**

sheim (21 April), Austria sued for peace and withdrew from the war (18 April 1797).

Neva ∎ 1240 ∎ Rise of Russia

Prince Alexander of Novgorod faced an advance on Novgorod by the outstanding Swedish General Birger Magnusson and his Danish allies. On the banks of the Neva near its junction with the Izhora he met and destroyed the invasion. Following his decisive victory, Alexander was recognised with the honorific Nevski. Two years later he achieved an even greater victory at **Lake Peipus**.

Nevel ∎ 1564 ∎ Livonian War

When war resumed between Russia and Poland over Livonia, Russia suffered a terrible loss south of Polotsk at **Chashniki** and the previously successful Russian General Andrei Kurbsky later met a Polish force at Nevel, north of Vitebsk. Kurbsky was ignominiously defeated and, fearing the wrath of Ivan IV "the Terrible," he defected to the Poles. The angry Tsar arrested and killed Kurbsky's family.

Neville's Cross ∎ 1346 ∎ Anglo-Scottish Border Wars

With Edward III occupied in France, David II of Scotland invaded England and was met just west of Durham at Neville's Cross by a large force under Ralph Baron Neville and Henry Percy of Alnwick. Despite the efforts of Robert the Steward and Sir William Douglas of Liddesdale, King David was defeated with terrible losses. He spent ten years as a prisoner in London (17 October 1346).

Nevis ∎ 1667 ∎ 2nd Dutch War

Threatened by Franco-Dutch forces in the West Indies, English Captain (later Admiral) John Berry in the frigate *Coronation* and a squadron of armed merchantmen attacked the rival fleet preparing to assault Nevis. After sharp action off Nevis Point, Dutch Commodore Abraham Crijnssen sailed north against Virginia and French Commander Joseph de La Barre withdrew to **Martinique** (20 May 1667).

Nevis ∎ 1799 ∎ Franco-American Quasi War

During America's undeclared war with Revolutionary France, the French frigate *L'Insurgente* (36) captured a schooner off **Guadeloupe**, but was later attacked off Nevis by Captain Thomas Truxton in *Constellation* (40). French Captain Michel Barreaut surrendered with 70 casualties after very heavy fighting. Truxton won another bloody action a year later off Guadeloupe (9 February 1799).

Newark ∎ 1644 ∎ British Civil Wars

After a rapid march to relieve Newark-upon-Trent, held by Royalist Sir Richard Byron, Prince Rupert launched a heavy attack against the Parliamentary siege force of General Sir John Meldrum, who commanded over 6,000 men. Facing heavy losses, Meldrum surrendered his Parliamentary troops and their siege train and the Royalists retained the strategic city (21 March 1644).

New Bern ∎ 1862 ∎ American Civil War (Eastern Theatre)

Union General Ambrose E. Burnside opened his coastal expedition against North Carolina by capturing **Roanoke Island** (8 February), then sailed south against General Lawrence O'Bryan Branch at New Bern on the Neuse. The Union captured the town after heavy fighting and held it for the rest of the war. Burnside then sent a force southeast against **Fort Macon** (14 March 1862).

New Britain ∎ 1943–1944 ∎ World War II (Pacific)

Determined to isolate Rabaul, on eastern New Britain, American forces landed at **Arawe** and **Cape Gloucester** to secure the western end of the island. Seizure of the **Admiralty Islands** to the west and **Green Islands** to the east further isolated over 100,000 Japanese at **Rabaul**, who were heavily bombed and remained cut off until surrender at the end of the war (December 1943–April 1944).

Newburn ∎ 1640 ∎ 2nd Bishops' War

In a renewed struggle against King Charles I trying to impose a new prayer book on Scotland, over 4,000 Scottish veterans under Sir Alexander Leslie invaded Northumbria. West of Newcastle at Newburn they met a Royalist force led by Edward Viscount Conway. The English fled under heavy artillery fire and the Scots occupied Durham before Charles sued for peace (28 August 1640).

Newbury ∎ 1643 ∎ British Civil Wars

King Charles I faced an approaching Parliamentary army under Robert Devereux Earl of Essex and raised his siege of **Gloucester** (6 September) to march south to Newbury, Berkshire, where Essex blocked the road to London. Despite a day of very heavy losses on both sides, the Royalists claimed the victory. However, they withdrew during the night to Oxford (20 September 1643).

Newbury ∎ 1644 ∎ British Civil Wars

Returning from victory in Cornwall at **Lostwithiel** in early September, King Charles I was blocked at Newbury, Berkshire, by the Parliamentary forces of Robert Devereux Earl of Essex, Edward Montagu Earl of Manchester, Sir William Waller and Oliver Cromwell. An indecisive action saw the King cut his way through, though Manchester refused to pursue and was replaced (27 October 1644).

New Carthage ∎ 209 BC ∎ 2nd Punic War

To avenge the death of his father and uncle in the **Baetis** Valley (211 BC), which cost Rome all of southern Spain, Publius Scipio the Younger took a large force against the great Carthaginian fortress at New Carthage (modern Cartagena). A brilliant assault gave him the city, along with its massive military stores. It was the first major victory for the 24-year-old, later famous as Scipio Africanus.

Newchwang ∎ 1895 ∎ Sino-Japanese War

See **Niuzhuang**

Newfoundland I 1812 I War of 1812

Emerging from Boston, the American frigate *Constitution* (Captain Isaac Hull) met and destroyed the British frigate *Guerrière* (Captain James Dacres) south of Newfoundland. With heavy losses the wounded Dacres surrendered his ship. The action is regarded as the first American naval victory of the war and earned *Constitution* the nickname "Old Ironsides" (19 August 1812).

New Georgia I 1943 I World War II (Pacific)

With **Guadalcanal** secured, Admiral Kelly Turner and General John Hester (later General Oscar Griswold) moved west against New Georgia, defended by General Noboru Sasaki. The guns at **Enogai Inlet** were destroyed (10 July) and Munda airfield fell after very heavy fighting (5 August). While the island was being cleared, attention turned to nearby **Vella Lavella** (2 July–25 August 1943).

New Hope Church I 1864 I American Civil War (Western Theatre)

Union commander William T. Sherman pursued General Joseph E. Johnston through Georgia towards **Atlanta**, advancing through **Adairsville**. He then circled west towards Dallas to outflank the Confederates at Allatoona. At New Hope Church, Johnston repulsed Union General Joseph E. Hooker, then beat another Union advance further northeast next day at **Pickett's Mill** (25–26 May 1864).

New Lisbon I 1863 I American Civil War (Western Theatre)

See **Salineville**

New Madrid I 1862 I American Civil War (Western Theatre)

See **Island Number Ten**

New Market I 1864 I American Civil War (Eastern Theatre)

In an attempted advance south along the Shenandoah Valley from Winchester towards **Lynchburg**, Union General Franz Sigel was blocked north of Staunton at New Market, Virginia, by General John C. Breckinridge and a mixed Confederate force. Sigel was badly beaten and withdrew, and was replaced by General David Hunter who soon resumed the offensive at **Piedmont** (15 May 1864).

New Market Heights I 1864 I American Civil War (Eastern Theatre)

Supporting the Union offensive in Virginia at **Poplar Springs Church**, Union General Benjamin F. Butler crossed the James, southeast of Richmond at Chaffins Bluff, against General Richard S. Ewell. He captured New Market Heights and nearby Fort Harrison, but a week later the Confederates counter-attacked at the **Darbytown** and **New Market Roads** (29–30 September 1864).

New Market Road I 1864 I American Civil War (Eastern Theatre)

When Union forces crossed the James River southeast of Richmond, Virginia, and seized **Fort Harrison**, Confederate General Robert E. Lee counter-attacked and repulsed General Augustus V. Kautz further north at the Darbytown Road. At the New Market Road, Union General David B. Birney held firm and Lee was forced to withdraw with over 1,300 casualties (7 October 1864).

New Orleans I 1815 I War of 1812

British General Sir Edward Pakenham led a southern offensive against the United States, taking a large force to capture New Orleans, held by General Andrew Jackson. A frontal assault cost the British over 2,000 casualties, including Pakenham killed, for minimal American losses. The British withdrew east and attacked **Fort Bowyer**, only to find peace had been signed in Europe (8 January 1815).

New Orleans I 1862 I American Civil War (Lower Seaboard)

Union Flag-Officer David G. Farragut advanced up the Mississippi past Confederate **Forts Jackson and St Philip**, and seized New Orleans, Louisiana, from General Mansfield Lovell (who was subsequently court-martialled).

Following capture of the downstream forts, the Confederate city formally surrendered and was occupied by General Benjamin F. Butler (25 April–1 May 1862).

Newport, Rhode Island I 1778 I War of the American Revolution

Supported by French ships, American General John Sullivan landed on **Rhode Island** to besiege Newport, held by General Sir Robert Pigot. After indecisive action between Admirals Charles-Hector d'Estaing and Sir Richard Howe (11 August), both fleets were dispersed by a storm. Following defeat on land (29 August), Sullivan withdrew from Rhode Island (29 July–31 August 1778).

Newport, Wales I 1265 I 2nd English Barons' War

After Simon de Montfort Earl of Leicester defeated and captured King Henry III at **Lewes** (May 1264), the King's son Prince Edward gathered a powerful army in the west and repulsed de Montfort north of the Bristol Channel at Newport. The Earl withdrew into Wales and when he re-crossed the Severn a month later against Edward, he was defeated and killed at **Evesham** (8 July 1265).

Newport News I 1862 I American Civil War (Eastern Theatre)
See **Hampton Roads**

New Providence I 1776 I War of the American Revolution

In a well co-ordinated operation, American Commodore Esek Hopkins and Marine Captain Samuel Nicholas sailed from Philadelphia to attack New Providence (modern Nassau) in the British West Indies. Forts Montague and Nassau were seized after only light resistance, along with many guns and mortars. Governor Montfort Browne was captured and later exchanged (3–4 March 1776).

New River Bridge I 1864 I American Civil War (Eastern Theatre)
See **Cove Mountain**

New Ross I 1798 I Irish Rebellion

The first major battle of the Rebellion saw a force of perhaps 30,000 insurgents under Bagenal Harvey attack New Ross, near Waterford, defended by 1,400 regulars under General Henry Johnson and Colonel Robert Crauford. Despite capturing part of the town, the rebels were repulsed, losing about 2,600 men and most of their field guns. Harvey was promptly deposed as leader (5 June 1798).

Newtonia I 1862 I American Civil War (Trans-Mississippi)

Six months after defeat at **Pea Ridge**, Confederate forces returned to southwest Missouri to threaten General James B. Blunt's Union army. At Newtonia, south of Carthage, Confederate cavalry led by Colonel Douglas H. Cooper defeated advance units under Colonel Friedrich Salomon. Cooper was then pursued west towards **Old Fort Wayne** by Blunt's approaching army (30 September 1862).

Newtonia I 1864 I American Civil War (Trans-Mississippi)

At the end of his bold expedition across Missouri, Confederate General Sterling Price retreated through defeat at **Mine Creek** and **Marmiton** to Newtonia, south of Carthage, where his shattered survivors were attacked by General James G. Blunt. With fresh Union forces arriving, Price withdrew west into Indian Territory, eluding pursuit until the end of the war (28 October 1864).

Newtown I 1779 I War of the American Revolution

American Generals John Sullivan and James Clinton led a punitive expedition against pro-British Indians, who had taken part in the **Wyoming** and **Cherry Valley** Massacres in 1778, and marched into New York State. At Newtown, near modern Elmira, they routed a joint force of Tories and Iroquois and over the next three months, they virtually destroyed the Iroquois nation (29 August 1779).

Newtown Butler I 1689 I War of the Glorious Revolution

A few days after James II failed at **Londonderry** in northern Ireland, he sent Justin Macarthy Viscount Mountcashel to conclude the siege of Protestant Enniskillen on Lough Erne. However, at nearby Newtown Butler, Macarthy's Catholics were routed by Colonel William Wolesley, losing over 1,000 killed, 500 captured and all their cannon. Enniskillen was saved (2 August 1689).

New Ulm I 1862 I Sioux Indian Wars

With Little Crow of the Santee Sioux wounded besieging **Fort Ridgely**, 500 warriors under Mankato attacked the German settlement at New Ulm, on the Minnesota. About 150 volunteers under Judge Charles Flandrau burned outlying buildings to deny the attackers cover. After very fierce fighting the Indians were driven off and withdrew with their prisoners and plunder (23 August 1862).

Nezeros I 1897 I 1st Greco-Turkish War

In response to Greek border incursions, Ottoman commander Edhem Pasha marched into Thessaly and in the east, sent forces through Analipsis towards Nezeros, where Colonel Louros and 1,200 Greeks defended Mount Annunciation and Marcasi Hill. While repeated assaults were repulsed, Crown Prince Constantine forbade an offensive action until the advance on **Vigla** (17–18 April 1897).

Nezhatina Niva I 1078 I Russian Dynastic Wars

When Sviatoslav of Kiev died, his brothers Iziaslav and Vsevolod attacked their nephews Oleg Sviatoslavich and Boris Vseslavich, who were threatening Chernigov. At nearby Nezhatina Niva, Boris was defeated and killed and Oleg fled. However, Iziaslav was also killed and Vsevolod became Grand Prince of Kiev. Oleg

returned from exile 15 years later to retake **Chernigov** (3 October 1078).

Nezib I 1839 I 2nd Turko-Egyptian War

Egyptian Viceroy Mohammed Ali renewed his war against Turkey by sending his son Ibrahim Pasha with a large force into northern Syria, where he defeated the Turkish army of Hafiz Pasha and Prussian advisor Helmuth von Moltke at Nezib, near Aleppo. Ottoman Sultan Mahmud II died a week later and when his fleet surrendered, European forces intervened at **Beirut** and **Acre** (24 June 1839).

Ngakyedauk I 1944 I World War II (Burma-India)

See **Admin Box**

Ngasaunggyan I 1277 I Mongol Wars of Kubilai Khan

While campaigning in southern Burma, the Mongol Kubilai Khan sent Nasir-al-din and 10,000 men against King Narathihapate of Pagan. In a decisive battle at Ngasaunggyan, the Mongols panicked the Burmese elephants with fire arrows and routed Narathihapate. A second expedition under Kubilai's grandson Esen Temur in 1287 forced the pliable new King Kyawswa to pay tribute.

Ngatapa I 1869 I 2nd New Zealand War

Hauhau rebel Te Kooti was pursued into the hills behind Poverty Bay to defeat at **Makaretu**, then withdrew southwest to his stockade at Ngatapa, where he was cornered by Colonel George Whitmore and friendly Maoris. A bloody siege and assault cost the Hauhau 136 men killed (many after being captured). However, Te Kooti escaped and attacked **Mohaka** in April (1–4 January 1869).

Nghia Lo I 1951 I French Indo-China War

Re-equipping during the rainy season after costly defeats in the **Red River Delta**, Viet Minh commander Vo Nguyen Giap crossed the upper Red River at Yen Bai and attacked Nghia

Lo, 75 miles northwest of Hanoi. However, daylight brought French air attack and paratroop reinforcements. Giap was badly defeated, encouraging a French offensive west of Hanoi at **Hoa Binh** (2–4 September 1951).

Nghia Lo | 1952 | French Indo-China War

General Vo Nguyen Giap resolved to draw French forces beyond defensive lines and attacked between the Black and Red Rivers around Nghia Lo (11 October). General Raoul Salan launched 30,000 men on Operation Lorraine, with a paratroop drop at Phu Doan. Viet Minh guerrilla attacks cost over 1,200 French casualties and Salan finally withdrew without success (29 October–17 November 1952).

Nguyen Hue | 1972 | Vietnam War
   See **Eastertide Offensive**

Nhembucu | 1867 | War of the Triple Alliance

On campaign in the Nhembucu district northeast of **Humaitá**, Allied forces led by Brazilian commander Jose Joaquim de Andrade Neves routed Paraguayan Colonel Gorgônio Rojas. Victory enabled Andrade Neves to seize the river port of Pilar on the Paraguay and he was created Baron de Triunfo. He defeated Rojas again in 1868 at the **Tebicauri**, but died at **Ita Ybate** (20 September 1867).

Nhu-Guacu | 1869 | War of the Triple Alliance
   See **Acosta-Ñu**

Niagara | 1759 | Seven Years War (North America)
   See **Fort Niagara**

Niagara | 1813 | War of 1812
   See **Fort Niagara**

Nianzhuang | 1948 | 3rd Chinese Revolutionary Civil War

As the Communist **Huaihai** offensive converged on Xuzhou, General Chen Yi attacked an approaching Nationalist force under Huang Bodao 20 miles east at Nianzhuang. A decisive defeat saw Huang's army surrounded and destroyed, with 90,000 men and over 1,000 guns lost. Huang committed suicide and Chen swung south towards **Shuangduiji** (7–22 November 1948).

Nibley Green | 1470 | Wars of the Roses

Amid anarchy caused by the war, a long-standing feud flared and the claimed last private battle fought in England was arranged between William Lord Berkeley and Thomas Talbot Viscount Lisle, grandsons of the great John Talbot Earl of Shrewsbury. At Nibley Green, near Berkeley Castle west of Stroud, Lisle was killed and his seat at Wotton Manor was plundered (20 March 1470).

Nicaea | 194 | Wars of Emperor Severus

Emperor Septimius Severus marched into Asia against Pescennius Niger and defeated his rival's army at **Cyzicus**, then pursued Niger himself into Bithynia. East of Nicaea, on modern Lake Iznik in northern Turkey, Niger was heavily defeated by the General Tiberius Claudius Candidus. Faced by the arrival of fresh Severan Legions, Niger withdrew to Antioch. He was routed later that year at **Issus**.

Nicaea | 1077 | Byzantine Wars of Succession

Political instability following Christian disaster at **Manzikert** (1071) saw Byzantine General Nicephorus Botaniates gather Turkish support and march against the army of Emperor Michael VII near Nicaea (modern Iznik). The Imperial troops were decisively defeated, after which Botaniates seized the throne in Constantinople as Nichephorus III. He turned on his rival Briennes in 1079 at **Calavryta**.

Nicaea | 1096 | 1st Crusade
   See **Xerigordon**

Nicaea | 1097 | 1st Crusade

In return for assistance while passing through Byzantium, Crusaders under Godfrey de Bouillon marched east to besiege Nicaea (modern Iznik) on behalf of Emperor Alexius. Kilij Arslan ibn-Suleiman, Sultan of Rum, failed in two attempts to raise the siege and eventually negotiated to surrender the city personally to Alexius to avoid a sack by the Crusaders (14 May–19 June 1097).

Nice I 1543 I Turkish-Habsburg Wars

Turkish Admiral Khair-ed-Din Barbarossa took his fleet to the French Riviera, then started home and attacked the port of Nice, held by Duke Emmanuel Philibert of Savoy, an ally of Emperor Ferdinand I. Nice surrendered after Turkish artillery smashed the city walls, though the citadel held out. Barbarossa then broke the terms of capitulation and sacked Nice before burning it to the ground.

Nicholson's Nek I 1899 I 2nd Anglo-Boer War

As Boer forces advanced deep into Natal, British commander Sir George White at Ladysmith attacked a small force at **Rietfontein**, then led a larger offensive northeast to Nicholson's Nek, attempting to emulate success at **Elandslaagte**. White was repulsed by Christiaan de Wet with humiliating losses (almost 1,000 men surrendered) and he fell back to **Ladysmith** (30 October 1899).

Nicomedia I 782 I Byzantine-Muslim Wars

In retaliation for the sack of **Hadath** in 779, Arab forces captured **Samalu**, then Caliph al-Mahdi sent his teenage son Harun al-rashid and General Yazid ibn Mayzad al-Shaybani on a second expedition into Byzantine Anatolia. Victory at Nicomedia (modern Izmit) enabled Harun to reach the Bosphorus and Empress Irene (Regent for Constantine VI) was forced to accept a humiliating peace.

Nicomedia I 1331–1337 I Byzantine-Ottoman Wars

Sultan Orkhan Gazi completed expansion of Ottoman power in northern Turkey by besieging Nicomedia (modern Izmit) on the eastern ex-

tremity of the Sea of Marmara. With the capture of **Brusa** (1326) and the surrender of Nicaea after **Pelacanon** (1328), the fall of this last remaining Byzantine outpost after a six-year siege effectively ended Imperial influence south of the Sea of Marmara.

Nicopolis, Armenia I 66 BC I 3rd Mithridatic War
See **Lycus**

Nicopolis, Armenia I 48 BC I Roman-Pontian Wars

Taking advantage of civil war in Rome, King Pharnaces of Bosporus attacked Rome in Asia Minor and marched into Cappadocia. In the Lycus Valley at Nicopolis (possibly modern Devriki, Turkey) he repulsed Julius Caesar's General Domitius Calvinus. The following year Caesar himself entered the war and destroyed Pharnaces at **Zela** (October 48 BC).

Nicopolis, Bulgaria I 1396 I Ottoman Conquest of the Balkans

Caught up in a surge of Crusading zeal against Turks in the Balkans, a massive multi-national army set out led by King Sigismund of Hungary and Count John of Nevers. Facing a large Ottoman force under Sultan Bayazid at Nicopolis (modern Nikopol, Bulgaria), the Crusaders were badly defeated then pursued and slaughtered, ending the so-called "Crusade of Nicopolis" (25 September 1396).

Nicopolis, Bulgaria I 1877 I Russo-Turkish Wars

Russian Grand Duke Nicholas led a surprise crossing of the Danube at **Svistov** (27 June), then marched upstream against the Turkish fortress at Nicopolis (modern Nikopol). A two-day artillery barrage convinced the garrison of 7,000 to surrender to General Nikolai Krudener, along with their 40 guns. The main Russian army then moved south against the key fortress at **Plevna** (15–16 July 1877).

Nicopolis ad Istrum | 250 |
1st Gothic War

When the Goth Kniva crossed the Danube in force, he led part of his army to besiege Nicopolis ad Istrum (modern Nikyup, north of Veliko Turnovo, Bulgaria). The new Emperor Decius himself marched north from Rome and near Nicopolis secured a major victory, inflicting heavy losses. Kniva turned south into Thrace and joined up with another part of his army that was besieging **Philippopolis**.

Nicosia | 1570 | Venetian-Turkish
War in Cyprus

Sultan Selim II renewed war against Venice and sent Lala Mustafa and 50,000 men to Cyprus to besiege the well-fortified city of Nicosia. Venetian Governor Nicolo Dandolo repulsed two assaults before he was overwhelmed and killed in a third massive attack. The population was massacred and the Turks then turned their attention to **Famagusta** (22 July–9 September 1570).

Niebla | 1811 | Napoleonic Wars
(Peninsular Campaign)

Facing a Spanish offensive in Andalusia led by General Joachim Blake, French Marshal Nicolas Soult marched south to relieve Niebla, west of Seville. He defeated the Spanish general and forced him to lift the siege. However, Allied naval control off southern Spain ensured Blake was able to withdraw by sea to **Cadiz** (2 July 1811).

Nieder-Sasbach | 1675 | 3rd Dutch War
See **Sasbach**

Niellim | 1899 | French Conquest
of Chad

While travelling along the Chari, southeast of Lake Chad, the military explorer Henri-Étienne Bretonnet and 50 riflemen were surrounded at Niellim, by about 3,500 supporters of Muslim leader Rabih az-Zubayr. While Rabih lost over 500 troops in a six-hour action, Bretonnet and all but three of his men were also killed. The French

were avenged in October at nearby **Kouno** (17 July 1899).

Nieman | 1914 | World War I
(Eastern Front)
See **Augustovo**

Nieman | 1920 | Russo-Polish War

Routed near **Warsaw** by Polish commander Josef Pilsudki (25 August), Russian General Mikhail Tukhachevski fought a bloody withdrawal northeast to the Nieman and attempted to make a stand around Grodno. Outflanked to the north, Tukhachevski suffered very heavy losses and sections of his retreating army were then defeated again further south on the **Szczara** (20–28 September 1920).

Nienchuang | 1948 | 3rd Chinese
Revolutionary Civil War
See **Nianzhuang**

Nieuport | 1600 | Netherlands War
of Independence

Prince Maurice of Orange invaded Flanders to besiege Nieuport, west of **Ostend**, then faced a large Spanish relief army under Archduke Albert, who heavily repulsed Allied (largely Scots) troops attempting to hold the line at the Yser. In the dunes near Nieuport Albert was wounded and routed. However, Maurice also suffered heavy casualties and raised the siege (2 July 1600).

Nieuport | 1653 | 1st Dutch War
See **Gabbard Bank**

Nieuport | 1794 | French Revolutionary
Wars (1st Coalition)

As he advanced against the remaining Allied strongholds in the Netherlands, French General Jean Victor Moreau captured Ostend then sent Dominique Vandamme's brigade west to besiege Nieuport. The port fell after two weeks, with the garrison of 2,000 Hanoverians taken prisoner. Further east ten days later, Moreau began his attack on **L'Ecluse** (4–18 July 1794).

Nijmegen I 1672 I 3rd Dutch War

French Marshal Henri de Turenne crossed the Rhine at **Tolhuis** and days later laid siege to Nijmegen, southwest of Arnhem, defended by Dutch General Jan van Welderen. Despite severe French losses during the siege, the city eventually surrendered, though the delay is said to have cost Turenne final victory on his resumed advance into the Dutch Republic (16 June–9 July 1672).

Nijmegen I 1944 I World War II (Western Europe)

See **Arnhem**

Nile I 47 BC I Wars of the First Triumvirate

With Julius Ceasar besieged by Egyptian forces at **Alexandria**, Mithridates of Pergamum raised a relief force in Syria but was blocked at the mouth of the Nile by an army under personal command of Egyptian ruler Ptolemy XII. When Caesar himself arrived with additional troops Ptolemy was defeated, then drowned while attempting to flee. Alexandria was relieved.

Nile I 1798 I French Revolutionary Wars (Middle East)

A month after disembarking the French army at **Alexandria**, Admiral Francois-Paul Brueys was attacked at Aboukir Bay, near the mouth of the Nile, by British Admiral Horatio Nelson. Brueys was killed in a brutal and decisive nighttime action and all but two French ships of the line were taken or destroyed. The great naval victory ensured British control of the Mediterranean (1 August 1798).

Nimach I 1857 I Indian Mutiny

Firoz Shah of Mandasur lost at **Jiran**, then joined Kusal Singh, Thakur of Awah, to attack Nimach. Up to 4,000 rebels secured the town, but the garrison under Captain Charles Bannister held the strongly fortified citadel. When a heavy assault was repulsed (19 November) Firoz withdrew. He soon lost at **Goraria** and abandoned Mandasur. The Thakur was later beaten at **Awah** (9–22 November 1857).

Nimaraq I 634 I Muslim Conquest of Iraq

Following defeat near **Babylon** in July, a fresh Sassanian Persian army under General Rustam advanced into Mesopotamia to retake **Hira**. Muslim commander Muthanna sent General Abu Ubayd, who defeated Rustam at Nimaraq, between the Euphrates and Tigris. The Persians also suffered a check at nearby Kaskar, but soon recovered for a great victory at the Battle of the **Bridge** (September 634).

Nimla I 1809 I Afghan Wars of Succession

Former Afghan Amir Mahmud Shah escaped from imprisonment and seized Kabul, then marched towards Peshawar against his brother Shah Shuja, whose advancing army made a stand at Nimla, near Gandamak, southwest of Jalalabad. Attacked by Mahmud Shah and his Vizier Fath Khan, Shah Shuja was utterly defeated and fled. Mahmud was then restored as ruler of Afghanistan.

Nineveh I 653 BC I Assyrian Wars

With Assyria distracted by war with **Babylon**, King Phraortes of Media, supported by Cimmeria, laid siege to the Assyrian capital at Nineveh. Phraortes was defeated and killed by Assyria's Scythian allies, who then ruled Media. However, the Scythians were subsequently overthrown by Phraortes' son Cyaxares, who joined with Babylon and returned 40 years later to destroy Nineveh.

Nineveh I 612 BC I Babylon's Wars of Conquest

King Nabopolassar of the Chaldeans overthrew Assyrian rule in **Babylon** (648 BC), then joined Cyaxares of Media and Scythian allies to attack the Assyrian capital Nineveh, defended by King Sin-shar-ishkun. After bloody assaults the city was taken by storm and sacked. The Assyrian Empire effectively died with the King in the flames of his palace, although some of the army escaped to **Harran**.

Nineveh I 627 I Byzantine-Persian Wars

Emperor Heraclius repulsed an Avar and Persian threat against **Constantinople** (August

626), then renewed his campaign against the empire with a crushing victory near the Tigris at Nineveh. Persian General Rhazates and most of his army were killed and, with Heraclius advancing on Ctesiphon, Shah Chosroes II was killed in a coup by his son Seoses, who quickly sued for peace (12 December 627).

Ningbo **I** 1842 **I** 1st Opium War

With the fall of Ningbo after **Zhenhai** (October 1841), new Chinese Commissioner Yijing—cousin of the Emperor—attempted a counter-attack at Ningbo. His forces broke into the city, but were driven out in bloody street fighting with over 400 killed. Yijing was also repulsed at Zhenhai and was recalled in disgrace. The British soon withdrew to support the attack on **Zhapu** (10 March 1842).

Ningbo **I** 1862 **I** Taiping Rebellion

While the Taiping besieged **Shanghai**, Allied forces supported former pirate Zhang Jingqu attacking the nearby treaty port of Ningbo, across Hangzhou Bay, seized by Taiping troops on 9 December 1861. Bombarded by four British and two French warships, Generals Huang Chengzhong and Fan Ruceng were defeated and withdrew. Zhang's men then sacked the city (10 May 1862).

Ningxia **I** 1227 **I** Conquests of Genghis Khan

See **Yellow River**

Ningxia **I** 1592 **I** Ningxia Mutiny

In the last Mongol resistance to Ming authority, former commissioner Pübei and his son Pu Cheng'en joined Ming officer Liu Dongyang in mutiny at the border city of Ningxia. Government forces under Li Rusong besieged the rebels and, despite Mongol aid, Ningxia fell after a river was diverted to destroy the walls. Pu and Liu were executed and Pübei killed himself (February–20 October 1592).

Ningyuan **I** 1626 **I** Manchu Conquest of China

Five years after securing Manchuria at **Shenyang**, Manchu leader Nurhachi advanced into China against Ningyuan (modern Xingcheng), the last Ming city outside the Great Wall, defended by Yuan Chonghuan. In a major setback, Nurhachi's bowmen were driven off by Imperial artillery and he died later of wounds. His successors seized **Beijing** and the throne in 1644 (February 1626).

Nipe **I** 1898 **I** Spanish-American War

American Admiral William T. Sampson destroyed the Spanish fleet off **Santiago Bay** in southern Cuba (3 July), then sent Commander John Hunker with four warships to capture Bahia de Nipe, on the north coast. A fierce exchange of gunfire saw the American squadron sink the Spanish warship *Jorge Juan* to secure the port for possible use by the army, but the war soon ended (21 July 1898).

Niquitao **I** 1813 **I** Venezuelan War of Independence

When Simón Bolívar returned to Venezuela to assume leadership of the Revolution, he sent José Félix Ribas against José Martí on the heights of Niquitao, south of Trujillo, where the larger Royalist force was decisively defeated. About 400 captured Americans joined the Patriot army, but many Spanish prisoners were executed. Ribas pursued other Royalists at **Los Horcones** (1 July 1813).

Nirmohgarh **I** 1702 **I** Mughal-Sikh Wars

The year after Mughal defeat in the northern Punjab at **Anandpur**, Emperor Aurangzeb sent a fresh army under Wazir Khan against Sikh Guru Gobind Singh. Reinforced by the hill Rajas, Wazir Khan met the Sikhs just outside Anandpur on the banks of the Sutlej at Nirmohgargh. The Imperial army was forced to withdraw after two days of fighting and heavy losses on both sides.

Nisa Col | 1895 | Chitral Campaign

A force of 400 Punjab Pioneers under Colonel James Kelly, advancing west from Gilgit to relieve a British force besieged by rebels in Chitral (in northern modern Pakistan), was blocked by 1,500 Chitralis under Muhammad Isa at the precipitous ravine of Nisa Col on the Mastuj River. Opening fire with his mountain batteries, Kelly drove the tribesmen off and relieved **Chitral** (14 April 1895).

Nish | 269 | 3rd Gothic War

After defeating the Alemanni at **Lake Benacus**, new Emperor Claudius II returned east to deal with the Goths, who had been checked at the **Nestus**. A decisive action at Nish, in modern Serbia, saw Claudius inflict a terrible defeat on the Goths, with a claimed 50,000 killed. Victory earned Claudius the honorific "Gothicus" and secured lasting stability in the Balkans, but he died soon afterwards of plague.

Nish | 1443 | Turkish-Hungarian Wars (Long Campaign)

As they led a determined advance across the Danube into Serbia, King Ladislas of Hungary and General Janos Hunyadi met Kasim Bey, Governor of Rumelia and Ishak Bey near Nish. Aided by Serbian forces, the Christians crushed the Turkish army and captured Kasim. They seized Nish and Pirot then traversed the Balkans to sack Sofia before being checked at **Zlatitsa** (3 November 1443).

Nish | 1689 | Later Turkish-Habsburg Wars

Sultan Suleiman II personally led another Ottoman advance into the Balkans, taking a fresh army as far as Sofia before sending part of his vanguard northwest to Nish, where they were attacked and routed by an Imperial force under Prince Louis of Baden. The alarmed Sultan withdrew through Philippopolis, but a renewed Turkish offensive regained **Nish** the following year (23 September 1689).

Nish | 1690 | Later Turkish-Habsburg Wars

Despite Turkish defeats at **Vienna**, **Harkany** and **Belgrade**, Grand Vizier Fazil Mustafa Pasha personally led a renewed Turkish offensive in Europe and marched against Nish, between Sofia and Belgrade. Following victory over Austrian General Ferdinand-Bernhard Seckendorf, Mustafa took Nish after a 23-day siege. He then went on to recapture Semendria and **Belgrade** (9 September 1690).

Nish | 1737 | Austro-Russian-Turkish War

A poorly organised expedition down the Morava from Belgrade saw Austrian Commander Count Friedrich von Seckendorff diverted by the flooded Danube from attacking Vidin and he instead besieged and captured Nish. However, when he marched into Bosnia, the Austrians were defeated at **Valjevo**. Nish was soon lost (20 October) to an Ottoman counter-offensive (1 August 1737).

Nish | 1809 | 1st Serbian Rising

A Patriot army under Milan Obrenovich and Peter Dobrynias advanced into Ottoman Serbia and took an entrenched position on the heights north of Nish, where they were attacked by a reported 80,000 Turks under Grand Vizier Yusuf Ziya Pasha. After heavy fighting and costly losses on both sides, Kara George arrived too late to help and the Serbs were forced to withdraw (19 May 1809).

Nishapur | 1037 | Seljuk Wars of Expansion

The Seljuk Turk brothers Toghril and Caghri Beg marched into Khorasan, in eastern Iran and northern Afganistan, and attacked the key city of Nishapur (modern Neyshabur) held for the Ghaznavid Sultan Masud ibn Mahmud of Afghanistan. The Seljuks heavily defeated a combined Persian-Afghan army then three years later they secured Khorasan with victory at **Dandanaqan**.

Nishapur ▌ 1221 ▌ Conquests of Genghis Khan

With the great Khwarezmian city of **Merv** destroyed, the Mongol Tolui (youngest son of Genghis Khan) took Balkh then marched against Nishapur in northeastern Iran, where his brother-in-law Toghachar Bahadur had been killed in an unsuccessful siege (November 1220). Tolui took Nishapur by storm, then massacred the entire population and destroyed the city (7–10 April 1221).

Nishapur ▌ 1750–1751 ▌ Persian-Afghan Wars

After the death of Nadir Shah of Persia (June 1747), the Afghan Ahmad Shah Durrani captured **Herat**, then besieged Nishapur (modern Neyshabur) defended by Jafar Khan Bayat and, when he was killed, by his teenage son Abbas Kuli Khan. While Ahmad withdrew in the face of an extreme winter, the following year he besieged Nishapur and took it by assault. He soon won again at **Torbat-i-Jam**.

Nisibis ▌ 338 ▌ Later Roman-Persian Wars

Following the death of Emperor Constantine in 337, Shapur II of Sassanid Persia invaded Roman Mesopotamia and laid waste to the country, then besieged Nisibis (modern Nusaybin, Turkey) with a huge army, including elephants and massive siege machine. Bishop Jacob inspired a brilliant defence and, after 70 days, Shapur was forced to withdraw. A three-month siege in 344 also failed.

Nisibis ▌ 350 ▌ Later Roman-Persian Wars

After failure in Roman Mesoptamia at **Singara** (348), Shapur II of Sassanid Persia again invaded and began a third siege of Nisibis (modern Nusaybin, Turkey). The Persians diverted the river Mygdonius around the city to bring water-borne siege machines closer and undermine the walls, but with limited success. Shapur failed once more and withdrew, agreeing to a truce with Emperor Constantius.

Nissan ▌ 1944 ▌ World War II (Pacific)
See **Green Islands**

Niumaozhai ▌ 1619 ▌ Manchu Conquest of China

On campaign in Manchuria against Manchu leader Nurhachi, Ming General Yang Hao's army was defeated piecemeal at **Sarhu** and **Siyanggiayan**, and Nurhachi's son Amba Beile marched southeast against Ming and Korean forces under Liu Ting. Beyond Yaku Pass at Niumaozhai the allies were routed (Liu Ting was killed) and Nurhachi captured **Shenyang** (later Mukden) in 1621 (20 April 1619).

Niuzhuang ▌ 1895 ▌ Sino-Japanese War

Japanese General Taro Katsura finally drove off the Chinese attacking **Haicheng**, in southern Manchuria, and soon advanced northwest against the well-defended city of Niuzhuang. Bloody house-to-house fighting cost the Chinese 1,800 killed and over 2,000 captured, as Katsura seized the city and its massive supplies. He then marched west against **Yingkou** (4 March 1895).

Nive ▌ 1813 ▌ Napoleonic Wars (Peninsular Campaign)

In the wake of victory in the **Pyrenees**, Arthur Wellesley Lord Wellington's Anglo-Portuguese army crossed the **Nivelle**, then advanced against Marshal Nicolas Soult in southern France, west of the Nive. Despite a courageous French counter-attack, Soult was defeated when his German troops changed sides. He then fell back through **St Pierre d'Irube** towards **Bayonne** (9–10 December 1813).

Nivelle ▌ 1813 ▌ Napoleonic Wars (Peninsular Campaign)

Following his victories in the Pyrenees at **Sorauren**, and the fall of **Pamplona** (31 October), Arthur Wellesley Lord Wellington advanced on Marshal Nicolas Soult across the River Nivelle near the Franco-Spanish border. Wellington succeeded right along the French lines with a cleverly planned attack and Soult fell back on **Bayonne**, west of the **Nive** (10 November 1813).

Nivelle Offensive ▌ 1917 ▌ World War I (Western Front)

New French commander Robert Nivelle was determined to break through on the Western Front and launched a massive assault along the **Aisne**, while further north the British attacked at **Arras**. Though the British secured some success, the Allies suffered 350,000 casualties and the Germans lost about 260,000. Nivelle was dismissed and the French army mutinied (9 April–17 May 1917).

Nizip ▌ 1839 ▌ 2nd Turko-Egyptian War

See **Nezib**

Noche Triste ▌ 1520 ▌ Spanish Conquest of Mexico

See **Tenochtitlan**

Noemfoor ▌ 1944 ▌ World War II (Pacific)

To prevent Japanese reinforcements to **Biak**, off northern New Guinea, General Edwin Patrick leapfrogged west to Noemfoor, held by Colonel Suesada Shimizu. The airfield was quickly seized, although there was severe fighting at Hill 201 (4–5 July) and prolonged mopping up before the island was secured at the cost of 66 Americans and about 1,800 Japanese killed (2 July–30 August 1944).

Nogent ▌ 486 ▌ Fall of the Western Roman Empire

See **Soissons**

Nohoroco ▌ 1713 ▌ Tuscarora Indian War

When Tuscarora Indians renewed attacks on settlers in North Carolina, after previous peace at **Cotechna**, Colonel James Moore led 30 whites and 1,000 Indian allies from South Carolina against the rebels at Nohoroco, north of modern Snow Hill. A three-day assault saw the Tuscarora fortress overrun, with 400 prisoners sold into slavery, leading to a humiliating peace (20–23 March 1713).

Noi Bang ▌ 1288 ▌ Mongol Wars of Kubilai Khan

Withdrawing from defeat at the **Bach Dang** in Annam (northern Vietnam), a Mongol army under Toghon (son of Kubilai Khan) was ambushed and suffered a bloody rout at the Noi Bang Pass. The vengeful Kubilai executed the surviving Mongol commanders and exiled his son for life, swearing to never again look on his face. The Khan soon made peace with Annam and neighbouring **Champa**.

Noiseville ▌ 1870 ▌ Franco-Prussian War

French Marshal Achille Bazaine attempted to break out of siege at **Metz**, leading a badly organised and confused night-time sortie northeast towards Noiseville. The French were driven back with more than 3,000 casualties, although Prince Friedrich Karl of Prussia lost almost as many men. The main French army was routed the same day at **Sedan** (31 August–1 September 1870).

Nojpeten ▌ 1698 ▌ Spanish-Itzá War

For 150 years after the Spanish Conquest of northern Yucatan, the Itzá Maya continued to resist in the forests around Lake Petén Itzá in modern Guatemala. After a prolonged campaign, a Spanish force under Martin de Ursua stormed the fortified island of Nojpeten (Spanish Tayasal, modern Flores) at the western end of the lake. The Itzá capital fell, and with it ended the last Maya Kingdom (13 March 1697).

Nola ▌ 216 BC ▌ 2nd Punic War

Recovering from Roman disaster at **Cannae**, Marcus Claudius Marcellus soon marched south to secure Nola, northeast of Naples, which was threatening to defect to Hannibal. When the great Carthaginian leader approached the city, Marcellus led a powerful sortie. Hannibal was defeated outside the walls of Nola and withdrew. A fresh attempt was made on Nola the following year.

Nola ▌ 215 BC ▌ 2nd Punic War

The Carthaginian General Hannibal was reinforced by his brother Hanno with fresh forces from North Africa and made a second attempt to capture the walled city of Nola, northeast of Naples, which was defended by the great Roman Marcus Claudius Marcellus. Very heavy losses in killed and prisoners forced Hannibal to return to his camp at Mount Tifata and he later withdrew into Apulia.

Nola ▌ 214 BC ▌ 2nd Punic War

Despite the terrible defeat of his brother Hanno at **Beneventum**, the great Carthaginian general Hannibal made a third attempt to capture Nola, northeast of Naples. In a bold counter-offensive, Marcus Claudius Marcellus marched west from Nola and attacked Hannibal's camp. Forced to depend on unreliable local levies, Hannibal had to retreat, though most historians regard it as a drawn action.

Nomonhan Incident ▌ 1939 ▌ Russo-Japanese Border Wars
See **Khalkan Gol**

Nompatelize ▌ 1870 ▌ Franco-Prussian War
See **Etival**

No Name Line ▌ 1951 ▌ Korean War

When the Communist Spring Offensive was checked at **Kapyong** and the **Imjin**, other Chinese forces further west attacked across the Soyang River in the eastern peninsula. While General James Van Fleet's so-called No Name Line was breached, reinforcements halted the Communist advance, which proved to be the last major Chinese offensive. Futile truce talks then began (15–20 May 1951).

Nong Bua Lamphu ▌ 1827 ▌ Siamese-Laotian Wars

King Chao Anou of Laos falsely believing British forces threatened Bangkok, rose against Siamese hegemony and invaded Siam. Forced to withdraw, he tried to shield his capital Vientiane against a large Siamese army by a brave stand on the Mekong at Nong Bua Lamphu. When he was defeated and fled, Vientiane was razed and Siam ruled until the French took over in 1893.

Nong Sarai ▌ 1593 ▌ Burmese-Siamese Wars

Ending his rising against Burmese rule (which began in 1585 at **Pa Mok**), Naresuan of Siam met Burmese Crown Prince Minkyizawa in a famous action at Nong Sarai, near modern Suphanburi. The Crown Prince was defeated and killed, reputedly in hand-to-hand combat with King Naresuan, who restored Siamese independence, then attacked his former ally Cambodia at **Lovek** (8 January 1593).

No-Niang ▌ 1598 ▌ Japanese Invasion of Korea
See **Noryang**

Nonne Boschen ▌ 1914 ▌ World War I (Western Front)

Two weeks after a German offensive along the Menin Road was checked at **Gheluvelt**, the elite Prussian Guard were sent to break the Allied line east of Ypres. In a remarkable victory near Hooge at Nonne Boschen, outnumbered British infantry threw back the attack. The ensuing attempt to "pinch out" the Ypres Salient failed and the front settled into trench warfare (11 November 1914).

Nooitgedacht ▌ 1900 ▌ 2nd Anglo-Boer War

Jacobus de la Rey captured a British supply convoy at **Buffelshoek** (3 December), then joined with Christiaan Beyers to attack General Ralph Clements in camp at Nooitgedacht Gorge, 20 miles southeast of Rustenberg. The Boers inflicted over 600 casualties and seized the British guns, but Clements defended nearby Yeomanry Hill, then cut his way out towards Pretoria (13 December 1900).

Noonday Creek ▌ 1864 ▌ American Civil War (Western Theatre)
See **Marietta**

Noordhorn ▌ 1581 ▌ Netherlands War of Independence

Following the death of Count Rennenberg after defeat at **Kollum**, new Spanish commander

Francisco Verdugo took a large force against Noordhorn, just northwest of Groningen, commanded by Sir John Norris and Count William Louis of Nassau. After initial success by Dutch cavalry, Verdugo's infantry began to prevail and the Dutch and English had to withdraw (30 September 1581).

Nördlingen I 1634 I Thirty Years War (Swedish War)

With **Regensberg** on the Danube secured, Imperial commander Ferdinand of Hungary was joined by Ferdinand Cardinal-Infante of Spain besieging the Swede Eric Debitz at Nördlingen, near Donauwörth. A decisive victory saw the Catholic Allies destroy a German-Swedish relief army under Bernard of Saxe-Weimar and Gustavus Horn. Nördlingen then surrendered (6 September 1634).

Nördlingen I 1645 I Thirty Years War (Franco-Habsburg War)

Marshal Henri de Turenne regrouped after **Mergentheim** (5 May) and was joined by Louis II Duke d'Enghien for a fresh advance into Bavaria. At the village of Allerheim, near Nördlingen, Imperial commander Baron Franz von Mercy was defeated and killed. However the Franco-Weimar army had suffered heavy losses attacking strongly entrenched positions and did not pursue (3 August 1645).

Noreia I 113 BC I Rome's Gallic Wars

When Cimbri and Teuton tribesmen spread south to the Danube and threatened the Taurisci (allies of Rome), Consul Papirius Carbo marched north of the Alps into Corinthia and met them at Noreia, near the Magdalensberg in modern Austria. The invaders won a decisive victory, but ignored Italy and turned west to Gaul, where they defeated the Romans in **Provence**, at **Aginnum** and **Arausio**.

Norfolk I 1776 I War of the American Revolution

Soon after defeat at **Great Bridge**, Virginian Governor John Murray Earl of Dunmore withdrew to ships in Norfolk Harbour while the town was occupied by American Colonels William Woodford and later Robert Howe. After failed talks, Dunmore bombarded and burned much of the town. However, British landing parties were repulsed and Dunmore withdrew north to **Gwynn Island** (1 January 1776).

Normandy I 1944 I World War II (Western Europe)

After massive bombing and airborne drops, Allied armies under Generals Omar Bradley and Sir Bernard Montgomery landed on Normandy in the D-Day invasion of Europe. Despite a tenacious defence under General Friedrich Dollman, the beachhead was secured, followed by bitter fighting at **Caen**, **Cherbourg** and **St Lo** before the breakout towards **Avranches** and **Falaise** (6 June 1944).

Norridgewock I 1724 I Dummer's War

During struggle between English and French settlers in New England, Governor William Dummer of Massachusetts sent about 200 men against the village of Norridgewock on the Kennebec in Maine, where the Abnaki were led by French Jesuit Sebastian Rasle. Unlike a failed raid in 1721, the Abnaki were surprised and routed, with Father Rasle and about 80 killed (23 August 1724).

Northallerton I 1138 I Anglo-Scottish Territorial Wars
See **Standard**

Northampton I 1264 I 2nd English Barons' War

In support of a fresh Baronial rebellion against Henry III by Simon de Montfort Earl of Leicester, the Earl's son Simon the Younger occupied Northampton, where he was besieged in Northampton Castle by the King and his son Prince Edward. Simon was captured when the garrison fell. He was freed a few weeks later after his father defeated the Royalists at **Lewes** (5 April 1264).

Northampton ∎ 1460 ∎ Wars of the Roses

On their return from France after fleeing at **Ludford Bridge** (October 1459), Richard Neville Earl of Warwick and Edward Earl of March (son of Richard Duke of York) secured **Sandwich**, then marched north against the approaching Lancastrian army. At Northampton the Yorkists won a decisive victory and Henry VI was taken prisoner. Richard of York was then proclaimed heir (10 July 1460).

North Anna ∎ 1864 ∎ American Civil War (Eastern Theatre)

Union commander Ulysses S. Grant continued his offensive in Virginia, moving south from **Spotsylvania Court House** to attack General Robert E. Lee's lines on the North Anna River near Hanover Junction, about 25 miles north of Richmond. Withdrawing after inconclusive fighting, Grant again attempted to turn the Confederate flank and was met at **Totopotomoy Creek** (23–26 May 1864).

North Brittany ∎ 1943 ∎ World War II (War at Sea)

A badly conceived night sortie from Plymouth saw the British anti-aircraft cruiser *Charybdis* (Captain George Voelcker) and six destroyers attempt to intercept the blockade-runner *Munsterland*. Tracked by German radar, they were ambushed off North Brittany by five fleet torpedo boats. *Charybdis* and the destroyer *Limbourne* were sunk with over 500 men lost (23 October 1943).

North Cape ∎ 1943 ∎ World War II (War at Sea)

When German Admiral Erich Bey took the battle-cruiser *Scharnhorst* against Russian convoy JW55B, he was ambushed off North Cape by Admiral Sir Bruce Fraser in the battleship *Duke of York* and the converging cruiser squadron of Admiral Robert Burnett. *Scharnhorst* was sunk in a dramatic night action and only 36 out of more than 1,800 crew survived to be rescued (26 December 1943).

North Foreland ∎ 1653 ∎ 1st Dutch War
See **Gabbard Bank**

North Foreland ∎ 1666 ∎ 2nd Dutch War

Just two months after losing the **Four Days Battle**, English Admiral George Monck broke through the Dutch blockade of the Thames. Between North Foreland and Orfordness, Admiral Mihiel de Ruyter lost two ships and heavy casualties (including Admirals Jan Evertsen and Tjerk Hiddes de Vries killed). Monck and Prince Rupert then drove him back to the Dutch coast (4–5 August 1666).

North Fork of the Red River ∎ 1872 ∎ Red River Indian War
See **McClellan Creek**

North Inch ∎ 1396 ∎ Scottish Clan Wars

To settle a long-running feud between the MacPherson and Davidson clans, dating back to **Invernahavon** (1370), Robert III of Scotland witnessed a judicial fight to the death between 30 champions from each side. The battle was fought on the North Inch of Perth and reputedly ended when only one Davidson escaped alive, leaving 11 injured MacPherson survivors (28 September 1396).

North Point ∎ 1814 ∎ War of 1812
See **Baltimore**

Northwest Africa ∎ 1942 ∎ World War II (Northern Africa)
See **Torch**

Northwich ∎ 1659 ∎ Royalist Rising
See **Winnington Bridge**

Norton St Philip ∎ 1685 ∎ Monmouth Rebellion

James Duke of Monmouth rebelled against his Catholic uncle James II, raising a Protestant revolt in the west and unsuccessfully attempting to capture Bath. While withdrawing at nearby Norton St Philip, Monmouth ambushed and defeated his half-brother Henry Fitzroy Lord Grafton, who escaped after great gallantry.

Monmouth was defeated ten days later at **Sedgemoor** (27 June 1685).

Norway | 1940 | World War II
(Northern Europe)

Determined to protect their northwest flank and secure iron-ore shipments from Sweden, German forces invaded Norway and seized **Oslo**. Despite costly German naval losses, the Norwegians and Anglo-French allies were defeated, including heavy action around **Andalsnes**, **Valdres** and **Narvik**. King Haakon left for Britain and his remaining forces surrendered (9 April–9 June 1940).

Norwich | 1075 | Norman Conquest
of Britain

When Ralph Guader Earl of Norfolk and his brother-in-law Roger Fitzwilliam Earl of Hereford rebelled against King William I, the Lords William Warenne Earl of Surrey and Baron Robert Malet imprisoned Hereford, then besieged Norfolk and his Breton allies in Norwich Castle. Three months later Norfolk and his Bretons surrendered on terms of banishment. Norfolk died on Crusade in 1099.

Norwich | 1549 | Kett's Rebellion

A landholder named Robert Kett led a rural insurrection from Norfolk and took a reputed 20,000 against the city of Norwich. William Parr Marquess of Northampton attempted to relieve the siege, but was easily defeated and his ally Edmund Lord Sheffield was killed. Northampton was then replaced by John Dudley Earl of Warwick, who defeated the rebels at **Dussindale** (1 August 1549).

Noryang | 1598 | Japanese Invasion
of Korea

As Japanese forces abandoned the last coastal fortresses in southern Korea, Konishi Yukinaga withdrew from **Sunchon**, supported by Shimazu Yoshihiro sailing west from **Sachon**. In the Noryang Strait, Chinese Admiral Chen Lin and Korean Yi Sun-shin attacked the Japanese as they withdrew, sinking over 200 ships. Yi was

killed in the moment of victory as the war ended (16 December 1598).

Noteborg | 1702 | 2nd "Great"
Northern War

Despite his terrible defeat at **Narva** (1700), Russian Tsar Peter I marched into Swedish Ingria and attacked the fortified island of Noteborg (Oreshka), where Lake Ladoga flows into the Neva near Novgorod. The tiny garrison fell to overwhelming assault and Peter changed its name to Schlusselberg (The Key). He then proceeded down the Neva to **Nyenskans** (September–October 1702).

Notium | 406 BC | Great
Peloponnesian War

Sparta recovered from disastrous defeat at **Cyzicus** (410 BC) and rebuilt her fleet at Ephesus, where it was threatened from nearby Notium by Athenian Admiral Alcibiades. Left in command of the Athenian fleet, Antiochius was lured into battle by Spartan leader Lysander and lost 15 ships. Alcibiades was replaced by Conon, who soon fought at **Arginusae** and **Aegospotami** (March 406 BC).

Nouakchott | 1976 | Western
Sahara Wars

When Polisario forces launched a large-scale offensive across 1,200 miles of desert to attack Nouakchott, capital of Mauritania, they shelled the city before being driven off. Attacked next day by reinforcements arriving from Zouerate, the Polisario suffered heavy losses, included Secretary General El-Ouali Mustapha Sayad killed. They returned a year later to shell Nouakchott again (8–9 June 1976).

Nouart | 1870 | Franco-Prussian War

French General Pierre-Louis de Failly was manoeuvering near the Meuse, southeast of **Sedan**, when he encountered advance units under Prince George of Saxony as the Prussian army advanced through the Ardennes. Both sides fell back after sharp fighting around the village of Nouart, though de Failly was attacked and heavily defeated next day at nearby **Beau-mont-en-Argonne** (29 August 1870).

Nova Carthago ❙ 209 BC ❙ 2nd Punic War
See **New Carthage**

Novara ❙ 1500 ❙ Italian War of Louis XII
Louis XII of France had secured northern Italy when Ludovico Sforza of Milan raised a rebellion in Lombardy and the French King sent an army under Louis de le Trémouille, heavily suppported by Swiss mercenaries. Duke Ludovico was defeated at Novara and taken to France, where he died after ten years captivity. Meanwhile the Emperor recognised French rule in Milan (8 April 1500).

Novara ❙ 1513 ❙ War of the Holy League
Fearful of French power in Italy, Pope Julius II recruited Germany and Switzerland to the Holy League and Swiss troops occupied Lombardy. After French under Prince Louis de la Trémouille captured Milan and besieged Novara, a Swiss relief force attacked after an overnight march. At the Riotta, near Novara, the French army was destroyed and withdrew from Italy (6 June 1513).

Novara ❙ 1821 ❙ Italian Revolt against Austria
Encouraged by a revolt in Naples which deposed Ferdinand IV, the Piedmontese unexpectedly revolted in the rear of the Austrian army which had marched south to defeat the Neapolitans at **Rieti**. An Austro-Sardinian force under Count Ferdinand Bubna crushed the Piedmontese at Novara, west of Milan, and the King was restored as Ferdinand I of the Two Sicilies (8 April 1821).

Novara ❙ 1849 ❙ 1st Italian War of Independence
Two days after defeat at **Mortara**, Charles Albert of Sardinia fought the decisive battle in Italy's resumed campaign for Independence from Austria. Taking a strong position between two small rivers at Novara, west of Milan,

Charles Albert and Polish commander Adalbert Chrzanowsky were routed by Austrian Marshal Josef Radetzky. The King abdicated to his son (23 March 1849).

Noveleta ❙ 1896 ❙ Philippines War of Independence
See **Binakayan**

Nove Zamky ❙ 1919 ❙ Hungarian-Czech War
On campaign in western Slovakia after victory further east at **Salgótarján**, Hungary's Red Army advanced towards Bratislava and took Nove Zamky (Ersekujvar). Czech forces under French General Eugène Mittelhauser then counter-attacked and bloody fighting saw Nove Zamky retaken. Dictator Béla Kun soon agreed to withdraw from Slovakia to defend **Budapest** (2–7 June 1919).

Novgorod ❙ 1456 ❙ Muscovite Wars of Expansion
Grand Prince Vasili II of Moscow was determined to punish Novgorod for sheltering his rival Dimitri Shemiaki and marched on the city with his 16-year-old son Ivan. The Archbishop of Novgorod's cavalry was routed by a much smaller Muscovite force, but the harsh peace terms imposed eventually drove Novgorod to support Lithuania. Ivan returned 15 years later to win again at the **Shelon**.

Novgorod ❙ 1471 ❙ Muscovite Wars of Expansion
See **Shelon**

Novgorod ❙ 1614 ❙ Russo-Swedish Wars
See **Bronnitsa**

Novgorod Seversk ❙ 1604 ❙ Russian Time of Troubles
At the start of his march on Moscow, a pretender claiming to be Dimitri—murdered son of former Tsar Ivan IV—led a Polish army into the Ukraine, where the "First False Dimitri" captured Chernigov, then besieged Novgorod Seversk. A large Tsarist army arrived under Fedor

Mstislavski, but was attacked and routed. Mstislavski was avenged a month later at **Dobrynitchi** (21 December 1604).

Novi Ligure ▌ 1799 ▌ French Revolutionary Wars (2nd Coalition)

A month after French defeat at the **Trebbia**, General Barthélemy Joubert concentrated in the hills north of Genoa at Novi Ligure against a massive force of Russians under General Alexander Suvorov and General Paul Kray's Austrians. Joubert was routed and killed and General Jean Victor Moreau resumed command to lead the defeated French out of the Piedmont (15 August 1799).

Noviodunum ▌ 369 ▌ 4th Gothic War

When Visigoths under Athanaric threatened northern Greece, the Eastern Emperor Valens initially repulsed the invaders at Daphne, after which he secured a decisive victory on the Danube at Noviodunum in Moesia Inferior. Athanaric accepted an advantageous treaty (September 369), but peace with the Goths was short-lived and Valens was killed ten years later at **Adrianople**.

Novi Slankamen ▌ 1691 ▌ Later Turkish-Habsburg Wars
See **Slankamen**

Novo Brdo ▌ 1455 ▌ Turkish-Hungarian Wars

Sultan Mehmed II and Isa Bey Evrenos launched a fresh invasion of southern Serbia, where they attacked the mountain fortress of Novo Brdo, on the Morava near Pristina, a wealthy Christian bastion in the southeast famous for its silver mines. Novo Brdo surrendered after siege guns destroyed its walls. Isa Bey then marched towards **Berat** while Mehmed soon captured **Belgrade** (May–1 June 1455).

Novocherkassk ▌ 1918 ▌ Russian Civil War

When a few White Cossacks seized Novocherkassk, northeast of Rostov (14 April), they were driven out after three days but regained the city a month later. Initially repulsed once more, they were reinforced by Colonel Mikhail Drozdovsky, who had led 1,000 men on a remarkable march from the Romanian front. The Red Cossacks and Red Guards were driven out (6–8 May 1918).

Novocherkassk ▌ 1920 ▌ Russian Civil War
See **Rostov**

Novorossisk ▌ 1920 ▌ Russian Civil War

As Red forces stormed into the Kuban through **Torgovaya**, White General Aleksandr Kutepov fell back on the Black Sea port of Novorosissk, where General Vladimir Sidorin tried to defend the perimeter. The defeated survivors of Anton Denikin's once-victorious White Army were evacuated to the Crimea in British ships and he was replaced by Pyotr Wrangel (27 March 1920).

Novorossisk ▌ 1943 ▌ World War II (Eastern Front)

While Soviet forces swept across the Ukraine, General Ivan Petrov sent General Konstantin Leselidze against the last German bridgehead in the Kuban around Novorossisk, which had been under virtual siege since September 1942. Very heavy fighting saw the Russians break through strong lines and General Erwin Jaenecke withdrew across the straits to **Kerch** (9–16 September 1943).

Nowo Georgiewsk ▌ 1915 ▌ World War I (Eastern Front)

Days after **Warsaw** fell, German General Hans von Beseler took his siege train against the huge fortress of Nowo Georgiewsk (later Modlin, modern Novy Dwor), west of the capital. Russian command believed the fortress could hold out, with 90,000 garrison, 1,600 guns and almost a million shells. But it was quickly forced to surrender, as was fortress **Kovno**, further north (8–19 August 1915).

Nowshera ▌ 1823 ▌ Afghan-Sikh Wars

The great Ranjit Singh threatened the Afghan-held city of Peshawar and faced a massive army under Vizier Mohammad Azim Khan, who unwisely permitted his force at nearby Nowshera to be divided by the Kabul River. As a result, the Afghan army was utterly routed. After Ranjit seized Peshawar, he gave the Governorship to Azim Khan's brother Sultan Mohammad Khan (14 March 1823).

Nowy Dwor I 1655 I 1st Northern War

With Warsaw captured by Charles X of Sweden after action at **Sobota**, Swedish General Gustav Otto Stenbock marched north against about 11,000 Poles under Jan Krasinksi near Pultusk, where the outnumbered Swedes secured a sharp victory in battle at Nowy Dwor. A few days later Charles himself decisively defeated John II Casimir southwest of Warsaw at **Opoczno** (20 September 1655).

Noyon I 1914 I World War I (Western Front)
See **Albert**

Noyon-Montdidier I 1918 I World War I (Western Front)

German commander Erich von Ludendorff won on the **Aisne**, then launched a fourth offensive between Noyon and Montdidier. While General Oscar von Hutier drove General Georges Humbert back ten miles, General Max von Boehn advancing from Soissons was checked by French and Americans under General Charles Mangin. Germany's last offensive was on the **Marne** (9–13 June 1918).

Ntombe I 1879 I Anglo-Zulu War
See **Myer's Drift**

Nuits Saint George I 1870 I Franco-Prussian War

While campaigning in eastern France, Prussian General Karl August von Werder sent General Adolf von Glumer and the Baden Division on a reconnaissance in force south of Dijon, where they met French General Camille Cremer marching north from Beaune. In heavy fighting near Nuits Saint George, both sides lost

about 1,000 men then withdrew to avoid further casualties (18 December 1870).

Nukumaru I 1865 I 2nd New Zealand War

With the religio-military Hauhau continuing to threaten Wanganui, despite a check at **Moutoa**, General Sir Duncan Cameron led 1,250 men to Nukumaru, 15 miles to the north, believing the Maoris would not attack. About 600 Hauhau were eventually repulsed in a bloody two-day action, though at a cost of 15 British killed and 31 wounded, and Cameron had to withdraw (24–25 January 1865).

Numa I 1086 I Later Three Years War

In renewed war in northeastern Japan, Minamoto Yoshiie turned against the Kiyohara, who had helped his father Yoriyoshi defeat the Abe at **Kuriyagawa**. Intervening in a clan feud, Yoshiie and 3,000 men besieged Kiyohara Iehira at Numa Stockade (southwest of modern Yokote in Akita), but were driven off by starvation and heavy snow. The next year he attacked again further north at **Kanazawa**.

Numantia I 133 BC I Numantian War

When Numantia, north of modern Soria, rebelled and humiliated a Roman force under Gaius Mancinus, the Senate sent a fresh army to Spain under Publius Scipio Aemilianus (famous for destroying **Carthage**). Scipio built a rampart around the city, which was starved into surrender after eight months. Numantia was then razed, with its population killed or enslaved, securing Roman rule in central Spain.

Numistro I 210 BC I 2nd Punic War

Shortly after destroying **Herdonea**, Carthaginian General Hannibal was attacked in camp at Numistro, southwest of Venusia in eastern Italy, by an avenging Roman force under the great Marcus Claudius Marcellus. The hard-fought action which followed is regarded as a narrow victory for Hannibal, though the Carthaginian declined further action next day and withdrew towards Tarentum.

Nundy Droog ∎ 1791 ∎ 3rd British-Mysore War

See **Nandi Drug**

Nuranang ∎ 1962 ∎ Sino-Indian War

See **Se La**

Nuremberg ∎ 1632 ∎ Thirty Years War (Swedish War)

See **Alte Veste**

Nuremberg ∎ 1944 ∎ World War II (Western Europe)

Britain's costliest air attack occured when 795 bombers sent against Nuremberg without long-range escort were hounded by German night-fighters to and from the target. Bomber Command lost 94 aircraft and a further 71 damaged at the cost of 500 killed, while fewer than ten German fighters were destroyed. Such raids ceased until long-range fighter escort became available (30–31 March 1944).

Nuuanu ∎ 1795 ∎ Hawaiian Wars

Kamehameha completed his conquest of Hawaii by assaulting Oahu, held by Kalanikupulu, who had been routed at **Kepaniwai** in 1790. Landing near modern Honolulu, Kamehameha attacked and destroyed his enemy on the cliff-tops at Nuuanu. Kalanikupulu fled (he was later captured and executed) and his ally Kaiana was killed. Kamehameha soon ruled a unified Hawaii (April 1795).

Nyborg ∎ 1659 ∎ 1st Northern War

Dutch ships intervening to support Denmark against Charles X of Sweden, defeated the Swedish navy in The **Sound**. Admiral Michael de Ruyter then transported Danish and Brandenburg troops to Funen, where Philip of Sulz-

bach was heavily entrenched at Nyborg. The Swedish invaders surrendered after Nyborg was stormed and war soon ended when Charles died (24 November 1659).

Nyenskans ∎ 1703 ∎ 2nd "Great" Northern War

Having captured the Swedish fortress at **Noteborg**, where Lake Ladoga flows into the Neva, Russian Tsar Peter I and Marshal Boris Sheremetev marched to the mouth of the Neva, where Nyenskans capitulated after a two-day bombardment. Peter thus gained his outlet to the Gulf of Finland and immediately began construction of the port of St Petersburg (11–12 May 1703).

Nyezane ∎ 1879 ∎ Anglo-Zulu War

On the same day as the British disaster at **Isandhlwana**, a column in the south under Colonel Charles Pearson was attacked at the Nyezane by perhaps 4,000 Zulus under Godide. In reputedly the first British battlefield use of the Gatling gun, the Zulus were driven off with about 400 men killed. Pearson then continued north to establish a fortified position at **Eshowe** (22 January 1879).

Nykarleby ∎ 1808 ∎ Napoleonic Wars (Russo-Swedish War)

After halting the Russian invasion of Finland at the **Siikajoki**, Swedish forces pursued the invaders down the west coast towards **Revolax** and attempted to surround the Russians at Nykarleby, northeast of **Vasa**. Swedish General Karl Adlercreutz found only a rearguard under General Ivan Fedorovich Jankovich, which fought briefly before being forced to evacuate the town (24 June 1808).

O

Oak Grove ▍ 1862 ▍ American Civil War (Eastern Theatre)

The first of the **Seven Days' Battles** saw Union commander George B. McClellan's attempt to close on the Confederate capital at Richmond blocked to the east at Oak Grove, Virginia, by a Confederate offensive under General Robert E. Lee. Both sides lost over 500 men in an inconclusive action and the following day Lee led a bold assault at **Beaver Dam Creek** (25 June 1862).

Oak Hills ▍ 1861 ▍ American Civil War (Trans-Mississippi)

See **Wilson's Creek**

Oaxaca ▍ 1865 ▍ Mexican-French War

Marshal Achille Bazaine led a French offensive south from **Puebla**, where he took 8,000 men against Oaxaca, held by 3,000 Mexicans under Porfirio Diaz. Taking time to build roads for his siege guns, Bazaine launched a terrible bombardment. Diaz surrendered after suffering heavy losses to casualties and desertion, though he later escaped from captivity (1 January–9 February 1865).

Oaxaca ▍ 1866 ▍ Mexican-French War

Republican General Porfirio Diaz advanced south from **Miahuatlán** and again besieged his birthplace, Oaxaca, held by Imperial commander Carlos Oroñoz. When a relief column was driven off at **La Carbonera**, Oroñoz surrendered his exhausted garrison of about 300—mainly Austrians, with some French and Mexicans. Diaz went on to secure Mazatalán and Jalapa (5–30 October 1866).

Oaxaca ▍ 1876 ▍ Diaz Revolt in Mexico

At the start of a new rising against President Sebastián Lerdo de Tejada, General Fidencio Hernandez and 2,000 rebels defeated a smaller force of Federal troops and national guards at San Felipe del Agua outside Oaxaca, capturing 2,500 rifles and half a million rounds. Hernandez then seized Oaxaca and proclaimed Porfirio Diaz Commander of a new revolutionary army (27 January 1876).

Oberalpsee ▍ 1799 ▍ French Revolutionary Wars (2nd Coalition)

See **Devil's Bridge**

Oberhollarbrunn ▍ 1805 ▍ Napoleonic Wars (3rd Coalition)

See **Hollarbrunn**

Ober-Kamlach ▍ 1796 ▍ French Revolutionary Wars (1st Coalition)

See **Mindelheim**

Oberndorf ▍ 1800 ▍ French Revolutionary Wars (2nd Coalition)

See **Biberach**

Obertyn ▍ 1531 ▍ Polish-Moldavian War

When Hospodar Petrylo of Moldavia invaded southern Poland over the disputed Hungarian succession, Polish Hetman Jan Tarnowski beat the invaders at **Gwozdiec** and soon after met their main army at nearby Obertyn, in modern Ukraine. Although massively outnumbered, Tarnowski held a defensive position. He then counter-attacked for a brilliant victory and Petrylo withdrew (22 August 1531).

Obidos I 1808 I Napoleonic Wars (Peninsular Campaign)

In a prelude to the battle at **Rolica**, a British force under General Sir Arthur Wellesley, which had landed at Mondego Bay in central Portugal, repulsed pickets sent out by General Henri Delaborde at Obidos, north of Rolica. While the skirmish was not significant, it was said to be the first action between British and French troops in the Peninsular Campaign (15 August 1808).

Obligada I 1845 I Argentine-Uruguayan War

See **Vuelte de Obligada**

Obrajuela I 1845 I Central American National Wars

When Honduras tried to restore President Francisco Malespín of El Salvador, a Salvadoran invasion was repulsed at **Comayagua**. Honduran General José Santos Guardiola then marched into El Salvador and seized La Union (5 July) and San Miguel (7 August). At Obrajuela, near Quelepa, General Nicolás Angulo repulsed the invasion, ending support for Malespín (15 August 1845).

Ocaña, Colombia I 1841 I Colombian War of Supreme Commanders

As newly elected President of Colombia, General Pedro Alcántara Herrán marched north against the rebel forces of General Lorenzo Hernández. Near Ocaña, Herrán won the last major victory of the northern campaign, effectively securing the Atlantic coast. He then returned to Bogotá to resume his official duties and the war ended early the following year (9 September 1841).

Ocaña, Spain I 1809 I Napoleonic Wars (Peninsular Campaign)

The Army of La Mancha under General Carlos Areizaga prepared a Spanish offensive from the south against French-held Madrid, assembling at Ocaña, south of Madrid beyond the Tagus. However, King Joseph Bonaparte and Marshal Nicolas Soult destroyed Areizaga in a bloody rout, capturing many men and guns, opening the way to French conquest of Andalusia (19 November 1809).

Occaneechee Island I 1676 I Bacon's Rebellion

When Governor Sir William Berkeley of Virginia declined to act against Indian tribes which had attacked settlers, Nathaniel Bacon led 70 colonists against the Susquehanna and the formerly friendly Occaneechee. In an unauthorised attack at Occaneechee Island, on the Roanoke, 130 Indians were killed. Bacon was declared a rebel and in September he attacked **Jamestown** (10 May 1676).

Ocean Pond I 1864 I American Civil War (Lower Seaboard)

See **Olustee**

Ochagavía I 1829 I Chilean Conservative Revolution

During disorder following the overthrow of Chilean Dictator Bernardo O'Higgins, rebellious Conservative General Joaquín Prieto met government troops led by General Francisco Lastra de la Sotta at Ochagavía, near Santiago. An armistice was agreed following indecisive action, though fighting soon broke out again and in April 1830 the government was routed at the **Lircay** (14 December 1829).

Ochakov I 1737 I Austro-Russian-Turkish War

Marshal Count Burkhard Christoph von Münnich led a major Russian offensive into the Turkish Ukraine, sweeping the Turks before his advance to the mouth of the Dnieper. There he inflicted a sharp defeat to storm and sack the key city of Ochakov. The Russian army was then halted by disease, delaying Münnich's advance into Moldavia, where he met the Turks in 1738 at **Bender** (July 1737).

Ochakov ∎ 1788 ∎ Catherine the Great's 2nd Turkish War

At the end of a lethargic siege of Ochakov at the mouth of the Dnieper, Russian General Prince Grigori Potemkin arrived and ordered a midwinter advance across a frozen marsh to take the Black Sea fortress by storm. The subsequent massacre is said to have cost 20,000 Turkish lives. The Russians then marched into Wallachia for victory at **Focsani** and **Rimnik** (June–17 December 1788).

Ochomogo ∎ 1823 ∎ Central American National Wars

Emperor Agustin Iturbide of Mexico tried to annex Costa Rica, supported by conservative forces in the capital Cartago. In battle on the nearby heights of Ochomogo, the Allies were defeated by Republican militia from San José and Alajuela under Gregorio José Ramirez. San José then became the capital of independent Costa Rica in the Central American Federation (5 April 1823).

Ochomogo ∎ 1948 ∎ Costa Rican Civil War

Following a disputed presidential election in Costa Rica, the Conservative José María Figueres Ferrer fought a 40-day war against the Christian Socialist government of Dr Rafael Calderón Guardia and Teodoro Picado. When Figueres seized Cartago and the nearby heights of Ochomogo, threatening San José, Picado surrendered and the Conservative Otilio Ulate became President (12 April 1948).

Ockley ∎ 851 ∎ Viking Raids on Britain
See **Aclea**

O'Connell Street ∎ 1922 ∎ Irish Civil War
Irish Republican forces seized key positions in Dublin and were driven out of the **Four Courts**, although they held "the block" of buildings in O'Connell Street against General Tom Ennis. Government artillery and heavy fighting forced the defenders to surrender with costly losses, including leader Cathal Brugha killed. The survivors withdrew towards **Limerick** (2–5 July 1922).

Octavem ∎ 1809 ∎ Napoleonic Wars (Peninsular Campaign)
See **Oitaven**

Odasu ∎ 1874 ∎ 2nd British-Ashanti War

Advancing inland against Ashanti forces threatening British territory in modern Ghana, General Sir Garnet Wolseley secured victory at **Abakrampa** and **Amoafo**, then crossed the Oda, just south of the capital Kumasi. At the village of Odasu just days later the Royal army was defeated. Wolseley entered Kumasi the same day, accepting the submission of King Kofi Karikari (4 February 1874).

Odawara ∎ 1590 ∎ Japan's Era of the Warring States

Hideyoshi Toyotomi conquered Kyushu at **Kagoshima** (July 1587) then turned east against the Hojo clan of Kanto. Hideyoshi besieged Odawara for months before Hojo Ujimasa finally yielded and was made to commit seppuku, while his son Ujinao was exiled. When Date Masamune of Matsu then quickly submitted, Hideyoshi had effectively completed unification of Japan (March–12 August 1590).

Odessa ∎ 1854 ∎ Crimean War

When Russian guns at the Black Sea port of Odessa reportedly fired on the frigate *Furious* under a flag of truce a week after war was declared, British Admiral Sir James Dundas took a fleet to bombard the military port. While an attempt was made to avoid damage to the commercial port and city, it was claimed that all but one of the Russian warships in harbour was destroyed (22 April 1854).

Odessa ▮ 1914 ▮ World War I (War at Sea)
See **Sevastopol**

Odessa ▮ 1919 ▮ Russian Civil War

Intervening to assist the White cause in the south, French General Philippe d'Anselm, aided by Greek units, landed at Odessa (18 December 1918) to support Governor Aleksei Grishin-Almazov. The campaign was a disorganised fiasco. With Red General Nikifor Grigorev advancing through Nikolayev, the French and others evacuated, abandoning their White allies (12 March–4 April 1919).

**Odessa ▮ 1941 ▮ World War II
(Eastern Front)**

As German forces swept across the Ukraine towards **Kiev**, the Romanian Fourth Army under General Nicolai Ciuperca (later Iosif Iacobini) besieged Odessa, cut off behind enemy lines. A bloody defence cost over 90,000 Romanian casualties and about 40,000 Russians before General Ivan Petrov withdrew. The Romanians took 12,000 prisoners and held Odessa until 1944 (5 August–16 October 1941).

**Odessa ▮ 1944 ▮ World War II
(Eastern Front)**

While the Russians attacked west through **Uman**, General Rodion Malinovsky circled south across the Bug towards the German and Romanian divisions on the Black Sea. Marshal Ewald von Kleist evacuated many men through Odessa before the key city fell with heavy losses, but he was dismissed after withdrawing across the Dniester to escape encirclement (6 March–10 April 1944).

**Oenoparas ▮ 145 BC ▮ Syrian
Dynastic War**

Ptolemy VI of Egypt married his daughter Cleopatra Thea to Alexander Balas, who seized Seleucid Syria at **Ptolemais**. However, Ptolemy later invaded against his son-in-law to support the legitimate heir, Demetrius. Alexander was killed in battle at the Oenoparas, near Antioch, but Ptolemy also died of wounds. The victor became Demetrius II Nicator, but was soon overthrown by Syrian Greeks.

**Oenophyta ▮ 457 BC ▮ 1st
Peloponnesian War**

Just two months after being heavily defeated at **Tanagra**, Athenian commander Myronides resumed the offensive to the north against Boeotia and, at Oenophyta, defeated a combined Theban-Boeotian army. The victory enabled Athens to extend control over central Greece, creating a sizeable land empire as a counter to the threat of a Spartan-led confederacy until defeat at **Coronea**.

**Ofen ▮ 1849 ▮ Hungarian
Revolutionary War**
See **Buda**

**Ogaden ▮ 1936 ▮ 2nd Italo-
Ethiopian War**

With the war effectively decided by Ethiopia's rout at **Maychew**, General Rodolfo Graziani attacked Ras Nasibu of the Ogaden in the triangle Dejeh Bur-Harar-Jijiga, east of Addis Ababa. Heavy fighting cost about 2,000 Italian casualties before Generals Guglielmo Nasi, Luigi Frusci and Augusto Augustini destroyed the "Hindenburg Wall." Graziani entered Harar on 5 May (15–25 April 1936).

Ogdensburg ▮ 1813 ▮ War of 1812

American Major Benjamin Forsyth crossed the frozen St Lawrence River to raid Morristown (7 February) and Canadian Colonel George Macdonell led the Glengarry Light Infantry Fencibles on a reprisal across the ice from Fort Wellington to attack Forsyth at Ogdensberg. When the Americans were defeated and fled, Macdonell destroyed the fort and withdrew (22 February 1813).

Ognon ▮ 1870 ▮ Franco-Prussian War
See **Chatillon-le-Duc**

**Ognot ▮ 1916 ▮ World War I
(Caucasus Front)**
See **Bitlis**

Ohaewai I 1845 I 1st New Zealand War

With Hone Heke defeated in New Zealand's far north at **Te Ahuahu**, Colonel Henry Despard led 600 soldiers and volunteers against Kawiti and Hone Heke's pa (fortified village) at Ohaewai, near Waimate. After a long bombardment, Despard lost 40 killed and 80 wounded in a suicidal assault before the Maoris slipped away. In December Despard attacked again at **Ruapekapeka** (23 June–1 July 1845).

Ohamakarai I 1904 I German Colonial Wars in Africa

See **Waterberg**

Ohud I 625 I Campaigns of the Prophet Mohammed

Despite his defeat at **Badr** (January 624), Abu Sufyan of Mecca took a large force of Koreish to attack **Medina**. On the nearby Mount of Ohud, the Prophet Mohammed and his heavily outnumbered warriors were almost defeated when the Prophet was wounded and thought to be dead. However, they regrouped and repulsed Abu Sufyan with heavy losses on both sides (21 March 625).

Oitaven I 1809 I Napoleonic Wars (Peninsular Campaign)

Facing a French offensive in northwestern Spain by Marshal Michel Ney, General Gaspar de Norona took a position with about 13,000 men behind the Oitaven Estuary near the city of Vigo. Several French attempts to force the bridge of San Payo were repulsed, though it was largely a feint to keep the Spanish occupied. Ney later withdrew to join Marshal Nicolas Soult at Zamora (8 June 1809).

Ojinaga I 1913–1914 I Mexican Revolution

Generals Pascual Orozco and José Inez Salazar were decisively defeated at **Tierra Blanca** and evacuated **Chihuahua**, withdrawing northeast to Ojinaga, the last garrison in northern Mexico loyal to President Victoriano Heurta. They stubbornly resisted revolutionary forces under Pánfilo Natera until Francisco (Pancho) Villa arrived and Ojinaga fell by storm (December 1913–10 January 1914).

Okaharui I 1904 I German Colonial Wars in Africa

Weeks after a bloody ambush at **Owikokorero**, northeast of Windhoek in German Southwest Africa, Major Franz-Georg Glasenapp and 300 Germans marched southwest from Onjatu towards **Onganjira** and were ambushed at Okaharui by about 1,000 Herero rebels. Glasenapp lost 32 killed and 17 wounded, and fell back on Onjatu, where his column was later decimated by typhus (3 April 1904).

Okaihau I 1845 I 1st New Zealand War

See **Puketutu**

Oka River I 1572 I Russian-Tatar Wars

See **Molodi**

Okehazama I 1560 I Japan's Era of the Warring States

Imagawa Yoshimoto of Mikawa marched on Kyoto with 25,000 Samurai, including the young Tokugawa Ieyasu, and was blocked by Oda Nobunaga of Owari, who attacked the invaders near Okehazama, east of Kyoto, with perhaps just 2,000 men. In a brief, bloody action Yoshimoto was defeated and killed. Ieyasu then joined Nobunaga, who eventually secured Kyoto (12 June 1560).

Okhmatov I 1644 I Polish-Tatar Wars

After decades of fighting Cossacks and Tatars, Polish Hetman Stanislas Koniecpolski again marched south to meet the Crimean Tatars he had repulsed at **Martynow** (1624) and **Kamieniec** (1633). Aided by Jeremi Wisniowiecki, he secured a savage victory over Tuhai-Bei at Okhmatov, south of Kiev, but died just two years later. Tuhai-Bei was avenged in 1648 at **Korsun** (30 January 1644).

Okhmatov I 1655 I Russo-Polish Wars

Following the fall of **Smolensk** (September 1654), Poland attacked in the Ukraine, where Stanislas Potocki and Stefan Czarniecki besieged Uman. To the north at Okhmatov, they were met by a massive Russian force under Vasili Sheremetev and the Cossack Bogdan Chmielnicki. Despite terrible Russian losses, the Poles were checked and in September Chmielnicki besieged **Lvov** (29 January 1655).

Okinawa ▎ 1945 ▎ World War II (Pacific)

When American General Simon Buckner led over 150,000 men to Okinawa, south of Japan, there was severe fighting against General Mitsuru Ushijima and also heavy losses at sea. The war's largest and bloodiest island campaign saw Okinawa secured at the cost of 12,500 American troops and sailors killed, over 100,000 Japanese soldiers killed and many civilians dead (1 April–21 June 1945).

Okita Nawate ▎ 1584 ▎ Japan's Era of the Warring States

The Shimazu of Satsuma secured southern Honshu at **Mimikawa** (1578) and **Minamata** (1581), and Shimazu Iehisa marched northwest to aid Arima Harinobu against Ryuzoji Takanobu of Saga, besieging Shimabara. At nearby Okita Nawate, Takanobu was defeated and killed. The Shimazu later began their fateful invasion of Bungo, leading to destruction in 1587 at **Kagoshima** (4 May 1584).

Okolona, Arkansas ▎ 1864 ▎ American Civil War (Trans-Mississippi)

See **Elkin's Ferry**

Okolona, Mississippi ▎ 1864 ▎ American Civil War (Western Theatre)

Union commander William T. Sherman marched east from Vicksburg towards **Meridian**, Mississippi, while General William S. Smith advanced southeast from Memphis in support. After running action against Confederate General Nathan B. Forrest, Smith turned back. At Okolona, Mississippi, Forrest inflicted a decisive defeat and Smith returned to Memphis (22 February 1864).

OK Pass ▎ 1919 ▎ Wars of the Mad Mullah

As war against Muhammad Abdullah Hassan of Somaliland dragged on after **Dul Madoba**, Major Charles Howard led an offensive northeast from Burao and left Captain Richard Simons to hold the OK Pass, where he was attacked by 400 Dervishes. In their worst defeat since **Jidballi** (1904) the Dervishes lost about 200 killed for just two British dead. Fighting continued until **Taleh** (1 March 1919).

Okpo ▎ 1592 ▎ Japanese Invasion of Korea

Japanese invaders secured **Pusan** before Korean naval commander Yi Sun-shin and Admiral Won Kyun attacked the Japanese supply fleet and troopships to the southwest off Okpo, on Kyo-che Island. Here, and in further fighting the same day at Happo and next day at Chokjinpo, Japanese commander Mori Terumoto lost 42 ships. Yi soon won again off **Sachon** (16–17 June 1592).

Oksnebjerg ▎ 1535 ▎ Danish Counts' War

In a dispute over the Danish throne following the death of Frederick I (1533), his Lutheran son Duke Christian initially lost to Catholic nobles and Lubeck forces under Count Christopher of Oldenberg. However with Swedish aid, Christian's General Johan Rantzau secured a decisive victory at Oksnebjerg near Assens. The Hanseatic navy was defeated days later off **Bornholm** (11 June 1535).

Oland (1st) ▎ 1564 ▎ Nordic Seven Years War

Swedish commander Jakob Bagge recovered from the costly drawn action off **Gotland** (September 1563) attacking a Danish-German flotilla off Oland, where intense gunfire sank the Swedish flagship Mars before Bagge was forced to withdraw with heavy losses. While defeat cost Bagge his command, Swedish naval forces were avenged three months later in the same waters (30–31 May 1564).

Oland (2nd) **I** 1564 **I** Nordic Seven Years War

Following Sweden's defeat in the eastern seas off Oland, new commander Klas Kristersson Horn attacked Danish and German ships in the same waters north of the strategic island, where a decisive victory by Horn prevented a naval attack on Stockholm. Meanwhile an advance on land ended when 300 Danish supply wagons were destroyed and Denmark's German mercenaries withdrew (14–15 August 1564).

Oland **I** 1566 **I** Nordic Seven Years War

In perhaps the decisive naval action of the war, Swedish Commander Klas Kristersson Horn took 68 ships from Stockholm to meet the Danish fleet north of Oland. After a heavy defeat, the Danes withdrew into Visby where a storm that night sank 15 ships and cost about 4,000 lives. Sweden regained control of the eastern seas, though war dragged on until the fall of **Varberg** in 1569 (26 July 1566).

Oland **I** 1676 **I** Scania War

Danish Admiral Niels Juel defeated a Swedish fleet at **Jasmund** and a week later, supported by Dutch Admiral Cornelius van Tromp, met the Swedes again south of Oland in southeast Sweden. Swedish Admiral Lorenz Creutz was killed in this second defeat, with three ships lost. Despite Danish defeats on land, Juel went on to further victory the following year off **Koge Bay** (1 June 1676).

Oland **I** 1789 **I** 2nd Russo-Swedish War

After defeat off **Bornholm** (26 June), Duke Charles of Sodermanland, brother of Gustav III of Sweden, sailed from Karlskrona in southeast Sweden and intercepted a small Russian squadron under Admiral Paul Vasili Tchitchakov off nearby Oland. In a disorganised action, the Swedes failed to inflict any major damage on the outnumbered Russians, squandering an invaluable opportunity (25 July 1789).

Old Baldy **I** 1952 **I** Korean War

A Chinese spring offensive to secure key outposts between the lines saw very heavy fighting for Old Baldy (Hill 266), west of Chorwon. After a failed first assault, the reinforced Chinese took the hill, then lost it. A third attempt after heavy bombardment saw the Chinese seize the crest before Allied tanks finally helped drive them off (26 June–3 July; 17 July–4 August & 18–21 September 1952).

Old Baldy **I** 1953 **I** Korean War

As peace talks dragged on, North Koreans renewed the attack on Old Baldy (Hill 266), west of Chorwon. A small force of Colombians was overwhelmed and American infantry suffered heavy losses failing to retake the hill. New commander General Maxwell Taylor decided Old Baldy was not worth more casualties, but it was later used by the Communists to attack **Pork Chop Hill** (23–26 March 1953).

Old Church **I** 1864 **I** American Civil War (Eastern Theatre)

While the Union and Confederate armies fought out an inconclusive confrontation northeast of Richmond at **Totopotomoy Creek**, Virginia, Union cavalry under General Alfred T. Torbert probed south and met Confederate General Wade Hampton at Old Church. Hampton was repulsed in a sharp action and fell back to help meet the Union army next day at nearby **Cold Harbour** (30 May 1864).

Old Fort Wayne **I** 1862 **I** American Civil War (Trans-Mississippi)

Union General James G. Blunt pursued Confederate Colonel Douglas H. Cooper out of southwestern Missouri after **Newtonia** and attacked him in Indian Territory at Old Fort Wayne, near Maysville, Oklahoma. Cooper and the Cherokee Chief Stand Watie were outnumbered and defeated, and Blunt soon entered northeastern Arkansas to fight at **Cane Hill** and **Prairie Grove** (22 October 1862).

**Oldorobo ▎ 1916 ▎ World War I
(African Colonial Theatre)**
  See **Salaita**

**Old River Lake ▎ 1864 ▎ American
Civil War (Trans-Mississippi)**
  Attacking the Confederates just west of the Mississippi, General Joseph A. Mower, supported by Colonel Lucius F. Hubbard, disembarked at Sunnyside Landing, then marched towards Lake Village, Arkansas. In a sharp action, with about 100 men lost on either side, he defeated Colonel Colton Greene and seized Lake Village, then returned to the Mississippi at Columbia (6 June 1864).

**Olinda ▎ 1630 ▎ Dutch-Portuguese
Colonial Wars**
  See **Recife**

**Olivento ▎ 1041 ▎ Norman Conquest of
Southern Italy**
  Norman forces on a fresh offensive in southern Italy secured Melfi, then joined with their Lombard allies to meet a large Byzantine army advancing from Bari under Michael Doukeianus. At the Olivento, near Venosa, the Greeks and their Varangian (Viking) mercenaries suffered a terrible defeat, with many drowned in the river. They were soon beaten again at **Montemaggiore** (17 March 1041).

**Olivenza ▎ 1811 ▎ Napoleonic Wars
(Peninsular Campaign)**
  Marshal Nicolas Soult was marching west from central Spain to support Marshal André Masséna in Portugal, when he attacked the small fortress of Olivenza, 15 miles southwest of Badajoz. Spanish commander Manuel Herck surrendered after 12 days and Soult moved on to besiege the major frontier fortress at **Badajoz** (11–22 January 1811).

**Oliwa ▎ 1627 ▎ 2nd Polish-
Swedish War**
  During Swedish blockade of **Danzig** (modern Gdansk) in Polish Prussia, ten Polish ships under

the Dane Arend Dickman made a surprise sortie against Swedish Admiral Nils Stiernskold. While four of his ships fled, Stiernskold was killed in the capture of his flagship off nearby Oliwa and a second Swedish vessel blew herself up. However, Danzig remained under blockade (28 November 1627).

**Olmedo ▎ 1445 ▎ Spanish Wars
of Succession**
  Castilian nobles rebelling against King Juan II of Castile and his unpopular Constable, Don Alvaro de Luna, were supported by an invasion by Henry of Aragon and his brother, Juan of Navarre. Taking the field in person, the King of Castile defeated the brothers at Olmedo, south of Valladolid, where Henry died of wounds. De Luna later fell from Royal favour and was beheaded for murder.

**Olmütz ▎ 1642 ▎ Thirty Years War
(Franco-Habsburg War)**
  Soon after victory at **Schweidnitz** in Silesia, Swedish Marshal Lennart Torstensson advanced into Moravia and seized and sacked the capital, Olmütz (modern Olomouc), 40 miles northeast of Brno. He then fortified the historic city, but with Archduke Leopold William and General Ottavio Piccolomini threatening, he was forced to withdraw into Saxony for his great victory at **Breitenfeld** (June 1642).

**Olmütz ▎ 1758 ▎ Seven Years War
(Europe)**
  Frederick II of Prussia campaigning against Moravia attempted to besiege Austrian General Ernst Dietrich von Marschall on the March at Olmütz (modern Olomouc, Czech Republic). However, Marshal Leopold von Daun maintained lines to the fortress and the day after a Prussian convoy was destroyed at **Domstadtl**, Frederick broke off the siege and withdrew (May–1 July 1758).

**Olpae ▎ 426 BC ▎ Great
Peloponnesian War**
  A fresh offensive in west-central Greece saw Peloponnesian forces under Spartan commander

Eurylochus join local Ambraciots to besiege Olpae, northeast of Argos. Arriving with an Athenian squadron, Demosthenes won a decisive victory against superior forces, with Eurylochus killed. Demosthenes returned to Athens in triumph and was later sent to fortify **Pylos-Sphacteria** (November 426 BC).

Oltenitza I 1853 I Crimean War

When Russia occupied Moldavia and Wallachia, Turkey sent Omar Pasha (Michael Lattas) north across the Danube. At its junction with the Arges near Oltenitza he overwhelmed Russian General Pyotr Andreevich Dannenberg. However, the Russians recovered and within six months counter-attacked across the Danube at **Silistria**, provoking British and French intervention (4 November 1853).

Olustee I 1864 I American Civil War (Lower Seaboard)

Determined to secure northern Florida, Union General Quincy Gillmore sent General Truman Seymour southwest from Jacksonville against Confederate forces under General Joseph Finegan at Olustee, just south of Ocean Pond. In the war's largest battle in Florida, Seymour attacked with over 5,000 men, but was repulsed with 1,800 casualties and withdrew to Jacksonville (20 February 1864).

Olympieum I 415 BC I Great Peloponnesian War

See **Syracuse**

Olynthus I 348 BC I 3rd Sacred War

Philip II of Macedon renewed his offensive against Greek cities in the northern Aegean after taking **Pagasae** and invaded Chalcidice to attack Olynthus, on the Gulf of Toroni, which had earlier helped him take **Potidaea**. Forces sent from Athens under Chares arrived too late and a pro-Macedonian faction surrendered the city. Olynthus was razed and her citizens were enslaved (September 348 BC).

Omaha Beach I 1944 I World War II (Western Europe)

See **D-Day**

Omata I 1860 I 2nd New Zealand War

See **Waireka**

Omdurman I 1898 I British-Sudan Wars

Moving up the Nile to reconquer the Sudan and avenge the death of General Charles Gordon at **Khartoum** in 1885, General Herbert Kitchener's British-Egyptian-Sudanese army defeated the Mahdists at the **Atbara**, then met the Khalifa Abdullah-al-Taaishi at Omdurman (Karala), near Khartoum. The Dervish army was destroyed—with perhaps 10,000 dead and 15,000 wounded (2 September 1898).

Omoa I 1853 I Central American National Wars

During a border war between Guatemala and Honduras, Guatemala won in the east at **Atulapa**, then Guatemalan President Rafael Carrera launched a surprise attack in the west, where Colonel José Victor Zalava landed from the sea to storm the Honduran fortress of Omoa. The combatants agreed to a truce to fight American Filibusters then in late 1856 resumed the war at **Masaguara** (19 August 1853).

Omsk I 1919 I Russian Civil War

Defeated in the Urals, White commander Admiral Aleksandr Kolchak lost a costly defensive action at the **Tobol**, then withdrew east to Omsk, where he had seized authority in November 1918. Massively defeated by General Mikhail Tukhachevski, Kolchak fled along the Trans-Siberian railway to Irkutsk, where he was later handed over to the Bolsheviks and executed (14 November 1919).

Oncativo I 1830 I Argentine Civil Wars

Federalist leader Juan Facundo Quiroga refused to sign the peace following his defeat at **La Tablada** (June 1829) and regrouped his forces, then attempted to invade Córdoba Province in western Argentina. He was again beaten by Unitarist General José Maria Paz in the valley of Oncativo, southeast of Córdoba, but recovered for victory a year later at **Rodeo de Chacón** (25 February 1830).

Ondini I 1883 I Zulu Civil War

When the British-restored Zulu King Cetshwayo returned to his kingdom, his uSuthu forces were routed at **Msebe**. A few months later the Mandlakazi faction under Zibebhu attacked the King's capital at Ondini. About 500 uSuthu died in a bloody battle and subsequent massacre, though Cetshwayo escaped. His son and successor Dinuzulu was avenged a year later at **Tshaneni** (21 July 1883).

Onganjira I 1904 I German Colonial Wars in Africa

On campaign against Herero rebels north of Windhoek, in German Southwest Africa, Colonel Theodor Leutwein relieved Okahanja then advanced northeast towards Onganjira. Ambushed by Samuel Maherero, Leutwein lost 14 killed and 12 wounded, though the Hereros suffered heavy casualties to artillery and machine-gun fire. The Germans soon marched on through **Oviumbo** (9 April 1904).

Ongon I 1900 I Russo-Chinese War

As Russian forces advanced into Manchuria along the Chinese Eastern Railway in the aftermath of the Boxer Rebellion, General Orlov attacked a large Chinese force at Ongon. With the Mongol cavalry defeated, Orlov seized the nearby city of Hailar, along with a massive supply of food and stores, then continued east along the railway towards **Xing-an** (30 July 1900).

Onitsha I 1967–1968 I Biafran War

After driving back a Biafran offensive through **Benin**, Nigerian Federal Colonel Murtala Mohammed rashly tried to storm the Niger against Onitsha, held by Colonel Joe Achuzie. Repulsed with severe losses, Mohammed failed twice more before crossing upstream to besiege Onitsha. Despite a deadly ambush at **Abagana**, the Federals finally seized the city (20 October 1967–21 March 1968).

Onon I 1410 I Ming Imperial Wars

Determined to avenge Chinese disaster on the **Kerulen** (September 1409), Ming Emperor Yongle led a claimed 300,000 men to attack the Eastern Mongols at the Onon River. Mongol Prince Bunyashiri suffered a bloody defeat and fled west (where he was killed by a rival two years later). His Chancellor Arughtai was pursued east to battle the following month at **Jing Luzhen** (15 June 1410).

Oomuli I 1560 I Livonian War

Ivan IV of Russia renewed his war against Livonia and sent Andrei Kurbsky, who captured Marienburg, while Alexei Adashov attacked the Livonian Order at Oomuli (north of Valga in modern Estonia). Landmarshal Philipp Schall von Bell overconfidently sortied and was defeated and captured, and later executed on orders from the Tsar. Kurbsky then besieged the knights at **Fellin** (2 August).

Oondwah Nullar I 1763 I Bengal War
See **Udaynala**

Oostend I 1601–1604 I Netherlands War of Independence
See **Ostend**

Opequon I 1864 I American Civil War (Eastern Theatre)

Two weeks after inconclusive action in the Shenandoah Valley near **Berryville**, Union commander Philip Sheridan advanced west on General Jubal A. Early's Confederate army on the Opequon Creek, in front of Winchester, Virginia. Early was decisively defeated after a costly battle of attrition and abandoned Winchester, retreating south to dig in at **Fisher's Hill** (19 September 1864).

Ophlimos I 622 I Byzantine-Persian Wars

To combat Persian occupation of Asia Minor, Byzantine Emperor Heraclius took a large army across the Sea of Marmara to Pylae (modern Yalova) to threaten the flank of Persian Shahbaraz in Armenia. Heraclius advanced to a good victory near Ophlimos in the Lycus Valley, but had to return to meet Avars in the Balkans. He renewed his eastern offensive two years later at **Dwin** (August 622).

Opoczno | 1655 | 1st Northern War

As he invaded Poland through **Ujscie** (15 July), Charles X of Sweden captured Warsaw after action at **Sobota**, then joined General Arvid Wittenberg against King John II Casimir to the southwest at Opoczno. Casimir was badly defeated and withdrew into Silesia. His forces were beaten again at **Nowy Dwor** and **Wojnicz**, before the Swedes were finally checked at **Jasna Gora** (6 September 1655).

Oporto (1st) | 1809 | Napoleonic Wars (Peninsular Campaign)

French Marshal Nicolas Soult invaded Portugal from the north, brushing aside Portuguese forces at **Chaves** and **Braga** in March and advancing to Oporto, where a large force of poorly armed militia and peasant levies tried to defend Portugal's second city. The Portuguese were routed in a one-sided disaster, with thousands drowned in the Duoro, and Soult seized Oporto (29 March 1809).

Oporto (2nd) | 1809 | Napoleonic Wars (Peninsular Campaign)

Six weeks after seizing Oporto, French Marshal Nicolas Soult's invasion of northern Portugal stalled as he faced a large-scale counter-offensive from Lisbon by Anglo-Portuguese forces under General Sir Arthur Wellesley. In a hard-fought battle, Wellesley drove Soult out of Oporto and then out of Portugal, capturing French guns and supplies as Soult withdrew to Spain (12 May 1809).

Oporto | 1832 | Miguelite Wars

After Don Miguel de Braganza usurped the throne of Portugal, his brother Don Pedro, father and Regent for the legitimate heir Maria da Gloria, raised an army with English support and invaded from the Azores. The Regent captured Oporto following a sharp battle and held it against the Miguelites until the usurper's navy was defeated a year later off **Cape St Vincent** (8 July 1832).

Orakau | 1864 | 2nd New Zealand War

When Rewi Maniapoto defiantly built a fortified pa at Orakau, six miles from Te Awamutu, General George Carey inflicted a heavy artillery bombardment, though his assault was repulsed. General Sir Duncan Cameron then brought up reinforcements and the Maoris fought their way out, losing 80 killed (including Rewi) and 40 wounded, and ending the Waikato War (31 March–2 April 1864).

Oran | 1509 | Spanish Colonial Wars in North Africa

After Ferdinand V completed the Reconquest of Spain at **Granada** (1492), Cardinal Francisco Jimenes de Cisneros captured **Mers el Kebir** (1505), then equipped and accompanied a larger force under Pedro Navarro against Oran, west of Algiers. The port was taken with heavy losses in killed and prisoners, and was held by Spain until 1708. The next year Navarro took **Bougie** and **Tripoli** (May 1509).

Oran | 1704–1708 | Spanish-Algerian Wars

Algerian commander Moustafa-bou-Chlarem took the offensive in North Africa, laying siege to the key Spanish-held port of Oran. After years of ineffective blockade, fresh Algerian forces with siege guns arrived under Ozen Hassan and bloody fighting secured four outlying forts before the citadel was taken by assault. The nearby harbour of Mers-el-Kébir fell a few months later (1704–2 January 1708).

Oran | 1732 | Spanish-Algerian Wars

Determined to retake Oran, west of Algiers, Spain sent Admiral Francisco Cornejo with 520 ships and 20,000 men led by José Carrillo de Albornoz Comte de Montemar. When Dey Abdi Pasha of Algiers was slow sending troops, Moustafa-bou-Chlarem was driven out. While aid finally arrived, the Algerian siege was repulsed with heavy losses on both sides and Spain held Oran (June 1732).

Oran | 1780–1791 | Spanish-Algerian Wars

With Spain distracted by European war, Mohammad-el-Kébir of Western Algeria besieged Oran, though he could not command the sea. Spain reacted by bombarding **Algiers**. Huge earthquakes in October 1790 caused terrible damage and casualties at Oran, but an Algerian offensive was driven off. Spain later agreed to evacuate Oran while retaining a bastion at Mers-el-Kébir (1780–September 1791).

Oran | 1940 | World War II (Northern Africa)

See **Mers el Kebir**

Oran | 1942 | World War II (Northern Africa)

As part of the **Torch** operations in French Northwest Africa, a flotilla from Britain under Admiral Thomas Troubridge discharged 31,000 Americans led by General Lloyd Fredenhall at the well-defended Vichy port of Oran. While the landing was largely unopposed, there was stiff opposition ashore for two days before Central Task Force secured the city's surrender (8–10 November 1942).

Oranik | 1456 | Albanian-Turkish Wars

Attempting to undermine George Kastriote Skanderbeg, Sultan Mehmed II sent 15,000 Turkish auxiliaries to support the Albanian leader's uncle, Musa Komninos Golem. In battle at Oranik, Skanderbeg defeated Komninos and took possession of Dibra, giving him most of upper Albania. Komninos was later pardoned and joined his nephew against the Turks (March 1456).

Oravais | 1808 | Napoleonic Wars (Russo-Swedish War)

Despite his successful summer offensive against the Russian invasion of Finland, Swedish commander Karl Adlercreutz was forced back to the coast and tried to halt the Russians at Oravais, northeast of **Vasa**. In the largest battle of the campaign, new Russian commander Nikolai Kamenski secured a decisive victory and forced the Swedes to withdraw through **Juthas** (14 September 1808).

Orbetello | 1646 | Thirty Years War (Franco-Habsburg War)

Prince Thomas of Savoy advanced into Tuscany with French support and besieged the Spanish-held fortress of Orbetello, in a lagoon on Italy's west coast south of Piombino. French Admiral Jean-Armande de Maillé-Brézé was killed fighting a Spanish relief fleet off **Isola del Giglio** and, when Spanish forces captured nearby Porto-Ecole, Thomas had to withdraw to Piedmont (June 1646).

Orbigo | 456 | Goth Invasion of the Roman Empire

With approval of the Western Emperor Avitus, Theodoric II the Visigoth took a massive army into northwest Spain and at the Orbigo near Astorga, beat his brother-in-law Rechiarius II of the Suevi to regain Spain for Rome. A year later, Theodoric captured and executed Rechiarius in Oporto. However, in 458 Theodoric was himself defeated in Gaul at **Toulouse** by the new Emperor Majorian.

Orbigo | 1811 | Napoleonic Wars (Peninsular Campaign)

Spanish commander José Maria Santocildes, marching through Leon, killed French General Jean-Andre Valletaux at **Benavides** (23 June), then advanced to the Orbigo, where Generals Jean-Pierre Bonet and Jean-Mathieu Seras attempted to hold a position. They were defeated and fell back to Leon, but a French counter-attack soon regained the river and Santocildes withdrew (2 & 18 July 1811).

Orbiso | 1835 | 1st Carlist War

Carlist commander Tomás Zumalacárregui recovered from a costly repulse at **Ormáiztegui** in Navarre and two weeks later attempted to intercept a Spanish Liberal army under General Manuel Lorenzo and Colonel Marcelino Oráa marching towards Maeztu. Zumalacárregui was driven off at Orbiso with about 400 men lost, but he soon had his revenge on Lorenzo at **Arquijas** (17 January 1835).

Orchanie | 1877 | Russo-Turkish Wars

On campaign south of the Danube to support the Russian siege of **Plevna**, General Osip Gourko and about 36,000 men surprised a Turkish force under Mehmed Ali Pasha crossing a pass in the Balkan Mountains, northeast of Sofia. Near Orchanie (modern Botevgrad) Gourko routed the Turks and captured supplies intended for Plevna, which fell a few weeks later (15 November 1877).

Orchomenus | 86 BC | 1st Mithridatic War

Pontic commander Archelaus was driven out of Greece at **Chaeronea**, but returned from Chalcis with reinforcements and, near Orchomenus, again faced Roman General Lucius Sulla. He was decisively beaten, with perhaps 15,000 killed, and the Pontic invasion of Greece was over. Following defeats at **Miletopolis** and **Tenedos** (85 BC), Mithridates VI of Pontus sued for peace.

Ordahsu | 1874 | 2nd British-Ashanti War
See **Odasu**

Ordal | 1813 | Napoleonic Wars (Peninsular Campaign)

With France facing defeat in northern Spain, Marshal Louis Suchet opened a new offensive southwest from Barcelona. Advancing through Molins de Rey, he surprised units of the Anglo-Spanish army at Ordal and Colonel Frederick Adam was routed. However, Suchet did not pursue his advantage and Allied commander Lord Frederick Bentinck was able to withdraw (13 September 1813).

Orduña | 1836 | 1st Carlist War

Spanish Liberal commander Baldomero Espartero, campaigning northwest from Vitoria in Navarre, advanced on Orduña where he was met by Carlist forces under Generals Joaquín Elío and Simon de La Torre. Heavy fighting cost the Carlists a decisive defeat and they retreated northeast towards Bilbao. A snowstorm prevented Espartero marching in pursuit (5 March 1836).

Orekhovo | 1769 | Polish Rebellion

Facing a Polish rebellion under Stanislas Poniatowski, Russian forces recaptured Warsaw, then Colonel Alexander Suvorov marched east against rebel leaders Francis and Casimir Pulawski. Suvorov surprised a much larger Polish force in a dawn attack near Orekhovo, killing more than 200, including Francis Pulawski. The survivors fled and Russia secured the region (1 September 1769).

Orel | 1919 | Russian Civil War

General Vladimir Mai-Maevski advanced towards Moscow through **Voronezh** before reaching Orel, defended by Red commander Aleksandr Yegorov. Very heavy fighting saw Orel taken (13 October) marking the northern limit of White expansion. It was soon lost in a bloody counter-offensive and White commander Anton Denikin began his withdrawal (20 October 1919).

Orel | 1941 | World War II (Eastern Front)
See **Bryansk**

Orel | 1943 | World War II (Eastern Front)

As the German offensive at **Kursk** ground to a halt, Soviet forces counter-attacked to the north against the Orel Salient, held by General Walther Model. With Russian General Markian Popov circling Orel itself and General Vasili Sokolovsky driving south into the German rear, Model's outnumbered force withdrew to avoid encirclement and fell back to Bryasnk (12 July–5 August 1943).

Orenburg | 1773–1774 | Pugachev Rebellion

When Cossack rebel Emelyan Pugachev and only 3,000 men failed to take the Ural city of

Orenburg by storm, he settled down to a siege and defeated relief columns from Simbirsk and Kazan. However, a third column with 2,400 men and 20 guns broke into Orenburg to reinforce Governor Ivan Reinsdorp. Pugachev was then defeated at nearby **Tatishchevo** (5 October 1773–22 March 1774).

**Orenburg I 1917–1918 I Russian
Civil War**
Near the start of the war, Orenburg Cossacks under Aleksandr Dutov seized the city from the Bosheviks (26 November 1917). They were driven out by Red Guards in late January 1918, then retook Orenburg in a counter-offensive (3 July 1918). With White defeat at **Omsk** in 1919, Dutov led the Orenburg Cossacks east to China, where he was assassinated in 1921 by one of his own men.

Oresund I 1658 I 1st Northern War
See **Sound**

**Orewin Bridge I 1282 I English
Conquest of Wales**
See **Aber Edw**

Orfordness I 1666 I 2nd Dutch War
See **North Foreland**

Oriamendi I 1837 I 1st Carlist War
On a fresh offensive against the Carlists near **San Sebastian**, Spanish forces and the British legion under General Sir George de Lacy Evans advanced on Hernani and captured the nearby Heights of Oriamendi. Next day they were attacked and routed by the approaching army of Carlist commander the Infante Sebastia, and withdrew with very heavy losses (15–16 March 1837).

**Oriskany I 1777 I War of the
American Revolution**
British Colonel Barry St Leger was besieging **Fort Stanwix**, on the Mohawk when he sent Chief Joseph Brant and about 400 Indians to intercept a relief column under General Nicholas Herkimer. About six miles downstream at Oriskany, the Indians ambushed and virtually destroyed the American militia and the survivors

retreated, with Herkimer fatally wounded (6 August 1777).

Orizaba I 1862 I Mexican-French War
Repulsed at **Puebla**, Charles Latrille Comte de Lorencez withdrew to Orizaba, where he was attacked by a large Mexican force under General Ignacio Zaragoza. In a brilliant night-time sortie led by French Captain Paul-Alexandre Détrie, the Mexicans were driven off nearby Cerro del Borrego with heavy losses. Orizaba was held until Napoleon III sent reinforcements (18 May 1862).

**Or-Kapi I 1736 I Austro-Russian-
Turkish War**
See **Perekop**

**Orlau-Frankenau I 1914 I World War I
(Eastern Front)**
While Russia's invasion of eastern Prussia stalled in the north after **Gumbinnen**, General Aleksander Samsonov to the south advanced against the German XX Corps of Friedrich von Scholtz at Orlau-Frankenau (near Olsztyn, Poland). After severe fighting, the Germans fell back southwest on **Tannenberg**, where von Scholtz's delaying action helped ensure a brilliant German victory (23–24 August 1914).

**Orleans I 451 I Hun Invasion of the
Roman Empire**
See **Chalons**

**Orleans I 463 I Goth Invasion of the
Roman Empire**
Twelve years after Theodoric the Visigoth died at **Chalons** supporting Rome against the Huns, his son Theodoric II renewed the Goth expansion across Gaul and was met at Orleans by the Roman-Frankish General Aegidus and the Salian Franks. Theodoric's army was heavily defeated, with his brother Frederic killed. Theodoric himself was assassinated a few years later.

**Orleans I 1428–1429 I Hundred
Years War**
In the wake of English repulse at **Montgisard**, Thomas Montacute Earl of Salisbury arrived

with fresh troops to besiege Orleans, where he was killed by a cannon shot, then succeeded by William de la Pole Earl of Suffolk. Orleans was then reinforced by Jean Count of Dunois, and Suffolk's besieging army withdrew after defeat by Jeanne d'Arc and Jean Duke of Alencon (12 October 1428–8 May 1429).

Orleans | 1563 | 1st French War of Religion

Catholic Francis Duke of Guise followed his great victory over the Huguenot forces of Louis I de Bourbon Prince of Condé at **Dreux** (December 1562), by moving south to besiege Orleans, where he was struck down by a Huguenot assassin. With his death and the capture of Catholic Commander Anne Duke of Montmorency at Dreux, the siege and the war came to an end (February 1563).

Orleans (1st) | 1870 | Franco-Prussian War

See **Artenay**

Orleans (2nd) | 1870 | Franco-Prussian War

See **Coulmiers**

Orleans (3rd) | 1870 | Franco-Prussian War

Recaptured after French victory at **Coulmiers**, Orleans was again threatened by the Germans under Prince Friedrich Karl of Prussia and Grand Duke Friedrich Franz II of Mecklenburg in the wake of French withdrawal after defeat around **Loigny**. The city capitulated following heavy fighting in the western suburbs, yielding a reported 10,000 prisoners and 60 guns (4–5 December 1870).

Ormáiztegui | 1835 | 1st Carlist War

Carlist commander Tomás Zumalacárregui followed success at **Arquijas** by marching north to Ormáiztegui, west of Beasain, to meet Spanish Liberal Generals Baldomero Espartero and José Carratalá. Costly fighting drove the Carlists back to Segura though both sides withdrew after scattered action next day. Two weeks later, Zu-

malacárregui was repulsed again at **Orbiso** (2–3 January 1835).

Ormoc Bay | 1944 | World War II (Pacific)

A Japanese destroyer squadron under Admiral Mikio Hayakawa attempting to escort munitions and reinforcements to the **Philippines** was attacked in Ormoc Bay, off **Leyte**, by aircraft from a carrier task force led by Admiral Frederick Sherman. Almost 350 sorties sank four destroyers, a minesweeper and five transports with heavy loss of life, including Hayakawa (11 November 1944).

Ormuz | 1507–1508 | Portuguese Colonial Wars in Arabia

See **Hormuz**

Ormuz | 1622 | Anglo-Portuguese Colonial Wars

See **Hormuz**

Orontes | 271 | Roman-Palmyrean War

See **Immae**

Orontes | 1098 | 1st Crusade

Just two days after capturing **Antioch** following a long siege, the Crusaders were in turn besieged by a massive relief army under Kerboga, Emir of Mosul. Inspired by discovery of the supposed Holy Lance, Bohemund of Taranto led a courageous counter-attack across the Orontes River. Kerboga's army was driven off with heavy casualties and Antioch was saved (5–28 June 1098).

Oropesa | 1811 | Napoleonic Wars (Peninsular Campaign)

As French forces advanced down the Valencia coast of Spain towards the siege of **Sagunto**, the road for Marshal Louis Suchet's siege guns was blocked by the ancient fortress of Oropesa. The British ship *Magnificent* arrived too late to help and, following a heavy artillery bombardment, Suchet forced the Spanish garrison to surrender. He was then able to move his guns south (11 October 1811).

Oroquieta ▌ 1872 ▌ 2nd Carlist War

In the vacuum following abdication of King Amadeo of Spain, Young Pretender Don Carlos VII raised volunteers at Oroquieta in Navarre and the government sent a small force under General Domingo Moriones. Despite greatly superior numbers, Don Carlos was routed and fled, leaving almost 50 dead and more than 700 prisoners. Moriones was created Marques de Oroquieta (4 May 1872).

Orsha ▌ 1514 ▌ 2nd Muscovite-Lithuanian War

Duke Basil III of Moscow campaigned in Lithuania to support Prince Mikhail Glinski against Sigismund I of Poland and in June 1514 recovered **Smolensk** after a three-year struggle. Sigismund sent Konstantine Ostrozhsky and, to the west at Orsha, Russian Prince Mikhail Golitz suffered a terrible defeat. While war dragged on until 1520, Moscow managed to hold Smolensk (8 September 1514).

Orsova ▌ 1738 ▌ Austro-Russian-Turkish War

On a fresh offensive on the Danube, Ottoman Grand Vizier Yeghen Mehmed Pasha besieged Orsova, 100 miles east of Belgrade, at the gorge known as the Iron Gates. A relief force under Count Lothar Königsegg defeated the Turks 30 miles away at Kornia. But facing the main Turkish army, and suffering heavy losses from disease, the Austrians retreated to Belgrade and Orsova fell.

Orsova ▌ 1788 ▌ Catherine the Great's 2nd Turkish War

In order to support Russia against Turkey, Austrian Baron Gideon Ernst von Laudon invaded Bosnia, where he quickly captured Dubitza and Novi. However, at the Danube River gorge near Orsova, he and General Leopold Wartensleben were heavily repulsed by the Turks. As a result, they were forced to withdraw until the following year's offensive took them to victory at **Belgrade** (9 August 1788).

Orsza ▌ 1514 ▌ 2nd Muscovite-Lithuanian War

See **Orsha**

Orthez ▌ 1569 ▌ 3rd French War of Religion

With the main Protestant army besieging Poitiers, a subsidiary force under Count Gabriel de Montgomery was detached to face a Royalist invasion of Navarre by Catholic commander Antoine de Lomagne, Vicomte de Terride. The Huguenots defeated Terride in the southwest at Orthez, but this modest success was soon followed by Protestant losses at **Poitiers** and **Moncontour** (24 August 1569).

Orthez ▌ 1814 ▌ Napoleonic Wars (Peninsular Campaign)

As the Allied siege closed on **Bayonne**, Arthur Wellesley Lord Wellington took his Anglo-Portuguese force further east against the French army in the field under Marshal Nicolas Soult. In the hills at Orthez, on the River Gave de Pau, Soult attempted to make a stand. He was driven off in a hard-fought action and withdrew to the Upper Adour and defeat at **Aire** (27 February 1814).

Ortigara ▌ 1917 ▌ World War I (Italian Front)

Italian General Ettore Mambretti led a determined offensive on the Trentino Plateau, seizing strategic Monte Ortigara. However, it was quickly retaken by Austrian General Artur von Mecenseffy in some of the bloodiest alpine fighting of the war. Austria lost 9,000 casualties and the Italians sacrificed over 23,000 men (2,800 killed) in the so-called "Calvary of the Alpini" (10–19 June 1917).

Ortona ▌ 1943 ▌ World War II (Southern Europe)

Driving north along Italy's Adriatic coast, General Sir Bernard Montgomery forced the Germans back from the **Sangro**, then crossed the Moro and sent Canadian General Christopher Vokes against the medieval seaport of Ortona. Brutal hand-to-hand street fighting saw almost

1,400 Canadians killed before Ortona fell. Montgomery then called off his offensive (20–27 December 1943).

Osage ▌ 1864 ▌ American Civil War (Trans-Mississippi)
See **Mine Creek**

Osaka Castle ▌ 1570 ▌ Japan's Era of the Warring States
See **Ishiyama Honganji**

Osaka Castle ▌ 1614–1615 ▌ Japan's Era of the Warring States
Tokugawa Ieyasu secured Japan at **Sekigahara** (1600) and finally moved against Toyotomi Hideyori (son of former ruler Hideyoshi) besieging him at Osaka castle. A brief truce intervened before the siege resumed and the castle fell by storm. Hideyori committed seppuku and Ieyasu reasserted his dominance (29 November 1614–22 January 1615 & 6 May–3 June 1615).

Osan ▌ 1950 ▌ Korean War
As North Korean forces seized **Seoul** and stormed the **Han**, about 500 green American troops under Colonel Brad Smith were thrown forward to delay the invaders at Osan. Outnumbered and without armour, Smith was overwhelmed by North Korean tanks with almost 200 casualties. The defeat shocked American confidence and Smith retreated through **Chochiwon** towards the **Kum** (5 July 1950).

Osel Island ▌ 1719 ▌ 2nd "Great" Northern War
Five months after Charles XII of Sweden died at **Fredrikshald**, Russian ships assumed the offensive and Captains Naum Sinyaven and Konon Zotov attacked Commodore Anton Johan Wrangel near Osel Island (modern Saaremaa, off Estonia). The Swedish flagship *Wachtmeister* and a frigate were captured in heavy fighting and another Russian victory off **Grengam** ended the war (24 May 1719).

Osijek ▌ 351 ▌ Later Roman Military Civil Wars
See **Mursa**

Oslo ▌ 1940 ▌ World War II (Northern Europe)
At the start of the lightning invasion of Norway, the German naval advance on Oslo was delayed when the cruiser *Blucher* was sunk in Oslofjord by land batteries. Meantime, an airborne attack seized the vital airport at Fornebu after sharp fighting, opening the way to the capital. Oslo surrendered and the Germans advanced northwest to meet Allied forces from **Andalsnes** (9 April 1940).

Osma ▌ 1813 ▌ Napoleonic Wars (Peninsular Campaign)
Arthur Wellesley Lord Wellington advanced across the Duoro towards **Vitoria** and sent General Sir Thomas Graham against Osma, where General Honoré Rielle was expecting reinforcements from General Antoine-Louis Maucune. However, Maucune was defeated the same day at **San Millan** and Rielle lost over 100 men before withdrawing to Espejo (18 June 1813).

Ostend ▌ 1601–1604 ▌ Netherlands War of Independence
Despite repulsing Archduke Albert of Spain at **Nieuport**, Prince Maurice of Orange could not prevent the siege of nearby Ostend, defended by Sir Horace Vere. After more than three years, General Ambrogio de Spinola forced Vere's successor Frederick van Dorp to surrender the ruined town. The siege reportedly cost the Dutch 30,000 men and the Spanish 70,000 (5 July 1601–20 September 1604).

Ostend ▌ 1918 ▌ World War I (War at Sea)
As part of the heroic failed raid on **Zeebrugge**, British forces also tried to block German destroyers and U-boats exiting Ostend. However, the two intended blockships were sunk by gunfire. A second attempt by Admiral Roger Keyes saw three Victoria Crosses won, but also

failed when one blockship broke down and the other was sunk in the wrong position (22–23 April & 9–10 May 1918).

Ostia I 409 I Goth Invasion of the Roman Empire

The great Goth leader Alaric's second invasion of Italy drove the Emperor Honorius to Ravenna then laid general siege to **Rome**. In support of his siege Alaric attacked nearby Ostia at the mouth of the Tiber and took the port, along with massive supplies of corn and other food destined for the capital. The fall of Ostia was followed the next year by the eventual capture of Rome itself.

Ostia I 849 I Byzantine-Muslim Wars

Three years after an Arab-Muslim force attacked Rome and sacked St Peter's Basilica, they threatened Rome again and Pope Leo IV sought aid from the Byzantine cities of Naples, Amalfi and Gaeta, which sent a large fleet under Neopolitan Admiral Caesarius to support the Pope's army. The alliance secured a great victory at the mouth of the Tiber off Ostia and the invaders were driven off.

Ostrach I 1799 I French Revolutionary Wars (2nd Coalition)

When Austrian forces advanced over the Lech, French General Jean-Baptiste Jourdan crossed the Rhine and was attacked at Ostrach, near Pfullendorf, by Archduke Charles Louis of Austria with massive strength. With his line too widely dispersed, Jourdan was heavily defeated, with General Francois Lefebvre wounded. He lost again four days later at **Stockach** (21 March 1799).

Ostrog I 1853 I Turko-Montenegran Wars

Concerned over growing Russian influence in Montenegro, a large Ottoman army invaded under Omar Pasha, and near the monastery at Ostrog he was attacked and heavily defeated by Prince Danilo II. While Austria and Russia intervened after three months to secure peace, Turkish demands for Russia to withdraw from the Balkans soon led to the Russo-Turkish War (20 January 1853).

Ostroleka I 1831 I Polish Rebellion

See **Ostrolenka**

Ostrolenka I 1807 I Napoleonic Wars (4th Coalition)

The small Prussian Corps of General Anton Lestocq was defeated by Napoleon Bonaparte's Grand Army in eastern Prussia at **Waltersdorf** and **Eylau** in early February and withdrew southeast to Ostrolenka, north of Warsaw, where they were again defeated. They and their Russian allies were driven out and both armies retired to winter quarters (16 February 1807).

Ostrolenka I 1831 I Polish Rebellion

Three months after repulsing a Russian invasion at **Praga** near Warsaw, Polish rebel forces under General Jan Skrzynecki met Russian Field Marshal Hans von Diebitsch 60 miles to the northeast, on the Narew at Ostrolenka. Both sides suffered heavy casualties in a long and bloody battle, but the Polish losses could not be sustained and the rebels retreated towards **Warsaw** (26 May 1831).

Ostrovo I 1043 I Later Byzantine Military Rebellions

While defeating Normans in Byzantine southern Italy at **Monopoli**, George Maniakes revolted against Constantine IX and, after allowing his troops to proclaim him Emperor, crossed to Epirus and marched on Thessalonica. He appeared to secure victory in battle against Imperial forces at Ostrovo in Bulgaria, but was killed by an arrow at his moment of triumph (May 1043).

Ostrovono I 1812 I Napoleonic Wars (Russian Campaign)

See **Ostrowno**

Ostrowno I 1812 I Napoleonic Wars (Russian Campaign)

As he advanced into Russia, Napoleon Bonaparte tried to prevent the junction of two

Russian armies under Prince Pyotr Bagration and General Mikhail Barclay de Tolly, defeating Bagration at **Mogilev**. In the north at Ostrowno, part of Barclay's force under Count Alexander Ostermann-Tolstoy was routed by Marshal Joachim Murat and forced back to **Smolensk** (25–26 July 1812).

Oswald's Cross I 634 I Anglo-Saxon Territorial Wars
See **Heavenfield**

Oswego I 1756 I Seven Years War (North America)
French commander Marquis Louis de Montcalm led a bold attack across Lake Ontario to besiege the British outpost at Oswego, inadequately defended by Forts Ontario, Oswego and George. Overwhelmed by artillery fire, the settlement surrendered after Commander Colonel James F. Mercer was killed. Montcalm captured massive military stores and destroyed the forts (11–14 August 1756).

Oswestry I 641 I Anglo-Saxon Territorial Wars
See **Maserfield**

Otapawa I 1866 I 2nd New Zealand War
At war with the religio-military Hauhau in South Taranaki, General Trevor Chute led Regular forces, Forest Rangers and Maori allies against the powerful Ngatiruanui fortified pa at Otapawa on the Tangahoe. In the last major Imperial campaign in New Zealand, the pa was stormed with 30 Hauhau and ten Europeans killed. Chute then fought his way north to New Plymouth (14 January 1866).

Otchakov I 1737 I Austro-Russian-Turkish Wars
See **Ochakov**

Otchakov I 1788 I Catherine the Great's 2nd Turkish War
See **Ochakov**

Oteiza I 1874 I 2nd Carlist War
Two months after government forces were repulsed from Carlist-held **Estella** in Navarre, Republican General Domingo Moriones made a fresh diversionary attack a few miles to the southeast at Oteiza. Heavy fighting secured Moriones a costly tactical victory over Carlist General Torcuato Mendíri, though the war continued another 18 months before **Estella** finally fell (11 August 1874).

Otford I 775 I Anglo-Saxon Territorial Wars
King Offa was determined to rebuild the power of Mercia, which had lost land north of the Thames after defeat at **Burford** (752), and moved first against Kent. Southeast of London at Otford, near Sevenoaks, the Kentish army was defeated securing Mercian overlordship of the kingdom. Four years later, Offa turned against Wessex and achieved a decisive victory at **Bensington**.

Othée I 1408 I Hundred Years War
Following the death of Duke Philip of Burgundy, his son John the Fearless arranged the murder of his rival, the Duke of Orleans (brother of King Charles VI), then turned against the people of Liège who had risen against his nominee as their bishop. The young noble crushed the Liègeois in a terrible defeat northeast of Liège at Othée, then made peace with the King (23 September 1408).

Otluk Beli I 1473 I Ottoman-Turkoman War
See **Erzincan**

Otranto I 1480 I Turkish Imperial Wars
While Ottoman forces were making their final unsuccessful assault on the Aegean island of **Rhodes**, Sultan Mehmed II sent Ahmad Gedik Pasha to launch a massive land and sea attack on the port of Otranto on the "heel" of Italy. The city fell by storm and 800 residents were executed. However, the Sultan died before he could

expand his bridgehead on the mainland of Italy (11 August 1480).

Otranto ∎ 1917 ∎ World War I (War at Sea)

With Austria determined to break the Otranto Barrage blocking the Adriatic, Captain Miklos Horthy took three cruisers and sank 23 drifters off Brindisi before being attacked by three Allied cruisers and destroyer escorts under Admiral Alfredo Acton. Although two of Horthy's ships were hit, the Allies withdrew with two destroyers sunk and a British cruiser badly damaged by a torpedo (15 May 1917).

Otrar ∎ 1219–1220 ∎ Conquests of Genghis Khan

One of the triggers for Genghis Khan's offensive against the Khwarezmian Empire was the massacre of a Mongol caravan on the Syr Darya at Otrar (modern Shaulder). Otrar was later besieged by the Conqueror's sons, Chagetai and Ogadei. After the city fell, Governor Inalchuq—who had instigated the massacre—surrendered the citadel and was tortured to death (September 1219–February 1220).

Otterburn ∎ 1388 ∎ Anglo-Scottish Border Wars

James Earl of Douglas had raided into County Durham and was beginning to withdraw, when he took a defensive position against the pursuing army of Sir Henry Percy (Hotspur), son of Earl of Northumberland. Douglas was killed repulsing a rash night attack on his camp at Otterburn, near the Rede north of Hexham, but Hotspur was captured in a costly English defeat (August 1388).

Otumba ∎ 1520 ∎ Spanish Conquest of Mexico

Spanish Conquistador Hernán Cortés was driven out of **Tenochtitlan** by the resistance known as the Noche Triste and retreated 30 miles northeast to Otumba, where he turned on the massive pursuing Aztec army. Cortés inflicted heavy losses in a hard-fought victory, then withdrew to Tlaxcala where he regrouped before returning a year later to destroy the Aztec capital (7 July 1520).

Ouaddai ∎ 1990 ∎ Chad Civil Wars

Defeated at **Iriba** in eastern Chad in April, Libyan-backed rebel Idriss Déby built up his forces in Darfur, Sudan, then marched into Chad's Ouaddai Prefecture. President Hissen Habré personally led his army to meet the rebels and was decisively defeated in several very bloody actions. Déby then took the capital N'Djamena unopposed, and Habré's eight-year rule was over (10–28 November 1990).

Ouadi Doum ∎ 1987 ∎ Libyan-Chad War

When Libya sent two columns 50 miles south from Ouadi Doum to retake **Fada**, both were routed with terrible losses and Chad's army advanced after brutal fighting to take Ouadi Doum and huge booty. The disaster cost Libya perhaps 3,000 killed and her occupation of northern Chad was effectively over. Further Libyan defeat at **Maaten-as-Sarra** in September ended the war (19–22 March 1987).

Oudenarde ∎ 1708 ∎ War of the Spanish Succession

Louis Duke de Vendôme and Louis Duke of Burgundy launched a renewed French offensive in the Netherlands, advancing through Ghent to besiege Oudenarde, 30 miles west of Brussels. A masterful assault river crossing by John Churchill Duke of Marlborough and Prince Eugène of Savoy saw the French driven off with very heavy losses and the Allies turned southwest against **Lille** (11 July 1708).

Oulart ∎ 1798 ∎ Irish Rebellion

At the start of the rising in Ireland, about 5,000 rebels under Father John Murphy at Oulart, a hill ten miles south of Gorey in County Wexford, were attacked by Colonel Foote of the North Cork Militia—with just 110 men and a handful of yeoman cavalry. Foote was predictably routed and he, a sergeant and three privates were said to be the only survivors (27 May 1798).

Oulo | 1918 | Finnish War of Independence

As the war began, White forces seized the area around Vaasa with little resistance, though further north at Ouolu, about 300 poorly armed Whites were heavily attacked by twice as many Red Guards and Russians. The first real battle of the war saw the defence hold firm until Colonel Hannes Ignatius arrived next day with artillery, persuading the main Russian force to capitulate (2–3 February 1918).

Oum Chalouba | 1983 | Chad Civil Wars

With their offensive towards Chad's capital N'Djamena blocked by French reinforcements, Libyan-backed rebels loyal to Goukouni Oueddei advanced southeast from **Faya Largeau** to attack Oum Chalouba. Government veterans under Idriss Déby and Ibrahim Itno repulsed the advance then counter-attacked, inflicting heavy losses and bringing a six-month pause in fighting (August 1983).

Oum Droussa | 1977 | Western Sahara Wars

When Morocco sent troops to assist Mauritania after the raid on **Zouerate** (1 May), they faced fierce attack by Polisario guerrillas from Western Sahara. One of the sharpest actions was further north at Oum Droussa, where two companies of Moroccan paratroops were ambushed with over 100 killed. Guerrilla pressure continued and Mauritania soon withdrew from the war (14 October 1977).

Ourcq | 1814 | Napoleonic Wars (French Campaign)

Prussian General Gebhard von Blucher was defeated in successive actions by Napoleon Bonaparte, then turned to attack Marshals Auguste Marmont and Édouard Mortier who had withdrawn behind the Ourcq near Meaux, northeast of Paris. Mortier repulsed Blucher at Lizy, while Marmont checked him at nearby May and Crouy, delaying his advance on **Soissons** (28 February–1 March 1814).

Ourcq | 1914 | World War I (Western Front)

As German commander Alexander von Kluck advanced through **Mons**, then wheeled north and east of Paris, French Generals Joseph Gallieni and Michel Manoury launched a bold flank attack along the Ourcq. Very intensive fighting saw von Kluck and Hans von Gronau finally beaten as part of the broader Battle of the **Marne** and they withdrew to the **Aisne** (5–9 September 1914).

Ourique | 1139 | Christian Reconquest of Portugal

At war with Muslims beyond the Tagus, the brilliant campaign of Afonso I Henriques, Count of Portugal, culminated in a massive battle near modern Ourique. Despite reinforcements from Africa, the Muslims were routed with five Walis (Kings) killed. Afonso was hailed as first King of independent Portugal and the next year he secured Galicia at **Arcos de Valdevez** (25 July 1139).

Ourthe | 1794 | French Revolutionary Wars (1st Coalition)

General Jean-Baptiste Jourdan advanced across the Meuse at Namur and sent General Barthélemy Schérer southeast in pursuit of Austrian Count Charles von Clerfayt, who had recently replaced Prince Friedrich Josias of Saxe-Coburg. Schérer defeated the Austrians at the River Ourthe and drove them back across the Ruhr towards the Rhine (18 September 1794).

Oveida | 1809 | Napoleonic Wars (Peninsular Campaign)

Having successfully dispersed the independent-minded local junta in the northern province of Asturia, Spanish General Pedro La Romana found himself facing a French offensive under Marshal Michel Ney. When La Romana and Asturian General Francisco Ballasteros attempted to hold Ney at the Nalon near Oveida, they were heavily repulsed. Ney then took Oveida and nearby Gijon (19 May 1809).

Oveida **|** 1936 **|** Spanish Civil War

At the start of the war, Liberal Colonel Antonio Aranda at Oveida in Asturias unexpectedly declared for the rebellion and his force of 3,000 quickly came under siege by about 15,000 miners. A Nationalist column finally fought its way through against heavy resistance to relieve the starving garrison, leaving **Maria de la Cabeza** as the last isolated rebel position (19 July–17 October 1936).

Oviumbo **|** 1904 **|** German Colonial Wars in Africa

On campaign north of Windhoek in German Southwest Africa, Colonel Theodor Leutwein fought a bloody action at **Onganjira** and was then ambushed at Oviumbo by Herero leader Samuel Haherero. Unable to use his firepower in dense bush, Leutwein was forced into a humiliating retreat. He was quickly replaced and his successor beat the Herero in August at **Waterberg** (13 April 1904).

Owerri **|** 1968–1969 **|** Biafran War

Nigerian Federal forces advanced north from **Port Harcourt** to capture Owerri (16 September 1968), then faced an unexpected Biafran counteroffensive under Colonel Ogbugo Kalu. After a long siege, Colonel E. A. Etuk led a brilliant breakout, which saved his brigade. A new Federal offensive retook Owerri (9 January 1970) and starving Biafra collapsed (December 1968–25 April 1969).

Owikokorero **|** 1904 **|** German Colonial Wars in Africa

Major Franz-Georg Glasenapp marched against Herero rebels northeast from Windhoek in German Southwest Africa, where he was ambushed at Owikokorero, losing 26 killed and five wounded out of just 230 men. However, the rebels suffered costly losses to artillery and machine-gun fire before Glasenapp fell back on Onjatu. The German was soon ambushed again at **Okaharui** (13 March 1904).

Oxford **|** 1141 **|** English Period of Anarchy

Amid anarchy following the death of Henry I in 1135, the Empress Matilda was defeated at **Winchester** by her cousin Stephen, who regained the throne and soon besieged her court at Oxford. Matilda fled and the city fell after three months. Her half-brother Robert of Gloucester fought on and won at **Wilton** (1143). But when he died Matilda retired to Normandy (October–21 December 1141).

Ox Ford **|** 1864 **|** American Civil War (Eastern Theatre)

See **North Anna**

Ox Hill **|** 1862 **|** American Civil War (Eastern Theatre)

See **Chantilly**

Oxnebjerg **|** 1535 **|** Danish Counts' War

See **Oksnebjerg**

Oyster River **|** 1694 **|** King William's War

In France's war against Colonial America, Claude-Sebastian de Villeu invaded New Hampshire but, lacking resources to attack **Pemaquid**, he fell on the small settlement of Oyster River (modern Durham). Supported by Abnaki Indians under Chief Taxous, he killed over 100 settlers, mainly women and children, before burning the houses and taking his captives to Quebec (July 1694).

Ozernoe **|** 1655 **|** Russo-Polish Wars

A Russian-Ukrainian army under Vasili Buturlin and Bogdan Chmielnicki withdrawing east from **Lvov**, was attacked southeast of Zborov at Ozernoe by Tatars, who had invaded the Ukraine. The Tatars and their Polish allies were badly defeated, and Crimean Khan Mehmet Girai agreed to withdraw. In 1658 Ukrainian Cossacks attacked Russia at **Poltava** and **Kiev** (10 November 1655).